T0183479

Lecture Notes in Computer Science 11918

Formal Methods

Subline of Lectures Notes in Computer Science

More information about this series at http://www.springer.com/series/7408

Wolfgang Ahrendt · Silvia Lizeth Tapia Tarifa (Eds.)

Integrated Formal Methods

15th International Conference, IFM 2019
Bergen, Norway, December 2–6, 2019
Proceedings

Editors
Wolfgang Ahrendt
Chalmers University of Technology
Gothenburg, Sweden

Silvia Lizeth Tapia Tarifa
University of Oslo
Oslo, Norway

ISSN 0302-9743 ISSN 1611-3349 (electronic)
Lecture Notes in Computer Science
ISBN 978-3-030-34967-7 ISBN 978-3-030-34968-4 (eBook)
https://doi.org/10.1007/978-3-030-34968-4

LNCS Sublibrary: SL2 – Programming and Software Engineering

This Springer imprint is published by the registered company Springer Nature Switzerland AG
The registered company address is: Gewerbestrasse 11, 6330 Cham, Switzerland

Preface

Broadening the adoption and applicability of formal methods hinges on being able to combine different formalisms and different analysis techniques, because different components may be more amenable to different techniques, or simply to express complex properties and to reason about complex systems. The Integrated Formal Methods (IFM) conference series aims to bring together researchers from the formal methods community, whose novel and combined approaches are targeting different formal and semi-formal methods for modeling and analysis. The conference covers a broad spectrum of topics: from language design, to verification and analysis techniques, to supporting tools and their integration into software engineering practice.

This volume contains the papers presented at IFM 2019, the 15th International Conference on integrated Formal Methods, which took place in Bergen, Norway, during December 2–6, 2019. The conference was hosted by the Western Norway University of Applied Sciences.

IFM 2019 solicited high-quality papers reporting research results and/or experience reports related to the overall theme of the conference. The Program Committee (PC) received 87 regular paper submissions, plus 8 short paper submissions. This is the second highest number of submissions in the history of IFM. After several weeks of reviewing, followed by a lively online discussion among PC members, we selected 28 contributions (25 regular papers and 3 short papers) for inclusion in this proceedings volume and presentation at the conference. This amounts to an acceptance rate of 29% (whether or not the short papers are included in the statistics).

The combination of topics covered by the selected papers includes both theoretical approaches and practical implementations, demonstrating that the underlying principle of integrating heterogeneous formal methods can buttress rigorous solutions in different domains and at different levels of abstraction.

In addition to the regular and short paper categories, IFM 2019 also allowed the submission of 'journal-first' papers, i.e., summaries of papers which were earlier published in a journal. The aim was to further enrich the program of IFM, as well as to provide an overall more flexible path to publication and dissemination of original research in formal methods. Seven 'journal-first' papers were submitted, out of which six were accepted for presentation at IFM.

The scientific program of IFM 2019 was completed by keynote talks given by three remarkable researchers:

- Jean-Christophe Filliâtre from Laboratoire de Recherche en Informatique, University of Paris-Sud, CNRS, Orsay, France
- Tiziana Margaria from University of Limerick and Confirm, Ireland
- Corina Păsăreanu from NASA Ames and Carnegie Mellon University, USA

We would like to thank our invited speakers for contributing exciting and inspiring presentations to the conference.

We also thank the PC members and the reviewers who helped them for their thorough reviewing work, and for animating a careful discussion of the merits of each submission. Their names are listed on the following pages. The EasyChair system provided indispensable practical support to the reviewing and discussion process.

The local organization in Bergen ensured a successful and enjoyable conference. We are grateful to all the organizers, and in particular to the general chair, Volker Stolz, and the local organization chairs, Violet Ka I Pun and Fazle Rabbi, who took care of all organizational aspects with great resourcefulness and punctuality. Our full-hearted thanks go also to the workshop chairs, Martin Leucker and Violet Ka I Pun, the PhD symposium chairs, Jacopo Mauro and César Sánchez, the financial chair, Pål Ellingsen, and the publicity chairs, Lars Michael Kristensen and Kristin Yvonne Rozier. Together, you made IFM 2019 a success.

Finally, we would like to express our gratitude to the organizations which generously sponsored the conference: the Research Council of Norway, the municipality of Bergen, and Springer.

October 2019

Wolfgang Ahrendt
Silvia Lizeth Tapia Tarifa

Organization

Program Committee

Erika Abraham	RWTH Aachen University, Germany
Wolfgang Ahrendt	Chalmers University of Technology, Sweden
Bernhard K. Aichernig	TU Graz, Austria
Borzoo Bonakdarpour	Iowa State University, USA
David Cok	CEA and Safer Software Consulting, France
Ferruccio Damiani	Università di Torino, Italy
Ornela Dardha	University of Glasgow, UK
Brijesh Dongol	University of Surrey, UK
Constantin Enea	IRIF, University Paris Diderot, France
Marie Farrell	The University of Liverpool, UK
Carlo A. Furia	Università della Svizzera Italiana, Italy
Susanne Graf	University of Grenoble Alpes, CNRS, Grenoble INP, VERIMAG, France
Dilian Gurov	KTH Royal Institute of Technology, Sweden
Ludovic Henrio	CNRS, France
Marieke Huisman	University of Twente, the Netherlands
Ralf Huuck	UNSW Sydney and LOGILICA, Australia
Einar Broch Johnsen	University of Oslo, Norway
Nikolai Kosmatov	CEA List, France
Laura Kovacs	Vienna University of Technology, Austria
Martin Leucker	University of Lübeck, Germany
Tiago Massoni	Universidade Federal de Campina Grande, Brazil
Larissa Meinicke	The University of Queensland, Australia
Rosemary Monahan	National University of Ireland Maynooth, Ireland
Luigia Petre	Åbo Akademi University, Finland
Nadia Polikarpova	University of California San Diego, USA
Philipp Rümmer	Uppsala University, Sweden
Cesar Sanchez	IMDEA Software Institute, Spain
Steve Schneider	University of Surrey, UK
Emil Sekerinski	McMaster University, Canada
Marjan Sirjani	Malardalen University, Sweden, and Reykjavik University, Iceland
Jorge Sousa Pinto	University of Minho, Portugal
Silvia Lizeth Tapia Tarifa	University of Oslo, Norway
Caterina Urban	Inria, France

Jüri Vain	Tallinn University of Technology, Estonia
Tomas Vojnar	Brno University of Technology, Czech Republic
Kirsten Winter	The University of Queensland, Australia
Naijun Zhan	Institute of Software, Chinese Academy of Sciences, China
Chenyi Zhang	Jinan University, China

Additional Reviewers

Abbaspour Asadollah, Sara
Ameur-Boulifa, Rabea
Andrei, Oana
Arnaud, Mathilde
Bacci, Giovanni
Backeman, Peter
Bannour, Boutheina
Belo Lourenço, Cláudio
Bubel, Richard
Coenen, Norine
Colvin, Robert
D'Osualdo, Emanuele
Dalvandi, Mohammadsadegh
Dang, Thao
Delbianco, Germán Andrés
Delmas, David
Dezani-Ciancaglini, Mariangiola
Dijk, Thomas C. Van
Dong, Naipeng
Eilers, Marco
Faghih, Fathiyeh
Fantechi, Alessandro
Feret, Jérôme
Fernando, Dileepa
Fiedor, Jan
Filipovikj, Predrag
Fowler, Simon
Francalanza, Adrian
Ghassemi, Fatemeh
Giannini, Paola
Habermehl, Peter
Hong, Chih-Duo
Iannetta, Paul
Jacobs, Swen
Joosten, Sebastiaan
Junges, Sebastian
Kamburjan, Eduard
Kapus, Timotej
Khosrowjerdi, Hojat
Kremer, Gereon
Le Gall, Pascale
Lemerre, Matthieu
Li, Qin
Li, Yangjia
Liang, Chencheng
Lidström, Christian
Lienhardt, Michael
Linker, Sven
Loow, Andreas
Loulergue, Frederic
Lu, Yi
Luckcuck, Matt
Lupp, Daniel P.
Luteberget, Bjørnar
Madelaine, Eric
Markin, Grigory
Miné, Antoine
Monti, Raúl E.
Moradi, Fereidoun
Mutluergil, Suha Orhun
Neves, Renato
Neykova, Rumyana
Noll, Thomas
Norman, Gethin
Nowotka, Dirk
Pedro, André
Perrelle, Valentin
Prabhakar, Pavithra
Proença, José
Pun, Ka I.
Pérez, Jorge A.
Rehak, Vojtech
Rogalewicz, Adam
Safari, Mohsen
Scheffel, Torben
Schlaipfer, Matthias

Schmitz, Malte
Sedaghatbaf, Ali
Sharifi, Zeinab
Signoles, Julien
Smrcka, Ales
Sproston, Jeremy
Steffen, Martin
Stoelinga, Marielle
Thoma, Daniel
Torfah, Hazem
Torta, Gianluca
Tyszberowicz, Shmuel
Voinea, A. Laura
Volk, Matthias
Vörös, András
Wang, Lingtai
Wang, Qiuye
Wang, Shuling
Wang, Yu
Xue, Bai
Zeljić, Aleksandar
Zhan, Bohua
Zhang, Miaomiao

Abstracts of Invited Talks

Deductive Verification of OCaml Libraries

Jean-Christophe Filliâtre

CNRS Lab. de Recherche en Informatique, Univ. Paris-Sud, 91405 Orsay

In this talk, we report on an on-going project, VOCaL, which aims at building formally-verified general-purpose OCaml libraries of data structures and algorithms. We present the various ingredients of this project. First, we introduce GOSPEL, a specification language for OCaml. It resembles existing behavioral specification languages (e.g. JML, ACSL, SPARK), yet departs from them on several points. Second, we describe techniques and tools to perform deductive verification of GOSPEL-specified OCaml code. Currently, this is built on top of three existing tools, namely Why3, CFML and Coq. Last, we report of the successful verification of the first OCaml modules of the VOCaL library. This includes general-purpose data structures such as resizable arrays, hash tables, priority queues, and union-find.

Safe Deep Neural Networks

Corina S. Păsăreanu

CyLab Carnegie Mellon University and NASA Ames, USA

Deep Neural Networks (DNNs) are increasingly used in a variety of applications that require high assurance guarantees. Verification and understanding of DNNs is hindered by their high complexity, their opaqueness and sensitivity to small adversarial perturbations and also by the lack of high-level formal specifications. In this talk I will describe recent research work which explores techniques and tools to ensure that DNNs and systems that use DNNs are safe, robust and interpretable. These include: symbolic execution for DNN analysis, compositional approaches to improve formal SMT-based verification, property inference for DNNs, adversarial training and detection, and probabilistic reasoning for DNNs. The techniques aim to provide guarantees wrt safety and robustness for DNNs, making them amenable for use in safety critical domains, particular autonomy. I will describe recent applications of the techniques to the analysis of deep neural networks designed to operate as controllers in the next-generation Airborne Collision Avoidance Systems for unmanned aircraft (ACAS Xu). Furthermore I will discuss analysis of image classification networks (MNIST, CIFAR) and sentiment networks (for text classification).

Contents

Invited Talk

The Digital Thread in Industry 4.0

Tiziana Margaria(✉) and Alexander Schieweck

Chair of Software Systems, University of Limerick, and Confirm, Limerick, Ireland
{tiziana.margaria,alexander.schieweck}@ul.ie

Abstract. Industry 4.0, the new wave of Smart Manufacturing in Europe and globally, relies on a Digital Thread to connect the data and processes for smarter products, smarter production, and smarter integrated ecosystems. But what is the Digital Thread?

We discuss a few key questions about modelling, the nature of models and the use of models that arose from the experience in the first two years of Confirm, the Irish Centre for Smart Manufacturing. We also provide an example of how the new model-powered and integrated thinking can disrupt the status quo, empower a better understanding, and deliver a more automatic management of the many cross-dimensional issues that future connected software and systems will depend upon.

1 From the Digital Twin to the Digital Thread

The Industry 4.0 movement towards smart advanced manufacturing presupposes a thorough revolution in the perception and practice of the "Art of Manufacturing" that shifts the innovation focus increasingly from the traditional crafts and engineering, like mechanical engineering, materials science and plants construction, to immaterial assets, like knowledge, flexibility and ultimately models for their exploration 'in silico'. The role of models is well understood for what concerns blueprints of facilities, CAD of machines and parts, P&IDs of various tooling processes in production [68], and various behavioural models like stress curves of materials, yield of various processes, and isolated simulations. The new trend of modelling concerns the *Digital Twin* of processes, machines and parts. That the essence of a Digital Twin is not yet stabilized is witnessed by the fact that everyone seems to have a different definition. For example, as of today Wikipedia [67] provides an own description (note: not a definition) as "*A digital twin is a digital replica of a living or non-living physical entity.*[1] *By bridging the physical and the virtual world, data is transmitted seamlessly allowing the virtual entity to exist simultaneously with the physical entity. Digital twin refers to a digital replica of potential and actual physical assets (physical twin), processes, people, places, systems and devices that can be used for various purposes.*" and "*Definitions of digital twin technology used in prior research emphasize two important characteristics. Firstly, each definition emphasizes the connection between the physical model and the corresponding virtual model or virtual counterpart.* [8] *Secondly, this connection is established by generating real time data using sensors.* [2]". Wikipedia then lists 10 different definitions, from

W. Ahrendt and S. L. Tapia Tarifa (Eds.): IFM 2019, LNCS 11918, pp. 3–24, 2019.
https://doi.org/10.1007/978-3-030-34968-4_1

2012 to 2019, that include references to as diverse concepts as multilevel, multiphysics, multiscale, real time, cloud platform, lifecycle, health condition, and many more. A recent, quite realistic and encompassing definition is by Ashtari et al. [65]: "*The Digital Twin is a virtual representation of a physical asset in a Cyber-Physical Production System (CPPS), capable of mirroring its static and dynamic characteristics. It contains and maps various models of a physical asset, of which some are executable, called simulation models. But not all models are executable, therefore the Digital Twin is more than just a simulation of a physical asset. Within this context, an asset can be an entity that already exists in the real world or can be a representation of a future entity that will be constructed.*"

In this context - an adaptation of Cyberphysical Systems to the production environment - most engineers accept the need of continuous models or discretized numerical simulation models like in finite element analysis. They are however not familiar with models for software, nor are they aware that software, and thus software correctness and thus software quality, are essential to the information propagation, aggregation, and analysis that combines collections of such models to deliver or at least enable the desired insight from those models. In other words, the **Digital Thread** that connects real things and their twin models, but also the communication networks, the decision algorithms, the visualisations needed to work in design, construction, and operation within a mature Industry 4.0 environment are still not in the sphere of awareness of the responsibles. Thus software in general and software models in particular are hopelessly underestimated in their relevance, complexity, challenges and cost.

The modern version of the Digital Thread can be seen as the information-relay framework which enables the holistic view and traceability of an asset along its entire lifecycle. This framework includes any data, behaviours, models, protocols, security, and their standards related to the asset as well as to the context where it is expected to operate. As such, it goes well beyond the customary understanding of the thread as mostly a collection of data, cast in terms of the Digital Twin as a new way of managing variants in a Product Line Engineering context and with the Digital Thread being the new counterpart of the established Product Lifecycle Management [13].

Being a Principal Investigator in Confirm responsible for the co-direction of the Cyberphysical Systems research hub, involved in the Virtual and Physical Testbeds hub, and working with Digital Twins to deliver the Confirm platform, the current unawareness in industry and academia alike about the high demands and enormous potential of the Digital Thread are a threat and an opportunity at the same time. We found out that the first step of communication needed to reach professionals who do not know much about software, less about models, and even less about (discrete) behavioural models for software and systems, is to build a micro-size demonstrator in exactly their domain.

In the rest of the paper we provide a description of the micro-demo we built this Summer, essentially a web based UR3 robot controller (Sect. 2), we give a little background on the Model-driven Integrated Development Environment

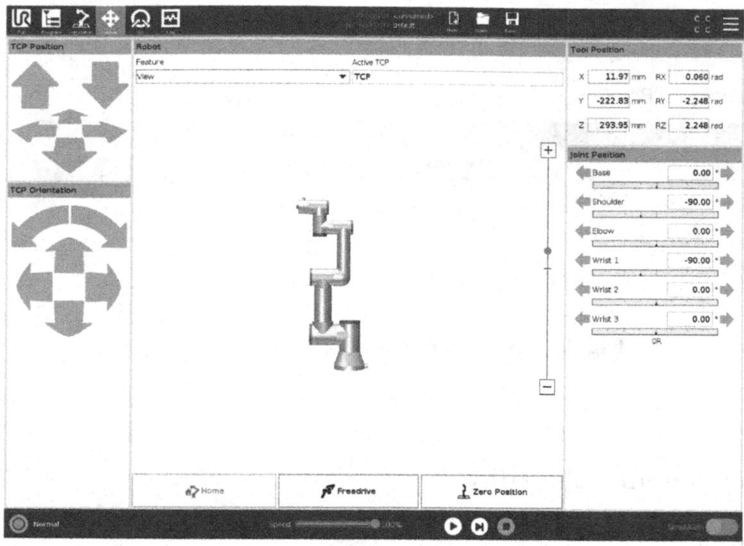

Fig. 1. The simulator provided by UR.

DIME [5] that we used to build it, and the Robotics DSL (domain specific language) we built to integrate robotics capabilities in DIME (Sect. 3). Then we provide some final considerations about the prospective of using this approach and framework as the technical platform to build the Confirm Digital Thread and Digital Twin shared assets (Sect. 4).

2 Bringing the UR3 Controller in the Web

The mini-project we identified as the first nugget of model driven design and development of a demonstrator in the robotic field for Confirm literally *unleashes* the normally tethered UR3 robot control. Universal Robots, an originally Danish company acquired in 2015 by Teradyne, is a leader in collaborative robots (cobots), i.e. robots that can work sharing the same space with humans, instead of having to be isolated from humans in shielded work cells. UR was the first company to deliver commercially viable collaborative robots. This ability to act next to or with humans enables advanced robotics to help with mixed product assembly, and is transforming companies and entire industries.

The UR3 is their smallest cobot model. It is a compact table-top robot for light assembly tasks and automated workbench scenarios. It weighs only 11 kg, but has a payload of 3 kg, 360-degree rotation on all wrist joints, and infinite rotation on the end joint. Confirm has bought one for demonstration and outreach purposes, and a few small applications have been built with it using the programming techniques offered by UR3.

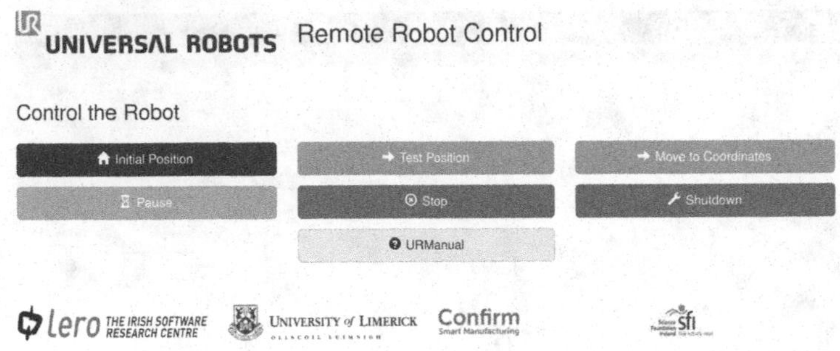

Fig. 2. UR3 web controller: the main page.

2.1 Programming the UR3

Polyscope GUI
A tablet with a graphical GUI for steering and commanding the robot is tethered to the robot. This Polyscope GUI interface is programmed using the touch screen of the tablet with URP files. Figure 1 shows the Polyscope GUI in the UR3 simulator environment: one can control the robot movements using the arrows on the left, or program waypoints by entering the coordinates on the right. It is also possible to upload scripts in the UR script language to the tablet.

UR Script Language
We used instead the UR script language. UR Script has variables, types, flow of control statements, function etc. In addition, UR Script has several built-in variables and functions which control the I/O and the movements of the robot. UR script commands can be sent from a host computer or PC via an Ethernet TCP socket connection directly to the UR robot, for motion and action control without using the tablet pendant. We use the UR simulator to execute .urp progams. At the bottom of Fig. 1 we see that the simulator screen provides buttons to go to a Home position, to perform Freedrive using the arrows, and to a Zero Position.

The RoboDK Simulator
RoboDK is a simulator and offline programming software for industrial robots. It can generate script and URP files which can be executed by a UR robot. Additionally, it is possible to execute programs on the robot from the RoboDK if the robot is connected to the computer. RoboDK can also import script files to the simulator. This allows to simulate existing script programs, modify them and re-export them.

2.2 Case Study: A Web UR3 Controller

We used the Script language and the TCP socket to program the UR3, creating a web based application that controls the robot in a very simple fashion. After having entered the IP of the robot in a first screen, Fig. 2 shows the main

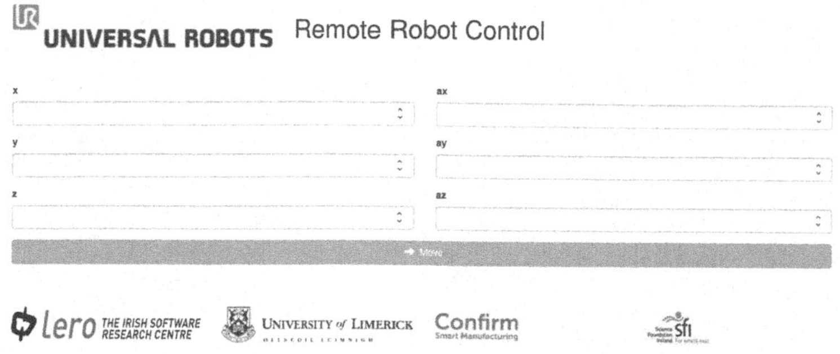

Fig. 3. UR3 web controller: the Move to Coordinates page

page of the controller: One can bring the robot to a predefined Initial Position (equivalent to the simulator's Home button), bring it to a predefined Test position (equivalent to the simulator's Zero Position), ask it to Move to Coordinates, Pause the robot, Stop it, and perform its Shutdown. All these buttons drive the simulator, or, alternatively, the real robot. The UR Manual button links to the online manual provided by UR. The only action that requires further inputs is Move to Coordinates: Fig. 3 shows the corresponding page.

As mentioned before, the Web application is connected per TCP to the Robot and the execution happens on the simulator or on the real UR3 cobot.

But how did we program the Web application?
This was started as this Summer as a small Proof of Concept demo by two interns from INSA Rouen in France, mathematics students after the 2nd year, not really familiar with programming, in particular not with Web programming, Java, nor deployment.

3 DIME as a Model Driven IDE for Robotics

The "program" that steers the UR3 controller application as well as the GUI layer for the Web are actually not hand-programmed in code at all. We see in Fig. 4 that models cover the complete web application design thanks to the use of DIME [5], the DyWA Integrated Modelling Environment [45], which is the currently most advanced and comprehensive Cinco-product [43]. DIME is a allows the integrated modelling of all the aspects needed for the design of a complete web application in terms of Graphical Domain-Specific Languages (GDSLs). Figure 4 shows that models capture the control flow as in the Service Logic Graphs of METAFrame [53,57] and jABC [36,44,61] before DIME. In DIME we have additionally also data models and UI models in the same Integrated Development Environment (IDE). In fact we see in this model:

- the **control flow**, showing that from the Start we proceed to the GetAddress page, with the symbol of a UI model, and then from there to the PublicHome page, another UI model, from which the control branches (solid arrows) lead

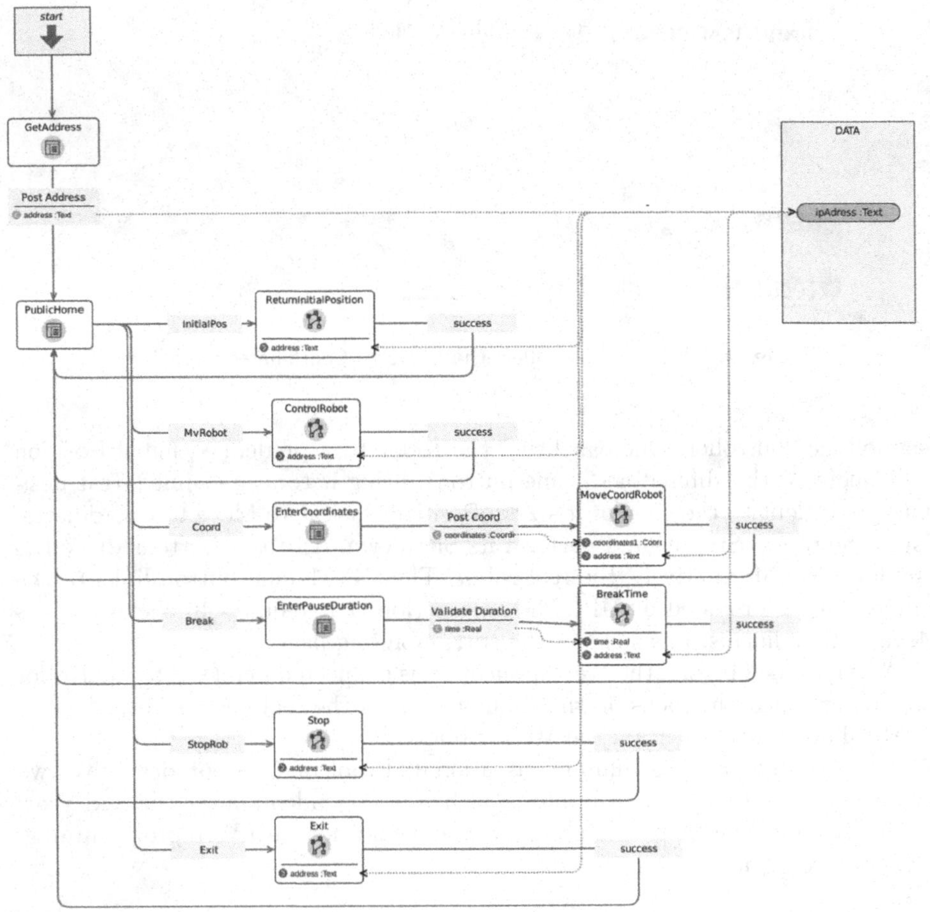

Fig. 4. The main workflow of the control application.

us to one of the successive actions: ReturnInitialPosition, ControlRobot, EnterCoordinates, EnterPauseDuration, Stop, Exit.

- the **data flow**, showing that there is a Data Context containing the data collected or used in the application. The data flow arrows are dotted, they connect the data from the output branches (like the IPaddress and their type, here text, the coordinates, and the pause time) to the data context, which models the store (i.e. the memory) and the data context to the inputs of the successive processes. For example the MoveCoordRobot process receives both the Coordinates and the IPaddress.
- the **subprocesses**, like ReturnInitialPosition, ControlRobot, which have own models,
- the **Web pages**, with GUI models, which are the only part the user experiences, as the processes work in the background.

- We also see that this is a **reactive application**: there is no End action, all the paths through the web application workflows lead back to the PublicHome main page of Fig. 2.

All these models are interdependently connected, shaping the 'one thing' [39, 62] global model in a manner which is formal, yet easy to understand and to use. The continuous and model driven deployment cycle is simplified to the extent that its code can be one-click-generated and deployed as a complete and ready to run web application. This happens along the methodology and process of [5].

3.1 Behavioural Models and Feature DSL

The power of DIME as a modelling and development tool for code-less [10] and even no-code development is connected with behavioral model-driven design as auspicated in [31] and [32]: the original DyWA was for the user a web-based definition facility for the type schema of any application domain of choice. Coupled with the defined types is the automatic generation of corresponding Create, Read, Update, Delete (CRUD) operations, so that application experts are able to model domain specific business processes which are directly executable in our modelling environment. Upon change, the prototype can be augmented or modified stepwise by acting on one or more types in the type schema, the corresponding data-objects, and the executable process models, while maintaining executability at all times. As every step is automated via a corresponding code generator, no manual coding is required.

In this case, we see that the main workflow includes various other process models, indicated by the little graph symbol. For example, the MoveCoordRobot subprocess that sends the coordinates to the robot is shown in Fig. 5. Upon start it receives the coordinates collected in the respective webpage (see Fig. 3), it prepares the UR script program that initialises the robot, instructs it to move to those coordinates, then sends the commands and shuts down the robot.

The collection of such processes is a **domain specific language (DSL)** at the **feature** [1,9,16,28] level: these process accomplish one user level intent each, which is the definition of feature. Additionally, these features are **behavioural**: the processes express operations of the UR3 (i.e., what it does) instead of static affordances (i.e., what are its components). We see in Fig. 6 the collection of subprocesses created for this application. Behavioural features are usually domain specific but application independent: we could easily reuse them to create a different demonstration with the UR3. As in DIME, we distinguish

- Basic processes, like CreateUser needed to log in and access the WebApplication. Basic processes are DIME-level processes, that deal with the essential elements of a web application, like creating users. This process has been in fact reused from a previous application, and not developed specifically for this demo.
- Interaction processes are executed client-side within the user's web browser. They define the immediate interaction between user and application and can be regarded as a site map.

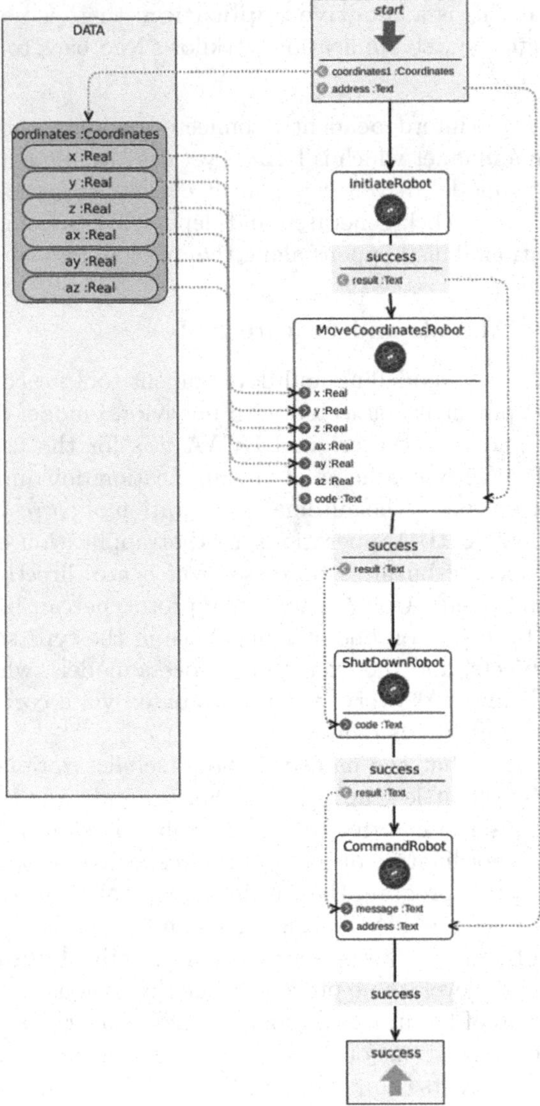

Fig. 5. Subprocess MoveCoordRobot: sends the Move command to the robot.

- Interactable processes are slightly restricted basic processes that are provided as REST services and can thus be included in interaction processes.

  Not used here are additionally

- Long running processes, that describe the entire lifecycle of entities. They integrate interactions with one or multiple users as well as business logic in the form of interactable and basic processes.

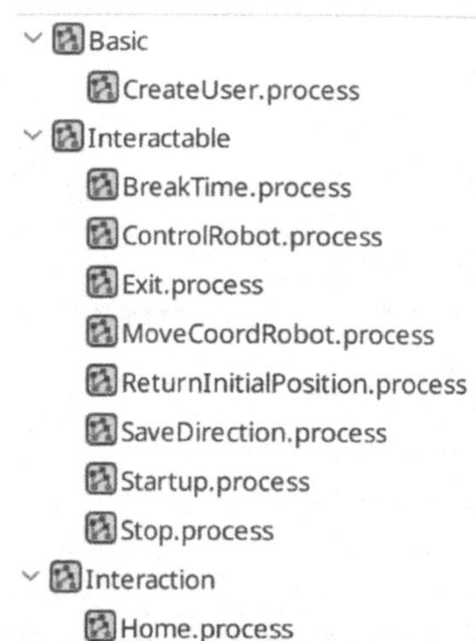

Fig. 6. Overview of the created processes: the behavioural Features DSL

- Security processes, that realise access control based on the specific user currently logged in and the association, e.g. in form of access rights, to other entities in the system.

It is also very likely that we could easily reuse the behavioural features in a demo for a different UR robot, like the larger UR5, even larger UR10, and the brand new UR16. In this particular case of the UR cobot family, they are built in a physically similar way, because they all have the same arm component types, only scaled dimensionally or made internally more robust, but they have the same functionalities and thus share the same list of behavioural capabilities. What makes a difference is the reach, own weight, maximum load, which impact the parameter (i.e., the concrete data) but not the collection of capabilities. As the workflows are parameterised in the data, they could be reused very likely as they are (Fig. 7).

3.2 The UR3 Native DSL

As we see in Fig. 4, the process models can contain other process models, hierarchically and also recursively, collected in this case in the Feature DSL of Fig. 6, but at some point processes also include atomic actions, like the InitiateRobot, MoveCoordinatesRobot, ShutdownRobot, and CommandRobot in Fig. 5. Figure 7 shows the collection of UR3-specific atomic actions (called SIBs, for service independent building blocks) used in this application. Notice the symbol of an atom, indicating their basic character, i.e. their referring to either native code, or an external API or service. This distinguishes them from the processes. While processes are models (Service Logic Graphs in our terminology) and are "implemented" by models and symbolised by a little graph icon, atomic SIBs are

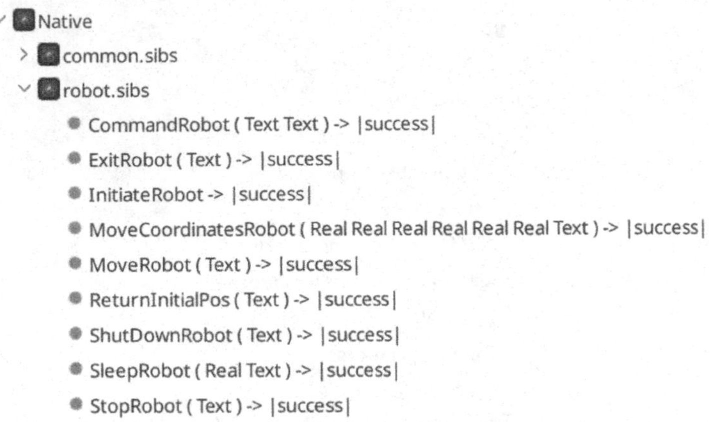

Fig. 7. Overview of the created SIBs: the native UR3 DSL

implemented by code. Therefore they are the basic units (thus "atoms") from a model point of view, and they embody and provide the link to the traditional programming level.

The native SIB palette robot.sibs encapsulates at the model level a subset of the native commands in the UR script programming language. There are more commands in the script language, and in order to use them in this or other applications they would need to be encapsulated similarly, to be included in the palette and made available to the application modellers.

Like the Feature DSL, also this DSL is reusable. While the Feature DSL is a collection of models, and thus it can change and evolve largely independently of programming artefacts in native code, the evolution of the Native DSLs depends on changes in the languages, APIs, and (service) interfaces they encapsulate. In this sense, the use of these layered DSLs provides also a very clean structure for organising and managing the domain and application evolution, which are usually in distinct areas of competence and responsibility:

- On the basis of the available Native DSLs, application designers can change, enrich and evolve their application, like our UR3 Controller demo, at pleasure without the need of programming. Modifications happen in the GUI or in the business logic, on the basis of existing native libraries and thus with the same code basis. The new workflows and GUI models are compiled to new application code and deployed without the need of any programming skills nor activity. In this sense, our XMDD approach [38,42] is a zero-code environment for this application design and evolution.
- If the UR script language changes, or an API or another interface, library, or code that are encapsulated in respective Native DSLs change, this happens in the decision and management sphere of the organisation or entity that is responsible for that platform or code. In such case it may be necessary to revisit the corresponding Native SIB DSL, and potentially take action.

In some cases, changes to implementations internal to a platform do not impact the interface. In that case the Native DSL is still valid as is. In case there are changes, they can lead to the addition, modification or deletion of operations, which may require the Native DSL manager to modify the palette accordingly. Potentially this can lead to versioning of atomic SIBs, because applications relying on the older palette may have to be retained running on the previous version. Modifications and deletions in a Native DSL may also have consequences for the applications that use them. This is however not different from the usual practice with any application relying on external code or libraries.

3.3 GUI Models and Their DSL

GUI models allow the definition of the user interface of the web application. As we see in Fig. 8 (right), they reflect the structure of the individual web pages. They can be included within the sitemap processes as an interaction point for the user, like in this case, or within other GUI models to reuse already modelled parts, as in the case of the Header GUI model at the top of the model, containing the UR logo and the top line (Remote Robot Control) that is the title of the demo, and the Footer GUI model, containing the logos of the university, Confirm, SFI etc.

On the right we see the GUI Native DSL of DIME. It is important to note that this GUI comes with DIME and is shared by all the applications, win whatever domain, built with DIME. Not only it ensures a common technological basis for all the DIME applications, it also enables application designers with no experience of GUI and web programming, like our interns, to create really nice applications without the need to learn the various server side and client side technologies, nor to have to deal with compilation and deployment stacks. In our application, the students concentrated their effort exclusively on the creation of the Native UR DSL, the conception of the application, and its design and debugging at the level of the (executable) models. If the common GUI palette is not enough there is a way to write Native Frontend Components, similar to the Java Native SIBs.

In the design, the connection between the different model types is evident in the combination of the GUI model of Fig. 8 (right) and the workflow model in Fig. 4. When composing the GUI model of the homepage, the designer drags and drops the various buttons and elements from the GUI palette onto the canvas, places them and defines their surface properties, like e.g. what's written on a button and its colour. Due to the knowledge about these models and model elements embedded in the DIME environment, for example adding a button to the page makes its GUI model add one outgoing branch with that name. As a consequence, once the designer has defined the Home GUI model in Fig. 8 (right), so that it now appears in the list of defined GUIs, and then drags it onto the Workflow canvas when composing the workflow model of Fig. 4, the symbol of the Home GUI automatically displays also the 6 outgoing branches, each labelled with the name of a button in the corresponding GUI model. This way

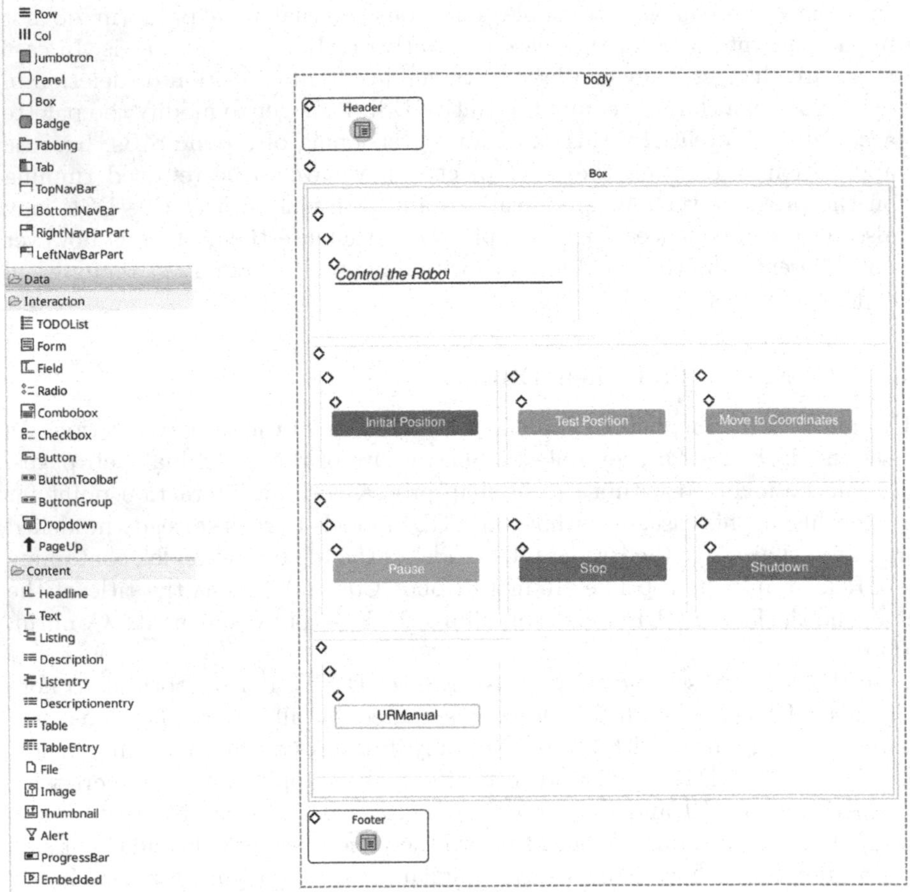

Fig. 8. The DIME GUI palette (left) and the GUI editor for the control page.

the consistency and correctness of the connections between different model types and different aspects and element of the application are enforced or supported by DIME in its nature as knowledge-infused IDE for models.

4 XMDD for the Digital Thread

The rising dependence on intersectoral knowledge and the convergence of economic sectors are being increasingly experienced in Industry 4.0. This happens internally due to the smart manufacturing model, which connects hardware, software, networks and communications, materials, business models, laws and regulations. It happens also externally, due to the manufacturing of all kinds of goods, in any sector, and the need to be more flexible in moving from one product or kind of products to another due to increased market demand fluctuations and opportunities.

As described last year in [32], referring to the Irish and global situation, a number of "needs" are mentioned over and over again:

- the need to integrate across specialisation domains, spanning across various disciplines of research and professions;
- the need to become increasingly agnostic about the specific technologies: the programming language, the operating system, the data management/information system, the communication networks, the runtime platforms, and more;
- the need to be future-ready: projects, collaborations, consortia and alliances change. No IT product can afford being locked into technological walled gardens, the need is voiced over and over again to be as technology- and as platform-independent as possible;
- the need to be able to try fast and improve fast: time to market is important, but time to test/time to retest are equally important. What is called "continuous development" or "continuous integration" needs to be supported as the new mainstream paradigm of system design and evolution.

The answer rests in the up-skilling of knowledge, at the same time trying to go to the essential bits, without lengthy and costly education paths. It seems the case that at the centre of the Smart Manufacturing movement lie the *increased use of models*, first and foremost the creation and adoption of the Digital Twin, and the *increased integration of heterogeneous models* in a Digital Thread, and this has to happen within the next few years, this will have to happen with the current labour force in the design and decision workshops. This population of selected experts is sectorally trained, sectorally competent, and unlikely to be able or willing to undergo significant retraining specifically in software.

The creation of a software or system is itself *innovation*, and the change or evolution of an existing system is innovation, too. Consistently with the widely successful school of *lean* approaches to innovation, one needs to *fail fast* and *eliminate waste*. The key is to recognise as early as possible that something is not as wished, possibly before investing time and resources into producing what will need to be amended, and make changes right away on the artefacts that are available at that stage. The systematic use of portable and reusable models, in a single paradigm, combined with generative approaches to code, has the potential to provide a Next Wave of IT that meets by and large the ambitious goals described above.

Revisiting some of the aspects mentioned in [32] after over one year of further interaction with various industries and more direct experience on what works and what is too complicated or looks too unfamiliar to be successful, we think that the approach described in the UR3 case study has a number of essential traits that make it attractive to the new public of Industry 4.0.

4.1 Innovation Directions

An efficient way to deal with this paradigm addresses a variety of aspects and innovation directions, that we briefly summarise.

The **cultural aspect** is made accessible by resorting to the description of artefacts within domain models, rather than code: the immediacy of understanding of these simple models has a chance to concretise "**what happens when**" (addressing comprehension, structure, documentation, training) and "**what happens if**" (covering simulation and prognosis) to a nearly haptic level. In discussions with engineers, they called the models and elements "blocks" of what happens, that one can assemble and construct in a virtual way but feel concrete and real. The concept of DSLs and domain specific Palettes of features and native SIBs in DIME covers this aspect in an intuitive way.

The **code aspect** is addressed by separating the (application specific or reusable) "logic" from the implementation of the operations and the system. What's native is system-side, and it encapsulates and integrates what's already there, reusing it and making it better understandable. Models, simulation environments, tools and machines, but also AI tools, visualisation tools and communication networks, IoT devices etc come with APIs amenable to the DSL transformation and integration as we just illustrated for the UR3. Here, the service oriented computing embraced by DIME and its underlying integration paradigm leverages component based design together with a high level description of the interfaces and properties of the components.

The **testing aspect** is streamlined and anticipated in the design lifecycle by choosing modelling languages that facilitate an early stage "checking" of the model structure, of the architectural and behavioural compatibilities. This is happening at the Digital Twin level with the choice of adequate simulation languages and environments. There is an interest spike for SysML due to the influence of the traditional UML community on the software engineering mainstream, but not without critics due to the heterogeneity and heavy weight approach to modelling it imposes. This is perceived as costly and bulky, so there is interest for lighter alternatives. On the software side, Architecture Analysis and Description Languages (AADLs) cover the architectural and static aspects, while the use of formal models like the KTS used in jABC [36], DIME [5] and in general graph-based models supported by Cinco [43] allow also a behavioural analysis. Early analysis capabilities, e.g. by model checking on the kind of models DIME provides, and in some cases a correct-by-construction synthesis of property-conform models seem to be useful to deliver the "speed" of early detection and even avoidance of errors that makes the successive testing on the (mostly generated) code much faster.

The **dissemination and adoption aspect** is going to be taken care of by sharing such models, for example within the Confirm community of practice. Such models are understandable to the domain experts, and to a good extent (at the level of the processes and features) independent of the specific technology of a vendor. In several cases it would be possible to share also the implementations of the building blocks, at the level of Native DSLs, using for instance Open

Source Software facilities and structures [64]. Libraries of services have been in use in the telecommunication domain since the '80s [59], they are increasingly in use in bioinformatics, geo-information systems, and are slowly taking a center stage attention also in the advanced manufacturing community, albeit mostly still in form of reference architectures and shared component models for which standards need to be developed.

The **speed to change** is accelerated by using generative approaches that transform the models into lower level descriptions, possibly into code. The speed and quality advantage of this demo in comparison with a handcrafted programmed version was immediately evident to all the non-software engineers who saw it. The core engine for this is the generative approach from models to code, and - also an aspect that arose by itself - to re-targetable code. In jABC, Cinco and DIME we use both model-to-model and model-to-code transformations, starting from the Genesys approach of [19] and [17], up to the generalized approach that Cinco adopts also at the tool metalevel [43].

The **rich description** of the single components, data, and applications is achieved by means of both domain-independent and domain-specific knowledge about the functionalities, the data and business objects, and the application's requirements and quality profile, as in language-oriented programming [11,66] or language-driven engineering [51]. The variety of vendor-specific robot programming languages, the individual APIs coming with sensors, actuators and IoT devices, in spite of standardisation efforts, are a well known obstacle to interoperability. The ease of mapping from abstract DSLs to native DSLs, via code or also via smaller adapter processes that manage the data and protocol adaptation, is possible and already experienced in DIME. It could bring here a significant relief.

The **scalability and speed of education** are supported by teaching domain specialists to deal with these domain specific models, their analysis and composition, and the validation using tools that exploit the domain-specific and contextual knowledge to detect the suitability or not of the current version of the application's models for solving a certain problem in a certain (regulatory, technological, economic) context. We have had successes in the context of school pupils, postgraduate students with a background in biology and geography [21]. We are now creating an online course that will provide a gentle introduction to these models and a number of e-tivities so that professionals and students alike will be able to self-pace and gain experience in the use of these models.

The **quick evolution** is delivered by means of integrated design environments that support the collaboration of all the professional profiles and stakeholders on the same set of models and descriptions, as in the XMDD [38,42] and One Thing Approach [39,62], applied to models of systems and of test cases [47].

The **structuring approaches** are based e.g. on hierarchy [54,55,58], on several notions of features like in [7,16,20,56], or contracts for abstraction and compositionality as in [14]. These structures allow a nice and incremental factoring of well characterised system components.This factoring aides the hierarchical and collaborative organisation of complex or large systems, while supporting the intuition of the domain experts. It also supports finding, maybe in approximations, the most opportune units of reuse (for development, evolution and testing), and units of localised responsibility, e.g. for maintenance, evolution and support.

4.2 Experiential Evidence so Far

We used DIME, Cinco or its predecessors in a large number of industry projects, research projects, and educational settings. Various aspects of the overall picture needed in a suitable and mature integrated modelling environment for the digital thread have been already exercised in those context. They focussed mostly on a single or a small number of aspects, due to the focus of the respective project, while a Confirm digital Thread platform would be required to match and surpass them all. Still, it is useful to summarise what we know that we can do.

The acceptance of formality as a means to clarify interfaces, behaviours and properties and as a precondition to verify and prevent, instead of implementing, testing, and then repairing case by case, is essential to meet the challenges and demands for the future platforms of IT provision and use. In this sense, we need both Archimedean points [63] and future oriented knowledge management for change management [31] for the fundamental attention to usability by non-IT specialists. With this work, we intend to leverage the XMDD approach [38,42] and the previous work on evolution-oriented software engineering, under the aspect of simplicity [41] and continuous systems engineering [40] especially from the perspective of reconciling domain experts and software professionals [30]. Models with a formal underpinning are likely to be central to the wish of many manufacturers to be able to reconfigure production, which demands simplicity and predictability in evolution and reconfiguration.

We build upon over a decade of previous experiences gathered in various application domains. Specifically, our own work in scientific workflows summarized in [27] included experiences gathered from the initial projects in 2006 [33] to building platforms for the access to complex genetic data manipulations in the bioinformatics domain (the Bio-jETI platform of [23,34] and the agile Gene-Fisher-P [24]). These platforms, and other similar experiences in geo-information systems, have proven that we are able to create platforms that virtualise and render interoperable collections of third-party services and tools that were not designed for interoperability. This happened with essentially the technology exemplified in the tiny UR3 remote controller. We hope that this previous experience may raise in manufacturing designers and producers the confidence that such a platform is indeed feasible also for the Digital Thread.

The tools we intend to use span from the Cinco-products [43] DIME and DyWA to the most work on DSLs for decision services [12]. The availability of well characterised service collections makes a semantic web-like approach feasible for these DSLs: their classification in terms of taxonomies and labelled properties brings semantics and semantics-based composition within reach. In these respects, we have a long experience of modelling, integration, and synthesis [35,37,60] up to entire synthesis-based platforms and applications [25,26] as well as benchmark generation platforms [52]. The domain specific knowledge captured in native DSLs and their taxonomic classification as well as the feature-level DSLs and collections of properties may in fact lead to synthesizable workflows and processes within the Digital Thread.

We have experience of various tool integration techniques [29] and service integration platforms, and in the Semantic Web Challenge [48,49]. This past experience has taught that various technology choices in the interfaces, design choices in and degrees of uniformity in the structure and presentation of APIs make a huge difference in the degree of automation of producing native DSLs from such native libraries and APIs. Here we expect unfortunately a large manual effort, as from the current experience with the IoT devices, sensors and actuators we expect to need bespoke solutions for each device, manufacturer, and constant changes across a product's evolution. Interfaces and APIs design appear today in fact almost accidental, they are at the moment one of the most severely undermanaged assets in the Industry 4.0 landscape.

We used features for a long time to model variability [20], introduced various categories of constraints to define structural and behavioural aspects of variability [18] and provided constraint-driven safe service customization adapting features to various contexts [6], up to higher order processes in [46]. On the effects of knowledge on testing, we addressed specifically efficient regression testing supported by models [15] and the hybrid test of web applications with various tools and approaches [50]. We used many techniques that leverage the mathematical nature of the models in order to prove the correctness of the dataflow [22], the control flow [3], the use of games to enhance diagnosis capabilities in model-driven verification [4]. We expect these techniques to be applicable also to the Digital Twin integration in a Digital Thread, and we expect that their impact on shorter design times (i.e., quick prototyping and validation of a new application) and increased quality (i.e. less testing) will lead to a significant speed up in comparison with the current patchwork of ad-hoc code.

We are convinced that all these abilities will be essential for the realisation of an integrated, efficient and correct Digital Thread for the connected and evolving industrial critical systems of tomorrow, to achieve true *Sustainable Computing in Continuous Engineering*[1] platforms for Industry 4.0.

Acknowledgments. Thanks are due to Romain Poussin and Jean-Baptiste Chanier, who implemented the Proof of Concept of the UR3 Controller demo.

This work was supported, in part, by Science Foundation Ireland grant 16/RC/3918 and co-funded under the European Regional Development Fund through the Southern & Eastern Regional Operational Programme to Confirm, the Smart Manufacturing SFI Research Centre (www.confirm.ie).

[1] For SCCE see https://scce.info.

References

1. Asirelli, P., ter Beek, M.H., Gnesi, S., Fantechi, A.: Formal description of variability in product families. In: 15th International Software Product Line Conference (SPLC 2011), pp. 130–139 (2011)
2. Bacchiega, G.: Creating an embedded digital twin: monitor, understand and predict device health failure. In: Inn4mech - Mechatronics and Industry 4.0 Conference Presentation (2018). https://irsweb.it/pdf/Embedded_Digital%20Twin_v2.pdf
3. Bakera, M., Margaria, T., Renner, C., Steffen, B.: Verification, diagnosis and adaptation: tool-supported enhancement of the model-driven verification process. In: Revue des Nouvelles Technologies de l'Information (RNTI-SM-1), pp. 85–98, December 2007
4. Bakera, M., Margaria, T., Renner, C., Steffen, B.: Tool-supported enhancement of diagnosis in model-driven verification. Innov. Syst. Softw. Eng. **5**, 211–228 (2009). https://doi.org/10.1007/s11334-009-0091-6
5. Boßelmann, S., et al.: DIME: a programming-less modeling environment for web applications. In: Margaria, T., Steffen, B. (eds.) ISoLA 2016. LNCS, vol. 9953, pp. 809–832. Springer, Cham (2016). https://doi.org/10.1007/978-3-319-47169-3_60
6. Braun, V., Margaria, T., Steffen, B., Yoo, H., Rychly, T.: Safe service customization. In: Intelligent Network Workshop, IN 1997, vol. 2, p. 4. IEEE, May 1997
7. Buckley, J., Rosik, J., Herold, S., Wasala, A., Botterweck, G., Exton, C.: FLINTS: a tool for architectural-level modeling of features in software systems. In: Proceedings of the 10th European Conference on Software Architecture Workshops, ECSAW 2016, pp. 14:1–14:7. ACM, New York (2016). https://doi.org/10.1145/2993412.3003390
8. Chhetri, M.B., Krishnaswamy, S., Loke, S.W.: Smart virtual counterparts for learning communities. In: Bussler, C., et al. (eds.) Web Information Systems - WISE 2004 Workshops WISE 2004. LNCS, vol. 3307, pp. 125–134. Springer, Heidelberg (2004). https://doi.org/10.1007/978-3-540-30481-4_12
9. Classen, A., Heymans, P., Schobbens, P.Y., Legay, A., Raskin, J.F.: Model checking lots of systems: efficient verification of temporal properties in software product lines. In: Proceedings of the 32nd ACM/IEEE International Conference on Software Engineering - Volume 1, ICSE 2010, pp. 335–344. ACM, New York (2010). https://doi.org/10.1145/1806799.1806850
10. Codeless, Platforms: Codeless platforms homepage. Technical report, ex Orbis Software (2019). https://www.codelessplatforms.com
11. Dmitriev, S.: Language oriented programming: the next programming paradigm. JetBrains onBoard Online Magazine(2004). http://www.onboard.jetbrains.com/is1/articles/04/10/lop/
12. Gossen, F., Margaria, T., Murtovi, A., Naujokat, S., Steffen, B.: DSLs for decision services: a tutorial introduction to language-driven engineering. In: Margaria, T., Steffen, B. (eds.) ISoLA 2018. LNCS, vol. 11244, pp. 546–564. Springer, Cham (2018). https://doi.org/10.1007/978-3-030-03418-4_33
13. Gould, L.S.: What are digital twins and digital threads? (2018)
14. Graf, S., Quinton, S., Girault, A., Gössler, G.: Building correct cyber-physical systems: why we need a multiview contract theory. In: Howar, F., Barnat, J. (eds.) FMICS 2018. LNCS, vol. 11119, pp. 19–31. Springer, Cham (2018). https://doi.org/10.1007/978-3-030-00244-2_2
15. Hagerer, A., Margaria, T., Niese, O., Steffen, B., Brune, G., Ide, H.D.: Efficient regression testing of CTI-systems: testing a complex call-center solution. Ann. Rev. Commun. Int. Eng. Consortium (IEC) **55**, 1033–1040 (2001)

16. Jonsson, B., Margaria, T., Naeser, G., Nyström, J., Steffen, B.: Incremental requirement specification for evolving systems. Nordic J. Comput. **8**, 65–87 (2001). http://dl.acm.org/citation.cfm?id=774194.774199
17. Jörges, S.: Construction and Evolution of Code Generators. LNCS, vol. 7747. Springer, Heidelberg (2013). https://doi.org/10.1007/978-3-642-36127-2
18. Jörges, S., Lamprecht, A.L., Margaria, T., Schaefer, I., Steffen, B.: A constraint-based variability modeling framework. Int. J. Softw. Tools Technol. Transf. (STTT) **14**(5), 511–530 (2012)
19. Jörges, S., Margaria, T., Steffen, B.: Genesys: service-oriented construction of property conform code generators. Innov. Syst. Softw. Eng. **4**(4), 361–384 (2008)
20. Karusseit, M., Margaria, T.: Feature-based modelling of a complex, online-reconfigurable decision support service. Electron. Notes Theor. Comput. Sci. **157**(2), 101–118 (2006). http://www.sciencedirect.com/science/article/pii/S1571066106002489
21. Lamprecht, A.-L., Margaria, T. (eds.): Process Design for Natural Scientists. CCIS, vol. 500. Springer, Heidelberg (2014). https://doi.org/10.1007/978-3-662-45006-2
22. Lamprecht, A.-L., Margaria, T., Steffen, B.: Data-flow analysis as model checking within the jABC. In: Mycroft, A., Zeller, A. (eds.) CC 2006. LNCS, vol. 3923, pp. 101–104. Springer, Heidelberg (2006). https://doi.org/10.1007/11688839_9
23. Lamprecht, A.L., Margaria, T., Steffen, B.: Bio-jETI: a framework for semantics-based service composition. BMC Bioinf. **10**(Suppl. 10), S8 (2009)
24. Lamprecht, A.L., et al.: variations of GeneFisher as processes in Bio-jETI. BMC Bioinf. **9**(Suppl. 4), S13 (2008). http://www.ncbi.nlm.nih.gov/pubmed/18460174
25. Lamprecht, A.L., Naujokat, S., Margaria, T., Steffen, B.: Synthesis-based loose programming. In: Proceedings of the 7th International Conference on the Quality of Information and Communications Technology (QUATIC 2010), Porto, Portugal, pp. 262–267. IEEE, September 2010
26. Lamprecht, A.L., Naujokat, S., Margaria, T., Steffen, B.: Semantics-based composition of EMBOSS services. J. Biomed. Seman. **2**(Suppl. 1), S5 (2011). http://www.jbiomedsem.com/content/2/S1/S5
27. Lamprecht, A., Steffen, B., Margaria, T.: Scientific workflows with the jABC framework - a review after a decade in the field. STTT **18**(6), 629–651 (2016). https://doi.org/10.1007/s10009-016-0427-0
28. Margaria, T.: Components, features, and agents in the ABC. In: Ryan, M.D., Meyer, J.-J.C., Ehrich, H.-D. (eds.) Objects, Agents, and Features. LNCS, vol. 2975, pp. 154–174. Springer, Heidelberg (2004). https://doi.org/10.1007/978-3-540-25930-5_10
29. Margaria, T.: Web services-based tool-integration in the ETI platform. Softw. Syst. Model. **4**(2), 141–156 (2005). https://doi.org/10.1007/s10270-004-0072-z
30. Margaria, T.: Service is in the eyes of the beholder. IEEE Comput. **40**(11), 33–37 (2007)
31. Margaria, T.: Knowledge management for inclusive system evolution. In: Steffen, B. (ed.) Transactions on Foundations for Mastering Change I. LNCS, vol. 9960, pp. 7–21. Springer, Cham (2016). https://doi.org/10.1007/978-3-319-46508-1_2
32. Margaria, T.: Generative model driven design for agile system design and evolution: a tale of two worlds. In: Howar, F., Barnat, J. (eds.) FMICS 2018. LNCS, vol. 11119, pp. 3–18. Springer, Cham (2018). https://doi.org/10.1007/978-3-030-00244-2_1
33. Margaria, T., Kubczak, C., Njoku, M., Steffen, B.: Model-based design of distributed collaborative bioinformatics processes in the jABC. In: Proceedings of the 11th IEEE International Conference on Engineering of Complex Computer Systems (ICECCS 2006), pp. 169–176. IEEE Computer Society, Los Alamitos, August 2006

34. Margaria, T., Kubczak, C., Steffen, B.: Bio-jETI: a service integration, design, and provisioning platform for orchestrated bioinformatics processes. BMC Bioinf. **9**(Suppl 4), S12 (2008)
35. Margaria, T., Steffen, B.: Backtracking-free design planning by automatic synthesis in metaframe. In: Astesiano, E. (ed.) FASE 1998. LNCS, vol. 1382, pp. 188–204. Springer, Heidelberg (1998). https://doi.org/10.1007/BFb0053591
36. Margaria, T., Steffen, B.: Lightweight coarse-grained coordination: a scalable system-level approach. Softw. Tools Technol. Transf. **5**(2–3), 107–123 (2004)
37. Margaria, T., Steffen, B.: LTL-guided planning: revisiting automatic tool composition in ETI. In: Proceedings of the 31st Annual IEEE/NASA Software Engineering Workshop (SEW 2007), Columbia, MD, USA, pp. 214–226. IEEE Computer Society (2007). http://portal.acm.org/citation.cfm?id=1338445.1338873&coll=GUIDE&dl=GUIDE
38. Margaria, T., Steffen, B.: Agile IT: thinking in user-centric models. In: Margaria, T., Steffen, B. (eds.) ISoLA 2008. CCIS, vol. 17, pp. 490–502. Springer, Heidelberg (2008). https://doi.org/10.1007/978-3-540-88479-8_35
39. Margaria, T., Steffen, B.: Business process modelling in the jABC: the one-thing-approach. In: Cardoso, J., van der Aalst, W. (eds.) Handbook of Research on Business Process Modeling. IGI Global (2009)
40. Margaria, T., Steffen, B.: Continuous model-driven engineering. IEEE Comput. **42**(10), 106–109 (2009)
41. Margaria, T., Steffen, B.: Simplicity as a driver for agile innovation. Computer **43**(6), 90–92 (2010)
42. Margaria, T., Steffen, B.: Service-orientation: conquering complexity with XMDD. In: Hinchey, M., Coyle, L. (eds.) Conquering Complexity, pp. 217–236. Springer, London (2012). https://doi.org/10.1007/978-1-4471-2297-5_10
43. Naujokat, S., Lybecait, M., Kopetzki, D., Steffen, B.: CINCO: a simplicity-driven approach to full generation of domain-specific graphical modeling tools. Softw. Tools Technol. Transf. **20**(2), 1–28 (2017)
44. Naujokat, S., Neubauer, J., Lamprecht, A.L., Steffen, B., Jörges, S., Margaria, T.: Simplicity-first model-based plug-in development. Softw. Pract. Exp. **44**(3), 277–297 (2013)
45. Neubauer, J., Frohme, M., Steffen, B., Margaria, T.: Prototype-driven development of web applications with DyWA. In: Margaria, T., Steffen, B. (eds.) ISoLA 2014. LNCS, vol. 8802, pp. 56–72. Springer, Heidelberg (2014). https://doi.org/10.1007/978-3-662-45234-9_5
46. Neubauer, J., Steffen, B., Margaria, T.: Higher-order process modeling: product-lining, variability modeling and beyond. Electron. Proc. Theor. Comput. Sci. **129**, 259–283 (2013)
47. Niese, O., Steffen, B., Margaria, T., Hagerer, A., Brune, G., Ide, H.-D.: Library-based design and consistency checking of system-level industrial test cases. In: Hussmann, H. (ed.) FASE 2001. LNCS, vol. 2029, pp. 233–248. Springer, Heidelberg (2001). https://doi.org/10.1007/3-540-45314-8_17
48. Petrie, C., Küster, U., Margaria, T., Zaremba, M., Lausen, H., Komazec, S.: Status, perspectives, and lessons learned. In: Semantic Web Services Challenge, Results from the First Year, pp. 275–284 (2009). https://doi.org/10.1007/978-0-387-72496-6_17
49. Petrie, C., Margaria, T., Lausen, H., Zaremba, M. (eds.): Semantic Web Services Challenge. Results from the First Year, Semantic Web and Beyond, vol. 8. Springer, US (2009)

50. Raffelt, H., Margaria, T., Steffen, B., Merten, M.: Hybrid test of web applications with webtest. In: TAV-WEB '08: Proceedings of the 2008 Workshop on Testing, Analysis, and Verification of Web Services and Applications, pp. 1–7. ACM, New York (2008)
51. Steffen, B., Gossen, F., Naujokat, S., Margaria, T.: Language-driven engineering: from general-purpose to purpose-specific languages. In: Steffen, B., Woeginger, G. (eds.) Computing and Software Science: State of the Art and Perspectives. LNCS, vol. 10000, pp. 311–344. Springer, Cham (2018). https://doi.org/10.1007/978-3-319-91908-9_17
52. Steffen, B., Isberner, M., Naujokat, S., Margaria, T., Geske, M.: Property-driven benchmark generation: synthesizing programs of realistic structure. Softw. Tools Technol. Transf. **16**(5), 465–479 (2014)
53. Steffen, B., Margaria, T.: METAFrame in practice: design of intelligent network services. In: Olderog, E.-R., Steffen, B. (eds.) Correct System Design. LNCS, vol. 1710, pp. 390–415. Springer, Heidelberg (1999). https://doi.org/10.1007/3-540-48092-7_17
54. Steffen, B., Margaria, T., Braun, V., Kalt, N.: Hierarchical service definition. Ann. Rev. Commun. ACM **51**, 847–856 (1997)
55. Steffen, B., Margaria, T., Claßen, A.: Heterogeneous analysis and verification for distributed systems. Softw. Concepts Tools **17**(1), 13–25 (1996)
56. Steffen, B., Margaria, T., Claßen, A., Braun, V.: Incremental formalization: a key to industrial success. Softw. Concepts Tools **17**(2), 78–95 (1996)
57. Steffen, B., Margaria, T., Claßen, A., Braun, V.: The METAFrame'95 environment. In: CAV, pp. 450–453 (1996)
58. Steffen, B., Margaria, T., Claßen, A., Braun, V., Nisius, R., Reitenspieß, M.: A constraint-oriented service creation environment. In: Margaria, T., Steffen, B. (eds.) TACAS 1996. LNCS, vol. 1055, pp. 418–421. Springer, Heidelberg (1996). https://doi.org/10.1007/3-540-61042-1_63
59. Steffen, B., Margaria, T., Claßen, A., Braun, V., Reitenspieß, M.: An environment for the creation of intelligent network services. In: Intelligent Networks: IN/AIN Technologies, Operations, Services and Applications - A Comprehensive Report, pp. 287–300. IEC: International Engineering Consortium (1996)
60. Steffen, B., Margaria, T., Freitag, B.: Module Configuration by Minimal Model Construction. Technical report, Fakultät für Mathematik und Informatik, Universität Passau (1993)
61. Steffen, B., Margaria, T., Nagel, R., Jörges, S., Kubczak, C.: Model-driven development with the jABC. In: Bin, E., Ziv, A., Ur, S. (eds.) HVC 2006. LNCS, vol. 4383, pp. 92–108. Springer, Heidelberg (2007). https://doi.org/10.1007/978-3-540-70889-6_7
62. Steffen, B., Narayan, P.: Full life-cycle support for end-to-end processes. IEEE Comput. **40**(11), 64–73 (2007)
63. Steffen, B., Naujokat, S.: Archimedean points: the essence for mastering change. LNCS Trans. Found. Mastering Change (FoMaC) **1**(1), 22–46 (2016)
64. Steinmacher, I., Robles, G., Fitzgerald, B., Wasserman, A.I.: Free and open source software development: the end of the teenage years. J. Internet Serv. Appl. **8**(1), 17:1–17:4 (2017). https://doi.org/10.1186/s13174-017-0069-9
65. Talkhestani, B.A., Jung, T., Lindemann, B., et al.: An architecture of an intelligent digital twin in a cyber-physical production system. Automatisierungstechnik **67**(9), 762–782. 101515/auto-2019-0039 2019
66. Ward, M.P.: Language oriented programming. Softw. Concepts Tools **15**(4), 147–161 (1994)

67. Wikipedia: Digital twin - including 10 definitions. https://en.wikipedia.org/wiki/Digital_twin
68. Wortmann, N., Michel, M., Naujokat, S.: A fully model-based approach to software development for industrial centrifuges. In: Margaria, T., Steffen, B. (eds.) ISoLA 2016. LNCS, vol. 9953, pp. 774–783. Springer, Cham (2016). https://doi.org/10.1007/978-3-319-47169-3_58

Regular Papers

Accelerating Parameter Synthesis Using Semi-algebraic Constraints

Nikola Beneš, Luboš Brim, Martin Geletka, Samuel Pastva(✉), and David Šafránek

Faculty of Informatics, Masaryk University, Brno, Czech Republic
{xbenes3,brim,xgeletka,xpastva,safranek}@fi.muni.cz

Abstract. We propose a novel approach to parameter synthesis for parametrised Kripke structures and CTL specifications. In our method, we suppose the parametrisations form a semi-algebraic set and we utilise a symbolic representation using the so-called cylindrical algebraic decomposition of corresponding multivariate polynomials. Specifically, we propose a new data structure allowing to compute and efficiently manipulate such representations. The new method is significantly faster than our previous method based on SMT. We apply the method to a set of rational dynamical systems representing complex biological mechanisms with non-linear behaviour.

Keywords: Parameter synthesis · Semi-algebraic set · CTL

1 Introduction

Computer-aided analysis of complex dynamical phenomena in real-world systems such as biological, biophysical processes, or networks involving economic and social interactions is inevitable for getting their understanding and enabling control of such systems. Formal methods make a necessary precursor for the robust design of reliable cyber-physical and cyber-biological systems such as synthetic design and control of living cells [33] or safe medical treatment [1].

Complex cyber-physical systems are typically formalised by means of *dynamical* or *hybrid systems* employing the framework of non-linear ordinary differential equations (ODE) that are highly parametrised. Parameters appear in functions determining the systems dynamics (defining the time derivatives of systems variables). In most cases, the model complexity, the number of *unknown parameters*, and the *non-linear dependency* of a system on these parameters do not allow to employ analytical methods. To that end, it seems to be unavoidable to develop and use fully automated (mechanised) formal methods to analyse such systems.

Phenomena occurring in the time domain of systems dynamics can be encoded in *temporal logics* (TL). TL allow a rigorous and abstract representation of the sequences of desired observable events in systems dynamics including

This work has been supported by the Czech Science Foundation grant No. 18-00178S.

W. Ahrendt and S. L. Tapia Tarifa (Eds.): IFM 2019, LNCS 11918, pp. 27–45, 2019.
https://doi.org/10.1007/978-3-030-34968-4_2

quantitative bounds on time and variable values [7,12,31] and can be combined with frequency-domain analysis [24]. Here, we work with the branching-time logic CTL.

A powerful formal verification method allowing algorithmic checking whether a system satisfies a given TL specification is *model checking*. In case of parametrised systems, model checking cannot be directly applied since the number of different settings of parameter values grows combinatorially with the number of unknown parameters and can be in general infinite (or even uncountable). To that end, several techniques of so-called *parameter synthesis* have been developed [5,7,11,14,20,23] allowing to compute (with exact or statistical guarantees) *all* parameter values that satisfy a given TL specification.

Discrete abstractions [3,7,21,28] are employed to work with finite quotients encoded as Kripke structures (KS), over-approximating the continuous state space. An important additional aspect of parameter synthesis methods for dynamical systems is the need to represent uncountable sets of parameter values symbolically. A parametrised dynamical system is abstractly captured by using a *parametrised Kripke structure* (PKS) that extends the standard KS with a parametrised transition relation. Abstraction techniques are typically complemented with some symbolic representation of parameters, e.g., in terms of BDDs (Binary Decision Diagrams) [6] (discrete parameters); intervals [4], first order real arithmetic formulae processed using Satisfiability Modulo Theories (SMT) [8] or polytopes [7,26] (continuous parameters). The role of such representations is to capture the system *parametrisation* (a mapping of parameters to values) with a compact encoding reflecting exactly the precision of the employed abstraction. Our algorithm presented in [8] employs a *semi-symbolic approach* – an explicit representation of KS is combined with a symbolic SMT-based representation of parameters.

There is a trade-off between the expressiveness of the chosen parameter representation and the complexity of basic operations performed over this representation. As an example, consider the interval-based representation [4] of parameter values, which allows for very efficient operation while disallowing parameter interdependency. In the case of polytopic representations [7,26], the operations are more computationally challenging, while linear parameter interdependencies are allowed; they are restricted to linear as each polytope has to have "flat" faces. Examples from the other side of the spectrum include the SMT-based approaches [8]. The encoding of parameter valuations into first-order formulae is very flexible but often results in very complex formulae challenging for the SMT solvers. The existing solutions to simplify SMT reasoning [17,27,29] are not yet well-established and do not significantly help. Furthermore, interpretation and visualisation of synthesis results can be difficult for such representations.

In this paper, we consider *semi-algebraic sets* of parametrisations. A semi-algebraic set can be defined as a finite sequence of intersections and unions of polynomial equalities and inequalities. Possible representations of semi-algebraic sets have been explored for example in [15,16]. These representations cover a wide-range of parametrised systems as they allow for arbitrary polynomial parameter interdependencies. Our method is based on *cylindrical algebraic decomposition (CAD)* [2], a general method used to represent semi-algebraic sets by decomposing the domain into sign-invariant regions. Additionally, we focus on open sets, which makes the problem computationally easier [37].

The key contribution of this paper is a *novel symbolic representation of parameters* in a PKS in terms of *semi-algebraic sets*. The representation provides a compact symbolic encoding of uncountable parameter sets and it allows to efficiently handle all operations used during parameter synthesis. The system dynamics can be *any rational polynomial function of the parameters*. To implement this concept, we design a flexible data structure – the *reduced cylindrical algebraic decomposition tree* – that forms the basis of our data-parallel semi-symbolic algorithm for parameter synthesis of PKSs with respect to a given CTL specification. Finally, we show that the method is significantly faster than our previous algorithm based on SMT [8]. We compare both approaches on real-world dynamical systems studied in cancer research and synthetic biology.

Possible applications of CAD to the analysis of dynamical systems, in particular to interrupt timed automata, have been considered in [10]. In our approach, we consider more general systems where the derivatives can be any rational polynomial functions, in contrast to timed automata where the derivatives are constant.

It is worth noting that monitoring based techniques [12,23,35,36] and linear-time TL have an advantage of considering the function defining the systems dynamics as a black box. This implies there is no limitation on the form of parametrisation. However, the main drawback of monitoring is the need to sample the parameter space while losing exact guarantees for the results. This drawback can be overcome by replacing numerical solvers with SMT solvers that can cope with non-linear functions and real domains up to required precision [25]. However, these techniques are limited to reachability analysis [30] and their extension to general TL specifications is a non-trivial task yet to be explored.

2 CTL Parameter Synthesis

In this section, we define the notion of parametrised Kripke structures and state the parameter synthesis problem for computation tree logic properties. Finally, we describe an adapted parallel lock-free algorithm which solves the problem.

In this paper, we consider the parametrised Kripke structure as a means of describing a finite state abstraction of continuous systems dynamics. In particular, we employ the method of rectangular abstraction [7]. The rectangular abstraction allows to conservatively transform a continuous-time dynamical system into a finite transition system that simulates the behaviour of the continuous system. The class of systems that can be abstracted that way is called piece-wise multi-affine (the derivative of the state variable x is required to be a piece-wise multi-affine function of x).

The abstraction is based on partitioning the bounded space of the (continuous) state variable into a finite set of adjacent regions. These regions induce a finite state space of the resulting transition system. Transitions are determined by evaluating the derivatives of the continuous state variable at the regions' vertices. In a parametrised system, the state variable partitioning induces a finite partitioning of the parametrisations into equivalence classes. Parametrisations in a given class form the same transition system. If the systems dynamics of each variable is given as a linear function of a single parameter (possibly different for each variable), the parametrisations' partitioning is rectangular (every equivalence class is a product of parameter intervals). Complex dependencies among parameters lead to non-regular shapes of the parametrisations' partitioning.

Definition 1. *Let AP be a set of* atomic propositions. *A* Parametrised Kripke Structure *(PKS) over AP is a tuple $K = (P, S, I, R, L)$ where:*

- *P is a set of parametrisations;*
- *S is a finite set of discrete states;*
- *$I \subseteq S$ is a set of initial states;*
- *$R \subseteq S \times P \times S$ is a total transition relation, meaning that for every $s \in S$ and $p \in P$, there exists $t \in S$ such that $(s, p, t) \in R$.*
- *$L : S \to 2^{AP}$ is a labelling of states with atomic propositions.*

We write $P(s,t)$ to denote the set of all parametrisations that allow the transition from s to t, i.e. $P(s,t) = \{p \in P \mid (s,p,t) \in R\}$. We also define $\mathtt{post}(s) = \{t \in S \mid \exists p \in P : (s,p,t) \in R\}$ and $\mathtt{pre}(t) = \{s \in S \mid \exists p \in P : (s,p,t) \in R\}$.

A set $X \subseteq \mathbb{R}^n$ is called *semi-algebraic* if it can be defined as a finite sequence of intersections and unions of polynomial equalities and inequalities (and is thus finitely representable). In the following definition, we introduce the class of semi-algebraic PKSs in which the parametrisations enabling any given transition are represented in terms of semi-algebraic sets.

Definition 2. *We say that a PKS $K = (P, S, I, R, L)$ is* semi-algebraic *(*has semi-algebraic parameter constraints*) if P is a product of n intervals $P = (a_1, b_1) \times \ldots \times (a_n, b_n)$ (*a rectangular set*) for some n, and for every s, $t \in S$, $P(s,t)$ is a semi-algebraic set.*

It is worth noting that PKSs obtained by using the rectangular abstraction procedure [7] can be directly considered (by construction) as semi-algebraic PKSs.

Fixing a parametrisation $p \in P$ reduces the PKS to a standard Kripke Structure $K_p = (S, I, R_p, L)$ where $R_p = \{(s,t) \mid (s,p,t) \in R\}$. A PKS can also be viewed as a Kripke Structure where the transitions are labelled with $P(s,t)$.

We use the standard branching time logic CTL to specify behaviour of PKSs. The abstract syntax of CTL formulae is defined as follows:

$$\varphi ::= a \mid \mathtt{tt} \mid \neg\varphi \mid \varphi_1 \wedge \varphi_2 \mid \mathbf{AX}\,\varphi \mid \mathbf{EX}\,\varphi \mid \mathbf{A}(\varphi_1\,\mathbf{U}\,\varphi_2) \mid \mathbf{E}(\varphi_1\,\mathbf{U}\,\varphi_2)$$

Here, a is an atomic proposition over AP. Additionally, we write $\mathbf{EF}\,\varphi \equiv \mathbf{E}(\mathtt{tt}\,\mathbf{U}\,\varphi)$, $\mathbf{AF}\,\varphi \equiv \mathbf{A}(\mathtt{tt}\,\mathbf{U}\,\varphi)$, $\mathbf{EG}\,\varphi \equiv \neg\,\mathbf{AF}\,\neg\varphi$, and $\mathbf{AG}\,\varphi \equiv \neg\,\mathbf{EF}\,\neg\varphi$

```
function SYNTHESIS(K, φ)
| for ψ_i ∈ sub(φ) do PROCESS(ψ_i)

function
  PROCESS(φ = A(φ_1 U φ_2))
| ∀s ∈ S : F_φ(s) ← F_φ2(s)
| W ← {s | F_φ2(s) ≠ ∅}
| parallel do
| | while t ← W.next() do
| | | for s ∈ pre(t) do
| | | | P ← ⋂_{t'∈post(s)} F_φ(t')
| | | | P ← P ∩ F_φ1(s) ∩ P(s,t)
| | | | UPDATE(φ, s, P, W)
| while not termination

function
  PROCESS(φ = E(φ_1 U φ_2))
| ∀s ∈ S : F_φ(s) ← F_φ2(s)
| W ← {s | F_φ2(s) ≠ ∅}
| parallel do
| | while t ← W.next() do
| | | for s ∈ pre(t) do
| | | | P ← F_φ(t) ∩ F_φ1(s) ∩ P(s,t)
| | | | UPDATE(φ, s, P, W)
| while not termination

function UPDATE(φ, s, P, W)
| do
| | Q ← F_φ(s)
| | if P ⊆ Q then return
| | P' ← P ∪ Q
| while ¬CaS(F_φ(s), Q, P')
| W.insert(s)
```

Fig. 1. Semi-symbolic parallel parameter synthesis algorithm for CTL.

to define other standard temporal operators. For a formula φ, we define an ordered set of sub-formulae, $sub(\varphi) = \{\psi_1, \ldots, \psi_n\}$, such that the sub-formulae are ordered from smallest to largest. We use $\models$ to denote the standard CTL property satisfaction relation on non-parametrised Kripke structures.

2.1 Parameter Synthesis Problem

Let $K = (P, S, I, R, L)$ be a PKS over a set of atomic propositions AP and φ be a CTL formula over the same AP set. The *parameter synthesis problem* is, given K and φ, to compute a function $\mathcal{F}_\varphi : S \to 2^P$ which assigns to every state of the PKS a subset of the parameter space for which the formula φ holds, formally: $\mathcal{F}_\varphi(s) = \{p \in P \mid (K_p, s) \models \varphi\}$. For easier visualisation and post-processing, one can also be interested in inspecting the set $P(\varphi) = \bigcup_{s \in S} \mathcal{F}_\varphi(s)$, i.e. the set of all parameters for which there is a state in which φ holds.

It is worth noting that in Definition 2 open intervals have been used to define a rectangular set of parametrisations. In fact, we consider an *almost all solution* to the parameter synthesis problem by working with open sets of parametrisations instead of closed sets. The reason for considering open sets is that set operations on open sets are significantly simpler while not harming the precision of the results. Intuitively, the space occupied by the border of a closed set of parametrisations is negligible with respect to the space occupied by its interior. The almost all solution simplification is sufficient in most real-world systems modelling scenarios.

Formally, we say that $\mathcal{F}'_\varphi$ is an *almost all solution to the parameter synthesis problem* if for every state $s \in S$, $\mathcal{F}'_\varphi(s)$ is a subset of $\mathcal{F}_\varphi(s)$ and the set of missing solutions, i.e. $\mathcal{F}_\varphi(s) \setminus \mathcal{F}'_\varphi(s)$, has zero volume in $\mathbb{R}^n$. This means that all full-dimensional subsets of the solution are correctly identified.

2.2 Parallel Lock-Free Algorithm

To solve the parameter synthesis problem, we employ a semi-symbolic approach as proposed in [8]. However, instead of using SMT for representation of parametrisations we utilise semi-algebraic sets. We assume a PKS such that the parameter sets can be represented symbolically with computable operations $\cup$, $\cap$, $\setminus$ and $\subseteq$. We then proceed by computing each $\mathcal{F}_{\psi_i}$ from the smallest to the largest sub-formulae ψ_i of φ. The ordering ensures that when we process ψ_i, synthesis for smaller formulas $\mathcal{F}_{\psi_{<i}}$ is already computed. An overview of the algorithm is given in Fig. 1.

Each operator in the formula is handled using a different parallel lock-free `Process` function. For Boolean operators and **X**, this process is trivial. For **EU** and **AU**, we show the respective algorithms in Fig. 1. We assume that the values of $\mathcal{F}_\varphi$ can be updated atomically using a `CaS` (compare and swap) instruction as is customary for shared-memory architectures. Furthermore, we assume a lock-free set `W` with two methods: `insert` inserts an element into the set, and `next` removes one arbitrary element from the set if available. The outer parallel loop is terminated once `W` is empty and no process is working (the termination condition). This avoids processes terminating prematurely when shortly no work is available.

Finally, note that on line 9, we compute the intersection over all the `post` states of s. For dense transition relations, this can be an expensive operation. However, the systems we encounter in practice typically have a low out-degree so the operation can be computed efficiently. In the case of a dense transition relation, we can reduce the complexity of the repeated updates by caching the partial results of the operation for each state in a tree-like structure. The standard sequential CTL model checking algorithms typically circumvent this problem by translating **AU** to **EG** and solving the formula using decomposition to strongly connected components. However, the problem of parallel SCC decomposition is not known to be solvable in linear time, and for systems with parameters, it can be hard to represent the whole component structure efficiently.

3 Semi-algebraic Sets as Cylindrical Decompositions

In the previous section, we have described a parameter synthesis algorithm for semi-symbolic parametrised Kripke structures. The algorithm relies on the assumption that we can efficiently compute operations over the parametrisation sets such as intersection, union or subset relation.

In this section, we describe how to compute such operations for semi-algebraic sets of parametrisations. In order to present the method rigorously we need some formal mathematical preliminaries.

3.1 Preliminaries

In order to avoid confusion between pairs and open intervals, we use $\langle a, b\rangle$ to denote pairs and write (a, b) for open intervals. In general, we use $\{\ \}$ for sets and $[\![\ ]\!]$ when referring to sequences which can be iterated in a fixed order and accessed using indices. For sequences, we also use $a \cdot b$ as concatenation. We use $|a|$ for both set cardinality and sequence length.

When we talk about the *volume* of a set $A \subseteq \mathbb{R}^n$, we refer to the standard *Lebesgue measure.* We also say that a set is *full-dimensional* if its volume is not zero. Additionally, we call the set A *open* if it does not contain any of its boundary points. Note that a non-empty open set is always full-dimensional.

A *univariate polynomial* p over a *ring* R is an expression $p = a_0 + a_1x + a_2x^2 + \ldots + a_nx^n$ such that $a_i \in R$ are the *coefficients*, x is the *indeterminate* and n is the *degree* of the polynomial. We denote the set of polynomials over R as $R[x]$. Note that $R[x]$ is also a ring. A polynomial $p \in R[x]$ defines a *polynomial function* $p : R \to R$; this can be extended to larger rings compatible with R.

In this paper, when talking about a univariate polynomial p, we typically mean $p \in \mathbb{Q}[x]$ evaluated over $\mathbb{R}$. For such a polynomial, we say that every $r \in \mathbb{R}$ satisfying $p(r) = 0$ is a *root* of the polynomial. While some roots may be rational numbers, in general, one cannot produce a formula describing all real roots of the polynomial exactly. However, one can approximate each root up to arbitrary precision using the technique of *root isolation* [19].

Since $R[x]$ in itself is a ring, we can also talk about *multivariate* polynomials $p \in R[x_1, \ldots, x_n]$ as univariate polynomials over a ring $R[x_1, \ldots, x_{n-1}]$ (i.e. the coefficients of the polynomial are polynomials of smaller dimensionality). Multivariate polynomials can also define functions or subsets of R^n; however, there is no similar root isolation method for $\mathbb{Q}[x_1, \ldots, x_n]$ since the set of "roots" is in general uncountable. In this paper, when we talk about multivariate polynomials, we typically refer to $\mathbb{Q}[x_1, \ldots, x_n]$. For a multivariate polynomial, we also define its *level*, which is the index of the last variable whose degree is greater than zero.

We write $p(s)$ for a polynomial $p \in \mathbb{Q}[x_1, \ldots, x_k]$ and a sequence of rational numbers s to denote the partial evaluation of p in the first $|s|$ variables (if $|s| = k$, the result is a rational number). We assume the existence of a procedure $\texttt{IsolateRoots}(s, L)$ which takes a set of multivariate polynomials $L \subseteq \mathbb{Q}[x_1, \ldots, x_{k+1}]$ where $k = |s|$, evaluates them at the point s (obtaining univariate polynomials) and returns an ordered sequence of their roots. Here, rational roots are given exactly and real roots are given using their isolating intervals. For simplicity, we do not differentiate between the two and we assume that the precision of the isolating interval is automatically adjusted on-the-fly to resolve ambiguities (for example when we compare a root with some rational number that belongs to the original isolating interval). For each such root r, we also define $\texttt{P}(r)$ to be the original polynomial $p \in L$ of which r is the root of.

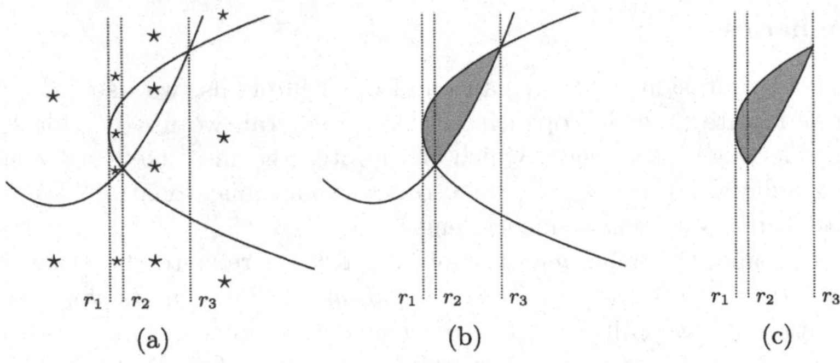

Fig. 2. (a) Example of an open CAD for polynomials $p_1 = (x + \frac{1}{2})^2 - y$ and $p_2 = (y - \frac{3}{4})^2 - x$. The dotted lines are the roots of the discriminant of p_2 and the resultant of p_1 and p_2, separating the four cylinders of the CAD. The stars define the individual open cells. (b) The semi-algebraic set $p_1 < 0$ and $p_2 < 0$, represented by the two CAD cells. (c) A reduced representation of the same set with the unnecessary cells removed.

3.2 Method Overview

Cylindrical Algebraic Decomposition (CAD) [2] is an exhaustive method for solving systems of polynomial inequalities by decomposing $\mathbb{R}^n$ into sign-invariant regions called *cells* $c \in \mathbb{N}_0^n$ (here, each cell is uniquely identified by its n-dimensional index vector) such that for each cell, a *sample point* $s \in \mathbb{R}^n$ (and the corresponding signs of considered polynomials) can be computed. This reduces the problem from uncountable space into a finite set of cells. Unfortunately, CAD is hard to use in practice as the complexity of the algorithm grows double-exponentially with n.

However, as shown in [32] and [37], one can significantly simplify the problem by only considering the open cells of the decomposition. We call such decomposition an *open* CAD (this represents an almost all solution to the satisfiability problem). The key property of the open CAD is that it represents almost all points since the omitted cells are not full-dimensional and therefore have zero volume. Figure 2 shows one such CAD and its usage as a semi-algebraic set representation.

Even in this simple example, we see that the CAD contains redundant information. First, the cylinders (extensions of lower-dimensional open sets to higher dimensions) on the very left and right ($< r_1$ and $> r_3$) contain no valid cells. Second, even for the two middle cylinders, some cells can be merged while preserving the represented set. In the end, we can simplify the set as shown in Fig. 2(c). This effect is even more pronounced if our space is bounded and we can thus eliminate cells and cylinders which fall outside of this bounded region.

Overall, our approach to semi-algebraic set representation can be summarised as follows: We organise the cells of the CAD in a tree, such that the leaves of the tree correspond to the fully determined open subsets. The nodes of the tree then represent the cylinders, each child of a cylinder being a cell in a higher dimension. On this representation, we define how to efficiently perform binary

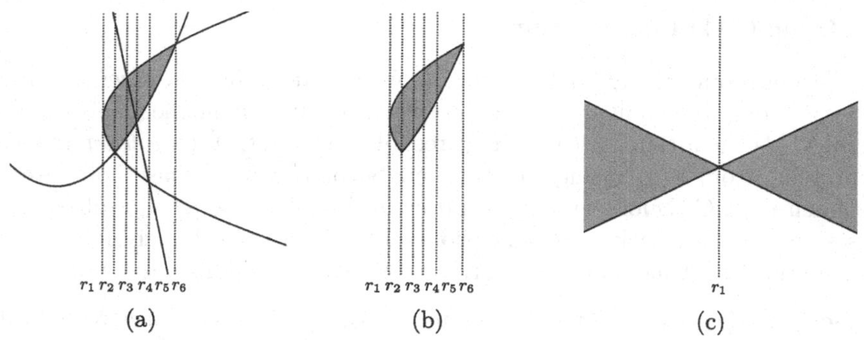

Fig. 3. Simplification criteria for semi-algebraic sets.

set operations and how to safely prune the tree to remove unnecessary cells and polynomials.

When computing binary operations, we have to keep in mind the possible new intersections of the polynomials representing the two sets. We see this situation in Fig. 2. If we consider p_1 alone, the CAD only needs to contain one cylinder with two cells (one below and one above the curve). If we consider p_2 alone, two cylinders separated by r_1 are needed. However, when considering both p_1 and p_2, four cylinders are needed since we also have to inspect their intersection.

After a set operation, our CAD tree can contain unnecessary cells or even cylinders. To prune such cells, we propose two reduction rules:

1. Whenever a cylinder only contains leaves of the same value, the cylinder can be replaced with a leaf of this value.
2. If two neighbouring sub-trees are similar (same tree structure and leaf values), one of them may be redundant. Specifically, a root that separates two sub-trees in the CAD is redundant if it is not an intersection or projection of some higher-dimensional polynomial in these two sub-trees.

In Fig. 3, we show how these rules can be applied. Imagine a semi-algebraic set similar to the one in Fig. 2, but extended with a polynomial $p_3 = 5x + y - \frac{5}{2}$ (Fig. 3(a)). We use the first reduction rule to remove the first and the last cylinder altogether as none of their leaves is in the set. We use the second reduction rule to merge cells in the remaining cylinders which separate equivalent leaves. We obtain a representation shown in Fig. 3(b). By pruning these cells, polynomial p_3 was eliminated. This allows us to apply the second rule again, merging cylinders separated by r_3, r_4 and r_5. Note that even if we were able to only remove some of the cells defined by p_3, it could still allow us to merge some cylinders (those that do not depend on the un-merged cells). It is critical to only merge cylinders which are free of dependencies. In Fig. 3(c), the two cylinders are completely equivalent (they have the same cell structure and same sample points); however, they cannot be merged because r_1 is a root of a dependent polynomial.

3.3 Open CAD Construction

Before we introduce the full data structure, we first describe how a general open CAD is computed to familiarise the reader with the underlying mechanisms. The general CAD algorithm proceeds in three phases: First, a *projection* reduces the problem from n to a single dimension. Second, a *base* phase computes a one-dimensional CAD for the reduced problem. Finally, an *extension* phase generalises the solution back to n dimensions. The description loosely follows the algorithm in [37]. A more detailed correctness analysis can also be found in [2].

Projection. Given a set of polynomials F, the projection phase recursively transforms F to remove variables from the polynomials until the whole system is one-dimensional. As a result, we obtain a sequence $[\![F_1, \ldots, F_n]\!]$ where $F_n = F$ and for each $f \in F_i$, the level of f is at most i. The process relies on projecting the critical points of each polynomial down to the lower dimension. Intuitively, the critical points are the places where the polynomials fold, intersect or form singularities.

Formally, given a set F_k (we assume all polynomials are square-free and relatively prime; if not, we first use multivariate factorisation to remove redundant factors), we define the set F_{k-1} as:

$$F_{k-1} = \{\texttt{ldc}(f) \mid f \in F_k\} \cup \{\texttt{res}(f,g) \mid f,g \in F_k\} \cup \{\texttt{dis}(f) \mid f \in F_k\}$$

Here, `ldc` denotes the leading coefficient of f with respect to variable x_k. By $\texttt{res}(f,g)$, we denote a polynomial *resultant*, i.e. a polynomial expression in $k-1$ variables which is zero iff f and g have a common root (creating an image of intersections between f and g). Finally, $\texttt{dis}(f)$ is a polynomial *discriminant*, i.e. a resultant with its own first derivative (producing an image of the folding points, as these are also zero in the derivative).

Note that for a general CAD, the projection phase typically includes additional items (depending on the specific projection operator) to correctly capture the lower-dimensional intersections and folds. However, this projection operator is sufficient to correctly produce all open cells [37,38].

Base Phase. In the base phase, we construct a one-dimensional open CAD for a set of univariate polynomials F_1 over x_1. We isolate all their roots, obtaining a sequence $r = [\![r_1, \ldots, r_l]\!]$. The open cells of the CAD are then given by the open intervals $(-\infty, r_1), (r_1, r_2), \ldots, (r_l, \infty) = \textsc{CellPairs}(r, (-\infty, \infty))$. Each cell has an ID which is its position within the sequence ($(-\infty, r_1)$ has ID 1, (r_1, r_2) has ID 2, etc.). For each cell c_i, we choose an arbitrary rational sample point s_i from the corresponding interval. Observe that for each cell, polynomials in F_1 are sign-invariant (to change sign, there has to be a root in between). So if a system of polynomial inequalities over F_1 holds in a cell, it has to hold in the whole cell.

Extension Phase. Now that we have a set of $(k-1)$-dimensional open cells $\langle c_i, s_i \rangle$, we construct for each cell a k-dimensional cylinder (extension) to the higher dimension. Let us fix a cell (c_i, s_i) and let $F_k(s_i)$ be the polynomials in

F_k, partially evaluated in the first $k-1$ variables using the sample point s_i. Observe that $F_k(s_i)$ is a set of univariate polynomials over x_k.

We can again compute the sequence of roots $r = [\![r_1, \ldots, r_l]\!]$ for the polynomials in $F_k(s_i)$. This defines a one-dimensional open CAD $[\![\langle 1, s'_1 \rangle, \ldots, \langle l+1, s'_{l+1} \rangle]\!]$. We then extend the $(k-1)$-dimensional cell $\langle c_i, s_i \rangle$ using these $l+1$ one-dimensional cells into a sequence of k-dimensional cells $[\![\langle c_i \cdot 1, s_i \cdot s'_1 \rangle, \ldots, \langle c_i \cdot (l+1), s_i \cdot s'_{l+1} \rangle]\!]$.

The same observations about sign invariance then follow inductively from the sign invariance in the first dimension and the fact that in the $(k-1)$-dimensional cell, the corresponding resultants and discriminants of the k-dimensional polynomials are also sign-invariant. By repeatedly extending each cell up to n dimensions, we can thus obtain sign-invariant open cells together with their sample points. However, in our data structure, we do not want to represent each cell explicitly.

3.4 Reduced CAD Tree

Here, we describe the specific operations that define the Reduced CAD Tree (RCT) structure of our bounded, semi-algebraic set. We assume that our universe consists of n-dimensional, rectangular, and bounded set of parametrisations $P = (l_1, h_1) \times \ldots (l_n, h_n)$. To implement all the necessary set operations over this universe of parametrisations, we define these base methods:

- IsEmpty($\mathtt{a}$) and IsUniverse($\mathtt{a}$) check the equality of $\mathtt{a}$ to $\emptyset$ and P;
- Invert($\mathtt{a}$) constructs a complement of the given set $\mathtt{a}$ with respect to the parametrisation set P;
- MakeSet(p) constructs the set of points $\{s \in P \mid p(s) > 0\}$ for a given multivariate polynomial p;
- Apply($\mathtt{a}, \mathtt{b}, \oplus$) constructs a semi-algebraic set that corresponds to the application of the Boolean function $\oplus$ to the cells of the two sets $\mathtt{a}$ and $\mathtt{b}$;
- Prune($\mathtt{a}$) performs the compaction of the tree, removing unnecessary cells and cylinders whenever possible (this also prunes the corresponding unnecessary polynomial constraints).

Using these methods, one can easily implement the standard operations over semi-algebraic sets: $\mathtt{a} \cap \mathtt{b} = \text{Apply}(\mathtt{a}, \mathtt{b}, \wedge)$, $\mathtt{a} \cup \mathtt{b} = \text{Apply}(\mathtt{a}, \mathtt{b}, \vee)$ and $\mathtt{a} \subseteq \mathtt{b} \equiv \text{IsUniverse}(\text{Apply}(\mathtt{a}, \mathtt{b}, \Rightarrow))$. To maintain a concise representation, we assume that after each Apply or MakeSet, the set is simplified using Prune.

Data Structure. The set representation is structured as a tree of *cells* of which there are two types. The first type is a Leaf($\mathtt{m}$) that stores an exact Boolean value m denoting whether this cell is part of the set. The second type is a Cylinder(`roots`, `cells`) that represents one cylinder of the open CAD. Specifically, `cells` is a sequence of higher-dimensional cells in the tree and `roots` contains the polynomial roots (evaluated at the sample point of this cylinder) that separate them. To simplify some operations, for each cell we define a Member function. For leaves, Member returns the corresponding Boolean value.

```
function MakeSet(p ∈ ℚ[x_1, ..., x_n])
    (F_1, ..., F_n) = Projection*(p)
    function MakeCell(s)
        if |s| = n then return Leaf(p(s) > 0)
        k = |s| + 1
        r = IsolateRoots(s, F_k)
        cells = ⟦ MakeCell(s · Sample(l, h)) | (l, h) ∈ CellPairs(r, (l_k, h_k)) ⟧
        return Cylinder(roots, cells)
    return MakeCell(⟦ ⟧)
```

Fig. 4. Algorithm for the MakeSet method.

For cylinders, it returns $\perp$ – a value which is neither `true` nor `false`. We also assume a method `Sample`(a, b) which returns some rational point from the interval (a, b). For a sequence $[\![r_1, \dots, r_k]\!]$, `CellPairs`$([\![r_1, \dots, r_k]\!], (l, h))$ denotes the sequence of subsequent pairs in the sorted sequence $[\![l, r_a, \dots, r_b, h]\!]$ where r_a is the smallest $l < r_i$ and r_b is the largest $r_i < h$.

IsEmpty, IsUniverse and Invert. To implement equality checking with $\emptyset$ and P, we simply have to traverse the leaves of the given tree, checking whether they are all `false` or `true`, i.e. IsEmpty(a) $\equiv \forall$c $\in$ Leafs(a) : $\neg$Member(c) and IsUniverse(a) $\equiv \forall$c $\in$ Leafs(a) : Member(c). Note that if such a set is pruned, it should be represented by a single Leaf. To implement Invert, we negate the Boolean value in each leaf. Observe that if the original set is pruned, after inversion, no pruning should be needed.

MakeSet. The algorithm for the construction of a semi-algebraic set from a given polynomial inequality is given in Fig. 4. We use Projection* to denote the sequence of polynomials obtained using the standard open CAD projection procedure.

Overall, the method is just a recursive construction of an open CAD over the given n-dimensional polynomial. Remember that for each $p' \in F_k$, we have level$(p') \leq k$, so the precondition for the IsolateRoots procedure is satisfied.

Apply. The main idea of Apply is to recursively zip the two given trees into one, applying a Boolean function to pairs of corresponding leaves. This procedure is described in Fig. 5. However, due to the nature of the considered problem, we cannot simply merge the two trees based on their structure. We also have to consider new intersections between the polynomials which might have appeared by interlaying the two sets. Due to these intersections, we may need to split the existing cylinder on the intersection boundaries.

First, Apply merges the root sequences from both a and b (here, Roots(c) for a leaf is an empty sequence and for a cylinder it is the corresponding `roots` sequence). Specifically, MergeRoots re-evaluates the roots from both a and b at the new sample point s and produces a unified sorted sequence of roots. The re-evaluation is necessary because the roots for a and b could have been originally computed in different sample points and might not be directly comparable. This

```
function APPLY(a, b, ⊕) return APPLY([[ ]], a, b, ⊕)
function APPLY(s, LEAF(m1), LEAF(m2), ⊕)
  | return LEAF(m1 ⊕ m2)
function APPLY(s, a, b, ⊕)
  | merged = MERGEROOTS(s, ROOTS(a), ROOTS(b))
  | roots' = [[ ]] ; cells' = [[ ]]
  | k = |s| + 1 ; i_a = 0 ; i_b = 0
  | for (l, h) ∈ CELLPAIRS(merged, (l_k, h_k)) do
  |   | c_a = LOOKUP(a, i_a) ; c_b = LOOKUP(b, i_b)
  |   | if P(h) ∈ {P(r) | r ∈ ROOTS(a)} then i_a = i_a + 1
  |   | if P(h) ∈ {P(r) | r ∈ ROOTS(b)} then i_b = i_b + 1
  |   | if c_a = LEAF(m_a) ∧ c_b = LEAF(m_b) then
  |   |   | roots' = roots' · l
  |   |   | cells' = cells' · LEAF(m_a ⊕ m_b)
  |   | else
  |   |   | cross = CYLINDERCROSS(k + 1, LEVELLIST(c_a), LEVELLIST(c_b))
  |   |   | for (ll, hh) ∈ CELLPAIRS(cross, (l, h)) do
  |   |   |   | roots' = roots' · ll ; s' = SAMPLEPOINT(ll, hh)
  |   |   |   | cells' = cells' · APPLY(k + 1, s · s', c_a, c_b, ⊕)
  | return CYLINDER(roots' \ l_k, cells')
```

Fig. 5. Algorithm for the APPLY method.

happens when existing cylinders are divided into more fine-grained ones and we need to produce a new root sequence specifically for the new cylinder. This can be done quite easily because (a) for each root, we keep the original multivariate polynomial P(r); (b) in each cylinder, all the corresponding polynomials are delineable, i.e. the multiplicity and the order of their roots do not change.

We then iterate over each cell of this merged root sequence, using i_a and i_b to keep track of the original cells in a and b that correspond to the current cell (l, h) (we define LOOKUP(c, i) as c for leaves and cells[i] for cylinders). If both original cells are leaves, we merge them immediately. Otherwise, we try to compute the possible intersections of the polynomials in a and b in higher dimensions which would cause this cell to split. Finally, we iterate over the roots of these cross polynomials to split the cell as much as needed.

To compute the cross polynomials, we could use the PROJECTION* operator as seen in the MAKESET procedure. However, it is possible (in fact, it is very common) that at this point, we have actually identified some of the polynomials given by PROJECTION* as unnecessary (i.e. they are not used as constraints anywhere in the set any more). To avoid re-introducing these constraints (and having to eliminate them again), we use a special projection operator CYLINDERCROSS which we define in Fig. 6.

For each cell, we define a LEVELLIST by merging the lists of polynomials in each cylinder at a specific level. Note that if a polynomial has been completely pruned from the specific cylinder, it is not going to appear in this list. We then compute a projection based on the open CAD projection operator, but we

```
function LevelList(Leaf c) return ⟦ ⟧
function LevelList(Cylinder(roots, cells))
  | return ⟦P(r) | r ∈ roots⟧ · Zip({LevelList(c) | c ∈ cells})
function CylinderCross(i, F = ⟦F_1, ..., F_k⟧, G = ⟦G_1, ..., G_l⟧)
  | if F = ∅ ∨ G = ∅ then return ∅
  | cross = CylinderCross(i + 1, ⟦F_2, ..., F_k⟧, ⟦G_2, ..., G_l⟧)
  | ldcf = {LDCF(p) | p ∈ cross}
  | dsc = {DSC(p) | p ∈ cross}
  | bound = {RES(p, P(l_i)) | p ∈ cross} ∪ {RES(p, P(h_i)) | p ∈ cross}
  | p_1 = {RES(p, q) | p ∈ cross, q ∈ (F_1 ∪ G_1)}
  | p_2 = {RES(p, q) | p ∈ (F_1 \ G_1), q ∈ G_1} ∪ {RES(p, q) | p ∈ (G_1 \ F_1), q ∈ F_1}
  | return ldcf ∪ dsc ∪ bound ∪ p_1 ∪ p_2
```

Fig. 6. Description of the intersection projection operator.

only compute new projections and intersections between the two level lists, not within the level lists themselves. This guarantees that a previously eliminated polynomial cannot be introduced unless it is needed.

```
1  function Prune(Leaf c) return c
2  function Prune(Cylinder(roots, cells))
3    | pruned = ⟦Prune(c) | c ∈ cells⟧
4    | if { Member(c) | c ∈ pruned } = {true} then return Leaf(true)
5    | if { Member(c) | c ∈ pruned } = {false} then return Leaf(false)
6    | roots' = ⟦ ⟧ ; cells' = ⟦ ⟧
7    | for i ∈ Indices(roots) do
8    |   | r = roots[i] ; a = pruned[i] ; b = pruned[i + 1]
9    |   | if a ≁ b ∨ P(roots[i]) ∈ (Dep(a) ∪ Dep(b)) then
10   |   |   | roots' = roots' · r ; cells' = cells' · a
11   | if cells' = ∅ ∧ Last(pruned) = Leaf(m) then return Leaf(m)
12   | else return Cylinder(roots', cells')
```

Fig. 7. Algorithm for the Prune method.

Prune. Finally, after applying an operation to the set, we would like to remove unnecessary polynomials. To this end, we use the procedure defined in Fig. 7. The goals of the procedure are twofold: (a) the contraction of unnecessary cylinders; (b) the pruning of unnecessary roots. The goal (a) is handled on lines 4 and 5. When the whole sequence of `pruned` cells represents the same value (`true` or `false`), we discard the whole sequence.

To achieve (b), we iterate the current sequence of roots and the cells they separate (`a` is separated from `b` using `r`). If the two sub-trees are not similar, the root is necessary (trees are similar if they have the same structure and the same Boolean values in their leaves – they can differ in their root sequences).

Model	n	Parameters	Degree	$\|S\|$	SMT	RCT
G_1/S cell cycle	2	ϕ_{E2F1}, k_1	1	$\approx 2^{13}$	376s	16s
G_1/S cell cycle	2	ϕ_{E2F1}, k_1, J_{11}	2	$\approx 2^{13}$	DNF	64s
G_1/S cell cycle	2	K_{m_2}, J_{12}	3	$\approx 2^{13}$	DNF	52s
Repressilator	2	k_1, ϕ_{x_1}	1	$\approx 2^{15}$	422s	29s
Repressilator	2	k_1, k_2, ϕ_{x_1}	1	$\approx 2^{15}$	DNF	659s
Repressilator	2	K_1, ϕ_{x_1}	6	$\approx 2^{15}$	DNF	101s
Repressilator	4	k_1, ϕ_{x_1}	1	$\approx 2^{17}$	1672s	267s
Repressilator	4	K_1, ϕ_{x_1}	6	$\approx 2^{17}$	DNF	306s
Repressilator	6	k_1, ϕ_{x_1}	1	$\approx 2^{19}$	2856s	573s
Carbon flux	4	$k_3, fast$	1	$\approx 2^{20}$	1265s	241s
Carbon flux	4	$k_2, fast$	2	$\approx 2^{20}$	3087s	498s
Carbon flux	4	$k_2, k_W, fast$	3	$\approx 2^{20}$	DNF	1093s

Fig. 8. Performance evaluation, comparing the RCT symbolic representation to SMT based approach in [8] using a time-out of one hour. The table lists the model, the number of variables (n), the chosen parameters, the maximum degree of polynomials appearing in the constraints, the approximate state space size of the Kripke structure ($|S|$), and the times measured for both methods (as an average of 5 runs).

We use $\textsc{Dep}(\mathtt{a})$ to denote all the polynomials that were introduced due to some higher-dimensional dependency in the subtree $\mathtt{a}$, i.e. those that were created as intersections or projections in some higher dimension. If the root is due to a dependent polynomial, we cannot remove it. Finally, when the trees are similar and the polynomial is not dependent, we can remove the root and one of the cells (by skipping it). Note that a dependent polynomial can become independent when all its dependencies are removed.

Implementing RCTs. We implement RCTs using the Rings library [34] which provides many useful features for symbolic polynomial manipulation. We have integrated the implementation within the Pithya [9] parameter synthesis tool, which provides the necessary algorithms.

Here, we simplify the algorithms to ease readability. In practice, we consider various performance bottlenecks. Specifically, we cache the computation of level lists and dependent sets within their associated cells. Additionally, the computation of resultants, discriminants, and even the root isolation can be performed repeatedly due to the iterative nature of the parameter synthesis algorithm. We use a least-recently-used cache to speed-up these operations. In our experience, such a cache can drastically improve performance with a hit rate often exceeding 99%. Finally, one can use fast approximation, such as interval arithmetic, to quickly eliminate polynomials not relevant in given bounds.

4 Evaluation

To evaluate our approach, we choose several rational ODE models from systems biology. First is the two-dimensional G_1/S cell cycle model from [39], the second is a repressilator motif studied in [13] which can be easily scaled in the number of dimensions. Third is a four-dimensional model of carbon fluxes in cyanobacteria [18]. We employ piece-wise multi-affine approximation [26] to obtain piece-wise multi-affine ODE models and subsequently the rectangular abstraction to obtain a parametrised Kripke structure. We compare the performance to the method presented in [8] which uses the SMT based set representation of parametrisations. As the SMT solver employed, we choose Microsoft Z3 [22]. We choose Z3 as it currently offers the best performance for both linear and non-linear real arithmetic (as shown at the SMT-COMP 2018 competition) together with a user-friendly API for manipulation and simplification of formulas.

The first two models exhibit bi-stable behaviour in `low` and `high` regions (for exact definition of these regions, see [8]). For the carbon flux model, there are also two interesting `low` and `high` regions of the $C_{CO_2}^{Carb}$ (specifically, $C_{CO_2}^{Carb}$ below and above $4 \cdot 10^{-6}$), however, no bi-stable behaviour occurs. We synthesise parametrisation sets where **AG** `low` or **AG** `high` holds (i.e. the regions are indeed stable) as well as the parametrisation set for which the bi-stability is present: **EF AG** `low` $\wedge$ **AG** `high` (expected to be empty for the carbon-flux model).

We present the results in Fig. 8, giving a performance comparison for selected combinations of parameters using a standard 4-core 3.2 Ghz desktop computer with 16 GB of RAM. In the table, we use the maximum degree of constraint polynomials to indicate the interdependence of selected parameters. For degree one, the constraints are linear. Observe that RCTs always significantly outperform the SMT based representation and even allow us to compute results which we would not be otherwise able to obtain. This difference is especially pronounced for models with high parameter interdependence, where the SMT approach times-out in most cases.

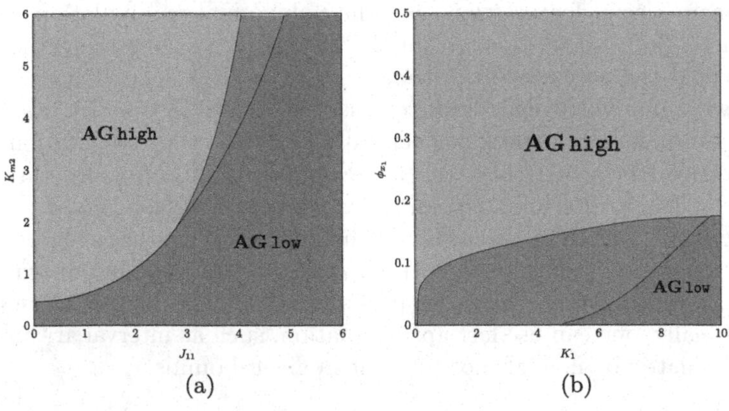

Fig. 9. Synthesis results for the G_1/S (a) and repressilator (b) models, showing the semi-algebraic sets of parameters where investigated properties hold. Green area represents the bi-stable regions of **EF AG** `high` $\wedge$ **AG** `low`. (Color figure online)

Finally, in Fig. 9, we visualise the results for two selected variants of the cell-cycle and repressilator models, showing the non-trivial parameter regions that the synthesis method needs to deal with. Note that to compute the figures, we do not need to employ sampling, we can instead traverse the RCT structure and directly obtain guaranteed intervals for every column of pixels.

5 Conclusions

Fully automatic parameter synthesis is essential to understand, develop, and tune realistic predictable models. Our new technique, reduced CAD trees, brings substantial improvement in this direction, providing a new data structure to represent non-trivial semi-algebraic sets of parameters. The method allows exploring models with complex non-linear parameter dependencies efficiently. Furthermore, the results in this form are much easier to visualise and post-process due to their regular structure. We compared this approach to an existing SMT based technique. Results demonstrate significant performance gains and we were able to compute even previously unsolvable parameter combinations.

References

1. Arney, D., Pajic, M., Goldman, J.M., Lee, I., Mangharam, R., Sokolsky, O.: Toward patient safety in closed-loop medical device systems. In: ICCPS 10, pp. 139–148. ACM (2010). https://doi.org/10.1145/1795194.1795214
2. Arnon, D.S., Collins, G.E., McCallum, S.: Cylindrical algebraic decomposition I: the basic algorithm. SIAM J. Comput. **13**(4), 865–877 (1984)
3. Asarin, E., Dang, T., Girard, A.: Hybridization methods for the analysis of non-linear systems. Acta Informatica **43**, 451–476 (2007)
4. Barnat, J., et al.: On parameter synthesis by parallel model checking. IEEE/ACM Trans. Comput. Biol. Bioinf. **9**(3), 693–705 (2012)
5. Bartocci, E., Bortolussi, L., Nenzi, L., Sanguinetti, G.: System design of stochastic models using robustness of temporal properties. TCS **587**, 3–25 (2015)
6. Batt, G., Page, M., Cantone, I., Goessler, G., Monteiro, P., de Jong, H.: Efficient parameter search for qualitative models of regulatory networks using symbolic model checking. Bioinformatics **26**(18), i603–i610 (2010)
7. Batt, G., Yordanov, B., Weiss, R., Belta, C.: Robustness analysis and tuning of synthetic gene networks. Bioinformatics **23**(18), 2415–2422 (2007)
8. Beneš, N., Brim, L., Demko, M., Pastva, S., Šafránek, D.: Parallel SMT-based parameter synthesis with application to piecewise multi-affine systems. In: Artho, C., Legay, A., Peled, D. (eds.) ATVA 2016. LNCS, vol. 9938, pp. 192–208. Springer, Cham (2016). https://doi.org/10.1007/978-3-319-46520-3_13
9. Beneš, N., Brim, L., Demko, M., Pastva, S., Šafránek, D.: Pithya: a parallel tool for parameter synthesis of piecewise multi-affine dynamical systems. In: Majumdar, R., Kunčak, V. (eds.) CAV 2017. LNCS, vol. 10426, pp. 591–598. Springer, Cham (2017). https://doi.org/10.1007/978-3-319-63387-9_29
10. Bérard, B., Haddad, S., Picaronny, C., El Din, M.S., Sassolas, M.: Polynomial interrupt timed automata. In: Bojańczyk, M., Lasota, S., Potapov, I. (eds.) RP 2015. LNCS, vol. 9328, pp. 20–32. Springer, Cham (2015). https://doi.org/10.1007/978-3-319-24537-9_3

11. Bogomolov, S., Schilling, C., Bartocci, E., Batt, G., Kong, H., Grosu, R.: Abstraction-based parameter synthesis for multiaffine systems. In: Piterman, N. (ed.) HVC 2015. LNCS, vol. 9434, pp. 19–35. Springer, Cham (2015). https://doi.org/10.1007/978-3-319-26287-1_2
12. Brim, L., Dluhoš, P., Šafránek, D., Vejpustek, T.: STL*: extending signal temporal logic with signal-value freezing operator. Inf. Comput. **236**, 52–67 (2014). Special Issue on Hybrid Systems and Biology
13. Brim, L., Demko, M., Pastva, S., Šafránek, D.: High-performance discrete bifurcation analysis for piecewise-affine dynamical systems. In: Abate, A., Šafránek, D. (eds.) HSB 2015. LNCS, vol. 9271, pp. 58–74. Springer, Cham (2015). https://doi.org/10.1007/978-3-319-26916-0_4
14. Brim, L., Češka, M., Dražan, S., Šafránek, D.: Exploring parameter space of stochastic biochemical systems using quantitative model checking. In: Sharygina, N., Veith, H. (eds.) CAV 2013. LNCS, vol. 8044, pp. 107–123. Springer, Heidelberg (2013). https://doi.org/10.1007/978-3-642-39799-8_7
15. Brown, C.W.: QEPCAD B: a program for computing with semi-algebraic sets using CADs. ACM SIGSAM Bull. **37**(4), 97–108 (2003)
16. Chen, C., Davenport, J.H., Moreno Maza, M., Xia, B., Xiao, R.: Computing with semi-algebraic sets represented by triangular decomposition. In: ISSAC 2011, pp. 75–82. ACM (2011)
17. Cimatti, A., Griggio, A., Sebastiani, R.: A simple and flexible way of computing small unsatisfiable cores in SAT modulo theories. In: Marques-Silva, J., Sakallah, K.A. (eds.) SAT 2007. LNCS, vol. 4501, pp. 334–339. Springer, Heidelberg (2007). https://doi.org/10.1007/978-3-540-72788-0_32
18. Clark, R.L., Cameron, J.C., Root, T.W., Pfleger, B.F.: Insights into the industrial growth of cyanobacteria from a model of the carbon? Concentrating mechanism. AIChE J. **60**(4), 1269–1277 (2014)
19. Collins, G.E., Akritas, A.G.: Polynomial real root isolation using Descarte's rule of signs. In: SYMSAC 1976, pp. 272–275. ACM (1976)
20. Dang, T., Dreossi, T., Piazza, C.: Parameter synthesis through temporal logic specifications. In: Bjørner, N., de Boer, F. (eds.) FM 2015. LNCS, vol. 9109, pp. 213–230. Springer, Cham (2015). https://doi.org/10.1007/978-3-319-19249-9_14
21. Dang, T., Guernic, C.L., Maler, O.: Computing reachable states for nonlinear biological models. Theor. Comput. Sci. **412**(21), 2095–2107 (2011)
22. de Moura, L., Bjørner, N.: Z3: an efficient SMT solver. In: Ramakrishnan, C.R., Rehof, J. (eds.) TACAS 2008. LNCS, vol. 4963, pp. 337–340. Springer, Heidelberg (2008). https://doi.org/10.1007/978-3-540-78800-3_24
23. Donzé, A., Krogh, B., Rajhans, A.: Parameter synthesis for hybrid systems with an application to simulink models. In: Majumdar, R., Tabuada, P. (eds.) HSCC 2009. LNCS, vol. 5469, pp. 165–179. Springer, Heidelberg (2009). https://doi.org/10.1007/978-3-642-00602-9_12
24. Donzé, A., Maler, O., Bartocci, E., Nickovic, D., Grosu, R., Smolka, S.: On temporal logic and signal processing. In: Chakraborty, S., Mukund, M. (eds.) ATVA 2012. LNCS, pp. 92–106. Springer, Heidelberg (2012). https://doi.org/10.1007/978-3-642-33386-6_9
25. Gao, S., Kong, S., Clarke, E.M.: dReal: an SMT solver for nonlinear theories over the reals. In: Bonacina, M.P. (ed.) CADE 2013. LNCS (LNAI), vol. 7898, pp. 208–214. Springer, Heidelberg (2013). https://doi.org/10.1007/978-3-642-38574-2_14
26. Grosu, R., et al.: From cardiac cells to genetic regulatory networks. In: Gopalakrishnan, G., Qadeer, S. (eds.) CAV 2011. LNCS, vol. 6806, pp. 396–411. Springer, Heidelberg (2011). https://doi.org/10.1007/978-3-642-22110-1_31

27. Guthmann, O., Strichman, O., Trostanetski, A.: Minimal unsatisfiable core extraction for SMT. In: FMCAD 2016, pp. 57–64. IEEE (2016)
28. de Jong, H., Gouzé, J., Hernandez, C., Page, M., Sari, T., Geiselmann, J.: Qualitative simulations of genetic regulatory networks using piecewise linear models. Bull. Math. Biol. **66**, 301–340 (2004)
29. Liffiton, M.H., Sakallah, K.A.: Algorithms for computing minimal unsatisfiable subsets of constraints. J. Autom. Reasoning **40**(1), 1–33 (2008)
30. Madsen, C., Shmarov, F., Zuliani, P.: `BioPSy`: an SMT-based tool for guaranteed parameter set synthesis of biological models. In: Roux, O., Bourdon, J. (eds.) CMSB 2015. LNCS, vol. 9308, pp. 182–194. Springer, Cham (2015). https://doi.org/10.1007/978-3-319-23401-4_16
31. Maler, O., Nickovic, D.: Monitoring temporal properties of continuous signals. In: Lakhnech, Y., Yovine, S. (eds.) FORMATS/FTRTFT -2004. LNCS, vol. 3253, pp. 152–166. Springer, Heidelberg (2004). https://doi.org/10.1007/978-3-540-30206-3_12
32. McCallum, S.: Solving polynomial strict inequalities using cylindrical algebraic decomposition. Comput. J. **36**(5), 432–438 (1993). https://doi.org/10.1093/comjnl/36.5.432
33. Milias-Argeitis, A., Engblom, S., Bauer, P., Khammash, M.: Stochastic focusing coupled with negative feedback enables robust regulation in biochemical reaction networks. J. Roy. Soc. Interface **12**(113) (2015)
34. Poslavsky, S.: Rings: an efficient Java/Scala library for polynomial rings. Comput. Phys. Commun. **235**, 400–413 (2019)
35. Raman, V., Donzé, A., Sadigh, D., Murray, R.M., Seshia, S.A.: Reactive synthesis from signal temporal logic specifications. In: HSCC 2015, pp. 239–248. ACM (2015)
36. Rizk, A., Batt, G., Fages, F., Soliman, S.: A general computational method for robustness analysis with applications to synthetic gene networks. Bioinformatics **25**(12) (2009)
37. Strzeboński, A.: Solving systems of strict polynomial inequalities. J. Symbolic Comput. **29**(3), 471–480 (2000)
38. Strzebonski, A.W.: An algorithm for systems of strong polynomial inequalities. Mathe. J. **4**(4), 74–77 (1994)
39. Swat, M., Kel, A., Herzel, H.: Bifurcation analysis of the regulatory modules of the mammalian G1/S transition. Bioinformatics **20**(10), 1506–1511 (2004)

Uniqueness Types for Efficient and Verifiable Aliasing-Free Embedded Systems Programming

Tuur Benoit[1(✉)] and Bart Jacobs[2]

[1] Siemens Industry Software, Leuven, Belgium
tuur.benoit@siemens.com

[2] Depatment of Computer Science, imec-DistriNet Research Group, KU Leuven, Leuven, Belgium
Bart.Jacobs@cs.kuleuven.be

Abstract. An important consequence of only having value types in an aliasing-free programming language is the significant reduction in annotation burden to verify programs using semi-automatic proof systems. However, values in such language are often copied implicitly which is detrimental to the execution speed and memory usage of practical systems. Moreover, embedded systems programmers need fine-grained control over the circumstances at which data is copied to be able to predict memory use and execution times.

This paper introduces a new approach to using uniqueness types to enable building efficient and verifiable embedded systems using an aliasing-free programming language. The idea is to use uniqueness types for enforcing at-most-once consumption of unique values. The proposed model of uniqueness of values enables compiler optimizations such as elimination of physical copies and in-place mutation. In addition, the proposed approach provides a lightweight notation for the programmer to control copying behavior.

We have implemented our method in Sim, a new language for the development of safety-critical software. Our validation cases suggest that our aliasing-free language allows one to verify the functional correctness of realistic embedded programs with only a small annotation overhead while keeping the run-time performance of the program up to par with hand-optimized code.

Keywords: Formal verification · Uniqueness types · Aliasing-free

1 Introduction

An aliasing-free language provides a compelling programming model for formal verification. Aliasing, more specifically mutable aliasing, prevents or complicates the use of semi-automatic proof systems. The reason is that in case of aliasing two variables can refer to the same object and modification of one variable might update the value of another variable outside the scope of a verification unit.

W. Ahrendt and S. L. Tapia Tarifa (Eds.): IFM 2019, LNCS 11918, pp. 46–64, 2019.
https://doi.org/10.1007/978-3-030-34968-4_3

There are two main approaches to addressing this problem. (1) Systems that allow unlimited aliasing but require relatively heavy annotations to detect cases of mutable aliasing. Examples are VeriFast [8] and Frama-C [2]. (2) Systems that exclude language constructs that introduce aliasing. Ada SPARK is a language which is *mostly* aliasing-free. However, Ada SPARK's `inout` parameters and global variables are sources of mutable aliasing [12].

We propose an approach based on Sim [3], a contract-based language designed for the development and formal verification of safety-critical software with a low annotation overhead. The Sim programming language is interesting because it is *entirely* aliasing-free. In this language, every variable and expression has a value type, including the built-in array type. In other words, there are no reference types such as pointers or classes. Moreover, function parameters are passed by value and cannot be modified.

As a consequence, every variable conceptually keeps a copy of the data. However, maintaining a physical copy for every variable might result in large memory usage and long execution times. This would prohibit the use of aliasing-free programming languages altogether in embedded systems programming where there are often constraints on system resources like memory size and processor speed.

To achieve the necessary performance characteristics for such programs, this paper proposes a type-based approach to ensuring that particular designated values are never copied implicitly. The fundamental idea is to statically enforce at-most-once consumption of these values by assigning permissions to variables and statically computing and checking the permissions of the variables at each program point. Our main goal is to reestablish control by the programmer over when a physical copy of a value is made and to open up opportunities for a compiler to perform optimizations like pass-by-reference and in-place mutation that result in more efficient system resource usage, using a lightweight notation for indicating *uniqueness*. Furthermore, with only slight adaptations our permissions system can also be used to statically detect use of uninitialized variables and reassignment of immutable variables.

Contribution. We introduce a syntax for indicating uniqueness of values and a type and permission system to ensure at-most-once consumption of unique values in an aliasing-free programming language. Our system removes an important limitation of the use of aliasing-free programming abstractions that are verifiable but performance-wise not efficient.

While treatment of uniqueness and permission systems exists, our approach takes a dual position to the approach taken e.g. by Rust, and a recent update of Ada SPARK [10]. These languages feature reference types and aliasing, but their type systems prevent mutable access to aliased names. In other words, Rust and Ada SPARK provide the programmer with a basic abstraction, i.e. reference types, to implement efficient data structures and algorithms while eliminating mutable aliasing of the references through their type system. Our approach on the other hand, starts from a programming model which is inherently aliasing-free by only allowing value types and pass-by-value, but which might be less efficient by default. Notwithstanding, our type system provides a means to regain efficiency by providing uniqueness information that the compiler and the programmer can exploit to optimize data structures and algorithms. This has several advantages: first, the absence of side effects caused by aliasing facilitates the use of semi-automatic proof tools in the context of program verification. Second, our approach provides the programmer with a lightweight syntax for controlling copying and allocation behavior of the program. Third, the uniqueness information can be exploited by a compiler for optimizations. This paper also contributes:

- A *formal model of the type and permission system.* We describe a formalization of the operational semantics our language and the type and permission system in Sect. 4 and prove that well-typed programs do not get stuck.
- A *validation on a realistic case study.* We validate our method by comparing the annotation overhead for programs written in Sim, with equivalent programs written in C and verified with VeriFast [8]. We demonstrate in Sect. 6 a reduction of the annotation burden by a factor of 4.6. In addition, we show that we can obtain performance similar to hand-optimized code that makes use of references.

Outline. The paper is organized as follows. Section 2 describes how aliasing-free programming reduces the annotation burden and how uniqueness types help in avoiding excessive copying. Section 3 introduces the type and permission system in an informal way. Section 4 presents a formalization of the syntax, operational semantics and type and permission system of our language. Section 5 discusses the implementation in the Sim compiler. Section 6 presents the validation case. Section 7 gives an overview of related work and Sect. 8 concludes.

2 Overview

2.1 Aliasing-Free Programming

In this section, we will explore uniqueness of values intuitively and how uniqueness types help in discovering excessive copying in resource-critical parts of the program and how to avoid it. Consider the function `shift` in Listing 1. It shifts the elements in a vector to the right by `n` steps, and fills the remaining elements with zero.

The contract on lines 2–4 describes the functional specification of the function. No additional annotations are needed since no aliasing is present in this example: the array type is a value type, function parameters are passed by value and function parameters are read-only. In a language with aliasing, for example C, this array would be passed by reference, and a tool like VeriFast or Frama-C would require extra annotations in separation logic [15] to indicate that the elements of the array are mutated in place. In Sect. 6.1 we show that our aliasing-free programming approach reduces the annotation burden by a factor of 4 to 5 compared to programs written in C and verified with VeriFast.

```
1  fn shift(vec: Array<float, ?>, n: int) -> shifted: Array<float, ?>
2      requires 0 <= n && n < length(vec, 0);
3      ensures forall j: int :: n <= j && j < length(vec, 0) ==> shifted[j] == vec[j - n];
4      ensures forall j: int :: 0 <= j && j < n ==> shifted[j] == 0.0;
5  {
6      let mut shifted = vec;
7      let mut i = 0;
8      while i < length(vec, 0)
9          invariant forall j: int :: n <= j && j < i ==> shifted[j] == vec[j - n];
10         invariant forall j: int :: 0 <= j && j < i && j < n ==> shifted[j] == 0.0;
11     {
12         shifted[i] = if i < n { 0.0 } else { vec[i - n] };
13         i = i + 1;
14     };
15     shifted
16 }
```

Listing 1. The function `shift` shifts the array elements to the right by `n` steps.

2.2 Uniqueness Types for High-Performance Aliasing-Free Programming

In an aliasing-free language, every variable conceptually keeps a copy of the data. However, maintaining a physical copy of the data for every variable might result in large memory usage and long execution times. For example, in Listing 1 at line 6, the value of `vec` is assigned to variable `shifted` to avoid allocation of a new array. However, this introduces an implicit copy of a potentially large array.

To achieve improved performance, a compiler could implement an optimization called *copy-on-write*, which stores equal variables at the same memory location until one is modified. However, in the case of Listing 1 such optimization only postpones the physical copy from line 6 to line 12.

This paper proposes a type-based approach to ensuring that particular designated values are never copied implicitly. The idea is that any type can be annotated with a `unique` modifier which instructs the compiler to enforce at-most-once use of values of that type. This way, the programmer regains control over when a physical copy of a value is made and it opens up opportunities for a compiler to perform optimizations like in-place mutation or passing values by reference. In case a unique value is used more than once, a compiler error is issued.

The example of Listing 1 can be adapted by adding a `unique` modifier to the type of the first input parameter and output parameter of the `shift` function, as follows:

```
fn shift(vec: unique Array<float, ?>, n: int) -> shifted: unique Array<float, ?>
```

However, with the `unique` modifiers in place, the following compilation error is issued for the code in Listing 1 at line 8 and line 12:

```
Variable ‘vec’ has no ‘Read’ permission.
```

The error diagnostic signals that the variable `vec` has been used already. Indeed, at line 6 `vec` was read and assigned to `shifted`.

```
1  fn shift(vec: unique Array<float, ?>, n: int) -> shifted: unique Array<float, ?>
2      requires 0 <= n && n < length(vec, 0);
3      ensures forall j: int :: n <= j && j < length(vec, 0) ==> shifted[j] == vec[j - n];
4      ensures forall j: int :: 0 <= j && j < n ==> shifted[j] == 0.0;
5  {
6      let mut shifted = vec;
7      let mut i = length(shifted, 0);
8      while i > 0
9          invariant forall j: int :: 0 <= j && j < i ==> shifted[j] == vec[j];
10         invariant forall j: int :: n <= j && j < length(vec, 0) && j >= i
11                                  ==> shifted[j] == vec[j - n];
12         invariant forall j: int :: 0 <= j && j < n && j >= i ==> shifted[j] == 0.0;
13     {
14         i = i - 1;
15         shifted[i] = if i < n { 0.0 } else { shifted[i - n] };
16     };
17     shifted
18 }
```

Listing 2. The parameters of the `shift` function have been annotated with `unique` modifiers and the algorithm is modified so no implicit copies are needed.

At this point, the programmer can reflect about their implementation. If they regard that a copy is justified at this point, then the error is eliminated by making an explicit clone of the array. For example by changing line 6 to `let mut shifted = clone(vec);`. Otherwise, if a copy is too expensive, the programmer might attempt to rewrite the algorithm. Listing 2 shows an alternative implementation of `shift` that iterates over the array from the back to the front as opposed to the forward iteration in Listing 1. Since the input parameter is declared as unique and no compilation errors are issued, it is guaranteed that the input argument is not copied implicitly.

Furthermore, since the compiler can assume uniqueness of the parameters, it can now perform an optimization such as passing the argument `vec` by reference instead of by value and mutating this variable in place instead of passing and returning a complete array. This optimization is transparent to the programmer. That means that one can benefit from performance improvements while keeping the ease of reasoning with value types.

Important to note is that nothing has to be changed on the caller-side because any value can always be cast to a unique value. As a matter of fact, one can always make a copy of a nonunique value and treat the copy as a unique value from that point on. Though, restructuring the code on the caller-side to take advantage of the uniqueness property might benefit performance even more.

Furthermore, remark that the function contract did not have to change either. The function contract of Listing 1 is exactly the same with and without the `unique` modifiers, as well as with a different implementation in Listing 2. Note also that a unique value can be used more than once in a specification context. This can be observed in Listing 2 on lines 9–11. The reason is that specifications such as loop invariants are not executed at run-time.

```
unique struct Circle {
    origin: Point,
    radius: int
}

unique struct Point {
    x: int,
    y: int
}

fn main() {
    let cl = Circle {
        origin = Point {
            x = 0,
            y = 1
        },
        radius = 5
    };

    let ra = cl.radius;
    let rb = cl.radius;
    let o = cl.origin;
    render(cl);  // ERROR
}
```

Listing 3. Using a unique value more than once results in an error.

3 Type and Permission System

The essence of our approach lies in the annotation of types with a `unique` modifier for which can be checked that values of the type are never copied implicitly. At the same time, the observable functional behavior of the program remains unchanged, though performance aspects of the program might be different. With slight adaptations to the permission system, the system can also be used for detecting the use of uninitialized variables and reassignment of immutable variables. This section describes the type and permission system informally.

3.1 Uniqueness Annotation

Two kinds of terms can be annotated with a `unique` modifier.

Modifier in a Type Declaration. This denotes that all values of the type must be treated as unique values, for which at-most-once use is enforced (e.g. `Circle` in Listing 3). Unique types may be composed of both unique and nonunique types, but the converse is not true. The reason is that a value of a nonunique type may be copied implicitly, which would violate the at-most-once use of a unique member.

Modifier in a Type Annotation. It is possible to locally turn a nonunique type into a unique type by adding the `unique` modifier in a type annotation (e.g. `unique Array<int, 10>` in Listing 2). This is particularly useful when the natural semantics of a type is that of nonuniqueness.

3.2 Uniqueness Semantics

In many aspects, unique types and nonunique types are exactly the same. Operations like creating instances, accessing members and mutating variables, have exactly the same result for both the unique and nonunique variant of some type. A value of a unique type can only be used once however, that is, if the value can be accessed through a path, the path becomes inaccessible for reading after it has been evaluated for reading.

The example in Listing 3 illustrates this idea. First a unique structure type, `Circle`, is declared that has two members of type `Point` and `int`. `Point` is another unique structure type. On line 16, a new (unique) `Circle` value is created and bound to the variable `cl`. Then, on line 24 and 25, the `radius` member of `cl` is used twice. Since a nonunique member can be freely copied, this does not produce an error. On line 26, `cl.origin` is assigned to `o`. At that point the unique `origin` field of `cl` has not been used before, so no error is produced. Finally, on line 27, an error is produced when one attempts to use `cl` since its unique `origin` field has been used already.

3.3 Permissions

In our system, each variable is guarded by a permission. Upon access of a variable (read or write), its permissions are checked. The permissions change throughout the program. The typing rules produce a set of permissions at each program point.

Scalar Permissions. A variable containing a value of a scalar type has a scalar permission. There are four scalar permissions: Read-Write (`RW`), Read-Only (`R`), Write-Only (`W`), No-Access (`NO`). Some compound types are also associated with a scalar permission. Arrays are an example thereof. The permission system does not distinguish between the different elements of an array and treats the array and its elements as a whole, carrying one scalar permission. That is, `v` and `v[0]` have the same scalar permission.

Compound Permissions. A compound permission is an aggregate of permissions. Compound permissions are associated with variables containing structure types. For a structure type the compound permission forms a tree. Each node in the permission tree corresponds to a member of the structure or the aggregate itself. Each node of the permission tree holds a scalar permission. Figure 1 shows an example of two permission trees.

Ordering of Permissions. Permissions are partially ordered according to a diamond lattice: $\texttt{NO} < \texttt{R} \mid \texttt{W} < \texttt{RW}$. The `NO` permission is the smallest permission. The `RW` permission is the largest permission. The `R` and `W` permission cannot be ordered with respect to each other.

3.4 Rules

Variable Introduction. Variables are introduced by let-statements. The permission of the variable is set initially to write-only (`W`). In case a variable of a structure type is introduced, a write-only scalar permission is associated with each member of the structure as well as with the top-level structure itself.

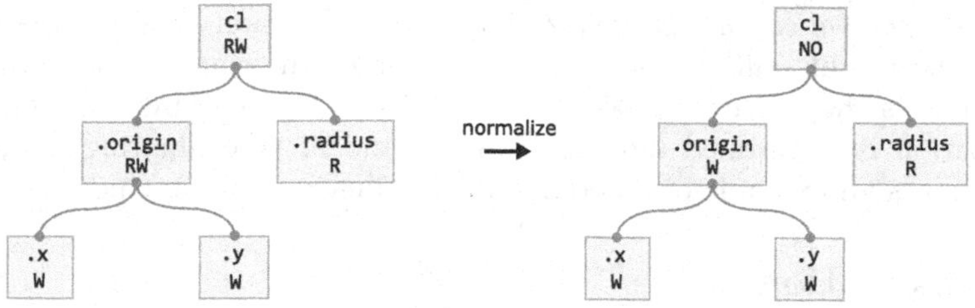

Fig. 1. Permission tree before and after normalization.

Assignment of Variables

- Before assignment, the variable must have a *writability* permission (`W` or `RW`).
- After assignment, the variable obtains the following permission:
  - If the variable is immutable, it gets a *read-only* (`R`) permission.
  - If the variable is mutable, it gets a *read-write* (`RW`) permission.
- After modification of the permissions, the permissions are normalized (ref. paragraph *Permission normalization*).

When assigning to a variable that contains a structure type, only the permission of the structure aggregate needs to be checked for writability permissions, since the permission tree is normalized at any point.

The rule for assignment ensures that no immutable variables are mutated, since immutable variables get a read-only permission after their first assignment.

Evaluation of Variables

- Before evaluation, the variable must have *readability* permissions (`R` or `RW`).
- After evaluation, the variable permissions are modified as follows:
  - Variables containing a value of a unique type lose their readability:
    * a `RW` permission becomes a `W` permission, and
    * a `R` permission becomes a `NO` permission.
  - For variables containing a value of a nonunique type, the permission remains unchanged.
  - Structure members get the same permission as the aggregate.
- After modification of the permissions, the permissions are normalized (ref. paragraph *Permission normalization*).

Since the permission tree is normalized, only the top-level permission of the structure needs to be checked for writability permissions.

The rule ensures at-most-once use of a unique value since readability permissions disappear after use for variables containing a unique type. The only way to regain readability permissions for that variable is through binding of a fresh value. This ensures that unique values move from one variable to another and no logical duplicates can be observed.

This rule, together with the rule of introducing variables, also ensures that no uninitialized variables are read. Since the variables start out with a write-only permission and readability permissions can only be obtained by assigning a value, it is ensured that no uninitialized variables are read.

Permission Normalization. Normalization of a permission tree corresponds to updating the permissions in such way that after normalization, the permission of each node is the Greatest Lower Bound (GLB) of its children's permissions. Normalization is performed after assignment and after evaluating a variable. Figure 1 shows an example of a permission tree before and after normalization.

4 Formalization

This section presents a formalization of the operational semantics and type and permission system of our language and a proof of soundness. A number of simplifications have been carried out without sacrificing expressiveness.

4.1 Syntax

Figure 2 shows the syntax of the language. A structure definition contains a modifier u, which indicates whether the structure is unique or nonunique. Expressions include standard primitive values, structure expressions, function calls, if-expressions, while-expressions, cast expressions and sequential compositions. In the formal language, struct expressions are labelled by a uniqueness u; in Sim, struct values adopt the uniqueness of the struct type by default. A path is either a variable identifier or a field selection on another path. A path expression reads the content of a variable or a (possibly nested) variable field. A let-expression introduces a new mutable or immutable variable into the scope before the execution of its body expression. The assignment expression binds the value of its right-hand side expression to the left-hand side path expression. A type is either a primitive type r or a type that consists of a user defined structure type s prepended by a modifier u that specifies whether the type is unique or nonunique.

$$
\begin{array}{rrl}
\text{structure} & st ::= & u\ \texttt{struct}\ s\ \{\ f : \tau, f : \tau\ \} \\
\text{function} & fn ::= & \texttt{fn}\ g(x : \tau) \to \tau\ \{\ e\ \} \\
\text{expression} & e ::= & b \in \mathbb{B} \mid z \in \mathbb{Z} \mid () \\
& & \mid \texttt{let}\ m\ x : \tau\ \texttt{in}\ e \mid e; e \\
& & \mid y \mid y := e \mid e\ \texttt{as}\ \tau \\
& & \mid u\ s\ \{\ f = e, f = e\ \} \mid g(e) \\
& & \mid \texttt{if}\ e\ \texttt{then}\ e\ \texttt{else}\ e \mid \texttt{while}\ e\ \texttt{do}\ e \\
\text{path} & y ::= & x \mid y.f \\
\text{type} & \tau ::= & r \mid u\ s
\end{array}
$$

$$
\begin{array}{ll}
x \in \mathit{Vars} & u \in \{\texttt{uniq}, \texttt{nonuniq}\} \\
s \in \mathit{Structs} & r \in \{\texttt{bool}, \texttt{int}, \texttt{unit}\} \\
f \in \mathit{Fields} & m \in \{\texttt{immut}, \texttt{mut}\} \\
g \in \mathit{Functions} &
\end{array}
$$

Fig. 2. Surface syntax.

4.2 Operational Semantics

We formalize the operational semantics as a small step relation $\Gamma \vdash \sigma; e \rightarrow \sigma'; e'$ and a head reduction relation $\Gamma \vdash \sigma; e \rightarrow_{\mathsf{h}} \sigma'; e'$. Head reduction steps only exist if the top-level expression itself can be reduced. Expressions e are reduced in a context consisting of a typing environment Γ, a store σ and an evaluation context K. Figure 3 shows their syntax. Values v in our language are scalar values w or structure values c. A structure value is labeled by a uniqueness u. The small step relation and the head reduction relation are defined mutually inductively by the rules shown in Fig. 4. Expressions are $\boxed{\text{boxed}}$. The rules are mostly standard aside from the treatment of unique values. The E-CONTEXT rule describes a reduction of an expression in an evaluation context K. A number of rules make use of the notations defined in Fig. 6, to recursively perform an operation. Well-formedness of types and values is defined in Fig. 5. The premise $u \leq u_s$ denotes that if u_s is unique then u must be unique as well. Furthermore we define $\mathsf{u}(r) = \texttt{nonuniq}$, $\mathsf{u}(u\ s) = u$, $\mathsf{u}(w) = \texttt{nonuniq}$, and $\mathsf{u}(u\ s\ \{\ f_1 = v_1, f_2 = v_2\ \}) = u$.

A call expression is reduced (E-FNCALL) by means of an intermediate, run-time-only expression of the form $\mathsf{with}(\Gamma, \sigma, e)$. A with-expression evaluates the given expression e under the given type environment Γ and store σ. The E-RETURN rule restores the original context. A let-expression introduces new variables in the type environment Γ (E-LET). We define $\Gamma \vdash y : m\ \tau$ in Fig. 6 to denote the typing of a variable field. Similar to function calls, E-LET makes use of a run-time-only with'-expression to model the scope of the variable. We define $\sigma|_{\mathsf{dom}(\Gamma)}$ as the restriction of σ to the domain of Γ. $\bot$ is stored in σ to distinguish initial assignment from reassignment in the assignment rule. Evaluating an assignment consists of the evaluation of the right-hand side expression (E-CONTEXT), followed by a binding of the obtained value to the path on the left-hand side (E-ASSIGNIMMUT, E-ASSIGNMUT). Immutable variables can only be assigned when they are uninitialized. A stub value $\circledast$ is stored at the structure top-level location. Evaluation of a path expression y is different for unique types and nonunique types. Evaluation of a path that has a unique type corresponds to a destructive read: the value is removed (recursively) from the store σ (E-EVALUNIQUE). For a nonunique type, the variable is read without removing it from the store (E-EVALNONUNIQUE); that is, it is copied. Evaluation gets stuck if the value or any of its (possibly nested) components is marked as unique. With the as-expression, any structure value can be cast to a unique structure value (E-AS).

4.3 Type and Permission System

Our operational semantics gets stuck if the program attempts to copy a value marked as unique, or if it tries to read from an uninitialized variable or mutate an initialized immutable variable. Our type and permission system ensures that a well-typed program does not get stuck. The judgment $\Sigma; \Delta \vdash e : \tau \rightsquigarrow \Delta'$ denotes that expression e is of type τ under type environment Σ and pre-state permission environment Δ, leading to post-state permission environment Δ'.

$$
\begin{array}{rl}
\text{value} & v ::= w \mid c \\
\text{scalar value} & w ::= b \mid z \mid () \\
\text{structure value} & c ::= u\ s\ \{\ f = v, f = v\ \} \\
\text{typing} & \Gamma ::= \emptyset \mid (\Gamma,\ x : m\ \tau) \\
\text{store} & \sigma ::= \emptyset \mid (\sigma,\ y \mapsto w) \mid (\sigma,\ y \mapsto u\ \circledast) \mid (\sigma,\ y \mapsto \bot) \\
\text{evaluation context} & K ::= [] \mid K; e \mid y := K \mid g(K) \mid K\ \mathtt{as}\ \tau \\
& \quad \mid u\ s\ \{\ f_1 = K, f_2 = e\ \} \mid u\ s\ \{\ f_1 = v, f_2 = K\ \} \\
& \quad \mid \mathtt{if}\ K\ \mathtt{then}\ e\ \mathtt{else}\ e \\
\text{expression} & e ::= \ldots \mid \mathsf{with}(\Gamma, \sigma, e) \mid \mathsf{with}'(\Gamma, \sigma, e)
\end{array}
$$

Fig. 3. Configuration for operational semantics.

The latter concepts are defined in Fig. 8. The typing judgment is defined by the rules in Fig. 7. We define $\pi(\mathtt{uniq}, \mathtt{RW}) = \mathtt{W}$, $\pi(\mathtt{uniq}, \mathtt{R}) = \mathtt{NO}$, $\pi(\mathtt{nonuniq}, p) = p$, $\rho(\mathtt{mut}) = \mathtt{RW}$ and $\rho(\mathtt{immut}) = \mathtt{R}$.

The typing rules for primitive values, expression sequences, struct expressions, function definitions, and function calls are standard. For if-expressions each branch is type checked separately in context of the state of the permission environment after type checking of the condition expression (T-If). We write $\Delta_t \Cap \Delta_f = \Delta'$ to denote that the resulting permission environment is the greatest lower bound of the permission environments of the branches. Similarly, for while expressions (T-While), we write $\Delta \leq \Delta_b$ to denote that the permission environment before type checking the condition expression is a lower bound on the permission environment after type checking the body. A structure can always be cast to a unique structure as described by (T-As).

In our system, the typing rules of only three kinds of expressions actively modify permissions, that is, let-expressions, assignments and path expressions. Creating a new variable with a let-expression (T-LetScalar) creates a new entry in the type environment Σ, which records the type and mutability of the variable. The premise $y \notin \text{dom}(\Sigma)$ denotes that y nor any of its fields are in the domain of Σ. The permission of the path is set initially to write-only in the permission environment Δ. In case a variable of a structure type is introduced, the type environment contains the uniqueness of the structure type as well, and the permission environment is set for the structure top-level, as well as for each member recursively (T-LetStruct).

The ability to assign a value to a variable is guarded by a writeability permission (T-Assign). A value can only be assigned to a variable if that variable has a write-only `W` or read-write `RW` permission. Only the top-level permission of the path need to be checked since the permission environment is normalized. Assignment (recursively) updates the permission of the variable (T-Delta, T-DeltaStruct). In case the variable is immutable, it obtains a read-only permission `R`, otherwise it obtains a read-write permission `RW`. The resulting permission environment is normalized.

Evaluation of a path expression (T-Eval) requires a readability permission (`R` or `RW`). Only the top-level permission of the path need to be checked since the

E-Context
$$\frac{\Gamma \vdash \sigma; \boxed{e} \to_{\mathsf{h}} \sigma'; \boxed{e'}}{\Gamma \vdash \sigma; \boxed{K[e]} \to \sigma'; \boxed{K[e']}}$$

E-Seq
$$\frac{}{\Gamma \vdash \sigma; \boxed{v; e} \to_{\mathsf{h}} \sigma; \boxed{e}}$$

E-EvalUnique
$$\frac{\Gamma \vdash y : m\ \tau \quad \sigma_\Gamma[y] = v \quad \mathsf{u}(v) = \mathtt{uniq} \quad \mathsf{wf}\ v}{\Gamma \vdash \sigma; \boxed{y} \to_{\mathsf{h}} \sigma -_\Gamma y; v}$$

E-FnCall
$$\frac{\mathtt{fn}\ g(x : \tau) \to \tau'\ \{\ e\ \}}{\Gamma \vdash \sigma; \boxed{g(v)} \to_{\mathsf{h}} \sigma; \boxed{\mathsf{with}((\emptyset, x : \mathtt{immut}\ \tau), \emptyset[x \mapsto v], e)}}$$

E-EvalNonunique
$$\frac{\Gamma \vdash y : m\ \tau \quad \sigma_\Gamma[y] = v \quad \mathsf{u}(v) = \mathtt{nonuniq} \quad \mathsf{wf}\ v}{\Gamma \vdash \sigma; \boxed{y} \to_{\mathsf{h}} \sigma; v}$$

E-With
$$\frac{\Gamma' \vdash \sigma'; \boxed{e} \to \sigma''; \boxed{e'}}{\Gamma \vdash \sigma; \boxed{\mathsf{with}(\Gamma', \sigma', e)} \to_{\mathsf{h}} \sigma; \boxed{\mathsf{with}(\Gamma', \sigma'', e')}}$$

E-Return
$$\frac{}{\Gamma \vdash \sigma; \boxed{\mathsf{with}(\Gamma', \sigma', v)} \to_{\mathsf{h}} \sigma; v}$$

E-IfTrue
$$\frac{}{\Gamma \vdash \sigma; \boxed{\mathtt{if\ true\ then}\ e_t\ \mathtt{else}\ e_f} \to_{\mathsf{h}} \sigma; \boxed{e_t}}$$

E-IfFalse
$$\frac{}{\Gamma \vdash \sigma; \boxed{\mathtt{if\ false\ then}\ e_t\ \mathtt{else}\ e_f} \to_{\mathsf{h}} \sigma; \boxed{e_f}}$$

E-While
$$\frac{}{\Gamma \vdash \sigma; \boxed{\mathtt{while}\ e_c\ \mathtt{do}\ e_b} \to_{\mathsf{h}} \sigma; \boxed{\mathtt{if}\ e_c\ \mathtt{then}\ e_b; \mathtt{while}\ e_c\ \mathtt{do}\ e_b\ \mathtt{else}\ ()}}$$

E-As
$$\frac{}{\Gamma \vdash \sigma; \boxed{u\ s\ \{f_1 = v_1, f_2 = v_2\}\ \mathtt{as\ uniq}\ s} \to_{\mathsf{h}} \sigma; \mathtt{uniq}\ s\ \{f_1 = v_1, f_2 = v_2\}}$$

E-Let
$$\frac{x \notin \mathrm{dom}(\Gamma) \quad \mathsf{wf}\ \tau}{\Gamma \vdash \sigma; \boxed{\mathtt{let}\ m\ x : \tau\ \mathtt{in}\ e} \to_{\mathsf{h}} \sigma; \boxed{\mathsf{with}'((\Gamma, x : m\ \tau), \sigma[x \mapsto_{(\Gamma, x:m\ \tau)} \bot], e)}}$$

E-With'
$$\frac{\Gamma' \vdash \sigma'; \boxed{e} \to \sigma''; \boxed{e'}}{\Gamma \vdash \sigma; \boxed{\mathsf{with}'(\Gamma', \sigma', e)} \to_{\mathsf{h}} \sigma; \boxed{\mathsf{with}'(\Gamma', \sigma'', e')}}$$

E-With'-Value
$$\frac{}{\Gamma \vdash \sigma; \boxed{\mathsf{with}'(\Gamma', \sigma', v)} \to_{\mathsf{h}} \sigma'|_{\mathrm{dom}(\Gamma)}; v}$$

E-AssignImmut
$$\frac{\Gamma \vdash y : \mathtt{immut}\ \tau \quad \sigma(y) = \bot \quad \mathsf{u}(v) = \mathsf{u}(\tau)}{\Gamma \vdash \sigma; \boxed{y := v} \to_{\mathsf{h}} \sigma[y \mapsto v]; \boxed{()}}$$

E-AssignMut
$$\frac{\Gamma \vdash y : \mathtt{mut}\ \tau \quad \mathsf{u}(v) = \mathsf{u}(\tau)}{\Gamma \vdash \sigma; \boxed{y := v} \to_{\mathsf{h}} \sigma[y \mapsto v]; \boxed{()}}$$

Fig. 4. Operational semantics.

W-StTy
$$\frac{u_s\ \mathtt{struct}\ s\ \{f_1 : \tau_1, f_2 : \tau_2\} \quad u \le u_s \quad \mathsf{wf}\ \tau_1 \quad \mathsf{wf}\ \tau_2 \quad u_s \le \mathsf{u}(\tau_1) \quad u_s \le \mathsf{u}(\tau_2)}{\mathsf{wf}\ u\ s}$$

W-Sc
$$\frac{}{\mathsf{wf}\ r}$$

W-StVal
$$\frac{u_s\ \mathtt{struct}\ s\ \{f_1 : \tau_1, f_2 : \tau_2\} \quad u \le u_s \quad \mathsf{wf}\ v_1 \quad \mathsf{wf}\ v_2 \quad \mathsf{u}(\tau_1) = \mathsf{u}(v_1) \quad \mathsf{u}(\tau_2) = \mathsf{u}(v_2)}{\mathsf{wf}\ u\ s\ \{f_1 = v_1, f_2 = v_2\}}$$

W-ScV
$$\frac{}{\mathsf{wf}\ w}$$

Fig. 5. Well-formedness of types and values.

D-GammaScalar
$$\frac{\Gamma(x) = m\ r}{\Gamma \vdash x : m\ r}$$

D-GammaStruct
$$\frac{\Gamma \vdash y : m\ u\ s \qquad u_s\ \texttt{struct}\ s\ \{\ f_1 : \tau_1, f_2 : \tau_2\ \}}{\Gamma \vdash y.f_i : m\ \tau_i}$$

D-Sigma
$$\sigma[y \mapsto w] = (\sigma, y \mapsto w)$$
$$\sigma[y \mapsto u\ s\ \{\ f_1 = v_1, f_2 = v_2\ \}] = (\sigma, y \mapsto u\ \circledast)[y.f_1 \mapsto v_1][y.f_2 \mapsto v_2]$$

D-SigmaBot
$$\frac{\Gamma \vdash y : m\ r}{\sigma[y \mapsto_\Gamma \bot] = (\sigma, y \mapsto \bot)}$$

D-SigmaBotStruct
$$\frac{\Gamma \vdash y : m\ u\ s \qquad u_s\ \texttt{struct}\ s\ \{\ f_1 : \tau_1, f_2 : \tau_2\ \}}{\sigma[y \mapsto_\Gamma \bot] = (\sigma, y \mapsto \bot)[y.f_1 \mapsto_\Gamma \bot][y.f_2 \mapsto_\Gamma \bot]}$$

D-SigmaMinusScalar
$$\frac{\Gamma \vdash y : m\ r}{\sigma -_\Gamma y = \sigma \setminus \{y\}}$$

D-SigmaMinusStruct
$$\frac{\Gamma \vdash y : m\ u\ s \qquad u_s\ \texttt{struct}\ s\ \{\ f_1 : \tau_1, f_2 : \tau_2\ \}}{\sigma -_\Gamma y = \sigma \setminus \{y\} -_\Gamma y.f_1 -_\Gamma y.f_2}$$

D-SigmaGetScalar
$$\frac{\Gamma \vdash y : m\ r \qquad \sigma(y) = w}{\sigma_\Gamma[y] = w}$$

D-SigmaGetStruct
$$\frac{\begin{array}{ccc}\Gamma \vdash y : m\ u\ s & u_s\ \texttt{struct}\ s\ \{\ f_1 : \tau_1, f_2 : \tau_2\ \} & \\ \sigma(y) = u\ \circledast & v_1 = \sigma_\Gamma[y.f_1] & v_2 = \sigma_\Gamma[y.f_2]\end{array}}{\sigma_\Gamma[y] = u\ s\ \{\ f_1 = v_1, f_2 = v_2\ \}}$$

Fig. 6. Definitions of $\Gamma \vdash y : m\ \tau$, $\sigma[y \mapsto v]$, $\sigma[y \mapsto_\Gamma \bot]$, $\sigma -_\Gamma y$, and $\sigma_\Gamma[y]$.

permission environment is normalized. After evaluation, the permission environment is updated recursively as follows: a path containing a unique type loses its readability permission, while for nonunique types permissions do not change. The resulting permission environment is normalized.

Normalization of the permission environment corresponds to updating the permissions in such way that after normalization, the permission of each variable field and the top-level variable is the greatest lower bound (*inf*) of its children's permissions (T-Normalize).

A program is well-typed if its struct definitions are well-formed, its function definitions are well-typed, and its main expression is well-typed.

4.4 Soundness

In this section, we show that well-typed Sim programs won't get stuck.

Theorem 1 (Type Safety). *If* $\Sigma; \Delta \vdash e : \tau \rightsquigarrow \Delta'$ *and* $\Sigma; \Delta \vdash \Gamma; \sigma$ *then* $\Gamma \vdash \sigma; e \to^* \sigma'; v$ *or the reduction diverges.*

In this theorem we say that when an expression e is well-typed, the expression will be reduced to a value v without getting stuck in a number of evaluation steps or otherwise diverges. We prove this type safety theorem by using the lemmas of progress and preservation. A complete proof of soundness appears in [4].

Lemma 1 (Progress). *If* $\Sigma; \Delta \vdash e : \tau \rightsquigarrow \Delta'$ *and* $\Sigma; \Delta \vdash \Gamma; \sigma$ *then either* $\exists v.\ e = v$*, or there is a reduction:* $\exists \sigma', e'.\ \Gamma \vdash \sigma; e \to \sigma'; e'$ *or* $\exists \sigma', e'.\ \Gamma \vdash \sigma; e \to_h \sigma'; e'$.

T-Bool
$$\frac{b \in \mathbb{B}}{\Sigma; \Delta \vdash \boxed{b} : \texttt{bool} \rightsquigarrow \Delta}$$

T-Int
$$\frac{z \in \mathbb{Z}}{\Sigma; \Delta \vdash \boxed{z} : \texttt{int} \rightsquigarrow \Delta}$$

T-Unit
$$\frac{}{\Sigma; \Delta \vdash \boxed{()} : \texttt{unit} \rightsquigarrow \Delta}$$

T-Fn
$$\frac{\mathsf{wf}\ \tau_i \qquad \mathsf{wf}\ \tau_o \qquad \emptyset; \emptyset \vdash \boxed{\texttt{let}\ x : \tau_i\ \texttt{in}\ e} : \tau_o \rightsquigarrow \Delta'}{\texttt{fn}\ g(x : \tau_i) \rightarrow \tau_o\ \{\ e\ \}}$$

T-Call
$$\frac{\texttt{fn}\ g(x : \tau_1) \rightarrow \tau_2\ \{\ e'\ \} \qquad \Sigma; \Delta \vdash \boxed{e} : \tau_1 \rightsquigarrow \Delta'}{\Sigma; \Delta \vdash \boxed{g(e)} : \tau_2 \rightsquigarrow \Delta'}$$

T-Seq
$$\frac{\Sigma; \Delta \vdash \boxed{e_1} : \tau_1 \rightsquigarrow \Delta_1 \qquad \Sigma; \Delta_1 \vdash \boxed{e_2} : \tau_2 \rightsquigarrow \Delta_2}{\Sigma; \Delta \vdash \boxed{e_1; e_2} : \tau_2 \rightsquigarrow \Delta_2}$$

T-As
$$\frac{\Sigma; \Delta \vdash \boxed{e} : u\ s \rightsquigarrow \Delta'}{\Sigma; \Delta \vdash \boxed{e\ \texttt{as uniq}\ s} : \texttt{uniq}\ s \rightsquigarrow \Delta'}$$

T-StructExpr
$$\frac{u_s\ \texttt{struct}\ s\ \{\ f_1 : \tau_1, f_2 : \tau_2\ \} \qquad u \le u_s \qquad \Sigma; \Delta \vdash \boxed{e_1} : \tau_1 \rightsquigarrow \Delta_1 \qquad \Sigma; \Delta_1 \vdash \boxed{e_2} : \tau_2 \rightsquigarrow \Delta_2}{\Sigma; \Delta \vdash \boxed{u\ s\ \{\ f_1 = e_1, f_2 = e_2\ \}} : u\ s \rightsquigarrow \Delta_2}$$

T-If
$$\frac{\Sigma; \Delta \vdash \boxed{e_c} : \texttt{bool} \rightsquigarrow \Delta_c \qquad \Sigma; \Delta_c \vdash \boxed{e_t} : \tau \rightsquigarrow \Delta_t \qquad \Sigma; \Delta_c \vdash \boxed{e_f} : \tau \rightsquigarrow \Delta_f \qquad \Delta_t \Cap \Delta_f = \Delta'}{\Sigma; \Delta \vdash \boxed{\texttt{if}\ e_c\ \texttt{then}\ e_t\ \texttt{else}\ e_f} : \tau \rightsquigarrow \Delta'}$$

T-While
$$\frac{\Sigma; \Delta \vdash \boxed{e_c} : \texttt{bool} \rightsquigarrow \Delta_c \qquad \Delta_b \le \Delta_c \qquad \Sigma; \Delta_c \vdash \boxed{e_b} : \tau \rightsquigarrow \Delta_b \qquad \Delta \le \Delta_b}{\Sigma; \Delta \vdash \boxed{\texttt{while}\ e_c\ \texttt{do}\ e_b} : \texttt{unit} \rightsquigarrow \Delta_b}$$

T-LetScalar
$$\frac{y \notin \mathrm{dom}(\Sigma) \qquad (\Sigma, y : m\ r); (\Delta, y \mapsto \texttt{W}) \vdash \boxed{e} : \tau \rightsquigarrow \Delta'}{\Sigma; \Delta \vdash \boxed{\texttt{let}\ m\ y : r\ \texttt{in}\ e} : \tau \rightsquigarrow \Delta'|_{\mathrm{dom}(\Sigma)}}$$

T-With'
$$\frac{\Sigma; \Delta \vdash \Gamma'|_{\mathrm{dom}(\Sigma)}; \sigma'|_{\mathrm{dom}(\Sigma)} \qquad \Sigma'; \Delta' \vdash \Gamma'; \sigma' \qquad \Sigma'; \Delta' \vdash \boxed{e} : \tau \rightsquigarrow \Delta''}{\Sigma; \Delta \vdash \boxed{\mathsf{with}'(\Gamma', \sigma', e)} : \tau \rightsquigarrow \Delta''|_{\mathrm{dom}(\Sigma)}}$$

T-LetStruct
$$\frac{y \notin \mathrm{dom}(\Sigma) \qquad u_s\ \texttt{struct}\ s\ \{\ f_1 : \tau_1, f_2 : \tau_2\ \} \qquad \mathsf{wf}\ u\ s \qquad (\Sigma, y : m\ u\ s); (\Delta, y \mapsto \texttt{W}) \vdash \boxed{\texttt{let}\ m\ y.f_1 : \tau_1\ \texttt{in let}\ m\ y.f_2 : \tau_2\ \texttt{in}\ e} : \tau \rightsquigarrow \Delta'}{\Sigma; \Delta \vdash \boxed{\texttt{let}\ m\ y : u\ s\ \texttt{in}\ e} : \tau \rightsquigarrow \Delta'|_{\mathrm{dom}(\Sigma)}}$$

T-Assign
$$\frac{\Sigma(y) = m\ \tau \qquad \Sigma; \Delta \vdash \boxed{e} : \tau \rightsquigarrow \Delta' \qquad \Delta'(y) \in \{\texttt{RW}, \texttt{W}\} \qquad \Delta'' = \mathsf{norm}(\Delta'[y \rightrightarrows_{\Sigma} \rho(m)])}{\Sigma; \Delta \vdash \boxed{y := e} : \texttt{unit} \rightsquigarrow \Delta''}$$

T-Eval
$$\frac{\Sigma(y) = m\ \tau \qquad \Delta(y) \in \{\texttt{RW}, \texttt{R}\} \qquad \Delta' = \mathsf{norm}(\Delta[y \rightrightarrows_{\Sigma} \pi(\mathsf{u}(\tau), \Delta(y))])}{\Sigma; \Delta \vdash \boxed{y} : \tau \rightsquigarrow \Delta'}$$

T-Normalize
$$\begin{array}{c}\mathsf{norm}(\Delta) = \Delta' \text{ such that} \\ \forall y \in \mathrm{dom}(\Delta).\ \Sigma(y) = m\ r \Rightarrow \Delta'(y) = \Delta(y) \\ \forall y \in \mathrm{dom}(\Delta).\ \Sigma(y) = m\ u\ s \wedge u_s\ \texttt{struct}\ s\ \{\ f_1 : \tau_1, f_2 : \tau_2\ \} \\ \Rightarrow \Delta'(y) = \mathit{inf}(\Delta(y.f_1), \Delta(y.f_2))\end{array}$$

T-Delta
$$\frac{\Sigma(y) = m\ r}{\Delta[y \rightrightarrows_{\Sigma} p] = (\Delta, y \mapsto p)}$$

T-With
$$\frac{\Sigma'; \Delta' \vdash \Gamma'; \sigma' \qquad \Sigma'; \Delta' \vdash \boxed{e} : \tau \rightsquigarrow \Delta''}{\Sigma; \Delta \vdash \boxed{\mathsf{with}(\Gamma', \sigma', e)} : \tau \rightsquigarrow \Delta}$$

T-DeltaStruct
$$\frac{\Sigma(y) = m\ u\ s \qquad u_s\ \texttt{struct}\ s\ \{\ f_1 : \tau_1, f_2 : \tau_2\ \}}{\Delta[y \rightrightarrows_{\Sigma} p] = (\Delta, y \mapsto p)[y.f_1 \rightrightarrows_{\Sigma} p][y.f_2 \rightrightarrows_{\Sigma} p]}$$

Fig. 7. Type and permission system.

$$\begin{aligned}
\text{type environment } \Sigma &::= \emptyset \mid (\Sigma,\ y : m\ \tau) \\
\text{permission environment } \Delta &::= \emptyset \mid (\Delta,\ y \mapsto p) \\
\text{scalar permission } p &::= \texttt{RW} \mid \texttt{R} \mid \texttt{W} \mid \texttt{NO} \\
\text{expression } e &::= \ldots \mid \texttt{let}\ m\ y : \tau\ \texttt{in}\ e
\end{aligned}$$

Fig. 8. Typing context for the type and permission system.

The progress lemma says that if an expression e is well-typed and the run-time configuration is consistent with the type and permission environment, then either the expression e is a value or we can take a step to an expression e'.

Lemma 2 (Preservation). *If $\Gamma \vdash \sigma; e \rightarrow \sigma'; e'$ or $\Gamma \vdash \sigma; e \rightarrow_h \sigma'; e'$ and $\Sigma; \Delta \vdash e : \tau \rightsquigarrow \Delta'$ and $\Sigma; \Delta \vdash \Gamma; \sigma$ then there is a Δ'', Δ''' such that $\Sigma; \Delta'' \vdash e' : \tau \rightsquigarrow \Delta'''$ and $\Sigma; \Delta'' \vdash \Gamma; \sigma'$ and $\Delta''' \geq \Delta'$.*

The preservation lemma says that if an expression e is well-typed, and the run-time configuration is consistent with the type and permission environment, and we can take a step to an expression e' then there exists a pre-state permission environment Δ'', and a post-state permission environment Δ''' under which the updated expression e' is also well typed.

5 Implementation

We have implemented our type and permission system in the Sim compiler. The compiler first performs the normal type checking on terms that are stripped of the uniqueness modifiers. Then, the permissions are checked on a control-flow graph representation of the code in an array static single assignment (Array SSA) form [14]. Array SSA form is a variant of SSA that allows partial assignment of variables and is well suited for the representation of assignments to structure fields and checking of permissions thereof.

For subsequent code generation, the compiler takes into account the uniqueness information provided in the code. If it detects a function that passes a unique value as input and it returns a unique value as output of the same type, it will generate code that passes the unique value by reference. In addition, it will generate code for the function implementation that dereferences the passed argument on reading, and it will mutate the referenced data in place instead of returning a new value. This is valid since the type and permission system guarantees that the value that was originally stored in the variable is never used again. The compiler generates Rust or C code depending on the backend used.

6 Validation

6.1 Annotation Overhead

We validated our claim that an aliasing-free language enables verification with a small annotation overhead, by comparing the verification of programs written in Sim, an aliasing-free programming language, with programs written in C and verified with VeriFast. VeriFast is a state-of-the-art verifier for C and represents the program's memory in separation logic [8].

Twenty-seven small programs (taken from [9]) and one larger program that is representative for a realistic embedded systems application ("fly_by_wire" on Fig. 9) have been written in both Sim and C [4]. The C-code has been decorated with VeriFast annotations.

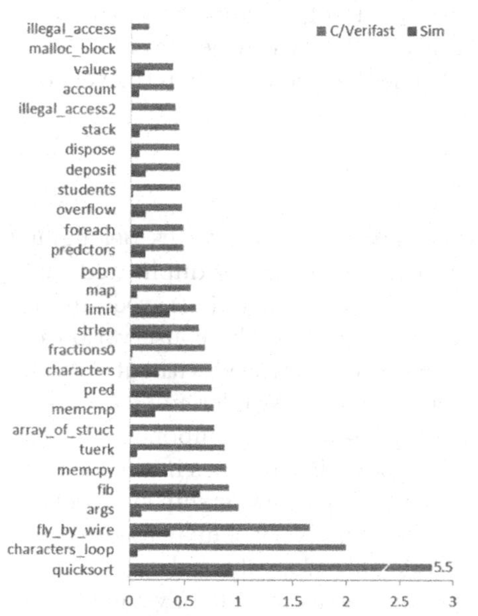

Fig. 9. Sim vs VeriFast-C: verification annotations per line of code.

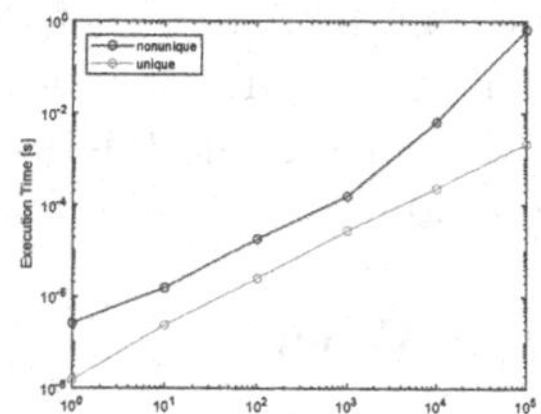

(a) Execution time vs. vector length

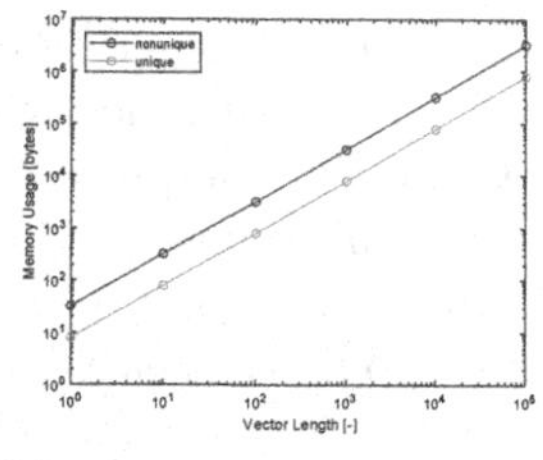

(b) Memory use vs. vector length

Fig. 10. Benchmark of the `shift` function of Listing 2.

The programs are subsequently verified with respectively the Sim verifier and VeriFast. Attention has been paid to write the code and annotations in an idiomatic way in both languages as well as making sure that the programs and proven properties in the two languages are equivalent.

For each program, the number of verification annotations and the number of executable lines of code are counted. The number of executable lines of code is similar for the two languages. Figure 9 shows the number of verification annotations per line of code (LOC) for each program. The average for VeriFast-C is *0.83* verification annotations per LOC, while for Sim *0.18* verification annotations per LOC are needed for the given programs. Compared to VeriFast-C, the annotation effort is reduced by a factor of *4.6* by writing the program in Sim.

6.2 Performance Benchmark

The `shift` function in Listing 2 is suited for optimization. We compiled two versions of the function: one where the `unique` modifiers are present and one where they are absent. Figure 10 shows the results of a benchmark of the execution time and memory use for different lengths of the array parameter that is passed.

From Fig. 10a, it can be observed that the execution time of the version with the `unique` modifiers is an order of magnitude lower than the version without the modifiers, for vector lengths lower or equal to 10^3. Above that, the difference in execution time increases to two and three orders of magnitude. Cache size limitations might explain this behavior. From Fig. 10b, it can be observed that the version with `unique` modifiers consumes 4 times less memory than the version without the modifiers.

7 Related Work

In line with Girard's linear logic [7], Wadler [17] notes that values belonging to a linear type must be used exactly once: a value cannot be duplicated and a value cannot be discarded: it must be explicitely used or destroyed. In [1] Baker describes the intuition behind linear types, that is, the conservation of physical matter - a linear object cannot be created or destroyed without special permission. Clean's [6] uniqueness type system is close to Wadler's linear types. Similar to Sim, a uniqueness type in Clean is a tuple of various components which can be decomposed or rebuilt. Cyclone C [11] supports linear types in the form of tracked pointers to make it easy to restrict aliasing. Rust's ownership system is a combination of linear types and a region-based system, very similar to the type system of Cyclone. In Rust types are unique by default. Copyable behavior is opt-in by implementing the `Clone` trait for a type. In contrast to Sim, Cyclone's and Rust's linear type system is primarily aimed at memory management without garbage collection and to ensure thread safety. Furthermore, Sim allows types to be declared locally unique, while in Rust uniqueness can only be defined at the type-definition level. In [10], Jaloyan et al. propose an extension of (a subset of) Ada SPARK with linear access types (Ada's pointers). Like Rust, the system is primarily aimed at aliasing control. Unlike Sim, the system cannot be used for resource management since no user-defined notion of uniqueness of a value is present. Munch-Maccagnoni [13] proposes a resource management model to extend OCaml with move semantics, destructors, and resource polymorphism. He describes a method for integrating garbage collected values with values of linear types. Pony is an actor-model programming language. Its main mechanism for ensuring data-race-freedom is the use of object capabilities and reference capabilities. Functional languages that include a uniqueness type system are Idris [5] and Alms [16].

8 Conclusion

We have introduced a new approach to using uniqueness types to enable building efficient and verifiable embedded software using an aliasing-free programming language. The proposed model enables compiler optimizations such as elimination of physical copies and in-place mutation. In addition, the proposed approach provides a lightweight notation for the programmer to control copying behavior. We show that the system increases the execution speed and reduces the memory use while keeping the ease of reasoning of value types, thereby considerably reducing the annotations required for semi-automatic formal verification.

References

1. Baker, H.G.: "Use-once" variables and linear objects: storage management, reflection and multi-threading. ACM SIGPLAN Not. **30**(1), 45–52 (1995)
2. Baudin, P., et al.: ACSL: ANSI/ISO C Specification Language Version 1.13, pp. 1–114 (2011)
3. Benoit, T.: Sim: a contract-based programming language for safety-critical software. In: Proceedings of the 38th Digital Avionics Systems Conference (DASC) (2019)
4. Benoit, T., Jacobs, B.: Uniqueness Types for Efficient and Verifiable Aliasing-Free Embedded Systems Programming - Extended Report. Technical report, Siemens Industry Software, Leuven, Belgium (2019). https://github.com/trbenoit/uniqueness-types
5. Brady, E.: Idris, a general-purpose dependently typed programming language: design and implementation. J. Funct. Program. **23**(05), 552–593 (2013)
6. Brus, T.H., van Eekelen, M.C.J.D., van Leer, M.O., Plasmeijer, M.J.: Clean — a language for functional graph rewriting. In: Kahn, G. (ed.) FPCA 1987. LNCS, vol. 274, pp. 364–384. Springer, Heidelberg (1987). https://doi.org/10.1007/3-540-18317-5_20
7. Girard, J.Y.: Linear logic. Theoret. Comput. Sci. **50**(1), 1–101 (1987)
8. Jacobs, B., Smans, J., Philippaerts, P., Vogels, F., Penninckx, W., Piessens, F.: VeriFast: a powerful, sound, predictable, fast verifier for C and Java. In: Bobaru, M., Havelund, K., Holzmann, G.J., Joshi, R. (eds.) NFM 2011. LNCS, vol. 6617, pp. 41–55. Springer, Heidelberg (2011). https://doi.org/10.1007/978-3-642-20398-5_4
9. Jacobs, B., Smans, J., Piessens, F.: The VeriFast Program Verifier: A Tutorial. Technical report, imec-DistriNet, Department of Computer Science, KU Leuven (2017)
10. Jaloyan, G.A., Moy, Y., Paskevich, A.: Borrowing safe pointers from rust in SPARK. In: International Conference on Computer-Aided Verification - 29th International Conference, Heidelberg, Germany (2018)
11. Jim, T., Morrisett, J.G., Grossman, D., Hicks, M.W., Cheney, J., Wang, Y.: Cyclone: a safe dialect of C. In: Proceedings of the USENIX Annual Technical Conference, pp. 275–288. USENIX Association, Berkeley, CA, USA (2002)
12. McCormick, J.W., Chapin, P.C.: Building High Integrity Applications with SPARK. Cambridge University Press, Cambridge (2015)
13. Munch-maccagnoni, G.: Resource Polymorphism (OCaml language with destructors, move semantics). Technical report (2018)
14. Rastello, F.: SSA-based Compiler Design. Springer Publishing Company, Incorporated, New York (2016)
15. Reynolds, J.C.: Separation logic: a logic for shared mutable data structures. In: Proceedings of the 17th Annual IEEE Symposium on Logic in Computer Science LICS 2002, pp. 55–74. IEEE Computer Society, Washington, DC, USA (2002)

16. Tov, J.A., Pucella, R.: Practical affine types. In: Proceedings of the 38th Annual ACM SIGPLAN-SIGACT Symposium on Principles of Programming Languages POPL 2011, New York, USA, pp. 447–458 (2011)
17. Wadler, P.: Linear types can change the world! In: IFIP Working Conference on Programming Concepts and Methods. Sea of Gallilee, Israel (1990)

Using Ontologies in Formal Developments Targeting Certification

Achim D. Brucker[1(✉)] and Burkhart Wolff[2]

[1] University of Exeter, Exeter, UK
a.brucker@exeter.ac.uk
[2] LRI, Université Paris-Saclay, Paris, France
wolff@lri.fr

Abstract. A common problem in the certification of highly safety or security critical systems is the consistency of the certification documentation in general and, in particular, the linking between semi-formal and formal content of the certification documentation.

We address this problem by using an existing framework, Isabelle/DOF, that allows writing certification documents with consistency guarantees, in both, the semi-formal and formal parts. Isabelle/DOF supports the *modeling* of document ontologies using a strongly typed ontology definition language. An ontology is then *enforced* inside documents including formal parts, e. g., system models, verification proofs, code, tests and validations of corner-cases. The entire set of documents is checked within Isabelle/HOL, which includes the definition of ontologies and the editing of integrated documents based on them. This process is supported by an IDE that provides continuous checking of the document consistency.

In this paper, we present how a specific software-engineering certification standard, namely CENELEC 50128, can be modeled inside Isabelle/DOF. Based on an ontology covering a substantial part of this standard, we present how Isabelle/DOF can be applied to a certification case-study in the railway domain.

Keywords: Certification of Safety-Critical Systems · CENELEC 50128 · Formal document development · Isabelle/DOF · Isabelle/HOL

1 Introduction

The initial motivation of this work lies in a failure: the second author was part of the theorem proving team of the EUROMILS project which attempted to certify the commercial operating system PikeOS 3.4 according to CC EAL5+ [12]. When the project came to an end, it became clear that the project would not achieve this goal.[1] The evaluator informed us about an embarrassing number of inconsistencies in the provided documents (written in Word, Excel, LaTeX, and

[1] The company SYSGO/Thales behind this initiative finally abandoned the approach and restarted a certification on a later version.

W. Ahrendt and S. L. Tapia Tarifa (Eds.): IFM 2019, LNCS 11918, pp. 65–82, 2019.
https://doi.org/10.1007/978-3-030-34968-4_4

documents generated from 3 000 lines of proof code written in Isabelle/HOL). While impressed by the proof work done, he pointed out that the overall inconsistency in the documents provided made an evaluation impossible. For example, he highlighted a number of informal definitions of the security target that did not fit to what was modeled, or that the implementation model did not fit to what was tested. He also made accurate comments on inconsistent references and terminologies.

This failure led the authors of this paper to the following insight: For a successful formal certification process, it is *by far not enough* to have abstract models and corresponding refinement proofs to some implementation model (or even, as is the case in [13] or the seL4 initiative [20], to realistic C code). Certification processes targeting higher-levels of assurance such as CENELEC 50128/SIL 4 [11] or CC EAL7 [12] are all requiring the use of formal methods. Therefore, they are a rewarding target for research in this domain. Their core concern, however, is the traceability of requirements, assumptions, application constraints of various nature, and the demonstration of evidence for their satisfaction. Proofs, as a means to connect models, are part of the solution; however the underlying notion of *evidence* in certifications comprises also tests, informal arguments or just references to an expert opinion.

In a wider perspective, it turns out to be a substantial problem in large, distributed development processes, to keep track of the evolution of project specific knowledge and to control the overall documentation effort.

In this paper, we present a methodology together with a set of mechanisms and techniques for an automated impact analysis of document changes in order to *achieve* coherence as well as to *maintain* it during evolution. For this purpose, we present

1. the formal development in Isabelle/HOL of an industrial case-study: the odometric function measuring position, speed, and acceleration of a train,
2. an ontology formalizing parts of the CENELEC 50128 standard in ODL, for which we use Isabelle/DOF [8,10], and
3. the methodology to annotate an Isabelle formal development with the concepts of this CENELEC in order to enforce coherence.

With respect to the formal development, we restrict ourselves to core aspects of this development, ranging from modeling the physics of a train over the physics of a measuring device down to a C implementation running on a Sabre-Light Card using seL4.

2 Background

In this section, we provide a guided tour through the underlying technologies of this paper: 1. Isabelle and Isabelle/HOL, 2. Isabelle/DOF and its Ontology Definition Language (ODL).

2.1 Isabelle and HOL

While still widely perceived as an interactive theorem proving environment, Isabelle [22] has become a generic system framework providing an infrastructure for plug-ins. This comprises extensible state components, extensible syntax, code-generation, and advanced documentation support. The plugin Isabelle/HOL offers a modeling language similar to functional programming languages extended by a logic and automated proof and animation techniques.

2.2 The Isabelle/DOF Framework

Isabelle/DOF [8–10] is a document ontology framework that extends Isabelle/HOL. We understand by a *document ontology* structured meta-data attached to an integrated document allowing classifying text-elements, connect them to typed meta-data, and establishing typed links between text- and formal elements (such as definitions, proofs, code, test-results, etc).

Isabelle/DOF offers basically two things: a language called ODL to *specify* a formal ontology, and ways to *annotate* an integrated document written in Isabelle/HOL with the specified meta-data. Additionally, Isabelle/DOF generates from an ontology a family of semantic macros—called *antiquotations* that may appear in text or code—allowing establishing machine-checked links between classified entities. Not unlike the UML/OCL meta-model, ODL offers class invariants as well as means to express structural constraints in documents. Unlike UML, however, Isabelle/DOF allows for integrated documents with informal and formal elements including the necessary management of logical contexts.

The perhaps most attractive aspect of Isabelle/DOF is its deep integration into the IDE of Isabelle (PIDE), which allows hypertext-like navigation as well as fast user-feedback during development and evolution of the integrated document. This includes rich editing support, including on-the-fly semantics checks, hinting, or auto-completion. Isabelle/DOF supports LaTeX-based document generation as well as ontology-aware "views" on the integrated document, i. e., specific versions of generated PDF addressing, for example, different stake-holders.

2.3 A Guided Tour Through ODL

Isabelle/DOF provides a strongly typed Ontology Definition Language (ODL) that provides the usual concepts of ontologies such as

- *document class* (using the `doc_class` keyword) that describes a concept,
- *attributes* specific to document classes (attributes might be initialized with default values),
- a special link, the reference to a super-class, establishes an *is-a* relation between classes;
- classes may refer to other classes via a regular expression in an optional *where* clause (a class with a where clause is called *monitor*);

The types of attributes are HOL-types. Thus, ODL can refer to any predefined type from the HOL library, e. g., `string`, `int` as well as parameterized types, e. g., `option`, `list`. As a consequence of the Isabelle document model, ODL definitions may be arbitrarily mixed with standard HOL type definitions. Document class definitions are HOL-types, allowing for formal *links* to and between ontological concepts. For example, the basic concept of requirements from CENELEC 50128 [11] is captured in ODL as follows:

```
doc_class requirement = text_element + (* derived from text_element     *)
          long_name    ::string option  (* an optional string attribute *)
          is_concerned::role set        (* roles working with this req. *)
```

This ODL class definition maybe part of one or more Isabelle theory–files capturing the entire ontology definition. Isabelle's session management allows for pre-compiling them before being imported in the actual target documentation required to be compliant to this ontology.

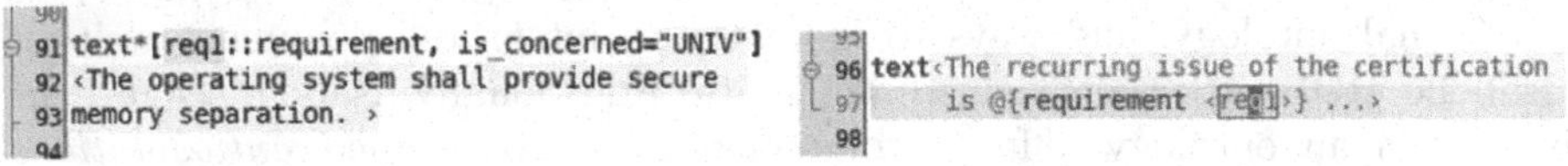

```
text*[req1::requirement, is_concerned="UNIV"]
‹The operating system shall provide secure
memory separation. ›
```

(a) A Text-Element as Requirement.

```
text‹The recurring issue of the certification
     is @{requirement ‹req1›} ...›
```

(b) Referencing a Requirement.

Fig. 1. Referencing a requirement.

Figure 1 shows an ontological annotation of a requirement and the referencing via an antiquotation `@{requirement ‹req1›}` generated by Isabelle/DOF from the above class definition. Undefined or ill-typed references were rejected, the high-lighting displays the hyperlinking which is activated on a click. Revising the actual definition of *requirement*, it suffices to click on its keyword: the IDE will display the class-definition and its surrounding documentation in the ontology.

Isabelle/DOF's generated antiquotations are part of a general mechanism of Isabelle's standard antiquotations heavily used in various papers and technical reports. For example, in the following informal text, the antiquotation `@{thm refl}` refers to the reflexivity axiom from HOL:

```
text‹According to the reflexivity axiom @{thm refl}, we obtain in Γ
      for @{term ‹fac 5›} the result @{value ‹fac 5›}.›
```

In the PDF output, this is represented as follows:

According to the reflexivity axiom $x = x$, we obtain in Γ for fac 5 the result 120.

The antiquotation `@{value ‹fac 5›}` refers to a function that is defined in the preceding logical context (and parsed as inner syntax) to compute the value of 5!, i. e., 120. Summing up, antiquotations can refer to formal content, can be type-checked before being displayed and can be used for calculations before actually being typeset. All these features can be used for the calculation of attribute values (as in Fig. 1, observe the value `UNIV` used to set the attribute `is_concerned` is a HOL-constant denoting the universal set).

Finally, for each ontological concept, a custom representation, using LaTeX notation, for the generated PDF document can be defined. The latter includes, e. g., the possibility to automatically generated glossaries or lists of concepts.

3 The Underlying Methodology

We assume that all documentation, models, proofs, test-execution scripts, and code are managed in an *integrated document*; Isabelle/DOF supports this approach by admitting an acyclic graph of sub-documents consisting of different type of files. We are well aware that this precondition will raise the question of scalability; however, the Isabelle system is based on a document model allowing for efficient, parallelized evaluation and checking of its document content (cf. [5,24,25] for the fairly innovative technologies underlying the Isabelle architecture). These technologies allow for scaling up to fairly large documents: we have seen documents with 150 files be loaded (excluding proof-checking) in about 4 min, and individual files—like the x86 model generated from Antony Fox's L3 specs—can have 80 kLOC and were loaded in about the same time.

Only *inside* an integrated document Isabelle/DOF can manage and check the mutual dependencies and give automated and fast feedback to the validity of ontological dependencies; document boundaries imply a drastically reduced information flow and the need for complex round-engineering techniques.

Methodologically, the integrated document is central; subsequent versions evolve from the informal to the formal, from unstructured to structured text.

We will use the odometry case-study as a show-case of our methodology, which consists of four (not necessarily sequential) phases:

1. *Textual Elicitation* of informal pre-documents into an integrated source,
2. *Formal Enrichment* of the integrated source with definitions in HOL, capturing the lexicon of concepts and notions concerning system environment, architecture, and required performances,
3. *Verification* of the theory resulting from these definitions; in our case, this comprises formal proofs of safety properties or refinements from high-level system models to design and from design to the code-level, and
4. *Ontological Embedding* of text-, model-, and evidence-elements in the integrated source into a concrete target ontology of a certification standard.

In the following, we will present selected snapshots of the document evolution covering the phases 1 to 3, while phase 4 is presented in Sect. 6.

4 A Case-Study: An Odometer-Subsystem

In our case study, we will follow the phases of analysis, design, and implementation of the odometry function of a train. This software processes data from an odometer to compute the position, speed, and acceleration of a train. This system provides the basis for many safety critical decisions, e. g., the opening of the doors. Due to its relatively small size, it is a manageable, albeit realistic target for a comprehensive formal development: it covers a physical model of the environment, the physical and architectural model of the odometer including the problem of numerical sampling, and the boundaries of efficient computations. The interplay between environment and measuring-device as well as the implementation problems on a platform with limited resources makes the odometer a fairly typical safety critical embedded system.

We start with our phase called *textual elicitation* of a number of informal documents available at the beginning of the development; since our approach assumes an integrated document for the entire project—only inside these documents, the checking if coherence is possible—all initial texts must be brought into this format. We selected a few text snippets from original documents and their treatment during this phase.

4.1 System Requirements Specification as an *Integrated Source*

Textual Elicitation of "Basic Principles of Motion and Motion Measurement." The motion of a train and the method for measuring the motion is textually described as follows: "A rotary encoder measures the motion of a train. To achieve this, the encoder's shaft is fixed to the trains wheels axle. When the train moves, the encoder produces a signal pattern directly related to the trains progress. By measuring the fractional rotation of the encoders shaft and considering the wheels effective ratio, relative movement of the train can be calculated."

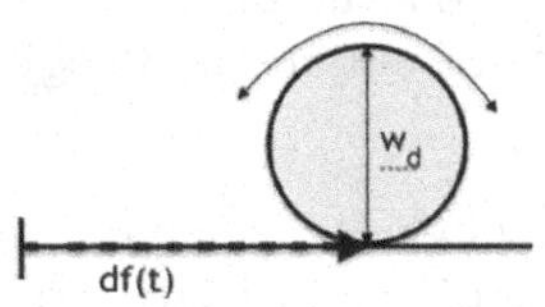

Fig. 2. Motion sensing via an odometer.

Figure 2 shows that we model a train, seen from a pure kinematics standpoint, as physical system characterized by a one-dimensional continuous distance function, which represents the observable of the physical system. Concepts like speed and acceleration were derived concepts defined as their (gradient) derivatives. We assume the use of the meter, kilogram, and second (MKS) system.

This model is already based on several fundamental assumptions relevant for the correct functioning of the system and for its integration into the system as a whole. In particular, we need to make the following assumptions explicit:

- that *a perfectly circular wheel profile* is assumed, with constant radius,
- that the *slip between the trains wheel and the track* is *negligible*,
- the distance between all teeth of a wheel is the same and constant, and
- the sampling rate of positions is a given constant.

These assumptions have to be traced throughout the certification process as *derived requirements* (or, in CENELEC terminology, as *exported constraints*), which is also reflected by their tracing throughout the body of certification documents. This may result in operational regulations, e. g., regular checks for tolerable wheel defects. As for the *no slip*-assumption, this leads to the modeling of constraints under which physical slip can be neglected: the device can only produce reliable results under certain physical constraints (speed and acceleration limits). Moreover, the *no slip*-assumption motivates architectural arrangements for situations where this assumption cannot be assured (as is the case, for example, of an emergency breaking) together with error-detection and error-recovery.

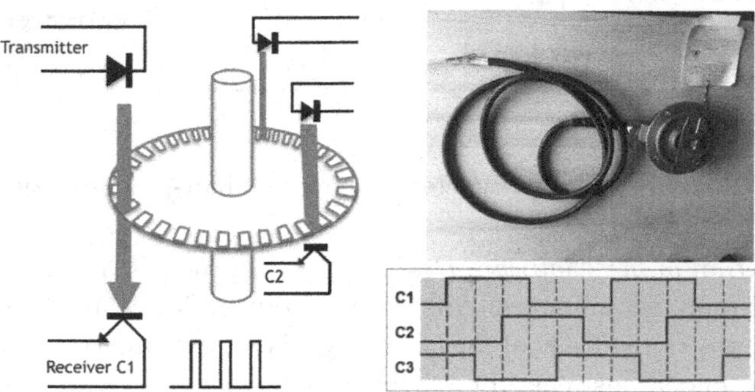

Fig. 3. An odometer with three sensors `C1`, `C2`, and `C3`.

Textual Elicitation of "System Architecture." The requirements analysis also contains a sub-document *interface data* which can be subsumed into the CENELEC notion *system architecture description.* It contains technical drawing of the odometer, a timing diagram (see Fig. 3), and tables describing the encoding of the position for the possible signal transitions of the sensors `C1`, `C2`, and $C3$.

Textual Elicitation of "System Interfaces." The initial document contains a section *Interface data* which is subsumed under the CENELEC notion *functions and interfaces* required as part of the requirements analysis. It describes the technical format of the output of the odometry function, e. g., specifies the output *speed* as given by a `int_32` to be the "Estimation of the speed (in mm/sec) evaluated over the latest N_{avg} samples" where the speed refers to the physical speed of the train and N_{avg} a parameter of the sub-system configuration.

Textual Elicitation of "Required Performances." The analysis documents were relatively implicit on the expected precision of the measurements; however, certain interface parameters like `Odometric_Position_TimeStamp` (a counter on the number of samplings) and `Relative_Position` are defined by an unsigned 32 bit integer. The textual elicitation phase even revealed minor errors in the consistent spelling of parameter names and a more severe ontological confusion between the *physical time* (i. e., *time* in the sense of the physical environment model) and the time measured by the device, which is not identical under all circumstances. These parameter definitions imply *exported constraints* (CENELEC notion) concerning the acceptable time of service as well the maximum distance before a necessary reboot of the subsystem. For our case-study, we assume maximum deviation of the `Relative_Position` to the theoretical distance.

The requirement analysis document describes the physical environment, the architecture of the measuring device, and the required format and precision of the measurements of the odometry function as represented (see Fig. 4).

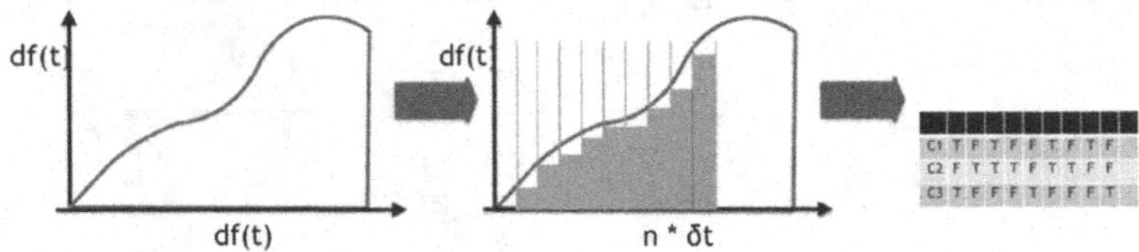

Fig. 4. Real distance vs. discrete distance vs. shaft-encoder sequence

Textual Elicitation of the "Software Design Spec" (Resume). The design provides a function that manages an internal first-in-first-out buffer of shaft-encodings and corresponding positions. Central for the design is a step-function analyzing new incoming shaft encodings, checking them and propagating two kinds of error-states (one allowing recovery, another one, fatal, signaling, e. g., a defect of the receiver hardware), calculating the relative position, speed and acceleration.

Textual Elicitation of the "Software Implementation" (Resume). While the design is executable on a Linux system, it turns out that the generated code from an Isabelle model is neither executable on resource-constraint target platform, an ARM-based Sabre-light card, nor certifiable, since the compilation chain via ML to C implies the inclusion of a run-time system and quite complex libraries. We adopted therefore a similar approach as used in the seL4 project [21]: we use a hand-written implementation in C and verify it via AutoCorres [17] against the design model. The hand-written C-source is integrated into the Isabelle/HOL technically by registering it in the build-configuration and logically by a trusted C-to-HOL compiler included in AutoCorres.

4.2 Formal Enrichment of the Software Requirements Specification

After the *eliciation*-phase, we turn now to *formal enrichment* phase. For example, the assumptions in the system architecture were formalized by the Isabelle/HOL definitions, which were added as close as possible to the informal text:

```
definition teeth_per_wheelturn::nat  (tpw) where tpw ≡ SOME x. x > 0
definition wheel_diameter::real (w_d) where w_d ≡ SOME x. x > 0
definition wheel_circumference::real (w_circ) where w_circ ≡ pi * w_d
definition δs_res::real where δs_res ≡ w_circ / (2 * 3 * tpw)
```

Here, `real` refers to the real numbers as defined in the HOL-Analysis library, which provides concepts such as Cauchy Sequences, limits, differentiability, and a very substantial part of classical Calculus. `SOME` is the Hilbert choice operator from HOL; the definitions of the model parameters admit all possible positive values as uninterpreted constants. Our perfect-wheel assumption is translated into a calculation of the circumference of the wheel, while δs_{res}, the resolution of the odometer, can be calculated from the these parameters. HOL-Analysis permits to formalize the fundamental physical observables:

```
type_synonym distance_function = real⇒real
definition Speed::distance_function⇒real⇒real where Speed f ≡ deriv f
definition Accel::distance_function⇒real⇒real
                                        where Accel f ≡ deriv (deriv f)
```

which permits to constrain the central observable `distance_function` in a way that they describe the space of "normal behavior" where we expect the odometer to produce reliable measurements over a `distance_function df`.

The essence of the physics of the train is covered by the following definition:

```
definition normally_behaved_distance_function :: (real ⇒ real) ⇒ bool
   where  normally_behaved_distance_function df =
           ( ∀ t. df(t) ∈ ℝ≥0  ∧  (∀ t ∈ ℝ≤0. df(t) = 0)
            ∧ df differentiable onR ∧ (Speed df)differentiable onR
            ∧ (Accel df)differentiable onR
            ∧ (∀ t. (Speed df) t ∈ {-SpeedMax .. SpeedMax})
            ∧ (∀ t. (Accel df) t ∈ {-|AccelMax| .. |AccelMax|}))
```

which constrains the distance functions in the bounds described of the informal descriptions and states them as three-fold differentiable function in certain bounds concerning speed and acceleration. Violations, in particular of the constraints on speed and acceleration, *do* occur in practice. In such cases, the global system adapts recovery strategies that are out of the scope of our model. Concepts like `shaft_encoder_state` (a triple with the sensor values `C1`, `C2`, `C3`) were formalized as types, while tables were defined as recursive functions:

```
fun phase0 :: nat ⇒ shaft_encoder_state   where
   phase0 (0) =  (| C1 = False, C2 = False, C3 = True |)
  |phase0 (1) =  (| C1 = True,  C2 = False, C3 = True |)
  |phase0 (2) =  (| C1 = True,  C2 = False, C3 = False|)
  |phase0 (3) =  (| C1 = True,  C2 = True,  C3 = False|)
  |phase0 (4) =  (| C1 = False, C2 = True,  C3 = False|)
  |phase0 (5) =  (| C1 = False, C2 = True,  C3 = True |)
  |phase0 x   =  phase0(x - 6)
definition Phase ::nat⇒shaft_encoder_state where Phase(x) = phase0(x-1)
```

We express the *shaft encoder sequences* as a translations of distance functions:

```
definition encoding::distance_function⇒nat⇒real⇒shaft_encoder_state
  where encoding df initpos ≡ λx. Phase(nat⌊df(x) / δsres⌋ + initpos)
```

where `initpos` is the initial position of the wheel. `sampling`'s were constructed from encoding sequences over discretized time points:

```
definition sampling::distance_function⇒nat⇒real⇒nat⇒shaft_encoder_state
  where sampling df initpos δt ≡ λn::nat. encoding df initpos (n * δt)
```

The sampling interval δt (the inverse of the sampling frequency) is a critical parameter of the configuration of a system.

Finally, we can formally define the required performances. From the interface description and the global model parameters such as wheel diameter, the number of teeth per wheel, the sampling frequency etc., we can infer the maximal time of service as well the maximum distance the device can measure. As an example configuration, choosing 1 m for w_d, 100 for tpw, 80 km/h $\texttt{Speed}_{\texttt{Max}}$, and 14400 Hz for the sampling frequency, results in an odometer resolution of 2.3 mm, a maximum distance of 9878 km, and a maximal system up-time of 123.4 h. The required precision of an odometer can be defined by a constant describing the maximally allowed difference between df(n*δt) and sampling df $\texttt{init}_{\texttt{pos}}$ δt n for all $\texttt{init}_{\texttt{pos}}$ ∈{0..5}.

4.3 Verification of the Software Requirements Specification

The original documents contained already various statements that motivate certain safety properties of the device. For example, the Phase-table excludes situations in which all sensors C1, C2, and C3 are all "off" or situations in which sensors are "on," reflecting a physical or electrical error in the odometer. It can be shown by a very small Isabelle case-distinction proof that this safety requirement follows indeed from the above definitions:

```
lemma Encoder_Property_1:(C1(Phase x) ∧ C2(Phase x) ∧ C3(Phase x))=False
  proof (cases x)
    case 0 then show ?thesis  by (simp add: Phase_def)
  next
    case (Suc n) then show ?thesis
      by(simp add: Phase_def,rule_tac n = n in cycle_case_split,simp_all)
  qed
```

for all positions x. Similarly, it is proved that the table is indeed cyclic: $\texttt{phase}_0$ x = $\texttt{phase}_0$(x mod 6) and locally injective: ∀x<6. ∀y<6. $\texttt{phase}_0$ x = $\texttt{phase}_0$ y ⟶ z = y. These lemmas, building the "theory of an odometer," culminate in a theorem that we would like to present in more detail.

```
theorem minimal_sampling :
  assumes * : normally_behaved_distance_function df
    and ** : δt * Speed_Max < δs_res
  shows ∀ δX≤δt. 0<δX ⟶
           ∃f. retracting (f::nat⇒nat) ∧
               sampling df init_pos δX = (sampling df init_pos δt) o f
```

This theorem states for normally_behaved_distance_functions that there is a minimal sampling frequency assuring the safety of the measurements; samplings on some df gained from this minimal sampling frequency can be "pumped up" to samplings of these higher sampling frequencies; they do not contain more information. Of particular interest is the assumption, labelled "**," which establishes a lower bound from w_{circ}, tpw, $Speed_{Max}$ for the sampling frequency. Methodologically, this represents an exported constraint that can not be represented *inside* the design model: it means that the computations have to be fast enough on the computing platform in order to assure that the calculations are valid. It was in particular this exported constraint that forced us to give up the original plan to generate the code from the design model and to execute this directly on the target platform.

For our example configuration (1 m diameter, 100 teeth per wheel, 80 km/h max), this theorem justifies that 14,4 kHz is indeed enough to assure valid samplings. Such properties are called "internal consistency of the software requirements specification" in the CENELEC standard [11], 7.2.4.22 and are usually addressed in an own report.

5 The CENELEC Ontology

Modeling an ontology from a semi-formal text such as [11] is, like any other modeling activity, not a simple one-to-one translation of some concepts to some formalism. Rather, implicit and self-understood principles have to be made explicit, abstractions have to be made, and decisions about the kind of desirable user-interaction may have an influence similarly to design decisions influenced by strengths or weaknesses of a programming language.

5.1 Tracking Concepts and Definitions

Isabelle/DOF is designed to annotate text elements with structured meta-information and to reference these text elements throughout the integrated source. A classical application of this capability is the annotation of concepts and terms definitions—be them informal, semi-formal or formal—and their consistent referencing. In the context of our CENELEC ontology, e. g., we can translate the third chapter of [11] "Terms, Definitions and Abbreviations" directly into our Ontology Definition Language (ODL). Picking one example out of 49, consider the definition of the concept "traceability" in paragraphs 3.1.46 (a notion referenced 31 times in the standard), which we translated directly into:

```
Definition*[traceability::concept]‹ degree to which relationship
  can be established between two or more products of a development
  process, especially those having a predecessor/successor or
  master/subordinate relationship to one another. ›
```

In the integrated source of the odometry study, we can reference in a text element to this concept as follows:

```
text*[...]‹  ... to assure @{concept traceability} for
  @{requirement bitwiseAND}, we prove ... ›
```

The presentation of this document element inside Isabelle/DOF is immediately hyperlinked against the `Definition*` element shown above; this serves as documentation of the standard for the development team working on the integrated source. The PDF presentation of such links depends on the actual configurations for the document generation; We will explain this later. CENELEC foresees also a number of roles, phases, safety integration levels, etc., which were directly translated into HOL enumeration types usable in ontological concepts of ODL.

```
datatype role =
   PM  (* Program Manager *) |  RQM (* Requirements Manager *)
 | DES (* Designer *)        |  IMP (* Implementer *)        |
 | VER (* Verifier *)        |  VAL (* Validator *)          | ...
datatype phase =
   SYSDEV_ext (* System Development *) | SPl (* Software Planning     *)
 | SR     (* Software Requirement    *) | SA  (* Software Architecture *)
 | SDES   (* Software Design         *) | ...
```

Similarly, we can formalize the Table A.5: Verification and Testing of [11]: a classification of *verification and testing techniques*:

```
datatype vnt_technique =
             formal_proof thm list    | stat_analysis
           | dyn_analysis dyn_ana_kind  | ...
```

In contrast to the standard, we can parameterize `formal_proof` with a list of theorems, an entity known in the Isabelle kernel. Here, Isabelle/DOF assures for text elements annotated with theorem names, that they refer indeed to established theorems in the Isabelle environment. Additional checks could be added to make sure that these theorems have a particular form, for example.

While we claim that this possibility to link to theorems (and test-results) is unique in the world of systems attempting to assure traceability, referencing a particular (proven) theorem is definitively not sufficient to satisfy the claimed requirement. Human evaluators will always have to check that the provided theorem *adequately* represents the claim; we do not in the slightest suggest that their work is superfluous. Our framework allows to statically check that tests or proofs have been provided, at places where the ontology requires them to be, and both assessors and developers can rely on this check and navigate through related information easily. It does not guarantee that intended concepts for, e. g., safety or security have been adequately modeled.

5.2 Major Ontological Entities: Requirements and Evidence

We introduce central concept of a *requirement* as an ODL `doc_class` based on some generic basic library `text_element` providing basic layout attributes.

```
doc_class requirement = text_element +
   long_name    :: string option
   is_concerned :: role set
```

where the `roles` are exactly the ones defined in the previous section and represent the groups of stakeholders in the CENELEC process. Therefore, the is_concerned-attribute allows expressing who "owns" this text-element. Isabelle/DOF supports a role-based presentation, e. g., different presentation styles of the integrated source may decide to highlight, to omit, to defer into an annex, text entities according to the role-set.

Since ODL supports single inheritance, we can express sub-requirements and therefore a style of requirement decomposition as advocated in GSN [19]:

```
doc_class sub_requirement =
  decomposes :: requirement
  relates_to :: requirement set
```

5.3 Tracking Claims, Derived Requirements and Evidence

As an example for making explicit implicit principles, consider the following statement [11], p. 25.:

> The objective of software verification is to examine and arrive at a judgment based on evidence that output items (process, documentation, software or application) of a specific development phase fulfill the requirements and plans with respect to completeness, correctness and consistency.

The terms *judgment* and *evidence* are used as a kind of leitmotif throughout the CENELEC standard, but they are neither explained nor even listed in the general glossary. However, the standard is fairly explicit on the *phase*s and the organizational roles that different stakeholders should have in the process. We express this key concept "judgment", by the following class:

```
doc_class judgement =
  refers_to      :: requirement
  evidence       :: vnt_technique list
  status         :: status
  is_concerned   :: role set <= {VER,ASR,VAL}
```

As one can see, the role set is per default set to the verification team, the assessors and the validation team.

There are different views possible here: an alternative would be to define evidence as ontological concept with vnt_technique's (rather than an attribute of judgement) and consider the basis of judgments as a relation between requirements and relation:

```
doc_class judgement =
  based_on       :: (requirement × evidence) set
  status         :: status
  is_concerned   :: role set <= {VER,ASR,VAL}
```

More experimentation will be needed to find out what kind of ontological modeling is most adequate for developers in the context of Isabelle/DOF.

6 Ontological Embedding and Compliance

From the variety of different possibilities for adding CENELEC annotations to the integrated source, we will, in the following, point out three scenarios from the phase *ontological embedding* (cf. Sect. 3).

Internal Verification of Claims in the Requirements Specification. In our case, the SR-team early on detected a property necessary for error-detection of the device (c.f. Sect. 4.3):

```
text*[encoder_props::requirement]‹ The requirement specification team ...
   C1 & C2 & C3  = 0   (bitwise logical AND operation)
   C1 | C2 | C3  = 1   (bitwise logical OR operation) ›
```

After the Isabelle proofs shown in Sect. 4.3, we can register the theorems directly in an evidence statement:

```
text*[J1::judgement, refers_to=@{docitem ‹encoder_props›},
     evidence=[formal_proof[@{thm ‹Encoder_Property_1›},
                                   @{thm ‹Encoder_Property_2›}]]]
  ‹The required encoder properties are in fact verified to be consistent
   with the formalization of @{term phase₀}.›
```

The references, @{ ... }, called antiquotation, allow us not only to reference to formal concepts, they are checked for consistency and there are also antiquotations that print the formally checked content (e. g., the statement of a theorem).

Exporting Claims of the Requirements Specification. By definition, the main purpose of the requirement specification is the identification of the safety requirements. As an example, we state the required precision of an odometric function: for any normally behaved distance function `df`, and any representable and valid sampling sequence that can be constructed for `df`, we require that the difference between the physical distance and distance calculable from the *Odometric-Position-Count* is bound by the minimal resolution of the odometer.

```
text*[R5::safety_requirement]‹We can now state ... ›
definition
Odometric_Position_Count_precise::(shaft_encoder_state list⇒output)⇒bool
where Odometric_Position_Count_precise odofunction ≡
      (∀ df. ∀S.  normally_behaved_distance_function df
               → representable S
               → valid_sampling S df
               → (let pos = uint(Odometric_Position_Count(odofunction S))
                    in |df((length S - 1)*δt_odo) - (δs_res * pos)| ≤ δs_res))

update_instance*[R5::safety_requirement,
      formal_definition:=[@{thm ‹Odometric_Position_Count_precise_def›}]]
```

By `update_instance*`, we book the property `Position_Count_precise_def` as `safety_requirement`, a specific sub-class of `requirements` requesting a formal definition in Isabelle.

Exporting Derived Requirements. Finally, we discuss the situation where the verification team discovered a critical side-condition for a major theorem necessary for the safety requirements; this was in our development the case for the condition labelled "**" in Sect. 4.3. The current CENELEC standard clearly separates "requirement specifications" from "verification reports," which is probably motivated by the overall concern of organizational separation and of document consistency. While this document organization is possible in Isabelle/DOF, it is in our experience often counter-productive in practice: organizations tend to defend their documents because the impact of changes is more and more difficult to oversee. This effect results in a dramatic development slow-down and an increase of costs. Furthermore, these barriers exclude situations where developers perfectly know, for example, invariants, but can not communicate them to the verification team because the precise formalization is not known in time. Rather than advocating document separation, we tend to integrate these documents, keep proof as close as possible to definitions, and plead for consequent version control of the integrated source, together with the proposed methods to strengthen the links between the informal and formal parts by anti-quotations and continuous ontological checking. Instead of separation of the documents, we would rather emphasize the *separation of the views* of the different document representations. Such views were systematically generated out of the integrated source in different PDF versions and for each version, document specific consistency guarantees can be automatically enforced.

In our case study, we define this condition as predicate, declare an explanation of it as `SRAC` (CENELEC notion for: safety-related application condition; ontologically, this is a derived class from `requirement`.) and add the definition of the predicate into the document instance as described in the previous section.

7 Generating Document Variants

Often in certification processes, traditional documents are required. Reasons for this include that traditional documents can ensure long-term archivability (which is much harder to ensure for a interactive document that requires Isabelle/HOL). Moreover, the requirements for reading and checking traditional documents are much smaller and no Isabelle expertise is required. To address these needs, Isabelle/DOF can generate a static certification document in the PDF/A format (i. e., the variant of PDF for archiving as defined in the ISO standard 19005)—reading these documents only requires a PDF reader, which one can expect to be available even 50 years from now.

In the context of the CENELEC 50128, we generate one document containing all sub-documents (including all formal proofs) and one document for reach role. The latter only contain the aspects relevant for this particular role (based on the `is_concerned` attribute). For each of the document variants, both semantical and syntactical consistency is checked and the PDF generation fails if these checks (e. g., due to dangling references in a sub-document) are not successful. In addition, we also generate role-specific (hyper-linked) glossaries and tables of relevant concepts (e.g., a table of all SRACs). The latter helps validators that either prefer to work with the final PDF instead of working with the interactive Isabelle/DOF system directly.

8 Related Work

Already in 1993, the need for an integrated and ontological under-pinned document model that are able to integrate formal verification aspects has been motivated by Rushby [23]. More recent reports on the industrial practice of high-assurance safety certifications, e.g., [14,16,18], show that not much has happened since the report from Rushby: certification processes still rely on a plethora of tools managing different aspects of the same system and/or model, and ensuring the consistency between the different tools and documents is a risk (and a significant cost factor in a certification).

The support for modeling ontologies in Isabelle/DOF shares similarities with existing ontology editors such as Protégé [4], Fluent Editor [1], NeOn [2], or OWLGrEd [3]. These editors allow for defining ontologies and also provide certain editing features such as auto-completion. In contrast, Isabelle/DOF does not only allow for defining ontologies, directly after defining an ontological concept, they can also be instantiated and their correct use is checked immediately.

Existing works on using ontologies as part of safety-critical (e.g., [7,26]) or security-critical (e.g., [15]) focus on using ontologies for structuring queries on the set of specifications documents. While not discussed in this paper, Isabelle/DOF supports this time of knowledge management as well: the Isabelle/DOF editor allows for interactively querying for instances of concepts defined in the underlying ontologies as well as for the formal artifacts (formal definitions, proofs, etc.). To our knowledge, none of the existing works provides a deep integration of formal and semi-formal content of certification documents.

9 Conclusion

We presented a methodology for developing certification documents including semi-formal and formal content by using Isabelle/DOF, a framework for ontological modeling and document enforcement. Isabelle/DOF is deeply integrated into Isabelle/PIDE, which allows for a particularly fluid development, immediate ontological feedback and a strong and efficient impact-analysis (already known from developments in interactive theorem proving).

We demonstrate the methodology by (a) modeling a non-trivial part of the CENELEC certification standard [11] in Isabelle/DOF ODL, and apply this (b) to a non-trivial formal development of a safety-critical component in railways systems. The study consists of five theories with about 4 000 LOC, consisting of documentation, definitions, proofs and test-executions of the model. Various PDF presentations of the integrated source were generated, depending on the different roles assumed in the process. The target C-code is about 300 LoC's, and has been integrated in an experimental continuous build-continuous integration environment on top of seL4 [6].

The approach offers mechanical checking of the links between formal and informal parts, technically assured traceability and, last but not least, fast impact analysis on changes, which is usually in the order of a few seconds. Experiments with the entire seL4-stack (100 theories, 200 000 LOC and 10 000 LOC of C code show that our approach can scale up to the size of integrated, medium-size critical software-subsystems [6].

Availability. The Isabelle/DOF framework [9], the discussed ontology definitions, and examples are available at https://git.logicalhacking.com/Isabelle_DOF/Isabelle_DOF/. Isabelle/DOF is licensed under a 2-clause BSD license (SPDX-License-Identifier: BSD-2-Clause).

Acknowledgments. This work has been partially supported by IRT SystemX, Paris-Saclay, France, and therefore granted with public funds of the Program "Investissements d'Avenir."

References

1. Fluent editor (2018). http://www.cognitum.eu/Semantics/FluentEditor/
2. The neon toolkit (2018). http://neon-toolkit.org
3. Owlgred (2018). http://owlgred.lumii.lv/
4. Protégé (2018). https://protege.stanford.edu
5. Barras, B., et al.: Pervasive parallelism in highly-trustable interactive theorem proving systems. In: Carette, J., Aspinall, D., Lange, C., Sojka, P., Windsteiger, W. (eds.) CICM 2013. LNCS (LNAI), vol. 7961, pp. 359–363. Springer, Heidelberg (2013). https://doi.org/10.1007/978-3-642-39320-4_29
6. Bezzecchi, S., Crisafulli, P., Pichot, C., Wolff, B.: Making agile development processes fit for V-style certification procedures. In: ERTS Conference Proceedings (2018)
7. Bicchierai, I., Bucci, G., Nocentini, C., Vicario, E.: Using ontologies in the integration of structural, functional, and process perspectives in the development of safety critical systems. In: Keller, H.B., Plödereder, E., Dencker, P., Klenk, H. (eds.) Ada-Europe 2013. LNCS, vol. 7896, pp. 95–108. Springer, Heidelberg (2013). https://doi.org/10.1007/978-3-642-38601-5_7
8. Brucker, A.D., Ait-Sadoune, I., Crisafulli, P., Wolff, B.: Using the isabelle ontology framework. In: Rabe, F., Farmer, W.M., Passmore, G.O., Youssef, A. (eds.) CICM 2018. LNCS (LNAI), vol. 11006, pp. 23–38. Springer, Cham (2018). https://doi.org/10.1007/978-3-319-96812-4_3
9. Brucker, A.D., Wolff, B.: Isabelle/DOF (2019).https://doi.org/10.5281/zenodo.3370483
10. Brucker, A.D., Wolff, B.: Isabelle/DOF: design and implementation. In: Ölveczky, P.C., Salaün, G. (eds.) SEFM 2019. LNCS, vol. 11724, pp. 275–292. Springer, Cham (2019b). https://doi.org/10.1007/978-3-030-30446-1_15
11. BS EN 50128:2011: Bs en 50128:2011: Railway applications - communication, signalling and processing systems - software for railway control and protecting systems. Standard, Britisch Standards Institute (BSI) (2014)

12. Common Criteria: Common criteria for information technology security evaluation (version 3.1), Part 3: Security assurance components (2006). CCMB-2006-09-003
13. Daum, M., Dörrenbächer, J., Wolff, B.: Proving fairness and implementation correctness of a microkernel scheduler. J. Autom. Reasoning **42**(2), 349–388 (2009). https://doi.org/10.1007/s10817-009-9119-8
14. Denney, E., Pai, G.: Evidence arguments for using formal methods in software certification. In: IEEE International Symposium on Software Reliability Engineering Workshops (ISSREW), pp. 375–380 (2013). https://doi.org/10.1109/ISSREW.2013.6688924
15. Ekclhart, A., Fenz, S., Goluch, G., Weippl, E.: Ontological mapping of common criteria's security assurance requirements. In: Venter, H., Eloff, M., Labuschagne, L., Eloff, J., von Solms, R. (eds.) SEC 2007. IIFIP, vol. 232, pp. 85–95. Springer, Boston, MA (2007). https://doi.org/10.1007/978-0-387-72367-9_8
16. Gleirscher, M., Ratiu, D., Schatz, B.: Incremental integration of heterogeneous systems views. In: 2007 International Conference on Systems Engineering and Modeling, pp. 50–59 (2007). https://doi.org/10.1109/ICSEM.2007.373334
17. Greenaway, D., Andronick, J., Klein, G.: Bridging the gap: automatic verified abstraction of C. In: Beringer, L., Felty, A. (eds.) ITP 2012. LNCS, vol. 7406, pp. 99–115. Springer, Heidelberg (2012). https://doi.org/10.1007/978-3-642-32347-8_8
18. Kaluvuri, S.P., Bezzi, M., Roudier, Y.: A quantitative analysis of common criteria certification practice. In: Eckert, C., Katsikas, S.K., Pernul, G. (eds.) TrustBus 2014. LNCS, vol. 8647, pp. 132–143. Springer, Cham (2014). https://doi.org/10.1007/978-3-319-09770-1_12
19. Kelly, T., Weaver, R.: The goal structuring notation - a safety argument notation. In: Dependable Systems and Networks (2004)
20. Klein, G.: Operating system verification – an overview. Sādhanā **34**(1), 27–69 (2009)
21. Klein, G., et al.: Comprehensive formal verification of an OS microkernel. ACM Trans. Comput. Syst. **32**(1), 2:1–2:70 (2014). https://doi.org/10.1145/2560537
22. Nipkow, T., Wenzel, M., Paulson, L.C. (eds.): Isabelle/HOL. LNCS, vol. 2283. Springer, Heidelberg (2002). https://doi.org/10.1007/3-540-45949-9
23. Rushby, J.: Formal methods and the certification of critical systems. Technical report SRI-CSL-93-7, Computer Science Laboratory, SRI International, Menlo Park, CA (1993). Also issued under the title Formal Methods and Digital Systems Validation for Airborne Systems as NASA Contractor Report 4551, December 1993
24. Wenzel, M.: Asynchronous user interaction and tool integration in Isabelle/PIDE. In: Klein, G., Gamboa, R. (eds.) ITP 2014. LNCS, vol. 8558, pp. 515–530. Springer, Cham (2014a). https://doi.org/10.1007/978-3-319-08970-6_33
25. Wenzel, M.: System description: Isabelle/jEdit in 2014. In: Proceedings Eleventh Workshop on User Interfaces for Theorem Provers, UITP 2014, Vienna, Austria, 17th July 2014, pp. 84–94 (2014b). https://doi.org/10.4204/EPTCS.167.10
26. Zhao, Y., Sanán, D., Zhang, F., Liu, Y.: Formal specification and analysis of partitioning operating systems by integrating ontology and refinement. IEEE Trans. Ind. Inf. **12**(4), 1321–1331 (2016)

A Program Logic for Dependence Analysis

Richard Bubel, Reiner Hähnle, and Asmae Heydari Tabar(✉)

Department of Computer Science, Technische Universität Darmstadt,
64289 Darmstadt, Germany
{bubel,haehnle,heydaritabar}@cs.tu-darmstadt.de

Abstract. Read and write dependences of program variables are essential to determine whether and how a loop or a whole program can be parallelized. State-of-the-art tools for parallelization use approaches that over- as well as under-approximate to compute dependences and they lack a formal foundation. In this paper, we give formal semantics of read and write data dependences and present a program logic that is able to reason about dependences soundly and with full precision. The approach has been implemented in the deductive verification tool KeY for the target language Java.

Keywords: Data dependence · Program verification · Static analysis

1 Introduction

In High-Performance Computing (HPC) one of the most important tasks is to find opportunities for parallelization of sequential programs, for example, of loop bodies. This requires to identify program segments that cannot possibly influence each other's outcome: a prerequisite for being able to run them in parallel without changing semantics. The central notion employed is an analysis of read and write data dependences.[1] For example, the absence of a read-after-write data dependence (termed `noRAW`) in a piece of code p with respect to a memory location x is defined as follows: for any possible execution sequence e of p started in an arbitrary state, no write access to x in e has a subsequent read access to x in e.

There is a large body of work on algorithms and tools that perform dependence analyses [3–5, 8, 10, 15–21, 23, 25, 27]. To the best of our knowledge, these approaches have two limitations: 1. They lack a rigorous, formal definition of dependences like `noRAW` which makes it impossible to formally argue for correctness. 2. They over- or under-approximate (or do both) the dependences present in a given piece of code.

[1] In the HPC community the term *dependence* (pl. *dependences*) is used rather than *dependency* / *dependencies*. We follow their convention.

This work was funded by the Hessian LOEWE initiative within the Software-Factory 4.0 project.

W. Ahrendt and S. L. Tapia Tarifa (Eds.): IFM 2019, LNCS 11918, pp. 83–100, 2019.
https://doi.org/10.1007/978-3-030-34968-4_5

We present an approach to dependence analysis that overcomes these restrictions: our first contribution is a *formal* trace semantics of read and write data dependences (Sect. 3.1). Second, we extend a program logic for deductive verification [1] that makes it possible to *formally verify* dependences (Sect. 3.3). As the program logic is sound and (relative to arithmetic) complete, we know that our analysis is sound and fully precise. Third, we made a first *implementation* based on the deductive verification tool KeY and experimentally demonstrate the viability of our approach. The target language is that of KeY, i.e. nearly all sequential JAVA programs [1]. Our experiments show that for loop-free program segments it is possible to obtain sound and precise analysis results in a highly automated manner.

The paper is structured as follows. In Sect. 2 we explain underlying program logic and calculus. Section 3 expands this program logic by making it dependence-aware. Section 4 contains experimental results of the defined which is implemented on top of the KeY verifier. Section 5 discusses related work. Section 6 concludes and provides ideas for possible future works.

2 Program Logic and Calculus

To reason about data dependences, we extend *Java Dynamic Logic* (JavaDL) [1], a program logic for sequential, deterministic Java programs. We introduce basic concepts of JavaDL to make the paper self-contained. While our presentation uses JavaDL as a logical framework, our approach can be easily transferred to other program logics for imperative languages.

2.1 Syntax

JavaDL extends first-order logic with the two modalities over programs $\langle\cdot\rangle\cdot$ ("diamond"), $[\cdot]\cdot$ ("box"). These take as first argument a program p and as second argument a JavaDL formula ϕ (possibly also containing modalities). Formula $pre \rightarrow [p]post$ is equivalent to the Hoare triple [12] $\{pre\}\ p\ \{post\}$ and expresses partial correctness of program p relative to precondition pre and postcondition $post$. Using the diamond instead of the box modality adds termination of p as a requirement and expresses total correctness. We define the syntax of JavaDL briefly (for a full account see [1]).

Definition 1 (Signature). *Given a* type hierarchy $\tau = (\mathsf{Sort}, \preceq)$ *with a set of type names* Sort *and a reflexive, transitive subtype relation* $\preceq: \mathsf{Sort} \times \mathsf{Sort}$. *The JavaDL signature* Σ_τ *for* τ *consists of*

- *a set* Pred *of typed predicate symbols* $p : T_1 \times \ldots T_n$ *with* $T_i \in \mathsf{Sort}$
- *a set* Func *of typed function symbols* $f : T_1 \times \ldots T_n \rightarrow T$ *with* $T, T_i \in \mathsf{Sort}$,
- *a set* LVar *of typed logical variables* $x : T$ *with* $T \in \mathsf{Sort}$
- *and a set of programs* Prg.

The set of types contains at least (i) $\top$, `Any`, `Heap`, `Field`, `LocSet`, `boolean`, `int`, where $\top$ is the unique root of τ and `Any` the supertype of all types except `Heap`, `Field`; (ii) any Java type declared or used in the program under verification (closed w.r.t. supertypes). Predicate and function symbols are partitioned into *rigid* (Pred_r, Func_r) and *non-rigid* (Pred_{nr}, Func_{nr}) symbols. The value of non-rigid symbols may depend on the state of the program under verification. Logic (first-order) variables are always rigid. Non-rigid constants (0-ary function symbols) are called *program variables.* We refer to the set of all program variables with ProgVSym.

Definition 2 (Syntax). *In addition to terms and formulas, JavaDL knows an additional syntactic category named* updates. *An* elementary update *is written as $v := t$ with $v : T \in \text{ProgVSym}$ and t a term of type S with $S \preceq T$. Given two updates u_1, u_2 then $u1 \| u2$ is called a* parallel update.

Terms and formulas are defined inductively as in standard typed first-order logic. We list only the non-standard cases:

- *If ϕ is a JavaDL formula and p a legal program fragment (sequence of statements) then $\langle p \rangle \phi$ and $[p]\phi$ are JavaDL formulas.*
- *If ϕ is a JavaDL formula, t a term of type T and u an update (elementary or parallel), then $\{u\}\phi$ is a JavaDL formula and $\{u\}t$ is a term of type T. We say "u is applied to ϕ (to t)".*

A signature's type hierarchy is extracted from the Java program under verification. From now on, with *program* we mean the context program including all declarations, as well as program fragments (sequence of statements).

Observe that JavaDL is closed under all first-order operators, quantifiers, and modalities. Program variables are modeled as non-rigid constant symbols and are disjoint from rigid logic (first-order) variables. The latter can be bound by quantifiers and may occur in programs. Program variables may occur in programs and first-order terms, but cannot be quantified over. We give examples of JavaDL formulas and their intuitive meaning:

Example 1. Let `i`, `j` be program variables, $\mathtt{i}_0$, $\mathtt{j}_0$ *rigid* constants of type `int`.

1. $(\mathtt{i} \doteq \mathtt{i}_0 \land \mathtt{j} \doteq \mathtt{j}_0) \rightarrow \langle \mathtt{i=i-j;j=i+j;i=j-i;} \rangle (\mathtt{i} \doteq \mathtt{j}_0 \land \mathtt{j} \doteq \mathtt{i}_0)$ means: if the program in the diamond is executed in an initial state, where `i`, `j` have the value $\mathtt{i}_0$, $\mathtt{j}_0$, then the program terminates and in its final state the program variables have their initial value swapped.
2. The evaluation of formula $\{\mathtt{i} := \mathtt{i} + 1\}(\mathtt{i} \geq 0)$ in a state s is equivalent to evaluating formula $\mathtt{i} \geq 0$ in the state s' that coincides with s except at `i`, whose value is increased by one relative to the value it had in s.
3. $(\mathtt{i} \doteq \mathtt{i}_0 \land \mathtt{j} \doteq \mathtt{j}_0) \rightarrow \{\mathtt{j} := \mathtt{i} \| \mathtt{i} := \mathtt{j}\}(\mathtt{i} \doteq \mathtt{j}_0 \land \mathtt{j} \doteq \mathtt{i}_0)$ means the same as the formula in 1, but expresses the effect of the program with a parallel update. Observe that the parallel update is executed simultaneously: The constituents of a parallel update do not influence each other.

2.2 Semantics

In classical first-order logic, a formula (or term) is evaluated relative to one interpretation (or model) that gives meaning to rigid symbols. JavaDL, like other modal logics, expresses properties relating execution states and has a big-step Kripke semantics. Each s in the set of states $\mathcal{S}$ of a given program can be seen as an interpretation of non-rigid symbols, specifically, of program variables. The definitions below are adapted from [1]:

Definition 3 (JavaDL Semantics). *Given a signature $\Sigma_\mathcal{T}$ for type hierarchy $\mathcal{T}$. JavaDL semantics is defined over (i) a* first-order structure $\mathcal{K} = (D, I)$, *consisting of a non-empty domain D and interpretation I, (ii) a set of states $\mathcal{S}$.*

- *I assigns to each type $T \in \mathsf{Sort}$ a domain $I(T) = D^T$ respecting the subtype relation, i.e. $D^T \subseteq D^S$ for $T \preceq S$.*
- *I assigns to each* rigid *function symbol $f : T_1 \times \ldots \times T_n \to T$ a function $I(f) : D^{T_1} \times \ldots \times D^{T_n} \to D^T$.*
- *I assigns to each* rigid *predicate symbol $p : T_1 \times \ldots \times T_n$ a relation $I(p) : D^{T_1} \times \ldots \times D^{T_n}$.*

States $s \in \mathcal{S}$ assign meaning to non-rigid *symbols analogously. A* variable assignment *$\beta : \mathsf{LVar} \to D$ maps logic variables to a value in their domain. For a logic variable $x : T$ and value $d \in D^T$ we define the* modification *of β at x as:* $\beta_x^d(y) := \begin{cases} d & , \text{ if } x = y \\ \beta(y) & , \text{ otherwise.} \end{cases}$

Definition 4 (Evaluation function *val*). *Let $\mathcal{K}$ be a first-order structure, s a state, β a variable assignment. Let f_r (f_{nr}) be a rigid (non-rigid) function symbol, t, t_i ($i \in \mathbb{N}$) terms, and $v, w \in$* ProgVSym. *The* evaluation function *$val_{\mathcal{K},s,\beta}$ maps terms and updates to states and is defined as follows:*

$$\begin{aligned}
val_{\mathcal{K},s,\beta}(f_r(t_1,\ldots,t_n)) &= I(f_r)(val_{\mathcal{K},s,\beta}(t_1),\ldots,val_{\mathcal{K},s,\beta}(t_n)) \\
val_{\mathcal{K},s,\beta}(f_{nr}(t_1,\ldots,t_n)) &= s(f_{nr})(val_{\mathcal{K},s,\beta}(t_1),\ldots,val_{\mathcal{K},s,\beta}(t_n)) \\
val_{\mathcal{K},s,\beta}(v := t)(s_1) &= s_2 \text{ with } s_2(w) = \begin{cases} val_{\mathcal{K},s,\beta}(t) & , w = v \\ s_1(v) & , \text{otherwise} \end{cases} \\
val_{\mathcal{K},s,\beta}(u_1 \| u_2)(s_1) &= val_{\mathcal{K},s,\beta}(u_2)(val_{\mathcal{K},s,\beta}(u_1)(s_1))
\end{aligned}$$

The overloaded evaluation function $val_{\mathcal{K},s,\beta} : Prg \to 2^{\mathcal{S}}$ maps programs p to sets of states. Programs are deterministic, so the result is either the empty set, when p does not terminate if started in s, otherwise, a singleton set with the final state reached by p started in s. We give exemplary definitions: Let se be a side effect-free expression, st_1, st_2 statements that either terminate normally (no thrown exception, no return, no break, etc.) or not at all:

$$val_{\mathcal{K},s,\beta}(v = se;) = \{s'\} \text{ with } s'(w) = \begin{cases} val_{\mathcal{K},s,\beta}(se) \text{ , } w = v \\ s(w) \text{ , otherwise} \end{cases} \quad (1)$$

$$val_{\mathcal{K},s,\beta}(st_1; st_2;) = \begin{cases} \mathrm{val}_{\mathcal{K},s',\beta}(st_2;) & \text{if } val_{\mathcal{K},s,\beta}(st_1;) = \{s'\} \\ \{\} & \text{if } val_{\mathcal{K},s,\beta}(st_1;) = \{\} \end{cases} \quad (2)$$

The semantics of parallel updates implies that when the same program variable is assigned more than once within a parallel update, then only the textually last assignment is relevant. For example, the update $\mathtt{i} := \mathtt{i} + 1 \| \mathtt{i} := \mathtt{i} + 2$ is equivalent to the elementary update $\mathtt{i} := \mathtt{i} + 2$.

The semantics of assignments with side effect-free right hand sides is identical to that of elementary updates. This becomes important in the calculus where updates are used to represent the effect of assignments.

Definition 5 (Validity). *$\mathcal{K}$ is a first-order structure, s a state, β a variable assignment. Let p_r (p_{nr}) be a rigid (non-rigid predicate symbol. We define the validity relation $\models$ for formulas:*

1. $\mathcal{K}, s, \beta \models p_r(t_1, \dots, t_n)$ *iff* $(val_{\mathcal{K},s,\beta}(t_1), \dots, val_{\mathcal{K},s,\beta}(t_n)) \in I(p_r)$
2. $\mathcal{K}, s, \beta \models p_{nr}(t_1, \dots, t_n)$ *iff* $(val_{\mathcal{K},s,\beta}(t_1), \dots, val_{\mathcal{K},s,\beta}(t_n)) \in s(p_{nr})$
3. $\mathcal{K}, s, \beta \models \neg\phi$ *iff* $\mathcal{K}, s, \beta \not\models \phi$
4. $\mathcal{K}, s, \beta \models \phi \wedge \psi$ *iff* $\mathcal{K}, s, \beta \models \phi$ and $\mathcal{K}, s, \beta \models \psi$ *(similar $\vee, \rightarrow, \dots$)*
5. $\mathcal{K}, s, \beta \models \forall x; \phi$ *iff for all* $d \in D^T$: $\mathcal{K}, s, \beta_x^d \models \phi$ *(similar $\exists x; \phi$)*
6. $\mathcal{K}, s, \beta \models \langle p \rangle \phi$ *iff* $val_{\mathcal{K},s,\beta}(p)(s) = \{s'\}$ and $\mathcal{K}, s', \beta \models \phi$ *(similar $[p]\phi$)*
7. $\mathcal{K}, s, \beta \models \{u\}\phi$ *iff* $\mathcal{K}, s', \beta \models \phi$ *with* $s' = val_{\mathcal{K},s,\beta}(u)(s)$

Write $\mathcal{K} \models \phi$ iff $\mathcal{K}, s, \beta \models \phi$ holds for all $s \in \mathcal{S}$ and all β. Formula ϕ is valid*, written $\models \phi$, iff $\mathcal{K} \models \phi$ holds for all first-order structures $\mathcal{K}$.*

The above semantics for diamond/box means that after executing p, there exists a state/for all states property ϕ holds, which is equivalent to total/partial correctness for deterministic programming languages like sequential Java.

2.3 Calculus

Reasoning about validity of formulas is done in a sequent calculus. A *sequent* $\phi_1, \dots, \phi_n \implies \psi_1, \dots, \psi_m$ consists of two sets of formulas and has the same meaning as $\bigwedge_{i=1,\dots,n} \phi_i \rightarrow \bigvee_{i=1,\dots,m} \psi_i$. The ϕ_i are called *antecedent*, the ψ_j *succedent* of the sequent, $n = 0$, $m = 0$ is possible. Calculus rules take the form

$$\mathsf{name}\ \frac{\overbrace{\Gamma_1 \implies \Delta_1 \qquad \cdots \qquad \Gamma_k \implies \Delta_k}^{\text{premises}}}{\underbrace{\Gamma \implies \Delta}_{\text{conclusion}}}$$

where Γ, Γ_i, Δ, Δ_i are schematic variables matching formula sets. Sequent calculus rules are applied bottom-to-top to construct a proof. A *proof* is a tree (i) whose nodes are labeled with a sequent and (ii) for each inner node n with children $n_1, \ldots, n_l$ there is a rule r with l premises such that r's conclusion matches the sequent of n and the sequent at child n_i is equal to the instantiated i-th premise of r. A proof is *closed* if at each of its leaves an axiom rule was applied, i.e., a rule without premises ($k = 0$). Figure 1 shows some calculus rules.

Schematic variables

x: logic (first-order) variable, v, $v1$, $v2$, b: program variables , $t, t_1, \ldots, t_n$: terms, ϕ, ψ: formulas, u, u_1, u_2: updates, s_1, s_2: statements, se: side effect-free expression

Calculus Rules

First-Order Rules

$$\text{andLeft}\ \frac{\Gamma, \phi, \psi \Longrightarrow \Delta}{\Gamma, \phi \wedge \psi \Longrightarrow \Delta} \qquad \text{andRight}\ \frac{\Gamma \Longrightarrow \phi, \Delta \qquad \Gamma \Longrightarrow \psi, \Delta}{\Gamma \Longrightarrow \phi \wedge \psi, \Delta} \qquad \text{allLeft}\ \frac{\Gamma, \forall\, x; \phi,\ \phi[t/x] \Longrightarrow \Delta}{\Gamma, \forall\, x; \phi \Longrightarrow \Delta}$$

$$\text{close}\ \frac{}{\Gamma, \phi \Longrightarrow \phi, \Delta}$$

Program Rules (Symbolic Execution Rules)

$$\text{ifThenElse}\ \frac{\Gamma, b \doteq \mathit{TRUE} \Longrightarrow [\pi\ s1;\ \omega]\phi, \Delta \qquad \Gamma, b \doteq \mathit{FALSE} \Longrightarrow [\pi\ s2;\ \omega]\phi, \Delta}{\Gamma \Longrightarrow [\pi\ \texttt{if}\ (b)\ \{\ s1;\ \}\ \texttt{else}\ \{\ s2;\ \}\ \omega]\phi, \Delta}$$

$$\text{assignLV}\ \frac{\Gamma \Longrightarrow \{v := se\}[\pi\omega]\phi, \Delta}{\Gamma \Longrightarrow [\pi\ v = se;\ \omega]\phi, \Delta}$$

Update-on-Term, -Formula

$$\{v1 := t\}v1 \rightsquigarrow t \qquad \{v1 := t\}v2 \rightsquigarrow v2, \text{ for } v2 \neq v1$$

$$\{u\}p(t_1, \ldots, t_n) \rightsquigarrow p(\{u\}t_1, \ldots, \{u\}t_n) \qquad \{u\}(\phi \circ \psi) \rightsquigarrow (\{u\}\phi) \circ (\{u\}\psi)$$

p is rigid predicate (similar for rigid functions), $\circ \in \{\wedge, \vee, \rightarrow, \ldots\}$

$$\{u\}[p]\phi \rightsquigarrow \{u\}[p]\phi$$

Update-on-Update

$$\{u_1\}\{u_2\}\phi \rightsquigarrow \{u_1 \| \{u_1\}u_2\}\phi \qquad \{u\}(v1 := t) \rightsquigarrow v1 := \{u\}t$$

Fig. 1. Selected sequent calculus and update simplification rules

The calculus rules for dealing with programs are designed following the symbolic execution paradigm [14], i.e. they behave like a symbolic interpreter. We explain the rules ifThenElse and assignLV rule in detail. The schematic variables π and ω match the *inactive prefix* (e.g., opening braces or labels) and the remaining program including closing braces, respectively. Rule ifThenElse symbolically executes a conditional statement. Schematic variable b matches a local program variable of type `boolean`. As b is symbolic and is evaluated to either true or false depending on the state, the calculus must consider both possibilities. The rule splits the proof into two branches, one where it assumes b to be true and the `then`-branch is executed, the other where b is assumed to be false and symbolic execution continues with the `else`-branch.

The calculus decomposes complex statements into simpler ones until the first active statement can be atomically executed, e.g., an assignment of a side effect-free expression to a local variable. Rule assignLV symbolically executes such an assignment by representing it in the logic as an *update*. For update simplification, there exist rules that allow any sequence of update applications to be rewritten into a single parallel update, for details see [1]. For example:

$$
\begin{array}{ll}
\mathtt{i} \doteq \mathtt{i_0}, \mathtt{j} \doteq \mathtt{j_0} \Longrightarrow [\mathtt{i=i-j;\ j=i+j;\ i=j-i;}]\mathtt{i} \doteq \mathtt{j_0} & \\
\mathtt{i} \doteq \mathtt{i_0}, \mathtt{j} \doteq \mathtt{j_0} \Longrightarrow \{\mathtt{i} := \mathtt{i-j}\}\{\mathtt{j} := \mathtt{i+j}\}\{\mathtt{i} := \mathtt{j-i}\}(\mathtt{i} \doteq \mathtt{j_0}) & (\mathsf{assignLV}) \\
\mathtt{i} \doteq \mathtt{i_0}, \mathtt{j} \doteq \mathtt{j_0} \Longrightarrow \{\mathtt{i} := \mathtt{i-j} \| \mathtt{j} := \mathtt{i} \| \mathtt{i} := \mathtt{j}\}(\mathtt{i} \doteq \mathtt{j_0}) & \text{(Update-on-Update, -Term)} \\
\mathtt{i} \doteq \mathtt{i_0}, \mathtt{j} \doteq \mathtt{j_0} \Longrightarrow \{\mathtt{j} := \mathtt{i} \| \mathtt{i} := \mathtt{j}\}(\mathtt{i} \doteq \mathtt{j_0}) & \text{(first update to } \mathtt{i} \text{ discarded)} \\
\mathtt{i} \doteq \mathtt{i_0}, \mathtt{j} \doteq \mathtt{j_0} \Longrightarrow \mathtt{j} \doteq \mathtt{j_0} & \text{(Update-on-Formula, -Term)}
\end{array}
$$

The final sequent can be discharged with close.

2.4 Memory Locations and Heap in JavaDL

Memory locations on the heap are modeled in JavaDL as follows: Type `Field` represents an object's field. Thus a memory location can be represented as a pair (obj, fld) with $obj : \mathcal{D}^{\mathtt{Object}}$ and $fld \in D^{\mathtt{Field}}$. Type `LocSet` models memory regions as location sets. Let o be a term of type `Object`, f a term of type `Field`, l_1, l_2 terms of type `LocSet`. The `LocSet` data type has constructors for singleton sets of memory locations $\{(o, f)\}$, for union $l_1 \cup l_2$, etc., as well as standard predicates like $l_1 \subseteq l_2$. The set `allLocs` denotes all possible locations.

The heap is modelled by type `Heap` in the theory of arrays with functions `select`, `store`, where $\mathtt{select}(h, o, f)$ looks up the value stored in heap h for field f of object o, while $\mathtt{store}(h, o, f, v)$ updates in heap h the value stored in field f of object o with value v. Programs access and modify the heap stored in the global program variable $\mathtt{heap} : \mathtt{Heap}$. Semantically, an element h of $D^{\mathtt{Heap}}$ is a function $h : D^{\mathtt{Object}} \times D^{\mathtt{Field}} \to D^{\mathtt{Any}}$, mapping memory locations to values. Let s be a state that maps program variable $o : \mathtt{Object}$ to some non-null value, v a program variable:

$$
val_{K,s,\beta}(o.f = v;) = \{s'\} \text{ with} \tag{3}
$$

$$
s'(w) = \begin{cases} s'(\mathtt{heap})(u, g) = \begin{cases} s(v)\,, & \text{if } u = s(o) \text{ and } g = s(f) \\ s(heap)(u, g)\,, & \text{otherwise} \end{cases} & , w = \mathtt{heap} \\ s(w) & , \text{otherwise} \end{cases}
$$

The calculus rules for reading from and writing to an object field are:

readAttribute

$$
\frac{\Gamma \Longrightarrow o \not\doteq \mathtt{null}, \Delta \qquad \Gamma, o \not\doteq \mathtt{null} \Longrightarrow \{v := \mathtt{select}(\mathtt{heap}, o, f)\}\langle\pi\omega\rangle\phi, \Delta}{\Gamma \Longrightarrow \langle\pi\, v = o.f;\ \omega\rangle\phi, \Delta}
$$

writeAttribute

$$
\frac{\Gamma \Longrightarrow o \not\doteq \mathtt{null}, \Delta \qquad \Gamma, o \not\doteq \mathtt{null} \Longrightarrow \{\mathtt{heap} := \mathtt{store}(\mathtt{heap}, o, f, se)\}\langle\pi\omega\rangle\phi, \Delta}{\Gamma \Longrightarrow \langle\pi\, o.f = se;\ \omega\rangle\phi, \Delta}
$$

3 Dependence-Aware Program Logic

3.1 Formal Semantics of Read and Write Dependences

A standard programming language semantics based on traces, i.e. finite or infinite sequences of states (see Sect. 2.2), is insufficient to characterize read and write dependences, as shown by a simple consideration: take two programs consisting of a single assignment $p \equiv$ `x = 42;` and $p' \equiv$ `x = y;`. if p, p' are started in state s with $s(\mathtt{y}) = 42$ both yield exactly the same trace, however, p' has a read access that p has not. *Traces do not record memory access.*

Rather than supplying a special purpose semantic construct, we decided to give a general solution. It is well-known (e.g., [2]) that *non-functional* properties (such as dependences) can often be formally specified with the help of *ghost variables*. These are memory locations not part of the program under verification that record meta properties of program execution (e.g., memory access). In our setting we add ghost variables r, w to states that record read and write access at each state change. For example, the state after executing p' in s is: $\{\mathtt{x} \mapsto 42, \mathtt{y} \mapsto 42, r \mapsto \{\mathtt{y}\}, w \mapsto \{\mathtt{x}\}\}$. This state can be distinguished from the state that results from executing p in s: $\{\mathtt{x} \mapsto 42, \mathtt{y} \mapsto 42, r \mapsto \{\}, w \mapsto \{\mathtt{x}\}\}$.

In our semantics we go a step further and introduce a *single* ghost variable ma (for *memory access*) that records the whole *history* of memory accesses in the current execution as a finite sequence of type `MASeq`. A single memory access is a pair `MAKind`×`LocSet`, where $D^{\mathtt{MAKind}} = \{r, w\}$. JavaDL has two rigid constants for `MAKind`: `read` with $I(\mathtt{read}) = r$ and `write` with $I(\mathtt{write}) = w$. In the semantics we use ϵ for the empty memory access sequence and $\circ$ for concatenation, e.g., $\langle(r, \{(o, f)\})\rangle \circ \langle(w, \{(u, g)\})\rangle$ for a sequence of length 2 with a read access to memory location (o, f) and a write access to location (u, g). We use $maSeq[i]$ to access the i-th element of sequence $maSeq$.

From now on we evaluate programs and formulas relative to states that contain ghost variable ma that records the trace of memory accesses during execution of a program. We only track heap memory access and not access to local program variables. One semantic rule (from Sect. 2.4) in need of modification is heap assignment (3):

$$val_{\mathcal{K},s,\beta}(o.f = v;) = \{s'\} \text{ with} \tag{4}$$
$$s'(w) = \begin{cases} s'(\mathtt{heap})(u, g) = \begin{cases} s(v)\,,\ \text{if } u = s(o) \text{ and } g = s(f) \\ s(heap)(u, g)\,,\ \text{otherwise} \end{cases} & , w = \mathtt{heap} \\ s'(\mathsf{ma}) = s(\mathsf{ma}) \circ (w, \{(s(o), s(f))\}) & , w = \mathsf{ma} \\ s(w) & , \text{otherwise} \end{cases}$$

The rule now records write access (read access is only to local variables). With the trace of memory accesses stored in ma it is possible to formally specify dependence properties like read-after-write as follows: Given a state s and a location set ls then there is a read-after-write iff there are i, j with $i < j$, $s(\mathsf{ma})[i] = (w, ls')$ and $s(\mathsf{ma})[j] = (r, ls'')$ such that $ls \cap ls' \cap ls'' \neq \emptyset$.

There is an advantage of maintaining the *whole* access history in each state: it is sufficient to know only the final state to define dependence. Hence, having the history in the final state makes it sufficient to look at a big-step semantic relation. This is important, because we base logical reasoning about dependences on the big-step program logic introduced in Sect. 2.3 and the existing tools.

3.2 Memory Access Updates

For efficiency the ghost program variable ma which keeps track of read and write dependences is not exposed in the JavaDL syntax. Instead, we introduce a new kind of update, called *memory access update*, to record changes to ma.

Memory access updates $\backslash\mathtt{ac}(ki,\ ls)$ keep track of read and write memory accesses. A memory access update takes two arguments: (i) a term ki of type `MAKind` to distinguish between read and write access, (ii) a term ls of type `LocSet` to capture the accessed memory locations. Its semantics is defined as:

$$val_{\mathcal{K},s,\beta}(\backslash\mathtt{ac}(ki, ls))(s_1) = s_2 \text{ where} \\ s_2(w) = \begin{cases} s_1(\mathsf{ma}) \circ \langle(s(ki), val_{\mathcal{K},s,\beta}(ls))\rangle, & w = \mathsf{ma} \\ s_1(w) & \text{, otherwise} \end{cases} \tag{5}$$

Several memory access updates mau_1, mau_2 can be *combined* and executed in the same program state s, written "mau_1, mau_2" with the meaning:

$$val_{\mathcal{K},s,\beta}(\backslash\mathtt{ac}(ki_1, ls_1),\ \backslash\mathtt{ac}(ki_2, ls_2))(s_1) = s_2 \text{ where} \\ s_2(w) = \begin{cases} s_1(\mathsf{ma}) \circ \langle(s(ki_1), val_{\mathcal{K},s,\beta}(ls_1))\rangle \circ \langle(s(ki_2), val_{\mathcal{K},s,\beta}(ls_2))\rangle, & w = \mathsf{ma} \\ s_1(w) & \text{, otherwise} \end{cases} \tag{6}$$

With memory access updates one can design assignment rules that reflect the semantics defined in Sect. 3.1. The rule from Sect. 2.3 for assigning a side effect-free expression se over local variables to a memory location (o, f) becomes:

writeAttribute

$$\frac{\begin{array}{l}\Gamma \Longrightarrow o \neq \mathtt{null}, \Delta \\ \Gamma, o \neq \mathtt{null} \Longrightarrow \{\mathtt{heap} := \mathtt{store}(\mathtt{heap}, o, f, se) \| \backslash\mathtt{ac}(\mathtt{write}, \{(o, f)\})\}\langle\pi\omega\rangle\phi, \Delta\end{array}}{\Gamma \Longrightarrow \langle\pi\ o.f = se;\ \omega\rangle\phi, \Delta}$$

Symbolic execution accumulates updates in front of the modality. To reason efficiently, we designed update simplification rules that allow to establish a normal form of the form: $u_1 \| \cdots \| u_n \| mau_1, \ldots, mau_m$, where

- u_i are state updates as introduced in Sect. 2.1.
- mau_j, mau_k are combined memory access updates with the property that if $j < k$ then mau_j was symbolically executed before mau_k.

In Fig. 2 some memory update simplification rules are shown. Central for establishing normal form is rule reorderUpdate that allows to swap state and memory access updates. The rule is sound, because state updates cannot change the value of ghost variable ma. We observe that all rules maintain the order of the memory access updates as required.

Schematic variables
u: any update, su: (parallel) update with no memory access updates,
mau: (combined) memory access update

Update Simplification Rules

sequentialToParallel1
$\{mau\}\{\backslash\mathtt{ac}(ki, ls)\}\phi \rightsquigarrow \{mau, \backslash\mathtt{ac}(\{mau\}ki, \{mau\}ls)\}\phi$

sequentialToParallel2
$\{mau\}\{su\}\phi \rightsquigarrow \{mau \| \{mau\}su\}\phi$

reorderUpdate
$\backslash\mathtt{ac}(ki, ls) \| su \rightsquigarrow su \| \backslash\mathtt{ac}(ki, ls)$

applyUpdateOnAc
$\{u\}\backslash\mathtt{ac}(ki, ls) \rightsquigarrow \backslash\mathtt{ac}(\{u\}ki, \{u\}ls)$

applyAcOnStateUpdate
$\{\backslash\mathtt{ac}(ki, ls)\}x := t \rightsquigarrow x := \{\backslash\mathtt{ac}(ki, ls)\}t$

Fig. 2. Selection of memory access update simplification rules

3.3 Specification of Data Dependence Properties

Memory access can be tracked in the ghost variable ma, but how are properties about the content of ma expressed, given that it is not directly accessible in the syntax? This is achieved with *non-rigid memory access predicates* that allow to express data dependence properties of locations:

$$\mathtt{noRAW} : \mathtt{LocSet},\ \mathtt{noWAR} : \mathtt{LocSet},\ \mathtt{noWAW} : \mathtt{LocSet},\ \mathtt{noR} : \mathtt{LocSet},\ \mathtt{noW} : \mathtt{LocSet}$$

These predicates take a location set ls as argument and evaluate to true iff in the memory access history of the current state for *no* location in ls there is a read-after-write, write-after-read, write-after-write, write or read, respectively. They allow us to express properties such as the following which says: if there was no read-after-write before execution of program p to the memory location $(\mathtt{o}, \mathtt{f})$ then there is no read-after-write after execution of p.

$$\mathtt{noRAW}(\{(\mathtt{o}, \mathtt{f})\}) \rightarrow \langle \mathtt{p} \rangle \mathtt{noRAW}(\{(\mathtt{o}, \mathtt{f})\})$$

Memory access predicates are non-rigid, because their value not only depends on the value of their argument, but also on the memory accesses recorded in ma. Consequently, semantic rules for these predicates define how ma affects evaluation. As an example, we give the semantics of noRAW. Let s be any state:

$$s(\mathtt{noRAW}) = \{ls \in D^{\mathsf{LocSet}} \mid ls \cap ls' \cap ls'' = \emptyset,\ \text{where}\quad s(\mathsf{ma})[i] = (w, ls'),\ s(\mathsf{ma})[j] = (r, ls'') \text{ and } i < j\} \tag{7}$$

In state s the extension of the memory access predicate are all location sets that contain only locations to which no read memory access happens after they have been written to.

3.4 Verification of Data Dependence Properties

The axiomatisation of memory access predicates in the calculus is given by rules for the application of memory access updates to memory access predicates. After the symbolic execution rules of the calculus have eliminated the program and updates have been normalized, what is left, are proof obligations of the form $\Gamma \Longrightarrow \{su \| mau\}\phi, \Delta$. Now one applies the memory access updates one by one from right to left. For the non-rigid memory access predicates one cannot use Update-on-Formula rules. Some of the specific update rules required are shown in Fig. 3 for memory access predicate noRAW:

Schematic variables: su: state update (no memory access update)

stateUpdateOnNoRAW

$$\frac{\Gamma \Longrightarrow \mathtt{noRAW}(\{su\}ls), \Delta}{\Gamma \Longrightarrow \{su\}\mathtt{noRAW}(ls), \Delta}$$

writeAcOnNoRAW

$$\frac{\Gamma \Longrightarrow \mathtt{noRAW}(\{\backslash\mathtt{ac}(\mathtt{write}, ls_1)\}ls_2), \Delta}{\Gamma \Longrightarrow \{\backslash\mathtt{ac}(\mathtt{write}, ls_1)\}\mathtt{noRAW}(ls_2), \Delta}$$

readAcOnNoRAW*

$$\frac{\begin{array}{l}\Gamma, ls_1 \cap \{mau\}ls_2 \not\doteq \emptyset \Longrightarrow \mathtt{noW}(\{mau\}ls_2) \wedge \mathtt{noRAW}((\{mau\}ls_2) \setminus ls_1), \Delta \\ \Gamma, ls_1 \cap \{mau\}ls_2 \doteq \emptyset \Longrightarrow \mathtt{noRAW}(\{mau\}ls_2), \Delta\end{array}}{\Gamma \Longrightarrow \{\underbrace{\backslash\mathtt{ac}(\mathtt{read}, ls_1)}_{mau}\}\mathtt{noRAW}(ls_2), \Delta}$$

knownNoRAW

$$\frac{\Gamma, \mathtt{noRAW}(ls1) \Longrightarrow \text{if } (ls2 \subseteq ls1) \text{ then (true) else } (\mathtt{noRAW}(ls2 \setminus ls1)), \Delta}{\Gamma, \mathtt{noRAW}(ls1) \Longrightarrow \mathtt{noRAW}(ls2), \Delta}$$

noWnoRAW

$$\frac{}{\Gamma, \mathtt{noW}(ls) \Longrightarrow \mathtt{noRAW}(ls), \Delta}$$

noRnoRAW

$$\frac{}{\Gamma, \mathtt{noR}(ls) \Longrightarrow \mathtt{noRAW}(ls), \Delta}$$

Fig. 3. Selected rules for dependence predicate noRAW

- stateUpdateOnNoRAW: a state update su cannot change the content of ghost variable ma. Consequently, the extension of predicate noRAW remains unchanged and the update can be propagated inwards.
- writeAcOnNoRAW: likewise, a write access applied to noRAW can also be propagated inwards. The justification is that we process the memory access list from the end, i.e. when applying the update we look at the final entry and in this case a write cannot invalidate the no read-after-write property.
- readAcOnNoRAW: in case of a read access $\backslash\mathtt{ac}(\mathtt{read}, ls_1)$, for $\mathtt{noRAW}(ls_2)$ to hold, one must prove that no write to any location in ls_2 happened before. There are two cases: ls_1, ls_2 contain common locations, i.e. there is a read from a location for which we want to show the no read-after-write property. This holds only if no write memory access happened before. For all other locations noRAW still must be shown. If ls_1, ls_2 contain no common locations, then the read memory access update does not affect the evaluation of the memory access predicate. In either case, the read memory access update mau is propagated inwards as it might affect the evaluation of ls_2.

- knownNoRAW: to show that $\mathtt{noRAW}(ls_2)$ holds it is sufficient to know that $\mathtt{noRAW}(ls_1)$ holds and ls_2 is a subset of ls_2, otherwise, one only needs to show the property for those locations in ls_2 not contained in ls_1.
- The final rules exploit that if there was no read (write) to any location in ls then there was also no read-after-write to any location in ls.

Except the rules mentioned above and a few related ones, only a few calculus rules of [1] needed to be modified. These were minor technical changes which we do not go into for space reasons. As an example, Fig. 4 shows the outline of a sequent calculus proof for the sequent:

$$\mathtt{o} \neq \mathtt{null},\ \mathtt{u} \neq \mathtt{null},\ \mathtt{o} \neq \mathtt{u},\ \mathtt{noW}(\{(\mathtt{o},\mathtt{a})\}) \Longrightarrow \langle \mathtt{o.a=v;\ z=u.a;} \rangle \mathtt{noRAW}(\{(\mathtt{o},\mathtt{a})\}).$$

It expresses that if we start in a state with no write access to `o.a`, and where `o` and `u` refer to different existing objects, then after executing `o.a=v; z=u.a;` there is still no read-after-write access to `o.a`. First, the program is symbolically executed and update normalization takes place. Subsequent update simplification eliminates state update su, as it does not affect the memory access property. This results in the sequent (abbreviations see figure):

$$\Psi \Longrightarrow \{ac_1, ac_2\}\mathtt{noRAW}(\{(\mathtt{o},\mathtt{a})\})$$

Now one can apply readAcOnNoRAW—which splits the proof—in a variant for combined memory access updates. One branch is closed immediately, because the intersection of the two location sets is provably empty. In the remaining branch the read access ac_2 can be removed, because its location set is disjoint with $(\mathtt{o},\mathtt{a})$.[2] Now write access update can be moved inwards with writeAcOnNoRAW. After further simplification we apply noWnoRAW (Ψ' contains $\mathtt{noW}(\mathtt{o},\mathtt{a})\}$) to close the proof.

4 Experiments

We implemented a proof-of-concept of our approach on top of the KeY verification system. We can (dis-)prove the existence of data dependence in the presence of aliasing, conditional statements, and loops. To be precise, what our tool does is dependence *checking*, because it is necessary to specify a conjecture in terms of memory access predicates. This is, however, not a real restriction: in practice, one starts with a proof attempt of the form $\mathtt{noRAW}(\mathtt{allLocs})$ (or any other memory access predicate), trying to prove that *no* location has a read-after-write. If this proof fails, from the models of unprovable goals it is possible to read off those locations ls where the predicate does not hold. Then one restarts the proof for $\mathtt{noRAW}(\mathtt{allLocs} \setminus ls)$.

Table 1 summarizes the results of our dependence analysis for six example programs. Their size is roughly ten lines of code each. Their relatively small

[2] This is easily justified formally by using $\{ac_1\}\{ac_2\}$ instead of $\{ac_1, ac_2\}$ and the original rule readAcOnNoRAW, but would result in a longer, more technical proof.

$$
\dfrac{\dfrac{\dfrac{\dfrac{\dfrac{\dfrac{\dfrac{\dfrac{*}{\Psi' \Longrightarrow \mathtt{noRAW}(\{(\mathtt{o},\mathtt{a})\})}}{\vdots}}{\Psi' \Longrightarrow \mathtt{noRAW}(\{ac_1\}\{(\mathtt{o},\mathtt{a})\})}}{\overbrace{\Psi, \{(\mathtt{u},\mathtt{a})\} \cap \{ac_1, ac_2\}\{(\mathtt{o},\mathtt{a})\} \doteq \emptyset}^{\Psi' :=} \Longrightarrow \{ac_1\}\mathtt{noRAW}(\{(\mathtt{o},\mathtt{a})\})} \quad \dfrac{*}{\vdots}}{\Psi \Longrightarrow \{ac_1, ac_2\}\mathtt{noRAW}(\{(\mathtt{o},\mathtt{a})\}}}{\vdots}}{\Psi \Longrightarrow \{su \| ac_1, ac_2\}\mathtt{noRAW}(\{(\mathtt{o},\mathtt{a})\})}}{\vdots}}{\underbrace{\mathtt{o} \not\doteq \mathtt{null}, \mathtt{u} \not\doteq \mathtt{null}, \mathtt{o} \not\doteq \mathtt{u}, \mathtt{noW}(\{(\mathtt{o},\mathtt{a})\})}_{\Psi :=} \Longrightarrow \langle \mathtt{o.a=v;\ z=u.a;} \rangle \mathtt{noRAW}(\{(\mathtt{o},\mathtt{a})\})}
$$

with

$$
\begin{aligned}
su &:= \mathtt{heap} := \mathtt{store}(\mathtt{heap}, \mathtt{o}, \mathtt{a}, \mathtt{v}) \,\|\, \mathtt{z} := \mathtt{select}(\mathtt{store}(\mathtt{heap}, \mathtt{o}, \mathtt{a}, \mathtt{v}), \mathtt{u}, \mathtt{a}) \\
ac_1 &:= \backslash\mathtt{ac}(\mathtt{write}, \{(\mathtt{o},\mathtt{a})\}) \\
ac_2 &:= \backslash\mathtt{ac}(\mathtt{read}, \{(\mathtt{u},\mathtt{a})\})
\end{aligned}
$$

Fig. 4. Example of a formal verification proof of a `noRAW` property

size is not a limitation *per se*: some of the programs are quite complex, contain arrays and nested loops. Also the main application of dependence analysis is parallelization which is performed on relatively small pieces of code, such as loops, i.e., our approach can be applied on these fragments only. Proof complexity is measured along the dimensions: number of interactive steps (cf. discussion below), number of nodes in proof tree, number of branches in proof tree.

Program `WtAliasing` models water flow between two tanks. It showcases that our approach works in the presence of aliasing. In case of an alias (source and target tank are identical), there is a read-after-write dependence and the proof stays open. In `WtNoAliasing` we exclude aliasing with a precondition which eliminates the read-after-write data dependence and the proof closes.

Program `WtConditional` has a write-after-read data dependence on one branch of a conditional statement, but not on the other. As expected, the proof stays open for the first branch. In addition, we can directly extract the path condition from the open proof goal, to be used for *conditional parallelization*: A compiler can add a check whether the condition is satisfied or not in an actual run and then decide whether to take the sequential or the parallelized version.

All programs so far are loop-free and the proofs are fully automatic. The remaining programs contain loops and required a small amount of interaction (see discussion below). Programs `ArrayAssignment` and `ArrayShift` manipulate arrays in a loop. The first writes to an array, while the second one shifts the

Table 1. Dependence analysis result

Program	Proof size		Interactive steps	Property to check	Proof status
	# Nodes	# Branches			
`WtAliasing`	467	11	0	`noRAW`	**Open**
`WtNoAliasing`	406	7	0	`noRAW`	Closed
`WtConditional`	710	15	0	`noWAR`	**Open**
`ArrayAssignment`	890	10	1	`noWAR`	Closed
`ArrayShift`	3129	38	6	`noRAW`	Closed
`Atax`	38491	200	14	`noRAW`(A)	Closed

The open proofs correspond to programs that exhibit a read-after-write dependence.

content of an array to the left by one, i.e. in each iteration it writes to the i-th array element and reads the $i + 1$-st element.

The `Atax` program is taken from the PolyBench 4.0 Kernel [26], a parallelization benchmark library widely used in HPC, and was translated from C to Java. It takes a matrix A, a vector x and computes $y = A^T(Ax)$. The whole program consists of four loops with a nesting depth of one.

We compared the performance of our prototype to a leading HPC parallelization tool called DiscoPoP [13]. While DiscoPoP replicates our result in the previous examples, the over-approximation its dependence analysis does report a spurious dependence: a read-after-write dependence for array `A` which in actuality is never written to (DiscoPoP discards this spurious dependence by a post-processing step later). In case of aliasing the `noRAW` property would actually not hold. Adding as a precondition the information that all arrays are disjoint allows our approach to prove it nevertheless. This shows an important advantage of using an expressive logic to perform dependence analysis: it is possible to instrument the analysis with complex assertions at arbitrary code locations.

DiscoPoP also (correctly) reported dependences for arrays `tmp` and `y` that are read from and written to in inner loops. These dependences do exist, because there is a read-after-write in each loop iteration, but they are too strong: To parallelize a loop it is sufficient to know that no dependence between two different loop iterations exists, while a local read-after-write dependence inside the loop body is permitted. To handle such situations, it is necessary to define refined dependence predicates that can distinguish between different loop iterations. This is perfectly possible in our approach and is a topic of future work.

In general, our approach is more precise than DiscoPoP (and related analyses that over-approximate), because, to the best of our knowledge, these always abstract a read-after-write dependence on a *single* array entry to a read-after-write on *all* array elements.

About Automation. To reason about loops, the user has to provide loop invariants. In future work we will investigate how to make use of loop invariant generation techniques to derive the necessary invariants automatically. As the domain is specific—loop invariants mainly capture properties about memory access—we expect to be able to use heuristics-driven techniques such as predicate abstraction [11] to achieve a high degree of automation [24]. All other interactive steps are due to the prototypic nature of our implementation and can be easily automatized. We could have achieved full automation already for the examples, by simply allowing the strategy to apply rules knownNoRaw and noWNoRAW/noRnoRAW automatically, but we prefer to implement a proper general strategy as future work.

All the examples in this section can be found at: www.key-project.org/a-program-logic-for-dependence-analysis-reviewers-only/

5 Related Work

There are many approaches to analyze data dependences [3–5, 8, 10, 15–21, 23, 25, 27]. They can be categorized into static and dynamic approaches.

Static dependence analyses [3–5, 8, 17, 19–21, 23] use several techniques: (i) systems of linear inequality constraints solved using integer programming [5, 8, 19, 20]; (ii) graph structures like reference trees [17] and program dependence graphs [9, 23]; (iii) renaming [3, 7]; (iv) symbolic value propagation [4]. These approaches are usually conservative and over-approximate data dependences, i.e. they might report false dependences, but do not miss existing ones [21]. In contrast, our approach is based on a fully precise and faithful program logic using symbolic execution interleaved with first-order reasoning to prove the absence of data dependences. In presence of loops, the user needs to provide loop invariants. We aim to reduce this need (see Sect. 6). Our logic is able to represent non-linear integer constraints and the calculus is able to prove some non-linear problems automatically. We have the possibility to export subgoals to be solved by SMT solvers [6]. Because of this, we can profit from the quickly evolving capabilities in the automated reasoning area.

Dynamic data dependence analyses [10, 15, 16, 27] provide probabilistic data about data dependence at runtime. These analyses are optimistic (under-approximating) as they rely on actual program runs. Kremlin [10] introduces hierarchical critical path analysis (HCPA) to make recommendations to the user about those parts of the code that should be parallelized first. Critical path analysis calculates parallelism by quantifying both the amount of work done and the minimum time needed to do that work. HCPA performs critical path analysis across many nested regions in a program. In addition to loop parallelism, Kremlin allows parallelism in serial program regions to be identified even if the program's current form does not expose it. Alchemist [27] introduces data dependence distance profiling. It detects code structures that can be run asynchronously in the dynamic context. DiscoPoP [15] is a generic data dependence profiler that is designed with a focus on scalability. It records memory accesses in signatures which is a data structure encoding an approximate representation of an unbound set of elements with a bounded amount of state [22]. Using signatures reduces memory overhead. POSH [16] combines static analysis to find data dependences with dynamic data dependence analysis to refine its choices.

Our approach is static, but it uses symbolic execution and in this way retains some advantages of the dynamic approaches: for example, it can distinguish between different symbolic execution paths. The advantage is that even for a failed proof attempt (caused by insufficient automation or by presence of data dependence), all path conditions from proven symbolic execution paths can be safely used in conditional parallelization by compilers.

6 Future Work and Conclusion

We presented a static approach to dependence analysis based on deductive verification in an expressive program logic. It deviates from existing approaches in several important respects: (i) dependence has a formal, mathematically rigorous semantic definition based on the standard trace semantics of programs; (ii) as a consequence, one can argue formally about soundness of the calculus for proving dependences which is inherited from the soundness of the program logic [1, Chap. 3]; (iii) it is possible to prove absence of dependences with full precision, i.e. without over- or under-approximation; (iv) dependence analysis with full precision in the presence of loops requires annotation with loop invariants, but at least it is *possible* to make a precise analysis which is not the case when working with a fixed abstraction; (v) from failed proof attempts one can extract path conditions under which the conjectured claim holds (to be used in conditional parallelization) and counter examples for when it does not (to be used to prove a refined claim).

We feel encouraged by the fact that already our prototype is able to replicate and even improve upon results obtained with a leading dependence analysis tool. The analysis of all loop-free examples was fully automatic. In the future, we plan to take our approach further:

Automation. As pointed out above, we are optimistic to be able to generate loop invariants mostly automatic via predicate abstraction, because in the specific domain of memory access predicates it is possible to discover well-founded abstract domains and effective search heuristics.

Parallelization. We will design refined memory access predicates that can distinguish between different iterations of a loop. This is a prerequisite for the analysis to be useful when parallelizing loops.

Interprocedural Analysis. One of the strengths of the deductive verification approach is that it is designed to work as an interprocedural analysis. Assume that we analyze a piece of code containing a call to a complex mathematical function. The approaches discussed in Sect. 5 have to *inline* the code, assuming it is even available. Our program logic allows the use of *contracts* [1, Chap. 9]. Like loop invariants, such *memory access contracts* have a specific form and are amenable to automatic generation. As for loops, it will be necessary to design refined memory access predicates that can distinguish executions outside and inside a method call.

Once the work sketched above is in place, we are in a position to perform extensive evaluation with industrial case studies, for example, based on [26].

Acknowledgment. We thank Prof. Felix Wolf, Mohammad Norouzi, and Arya Mazaheri for providing us with DiscoPoP and for helpful discussions about data dependence analysis.

References

1. Ahrendt, W., Beckert, B., Bubel, R., Hähnle, R., Schmitt, P.H., Ulbrich, M. (eds.): Deductive Software Verification – The KeY Book: From Theory to Practice. LNCS, vol. 10001. Springer, Cham (2016). https://doi.org/10.1007/978-3-319-49812-6
2. Albert, E., Bubel, R., Genaim, S., Hähnle, R., Díez, G.R.: A formal verification framework for static analysis–as well as its instantiation to the resource analyzer COSTA and formal verification tool KeY. Softw. Syst. Model. **15**(4), 987–1012 (2016)
3. Allen, F.E., Burke, M.G., Cytron, R., Ferrante, J., Hsieh, W.C.: A framework for determining useful parallelism. In: Lenfant, J. (ed.) Proceedings of the 2nd International Conference on Supercomputing, pp. 207–215. ACM (1988)
4. Amme, W., Braun, P., Thomasset, F., Zehendner, E.: Data dependence analysis of assembly code. Int. J. Parallel Program. **28**(5), 431–467 (2000)
5. Banerjee, U.: An introduction to a formal theory of dependence analysis. J. Supercomput. **2**(2), 133–149 (1988)
6. Barrett, C., Fontaine, P., Tinelli, C.: The Satisfiability Modulo Theories Library (SMT-LIB) (2016). www.SMT-LIB.org
7. Cytron, R., Ferrante, J.: What's in a name? -or- the value of renaming for parallelism detection and storage allocation. In: International Conference on Parallel Processing, pp. 19–27. Pennsylvania State University Press (1987)
8. Feautrier, P.: Dataflow analysis of array and scalar references. Int. J. Parallel Program. **20**(1), 23–53 (1991)
9. Ferrante, J., Ottenstein, K.J., Warren, J.D.: The program dependence graph and its use in optimization. ACM Trans. Program. Lang. Syst. **9**(3), 319–349 (1987)
10. Garcia, S., Jeon, D., Louie, C.M., Taylor, M.B.: Kremlin: rethinking and rebooting gprof for the multicore age. In: Hall, M.W., Padua, D.A. (eds.) 32nd ACM SIGPLAN Conference on Programming Language Design and Implementation, pp. 458–469. ACM (2011)
11. Graf, S., Saidi, H.: Construction of abstract state graphs with PVS. In: Grumberg, O. (ed.) CAV 1997. LNCS, vol. 1254, pp. 72–83. Springer, Heidelberg (1997). https://doi.org/10.1007/3-540-63166-6_10
12. Hoare, C.A.R.: An axiomatic basis for computer programming. Commun. ACM **12**(10), 576–580 (1969). https://doi.org/10.1145/363235.363259
13. Huda, Z.U., Atre, R., Jannesari, A., Wolf, F.: Automatic parallel pattern detection in the algorithm structure design space. In: 30th IEEE International Parallel and Distributed Processing Symposium, pp. 43–52. IEEE Computer Society (2016)
14. King, J.C.: Symbolic execution and program testing. Commun. ACM **19**(7), 385–394 (1976). https://doi.org/10.1145/360248.360252
15. Li, Z., Jannesari, A., Wolf, F.: An efficient data-dependence profiler for sequential and parallel programs. In: IEEE International Parallel and Distributed Processing Symposium, pp. 484–493. IEEE Computer Society (2015)

16. Liu, W., et al.: POSH: a TLS compiler that exploits program structure. In: Torrellas, J., Chatterjee, S. (eds.) ACM SIGPLAN Symposium on Principles and Practice of Parallel Programming, PPOPP, pp. 158–167. ACM (2006)
17. Maydan, D., Amarsinghe, S., Lam, M.: Data dependence and data-flow analysis of arrays. In: Banerjee, U., Gelernter, D., Nicolau, A., Padua, D. (eds.) LCPC 1992. LNCS, vol. 757, pp. 434–448. Springer, Heidelberg (1993). https://doi.org/10.1007/3-540-57502-2_63
18. von Praun, C., Bordawekar, R., Cascaval, C.: Modeling optimistic concurrency using quantitative dependence analysis. In: Chatterjee, S., Scott, M.L. (eds.) 13th ACM SIGPLAN Symposium on Principles and Practice of Parallel Programming, PPOPP, pp. 185–196. ACM (2008)
19. Pugh, W.: The omega test: a fast and practical integer programming algorithm for dependence analysis. In: Martin, J.L. (ed.) Proceedings Supercomputing 1991, pp. 4–13. ACM (1991)
20. Pugh, W., Wonnacott, D.: An exact method for analysis of value-based array data dependences. In: Banerjee, U., Gelernter, D., Nicolau, A., Padua, D. (eds.) LCPC 1993. LNCS, vol. 768, pp. 546–566. Springer, Heidelberg (1994). https://doi.org/10.1007/3-540-57659-2_31
21. Pugh, W., Wonnacott, D.: Static analysis of upper and lower bounds on dependences and parallelism. ACM Trans. Program. Lang. Syst. **16**(4), 1248–1278 (1994)
22. Sánchez, D., Yen, L., Hill, M.D., Sankaralingam, K.: Implementing signatures for transactional memory. In: 40th Annual IEEE/ACM International Symposium on Microarchitecture, pp. 123–133. IEEE Computer Society (2007)
23. Snelting, G., et al.: Checking probabilistic noninterference using JOANA. it - Inf. Technol. **56**(6), 280–287 (2014)
24. Wasser, N., Bubel, R., Hähnle, R.: Abstract interpretation. In: Ahrendt et al. [1], chap. 6, pp. 167–189
25. Wu, P., Kejariwal, A., Caşcaval, C.: Compiler-driven dependence profiling to guide program parallelization. In: Amaral, J.N. (ed.) LCPC 2008. LNCS, vol. 5335, pp. 232–248. Springer, Heidelberg (2008). https://doi.org/10.1007/978-3-540-89740-8_16
26. Yuki, T., Pouchet, L.N.: Polybench/c 4.1 (2015). http://web.cse.ohio-state.edu/~pouchet.2/software/polybench/
27. Zhang, X., Navabi, A., Jagannathan, S.: Alchemist: a transparent dependence distance profiling infrastructure. In: The Seventh International Symposium on Code Generation and Optimization, pp. 47–58. IEEE Computer Society (2009)

Evaluation of Program Slicing in Software Verification

Marek Chalupa and Jan Strejček(✉)

Masaryk University, Brno, Czech Republic
{chalupa,strejcek}@fi.muni.cz

Abstract. There are publications that consider the use of program slicing in software verification, but we are aware of no publication that thoroughly evaluates the impact of program slicing on the verification process. This paper aims to fill in this gap by providing a comparison of the effect of program slicing on the performance of the reachability analysis in several state-of-the-art software verification tools, namely CPAchecker, DIVINE, KLEE, SeaHorn, and SMACK. The effect of slicing is evaluated on the number of solved benchmarks and running times of the tools. Experiments show that the effect of program slicing is mostly positive and can significantly improve the performance of some tools.

1 Introduction

Program slicing [36] is a method that takes a program and extracts a subprogram called *sliced program* or simply *slice* that contains only statements relevant for a given *slicing criterion*. In this paper, we consider static backward slicing with slicing criterion given as some statement of the program. The slice comprises the program statements that have some influence on the reachability or the arguments of the slicing criterion.

Program slicing has applications in many areas of computer science including (but not limited to) program debugging, code comprehension, code maintenance and re-engineering, regression testing, and software verification. Many applications are mentioned in several program slicing surveys [6,15,27,28,31,37].

This paper is concerned with the last mentioned use case. In software verification, program slicing has been usually used simply as a preprocessing step. That is, the program is sliced with respect to the verified property before the actual verification process starts. Nevertheless, the impact of applying program slicing in such settings was usually certified by only few examples, if any. This paper aims to evaluate the impact of applying program slicing before verification on a large number of benchmarks.

We took the Symbiotic framework [9], which has the capability of slicing LLVM [24] bitcode, and integrated several state-of-the-art software verification tools processing LLVM bitcode into this framework. The tools, namely

This work has been supported by the Czech Science Foundation grant GA18-02177S.

W. Ahrendt and S. L. Tapia Tarifa (Eds.): IFM 2019, LNCS 11918, pp. 101–119, 2019.
https://doi.org/10.1007/978-3-030-34968-4_6

CPAchecker [4], DIVINE [25], KLEE [7], SeaHorn [14], and SMACK [8], were selected such that each uses a different verification approach.

We conducted experiments on benchmarks from Software Verification Competition (SV-COMP) [3]. More precisely, we took more than 6500 benchmarks, which are sequential C programs concerned with the reachability of a specified error location. Reachability of an error location represents probably the most common verification task, which may be used for verification of assertion validity, absence of division by zero, etc.

Each tool was run in three configurations. The first configuration does not use any slicing. The second configuration uses a slicing originally designed for terminating programs. This slicing can remove potentially non-terminating loops. As a result, a sliced program may contain a reachable error location that is not reachable in the original program. Therefore, if the sliced program contains no reachable error location, then the original program has no reachable error location as well, but the opposite implication does not hold. The third configuration uses a less aggressive slicing that preserves termination properties of program loops. The experiments show that the application of program slicing has a positive effect as it increases the number of decided benchmarks and often speeds up the whole verification process.

The rest of the paper is organized as follows. In the next subsection, we summarize the related literature. Details on program slicing and its use in software verification is the content of Sect. 2. Section 3 deals with the relevant aspects of tools we used to evaluate the effect of slicing on the reachability analysis. In particular, we describe the slicing functionality of Symbiotic and how we integrated the tools CPAchecker, DIVINE, KLEE, SeaHorn, and SMACK into the Symbiotic framework. Section 4 presents the experiments and discusses their results. The last section concludes the paper.

1.1 Related Work

There are many papers that present some use of program slicing in software verification but without any analysis of the contribution of program slicing to the efficiency of the considered verification approach [2,16,19–21,23,26]. In the following, we mention papers that provide some evaluation of the effect of program slicing.

Vasudevan et al. [33,34] use program slicing to speed-up LTL bounded model checking of Verilog models. The authors leverage the information from the LTL specification to improve the effectiveness of slicing over standard static backward slicing. Improvements over plain bounded model checking as well as over bounded model checking preceded by standard static backward slicing are reported. The authors evaluated the contribution of program slicing during bounded model checking (with bound 24) of 9 different LTL properties on a Verilog implementation of USB 2.0 Function Core.

Dwyer et al. [12] study the effect of applying program slicing in model checking of concurrent object-oriented programs. The work shows that slicing brings an additional reduction to partial order reduction, but no significant gain was achieved for simple assertion checking. The authors suggest that it may have been caused by the structure of the 10 benchmarks used in the study.

Wang et al. [35] use slicing to reduce a given program before model checking it for buffer overrun. The authors report significant performance gain due to slicing, but they witness it only by verification of 5 assertions in *minicom* program.

Sabouri and Sirjani [30] use program slicing to slice Rebeca models of concurrent programs before model checking. The evaluation is provided for 9 benchmarks, each parametrized with several properties. One property was always the presence of a deadlock and the other properties were unspecified. The authors conclude that slicing reduces state space of the models and can significantly help reducing the time of model checking.

Chebaro et al. [10,11] combine a fast static analysis with program slicing and concolic testing. The fast static analysis finds possible bugs in the program, program slicing then reduces the program with respect to these bugs (either to all of them or to a selected subset), and concolic testing tries to confirm whether the bug is real. In the two publications, the authors show the positive effect of slicing on 5 and 9 programs, respectively.

Trabish et al. [32] evaluate the use of program slicing during *chopped symbolic execution*. Chopped symbolic execution executes some (pre-determined) functions only on-demand when needed. Program slicing is used to further lower the cost of the execution of these functions, so it is also invoked on-demand during the analysis. The evaluation was done on 6 security vulnerabilities, each parametrised by 3 different search heuristics. The authors report that program slicing can significantly help their technique in some cases, but report also a slowdown in some other cases. They planned to avoid this problem by an automatic analysis which decides when to use program slicing.

2 Program Slicing

Program slicing was introduced by Mark Weiser in 1980's as a code decomposition technique for debugging [36]. The Weiser's algorithm is based on a backward data-flow analysis [36]. Ferrante et al. advocated using *program dependence graph* (PDG) for program slicing [13]. Their algorithm was extended by Horwitz et al. to programs with function calls [18] using so-called *system dependence graph* (SDG). The algorithms based on PDG/SDG gained on popularity as they are more intuitive and flexible. Research in the area of program slicing therefore focuses mainly on algorithms based on dependence graphs.

Now we describe slicing algorithms based on dependence graphs and discuss obstacles connected with program slicing in the context of program verification.

2.1 Slicing Programs Using Dependence Graphs

Slicing algorithms based on dependence graphs first build a dependence graph and then compute a slice from the graph. Nodes of the dependence graph correspond to program statements and edges capture all dependencies among these statements. Two basic kinds of dependence are *data* and *control dependence*.

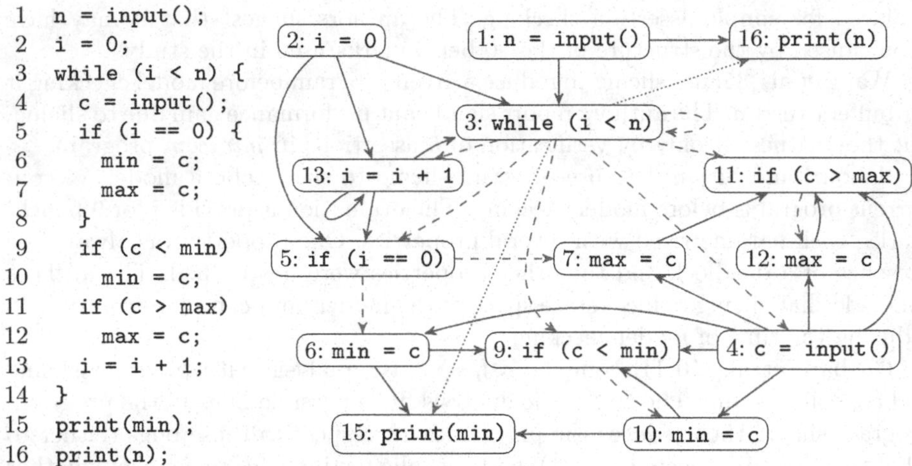

1 n = input();
2 i = 0;
3 while (i < n) {
4 c = input();
5 if (i == 0) {
6 min = c;
7 max = c;
8 }
9 if (c < min)
10 min = c;
11 if (c > max)
12 max = c;
13 i = i + 1;
14 }
15 print(min);
16 print(n);
2: i = 0
1: n = input()
16: print(n)
3: while (i < n)
13: i = i + 1
11: if (c > max)
5: if (i == 0)
7: max = c
12: max = c
6: min = c
9: if (c < min)
4: c = input()
15: print(min)
10: min = c

Fig. 1. A program (left) and its program dependence graph (right). Solid blue edges are data dependencies. Dashed red edges are control dependencies. The dotted red edges are extra control dependence edges added when using non-termination sensitive control dependence. (Color figure online)

Data dependence may arise between two statements of a program that work with the same memory. More precisely, a statement s_r is dependent on a statement s_w if there exists a program execution where the statement s_r reads a value that has been written by the statement s_w. For example, consider the program in Fig. 1 (left). The statement on line 3 is data dependent on the statement on line 2 because the value of variable `i` written on line 2 is read on line 3. Because the value of `i` read on line 3 may have been written also by the statement on line 13, the statement on line 3 is data dependent also on the statement on line 13. All data dependencies of the program are shown by solid blue edges in the graph of Fig. 1 (right).

The notion of control dependence is more complicated since there are several definitions that can be used, each of them leading to slices with different properties. We introduce two of them. The first one is *standard control dependence* as defined by Ferrante et al. [13] and the other is *non-termination sensitive control dependence* introduced by Ranganath et al. [29].

Before defining the mentioned forms of control dependence, we must recall some of the standard concepts from program analysis. A *path* in a directed graph $G = (V, E)$ is a nonempty finite or infinite sequence $n_1, n_2, ...$ of nodes from V such that for each pair n_i, n_{i+1} of consecutive nodes it holds $(n_i, n_{i+1}) \in E$. A path is *non-trivial* if it has at least two nodes. *Maximal path* is an infinite path or a path whose last node has no successors (i.e., a path that cannot be prolonged). If there exists a path starting in a node n that contains a node m, we say that m is *reachable* from n. *Control flow graph* (CFG) is a directed graph where nodes represent statements of a program and edges represent possible flow of control between statements in the program. We assume that a CFG has a distinguished *entry* node with no predecessors, from which all nodes are reachable. If a CFG contains also a unique *exit* node that has no successors and is reachable from any other node, we say that the CFG has the *unique exit property*. In such control flow graphs, we can define the post-dominance relation: we say that a node n *post-dominates* a node m if n appears on every path from m to the exit node. If, additionally, $n \neq m$, we say that n strictly post-dominates m.

Definition 1 (Standard control dependence). *Consider a CFG with the unique exit property. We say that a node n is* control dependent *on a node b if*

1. *there exists a non-trivial path π from b to n with any node on π (excluding b) post-dominated by n, and*
2. *b is not strictly post-dominated by n.*

In other words, a statement n is control dependent on a statement b if b is the "closest" point where the program may go some way that misses n. Figure 1 (right) depicts standard control dependencies as dashed red edges.

The standard control dependence is sufficient for the most of use cases, but it is problematic in several ways. First, it is not applicable to CFG without the unique exit property. Second, this definition of control dependence does not take into account the fact that loops may not terminate (as post-dominance considers only the paths that actually reach the exit node). That may result in incorrect slices where a non-terminating loop is sliced away making a previously unreachable code reachable. Both these problems can be solved by using *non-termination sensitive control dependence* [29]:

Definition 2 (Non-termination sensitive control dependence). *Given a CFG, a node n is* non-termination sensitive control dependent *on a node b if b has successors s_1 and s_2 such that*

1. *n occurs on all maximal paths form s_1, and*
2. *there exists a maximal path from s_2 on which n does not occur.*

For any CFG with the unique exit property, the definition actually extends the standard control dependence in the sense that if a node n is control dependent on a node b, then n is also non-termination sensitive control dependent b. The opposite implication does not hold. Figure 1 (right) depicts the additional non-termination sensitive control dependencies as dotted red edges.

Using non-termination sensitive control dependence improves the applicability of program slicing to a greater class of programs, but may be sometimes too strict – it results in keeping all loops of the program from which the slicing criterion is reachable in the slice. We elaborate on this matter later in Sect. 2.2.

Having a PDG and a slicing criterion, slicing the PDG is as easy as collecting all the nodes that are backward reachable through dependence edges from the node of the slicing criterion statement. For example, Fig. 2 shows slices of the

```
n = input();
i = 0;
while (i < n) {
  c = input();
  if (i == 0) {
    min = c;
  }
  if (c > min)
    min = c;
  i = i + 1;
}
print(min);
```

```
n = input();
print(n);
```

```
n = input();
i = 0;
while (i < n) {
  i = i + 1;
}
print(n);
```

Fig. 2. Slices of the program from Fig. 1 for slicing criterion `print(min)` using standard control dependence (left), for `print(n)` using standard control dependence (middle), and for `print(n)` using non-termination sensitive control dependence (right).

program in Fig. 1 for slicing criteria `print(min)` (on the left) and `print(n)` (in the middle) using standard control dependence. The slice on the right considers also slicing criterion `print(n)`, but non-termination sensitive control dependence is used. In contrast to the slice in the middle, the slice on the right obtained using non-termination sensitive control dependence keeps also the header and the counter of the loop, as the slicing criterion is never reached if the loop does not terminate. Note that a program can be sliced with respect to more slicing criteria at once. Such slice consists of all nodes of the dependence graph that are backward reachable from at least one of the slicing criteria nodes.

If a program is structured into procedures and contains call statements, one can naturally build a single PDG for the program by working with *interprocedural control flow graph (ICFG)* instead of isolated control flow graphs for each procedure. An ICFG is a graph containing a CFG for each procedure and edges that go from call sites to entry points of procedures and from exits from procedures to return sites. This approach is comfortable as it does not require any changes in the PDG construction or in the slicing algorithm. Nevertheless, there are better algorithms (i.e., producing smaller slices) that work on system dependence graphs [6, 18] instead of on PDG. We do not go into details of these algorithms as we do not use them.

2.2 Program Slicing in Verification

In this section, we describe several obstacles that must be considered when applying program slicing before reachability analysis in software verification. These are mainly the use of user-defined assumptions and possibly non-terminating loops.

Assumptions. If the analyzed code contains user-defined assumptions (further represented as calls to function `assume()`), a special care must be taken to slice the program correctly. The reason is that slicing criteria are not dependent on

```
1 int x = nondet();
2 assume(x > 0);
3 assert(x > 0); // slicing crit.
```

```
1 int x = 0;
2 assume(x == 1);
3 assert(0); // slicing crit.
```

Fig. 3. The code on the left contains an assumption that behaves like a modifier to the data and the code on the right shows an assumption that changes the control flow. In both cases, the assertion is neither control nor data dependent on the assumption and thus the assumption would be sliced out if the assertion is taken as the slicing criterion. However, slicing the assumption away would introduce an error in the program.

assumptions as an assumption only reads values of variables. However, assumptions can influence a program execution in two ways:

- Assumptions can restrict the value of non-deterministic variables and thus act in a sense as a write to the variable.
- Assumptions can change the control flow of the program (e.g., execution is terminated if an assumption is not satisfied).

An example of such effects can be seen in Fig. 3. On the left, the call to `assert` is dependent only on the statement on line 1 as the call to `assume` on line 2 only reads the variable `x` and does not modify it. However, if we would slice away the call to `assume`, we introduce an error to the program as the assertion on line 3 could be violated. Similar problem is shown in the code on the right, where the assertion on line 3 is independent of the rest of statements, but because of the unsatisfied assumption it is unreachable. Slicing away the assumption again introduces an error.

A simple solution, that we utilized also in our experiments, is to set the assumption statements as additional slicing criteria. This solution is imprecise – many of the assumptions that are left in the code along with their dependencies may be in fact irrelevant to the verified property. However, because the assumptions are usually localized to the beginning of the program where they constrain possible inputs, the increase of the slice size is mostly small.

The Choice of Control Dependence. Here we discuss advantages and disadvantages of the two definitions of control dependence provided in Sect. 2.1.

Using the standard control dependence (Definition 1) may result in slicing away non-terminating loops and thus making previously unreachable code reachable. In particular, it may transform an unreachable error location into a reachable one. For example, consider the program in Fig. 3 (right) with the error location `assert(0)` and replace the call `assume(x == 1)` by `while(1)`. The error location is unreachable due to the infinite loop, but if we slice the program with respect to the assertion as the slicing criterion, we get just the last line. Hence, the whole process of slicing and program verification can report spurious errors. On the positive side, when using error locations as slicingcriteria, slicing with standard control dependence cannot transform a reachable error location into unreachable one. Hence, if a slice is correct (i.e., it does not contain any reachable error location), then the original program is correct as well. Moreover, slices obtained with standard control dependence are smaller than these obtained with non-termination sensitive control dependence.

The non-termination sensitive control dependence (Definition 2) does not allow to slice away a loop (more precisely, its header and counters) if the loop may cause the unreachability of a slicing criterion by cycling forever. From the correctness point of view, one must therefore choose the non-termination sensitive control dependence. However, the price for this correctness is relatively high as only the loops that do not lie on a path in CFG from the entry node to any slicing criterion can be sliced away from the program.

To sum up, the main disadvantage of standard control dependence over non-termination sensitive control dependence is potential introduction of spurious errors by slicing away some non-terminating loops. Because these spurious errors can be ruled out by trying to reproduce each discovered error trace in the original program, we believe that using standard control dependence is also meaningful. In our experiments, we therefore consider both standard and non-termination sensitive control dependence and we report the numbers of correct as well as incorrect results.

3 Considered Tools

To evaluate the effect of program slicing on efficiency of reachability analysis, we integrated five state-of-the-art verification tools into the Symbiotic framework that has the capability of slicing programs. This section briefly describes Symbiotic, the implementation of the slicing procedure, and the five verification tools including important details about integration of these tools.

3.1 Symbiotic

Symbiotic [9] is a verification framework that applies program slicing to reduce the analyzed program before passing it to a verification backend. Slicing in Symbiotic works on programs in LLVM [24], which is an assembly-like language extended with types. An LLVM bitcode file is divided into functions. Instructions in a function are composed into basic blocks that form the control flow graph of the function. Memory manipulations (reads and writes) are done via pointers.

The workflow of Symbiotic when deciding reachability of an error location is straightforward. Symbiotic takes as input a list of C sources and compiles them into a single LLVM bitcode file (if the input is not already an LLVM bitcode). As the next step, the bitcode is optimized using the LLVM infrastructure, then it is sliced with error locations as slicing criteria, and optimized again. Finally, the sliced and optimized bitcode is passed to a selected verification tool. In this paper, we do not use the two optimization steps as we want to observe the pure effect of slicing. Note that the optimization steps can substantially improve efficiency of the verification process, but some care must be taken not to introduce unsoundness in the case the program contains undefined behavior.

3.2 Slicing Algorithm

The slicing procedure implemented in SYMBIOTIC is based on dependence graphs capturing dependencies between LLVM instructions. To compute dependencies for LLVM bitcode, one must

- perform *pointer analysis*,
- compute data dependencies by computing *reaching definitions*, and
- compute control dependencies from the bitcode structure.

Pointer analysis is needed to identify what memory is accessed by memory-manipulating instructions. SYMBIOTIC provides several pointer analyses with various precision and computation cost. Here we use interprocedural flow-insensitive field-sensitive inclusion-based pointer analysis [17] to compute information about pointers.

The information about pointers and the knowledge about the control flow of the analyzed program are then used in the (interprocedural) *reaching definitions analysis*. For each instruction that reads from memory, the analysis computes which instructions may have written the values read by the reading instruction. SYMBIOTIC applies the classic data-flow approach to reaching definitions computation [1]. With the results of reaching definition analysis, data dependencies can be computed easily.

Control dependencies (either standard or non-termination sensitive) are computed on the basic block level. Since computing control dependencies on ICFG can be impractical for big programs and programs that contain multiple calls of a function (which create a loop in ICFG), SYMBIOTIC computes control dependencies only intraprocedurally. Interprocedural control dependencies that arise from the possibility of not returning from a called function (e.g., when the function calls `exit` or `abort`, or loops indefinitely) are then filled in by post-processing.

When the algorithm computing standard control dependencies is used and the analyzed CFG does not have the unique exit property because it has multiple exit nodes, we establish the property by adding an artificial exit node that is the immediate successor of all original exit nodes. If the original CFG does not have the property because it has no exit node, then we conservatively make all instructions of each basic block control dependent on instructions immediately preceding the basic block.

SYMBIOTIC builds a single PDG for the whole bitcode. The slice is then computed as all instructions that are backward reachable from the slicing criteria nodes. The current slicing procedure in SYMBIOTIC cannot handle calls to `setjmp` and `longjmp` functions. However, these appear only rarely and do not appear in our benchmarks.

3.3 Verification Tools and Their Integration

In order to evaluate the effect of program slicing on reachability analysis, we integrated several state-of-the-art verification tools that can work with LLVM into SYMBIOTIC framework. Besides the symbolic executor KLEE, which has been used as SYMBIOTIC's verification back end for many years, the framework now supports also CPACHECKER, DIVINE, SEAHORN, and SMACK. The tools were integrated using *BenchExec* [5] tool-info modules that take care of assembling command line for a given tool setup.

Some of the tools have particular requirements on the input bitcode, e.g., that the bitcode does not contain any switch instructions. These requirements had to be addressed during the integration. We briefly describe the integrated tools along with the extra steps where the integration of the tool differs from the default configuration.

CPAchecker. [4] is a configurable program analysis framework implementing many modern program analysis algorithms. For experiments, we used our fork of CPACHECKER that contains several fixes for the LLVM backend [1] and SV-COMP 2019 configuration (`-svcomp19` option). This configuration runs several analyses sequentially chained one after each other (each with a given time budget). The actual sequence of the analyses depends on the structure of the program and include, for instance, bounded model checking, explicit value analysis, predicate abstraction, and k-induction.

Note that the support for LLVM in CPACHECKER is still experimental. The required version of LLVM is 3.9.1.

DIVINE. [25] is an explicit model checker that have recently added a support for verifying programs with inputs via instrumenting the symbolic computation directly into the analyzed program. Symbolic computations in DIVINE do not support 32-bit bitcode, therefore all the experiments with DIVINE assumed that the programs are written for 64-bit architectures. This assumption is void for most of the benchmarks that we used, but there are several cases where it led to an incorrect result.

We used DIVINE 4.3.1 (the static binary downloaded from DIVINE's web page) in experiments. The required LLVM version is 6.

KLEE. [7] is a highly optimized symbolic executor. Before passing a bitcode to KLEE, SYMBIOTIC makes external globals internal, and replaces undefined functions with functions that return non-deterministic values (which should have no effect in our experiments). Also, SYMBIOTIC transforms standard SV-COMP functions that model non-determinism (named `__VERIFIER_*`) to ones that call KLEE's internal functions with equivalent semantics.

SYMBIOTIC has its own fork of KLEE based on KLEE 2.0. The fork differs from the mainstream version mainly by the ability of handling memory alloca-

[1] https://github.com/mchalupa/cpachecker/tree/llvm-fixes2.

tions of symbolic size. We used this fork of KLEE built for LLVM in version 8.0.0 in our experiments.

SeaHorn. [14] is a modular verification framework that uses constrained Horn clauses as the intermediate verification language. The verification condition is model checked using PDR/IC3.

We used the nightly build in version `0.1.0-rc3-61ace48` obtained from the docker image. The LLVM version is 5.0.2.

SMACK. [8] is a bounded model checker that internally compiles the program into Boogie and then uses Corral [22] to perform the analysis.

We used the version of SMACK that competed in SV-COMP 2019. The required LLVM version is 3.9.1.

4 Experiments and Evaluation

We conducted a set of experiments on 6571 benchmarks from Software Verification Competition (SV-COMP) 2019 [3], namely all benchmarks from the category *ReachSafety* and from the subcategory *LinuxDeviceDrivers64* of the category *Systems*. Each of these benchmarks is a sequential C program that contains some marked error location. Moreover, each benchmark comes with the information whether at least one of its error locations is reachable or not.

The *ReachSafety* category contains several thematically focused subcategories like *Arrays*, *BitVectors*, and *Floats* with rather small programs. Then there is the subcategory *ProductLines* of generated models for e-mail communication, elevator, and mine pump, the subcategory *Sequentialized* of sequentialized parallel programs which often contian non-terminating loops, and the subcategory *ECA* of huge, synthetic benchmarks with extensive branching. Finally, *LinuxDeviceDrivers64* is a category of benchmarks generated from real Linux kernel device drivers.

The experiments were run on machines with *Intel Core i7-8700* CPU running at 3.20 GHz and 32 GB RAM. Each run was restricted to a single core, 8 GB of memory, and 15 min of CPU time. The presented times are running times of the whole process including compilation to LLVM and program slicing (if applied).

Each tool was run on each benchmark in three configurations:

- without any slicing (referred as *No slicing*),
- with slicing using standard control dependencies (*Standard CD*), and
- with slicing using non-termination sensitive control dependencies (*NTS CD*).

Table 1. Numbers of decided benchmarks by the considered tool configurations. The columns *correct* and *wrong* present the numbers of correctly and incorrectly decided benchmarks, respectively. The columns marked with ✓ (resp. ×) contain the number of benchmarks where the decision of the tool was that error locations are unreachable (resp. reachable). For each tool, the highest numbers of correctly decided benchmarks with and without reachable error locations are typeset in bold.

	No slicing				Standard CD				NTS CD			
	correct		wrong		correct		wrong		correct		wrong	
Tool	✓	×	✓	×	✓	×	✓	×	✓	×	✓	×
CPAchecker	673	666	72	13	**976**	**690**	75	44	841	672	71	14
DIVINE	727	458	0	1	**804**	**610**	0	35	799	518	0	4
KLEE	799	**1173**	45	0	**1364**	1138	46	43	1102	1007	4	4
SeaHorn	2222	874	23	580	**2460**	**933**	32	627	2264	898	21	589
SMACK	**2165**	969	2	235	2076	**1059**	5	282	1984	1039	3	259

Table 1 shows the numbers of decided benchmarks by each tool configuration summarized over all considered benchmarks.[2] It can be clearly seen that the configurations with slicing decide in all but one case more benchmarks than the corresponding configuration without slicing. As expected, *Standard CD* usually decides more benchmarks than *NTS CD*. In fact, slicing helps the most in *ProductLines* subcategory (this holds namely for SMACK and DIVINE) and *LinuxDeviceDrivers64* subcategory (CPAchecker, KLEE, and SeaHorn). This is not surprising as other subcategories contain usually small programs, which were often designed for testing of some verification tool, and thus slicing does not significantly change the complexity of these benchmarks.

There are only two cases when a tool in *Standard CD* configuration correctly decided less benchmarks than without slicing. The first case is KLEE on benchmarks with a reachable error location. The reason is that there are about 40 such benchmarks in the *ECA* subcategory that can be decided by KLEE without slicing, but not by the other configurations as slicing runs out of memory. The second case is SMACK and the explanation for this case is provided later at the description of Fig. 4.

The results also show that all configurations produce some incorrect answers. There are several potential sources of these answers including bugs in verification tools, bugs in slicing, and maybe also wrongly marked benchmarks. Nevertheless, one can clearly see that *NTS CD* produces very similar (and sometimes even lower) number of incorrect answers as the tools without any slicing. *Standard CD* produces noticeably more incorrect answers. Most of these incorrect answers

[2] Detailed numbers for each configuration and subcategory can be found at: https://github.com/staticafi/symbiotic/releases/tag/ifm2019.

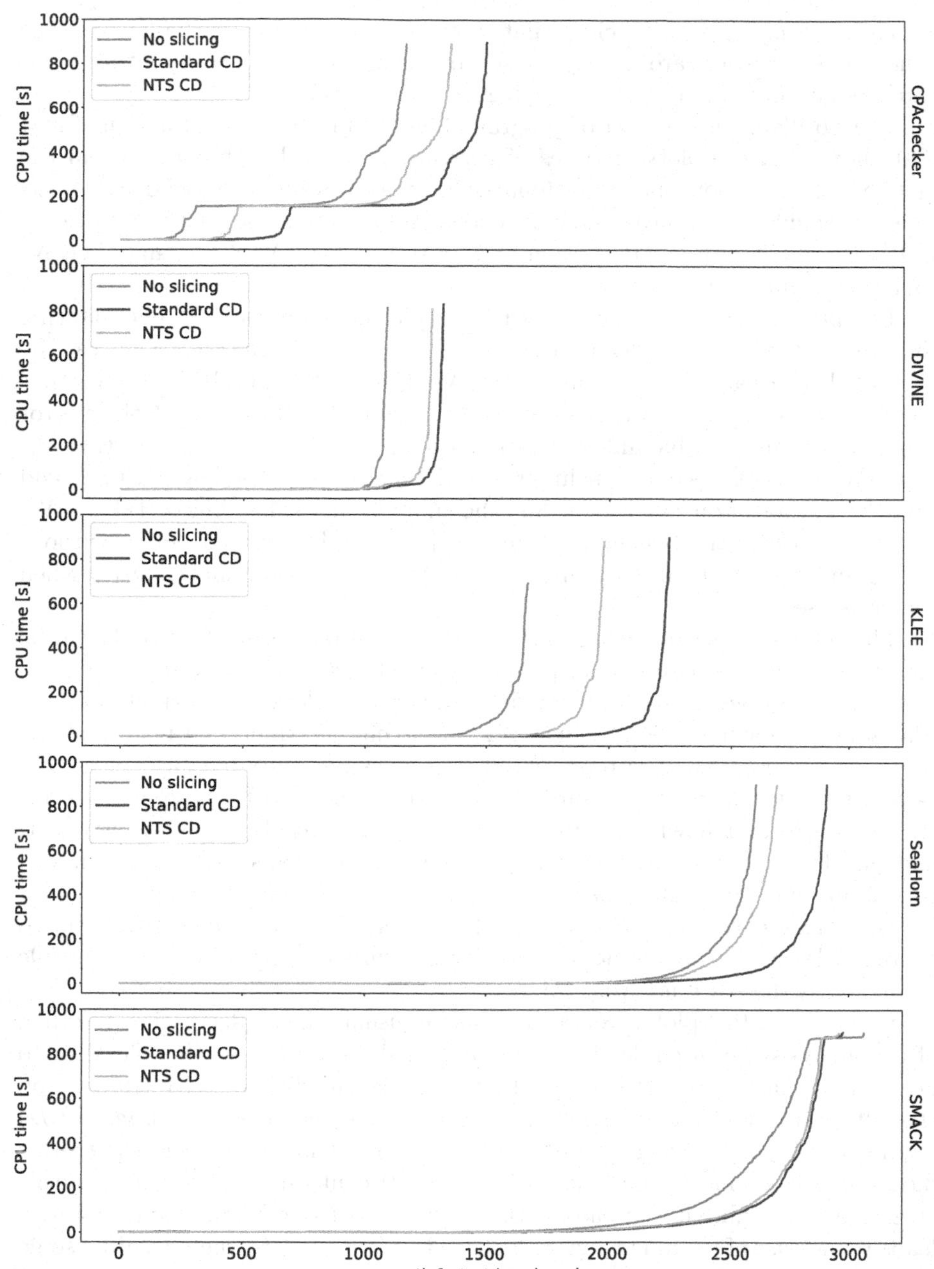

Fig. 4. Quantile plots of CPU time of correctly decided benchmarks. On x-axis are benchmarks sorted according to CPU time (on y-axis) in ascending order.

are negative, i.e., the tool decides that some error location is reachable even if it is not. These answers are mostly caused by slicing away non-terminating loops and are distributed mainly in the category *Sequentialized*.

The positive contribution of program slicing can be observed also in Fig. 4 that shows quantile plots of times of correctly decided benchmarks. From the plots, we can read how many benchmarks (on x-axis) would the tool decide if the timeout would be set to the value on y-axis. We see the same pattern: *Standard CD* is the best (with the exception of SMACK), then *NTS CD* and then *No slicing* configuration.

The plots for SMACK have a very specific shape on its right end showing that many benchmarks are decided shortly before the timeout. This can be explained by a careful optimization of SMACK for SV-COMP: it seems that for many benchmarks the tool says shortly before the timeout that their error locations are unreachable unless it proves the opposite until then. Note that our experiments use the same benchmarks and time limit as the competition, and that this optimization can also explain the anomaly on the last line of Table 1. We manually checked the benchmarks on which SMACK behaved better without slicing and most of them crash after *exactly* 880 s with a compilation error when slicing is used.

The positive effect of slicing to running times of the verification tools can be also seen in Fig. 5, where scatter plots on the left compare *No slicing* configuration against *Standard CD* configuration, and scatter plots on the right compare *Standard CD* configuration against *NTS CD* configuration. The results of the configuration on x-axis are represented by shapes and on y-axis by colors. For x-axis, circle means correct result, cross wrong result, and triangle other result (timeout, error, unknown). For y-axis, green is correct result, red is wrong result, and purple is other result. For example, green circle means that the result was correct for both configurations and red triangle means that the result was other for the x-axis configuration but turned to wrong for y-axis configuration. To decrease the clutter in the plots, we omitted results of type other-other (purple triangles) as these are not very interesting.

From the scatter plots, we see that slicing usually helps decreasing the time of the analysis (green circles below the diagonal on the left scatter plots) or to decide new benchmarks that were not decided without slicing (green triangles on the left scatter plots). Slicing with standard control dependence (*Standard CD*) can introduce some wrong answers (red circles and triangles on the left scatter plots), which are mostly eliminated in *NTS CD* configuration (green or purple crosses on the right scatter plots). Using the *NTS CD* configuration, however, leads to increase of running times compared to *Standard CD* when deciding some benchmarks (green circles above the diagonal on the right).

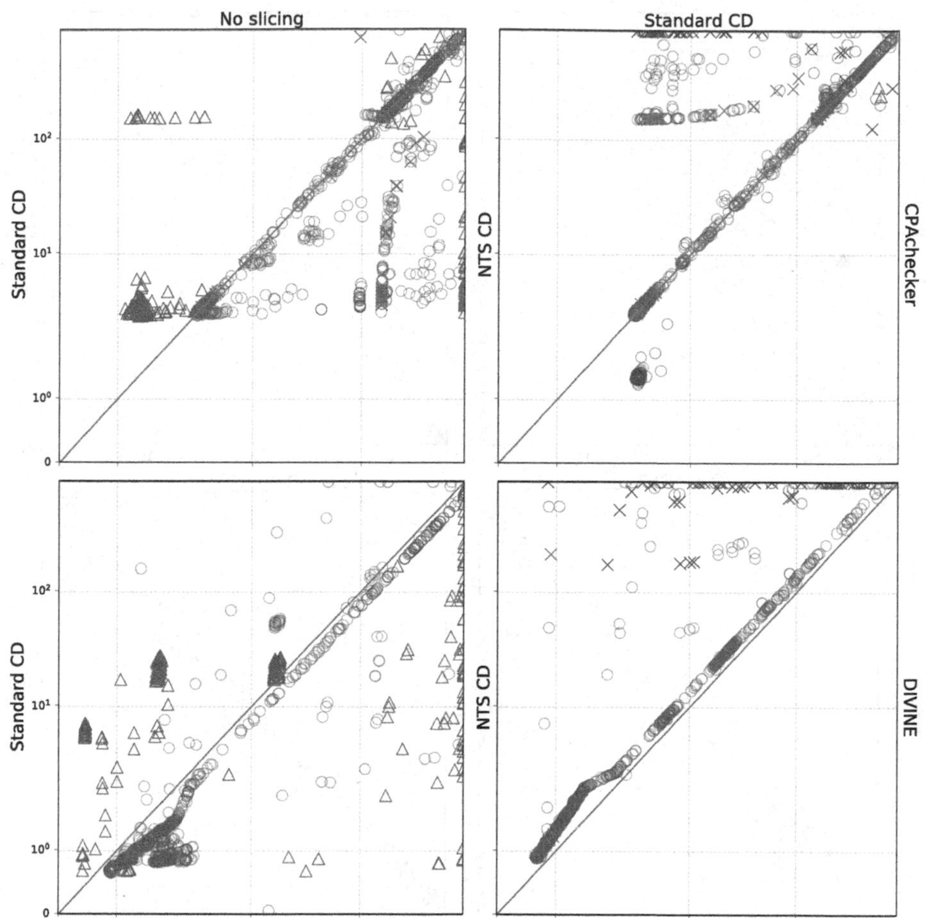

Fig. 5. Scatter plots that compare running time (in seconds) of *No slicing* and *Standard CD* configurations (left), and *Standard CD* and *NTS CD* configurations (right). Circle represents a correct result by the configuration on x-axis, cross a wrong result, and triangle other result (timeout, error, or unknown). Green color represents a correct result by the configuration on y-axis, red color a wrong result, and purple color other result. Purple triangles were omitted to reduce clutter. (Color figure online)

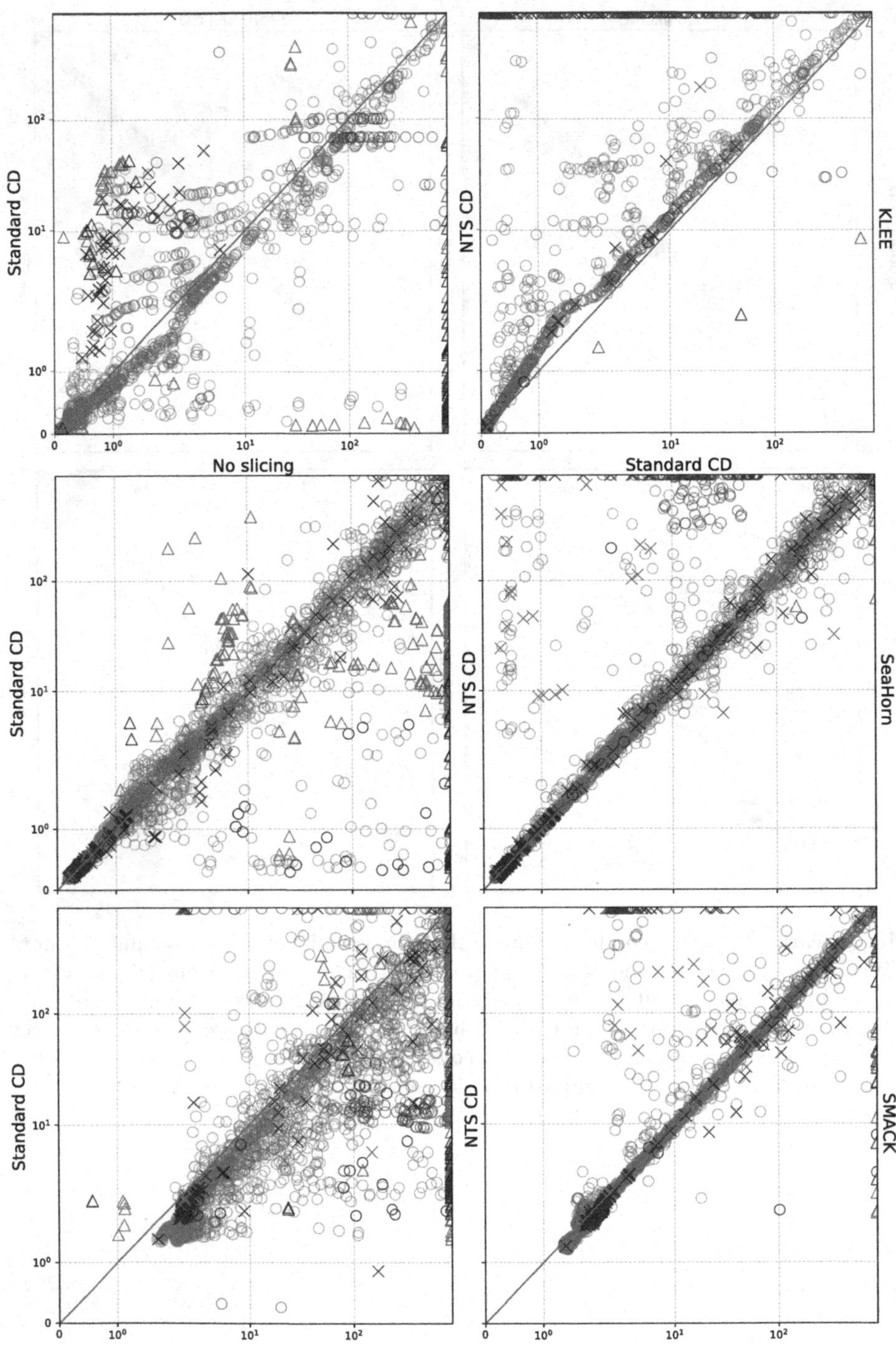

Fig. 5. *(continued)*

5 Conclusion

We provided an intensive evaluation of the impact of program slicing on performance of software verification tools in reachability analysis. The experiments used a huge set of 6571 benchmarks, namely the *ReachSafety* category and *LinuxDeviceDrivers64* subcategory of SV-COMP 2019 benchmarks.

We confirmed several previous observations that program slicing can be effective in reducing the verification time. Further, we showed that it is worth considering the use of standard control dependence when slicing a program before its verification. This follows from the fact that the increase of the number of false positive answers is typically small (and we can get rid of them by trying to replay the found error trace, but we have not included this part in our experiments). Using non-termination sensitive control dependence may increase the analysis time compared to using standard control dependence, but it is still better than not using program slicing at all.

References

1. Aho, A.V., Sethi, R., Ullman, J.D.: Compilers: Principles, Techniques, and Tools. Addison-Wesley Series in Computer Science/World Student Series Edition. Addison-Wesley, Boston (1986). http://www.worldcat.org/oclc/12285707
2. Backes, J.D., Person, S., Rungta, N., Tkachuk, O.: Regression verification using impact summaries. In: Bartocci, E., Ramakrishnan, C.R. (eds.) SPIN 2013. LNCS, vol. 7976, pp. 99–116. Springer, Heidelberg (2013). https://doi.org/10.1007/978-3-642-39176-7_7
3. Beyer, D.: Automatic verification of C and Java programs: SV-COMP 2019. In: Beyer, D., Huisman, M., Kordon, F., Steffen, B. (eds.) TACAS 2019, Part III. LNCS, vol. 11429, pp. 133–155. Springer, Cham (2019). https://doi.org/10.1007/978-3-030-17502-3_9
4. Beyer, D., Keremoglu, M.E.: CPAchecker: a tool for configurable software verification. In: Gopalakrishnan, G., Qadeer, S. (eds.) CAV 2011. LNCS, vol. 6806, pp. 184–190. Springer, Heidelberg (2011). https://doi.org/10.1007/978-3-642-22110-1_16
5. Beyer, D., Löwe, S., Wendler, P.: Reliable benchmarking: requirements and solutions. STTT **21**(1), 1–29 (2019)
6. Binkley, D.W., Gallagher, K.B.: Program slicing. In: Advances in Computers, vol. 43, pp. 1–50 (1996)
7. Cadar, C., Dunbar, D., Engler, D.R.: KLEE: unassisted and automatic generation of high-coverage tests for complex systems programs. In: OSDI 2008, pp. 209–224. USENIX Association (2008)
8. Carter, M., He, S., Whitaker, J., Rakamaric, Z., Emmi, M.: SMACK software verification toolchain. In: ICSE 2016, pp. 589–592. ACM (2016)
9. Chalupa, M., Vitovská, M., Strejček, J.: SYMBIOTIC 5: boosted instrumentation. In: Beyer, D., Huisman, M. (eds.) TACAS 2018. LNCS, vol. 10806, pp. 442–446. Springer, Cham (2018). https://doi.org/10.1007/978-3-319-89963-3_29
10. Chebaro, O., Kosmatov, N., Giorgetti, A., Julliand, J.: Program slicing enhances a verification technique combining static and dynamic analysis. In: SAC 2012, pp. 1284–1291. ACM (2012)

11. Chebaro, O., et al.: Behind the scenes in SANTE: a combination of static and dynamic analyses. Autom. Softw. Eng. **21**(1), 107–143 (2014)
12. Dwyer, M.B., Hatcliff, J., Hoosier, M., Ranganath, V.P., Robby, Wallentine, T.: Evaluating the effectiveness of slicing for model reduction of concurrent object-oriented programs. In: Hermanns, H., Palsberg, J. (eds.) TACAS 2006. LNCS, pp. 73–89. Springer, Heidelberg (2006). https://doi.org/10.1007/11691372_5
13. Ferrante, J., Ottenstein, K.J., Warren, J.D.: The program dependence graph and its use in optimization. ACM Trans. Program. Lang. Syst. **9**(3), 319–349 (1987)
14. Gurfinkel, A., Kahsai, T., Komuravelli, A., Navas, J.A.: The SeaHorn verification framework. In: Kroening, D., Păsăreanu, C.S. (eds.) CAV 2015. LNCS, vol. 9206, pp. 343–361. Springer, Cham (2015). https://doi.org/10.1007/978-3-319-21690-4_20
15. Harman, M., Hierons, R.M.: An overview of program slicing. Softw. Focus **2**(3), 85–92 (2001)
16. Hatcliff, J., Dwyer, M.B., Zheng, H.: Slicing software for model construction. Higher-Order Symb. Comput. **13**(4), 315–353 (2000)
17. Hind, M.: Pointer analysis: haven't we solved this problem yet? In: PASTE 2001, pp. 54–61. ACM (2001)
18. Horwitz, S., Reps, T.W., Binkley, D.W.: Interprocedural slicing using dependence graphs. ACM Trans. Program. Lang. Syst. **12**(1), 26–60 (1990)
19. Ivancic, F., et al.: Model checking C programs using F-SOFT. In: ICCD 2005, pp. 297–308. IEEE Computer Society (2005)
20. Ivančić, F., Yang, Z., Ganai, M.K., Gupta, A., Shlyakhter, I., Ashar, P.: F-Soft: software verification platform. In: Etessami, K., Rajamani, S.K. (eds.) CAV 2005. LNCS, vol. 3576, pp. 301–306. Springer, Heidelberg (2005). https://doi.org/10.1007/11513988_31
21. Ivancic, F., Yang, Z., Ganai, M.K., Gupta, A., Ashar, P.: Efficient SAT-based bounded model checking for software verification. Theor. Comput. Sci. **404**(3), 256–274 (2008)
22. Lal, A., Qadeer, S., Lahiri, S.K.: A solver for reachability modulo theories. In: Madhusudan, P., Seshia, S.A. (eds.) CAV 2012. LNCS, vol. 7358, pp. 427–443. Springer, Heidelberg (2012). https://doi.org/10.1007/978-3-642-31424-7_32
23. Lange, T., Neuhäußer, M.R., Noll, T.: Speeding up the safety verification of programmable logic controller code. In: Bertacco, V., Legay, A. (eds.) HVC 2013. LNCS, vol. 8244, pp. 44–60. Springer, Cham (2013). https://doi.org/10.1007/978-3-319-03077-7_4
24. Lattner, C., Adve, V.S.: LLVM: a compilation framework for lifelong program analysis & transformation. In: CGO 2004, pp. 75–88. IEEE Computer Society (2004)
25. Lauko, H., Štill, V., Ročkai, P., Barnat, J.: Extending DIVINE with symbolic verification using SMT. In: Beyer, D., Huisman, M., Kordon, F., Steffen, B. (eds.) TACAS 2019. LNCS, vol. 11429, pp. 204–208. Springer, Cham (2019). https://doi.org/10.1007/978-3-030-17502-3_14
26. Li, X., Hoover, H.J., Rudnicki, P.: Towards automatic exception safety verification. In: Misra, J., Nipkow, T., Sekerinski, E. (eds.) FM 2006. LNCS, vol. 4085, pp. 396–411. Springer, Heidelberg (2006). https://doi.org/10.1007/11813040_27
27. Lucia, A.D.: Program slicing: methods and applications. In: SCAM 2001, pp. 144–151. IEEE Computer Society (2001)
28. Mohapatra, D.P., Mall, R., Kumar, R.: An overview of slicing techniques for object-oriented programs. Informatica (Slovenia) **30**(2), 253–277 (2006)

29. Ranganath, V.P., Amtoft, T., Banerjee, A., Dwyer, M.B., Hatcliff, J.: A new foundation for control-dependence and slicing for modern program structures. In: Sagiv, M. (ed.) ESOP 2005. LNCS, vol. 3444, pp. 77–93. Springer, Heidelberg (2005). https://doi.org/10.1007/978-3-540-31987-0_7
30. Sabouri, H., Sirjani, M.: Slicing-based reductions for Rebeca. Electr. Notes Theor. Comput. Sci. **260**, 209–224 (2010)
31. Tip, F.: A survey of program slicing techniques. J. Prog. Lang. **3**(3), 121–189 (1995)
32. Trabish, D., Mattavelli, A., Rinetzky, N., Cadar, C.: Chopped symbolic execution. In: Proceedings of the 40th International Conference on Software Engineering, ICSE 2018, Gothenburg, Sweden, 27 May–03 June 2018, pp. 350–360. ACM (2018). https://doi.org/10.1145/3180155.3180251
33. Vasudevan, S., Emerson, E.A., Abraham, J.A.: Efficient model checking of hardware using conditioned slicing. Electr. Notes Theor. Comput. Sci. **128**(6), 279–294 (2005)
34. Vasudevan, S., Emerson, E.A., Abraham, J.A.: Improved verification of hardware designs through antecedent conditioned slicing. STTT **9**(1), 89–101 (2007)
35. Wang, L., Zhang, Q., Zhao, P.: Automated detection of code vulnerabilities based on program analysis and model checking. In: SCAM 2008, pp. 165–173. IEEE Computer Society (2008)
36. Weiser, M.: Program slicing. IEEE Trans. Softw. Eng. **10**(4), 352–357 (1984)
37. Xu, B., Qian, J., Zhang, X., Wu, Z., Chen, L.: A brief survey of program slicing. ACM SIGSOFT Softw. Eng. Notes **30**(2), 1–36 (2005)

Integrated Model-Checking for the Design of Safe and Efficient Distributed Software Commissioning

Helene Coullon[1,4(✉)], Claude Jard[3,4], and Didier Lime[2,4]

[1] IMT Atlantique, Inria, Nantes, France
helene.coullon@imt-atlantique.fr
[2] École Centrale de Nantes, Nantes, France
didier.lime@ec-nantes.fr
[3] Université de Nantes, Nantes, France
claude.jard@univ-nantes.fr
[4] LS2N, CNRS, Nantes, France

Abstract. We present MADA, a deployment approach to facilitate the design of efficient and safe distributed software commissioning. MADA is built on top of the Madeus formal model that focuses on the efficient execution of installation procedures. Madeus puts forward more parallelism than other commissioning models, which implies a greater complexity and a greater propensity for errors. MADA provides a new specific language on top of Madeus that allows the developer to easily define the properties that should be ensured during the commissioning process. Then, MADA automatically translates the description to a time Petri net and a set of TCTL formulae. MADA is evaluated on the OpenStack commissioning.

Keywords: Distributed software commissioning · Deployment · Model checking · Safety · Liveness · Efficiency · Component models · Petri nets

1 Introduction

This paper focuses on one specific challenge related to distributed software deployment: *distributed software commissioning*. By software commissioning we mean the complete installation, configuration and testing process when deploying distributed software on physical distributed resources, with or without a virtualization layer in between. This process is complex and error-prone because of the specificity of the installation process according to the operating system, the different kinds of virtualization layers used between the physical machines and the pieces of software, the amount of possible configuration options [23]. Recently, commissioning (or configuration) management tools such as Ansible[1],

[1] https://www.ansible.com/.

W. Ahrendt and S. L. Tapia Tarifa (Eds.): IFM 2019, LNCS 11918, pp. 120–137, 2019.
https://doi.org/10.1007/978-3-030-34968-4_7

or Puppet[2], have been widely adopted by system operators. These tools commonly include good software-engineering practices such as code reuse and composition in management and configuration scripts. It is nowadays possible to build a new installation by assembling different pieces of existing installations[3, 4] which improves the productivity of system operators and prevents many errors. Many distributed software commissionings are nowadays written with one the two above tools and by using containers between the host operating system and the pieces of software, such that portability of installations is improved. For instance, OpenStack, which is the de-facto open source operating system of Cloud infrastructures, can be automatically installed on clusters by using the *kolla-ansible* project, which uses both Docker containers and Ansible.

Yet, even for such well-established software, there is still much room for improving the efficiency of the commissioning process (i.e., reducing deployment times, minimizing services interruptions etc.). As manually coding parallelism into commissioning procedures is technically difficult and error prone, automated parallelism techniques should be introduced. To this purpose, not only dedicated tools, including Puppet, but also academic prototypes such as Aeolus [12] and Madeus [9], introduce parallelism capabilities within software commissioning, at different levels and by using different techniques more or less transparent for the user. For instance, we have observed a performance gain of up to 47% by using Madeus over the *kolla-ansible* reference approach (conducted on the Taurus cluster of the Grid'5000 experimental platform).

Madeus[5] is the commissioning model offering the highest parallelism level [9] in the literature, while offering a formal operational semantics. This makes Madeus the ideal candidate to further study challenges of efficient and safe distributed software commissioning. Madeus automatically handles the intricate details of parallelism coordination, by managing threads and their synchronizations for the user. However, users still have to design their parallel procedures, thus raising the following questions: (1) how to divide existing intricate commissioning scripts in interesting subtasks to introduce parallelism? (2) how to find correct dependencies between commissioning tasks? and (3) how to avoid safety issues such as deadlocks, wrong order of configurations etc.?

We study the feasibility of using model checking techniques to help in the three above challenges in the design of safe and efficient distributed software commissioning. To this purpose we present MADA, an extension of Madeus that brings the following contributions: (1) the automatic transformation process from a Madeus commissioning to an equivalent time Petri net; (2) a domain specific language on top of Madeus to easily express qualitative and quantitative properties related to both safety and efficiency; (3) the automatic translation of MADA properties to temporal logic properties, including liveness, observers and

[2] https://puppet.com.
[3] https://galaxy.ansible.com/.
[4] https://forge.puppet.com/.
[5] https://gitlab.inria.fr/Madeus/mad.

causality, which is uncommon for software commissioning; and (4) an evaluation of MADA on the real case study OpenStack[6] and compared to real experiments.

The rest of this paper is organized as follows. Section 2 introduces the related background. Section 3 presents MADA that is evaluated in Sect. 4 on the real commissioning of OpenStack. Finally, Sect. 5 comments the related work, and Sect. 6 concludes this work and opens some perspectives.

2 Madeus and Petri Nets

Madeus [9] is a component-based model where a component represents the configuration and the installation of a software module of a distributed system. A component contains a set of places that represent milestones of the deployment, and a set of transitions that connect the places together and represent actions to be performed between milestones (e.g., `apt-get install`).

The internal commissioning behavior of a Madeus component is called in the rest of this paper an internal-net. In Madeus, a transition is attached to output and input docks of places, which are used to properly manage parallel actions in the operational semantics. Madeus components expose ports that represent connection points with other components. Four kinds of ports are available: *service-provide* and *service-use* ports to provide (resp. require) a service, and *data-provide* and *data-use* ports to provide (resp. require) a piece of data. Provide ports (service or data) are bound to one or more places (i.e., called *groups*), illustrating the set of milestones where the component is able to provide a service or data. Use ports (service or data) are bound to one or more transitions where services or data are actually used. A component *assembly* (also sometimes called a *configuration*), is made of component instances and connections between ports.

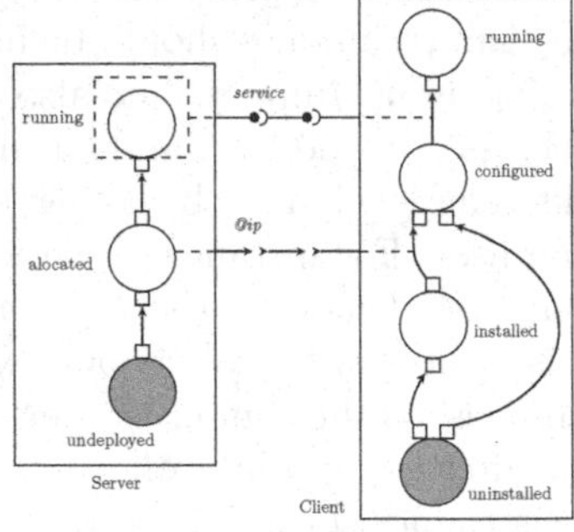

Fig. 1. A Madeus assembly of a server-client software commissioning. Each component (Server and Client) is composed of an internal-net associated to ports.

Figure 1 shows an assembly composed of two components. The internal-net of the *Server* component (on the left) is composed of three places (circles) and two transitions (arrows). The Server's *allocated* place is bound to the *ip* data-provide port (outgoing arrow), while the *running* place is within a group bound to the *service-provide* port (small black circle). The internal-net of the *Client* component (on the right) is composed of four places and four transitions, two of them being bound to (respectively) a *data-use* (incoming arrow) and a *service-use* (semi circle) ports. The ports of *Server* and *Client* are connected within the assembly forming data and service connections (i.e., dependencies).

The evolution of a Madeus deployment is modeled by a set of moving tokens within the internal-nets of components. The evolution of these tokens is handled

[6] https://www.openstack.org/.

by seven operational semantics rules which are specific to software commissioning procedures. Hereafter is an overview of these rules, which are formally detailed in [9]. Each initial place of a component (represented with a gray background in Fig. 1) initially contains a single token. The token is allowed to leave a place belonging to a group only if this would not deactivate a service provide port with an active connection (i.e., under use). If so, and if the outgoing transition of a place is not bound to a use port, the token is directly able to move from the place to the transition. Otherwise, all the use ports have to be *ready* before the move can happen, which is the case when the associated use-provide connections are *activated.* When a token reaches a transition the associated deployment action is started. Several transitions can be fired simultaneously (e.g., *Client* in Fig. 1). In this case, the token is duplicated on each transition. As soon as all the input transitions of a place have ended, their tokens are merged and go to the place. When a token moves to a place in a group that is bound to a provide port, the associated connection is activated, which eventually unlocks use ports of other components. Unlike the service-provide port, the data-provide port acts as a register and will never be disabled once being activated.

Petri nets [22] are a classic formalism for the modeling of concurrent systems. We recall here the basic definition. A *Petri net* (PN) is a 3-tuple (P, T, F), where P is finite set of *places*; T is finite set of *transitions*, with $P \cap T = \emptyset$; and $F : (P \times T) \cup (T \times P) \to \mathbb{N}$ is the *flow function* that defines *weighted arcs* between places and transitions. A *marking* of a net (P, T, F) is a function $m : P \to \mathbb{N}$. For a given marking m, we say that place p contains $m(p)$ *tokens.* A pair $(\mathcal{N}, m_0)$, where $\mathcal{N}$ is a Petri net and m_0 is a marking, is called a *marked* Petri net, which we often call just Petri net, when clear from the context. Marking m_0 is called the *initial marking* of $\mathcal{N}$. A transition t is said to be *enabled* by marking m, when $\forall p \in P, m(p) \geq F(p, t)$. A transition t enabled at marking m can be *fired*, producing the new marking m' defined by: $\forall p \in P, m'(p) = m(p) - F(p, t) + F(t, p)$.

We also consider *time Petri nets* [21], in which a time interval is attached to each transition. A transition can then only be fired (and must be fired or be disabled) after being continuously enabled for a duration in that interval. See [5] for details.

At first sight a Madeus assembly looks fairly close to a Petri net. However, compared to Petri nets, Madeus assembly falls into the category of Domain Specific Languages (DSL) to model and execute distributed software commissioning. It therefore has a few high-level specific primitives, adapted to developers and system administrators, that do not have direct equivalent in Petri nets.

3 MADA

Madeus automatically handles the intricate details of parallelism coordination, by managing threads and their synchronizations for the user. However, users still have to design their parallel procedures. MADA (*MADeus Analyzer*) uses model-checking to help Madeus users design their safe and efficient commissioning. First, MADA is responsible for the automatic transformation from a Madeus assembly to a time Petri net. Second, MADA offers a set of high level qualitative and quantitative properties that are automatically transformed to Timed Computational Tree Logic (TCTL) formulae.

3.1 From Madeus to Petri Nets

Table 1 show the five rules that illustrate the complete translation from Madeus assemblies to (time) Petri nets. Since the terminologies are similar we distinguish between *m-place* and *m-transition* for Madeus assemblies and *pn-place* and *pn-transition* for Petri nets. As docks, ports and connections only concern Madeus, no special notations are introduced for them.

The first and second rule of Table 1 illustrate the basic constructions, when Madeus port are not involved in the component (i.e., no synchronization). One pn-place is created for each dock, one for each m-place, and one for each m-transition. Those are connected straightforwardly to ensure the Madeus sequence <source m-place, output dock, m-transition, input dock, target m-place>. When considering time, all pn-transitions are executed immediately (interval $[0, 0]$) except the *end* pn-transitions that bear the execution time interval of the associated m-transition, thus representing the time needed for the commissioning action.

Each provide port of Madeus is modeled by a dedicated pn-place. Thus, connections related to this provide port are available if and only if that pn-place is non-empty. Rule (3) models how the pn-place modeling m-transition t, that uses two provide ports $port_1$ and $port_2$, checks for the connections availability by testing the non-emptiness of pn-places $port_1$ and $port_2$. Note that for service-provide it is necessary to know whether some transition is currently using the port (as explained below). We therefore add two pn-places for each provide port, that are marked in exclusion, one to mark that a port is under use, the other one to mark the opposite: $port_1\_in\_use$ and $port_1\_not\_used$ in Table 1 (rule (3)), for instance. With this construction, the following property holds, thus respecting the Madeus semantics:

Property 1. For any provide port *port*, pn-place *port_in_use* contains as many tokens as there are marked pn-places representing an m-transition that currently uses *port*. The total number of tokens in port_in_use and port_not_used is always the total number of m-transitions that require *port*.

Rule (4) of Table 1 models the activation of a data-connection. In Madeus as soon as m-place P is reached, the connection associated to the provide port $port_2$ is activated. Since a data-connection once activated will always remain so, in the equivalent Petri net a token is added in the pn-place $port_2$ once and for all at the same time as the pn-place P is marked. With this construction the following property holds:

Property 2. The number of tokens in a pn-place modeling a data-provide port is equal to the number of pn-places modeling m-places bound to that port that has been marked.

Finally, rule (5) models the most complex part of the transformation: a group of m-places that provides a service. In this case, we must first ensure that the connection is activated if and only if a m-place in the group is active, or a dock or a m-transition between two such m-places is active. In the Petri net, this is ensured in the following way: (1) whenever a pn-transition entering the group is executed, a token is added to the pn-place modeling the Madeus provide port (e.g., pn-transitions $enter_{P_1}$ and $enter_{P_2}$); (2) whenever a pn-transition leaving the group is executed (i.e., from one of the last m-place of the group), a token is removed from the pn-place modeling the Madeus provide port (e.g., pn-transitions $exit_{P'_1}$ and $exit_{P'_2}$); (3) whenever a pn-transition within the group (i.e., source and destination pn-places within the group) that goes to or comes from a pn-place modeling a m-place is executed, we accordingly remove in the

Table 1. Set of transformations from Madeus to Petri nets: (1) basic construction of a m-place and its associated docks, (2) basic construction of a m-transition and its source and destination docks, (3) *data-use* and *service-use* ports bound to a transition t, (4) *data-provide* port provided by a place P, (5) group of places bound to a *service-provide* port

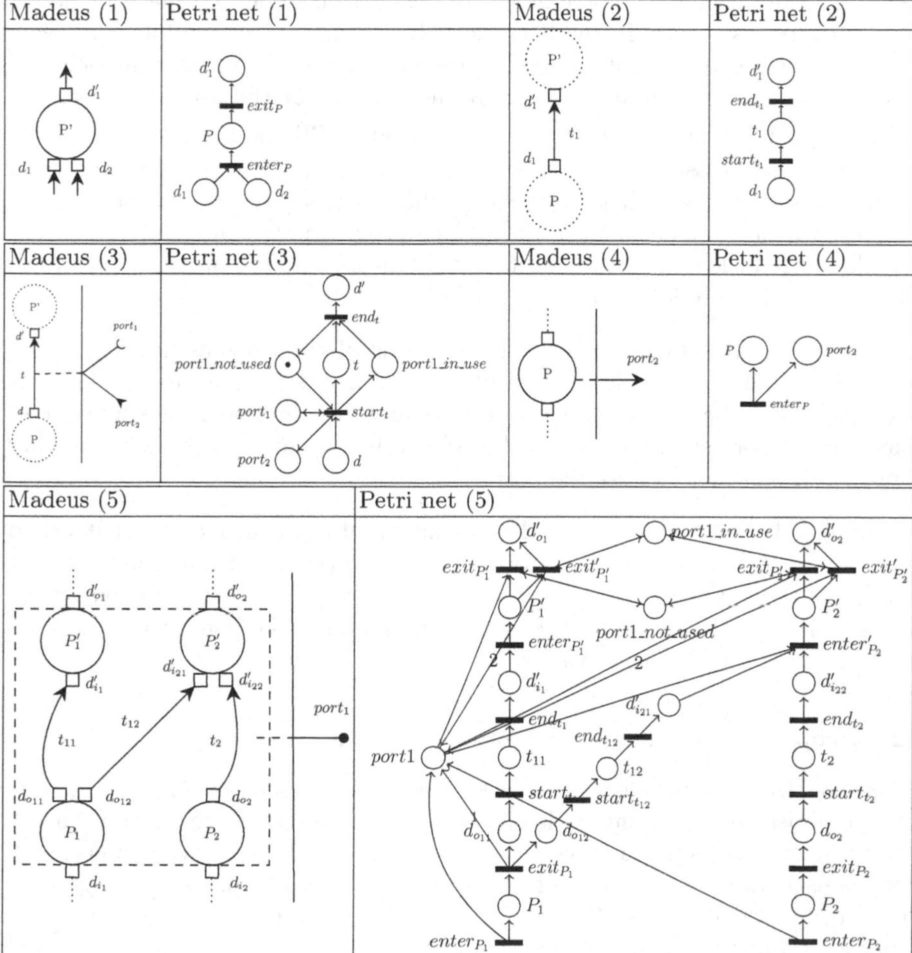

provide port pn-place as many tokens as input docks, and add in the same provide port pn-place as many tokens as output docks. Note that, in order to minimize the number of arcs in the Petri net, we actually compute the net effect on the port pn-place so that most transitions (leaving one dock for a place, or one place for a dock) do not modify the number of tokens in the port pn-place. Thus, only forks and joins within the group add and remove tokens in the port pn-place (e.g., $exit_{P_1}$ and $enter_{P_2'}$ in Table 1, rule (5)). With this construction the following property holds:

Property 3. The number of tokens in a pn-place modeling a service-provide port is equal to the number of marked pn-places modeling either active m-places or m-transitions or docks in the group.

Once the port activated, we need to keep it active until all m-transitions using the port are completed. Thus there are two ways to leave a group from a pn-place, first if the provide port is not used, and second if it is used but leaving the pn-place does not remove the last token of the pn-place modeling the service-provide port. In the Petri net, this is ensured in the following way: (1) two outgoing pn-transitions are represented for each pn-place modeling a m-place that leaves a group (e.g., $exit_{P_1'}$ and $exit'_{P_1'}$ for the m-place P_1', $exit_{P_2'}$ and $exit'_{P_2'}$ for the m-place P_2', rule (5) of Table 1): (2) the first one tests if the pn-place *not_used* associated to the service-provide port is equal to the total number of m-transition that may require this port; (3) the second one tests if the pn-place *in_use* associated to the service-provide port is marked and checks that there are at least two tokens left in the pn-place of the provide port. With this construction the following property holds:

Property 4. (1) At any given time, at most one of the two pn-transitions that go outside a pn-place modeling a m-place that leaves is enabled. (2) The pn-place modeling the service-provide port cannot be emptied if the number of tokens in the corresponding *not_used* pn-place is not equal to the total number of m-transitions that can use the port.

We have focused on a high-level explanation of the translation but it would not be difficult, if a bit tedious, to formally prove a (weak) bisimulation between the formal semantics of Madeus given in [9] and the Petri net obtained by the process outlined above. We leave it out of the scope of the paper to improve its readability and due to space concerns.

3.2 Property Language and Temporal Logic

Using MADA, an equivalent Petri net of a given Madeus assembly, i.e., software commissioning, is automatically generated. This saves the user from the transformation burden and prevents possible errors in this process. Furthermore, Madeus users are not familiar with Petri nets. This also holds for the properties on the generated Petri net. For this reason, MADA extends Madeus with a set of property functions that abstract away from the user the details of temporal logic and that are easy to understand for systems operators.

```
def set_interval(self, component, transition, min, max)
def add_deployment(self, name, dict_components_places)
def deployability(self, deployment_name, with_intervals)
def sequentiality(self, ordered_list_components_transition)
def forbidden(self, list_marked, list_unmarked)
def parallelism(self, full_assembly, list_components)
def gantt_boundaries(self, deployment_name, mini, maxi, critical)
```

Fig. 2. Methods signatures for MADA's `Properties`.

Figure 2 shows the set of functions offered by MADA in Python. First, a time interval can be associated to each m-transition of the Madeus assembly. A default interval is set to $[1, 100]$ and can be updated by the user. The interval of each m-transition can be specified by the user with the function `set_interval`.

Once an interval is declared for each m-transition, a set of *deployments* can be defined by the user. A deployment is identified by a name and a set of places to reach. Then the library offers five properties divided in two categories: qualitative properties and quantitative properties. Quantitative properties are only available if intervals have been indicated in the time Petri net as they offer results related to time spent in m-transition. However, as it will be shown in Sect. 4 these intervals do not necessarily have to be precise.

Qualitative Properties. Three such properties are available in MADA. First, for a given deployment D, its *deployability* is the property that all of the (modeled) paths eventually lead to D. The associated syntax is illustrated on the line 4 of Fig. 2. In the Petri net, the deployability property can be verified as an inevitability property, that is an AF property in TCTL [1]. Secondly, if an assembly is well defined by the developer with the needed connections between components and the right synchronization of transitions, the sequential orders between transitions will be true by construction. However, designing a Madeus assembly could become tricky for large distributed software, and the resulting high concurrency level could lead to unwitting errors. For this reason, MADA offers a way to define with an easy syntax the sequential orders that must be ensured between transitions of the assembly. The function `sequentiality` takes an ordered list of tuples as input, where each tuple contains a component name and its transition name. The order in which are given the tuples is the sequence to check. Sequentiality is a safety property that can be checked in Petri nets using an observer subnet: add an error pn-place p_{err} to the Petri net. Add also, for each pn-transition pnt_t modeling the end of a m-transition t (i.e., timed pn-transition), a pn-place p_t, initially not marked and a pn-place $p_{\neg t}$, initially with one token. pn-transition pnt_t moves the token from $p_{\neg t}$ to p_t. Then for each ordered relation of m-transitions $t \ll t'$, a pn-transition is added from $p_{\neg t}$ and $p_{t'}$ to p_{err}. That transition will be firable only if t' has fired but t has not fired. Sequentiality is therefore equivalent to the impossibility of putting tokens in p_{err}, which is a basic safety property: $\mathsf{AG}\ p_{err} = 0$ in TCTL. Finally, systems operators may want to ensure that a given configuration is not reachable during the software commissioning. To this purpose the method `forbidden` is available in MADA and checks that the following invariant holds: we always have at least one of the elements in `list_marked` that is not marked or one of the elements in `list_unmarked` that is marked. In the Petri net, the `forbidden` property is a basic safety property (AG). One can note that the opposite property could be easily added.

Quantitative Properties. When a Madeus assembly is designed it is not necessarily easy, because of the global coordination with connections between components, to understand the level of parallelism reached during the execution. The method `parallelism` on line 6 of Fig. 2 returns the level of parallelism achieved when executing the Petri net. It takes as arguments, first, a boolean indicating if the maximum parallelism level of the entire assembly has to be computed, and second, the list of components for which the parallelism has to be studied separately. To compute the (maximum) level of parallelism, we compute all the reachable markings and then compute for all of them the sum of all tokens in pn-places corresponding to m-transitions belonging to the components to check. The number we want is the maximum of those. The level of parallelism can be completed by a full Gantt diagram of all m-transitions execution. This result is longer to compute but offers a clear view of the behavior of the software commissioning. The function `gantt_boundaries` takes the name of the deployment to check as input, as well as two booleans `mini` and `maxi`. In facts, a Gantt diagram can be computed and drawn by computing either the minimum or the maximum time to reach some markings in the Petri net [6] and by asking the model checker to keep absolute time information in its trace. As a result, computation of a Gantt diagram also computes the minimum and/or the maximum boundaries of the software commissioning. One can note that the trace returned by the model checker has to be processed to be able to draw the Gantt diagram. Moreover, by starting with the last m-transition to execute and backtracking in the Gantt diagram, a clear causality trace can be obtained to identify the critical path that has led to the minimum or maximum execution time [4]. For this reason, the last input of `gantt_boundaries` is a boolean indicating if the critical path has to be extracted from the trace.

4 Evaluation

In this section, we describe how MADA has been used to build the Madeus OpenStack commissioning mentioned in Sect. 1 from a sequential original one. Before reaching the final efficient and safe version, a total of four versions have been incrementally written by using MADA. Thus, the goal of this evaluation is to illustrate on a real use-case how MADA can be used by a user to avoid safety issues and to identify where efficiency improvements can be performed thanks to quantitative properties. Finally, this section discusses the feasibility of the approach.

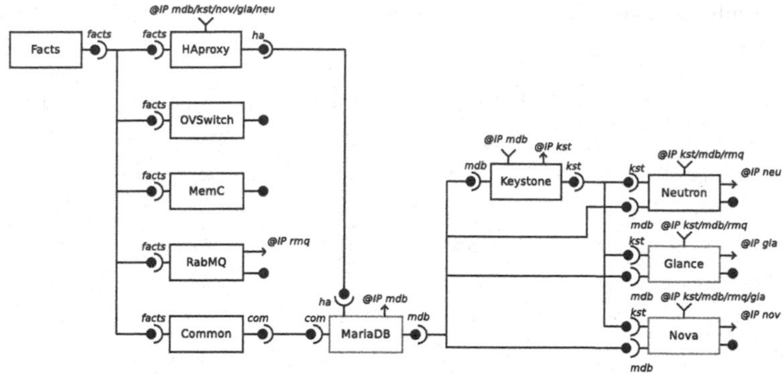

Fig. 3. Coarse-grain Madeus assembly of the OpenStack commissioning.

OpenStack is the de-facto open source solution to address the IaaS (*Infrastructure as a Service*) level of the Cloud paradigm. In other words, OpenStack is the operating system of the Cloud responsible for the management of physical resources of a set of clusters, as well as the management of virtual machines and their life cycle. Following the Ansible installation procedure defined in Kolla, a popular tool to deploy OpenStack[7], we have defined 11 Madeus components: *Nova, Glance, Neutron, Keystone, MariaDB, RabbitMQ, HAProxy, OpenVSwitch, Memcached, Facts, Common.* The coarse grain commissioning of OpenStack is depicted in Fig. 3, without the detailed internal-nets of components.

All results are shown in Table 2 where the initial Madeus number of elements, the resulting number of elements in the generated Petri net, as well as the execution time of the transformation are given. For space reasons, this evaluation focuses on the most original properties of MADA compared to the related work: `deployability` that checks the inevitable end of the deployment, and the two quantitative properties `parallelism` and `gantt_boundaries` related to the use of time Petri nets. The result of each property as well as its computation time are also shown Table 2. Each Gantt diagram is depicted in separated figures indicating in its caption the obtained critical path. The time intervals used in the experiments have been chosen according to real observed execution time traces. We have used the Roméo model checker for time Petri nets [20] in our experiments. Finally, all the materials used for these experiments are available online[8] (i.e., MADA python files, Petri nets and results).

4.1 MADA Evaluation

The first version (*0-deadlock*) has been designed by introducing three straightforward parallel tasks in the three components *Glance*, *Neutron* and *Nova*. The same parallel tasks have been used in these components: pulling the docker image

[7] https://docs.openstack.org/kolla-ansible/latest/.
[8] https://gitlab.inria.fr/hcoullon/mada.

Table 2. Results by using MADA on five different versions of OpenStack commissioning in Madeus.

	0-deadlock	1-naive	2-nova	3-nova	4-nova-mdb
Madeus places	27	27	28	28	29
Madeus transitions	22	22	25	25	28
Madeus connections	30	30	30	30	30
Petri net places	113	113	124	124	134
Petri net transitions	75	75	84	84	92
Transf. time (ms)	1.6	1.6	1.8	1.7	1.5
Deployability *Computation time (s)*	False *0*	True *41.6*	True *78.7*	True *88.7*	True *152.6*
Parallelism nova *Computation time (s)*	– –	1 *42.1*	2 *82.7*	2 *93.6*	2 *154.3*
Parallelism full *Computation time (s)*	– –	10 *43.2*	11 *86.1*	11 *98.4*	12 *162.9*
Gantt & critical path *Computation time (s)*	– –	Figure 5a *130.1*	Figure 5b *266.9*	Figure 5c *275.4*	Figure 5d *588.1*
Boundaries *Computation time (s)*	– –	[575, 615] *130.1, 128.8*	[518, 554] *266.9, 269.7*	[400, 423] *275.4, 267.6*	[377, 398] *588.1, 580.8*

from the Docker registry at the same time as preparing the configuration of the container, and at the same time as registering the service to the *Keystone* component. This parallelism pattern is illustrated for the component *Nova* on the left of Fig. 4.

An error was accidentally introduced in this first version of the Madeus OpenStack commissioning (*0-deadlock*). This error was due to the label "register" of a transition in the component *MariaDB*. In all components containing the same label as a transition, this transition was using the service of the *Keystone* component (for service authentication). However, in *MariaDB* this registering step has to be performed with the component *Common*. In fact *MariaDB* is globally installed before *Keystone*. For this reason, an incorrect sub-assembly has been accidentally built. By executing MADA on the Madeus assembly the deadlock has been detected and a clear trace leading to the problem has been returned. This problem occurs when both *MariaDB* and *Keystone* are waiting for each other.

The version *1-naive* solves the deadlock detected by MADA in *0-deadlock* and keeps the exact same set of components as well as the same assembly. By using MADA it appears that such a design is quite naive as the maximum level of parallelism in *Nova* is actually 1 while we were expecting 3 (Table 2). The Gantt diagram generated by MADA, shown in Fig. 5a, explains that the transition *Nova config* cannot be executed at the same time as *Nova pull* because it has to wait for *MariaDB deploy* that ends after *Nova pull*. Similarly, the transition *Nova register* cannot be executed at the same time as the two other tasks because it has to wait for *Keystone deploy* that ends after both *Nova pull* and *Nova config*. Furthermore, thanks to the MADA critical path (indicated in the caption of Fig. 5b), one can note that *Nova deploy* plays an important part in the overall execution time and could probably be divided into parallel subtasks. This information offers a very useful help to the user to know where to look first in order to improve the efficiency of the commissioning. Without these pieces of information we could have wasted time to understand scripts of *Glance deploy* while it is not in the critical path.

Then, the second version *2-nova* focuses on dividing the transition *Nova deploy* in parallel tasks. It appears that two long tasks responsible for database schemes can be performed in parallel, namely *Nova upg_api_db* and *Nova upg_db*. Moreover, one subtask of *Nova deploy* is independent from the other and can be added as a parallel task with *Nova config*, namely *Nova create-db* (see Fig. 4). By using MADA, we verify that the level of parallelism in *Nova* is increased to 2. The Gantt diagram of Fig. 5b obtained by MADA shows that both *Nova upg_api_db* and *Nova upg_db* wait for *Nova register* to end which is the reason why *Nova deploy* starts very late. One can also note that *Nova register* is in the critical path. Thanks to these results we have noticed that the dependencies of the parallel task *Nova register* were not well defined as it is entirely independent from other tasks except the last one *Nova deploy*.

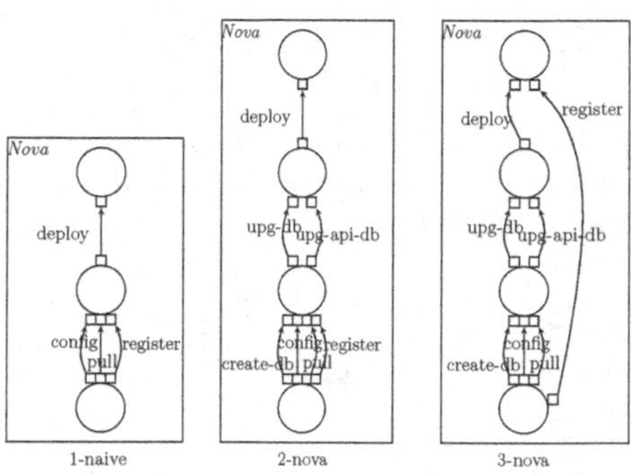

Fig. 4. Nova component evolution thanks to the analysis with MADA.

In the third version *3-nova* we have solved this issue as illustrated in Fig. 4, by defining *Nova register* as an overall parallel task. The Gantt diagram shown in Fig. 5c demonstrates that tasks of *Nova* are no longer in the critical path. As shown in Table 2 the expected boundaries (i.e., according to time intervals) were [575, 615] for *1-naive* and are [400, 423] for *3-nova*. Finally, in the Gantt diagram and critical path of Fig. 5c one can note that the transition *MariaDB deploy* is responsible for the delay of many other tasks such as *Keystone deploy*, for instance.

In the fourth version of the commissioning *4-nova-mdb* the parallelization of *MariaDB deploy* has been studied. This task has been divided in four tasks namely *MariaDB bootstrap*, *MariaDB restart*, *MariaDB register* and *MariaDB check*. The transition *MariaDB bootstrap* can be run at the same time as the already defined *MariaDB pull* transition. Moreover, *MariaDB register* and *MariaDB check* can be executed simultaneously. The resulting Gantt diagram is depicted in Fig. 5d with the following expected boundaries: [377, 398]. These boundaries are much better than the observed execution time, greater than 750 seconds, of the reference Kolla scripts.

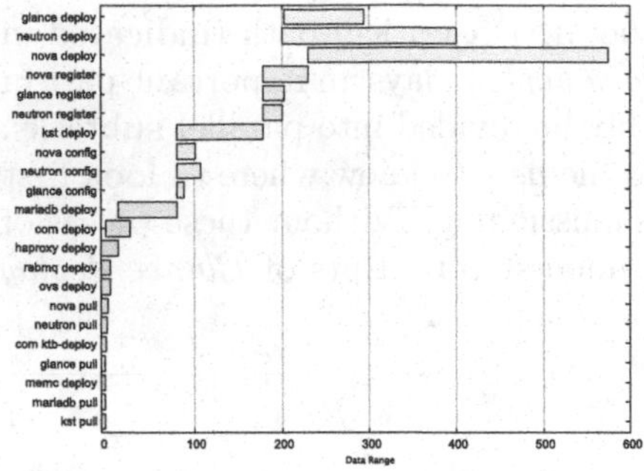

(a) 1-naive with critical path: *nova deploy, nova register, kst deploy, mariadb deploy, haproxy deploy*

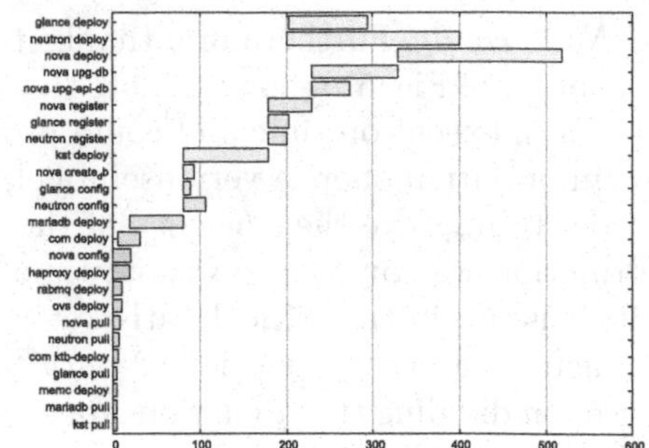

(b) 2-nova with critical path: *nova deploy, nova upg-db, nova register, kst deploy, mariadb deploy, haproxy deploy*

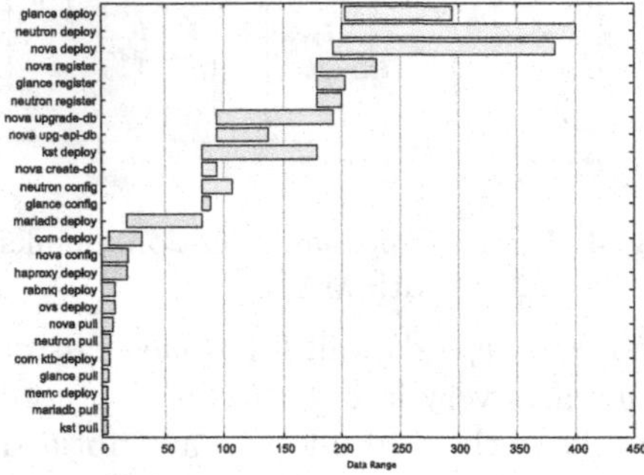

(c) 3-nova with critical path: *neutron deploy, neutron register, kst deploy, mariadb deploy, haproxy deploy*

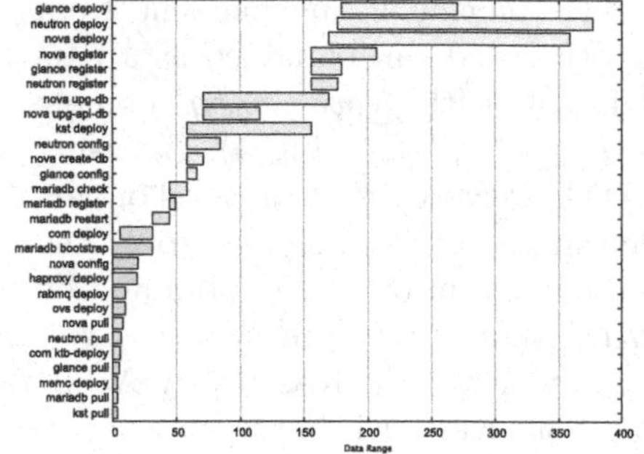

(d) 4-nova-mdb with critical path: *neutron deploy, neutron register, kst deploy, mariadb check, mariadb restart, mariadb bootstrap*

Fig. 5. Gantt diagrams generated by the *gantt_boundaries* property of MADA

4.2 Discussion

Does it Work? To answer this question we have conducted real experiments on the OpenStack commissioning. Figure 6a shows the Gantt diagram generated from the traces of one of the real experiments on *4-nova-mdb* (same as the one mentioned in Sect. 1). One can note that the obtained diagram is very close to the one computed by MADA with time intervals in Fig. 5d and that the obtained critical path fits perfectly with the one returned by MADA. This result is also observed for other versions of the commissioning *1-naive*, *2-nova* and *3-nova*, available in the git repository previously indicated. Moreover, the computed boundaries for all versions also perfectly match the real experiments. For instance, the boundaries of *4-nova-mdb* are [377, 398] and the execution time of the run of Fig. 6a is 389.8. This confirms that the approach works and that the transformation is valid as well as its implementation. In addition, we would like to emphasize once again that MADA has been very useful in working in the right direction, where tasks can be divided, saving time by avoiding the unnecessary exploration of complex scripts. Finally, by using MADA a separation of concerns is possible between the design phase and the experimental phase of the commissioning. Thus, MADA could be considered as a formal simulator to help the user in the design phase that avoids the burden of real experiments and associated technical issues (e.g., machines provisioning, commands errors, timeouts etc.).

Time Intervals. The goal of MADA is not to precisely compute the execution time of the distributed software commissioning but to help identify where efficiency improvements could be made. Accordingly, it is not necessary to be precise about time intervals. However, to provide a good insight of possible efficiency improvements to MADA users, the order of magnitude for each transition is needed. To illustrate this claim, Fig. 6b shows the Gantt diagram obtained by using MADA on *4-nova-mdb* with additional errors on the time intervals. Errors are introduced as follows: for tasks representing less than 5% of the total execution time (11 tasks) we have introduced 95% of error on the duration of the interval (e.g., $[6, 7]$ becomes $[3, 10]$). Similarly, for tasks representing respectively between 5–10% (11 tasks), 10–20% (2 tasks), 20–30% (3 tasks), 30–60% (2 tasks) of the execution time we have introduced 90%, 80%, 70%, 40% of error on the duration of the interval (e.g., $[98, 106]$ becomes $[61, 143]$). This method introduces an error that may be substantial (up to 95%) but that does not change the order of magnitude of intervals. One can note that even with this high error on time intervals the Gantt diagram has almost the same shape and the critical path of the execution stays valid. We think that it may be difficult for systems operators to give a precise execution time for a given task. However, giving an order of magnitude through a time interval is much easier as most software installation scripts contain the same types of commands (human expertise). Furthermore, thanks to the high frequency with which system commands appear, machine learning algorithms could also be designed.

Scalability. Most computations performed on bounded Petri nets (with or without time) have a PSPACE worst-case complexity. This can be observed in Table 2 where execution time of properties are depicted for each version according to its size. For an increase of the number of places and transitions in the Petri net of 15% the execution time of the *deployability* increases of 73%. We have however to consider a few additional elements in our assessment of the usability of the approach. First, OpenStack is a large system, thus many existing distributed systems can certainly be analyzed with this approach. Second, the generated Petri net itself can be made easier to analyze, depending on the property of interest. Third, the MADA approach is largely independent of the model checker used, and many techniques from the model checking community can be leveraged to improve performance such as partial orders [16], BDD-like data structures [8], SMT-based techniques [10], and lazy model checking [17] for instance. A complete scalability study is left to future work. Finally, compared to the few contributions

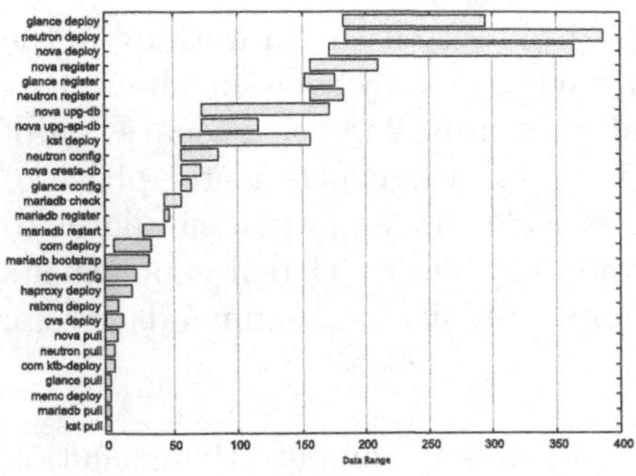

(a) Real experiment of 4-nova-mdb on Grid'5000 with critical path: *neutron deploy, neutron register, kst deploy, mariadb check, mariadb restart, mariadb bootstrap*

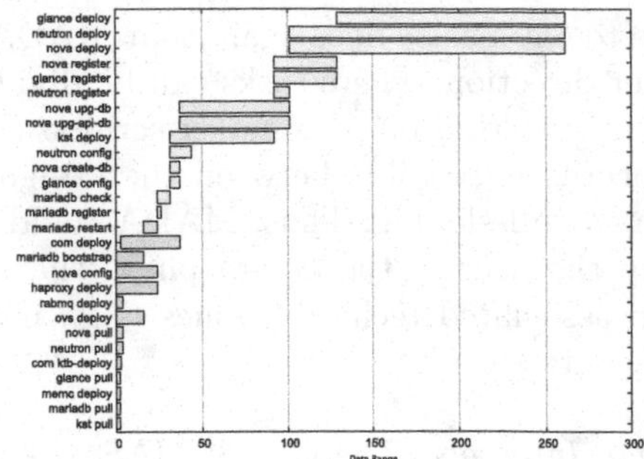

(b) MADA 4-nova-mdb with errors on time intervals with critical path: *neutron deploy, neutron register, kst deploy, mariadb check, mariadb restart, mariadb bootstrap*

Fig. 6. Experiment on Grid'5000 and experiment with errors on intervals.

of the related work that provide some model checking execution time [14,15] (50 min for BPEL, up to 47 min for Vercors), MADA execution times can be fairly considered acceptable compared to the burden of testing real experiments on infrastructures each time a modification is made in the assembly (up to 600 seconds). This is due to the fact that Madeus is a relatively small language compared to BPEL and Vercors because of its specificity for distributed software commissioning.

5 Related Work

MADA is specifically conceived to help in the design of safe and efficient distributed software commissioning on top of Madeus. Indeed, concurrency and parallelism introduced by Madeus comes at a price. First, parallelism can introduce liveness violation such as deadlocks. Secondly, even if the parallelism *coordination* is ensured by Madeus, designing a parallel software commissioning from a sequential one is difficult. Indeed, subtasks of the commissioning procedures and dependencies between subtasks and software components have to be identified while their exact internal behavior are not well known by operators, because implemented by other developers. Moreover, most of the time commissioning scripts are difficult to read and system commands do not clearly expose their behaviors and functionalities. As far as we know, no existing software commissioning tool or academic model is equipped with a formal way to help the user solving such problems when designing installation procedures. This is in line with the fact that the parallelism capabilities of existing tools and models for automatic software commissioning are very limited compared to Aeolus and Madeus, almost sequential in fact. Thus, in this context liveness issues are impossible, and finding subtasks and dependencies is useless. The contribution of this paper could partially be useful and applicable to Aeolus. However, Aeolus and its satellites [11] are not maintained and were not equipped with such integrated model checking.

Yet, using model checking to help in the design of safe distributed software (not software commissioning) has been extensively studied in the literature. For instance, formal methods have been used in the domain of software components. The *Vercors* framework [2,14] uses parameterized networks of asynchronous automata (pNets) as an intermediate formalism representing behaviors of distributed software components, statically analyzed by the CADP model checker. *BIP* [3] (Behavior, Interaction, Priority) was initially a component-based model for heterogeneous real-time and reactive systems, and has been extended for distributed systems with heterogeneous interactions through *HDBIP* [19]. In BIP, finite state automata are used to represent the behavior of components and their composition. In these contributions, formal methods are used to verify the functional behavior of distributed systems, which is very different from modeling and checking the execution and coordination of software commissioning procedures. In particular, MADA offers quantitative properties related to the concurrency and parallelism introduced within a commissioning execution. This cannot be modeled by Vercors nor BIP. Moreover, this kind of properties can be expressed by using time Petri nets as an intermediate representation of the commissioning execution semantics. Finally, neither Vercors nor BIP clearly explain how verification formulae are expressed by users while MADA automatically generates TCTL formulae from function calls.

Some languages for defining business processes, BPEL [15] and BPMN [13] for instance, have been straightforwardly translated to Petri nets such that a formal semantics can be offered to the user instead of natural language and UML-like semantics. In both of these contributions the Petri net translation has also been used to check liveness and safety properties to detect bugs in user-defined processes. However, quantitative properties such as the one proposed by MADA are not offered because helping the user to improve the process efficiency is not a goal. Moreover, details are missing regarding how translations and properties are integrated in a user-friendly framework.

MACE [18] is another language example that uses formal methods. MACE combines *objects*, *events* and *aspects* programming to address in a single framework concurrency and failures when designing distributed software. Guiding the users in their task and hiding from them the intricate details of static analysis is in line with MADA. However, MACE is more complete and complex than MADA and addresses many different problems at the same time thus raising the complexity of the overall framework. In other words, MADA is specific to software commissioning while MACE solves multiple issues related to distributed software design. The model checking in MACE targets liveness violation only. Causality is addressed by MACE to find failures origins, however, this causality is based on automatic logging instead of model checking. MADA offers an interesting separation of concerns between the design phase and the testing phase on real infrastructures. Quantitative information such as the critical paths for efficiency analysis are studied through model checking thanks to time Petri nets.

Finally, related work has studied how to simplify for a non expert the way properties could be expressed. This is for example one of the contributions around Statemate [7] where timing diagrams are used to generate CTL formulae for verification on reactive systems. The two main differences with MADA are: first the generalization of properties thanks to five function signatures instead of defining one timing diagram for each property to check in Statemate, and second the specific application domain of MADA to distributed software commissioning.

6 Conclusion

In this paper MADA has been presented as a useful approach for introducing model checking to help system operators design their parallel distributed software commissioning. MADA has been evaluated on the real use case of OpenStack which is a very large and complex distributed system. Moreover, comparisons with experiments on real infrastructures have shown the feasibility of the approach. Future work will be focused on using other model checking algorithms to improve the scalability of MADA. Moreover, MADA will be extended to help the user build fault-tolerant distributed software commissioning.

References

1. Alur, R., Courcoubetis, C., Dill, D.: Model-checking in dense real-time. Inf. Comput. **104**(1), 2–34 (1993)
2. Barros, T., Cansado, A., Madelaine, E., Rivera, M.: Model-checking distributed components: the vercors platform. Electron. Notes Theor. Comput. Sci. **182**, 3–16 (2007). Proceedings of the Third International Workshop on Formal Aspects of Component Software (FACS 2006)
3. Basu, A., Bozga, M., Sifakis, J.: Modeling heterogeneous real-time components in BIP. In: Proceedings of the Fourth IEEE International Conference on Software Engineering and Formal Methods, SEFM 2006, pp. 3–12. IEEE Computer Society, Washington, DC (2006)
4. Beer, I., Ben-David, S., Chockler, H., Orni, A., Trefler, R.: Explaining counterexamples using causality. Form. Methods Syst. Des. **40**(1), 20–40 (2012)
5. Berthomieu, B., Diaz, M.: Modeling and verification of time dependent systems using time Petri nets. IEEE Trans. Soft. Eng. **17**(3), 259–273 (1991)
6. Boucheneb, H., Lime, D., Parquier, B., Roux, O.H., Seidner, C.: Optimal reachability in cost time Petri nets. In: Abate, A., Geeraerts, G. (eds.) FORMATS 2017. LNCS, vol. 10419, pp. 58–73. Springer, Cham (2017). https://doi.org/10.1007/978-3-319-65765-3_4
7. Brockmeyer, U., Wittich, G.: Tamagotchis need not die—verification of statemate designs. In: Steffen, Bernhard (ed.) TACAS 1998. LNCS, vol. 1384, pp. 217–231. Springer, Heidelberg (1998). https://doi.org/10.1007/BFb0054174
8. Bryant, R.E.: Graph-based algorithms for Boolean function manipulation. IEEE Trans. Comput. **C–35**(8), 677–691 (1986)
9. Chardet, M., Coullon, H., Pertin, D., Pérez, C.: Madeus: a formal deployment model. In: 4PAD 2018 - 5th International Symposium on Formal Approaches to Parallel and Distributed Systems (Hosted at HPCS 2018) (2018)

10. Cimatti, A., Griggio, A.: Software model checking via IC3. In: Madhusudan, P., Seshia, S.A. (eds.) CAV 2012. LNCS, vol. 7358, pp. 277–293. Springer, Heidelberg (2012). https://doi.org/10.1007/978-3-642-31424-7_23
11. Di Cosmo, R., Eiche, A., Mauro, J., Zacchiroli, S., Zavattaro, G., Zwolakowski, J.: Automatic deployment of services in the cloud with aeolus blender. In: Barros, A., Grigori, D., Narendra, N.C., Dam, H.K. (eds.) ICSOC 2015. LNCS, vol. 9435, pp. 397–411. Springer, Heidelberg (2015). https://doi.org/10.1007/978-3-662-48616-0_28
12. Di Cosmo, R., Mauro, J., Zacchiroli, S., Zavattaro, G.: Aeolus: a component model for the cloud. Inf. Comput. **239**, 100–121 (2014)
13. Dijkman, R.M., Dumas, M., Ouyang, C.: Formal semantics and analysis of BPMN process models using Petri nets. Technical report, Queensland University of Technology (2007)
14. Henrio, L., Kulankhina, O., Li, S., Madelaine, E.: Integrated environment for verifying and running distributed components. In: Stevens, P., Wąsowski, A. (eds.) FASE 2016. LNCS, vol. 9633, pp. 66–83. Springer, Heidelberg (2016). https://doi.org/10.1007/978-3-662-49665-7_5
15. Hinz, S., Schmidt, K., Stahl, C.: Transforming BPEL to Petri nets. In: van der Aalst, W.M.P., Benatallah, B., Casati, F., Curbera, F. (eds.) BPM 2005. LNCS, vol. 3649, pp. 220–235. Springer, Heidelberg (2005). https://doi.org/10.1007/11538394_15
16. Holzmann, G.J., Peled, D.: An improvement in formal verification. Formal Description Techniques VII. IAICT, pp. 197–211. Springer, Boston, MA (1995). https://doi.org/10.1007/978-0-387-34878-0_13
17. Jezequel, L., Lime, D.: Lazy reachability analysis in distributed systems. In: Desharnais, J., Jagadeesan, R. (eds.) CONCUR 2016. LIPIcs. Dagstuhl Publishing, Québec City (2016)
18. Killian, C.E., Anderson, J.W., Braud, R., Jhala, R., Vahdat, A.M.: Mace: language support for building distributed systems. In: Proceedings of the 28th ACM SIGPLAN Conference on Programming Language Design and Implementation, PLDI 2007. ACM (2007)
19. Kobeissi, S., Utayim, A., Jaber, M., Falcone, Y.: Facilitating the implementation of distributed systems with heterogeneous interactions. In: Furia, C.A., Winter, K. (eds.) IFM 2018. LNCS, vol. 11023, pp. 255–274. Springer, Cham (2018). https://doi.org/10.1007/978-3-319-98938-9_15
20. Lime, D., Roux, O.H., Seidner, C., Traonouez, L.-M.: Romeo: a parametric model-checker for petri nets with stopwatches. In: Kowalewski, S., Philippou, A. (eds.) TACAS 2009. LNCS, vol. 5505, pp. 54–57. Springer, Heidelberg (2009). https://doi.org/10.1007/978-3-642-00768-2_6
21. Merlin, P.M.: A study of the recoverability of computing systems. Ph.D. thesis, Department of Information and Computer Science, University of California, Irvine, CA (1974)
22. Petri, C.A.: Kommunikation mit Automaten. Dissertation, schriften des iim, Rheinisch-Westfälisches Institut für Instrumentelle Mathematik an der Universität Bonn, Bonn (1962)
23. Xu, T., Zhou, Y.: Systems approaches to tackling configuration errors: a survey. ACM Comput. Surv. **47**(4), 70:1–70:41 (2015)

Learning to Reuse: Adaptive Model Learning for Evolving Systems

Carlos Diego N. Damasceno[1,2(✉)], Mohammad Reza Mousavi[2(✉)], and Adenilso da Silva Simao[1(✉)]

[1] University of Sao Paulo (ICMC-USP), São Carlos, SP, Brazil
damascenodiego@usp.br, adenilso@icmc.usp.br
[2] University of Leicester, Leicester, UK
mm789@leicester.ac.uk

Abstract. Software systems undergo several changes along their life-cycle and hence, their models may become outdated. To tackle this issue, we propose an efficient algorithm for adaptive learning, called partial-Dynamic $\mathtt{L}^*_\mathtt{M}$ ($\partial\mathtt{L}^*_\mathtt{M}$) that improves upon the state of the art by exploring observation tables *on-the-fly* to discard *redundant* prefixes and *deprecated* suffixes. Using 18 versions of the OpenSSL toolkit, we compare our proposed algorithm along with three adaptive algorithms. For the existing algorithms in the literature, our experiments indicate a strong positive correlation between number of membership queries and temporal distance between versions and; for our algorithm, we found a weak positive correlation between membership queries and temporal distance, as well, a significantly lower number of membership queries. These findings indicate that, compared to the state-of-the-art algorithms, our $\partial\mathtt{L}^*_\mathtt{M}$ algorithm is less sensitive to software evolution and more efficient than the current approaches for adaptive learning.

Keywords: Active learning · Mealy machines · Software evolution · Software reuse · Reactive systems

1 Introduction

According to Binder [3], software analysis is necessarily a *model-based* activity, whether models are in engineers' minds, informally sketched on papers or formally denoted as an explicit model [4]. Nevertheless, as requirements change and systems evolve, model maintenance is often neglected due to its high cost and models are rendered outdated [33]. To tackle this issue, active model learning [1] has been increasingly used to automatically derive behavioral models [15,21,30]. Active model learning aims at building a hypothesis $\mathcal{H}$ about the "language" (i.e., the set of possible behaviors) of a system under learning (SUL) by iteratively providing input sequences and observing outputs [30]. To formulate a hypothesis model $\mathcal{H}$, the learning algorithm searches for specific pairs of sequences to reach and distinguish states, i.e., called *transfer* and *separating* sequences, respectively.

W. Ahrendt and S. L. Tapia Tarifa (Eds.): IFM 2019, LNCS 11918, pp. 138–156, 2019.
https://doi.org/10.1007/978-3-030-34968-4_8

Applying model learning to industrial systems is hampered by scalability issues [8] as well as the constant changes along their life-cycle [5] that may require *learning from scratch*. Adaptive learning [10] is an approach that attempts to speed up learning by reusing the knowledge from existing models. Studies [5, 10, 13, 35] have shown that pre-existing models can steer learning by reusing the sequences applied in the past queries and hence, reduce the cost for re-inferring models from different versions. However, after several changes, old separating sequences may no longer be able to distinguish states, and lead to *deprecated* queries. Similarly, transfer sequences may not lead to different states anymore, and become *redundant*. These are known to be major threats to adaptive learning [13].

In this paper, we address the issues of redundant and deprecated sequence. To mitigate the aforementioned issues, we introduce `partial-Dynamic` $\mathtt{L}^*_{\mathtt{M}}$ ($\partial\mathtt{L}^*_{\mathtt{M}}$), an adaptive algorithm where the cost for active model learning is reduced by exploring observation tables *on-the-fly* for discarding *redundant* and *deprecated* sequences. Moreover, we present an experiment to compare our technique against three state-of-the-art adaptive algorithms and evaluate how these sequences can hamper learning. By this experiment, we answer the following questions:

(RQ1) Is our on-the-fly adaptive technique more efficient than the state-of-the-art adaptive learning techniques?
(RQ2) Is the effectiveness of adaptive learning strongly affected by the temporal distance between versions?

In our experiment, we reused 18 Mealy machines from a large-scale analysis of several versions of the OpenSSL project [26], an open-source and commercial-grade cryptographic toolkit [23]. To answer RQ1, we used the number of membership queries (`MQ`) to learn models with a fixed level of accuracy as a measure of effectiveness. To answer RQ2, we used the temporal distance between versions, denoted by the difference between their release dates as measure of software evolution because structural changes (e.g., changed transitions) in black-box setting are often unknown and behavioral metrics (e.g., percentage of failed tests) may mislead minor modifications closer to initial states compared to major changes.

Based on our experiments, we find that our $\partial\mathtt{L}^*_{\mathtt{M}}$ algorithm presented weak positive correlation between `MQ`s and temporal distance. These findings support the answer to **RQ1** that our algorithm is less sensitive to model evolution and more efficient than the state-of-the-art adaptive algorithms. On the other hand, we found that existing adaptive algorithms can have a strong positive correlation between `MQ`s and the temporal distance between the SUL and reused version. These findings affirmatively answer **RQ2** for existing techniques; and corroborate previous studies [13] where the quality of the reused models is shown as a factor that affects adaptive learning.

Our Contributions: (1) We introduce the $\partial\mathtt{L}^*_{\mathtt{M}}$ algorithm to mitigate the cost for re-inferring Mealy machines from evolving systems; and (2) We present an experiment comparing our proposal to three state-of-the-art adaptive learning algorithms [5, 13] to show that the side-effects of *redundant* and *deprecated* sequences can be mitigated by exploring reused observation tables on-the-fly. To date, there is a lack of studies about the pros and cons of adaptive learning and how much extra (and irrelevant) effort it may take if low-quality models are re-used, our second contribution provides essential insights to fill in this gap.

The remaining of this paper is organized as follows: In Sect. 2, we introduce the concepts of finite state machines, model learning and adaptive learning; In Sect. 3, we present the $\partial \mathtt{L}^*_\mathtt{M}$ algorithm; In Sect. 4, we design an experiment to evaluate and analyze the effect of reuse and its correlation with model quality; and, In Sect. 5, we draw some conclusions and pointout some avenues for future work. For the sake of reproducibility and repeatability, a lab package is available at https://github.com/damascenodiego/DynamicLstarM.

2 Background

In this section, we focus on model learning based on complete deterministic Mealy machines [4,27], hereafter called finite state machines (FSM). FSMs have been successfully used to learn models of hardware [8], software [13] and communication protocols at an abstract level [26].

2.1 Finite State Machines

Definition 1 *(Complete Deterministic FSM). An FSM $\mathcal{M} = \langle S, s_0, I, O, \delta, \lambda \rangle$ is a 7-tuple where S is the finite set of states, $s_0 \in S$ is the initial state, I is the set of inputs, O is the set of outputs, $\delta : S \times I \rightarrow S$ is the transition function, and $\lambda : S \times I \rightarrow O$ is the output function.*

Initially, an FSM is in the initial state s_0. Given a current state $s_i \in S$, when a defined input $x \in I$, such that $(s_i, x) \in S \times I$, is applied, the FSM responds by moving to state $s_j = \delta(s_i, x)$ and producing output $y = \lambda(s_i, x)$. The concatenation of two inputs α and ω is denoted by $\alpha \cdot \omega$. An input sequence $\alpha = x_1 \cdot x_2 \cdot \ldots \cdot x_n \in I^*$ is defined in state $s \in S$ if there are states $s_1, s_2, \ldots, s_{n+1}$ such that $s = s_1$ and $\delta(s_i, x_i) = s_{i+1}$, for all $1 \leq i \leq n$. Transition and output functions are lifted to input sequences, as usual. For the empty input sequence ϵ, $\delta(s, \epsilon) = s$ and $\lambda(s, \epsilon) = \epsilon$. For a non-empty input sequence $\alpha \cdot x$ defined in state s, we have $\delta(s, \alpha \cdot x) = \delta(\delta(s, \alpha), x)$ and $\lambda(s, \alpha \cdot x) = \lambda(s, \alpha)\lambda(\delta(s, \alpha), x)$. An input sequence α is a prefix of β, denoted by $\alpha \leqslant \beta$, when $\beta = \alpha \cdot \omega$, for some sequence ω. An input sequence α is a proper prefix of β, denoted by $\alpha < \beta$, when $\beta = \alpha \cdot \omega$, for $\omega \neq \epsilon$. The prefixes of a set T are denoted by $pref(T) = \{\alpha | \exists \beta \in T, \alpha \leq \beta\}$. If $T = pref(T)$, it is *prefix-closed.*

An input sequence $\alpha \in I^*$ is a transfer sequence from s to s', if $\delta(s, \alpha) = s'$. An input sequence γ is a separating sequence for $s_i, s_j \in S$ if $\lambda(s_i, \gamma) \neq \lambda(s_j, \gamma)$. Two states $s_i, s_j \in S$ are equivalent if, for all $\alpha \in I^*$, $\lambda(s_i, \alpha) = \lambda'(s_j, \alpha)$, otherwise they are distinguishable. An FSM is *deterministic* if, for each state s_i and input x, there is at most one possible state $s_j = \delta(s_i, x)$ and output $y = \lambda(s_i, x)$. Notice that our definition only allows for complete deterministic

FSMs, which are the focus of this paper. If all states of an FSM are pairwise distinguishable, then the FSM is *minimal*.

A set Q of input sequences is a *state cover* for $\mathcal{M}$ if $\epsilon \in Q$ and, for all $s_i \in S$, there is an $\alpha \in Q$ such that $\delta(s_0, \alpha) = s_i$. A set P of input sequences is a *transition cover* for $\mathcal{M}$ if $\epsilon \in P$ and, for all $(s, x) \in S \times I$, there are $\alpha, \alpha x \in P$, such that $\delta(s_0, \alpha) = s$, $x \in I$. A set W of input sequences is *characterization set* for $\mathcal{M}$ if for all $s_i, s_j \in S$ such that, with $s_i \neq s_j$, there is an $\alpha \in W$ where $\lambda(s_i, \alpha) \neq \lambda(s_j, \alpha)$.

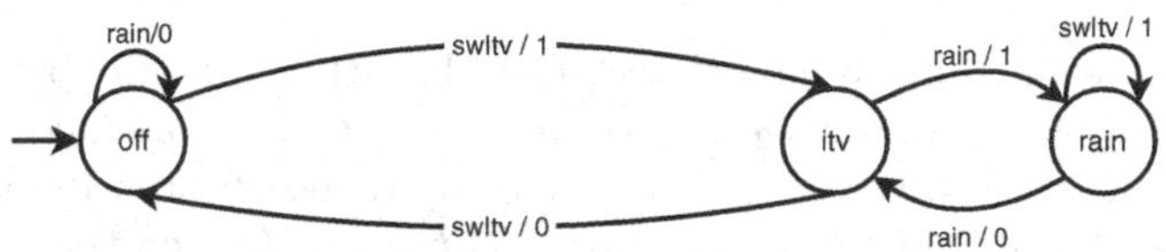

Fig. 1. The windscreen wiper FSM

Example 1 (The windscreen wiper FSM). Figure 1 depicts a windscreen wiper system supporting intervaled and fast wiping, if any raindrop is sensed, such that $S = \{off, itv, rain\}, I = \{rain, swItv\}$ and $O = \{0, 1\}$. Transition and output functions are represented by directed edges labeled with input/output symbols.

2.2 Model Learning

Coined by Angluin [1], active model learning was originally designed to formulate a hypothesis $\mathcal{H}$ about the behavior of a SUL as a deterministic finite automaton (DFA). Model learning has been adapted to several notations [30] and is often described in terms of the Minimally Adequate Teacher (MAT).

In the MAT framework [30], there are two phases:(i) *hypothesis construction*, where a learning algorithm poses Membership Queries (`MQ`) to gain knowledge about the SUL using `reset` operations and input sequences; and (ii) *hypothesis validation*, where based on the model learnt so far a hypothesis $\mathcal{H}$ about the "language" of the SUL is formed and tested against the SUL using Equivalence Queries (`EQ`). The results of the queries are organized in that is iteratively refined and used to formulate $\mathcal{H}$.

Definition 2 *(Observation Table). An observation table* `OT` $= (S_M, E_M, T_M)$ *is a triple, where* $S_M \subseteq I^*$ *is a prefix-closed set of transfer sequences (i.e., prefixes);* $E_M \subseteq I^+$ *is a set of separating sequences (i.e., suffixes); and* T_M *is a table where rows are labeled by elements from* $S_M \cup (S_M \cdot I)$*, columns are labeled by elements from* E_M*, such that for all* $pre \in S_M \cup (S_M \cdot I)$ *and* $suf \in E_M$*,* $T_M(pre, suf) = \lambda(\delta(q_0, pre), suf)$ *where* q_0 *is the initial state.*

Two rows $pre_1, pre_2 \in S_M \cup (S_M \cdot I)$ are equivalent, denoted by $pre_1 \cong pre_2$, when for all $suf \in E_M$ it holds that $T_M(pre_1, suf) = T_M(pre_2, suf)$. The equivalence class of a row r is denoted by $[r]$.

The $\mathtt{L}^*_\mathtt{M}$ Algorithm. Traditionally, the $\mathtt{L}^*_\mathtt{M}$ algorithm [27] starts with the sets of prefixes $S_M = \{\epsilon\}$ and suffixes $E_M = I$ so that it can reach the initial state and observe the outputs of the outgoing transitions, respectively. Afterwards, it poses MQs until the properties of closedness and consistency hold:

Definition 3 *(Closedness property). An observation table* OT *is closed if for all $pre_1 \in (S_M \cdot I)$, there is a $pre_2 \in S_M$ where $pre_1 \cong pre_2$.*

Definition 4 *(Consistency property). An observation table* OT *is consistent if for all $pre_1, pre_2 \in S_M$, such that $pre_1 \cong pre_2$, it holds that $pre_1 \cdot \alpha \cong pre_2 \cdot \alpha$, for all $\alpha \in I$.*

If an observation table is not closed, the algorithm finds a row $s_1 \in S_M \cdot I$, such that $s_1 \ncong s_2$ for all $s_2 \in S_M$, moves it to S_M, and completes the observation table by asking MQs for the new rows. If the observation table is not consistent, the algorithm finds $s_1, s_2 \in S_M, e \in E_M, i \in I$, such that $s_1 \cong s_2$ but $T_M(s_1 \cdot i, e) \neq T_M(s_2 \cdot i, e)$, adds $i \cdot e$ to E_M, and completes the observation table by asking MQs for the new column. Given a *closed* and *consistent* observation table, the $\mathtt{L}^*_\mathtt{M}$ formulates a hypothesis $\mathcal{H} = (Q_M, q_{0_M}, I, O, \delta_M, \lambda_M)$ where $Q_M = \{[pre] | pre \in S_M\}$, $q_{0_M} = [\epsilon]$ and, for all $pre \in S_M$, $i \in I$, $\delta_M([pre], i) = [pre \cdot i]$ and $\lambda_M([pre], i) = T_M(pre, i)$.

After formulating $\mathcal{H}$, $\mathtt{L}^*_\mathtt{M}$ works under the assumption that an EQ can return either a counterexample (CE) exposing the non-conformance, or yes, if $\mathcal{H}$ is indeed equivalent to the SUL. When a CE is found, a CE processing method adds prefixes and/or suffixes to the OT and hence refines $\mathcal{H}$. The aforementioned steps are repeated until EQ = yes. For black-box systems, EQs are often approximated using random walks [1,12], conformance testing [6,9,32], or both [17,22].

Example 2 (OT from the windscreen wiper FSM). In Table 1, we show an observation table built using $\mathtt{L}^*_\mathtt{M}$, a CE = swItv · rain · rain · rain and the Rivest and Schapire method [25], that uses binary search to find the shortest suffix from CE that refines a hypothesis. The cost to build this OT is 24 MQs and 1 EQ.

Table 1. OT extracted from the windscreen wiper FSM

		rain	*swItv*	*rain · rain*
S_r	ϵ	0	1	0 · 0
	swItv	1	0	1 · 0
	swItv · rain	0	1	0 · 1
$S_r \cdot I_r$	*rain*	0	1	0 · 0
	swItv · swItv	0	1	0 · 0
	swItv · rain · rain	1	0	1 · 0
	swItv · rain · swItv	0	1	0 · 1

The worst-case complexity of the $\mathtt{L}^*_\mathtt{M}$ algorithm for the number of MQs is $\mathcal{O}(|I|^2 mn + |I| mn^2)$ parameterized on the size of the input domain I, the length

m of the longest CE and the number of states n of the minimal FSM describing the SUL. Motivated by the impact of CEs on the complexity of L^*_M, a wide range of processing methods are found in the literature [15]. Another important component for model learning is cache filter which can pre-process queries to eliminate redundancy [20].

2.3 Adaptive Learning

Adaptive learning is a variant of model learning which attempts to speed up learning by reusing pre-existing models from previous/alternative versions [10]. In adaptive learning, transfer and/or separating sequences built from pre-existing models are used to initialize learning algorithms with sets of prefixes and suffixes (possibly) better than the traditional sets of sequences to reach the initial state (i.e., $S_M = \{\epsilon\}$) and collect outputs from outgoing transitions (i.e., $E_M = I$). Thus, a reduction on the number of MQs and EQs may be obtained. In this context, we are aware of four studies that address adaptive learning [5,10,13,35].

Groce, Peled and Yannakakis [10] introduce an approach where inaccurate (but not completely irrelevant) models are reused to reduce the time spent on model learning and model checking. They evaluate the benefits of reusing either transfer sequences, or separating sequences, or both; compared to *learning from scratch*. Their results indicate that adaptive learning is useful especially when modifications are minor or when they may have a very limited effect on the correctness of properties checked.

Windmüller, Neubauer, Steffen, Howar and Bauer [35] present an adaptive learning technique which periodically infers automata from evolving complex applications. Moreover, they show that learning algorithms which reuse separating sequences from models of previous versions are capable of finding states maintained in newer versions.

Huistra, Meijer and van de Pol [13] show that the benefits of adaptive learning are influenced by (i) the complexity of the SUL, (ii) differences between the reused version and the SUL, and (iii) the quality of the suffixes. Thus, if a set of reused separating sequences has bad quality (i.e., low ability to re-distinguish states), irrelevant queries may be posed, and hence extra effort will be required. To mitigate that, the authors suggest that calculating a subset of good separating sequence should provide a reduction on the number of deprecated sequences.

Chaki, Clarke, Sharygina and Sinha [5] introduce *DynamicCheck*, an approach to reduce the cost for model checking software upgrades. Central to their approach is Dynamic L*, an adaptive learning algorithm which reuses observation tables from previous versions for inferring DFAs [1]. As result, upgrade checking can succeed in a small fraction of the time to verify its reference version [5]. Next, we briefly present Dynamic L* in terms of Mealy machines.

Dynamic L^*. Normally, L^*_M starts with $S = \{\epsilon\}$, $E = I$ and, if there is any previously learnt model from some reference version v_{ref}, it misses opportunities for optimizing the learning process. To this end, DynamicL* restores the *agreement* of an outdated table $OT_o = (S_r, E_r, T_o)$ built from v_{ref} by re-posing MQs to the updated release v_{updt} to build an updated observation table $OT_r = (S_r, E_r, T_r)$.

Definition 5 *(Agreement). An* $\mathtt{OT}_r = (S_r, E_r, T_r)$ *agrees with* v_{updt} *if and only if, for all* $s \in (S_r \cup S_r \cdot I_u)$ *and* $e \in E_r$*, it holds that* $T_r(s, e) = \lambda_u(s, e)$*, such that* λ_u *is the output function of* v_{updt}*.*

After restoring the agreement, the observation table $\mathtt{OT}_r$ may have redundant prefixes and deprecated suffixes. To discard them, the `Dynamic` $\mathtt{L}^*$ searches for a smaller $S_R \subseteq S_r$ with the same state coverage capability but less prefixes, referred to as *well-formed cover* [5].

Definition 6 *(Well-Formed cover subset). Let* S_r *be the set of prefixes from an observation table* $\mathtt{OT}_r$ *in agreement with* v_{updt}*; a subset* $S_R \subseteq S_r$ *is well-formed cover, if and only if (i)* S_R *is prefix-closed, (ii) for all* $s1, s2 \in S_R$*, it holds that* $s1 \not\cong s2$*, and (iii)* S_R *is a maximal subset from* S_r*.*

After finding a $S_R \subseteq S_r$, we use a *Column function* to group prefixes into equivalence classes given a subset of suffixes.Thus, we search for an optimal subset of suffixes $E_R \subseteq E_r$, referred to as the *experiment cover* [5].

Definition 7 *(Column Function). Let* S_R *be well-formed cover, an observation table* $\mathtt{OT}_{R'} = (S_R, E_r, T_{R'})$ *derived from* $\mathtt{OT}_r$*, the input set* I_u *of* v_{updt}*, and an* $e \in E_r$*; the column function is* $Col(S_R, e) : S_R \times E_r \to \{B_1, B_2, \ldots, B_n\}$ *where* B_i *are non-empty partitions of* S_R *(i.e.,* $B_i \subseteq S_R$*),* $\cap_{i=1}^{n} B_i = \emptyset$*,* $\cup_{i=1}^{n} B_i = S_R$*,* $Col(S_R, \epsilon) = \{S_R\}$ *and* $x, y \in B_i$ *if and only if* $T(x, e) = T(y, e)$*.*

An $E_R \subseteq E_r$ is an experiment cover subset iff for all distinct $e_1, e_2 \in E_R$, it holds that $Col(S_R, e_1) \neq Col(S_R, e_2)$ and for all $e' \in E_R$ there is an $e \in E_r$ where $Col(S_R, e) = Col(S_R, e')$. Finally, $\mathtt{L}^*_\mathtt{M}$ is initialized with the subsets S_R and E_R. Thus, the time for upgrade model checking can be reduced to a small fraction of the time needed to verify its reference version from the scratch [5].

3 The `partial-Dynamic` $\mathtt{L}^*_\mathtt{M}$ Algorithm

For evolving systems, significant updates can lead adaptive learning to pose several irrelevant queries composed by redundant and deprecated sequences. Thus, calculating a "useful" subset of sequences should mitigate this risk [13]. To achieve this goal, we introduce `partial-Dynamic` $\mathtt{L}^*_\mathtt{M}$ ($\partial\mathtt{L}^*_\mathtt{M}$), an extension of the adaptive algorithm proposed in [5] and briefly described in Sect. 2.3. Our algorithm improves upon the state-of-the-art by exploring observation tables on-the-fly to avoid irrelevant queries rather than indiscriminately re-asking `MQ`s.

The term *partial* applies as the $\partial\mathtt{L}^*_\mathtt{M}$ algorithm copes with reused observation tables by exploring them using depth-first search (DFS) to find redundant prefixes; and breadth-first search (BFS) to find deprecated suffixes. Our $\partial\mathtt{L}^*_\mathtt{M}$ algorithm comprises three sequential steps which are discussed in the next subsections using two versions of the windscreen wiper as running examples.

Example 3 (Updated windscreen wiper). Let the FSMs in Figs. 1 and 2 be the reference version v_{ref} and updated release v_{updt} of an evolving system, respectively. Added elements are shown in dotted lines.

We refer to their representation as minimal FSMs and counterpart elements as $M_r = \langle Q_r, q_{0_r}, I_r, O_r, \delta_r, \lambda_r \rangle$ and $M_u = \langle Q_u, q_{0_u}, I_u, O_u, \delta_u, \lambda_u \rangle$.

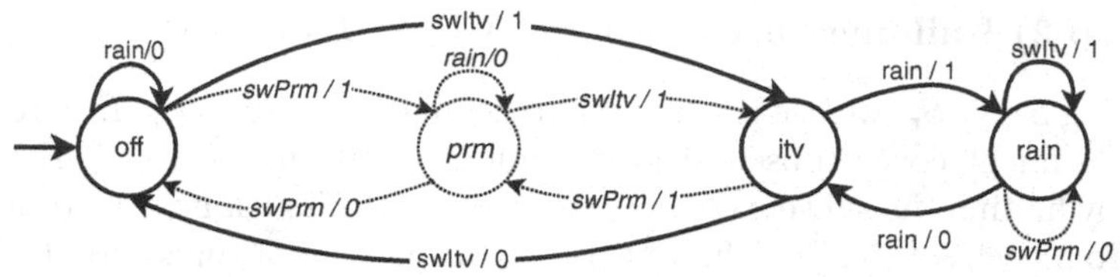

Fig. 2. Windscreen wiper with permanent movement

3.1 (Step 1) On-the-Fly Exploration of the Reused Table

Let S_r and E_r be prefixes and suffixes of an observation table $\texttt{OT}_r = (S_r, E_r, T_r)$. Since we do not know how the states may have changed, $\texttt{OT}_r$ may be outdated, redundant prefixes may emerge from S_r and no longer reach the same states [13], respectively. Thus, an updated observation table $\texttt{OT}_{R'} = (S_R, E_r, T_{R'})$ has to be built by restoring the agreement of $\texttt{OT}_r$ to v_{updt}. To achieve this, instead of indiscriminately re-asking queries, we explore the tree representation of $S_r \cdot I_u$ on-the-fly using depth-first search (DFS) to pose MQs and build an updated table $\texttt{OT}_{R'}$. In this tree representation, paths leading from root to nodes represent elements from $S_r \cdot I_u$ and nodes are annotated using rows of the updated observation table $\texttt{OT}_{R'}$. Thus, we can identify prefixes leading to states already discovered by E_r and find a well formed cover subset $S_R \subseteq S_r$.

Example 4 (Well-formed cover). Figure 3 shows parts of the tree representation of an $\texttt{OT}_{R'}$ built from an outdated observation table with prefixes and suffixes $S_r = \{\epsilon, swItv, swItv \cdot rain, swItv \cdot rain \cdot rain, wItv \cdot rain \cdot rain \cdot swItv, rain\}$ and $E_r = \{rain, swItv, swPrm, rain \cdot rain\}$, respectively.

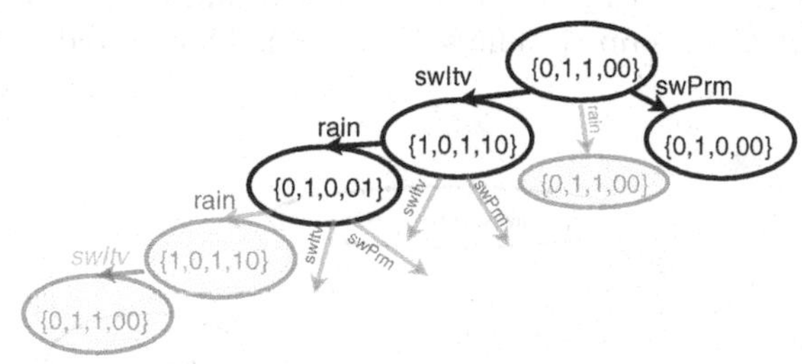

Fig. 3. Well-formed cover subset S_R generated from S_r

The well-formed cover subset is denoted by black arrows and discarded prefixes are in gray. The cost to find this well-formed cover subset is 40 MQs, in contrast to 76 MQs to completely restore the agreement of $\texttt{OT}_r$ to v_{updt}.

3.2 (Step 2) Building an Experiment Cover Tree

After finding $S_R \subseteq S_r$, we use the upper part from $\mathtt{OT}_{R'} = (S_R, E_r, T_{R'})$ to search for an experiment cover subset. An experiment cover subset $E_R \subseteq E_r$ can be obtained by finding the subsets of equivalent suffixes and picking a representative element from each set [5]. To achieve this, we propose an optimization technique that runs a breadth first search (BFS) on a tree representation of E_r, referred to as *experiment cover tree*, in a similar fashion to homing trees [4].

Definition 8 *(Experiment cover tree). Consider the updated observation table* $\mathtt{OT}_{R'} = (S_R, E_r, T_{R'})$ *and an input domain* I_u*; an experiment cover tree is a rooted tree that satisfies the following constraints:*

1. *The root node is labeled as* $lbl(root) = Col(S_R, \epsilon)$*;*
2. *Each edge* e *is labeled with one suffix* $e \in E_r$*;*
3. *Each node* n *linked to parent* n_p *by edge* e *is labeled as* $lbl(n) = Col(lbl(n_p), e)$*;*
4. *Non-leaf nodes* n *have outgoing edges for all suffixes* $E_r \backslash E_{R(n)}$*, where* $E_{R(n)}$ *is the set of suffixes labeling the edges in the path from root to* n*;*
5. *A node* n *is leaf iff*
   (a) *for all* $B_i \in lbl(n)$, $|B_i| = 1$*; or*
   (b) *there is a lower node* n_l *where* $lbl(n) = lbl(n_l)$*.*

The *experiment cover tree* is built using BFS and, if a node d satisfying *5a* is found, the suffixes labeling the path from *root* to d is returned as the experiment cover subset E_R. Otherwise, we traverse the whole experiment cover tree and the first node d found with maximum separating capability is selected as the E_R, i.e., $max(|Col(S_R, E_{R(d)})|)$. Neither MQs nor EQs are posed in this step.

Example 5 (Experiment cover). Figure 4 shows a fragment of the experiment cover tree generated from the subset S_R in Fig. 3 and the set of suffixes $E_r = \{rain, swItv, swPrm, rain \cdot rain\}$. The subset E_R is highlighted in black.

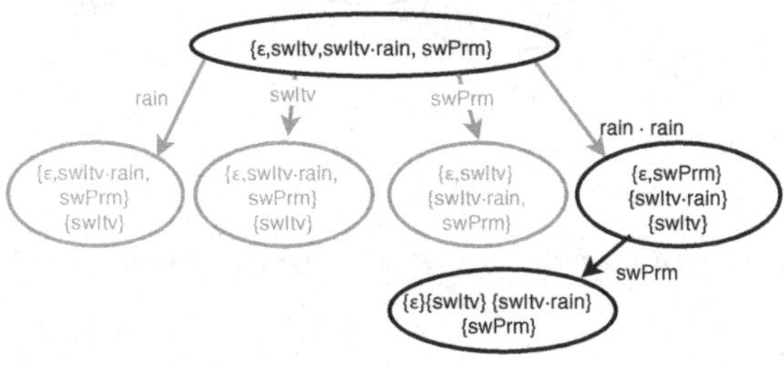

Fig. 4. Experiment cover tree

3.3 (Step 3) Running $\mathtt{L}^*_\mathtt{M}$ Using the Outcomes of $\partial\mathtt{L}^*_\mathtt{M}$

At this point, redundant prefixes and deprecated suffixes are discarded and we initialize the $\mathtt{L}^*_\mathtt{M}$ algorithm using the well-formed and experiment cover subsets, rather than $S_u = \{\epsilon\}$ and $E_u = I$. As results, we expect to build in the first iteration an observation table with higher state discovery capability at a reduced number of queries, especially if v_{ref} and v_{updt} are not drastically different.

Example 6. In Table 2, we summarize the number of `MQ`s and `EQ`s posed to the SULs in Figs. 1 and 2 by five model learning algorithms: $\mathtt{L}^*_\mathtt{M}$; our $\partial\mathtt{L}^*_\mathtt{M}$; an adaptive approach, referred to as `Adp`, where $\mathtt{L}^*_\mathtt{M}$ starts with suffixes from a previous version [13]; and two straightforward implementations of the `Dynamic L`* algorithm for Mealy machines, referred to as $\mathtt{DL}^*_\mathtt{M}$ and $\mathtt{DL}^*_{\mathtt{M}+}$. The latter differs by restoring the properties of closedness and consistency to avoid the loss of prefixes $s_1, s_2 \in S_R$ where $s_1 \cong s_2$ and $\exists(i,e) \in (I_u, E_r), T_{R'}(s_1 \cdot i, e) \neq T_{R'}(s_2 \cdot i, e)$. In this example, the $\partial\mathtt{L}^*_\mathtt{M}$ algorithm posed the lowest number of `MQ`s.

Table 2. Reuse approaches and number of queries

Algorithm	Reuse		Restore properties	SUL	OT	Number of	
	Prefixes	Suffixes				MQs	EQs
L^*_M [27]	–	–	–	v_{ref}	–	18	2
				v_{updt}	–	48	2
`Adp` [13]	No	Complete	No	v_{updt}	$\mathtt{OT}_r$	48	1
$\mathtt{DL}^*_\mathtt{M}$ [5]	Indiscriminate		No	v_{updt}	$\mathtt{OT}_r$	76	2
$\mathtt{DL}^*_{\mathtt{M}+}$			Yes	v_{updt}	$\mathtt{OT}_r$	81	1
$\partial\mathtt{L}^*_\mathtt{M}$	On-the-fly		No	v_{updt}	$\mathtt{OT}_r$	43	1

4 Empirical Evaluation

According to Huistra et al. [13], the more the states of a SUL have been changed, the lower is the number of suffixes with good quality. Therefore, we expect a higher number of irrelevant queries from state-of-the-art adaptive learning algorithms when older versions are re-used.

4.1 Research Questions

To evaluate adaptive learning in different settings, we extended the LearnLib framework [17] with the algorithms in Table 2. Thus, we investigated if our $\partial\mathtt{L}^*_\mathtt{M}$ algorithm is more efficient than three state-of-the-art adaptive algorithms (RQ1) and the impact of the temporal distance in their effectiveness (RQ2).

As a measure of software evolution, we opted for the temporal distance between the versions in terms of their release dates as structural changes (e.g., changed transitions) in black-box setting are often unknown; and behavioral metrics (e.g., percentage of failed test cases) may mislead minor modifications closer to initial states compared to major changes [34]. As a measure of effectiveness, we used the number of MQs and EQs posed by each adaptive learning algorithm compared to traditional learning using the L^*_M algorithm [27].

In Table 3, we formulated hypotheses about the influence of the temporal distance on the number of queries, denoted by ΔT; and the average difference between the number of MQs and EQs posed by the adaptive learning and L^*_M, denoted by μMQ and μEQ.

Table 3. Hypotheses

Measure	Hypotheses	Description
μMQ	$H_0^{\mu MQ}$	The ∂L^*_M requires an equivalent μMQ
	$H_1^{\mu MQ}$	The ∂L^*_M requires a higher μMQ
	$H_2^{\mu MQ}$	The ∂L^*_M requires a lower μMQ
μEQ	$H_0^{\mu EQ}$	The ∂L^*_M requires an equivalent μEQ
	$H_1^{\mu EQ}$	The ∂L^*_M requires a higher μEQ
	$H_2^{\mu EQ}$	The ∂L^*_M requires a lower μEQ
ΔT	$H_0^{\Delta T}$	The ∂L^*_M is influenced by the temporal distance
	$H_1^{\Delta T}$	The ∂L^*_M is not influenced by the temporal distance

For each scenario $\langle v_l, OT_r \rangle$, such that v_l is a SUL and OT_r is an observation table built from a reference version v_r, we used the Mann-Whitney-Wilcoxon (MWW) to check if there was *statistical significance* ($p < 0.01$) between the number of queries posed by the adaptive algorithms. To measure the *scientific significance* of our results [18], we used the Vargha-Delaney's $\hat{A}_{c,t}$ effect size [31,36] to assess the probability of one algorithm outperforming another [2]. If $\hat{A}_{c,t} < 0.5$, then the treatment t poses more queries than, the control c. If $\hat{A}_{c,t} = 0.5$, they are equivalent. To categorize the magnitude, we used the intervals between $\hat{A}_{c,t}$ and 0.5 suggested by [11,29]: $0 \leq$ *negligible* $< 0.147, 0.147 \leq$ *small* $< 0.33, 0.33 \leq$ *medium* < 0.474 or $0.474 \leq$ *large* ≤ 0.5. Finally, we used the Pearson's correlation coefficient to evaluate the relationship between the temporal distance between versions $\langle v_l, v_r \rangle$ to the numbers of MQs and EQs.

4.2 Subject Systems

As evolving system, we reused 18 Mealy machines learned in a large scale analysis of several versions of OpenSSL [26], an open-source and commercial-grade cryptographic toolkit [23]. In Fig. 5, we depict over 14 years of development branches from the server-side of OpenSSL. SULs are denoted by white boxes with arrows pointing out to their previous release in the branch, the number of implemented states in parentheses, and behavioral overlaps (i.e., equivalent FSMs) are grouped by dashed areas.

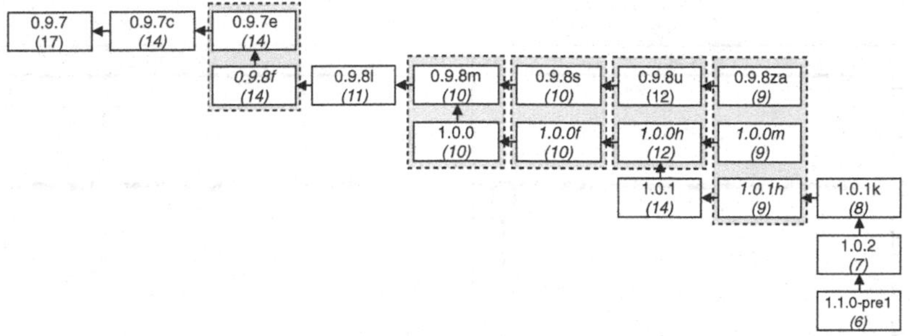

Fig. 5. OpenSSL server-side: 18 FSMs versions used as SUL

4.3 Experiment Design

Let $\langle v_l, \mathtt{OT}_r \rangle$ be a learning scenario where v_l is the SUL, and $\mathtt{OT}_r$ is an observation table built from a reference version v_r. For all 18 versions and their precedents, we measured the difference between the numbers of MQs and EQs posed by each adaptive algorithm and $\mathtt{L}^*_{\mathtt{M}}$, such that positive values denote *adaptive learning posing more queries*; and their temporal distance in years. For each version v_r, we built 500 different $\mathtt{OT_r} = (S_r, E_r, T_r)$ with prefix-closed state cover sets S_r created using randomized DFS and $E_r = I_u \cup W_r$, such that W_r is a W set for v_r; and calculated the μMQs and μEQs. For processing CE, we used the *Suffix1by1* [14], and the CLOSE_FIRST strategy to close tables [19]. To build EQs, we used the Wp method for conformance testing [9] with an upper bound $m = 2$.

4.4 Analysis of Results

In this section, we analyze the μMQs and μEQs posed by the adaptive algorithms and their relationship to the temporal distance within $\langle v_l, v_r \rangle$. For the averages, we calculated the difference between the numbers of MQs and EQs posed by each adaptive algorithm and learning from scratch using the $\mathtt{L}^*_{\mathtt{M}}$ algorithm.

By analyzing the release dates for all versions [24], we found a strong positive correlation ($r = 0.72$) between the temporal distance and difference of numbers of states implemented in each pair of versions. These findings corroborate de Ruiter [26] findings that OpenSSL improved over time and recent versions were more succinct (i.e., had fewer states). Moreover, they also indicate that the OpenSSL server-side represents an evolving system that can pose interesting challenges to adaptive learning algorithms, e.g., the reuse of larger and older versions may impact the benefits of adaptive learning.

Average Difference of EQs. In Fig. 6, we depict boxplots for the μEQs as a function of the temporal distance within $\langle v_l, v_r \rangle$. To keep the figure uncluttered, we calculated the boxplots for time windows of one year. Outliers are depicted as red dots.

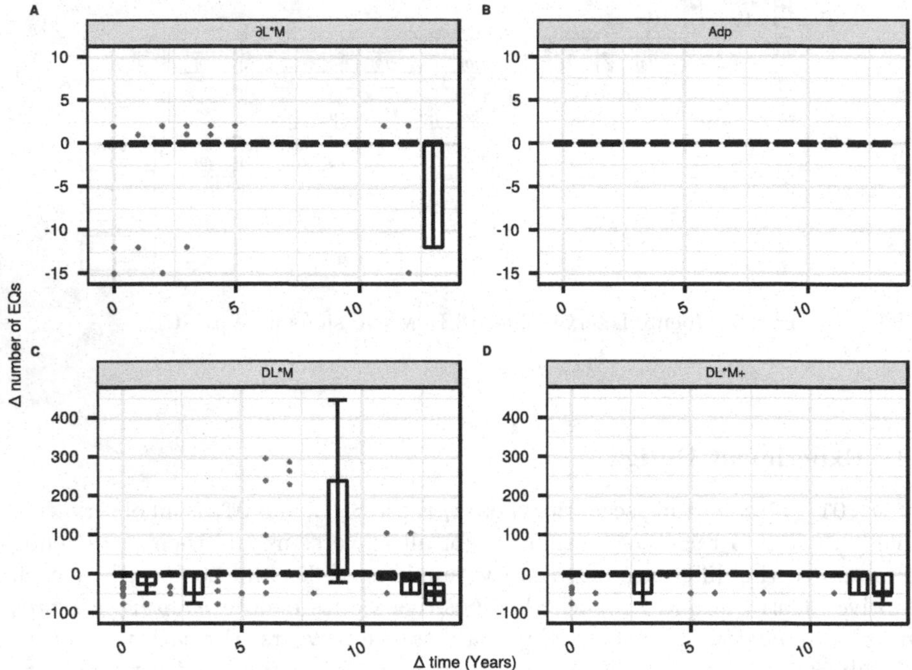

Fig. 6. Boxplots of the μEQs posed by adaptive and traditional learning (Color figure online)

By analyzing the μEQs and the learnt observation tables, we found that I_u turned out to be a good set of separating sequences. The I_u set allowed to discover most of the states from OpenSSL and, since the reused observation tables included I_u, the resulting μEQs happened to be quite similar, and whiskers turned out to be very close to their boxes.

In Fig. 7, we show histograms to the effect size for EQs, where $\partial \mathtt{L}^*_{\mathtt{M}}$ is the control method, i.e., $\hat{A} < 0.5$ means that the $\partial \mathtt{L}^*_{\mathtt{M}}$ algorithm posed less queries than the other adaptive algorithm. The MWW test indicated a statistically significant difference ($p < 0.01$) between $\partial \mathtt{L}^*_{\mathtt{M}}$ and the other adaptive algorithms; however, as the histograms indicate, the effect sizes were mostly categorized as *negligible*.

Added to this, the Pearson's correlation coefficient indicated a *very weak* to *no correlation* between μEQs and temporal distance. The number of rounds also happened to be approximately the same, i.e., *one* round for all versions with

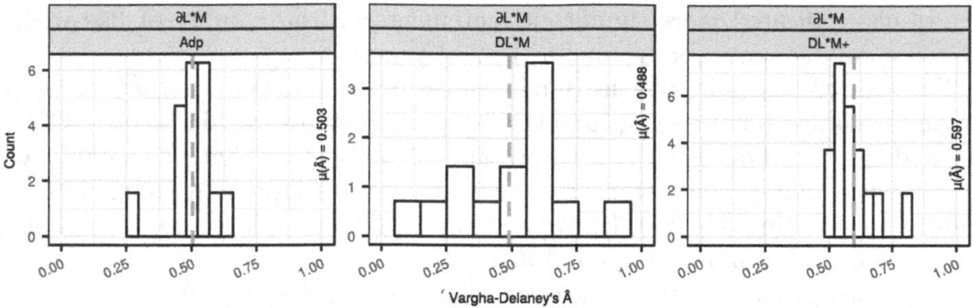

Fig. 7. Histograms of the effect sizes for EQs posed by the adaptive algorithms

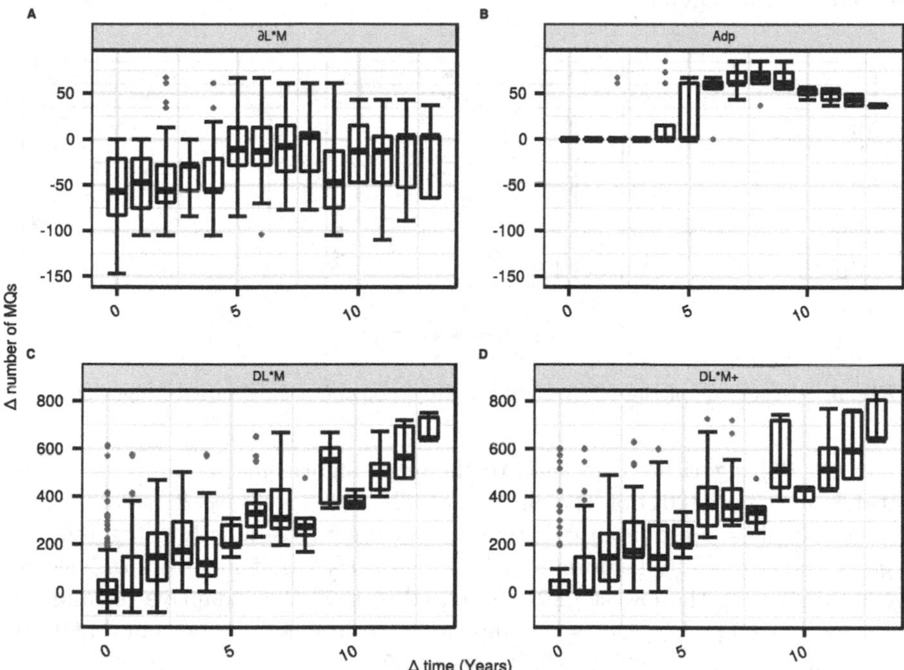

Fig. 8. Boxplots of the μMQs posed by adaptive and traditional learning

less than 14 states and *two to five* for all other versions. These findings support the hypothesis $H_0^{\mu \mathtt{EQ}}$ that our adaptive learning algorithm $\partial \mathtt{L}^*_{\mathtt{M}}$ required an μEQs similar to traditional learning.

Average Difference of MQs. In Fig. 8, we depict boxplots for the μMQs as a function of the temporal distance between v_l and v_r. To keep the figure uncluttered, we calculated one boxplot for each time window of a year.

By analyzing the μMQs, we found that Adp posed around 50 additional MQs when versions older than four years were reused. An increment on the μMQs also emerged for the $\mathtt{DL}^*_{\mathtt{M}}$ and $\mathtt{DL}^*_{\mathtt{M+}}$ where up to 800 extra MQs occurred to be required.

Our results indicated more significant increments on the number of MQs when the temporal distance was maximum (i.e., 14 years).

For the existing adaptive learning algorithms, we found a *strong* to *very strong* correlation between μMQs and the temporal distance within $\langle v_l, v_r \rangle$. Thus, our findings corroborate to Huistra et al. [13] indicative that the quality of the reused sequences is a factor that can underpower adaptive learning. Consequently, the existing adaptive learning algorithms posed a large number of MQs composed by *redundant* prefixes and *deprecated* suffixes.

Differently from the state-of-the-art adaptive learning algorithms, our $\partial\mathtt{L}^*_\mathtt{M}$ algorithm turned out to be more robust than the other algorithms. In Fig. 9, we show histograms for the effect sizes of the $\partial\mathtt{L}^*_\mathtt{M}$ algorithm compared to the three other adaptive techniques.

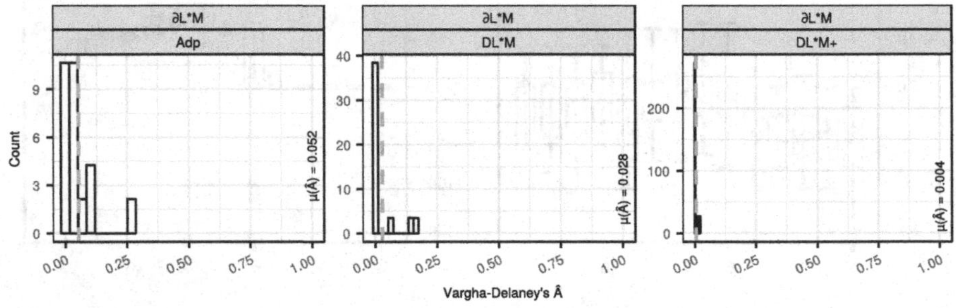

Fig. 9. Histograms of the effect sizes for MQs posed by the adaptive algorithms

For the $\partial\mathtt{L}^*_\mathtt{M}$ algorithm compared to the other algorithms, we found a significant difference ($p < 0.01$) on the number of MQs, and a *weak positive* correlation between the μMQs and temporal distance, with effect sizes mostly categorized as *large*. Thus, our results favoured the hypothesis $H_2^{\mu\mathtt{MQ}}$ that identifies $\partial\mathtt{L}^*_\mathtt{M}$ as the algorithm showing the lowest μEQs compared to the other adaptive techniques, and answered **RQ1** by placing our on-the-fly technique as more efficient than the existing adaptive algorithms in terms of MQs.

Benefits of Adaptive Learning vs. Temporal Distance. For all the adaptive learning algorithms, the Pearson's correlation coefficients indicated *very weak* positive correlation ($\leq$0.20) between number of EQs and temporal distance. These findings corroborate the mostly constant μEQ seen in Fig. 6.

For the algorithms Adp, $\mathtt{DL}^*_\mathtt{M}$ and $\mathtt{DL}^*_{\mathtt{M}+}$, we observed the Pearson's coefficients indicated strong positive correlations (0.73, 0.78 and 0.80, respectively) between number of MQs and temporal distance. Alternatively, for our $\partial\mathtt{L}^*_\mathtt{M}$ algorithm, we observed weak positive correlation (0.33) between number of MQs and temporal distance. Thus, we confirm the hypothesis $H_1^{\Delta\mathtt{T}}$ that the $\partial\mathtt{L}^*_\mathtt{M}$ algorithm is not influenced by the temporal distance between versions and affirmatively answer **RQ2** by showing that the effectiveness of existing adaptive learning techniques are indeed affected by the temporal distance between versions.

4.5 Threats to Validity

Internal Validity: Threats to internal validity concern with the influences that can affect the casual relationship between the treatment and outcomes. One element that forms a threat to internal validity is the temporal distance between versions as a measure of software evolution. We found a strong positive correlation ($r = 0.72$) between temporal distance and difference in the numbers of states of the underlying FSMs. Hence, we found the temporal distance as a reasonable measure, at least for this particular case. Failed test-cases may not be good measures, as they do not reflect the point of failure in the SUL semantics, e.g., minor changes close to initial states against major changes on the language.

External Validity: Threats to external validity concern with generalization. To guarantee the reliability of our experiment results, we relied on the LearnLib framework [17] to implement adaptive learning algorithms. Our study is based essentially on the OpenSSL toolkit; and this poses a threat to external validity. However, since the OpenSSL has realistic size and structure, we believe that our findings are generalizable to other real systems. We plan to mitigate this by extending our study to other systems, such as software product lines [7].

5 Conclusions and Future Work

Real systems pass through many changes along their life-cycle and, as we often do not know how states may have changed, behavioral models tend to become outdated, incomplete, or even deprecated. To deal with these issues, several studies have proposed the application of active model learning to automatically derive behavioral models.

Particularly, adaptive model learning is a variant of active learning which has been studied to speed up model inference by reusing transfer and separating sequences from previously learnt observation tables. However, software evolution may degrade the quality of existing artifacts so that they may no longer distinguish states and compose *redundant* and *deprecated* sequences. To date, there is a limited number of studies about the pros and cons of adaptive model learning and how much extra effort it may pose if low-quality models are re-used.

To mitigate these problems, we introduced a novel adaptive algorithm that explores observation tables *on-the-fly* to avoid irrelevant MQs, called $\partial \mathtt{L}^*_{\mathtt{M}}$. Using 18 versions of the OpenSSL toolkit, we showed that state-of-the-art adaptive algorithms mostly show a strong positive correlation between the number of MQs and temporal distance between the reused and learnt versions.

Alternatively, our $\partial \mathtt{L}^*_{\mathtt{M}}$ algorithm presented a weak positive correlation between temporal distance and MQs. Thus, our algorithm turned out to be less sensitive to software evolution and more efficient than current approaches for adaptive learning. Also, $\partial \mathtt{L}^*_{\mathtt{M}}$ posed fewer MQs compared to three state-of-the-art adaptive learning algorithms. In this study, we move towards solving this issue by evaluating adaptive learning algorithms for evolving systems and how *redundant* and *deprecated* sequences can undermine the benefits of these algorithms.

As future work, we plan to investigate the problem of learning behavioral models of software product lines (SPL) [7]. Recently, we have investigated the problem of combining models from product families into a single representation, referred to as *family model* [7]. Family models differs from traditional notations by including propositional logic formulae to express the combination of features involved in the concerned states/transitions of the model [28]. In our investigations, we have found that although traditional model learning can be applied to SPLs in an exhaustive way, it can be prohibitive due to redundant queries performed over products sharing behavior and non-trivial due to differences in the input domains of their products. Thus, we believe that ∂L_M^* can be improved for learning models of SPLs in a efficient and effective way. Another branch of future research forms to extending adaptive learning to *discrimination tree*-based algorithms, such as TTT [16]. These algorithms compose an interesting domain due to their redundancy-free nature and improved space complexity.

Acknowledgment. This study was financed in part by the Coordenação de Aperfeiçoamento de Pessoal de Nível Superior - Brasil (CAPES) - Finance Code 001, and University of Leicester, College of Science & Engineering. Research carried out using the computational resources of the Center for Mathematical Sciences Applied to Industry (CeMEAI) funded by FAPESP (grant 2013/07375-0). The authors are also grateful to the anonymous reviewers; the *VALidation and Verification* (VALVE) research group at the University of Leicester; and *Laboratory of Software Engineering* (LabES) at the University of Sao Paulo (ICMC-USP) for their insightful comments and suggestions.

References

1. Angluin, D.: Learning regular sets from queries and counterexamples. Inf. Comput. **75**, 87–106 (1987)
2. Arcuri, A., Briand, L.: A practical guide for using statistical tests to assess randomized algorithms in software engineering. In: Proceedings of the 33rd International Conference on Software Engineering, ICSE 2011, pp. 1–10. ACM (2011)
3. Binder, R.V.: Testing Object-Oriented Systems: Models, Patterns, and Tools. Addison-Wesley Longman Publishing Co. Inc., Boston (1999)
4. Broy, M., Jonsson, B., Katoen, J.-P., Leucker, M., Pretschner, A.: Part I. Testing of finite state machines. In: Broy, M., Jonsson, B., Katoen, J.-P., Leucker, M., Pretschner, A. (eds.) Model-Based Testing of Reactive Systems. LNCS, vol. 3472, pp. 1–3. Springer, Heidelberg (2005). https://doi.org/10.1007/11498490_1
5. Chaki, S., Clarke, E., Sharygina, N., Sinha, N.: Verification of evolving software via component substitutability analysis. Form. Methods Syst. Des. **32**(3), 235–266 (2008)
6. Chow, T.S.: Testing software design modeled by finite-state machines. IEEE Trans. Softw. Eng. **SE–4**(3), 178–187 (1978)
7. Damasceno, C.D.N., Mousavi, M.R., da Silva Simao, A.: Learning from difference: an automated approach for learning family models from software product lines. In: Proceeedings of the 23rd International Systems and Software Product Line Conference, SPLC 2019, vol. 1. ACM Press, Paris (2019)

8. al Duhaiby, O., Mooij, A., van Wezep, H., Groote, J.F.: Pitfalls in applying model learning to industrial legacy software. In: Margaria, T., Steffen, B. (eds.) ISoLA 2018. LNCS, vol. 11247, pp. 121–138. Springer, Cham (2018). https://doi.org/10.1007/978-3-030-03427-6_13
9. Fujiwara, S., Bochmann, G.V., Khendek, F., Amalou, M., Ghedamsi, A.: Test selection based on finite state models. IEEE Trans. Softw. Eng. **17**(6), 591–603 (1991)
10. Groce, A., Peled, D., Yannakakis, M.: Adaptive model checking. In: Katoen, J.-P., Stevens, P. (eds.) TACAS 2002. LNCS, vol. 2280, pp. 357–370. Springer, Heidelberg (2002). https://doi.org/10.1007/3-540-46002-0_25
11. Hess, M.R., Kromrey, J.D.: Robust confidence intervals for effect sizes: a comparative study of Cohen'sd and Cliffs delta under non-normality and heterogeneous variances. In: Annual Meeting - American Educational Research Association (2004)
12. Howar, F., Steffen, B., Merten, M.: From ZULU to RERS. In: Margaria, T., Steffen, B. (eds.) ISoLA 2010. LNCS, vol. 6415, pp. 687–704. Springer, Heidelberg (2010). https://doi.org/10.1007/978-3-642-16558-0_55
13. Huistra, D., Meijer, J., van de Pol, J.: Adaptive learning for learn-based regression testing. In: Howar, F., Barnat, J. (eds.) FMICS 2018. LNCS, vol. 11119, pp. 162–177. Springer, Cham (2018). https://doi.org/10.1007/978-3-030-00244-2_11
14. Irfan, M.N., Oriat, C., Groz, R.: Angluin style finite state machine inference with non-optimal counterexamples. In: Proceedings of the First International Workshop on Model Inference In Testing, MIIT 2010, pp. 11–19. ACM, New York (2010)
15. Irfan, M.N., Oriat, C., Groz, R.: Chapter 3 - Model inference and testing. In: Advances in Computers, vol. 89, pp. 89–139. Elsevier (2013)
16. Isberner, M., Howar, F., Steffen, B.: The TTT algorithm: a redundancy-free approach to active automata learning. In: Bonakdarpour, B., Smolka, S.A. (eds.) RV 2014. LNCS, vol. 8734, pp. 307–322. Springer, Cham (2014). https://doi.org/10.1007/978-3-319-11164-3_26
17. Isberner, M., Howar, F., Steffen, B.: The open-source LearnLib. In: Kroening, D., Păsăreanu, C.S. (eds.) CAV 2015. LNCS, vol. 9206, pp. 487–495. Springer, Cham (2015). https://doi.org/10.1007/978-3-319-21690-4_32
18. Kampenes, V.B., Dyb, T., Hannay, J.E., Sjberg, D.I.: A systematic review of effect size in software engineering experiments. Inf. Softw. Technol. **49**(11), 1073–1086 (2007)
19. LearnLib: LearnLib 0.13 - Javadoc (2018). http://learnlib.github.io/learnlib/maven-site/0.13.0/apidocs/. Accessed 06 Aug 2018
20. Margaria, T., Raffelt, H., Steffen, B.: Knowledge-based relevance filtering for efficient system-level test-based model generation. Innov. Syst. Softw. Eng. **1**(2), 147–156 (2005)
21. Mariani, L., Pezz, M., Zuddas, D.: Chapter 4 - Recent advances in automatic black-box testing. In: Advances in Computers, vol. 99, pp. 157–193. Elsevier (2015)
22. Meinke, K., Sindhu, M.A.: Incremental learning-based testing for reactive systems. In: Gogolla, M., Wolff, B. (eds.) TAP 2011. LNCS, vol. 6706, pp. 134–151. Springer, Heidelberg (2011). https://doi.org/10.1007/978-3-642-21768-5_11
23. OpenSSL Foundation Inc.: OpenSSL - Cryptography and SSL/TLS toolkit (2018). https://www.openssl.org/. Accessed 21 Aug 2018
24. OpenSSL Foundation Inc.: OpenSSL releases at Github (2018). https://github.com/openssl/openssl/releases. Accessed 26 Aug 2018
25. Rivest, R.L., Schapire, R.E.: Inference of finite automata using homing sequences. Inf. Comput. **103**(2), 299–347 (1993)

26. Ruiter, J.: A tale of the OpenSSL state machine: a large-scale black-box analysis. In: Brumley, B.B., Röning, J. (eds.) NordSec 2016. LNCS, vol. 10014, pp. 169–184. Springer, Cham (2016). https://doi.org/10.1007/978-3-319-47560-8_11
27. Shahbaz, M., Groz, R.: Inferring mealy machines. In: Cavalcanti, A., Dams, D.R. (eds.) FM 2009. LNCS, vol. 5850, pp. 207–222. Springer, Heidelberg (2009). https://doi.org/10.1007/978-3-642-05089-3_14
28. Thüm, T., Apel, S., Kästner, C., Schaefer, I., Saake, G.: A classification and survey of analysis strategies for software product lines. ACM Comput. Surv. **47**, 6:1–6:45 (2014)
29. Torchiano, M.: Effsize: efficient effect size computation (v. 0.7.1). CRAN package repository, March 2017. https://cran.r-project.org/web/packages/effsize/effsize.pdf. Accessed 20 Nov 2017
30. Vaandrager, F.: Model learning. Commun. ACM **60**(2), 86–95 (2017)
31. Vargha, A., Delaney, H.D.: A critique and improvement of the CL common language effect size statistics of McGraw and Wong. J. Educ. Behav. Stat. **25**(2), 101–132 (2000)
32. Vasilevskii, M.P.: Failure diagnosis of automata. Cybernetics **9**(4), 653–665 (1973)
33. Walkinshaw, N.: Chapter 1 - Reverse-engineering software behavior. In: Memon, A. (ed.) Advances in Computers, vol. 91. Elsevier (2013)
34. Walkinshaw, N., Bogdanov, K.: Automated comparison of state-based software models in terms of their language and structure. ACM Trans. Softw. Eng. Methodol. **22**(2), 1–37 (2013)
35. Windmüller, S., Neubauer, J., Steffen, B., Howar, F., Bauer, O.: Active continuous quality control. In: Proceedings of the 16th International ACM Sigsoft Symposium on Component-Based Software Engineering, CBSE 2013, pp. 111–120. ACM, New York (2013)
36. Wohlin, C., Runeson, P., Höst, M., Ohlsson, M.C., Regnell, B., Wesslén, A.: Systematic literature reviews. In: Wohlin, C., Runeson, P., Höst, M., Ohlsson, M.C., Regnell, B., Wesslén, A. (eds.) Experimentation in Software Engineering, pp. 45–54. Springer, Heidelberg (2012). https://doi.org/10.1007/978-3-642-29044-2_4

Axiomatic Characterization of Trace Reachability for Concurrent Objects

Frank S. de Boer and Hans-Dieter A. Hiep(✉)

Centrum Wiskunde & Informatica, Science Park 123,
1098 XG Amsterdam, The Netherlands
{frb,hdh}@cwi.nl

Abstract. In concurrent object models, objects encapsulate local state, schedule local processes, interact via asynchronous method calls, and methods of different objects are executed concurrently. In this paper, we introduce a compositional trace semantics for concurrent objects and provide an axiomatic characterization of the general properties of reachable traces, that is, traces that can be generated by a concurrent object program. The main result of this paper is a soundness and completeness proof of the axiomatic characterization.

Keywords: Concurrency · Compositionality · Completeness · Program synthesis

1 Introduction

A formal approach for performing verification of large and complex computer systems is compositional when a large system can be decomposed into separate components, each verified independently. Complex systems are constructed by composing verified components together; compositionality ensures that verified properties are preserved in such compositions [4]. Independent verification of components makes the verification work of a whole system divisible, verified components are reusable thus eliminating repeatable work, and therefore this approach is amenable for practical application.

In practice, large-scale computer systems typically consist of many spatially distributed processing units, each with independent and isolated computing and storage capabilities, interconnected by networks. Processing units are dynamically provisioned and interact asynchronously. Such systems are naturally modelled as concurrent object-oriented systems, in which concurrent objects are representing such processing units [7]. Classes of concurrent objects comprise object behaviors that share common behavioral properties, as specified by a concurrent object program. As such a program is executed, configuration and state changes, and a trace of interactions/communications between objects is generated. In general, for concurrent programs, such traces provide the semantic basis for compositional verification and abstraction from internal implementation details [4].

W. Ahrendt and S. L. Tapia Tarifa (Eds.): IFM 2019, LNCS 11918, pp. 157–174, 2019.
https://doi.org/10.1007/978-3-030-34968-4_9

Properties of traces can be expressed in some logical system, say first-order logic. We assume the logic has a satisfaction relation $\theta \models \phi$ which states that the trace θ of communications satisfies the property ϕ. The main contribution of this paper is an axiomatization of the class of properties which hold for any reachable trace describing the interaction between concurrent objects. Thus, properties that hold for every reachable trace can be established axiomatically, abstracting from the programming language semantics.

In this work, specifically, we give a finite axiomatization **Ax** of traces that can be generated by a concurrent object program, and show both *soundness* and *completeness*. The main structure of the completeness proof is as follows.

The semantic consequence relation $\psi \models \phi$ states that any trace θ which satisfies the property ψ, also satisfies property ϕ. That is, $\theta \models \psi$ implies $\theta \models \phi$. Not all traces follow from the axiomatization **Ax**, that is, there are traces θ such that $\theta \not\models \mathbf{Ax}$. Completeness means that a property that holds for all reachable traces, also follows from the axioms. Spelled out this amounts to the following statement: if for every program P and trace θ generated by P we have $\theta \models \phi$, then $\mathbf{Ax} \models \phi$. Assume that for every program P and trace θ of P, we have $\theta \models \phi$. To show that $\mathbf{Ax} \models \phi$, it suffices to show that for *any* trace θ which satisfies all the properties of **Ax** there exists a program P that generates θ (because by the assumption we then have that $\theta \models \phi$). At the heart of the completeness proof therefore lies the synthesis problem which consists of constructing for any trace that satisfies all the properties of **Ax**, a program that generates it.

To illustrate the main ideas underlying the program synthesis, we focus in this paper on an asynchronous active (concurrent) object language [3] that features classes, dynamic object creation, and asynchronous method calls which are immediately stored in a FIFO queue of the callee, later to be dequeued for execution by the callee in a run-to-completion mode. Further, each object encapsulates its local state and executes at most one method at a time.

Plan of the Paper. We first describe the programming language and its semantics in Sect. 2. We introduce the axiomatization and discuss soundness in Sect. 3. Section 4 describes the program synthesis and its use in the completeness proof. In Sect. 5, we sketch out how to extend our result to include futures and cooperative scheduling of method invocations as supported by the Abstract Behavioral Specification language (ABS, see [10]). We will discuss related and future work in Sect. 6.

2 The Programming Language

A *signature* is a finite set of *classes* $\mathcal{C}$, disjoint of a finite set of *methods*, and a map associating methods with classes. A *program* P of some signature consists of a set of class definitions and a designated main class. A *class definition* **class** C $\{\ldots\}$ consists of a class C, a constructor definition $C(\mathbf{arg}) :: s$ and a set of method definitions. A *method definition* $m(\mathbf{arg}) :: s$ consists of a method m and a statement s. Every constructor and method has precisely one argument. Although programs can be supplied with typing information, we do not deal with type annotations in this paper. We assume that every class C has a unique class definition in program P, and that it contains a unique method definition for every method associated to C. Let α be either a method m or a class C, then we write $P(\alpha :: s)$ to mean there is a definition $\alpha(\mathbf{arg}) :: s$ in program P.

The set of *statements* with typical element s is defined as follows: $s ::= (\mathbf{if}\ e\ \mathbf{then}\ s\ \mathbf{else}\ s) \mid (\mathbf{while}\ e\ s) \mid (s; s) \mid w := e \mid w := \mathbf{new}\ C(e) \mid e!m(e') \mid \mathbf{skip}$ It consists of standard control structures and assignments, and object creations ($w := \mathbf{new}\ C(e)$) and asynchronous method calls ($e!m(e')$), where w stands for either an instance variable or a local variable, and e for an expression. We treat statements syntactically equivalent up to associativity $(s; (s'; s'')) \equiv ((s; s'); s'')$, and identity $(\mathbf{skip}; s) \equiv s \equiv (s; \mathbf{skip})$, and drop parentheses if not ambiguous.

The variables of a program are drawn from three disjoint sets of *variables*: instance variables with typical element x, local variables with typical element k, and special variables. Variables lack variable declarations in programs, and instance and local variables have an undefined initial value. We further distinguish the special instance variable **this**, which denotes the currently executing object, and the special argument variable **arg**, which denotes the argument to the constructor or method.

By e we denote an arbitrary (side-effect free) *expression*. We have constant terms **null**, **true** and **false**, an equality operator, standard Boolean operators, and w, **this** and **arg** may occur as variable terms.

We present our semantics as a calculus of *finite* sequences of objects and events. The semantics is given with respect to a program P of some fixed signature. There is a countably infinite set O_C of *(object) references* for each class C, such that all O_C are disjoint. We denote by O their union. Thus, all references $o \in O$ have a unique class C such that $o \in O_C$. By V we denote an arbitrary set of *values*, such that $O \subseteq V$ and there are distinct values $\mathbf{null}, \mathbf{true}, \mathbf{false} \in V$ that are not references.

Assignments are partial maps of variables to values. By σ (resp. τ) we denote an assignment of instance (resp. local) variables to values, where **this** (resp. **arg**) is treated as a special variable standing for an object's identity (resp. a method's argument). We say σ is an *object assignment*, and τ is a *local assignment.* We write $[v/\mathbf{this}]$ (resp. $[v/\mathbf{arg}]$) for an *initial* assignment, which assigns **this** (resp. **arg**) to value $v \in V$ and all instance (resp. local) variables are undefined. Furthermore, $\sigma[v/x]$ (resp. $\tau[v/k]$) denotes the *update* of an assignment that assigns instance variable x (resp. local variable k) to value v. So, **this** and **arg** are never updated after their initial assignment.

By $V_{\sigma,\tau}(e)$ we denote the result of evaluating expression e under the assignments σ and τ as usual, and we write $V(e)$ if the subscript is obvious. We assume every non-reference value is *expressible*, that is, for every $v \in V \setminus O$ there is an e such that $V_{\sigma,\tau}(e) = v$ for every assignment σ and τ.

An *object* is either *stable* σ or *active* (σ, τ, s), where σ is an object assignment, τ is a local assignment and s a statement. Stable objects are sometimes also called passive or waiting: they have no active statement and local assignment. For object ξ, by $\xi(\mathbf{this})$ we mean $\sigma(\mathbf{this})$ in either case, and by $(\sigma, \tau, s)[v/w]$ we mean either $(\sigma[v/x], \tau, s)$ or $(\sigma, \tau[v/k], s)$, in case w is an instance variable x or a local variable k, respectively.

A *(global) configuration* is a sequence of objects separated by $\cdot$ dots. By $\Gamma \cdot \xi$ we mean a global configuration which consists of appending the object ξ to the (possibly empty) global configuration Γ. We treat global configurations syntactically equivalent up to commutativity of its objects.

Events record interactions/communications between objects, and are either:

1. *asynchronous method calls* $o' \rightsquigarrow o.m(v)$,
2. *object creations* $o' \rightsquigarrow o.C(v)$,
3. *root object creations* $\top \rightsquigarrow o.C(v)$,
4. *method selections* $o.m(v)$,
5. *constructor selections* $o.C(v)$,

where o, o' are object references, and v an *argument* value. A *trace* is a sequence of events separated by $\cdot$ dots. Let θ be such a trace, then $|\theta|$ denotes its length.

An asynchronous method call or (root) object creation is an *output* event, and a method or constructor selection is an *input* event. The *(callee) site* of any event is just $o.m(v)$ or $o.C(v)$. We write $o.\alpha(v)$ where α stands for either method m or class C. An output event *corresponds* to an input event if they have the same site. For every site, we assume that method m is associated to the class of o, and that C is the class of o. We leave argument v unrestricted, except for root object creations where we assume $v \notin O$.

We introduce two projections $\theta!o$ and $\theta?o$ which denote the sequence of output events with o as callee, and the sequence of input events with o as callee. The underlying FIFO discipline of processing calls ensures that $\theta?o$ is a prefix of the sites of $\theta!o$. We then define the next site to be executed by an object o, denoted by $Sched(\theta, o)$, as the first site in $\theta!o$ that is not in $\theta?o$, if it exists.

Derivability of $P \Rightarrow (\Gamma, \theta)$ (Definition 1) means that within an execution of program P we can reach configuration Γ by generating the (*global*) trace θ.

The rules operate on two levels: on the global level, the Q-rules activate objects by handling input events, and take active objects back to a stable state. On the local level, the S-rules perform the local computational steps of an active object. The calculus is non-deterministic: multiple choices are allowed by commutativity of global configurations, and picking a fresh reference for objects created by the S_{new} rule.

The rules S_{if}, S_{while} and S_{update} are standard for control structures, modifying the active object in its place. The two S_{if} rules do not apply if $V(e)$ is not **true** and not **false**. Rules S_{asyn} and S_{new} are essentially capturing communication between concurrent objects. Rule S_{asyn} does not apply if $V(e)$ is not a reference, or method m is not associated to the class of $V(e)$. Rule S_{new} creates a new object where $o \in O_C$ is an arbitrary *fresh* reference, that does not occur in the prior configuration or trace. The rule Q_{select} takes a stable object and results in an active object: it applies to both constructor and method selection events, and selects the first pending site after we look up in program P the corresponding method or constructor definition $\alpha :: s$. Rule Q_{skip} takes an active object and results in a stable object: finished continuations are discarded.

The initial configuration consists of a single object $[o/\textbf{this}]$, and the initial trace consists of a root object creation of the the main class of P. One may think of $\top$ as a dummy reference, but formally $\top \notin O$.

Definition 1. We inductively define $P \Rightarrow (\Gamma, \theta)$ as follows:

$$\frac{P \Rightarrow (\Gamma \cdot (\sigma, \tau, (\textbf{if } e \textbf{ then } s_1 \textbf{ else } s_2); s)\,,\ \theta) \quad V_{\sigma,\tau}(e) = \textbf{true}}{P \Rightarrow (\Gamma \cdot (\sigma, \tau, s_1; s)\,,\ \theta)}\ S_{\text{if-true}}$$

$$\frac{P \Rightarrow (\Gamma \cdot (\sigma, \tau, (\textbf{if } e \textbf{ then } s_1 \textbf{ else } s_2); s)\,,\ \theta) \quad V_{\sigma,\tau}(e) = \textbf{false}}{P \Rightarrow (\Gamma \cdot (\sigma, \tau, s_2; s)\,,\ \theta)}\ S_{\text{if-false}}$$

$$\frac{P \Rightarrow (\Gamma \cdot (\sigma, \tau, (\textbf{while } e \textbf{ do } s'); s)\,,\ \theta)}{P \Rightarrow (\Gamma \cdot (\sigma, \tau, \textbf{if } e \textbf{ then } (s'; \textbf{while } e \textbf{ do } s'); s \textbf{ else } s)\,,\ \theta)}\ S_{\text{while}}$$

$$\frac{P \Rightarrow (\Gamma \cdot (\sigma, \tau, w := e; s)\,,\ \theta)}{P \Rightarrow (\Gamma \cdot (\sigma, \tau, s)[V_{\sigma,\tau}(e)/w]\,,\ \theta)}\ S_{\text{update}}$$

$$\frac{P \Rightarrow (\Gamma \cdot (\sigma, \tau, e!m(e'); s)\,,\ \theta) \quad V_{\sigma,\tau}(e) \in O_C}{P \Rightarrow (\Gamma \cdot (\sigma, \tau, s)\,,\ \theta \cdot \sigma(\textbf{this}) \rightsquigarrow V_{\sigma,\tau}(e).m(V_{\sigma,\tau}(e')))}\ S_{\text{asyn}}$$

$$\frac{P \Rightarrow (\Gamma \cdot (\sigma, \tau, w := \textbf{new } C(e); s)\,,\ \theta) \quad \text{where } o \text{ is fresh}}{P \Rightarrow (\Gamma \cdot (\sigma, \tau, s)[o/w] \cdot [o/\textbf{this}]\,,\ \theta \cdot \sigma(\textbf{this}) \rightsquigarrow o.C(V_{\sigma,\tau}(e)))}\ S_{\text{new}}$$

$$\frac{P \Rightarrow (\Gamma \cdot \sigma\,,\ \theta) \quad \mathit{Sched}(\theta, \sigma(\textbf{this})) = o.\alpha(v) \quad P(\alpha :: s)}{P \Rightarrow (\Gamma \cdot (\sigma, [v/\textbf{arg}], s)\,,\ \theta \cdot o.\alpha(v))}\ Q_{\text{select}}$$

$$\frac{P \Rightarrow (\Gamma \cdot (\sigma, \tau, \textbf{skip})\,,\ \theta)}{P \Rightarrow (\Gamma \cdot \sigma\,,\ \theta)}\ Q_{\text{skip}} \qquad \frac{o \in O_C \quad C \text{ is main class}}{P \Rightarrow ([o/\textbf{this}]\,,\ \top \rightsquigarrow o.C(v))}\ O_{\text{init}}$$

We say $P \Rightarrow (\Gamma, \theta)$ is *derivable* if it can be obtained from above rules.

Our calculus is a "big-step" semantics. To see how our calculus is a trace semantics, we abstract from particular configurations to describe trace reachability:

Definition 2. $T(P)$ denotes the set of reachable traces of program P, that is, $\theta \in T(P)$ iff there is a stable configuration Γ such that $P \Rightarrow (\Gamma, \theta)$ is derivable. A trace θ is *reachable* if there exists a program P such that $\theta \in T(P)$.

A *stable configuration* is a configuration where every object is stable. This technical requirement simplifies the formulation of Axiom 4 in Sect. 3 considerably: otherwise we cannot splice a trace into its segments of input events followed by *all* output events and have to deal with methods that have not yet completed. Moreover, every non-stable configuration can be turned into a stable configuration if every method terminates: let active objects run to completion until a stable configuration is obtained.

For each derivable $P \Rightarrow (\Gamma, \theta)$ and for every reference o, there is at most one object ξ in configuration Γ such that $\xi(\mathbf{this}) = o$. Thus we may treat Γ as a partial map of references to objects, and write $\Gamma(o)$ to denote the unique object ξ for which $\xi(\mathbf{this}) = o$ if it exists. Further, $\Gamma[\xi/o]$ denotes the configuration one obtains from Γ where the object $\Gamma(o)$ is replaced by ξ.

A *local trace* θ_o of a reference o is obtained by the projection of a trace θ to only the events concerning local behavior of o.

$$\begin{aligned}(o \rightsquigarrow o'.\alpha(v) \cdot \theta)_o &= o \rightsquigarrow o'.\alpha(v) \cdot \theta_o \\ (o' \rightsquigarrow o''.\alpha(v) \cdot \theta)_o &= \theta_o \text{ if } o \neq o' \\ (o.\alpha(v) \cdot \theta)_o &= o.\alpha(v) \cdot \theta_o \\ (o'.\alpha(v) \cdot \theta)_o &= \theta_o \text{ if } o \neq o'\end{aligned} \tag{1}$$

This projection records all the outgoing calls generated by o as a caller and all its method and constructor selections. It abstracts from (pending) incoming calls generated by other objects (see Eq. (1) when $o = o''$).

Informally, objects are globally indistinguishable when generating the same local trace (see [2] for a formal treatment). For this, we consider two (local or global) traces *equivalent modulo renaming* when there exists a renaming that makes one of the traces equal to the other. A *renaming* λ is a family of bijections $\{f : O_C \to O_C\}_{C \in \mathcal{C}}$. By applying a renaming to configurations and traces, we substitute every occurrence of a reference $o \in O_C$ by $f(o)$ for the corresponding $f : O_C \to O_C$ in λ. For example, for distinct $o, o', o'' \in O$, the global traces

$$\begin{gathered}\top \rightsquigarrow o.C(\mathbf{true}) \cdot o.C(\mathbf{true}) \cdot o \rightsquigarrow o'.C(\mathbf{false}) \cdot o \rightsquigarrow o'.m(o') \cdot o'.C(\mathbf{false}) \\ \top \rightsquigarrow o'.C(\mathbf{true}) \cdot o'.C(\mathbf{true}) \cdot o' \rightsquigarrow o.C(\mathbf{false}) \cdot o' \rightsquigarrow o.m(o) \cdot o.C(\mathbf{false})\end{gathered}$$

are equivalent modulo renaming. The dummy reference is never renamed. Since we have that the set O of object references is countable, there exists a natural way of mapping references to natural numbers. Consider an encoding of traces, à la N.G. de Bruijn, that incrementally replaces every distinct reference by an index. For example, both traces above have the following encoding:

$$\top \rightsquigarrow \mathbf{1}.C(\mathbf{true}) \cdot \mathbf{1}.C(\mathbf{true}) \cdot \mathbf{1} \rightsquigarrow \mathbf{2}.C(\mathbf{false}) \cdot \mathbf{1} \rightsquigarrow \mathbf{2}.m(\mathbf{2}) \cdot \mathbf{2}.C(\mathbf{false})$$

In different local traces, the indices that encode the same reference may differ depending on the position where it occurs first in a local trace. The same index may be used to encode different references in different traces. In non-empty local traces of a reachable trace, indices of created object are never **1**, and **1** always encodes **this**.

3 Axiomatization

The following general properties describe the FIFO ordering between corresponding events, uniqueness of object creation, consistent data flow, and determinism.

The following axiom states that method calls are selected for execution in a FIFO manner: every input event corresponds to a unique prior output event.

Axiom 1 (FIFO). Let **F** denote the property such that $\theta \models \mathbf{F}$, if for every object reference o and every prefix θ' of θ, it holds that $\theta'?o$ is a prefix of $\theta'!o$.

An object reference o is created by an event $o' \rightsquigarrow o.C(v)$ (or by $\top \rightsquigarrow o.C(v)$, in case of the root object), and we then say that o' created o. We have the following axiom which guarantees uniqueness of object references.

Axiom 2 (Creation). Let **C** denote the property such that $\theta \models \mathbf{C}$, if: (1) the first and only the first event of θ is a root object creation, (2) all references o occurring in θ have been created exactly once, (3) an object cannot create other objects before it has been created itself, and (4) an object cannot create itself.

It is worthwhile to note that the FIFO axiom alone does not rule out that an object can create other objects before it has been created itself. Moreover, we will argue later that the FIFO and Creation axioms together with the following axiom rule out any calls by an object before it has been created.

Let $K_o(\theta)$ denote all the object references that o has created in θ or occur in $\theta?o$. The following axiom captures that every outgoing call of an object contains only prior information about objects that o has created, or that have been acquired by the parameter of a method selection.

Axiom 3 (Knowledge). Let **K** denote the property such that $\theta \models \mathbf{K}$, if for every trace θ' and every reference o, o', o'' and value $v \notin O$ the following holds: (1) if $\theta' \cdot o \rightsquigarrow o'.m(v)$ is a prefix of θ then o' is in $K_o(\theta')$, (2) if $\theta' \cdot o \rightsquigarrow o'.m(o'')$ is a prefix of θ then both o' and o'' are in $K_o(\theta')$, and (3) if $\theta' \cdot o \rightsquigarrow o'.C(o'')$ is a prefix of θ then o'' is in $K_o(\theta')$.

The final axiom describes the local determinism of objects, namely, that output behavior of objects is completely determined by its inputs. To formulate this axiom, consider that every local trace θ_o can be sliced into segments, such that each *segment* starts with an input event followed by as many output events as possible: all segments put back in order forms the local trace we started with. The number of input events of $\theta?o$ is equal to the number of segments of θ_o.

Axiom 4 (Determinism). Let **D** denote the property such that $\theta \models \mathbf{D}$, if for every object reference o', o'' and every trace θ', θ'' such that θ' is a prefix of $\theta?o'$ and θ'' is a prefix of $\theta?o''$ and θ' is equivalent modulo renaming to θ'', the first $|\theta'|$ segments of $\theta_{o'}$ and $\theta_{o''}$ are equivalent modulo renaming.

We illustrate the use of the above axioms by the following properties.

Proposition 1. *For every reference o occurring in θ, there is no output event with o as caller or input event with o as callee* before *the creation event of o.*

Proof. Suppose that o calls a method on another object o', before it has been created. By the Knowledge axiom, o' either must have been created by o or received as parameter before the outgoing method call by o. That o creates another object o' before it has been created itself is ruled out by the Creation axiom. So o must have received o' as a parameter before the outgoing call, and thus before it has been created. But the selection of a method by o *before* the creation event of o leads to an infinite regression: first observe that the FIFO axiom implies the existence of a corresponding (preceding) method call. The Creation and Knowledge axioms in turn imply that the caller of that method call to o has received o as a parameter of a previous method selection. This leads to an infinite sequence of method calls which is obviously impossible as each trace has only a finite number of events. □

Proposition 2. *For every reference appearing in θ, only the first event of its local trace is a constructor selection.*

Proof. If θ_o is empty, we are done. So suppose θ_o is non-empty, and consider its first event. It cannot be an asynchronous call with o as caller, nor the selection of an incoming call to o before its creation event, as these cases are ruled out by Proposition 1. When there is a pending call to o that call must be performed after the creation event of o, and by the FIFO axiom, the first event is the constructor selection. □

Proposition 3. *For every prefix of θ that ends with an object creation of o', there is no occurrence of o' before that creation event.*

Proof. By contradiction: suppose o' occurs in an event before $o \rightsquigarrow o'.C(v)$. It cannot occur as the callee of a creation event by Creation axiom, it cannot occur as an argument of an output event or as the callee of a method call as o' cannot appear in the learned knowledge of any other object before its creation event, and it cannot occur as the caller of an output event or as callee of an input event by Propositions 1 and 2 and the FIFO axiom. These are all possible cases. □

By axiomatization **Ax** we mean the above axioms: **F**, **C**, **K**, **D**. Let ϕ be a property, i.e. a predicate on *arbitrary* traces. A property ϕ is *R-valid* if $\theta \models \phi$ for every *reachable* trace θ (see Definition 2). We have the main soundness theorem.

Theorem 4 (Soundness). *All the axioms of* **Ax** *are R-valid.*

Assuming an arbitrary program it suffices to show that all its reachable traces satisfy the axioms of **Ax**, which can be established by a straightforward though tedious induction on the length of the derivation. As a corollary we infer that **Ax** $\models \phi$ implies that ϕ is R-valid. In other words, every property that follows from the axioms holds for every reachable trace.

4 Program Synthesis

The synthesis problem is to construct a program from a trace which satisfies the axioms **Ax**, such that the program witnesses that the given trace is *reachable*. We assume well-typed traces so that the class and method signature of the synthesized program coincides with the given trace. From the trace we then need to synthesize the method bodies (including the bodies of the constructors) which are expected to provide a general template for all the individual object behaviors as they appear in the trace.

We observe that each local trace, that is the individual object behavior, can be sliced into a number of segments, which consist of an input event followed by a largest possible sequence of consecutive output events. Since every method runs to completion, the output of a segment following an input event must be generated by the method selected by that input event. So we must define a method body in some way as a *choice* between *all* it corresponding segments. This choice requires knowledge of the executing object and the position of each segment in its local trace, which we will represent by an instance variable that serves as a program counter.

A large part of difficulty in solving the synthesis problem comes from the fact that traces contain object references, while programs never directly access such references. However, our programming language does have an equality operator suitable for checking whether two object references are equal. An object may thus learn of the existence of a new object reference, acquired by the argument of a method selection, by comparing it with any other reference it has encountered before. Moreover, values that are not references can be synthesized directly, by the assumption that such values are expressible.

The notion of knowledge is local to an object, since the knowledge of one object is not directly accessible to another object. When an object receives an unknown reference, it cannot determine its exact identity. Thus, under similar circumstances, two objects of the same class that both receive two unknown references that are actually different must be treated as if they were identical, since there is no expression that can tell the actual identity of an object.

An object may perform an outgoing call with as argument a reference that it learned by the argument of any of its previous method selections or by the creation of a new object. We need to ensure that the state of an object, the assignment σ of instance variables to values, reflects the current knowledge of an object. To do so, we update instance variables whenever a (previously unknown) reference is encountered: this happens possibly after a method selection and definitely after object creation. However, how do we determine in what instance variables such learned references are stored?

In order to abstract from the actual object references as they appear in a given trace, the program is synthesized using the above De Bruijn-like encoding[1] for the definition of its (object) instance variables. The encoding gives to each object reference a unique index: obtained by the first occurrence of that reference, counting from left-to-right. An encoded local trace represents an equivalence class of the local behavior of objects. Although two objects can have different behavior, their local behavior may differ only after a number of input events. For the time where the two objects have received equivalent input, the behavior of the two objects must be the same too, since they run the same method bodies to completion. For that reason, our encoding coincides on two equivalent prefixes of local traces.

[1] We say De Bruijn-*like* to mean the same purpose that De Bruijn had in Automath [5]: namely to identify two renaming-equivalent terms. The technical nature of De Bruijn-indices, e.g. in lambda calculus, is different than from here.

Each class C uses the instance variable x_{pc} for the program counter which value corresponds to the current segment. It further uses $x_1, \ldots, x_n$ instance variables, where n is the maximum number of object references which appear in a local trace of an instance of C. The variable x_i represents the storage of an object reference that was encoded by the index i.

The above leads to the following program synthesis. Let θ be a given trace that satisfies the axioms, i.e. $\theta \models \mathbf{Ax}$. By $P(\theta)$ we then denote the resulting synthesized program, that is constructed as follows:

1. For each class C, we collect all prefixes of its local traces in the set $T(\theta, C)$. Formally, $\theta' \in T(\theta, C)$ iff θ' is a prefix of θ_o for some $o \in O_C$.
2. Apply the De Bruijn-like encoding to every trace in $T(\theta, C)$.
3. Construct a forest from the set $T(\theta, C)$ by the prefix order on encoded traces.
4. In the forest, give a unique label to each input event.
5. We then synthesize the constructor and method bodies:
   (a) Do a case distinction on the current position and argument.
   (b) Set the new current position, based on testing the argument.
   (c) Store newly learned knowledge from argument in the state.
   (d) Realize output events of the segment corresponding to current position.
   (e) Store new knowledge from created objects in the state.
6. Declare the class of the root object creation event the main class.

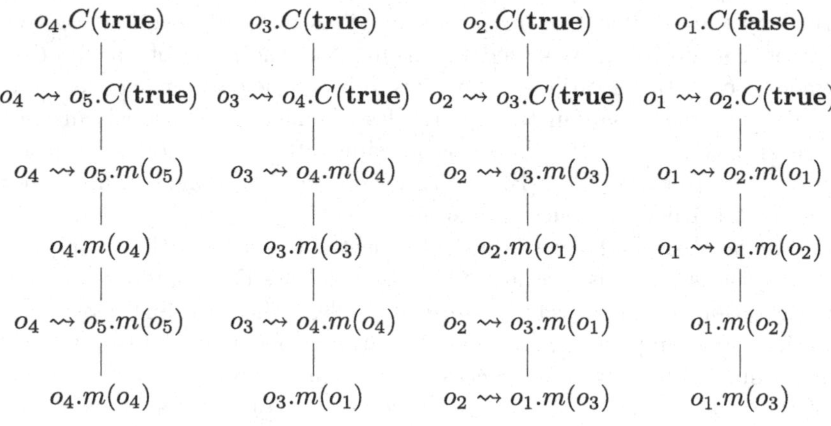

Fig. 1. Example local traces: $\theta_{o_4}, \theta_{o_3}, \theta_{o_2}, \theta_{o_1}$.

We explain the steps of our construction in more detail below, alongside an example trace θ. In our example we deal with only one class: in general, for each class a similar treatment is given. The trace θ starts with the root object creation $\top \rightsquigarrow o_1.C(\mathbf{false})$, and has non-empty local traces $\theta_{o_1}, \theta_{o_2}, \theta_{o_3}, \theta_{o_4}$, and the other local trace, θ_{o_5}, is empty. Only the local traces are shown in Fig. 1. This is also the result of collecting the local traces per class (Step 1).

(Step 2) We bring the local traces in a particular form: we apply an encoding to ensure that two local traces that are equivalent modulo renaming are identified. By the way we encode each object reference with an increasing index, it is ensured that two local traces that have a common prefix modulo renaming have the same encoding on that prefix. Figure 2 shows the encoded traces of the local traces of Fig. 1. These encodings have different interpretations per local trace: e.g. in θ_{o_1} we have $\mathbf{1} \mapsto o_1$, $\mathbf{2} \mapsto o_2$, $\mathbf{3} \mapsto o_3$, but in θ_{o_2} we have a different one: $\mathbf{1} \mapsto o_2$, $\mathbf{2} \mapsto o_3$, $\mathbf{3} \mapsto o_1$.

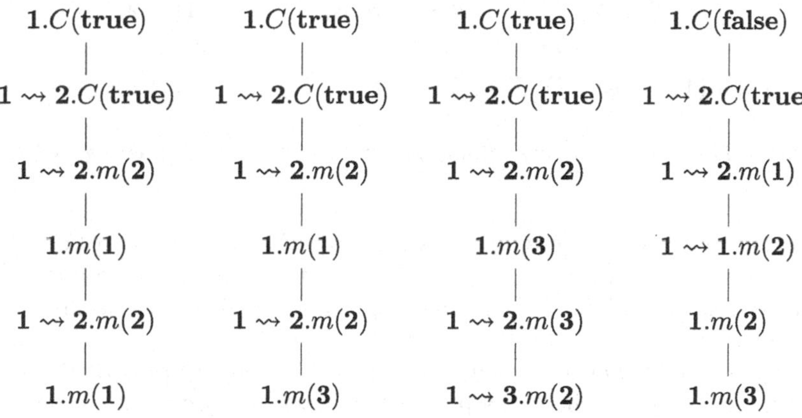

Fig. 2. Result of the encoding of the local traces of Fig. 1.

(Step 3) The set of local traces $T(\theta, C)$ allows us to construct a forest: nodes correspond to events, edges describe the order between events within a local trace. Roots correspond to a constructor selection event, and every path from a root to a leaf corresponds to a local trace. Every two traces that have a common prefix also have a common ancestor in the forest: the last event of the common prefix. It is crucial to construct the forest only *after* encoding the local traces. Figure 3 shows the forest upside down.

(Step 4) We find a labeling of every input event in the forest, by numbering input events in a breath-first left-to-right manner (as shown in Fig. 3 by the circled numbers). Observe that each segment of a local trace corresponds to a path segment in the forest, since it comprises the same events. This correspondence becomes important later, when we realize the output events. Our labeling is used as a *program counter*, to keep track of the possible local traces that an object simulates: at any prefix the object may not yet know which path it will take in the future. In other words, if two different paths from root to leaf have a common ancestor, the object that simulates either of them does not yet know which object it simulates until a choice is made after the common ancestor.

(Step 5) For a given class, we now synthesize its constructor and method bodies. We first describe snippets of statements that implement a particular feature of the construction, and then give the overall construction of class definitions

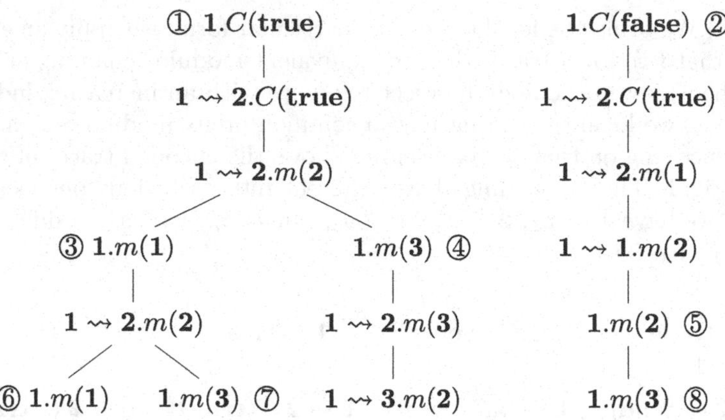

Fig. 3. Forest with shared common prefixes and numbered input events.

as a scheme that pastes these snippets together. As already described above, each class uses the following instance variables: x_1 up to x_n corresponding to encoded references, and x_{pc} for the program counter which value is the current path segment.

Testing the state and argument and set the current position in the forest: after an input event, we check the program counter and argument to decide at which place in the forest the object currently is. After a constructor selection, the program counter has an undefined initial value, and we only inspect the argument. For our example we have these tests:

$$\begin{aligned}
&\mathit{test}_C = \mathbf{if}\ \mathbf{arg} = \mathbf{true}\ \mathbf{then}\ x_{\mathrm{pc}} := 1\\
&\quad \mathbf{else\ if}\ \mathbf{arg} = \mathbf{false}\ \mathbf{then}\ x_{\mathrm{pc}} := 2\\
&\quad \mathbf{else\ skip}
\end{aligned}$$

$$\begin{aligned}
&\mathit{test}_m = \mathbf{if}\ x_{\mathrm{pc}} = 1 \wedge \mathbf{arg} = \mathbf{this}\ \mathbf{then}\ x_{\mathrm{pc}} := 3\\
&\quad \mathbf{else\ if}\ x_{\mathrm{pc}} = 1 \quad \mathbf{then}\ x_{\mathrm{pc}} := 4\\
&\quad \mathbf{else\ if}\ x_{\mathrm{pc}} = 2 \wedge \mathbf{arg} = x_2 \quad \mathbf{then}\ x_{\mathrm{pc}} := 5\\
&\quad \mathbf{else\ if}\ x_{\mathrm{pc}} = 3 \wedge \mathbf{arg} = \mathbf{this}\ \mathbf{then}\ x_{\mathrm{pc}} := 6\\
&\quad \mathbf{else\ if}\ x_{\mathrm{pc}} = 3 \quad \mathbf{then}\ x_{\mathrm{pc}} := 7\\
&\quad \mathbf{else\ if}\ x_{\mathrm{pc}} = 5 \quad \mathbf{then}\ x_{\mathrm{pc}} := 8\\
&\quad \mathbf{else\ skip}
\end{aligned}$$

There are three kinds of tests on arguments: a value tested for equality (e.g. $\mathbf{arg} = \mathbf{true}$), a known reference is checked (e.g. $\mathbf{arg} = \mathbf{this}$ or $\mathbf{arg} = x_2$), or a reference is unknown (e.g. when $x_{\mathrm{pc}} = 1$ or 3 or 5). The last kind of test is checked after all known references are checked, since if all tests of known references fail the reference must be unknown. For method selections, we check the previous value of the program counter to decide which conditions to check (e.g. for $x_{\mathrm{pc}} = 1$ only the input events 3 and 4 could match). We never test for possibilities that do not occur in our forest.

Case distinction on the current position: after the former step of deciding the current position, we will perform three other tasks: if applicable, store the newly learned knowledge from the argument in an instance variable. Then we perform the output events by asynchronous method calling and object creation statements, and further store the newly learned knowledge from object creations in instance variables. The purpose of performing a case distinction on the current position is to realize output events that correspond to a segment. For example:

$$
\begin{array}{l}
out_C = \textbf{if } x_{\mathrm{pc}} = 1 \textbf{ then}\\
\quad\quad x_2 := \textbf{new } C(\textbf{true});\\
\quad\quad x_2!m(x_2)\\
\quad \textbf{else if } x_{\mathrm{pc}} = 2 \textbf{ then}\\
\quad\quad x_2 := \textbf{new } C(\textbf{true});\\
\quad\quad x_2!m(\textbf{this});\\
\quad\quad \textbf{this}!m(x_2)\\
\quad \textbf{else skip}
\end{array}
\qquad
\begin{array}{l}
out_m = \textbf{if } x_{\mathrm{pc}} = 3 \textbf{ then}\\
\quad\quad x_2!m(x_2)\\
\quad \textbf{else if } x_{\mathrm{pc}} = 4 \textbf{ then}\\
\quad\quad x_3 := \textbf{arg};\\
\quad\quad x_2!m(x_3);\\
\quad\quad x_3!m(x_2)\\
\quad \textbf{else if } x_{\mathrm{pc}} = 5 \textbf{ then}\\
\quad\quad \textbf{skip}\\
\quad \textbf{else if } x_{\mathrm{pc}} = 6 \textbf{ then}\\
\quad\quad \textbf{skip}\\
\quad \textbf{else if } x_{\mathrm{pc}} = 7 \textbf{ then}\\
\quad\quad x_3 := \textbf{arg}\\
\quad \textbf{else if } x_{\mathrm{pc}} = 8 \textbf{ then}\\
\quad\quad x_3 := \textbf{arg}\\
\quad \textbf{else skip}
\end{array}
$$

For object creation events we synthesize a **new**-statement and store the reference in the instance variable corresponding to the encoded index as it occurs the local trace. For asynchronous method calls, we simply perform that action. For both output events, argument values are synthesized by constants, and argument references (and the callee reference) are looked up by its corresponding instance variable (or the special **this**-variable for the first occurrence **1**, that always refers to the reference of the object itself). Note how segments 4, 7, 8 first store the argument, before realizing any output (if any).

The synthesized program has a unique class definition for every class C: we take $C(\textbf{arg}) :: test_C; out_C$ as constructor definition and $m(\textbf{arg}) :: test_m; out_m$ as method definition for each method m. Finally, the class that appears in the root object creation of our trace will be taken as main class of the program.

Completeness. Correctness of the above construction requires the following auxiliary notions which allow us to construct explicitly the global configuration that is used as witness for reachability. For every object reference o that occurs in a global trace θ, we know that the local trace θ_o can be encoded in a De Bruijn-like way as described above. Formally, by $e(\theta, o) : O \to I$ we denote the partial function that encodes the occurring references in θ_o as an index, and by

$d(\theta, o) : I \to O$ we denote the partial function that decodes the indices to the actual object reference, such that $d(e(o')) = o'$ for every reference o' that occurs in θ_o, where we write $e(\theta, o)$ and $d(\theta, o)$ simply as e and d since θ and o are clear from context.

Also for every object reference o of class C that occurs in θ, there is a path θ_o from root to leave in the forest $T(\theta, C)$. As explained above, the forest $T(\theta, C)$ associates to each input event node a unique label: by $\ell(\theta' \cdot o.\alpha(v))$ we denote that label for each prefix $\theta' \cdot o.\alpha(v)$ of θ_o. The construction of this forest has the property that there are only choice branches *before* input events: this property follows from Determinism Axiom 4.

The function f will construct the local state of object o, which will be contained in a global configuration corresponding to the trace θ. Recall that for each index $i \in I$ there is an instance variable x_i, and x_{pc} is the program counter. We treat the first occurrence in a local trace specially, as it can always be retrieved by **this**. In the following, let ϵ be the empty trace:

$$f(\theta_o \cdot o \rightsquigarrow o'.D(v)) = f(\theta_o)[o'/x_{e(o')}]$$
$$f(\theta_o \cdot o \rightsquigarrow o'.m(v)) = f(\theta_o)$$
$$f(\theta_o \cdot o.\alpha(v)) = \begin{cases} f(\theta_o)[\ell(\theta_o \cdot o.\alpha(v))/x_{\text{pc}}][v/x_{e(v)}] & \text{if } v \in O \\ f(\theta_o)[\ell(\theta_o \cdot o.\alpha(v))/x_{\text{pc}}] & \text{otherwise} \end{cases}$$
$$f(\epsilon) = [o/\mathbf{this}]$$

The above function results in stable objects. Furthermore, f is also well-defined for all prefixes of local traces. We have that for any *non-empty* prefix θ' of θ_o, the set of references contained in object $f(\theta')$ equals the set $K_o(\theta')$. Note that for objects that are created but have not yet selected the constructor, their knowledge set is empty but their state is already $[o/\mathbf{this}]$.

Lemma 5. *Every trace θ for which $\theta \models$* **Ax** *holds, is reachable.*

Proof. We assume $\theta \models \mathbf{Ax}$ holds. To show that θ is reachable, we show there exists a stable configuration Γ such that $P(\theta) \Rightarrow (\Gamma, \theta)$, where $P(\theta)$ denotes the synthesized program, as described above. We construct a particular global configuration out of objects which are obtained by the above function of local traces, and use that as witness for Γ. In particular, that configuration consists of a sequence of objects $f(\theta_o)$ for every reference o that occurs in θ.

What remains is to show that $P(\theta) \Rightarrow (\Gamma, \theta)$ is derivable (see Definition 1). We prove the existence of such a derivation by induction of the length of θ. By the Creation Axiom 2, the base case is captured by an application of the rule O_{init} that generates the root object creation and the initial configuration.

For any proper prefix θ' of θ, the induction hypothesis states the existence of a derivation $P(\theta) \Rightarrow (\Gamma', \theta')$, such that for each object reference o in θ' there is an object $\Gamma'(o)$. In either case that $\Gamma'(o) = \sigma$ or $\Gamma'(o) = (\sigma, \tau, s)$, we have that $\sigma = f(\theta'_o)$, meaning that the object is in a well-known state as constructed from its local trace. If the local trace is empty, the object has not yet selected its constructor. Otherwise, we know that its state has a valid program counter: this points to a particular input node in the forest, corresponding to the last selected input event. For active objects, we can relate the current statement even further to an output node in the forest, since the synthesized program is constructed along the same forest. For stable objects, there is no next output node and the object waits for the next method selection. Note that although our goal configuration Γ is stable, the intermediary Γ' is not necessarily stable. The induction step consists of a case analysis of the different next events.

1. The next event is either a constructor selection $o.C(v)$ or method selection $o.m(v)$. By FIFO Axiom 1, we know the construction selection corresponds to a prior creation event that is pending. There exists a stable object configuration $\Gamma(o)$ on which we apply the rule Q_{select} to generate the selection event. In case of a method selection, we know that the current program counter value is defined: the synthesized program first checks which branches in the forest have to be checked (as described in detail above). After running the synthesized body until its first output event or until completion, we have assigned the program counter and updated the knowledge acquired by the argument if v was a reference and not encountered before.
2. The next event is $o \rightsquigarrow o'.m(v)$. By Proposition 1, we know that o must have been created before this output event. Moreover, the object $\Gamma(o)$ is an active object, where the next statement is an asynchronous method call by construction: we apply the rule S_{asyn}, where we evaluate the callee expression and argument expression. By Knowledge Axiom 3, we know that o' is in $K_o(\theta')$ and since the local history of θ_o is non-empty, this equals $f(\theta'_o)$. Hence, the callee expression $x_e(o')$ results in the object reference o'. Similar for argument references.
3. The next event is $o \rightsquigarrow o'.C(v)$. The object $\Gamma(o)$ is an active object, where the next statement is an object creation statement by construction: the resulting reference will be stored in the corresponding instance variable $x_e(o')$. We know that o' is fresh in the current trace by the FIFO axiom, Creation axiom and Knowledge axiom. Thus we can apply S_{new}, where we choose o' as fresh reference, to add $[o'/\textbf{this}]$ to the global configuration (being $f(\epsilon)$ for o'). For the argument, similar as above. □

Finally, we can state our completeness result with a straightforward proof.

Theorem 6 (Completeness). *If ϕ is R-valid then* $\mathbf{Ax} \models \phi$.

Proof. Let ϕ be R-valid. We have to show that $\mathbf{Ax} \models \phi$. Assume $\theta \models \mathbf{Ax}$. Now, by Lemma 5, trace θ is reachable. Since ϕ is R-valid, we conclude that $\theta \models \phi$. □

5 Future Extensions

In this section we sketch how to extend our axiomatization to cooperative scheduling and futures. First, we consider cooperative scheduling by means of

Boolean **await**-statements. Semantically such statements require the inclusion of a set Q of suspended processes (τ, s): an object ξ is either stable (Q, σ) or active (Q, σ, τ, s). We have the following semantic rules rules Q_{await} and Q_{resume} for the suspension and resumption of processes:

$$\frac{P \Rightarrow (\Gamma \cdot (Q, \sigma, \tau, \textbf{await } e; s), \theta)}{P \Rightarrow (\Gamma \cdot (Q \cup \{(\tau, \textbf{await } e; s)\}, \sigma, \theta)} \; Q_{\text{await}}$$

$$\frac{P \Rightarrow (\Gamma \cdot (Q \cup \{(\tau, \textbf{await } e; s)\}, \sigma), \theta) \quad V_{\sigma,\tau}(e) = \textbf{true}}{P \Rightarrow (\Gamma \cdot (Q, \sigma, \tau, s), \theta)} \; Q_{\text{resume}}$$

Clearly the extended language gives rise to non-determinism in the sense that the input events no longer determine the local behavior of an object because of the non-deterministic internal scheduling of the methods. We must therefore weaken Axiom 4 to apply only for the first segment. Note that the first segment corresponds to outputs which can be generated by the constructor method only and these outputs only depend on the input parameter. The main construction underlying the above program synthesis crucially exploits the general determinism. Therefore, instead of synthesizing the individual method bodies in terms of the output events of the given trace, all the output behavior of all the instances of a given class is synthesized in the body of the constructor. The body of the constructor is in this setting a loop, in which the statement $b := \textbf{true}; \textbf{await true}; b := \textbf{false}$ precedes a large case distinction on the program counter, and each case consists of a sequence of method calls (corresponding to the sequence of output events of a segment). The Boolean instance variable b controls the internal scheduling, as described below. When the constructor releases control, a new method can be selected (as expected by the given trace) which first checks and updates the local state as before. After that, the method enters a loop the body of which consists of an update of the program counter followed by an **await true** statement, which may release control. The loop condition is simply $b = \textbf{true}$. The updates of the program counter systematically generates all its possible values (as generated from the given trace). As soon as the constructor method is scheduled again, it thus can proceed with a non-deterministically generated value of the program counter (which corresponds to the number of iterations of the above loop). Note that when the method is scheduled again the above loop will terminate. In showing reachability, one can steer towards the right number of times a method is (re)scheduled to set the counter to the right value.

Next, we briefly sketch the extension to futures, as employed by the ABS language (see also [1]), where futures are dynamically generated references to return values and as such provide an asynchronous communication of these values. This extension consists of a further refinement of the above scheme. It introduces two kinds of events: the completion of a future (by a return statement) and a successful **get** operation on a future. Both input and output events record as additional parameter the future which uniquely identifies the event. Further, we have additional axioms which state that a completion of a future has to be preceded by the corresponding method selection, and that a get event is preceded by the corresponding completion event. The Creation axiom has also to be extended to ensure the uniqueness of futures, so that every future recorded in an asynchronous method call is unique.

In solving the synthesis problem, futures can only be completed by the return statement of the corresponding method. But as output behavior is realized within the constructor, the constructor method has to release control back to the corresponding method. Each method body is augmented with an "exit protocol" which precedes the return statement and which consists of the statement **await** $r = d$, where r is an instance variable which is set by the constructor and which stores the future that should be completed. The local variable d, the so-called destiny variable, is an implicit formal parameter of every method which hold its own future, that is, the unique future for returning a value.

A more formal treatment of these extensions is left for future work.

6 Discussion

To the best of our knowledge this is a first sound and complete axiomatization of trace reachability for concurrent objects. Doveland et al. [7] present a proof theory for concurrent objects that uses traces for compositional reasoning. Their traces satisfy certain well-formedness conditions, but completeness of their well-formedness conditions is not mentioned. Din and Owe [6] present a soundness and completeness of a proof system for reasoning about asynchronous communication with shared futures. Their proof system also is based on well-formed traces, but soundness and completeness focuses on program correctness instead.

It is worthwhile to note the analogy between our completeness proof and existing completeness proofs of a variety of logics (first-order logic, modal and intuitionistic logics) which in general are based on the so-called "model existence theorem" (see [9]). In our completeness proof the program synthesis corresponds to such a theorem which states the existence of a model for a theory which satisfies certain consistency requirements.

We are currently working on mechanically verifying the established results, formalizing the presented results in the context of the Lean interactive theorem prover. The bulk of this on-going work comprises proving soundness of the axioms, and proving our solution to the synthesis problem correct.

Further ahead is a trace logic that allows the formulation of user-defined class specifications and global invariants. This requires formalization of the trace logic itself, resulting in a trace specification language. The axioms as given above can be formulated in the trace logic, and a corresponding proof system can then establish general properties of reachable traces. Such a system can be integrated with proof methods for verifying the correctness of concurrent object programs, where class definitions are annotated with invariants on the properties of local traces of its objects, and a user-defined global invariant that describes properties of global traces. Any property that follows from the axioms can thus be inferred directly, without requiring such properties to be encoded in global invariants.

Our program synthesis is a step towards the full abstraction problem, that yet remains to be addressed for active object languages. Another application of the program synthesis is to provide a formal model for generating testing environments. A test case describes the desirable properties of traces, similar to Ducasse et al. [8] By synthesizing a program that reproduces a trace that satisfies the desirable property, and substituting in the resulting program a class under test, allows one to test a class definition in isolation of the rest of a system: we can test whether the desired trace is indeed reachable after such a substitution. This could lead to practical applications by the integration of above methods.

Acknowledgements. Thanks to Lars Tveito for visiting our research group and for having many interesting discussions, Roy Overbeek for reading a draft, and the anonymous referees for their suggestions.

References

1. de Boer, F.S., Clarke, D., Johnsen, E.B.: A Complete guide to the future. In: De Nicola, R. (ed.) ESOP 2007. LNCS, vol. 4421, pp. 316–330. Springer, Heidelberg (2007). https://doi.org/10.1007/978-3-540-71316-6_22
2. de Boer, F.S., de Gouw, S.: Compositional semantics for concurrent object groups in ABS. Principled Software Development, pp. 87–98. Springer, Cham (2018). https://doi.org/10.1007/978-3-319-98047-8_6
3. de Boer, F.S., et al.: A survey of active object languages. ACM Comput. Surv. **50**(5), 76:1–76:39 (2017)
4. de Roever, W.P., et al.: Concurrency Verification: Introduction to Compositional and Noncompositional Methods. Cambridge Tracts in Theoretical Computer Science, vol. 54. Cambridge University Press, Cambridge (2001)
5. Dechesne, F., Nederpelt, R.: N.G. de Bruijn (1918–2012) and his road to automath the earliest proof checker. Math. Intell. **34**(4), 4–11 (2012)
6. Din, C.C., Owe, O.: A sound and complete reasoning system for asynchronous communication with shared futures. J. Logical Algebraic Methods Program. **83**(5), 360–383 (2014)
7. Dovland, J., Johnsen, E.B., Owe, O.: Verification of concurrent objects with asynchronous method calls. In: IEEE International Conference on Software - Science, Technology and Engineering (SwSTE 2005), 22–23 February 2005, Herzelia, Israel, pp. 141–150 (2005)
8. Ducasse, S., Girba, T., Wuyts, R.: Object-oriented legacy system trace-based logic testing. In: Conference on Software Maintenance and Reengineering (CSMR 2006), pp. 37–46. IEEE (2006)
9. Fitting, M.: Proof methods for modal and intuitionistic logics. J. Symbolic Logic **50**(3), 855–856 (1985)
10. Johnsen, E.B., Hähnle, R., Schäfer, J., Schlatte, R., Steffen, M.: ABS: a core language for abstract behavioral specification. In: Aichernig, B.K., de Boer, F.S., Bonsangue, M.M. (eds.) FMCO 2010. LNCS, vol. 6957, pp. 142–164. Springer, Heidelberg (2011). https://doi.org/10.1007/978-3-642-25271-6_8

Dynamic Reconfigurations in Frequency Constrained Data Flow

Paul Dubrulle[1(✉)], Christophe Gaston[1], Nikolai Kosmatov[1,2], and Arnault Lapitre[1]

[1] CEA, List, 91191 Gif-sur-Yvette, France
{paul.dubrulle,christophe.gaston, nikolai.kosmatov,arnault.lapitre}@cea.fr

[2] Thales Research and Technology, Palaiseau, France

Abstract. In Cyber-Physical Systems, the software components are often distributed over several computing nodes, connected by a communication network. Depending on several factors, the behavior of these components may dynamically change during its execution. The existing data flow formalisms for the performance prediction of dynamic systems do not cover the real-time constraints of these systems, and suffer from complexity issues in the verification of mandatory model properties. To overcome these limitations, we propose a dynamic extension to Polygraph, a static data flow formalism covering the real-time behavior of the CPS components. We also propose a verification algorithm to determine if the transitions between different modes are well-defined for a given model. Initial experiments show that this algorithm can be efficiently applied in practice.

1 Introduction

Context. Cyber-Physical Systems (CPS) are increasingly present in everyday life. These systems are often distributed over several computing nodes, connected by a communication network. For example, the next generation of autonomous vehicles will heavily rely on sensor fusion systems to operate the car. Sensors and actuators are distributed over the car, in places where their measure or action makes sense, while fusion kernels operate on high-performance computation platforms. A network connects these elements together, and in some cases the computation kernels can even be off-loaded to remote servers over wireless connections.

Depending on several factors, the behavior of the software components of a CPS may change during its execution. The algorithms used to process data may change depending on the nature of the input data, and a component may even be deactivated due to an external factor. In an autonomous car for example, the components implementing a parking assistance functionality relying on a rear-view camera may operate at a lower resolution while driving on a highway, or even be deactivated completely.

W. Ahrendt and S. L. Tapia Tarifa (Eds.): IFM 2019, LNCS 11918, pp. 175–193, 2019.
https://doi.org/10.1007/978-3-030-34968-4_10

When network communication is involved, an analysis of the communications between the components is necessary to determine the bandwidth and memory necessary to respect the application's real-time requirements. Dynamic variations in execution time and bandwidth usage due to changes in the behavior of the components must be taken into account in the performance prediction.

Several extensions to static data flow formalisms [2,9] can be used to perform this kind of performance analysis, taking dynamic reconfigurations into account [6,7,11,14,15]. In general for data flow formalisms, a prerequisite to analyze a model is the existence of a periodic schedule in bounded memory without deadlock, sometimes called an admissible schedule.

Motivation and Goals. Dynamic data flow models are adapted to capture reconfigurations in a CPS, but they lack expressiveness regarding the real-time synchronization of the components interfaced with the physical world. Recent research introduced Polygraph, a new static data flow formalism that covers such synchronous behavior [5], while allowing asynchronous behavior for computation kernels. Our goal is to extend Polygraph to support the expression of dynamic reconfigurations, describing more precisely the behavior of distributed CPS, thus allowing a refinement of the static performance analysis of the resulting models.

Approach and Main Results. This paper proposes to extend Polygraph models with the specification of different operational modes, in a way inspired by the well-known Scenario-Aware Data Flow (SADF) [14]. We rely on additional type information on the communication data to dynamically change the execution mode of the components that receive it, allowing for a distributed control of the current operational modes in the system. With our approach, if there is an admissible schedule for a polygraph model without any mode extension, this schedule is admissible for any of its extended versions. For a given model, this property allows to specify as many modes as required by the real-life system, without impacting the cost of the verification of the existence of such a schedule. In addition, we propose an algorithm to check that the dynamic changes in the modes of the components never lead to incoherent states where a component is supposed to execute in two different modes.

The contributions of this work include:

- an extension to the Polygraph data flow formalism, to support dynamic changes between static configurations of the modeled system;
- a proof of additional properties on the executions of non-extended polygraphs, and properties on their extended executions; these properties are proved in all generality, for an arbitrary reconfiguration strategy;
- an algorithm that, given an extended polygraph with an admissible schedule, checks that the current mode of the polygraph is always defined;
- an implementation of that algorithm in the DIVERSITY tool, and initial experiments to validate this approach.

Outline. The remainder of this paper is organized as follows. Section 2 gives an informal introduction to the proposed modeling approach. In Sect. 3, we remind the formalization of Polygraph, prove additional execution properties, and formalize the extension. Section 4 presents the verification algorithm and an initial evaluation of its implementation. In Sect. 5, we discuss related work, while Sect. 6 presents conclusion and perspectives.

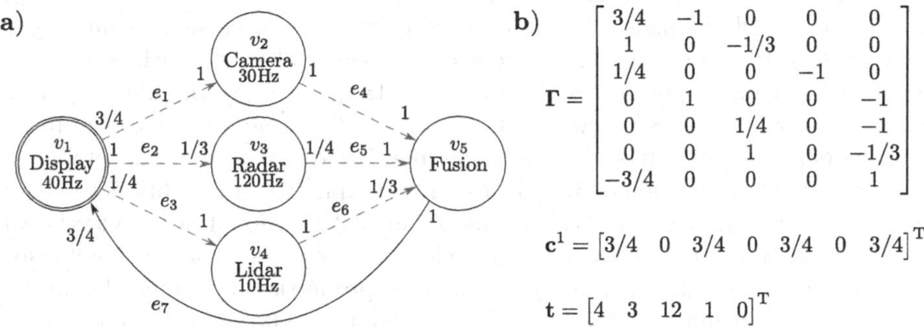

Fig. 1. (a) A cockpit display system modeled as a polygraph denoted $\mathcal{P}_1$, and (b) its topology matrix $\mathbf{\Gamma}$, initial channel state $\mathbf{c}^1$, and vector of synchronous constraints $\mathbf{t}$.

2 Motivation

To introduce the dynamic extension to Polygraph, we use a toy example of a data fusion system that could be integrated into the cockpit display of a car, depicted in Fig. 1. The system is composed of three sensors producing data samples to be used by a data fusion component, and a display component. The first sensor component is a video camera producing frames. The other two sensor components analyze radar and lidar based samples to produce a descriptor of the closest detected obstacles. The fusion component uses this information to draw the obstacle descriptors on the corresponding frame. The display component is a touch screen, and the driver can choose to activate or deactivate the rendering of the enhanced camera feed through an interface on the screen. The driver can also choose to deactivate only the lidar. This leads to three different configurations for the fusion sub-system: all the components are active (denoted *all*), all the components are active except the lidar (denoted *no lidar*), and the three sensor components are inactive (denoted *none*).

Existing Semantic. The Polygraph language is a data flow formalism enabling static performance analysis of systems mixing real-time and compute intensive components. Compared to existing static data flow formalisms [2,9,10], Polygraph mixes synchronous and asynchronous constraints for the execution of a model, and is well-suited to capture the real-life constraints of the CPS.

The core element of Polygraph is a *system graph*, capturing data dependencies between the components. Each vertex of this graph models an *actor*, an abstract entity representing the function of a component. Each directed edge of the graph models a communication *channel*, the source actor being the producer of data consumed by the destination actor. The communication policy on the channels is First-In First-Out (FIFO), the write operation is non-blocking, and the read operation is blocking. The actors communicate by *firing*, an atomic process during which they consume and produce a certain number of data *tokens* on the connected channels. The number of tokens produced or consumed per firing of an actor on a channel is specified by a rational *rate*, which is adapted to capture resampling of data streams. Figure 1a gives an example of a system graph with rational rates (shown near the ends of the edges) for our example.

Considering only the modeling elements mentioned so far, the model of Fig. 1a is equivalent to a Fractional Rate Data Flow graph [10]. In addition to these elements, Polygraph introduces a specific semantic for rational rates, whose goal is to approximate a non-linear behavior with integer rates by a linear behavior with rational rates, and thus to gain the good properties of a linear behavior. It allows rational initial conditions on the channels. The detailed semantic is recalled in Sect. 3.1.

The main advantage of Polygraph is the capability to label a subset of actors with *frequencies*, corresponding to the real-life constraints imposed for example by the sampling rates of the sensors (see the frequency labels on v_1, v_2, v_3, and v_4 in Fig. 1a). The actors that do not have a specified frequency correspond to computation kernels, which in real-life systems often compute as soon as enough input data is available (notice the absence of a frequency label on v_5 in Fig. 1a). A *global clock* provides *ticks* to synchronize the firings of frequency labeled actors, introducing global synchronous behavior in the data flow graph.

A prerequisite to analyze the performance of a Polygraph model is the existence of a periodic schedule with two properties. The first property, *consistency*, requires that the sizes of communication buffers remain bounded for an unbounded execution of the periodic schedule. In practice, if a model is not consistent, it is not possible to implement the communications without losing data samples. The second property, *liveness*, requires the absence of deadlocks in the schedule. The semantic of Polygraph is detailed in [5], including a proof that the existence of an *admissible schedule* with both consistency and liveness properties is decidable and can be checked in practice.

Dynamic Extension. The different configurations of our fusion example could be captured by the scenario concept introduced in Scenario Aware Data Flow (SADF) [14], which encompasses the semantic of many other dynamic data flow formalisms (see Sect. 5). In SADF, some actors receive the role of detector, and are in charge of broadcasting the current scenario to other actors. Each actor impacted by the decisions of a detector has a different rate specification and execution time per possible scenario. Before firing, such an actor reads the scenario information received from the detector and then fires with the appropriate rates and execution time. Special care is required from the designer when specifying the alternative rates, to avoid situations where an actor consumes tokens produced in two different scenarios, that we call an *indecision*. An SADF model with no indecision is said to be *strongly consistent* (see [14] for more detail).

In our context, there are several issues that do not allow for a direct reuse of this concept. First of all, unlike Polygraph, SADF does not capture synchronous constraints for a subset of actors. Second, since the rates are the main parameter influencing the existence of an admissible schedule, a separate check is required for each possible combination of scenarios, which does not scale up well for real-life systems with many configurations. Finally, the broadcasting of the detected scenario has several disadvantages. Additional channels impede the model's readability, and increase the modeling complexity, since the designer needs to know the number of firings of each scenario-dependent actor in a schedule to specify appropriate output rates on the control channels. In addition, the idea of a centralized orchestrator implies additional synchronizations, with a negative impact on the overall performance for distributed architectures. Our proposal extends Polygraph with similar concepts, preserving the support of synchronous constraints, and trying to overcome these limitations.

Modes. We introduce the notion of *modes* for a polygraph. A mode is decided for each firing of an actor, and it is similar to a scenario. The main difference is that the rates do not change in different modes. Instead, a mode change implies a change in the contents of produced data tokens. For example, for the three aforementioned configurations in Fig. 1, the firing of each actor can have one of three user-defined modes λ_1 (*all*), λ_2 (*no lidar*), λ_3 (*none*), which can be used to enable a non-trivial behavior. For one firing of the lidar actor, it will produce 1 token regardless of the decided mode of that firing. The produced token will hold an obstacle descriptor if the firing has mode λ_1. For the other modes λ_2 and λ_3, since the lidar is disabled in the corresponding configurations, the produced token will hold an empty descriptor. With scenarios, a similar behavior would require rate 1 in scenario *all* and 0 in the other scenarios.

The fact that the rates are fixed, regardless of the mode of a firing, brings an important benefit. The existence of an admissible schedule for an extended polygraph can be verified once and for all, by considering the polygraph without modes. We show that by construction of the extension in Sect. 3.3.

Modes allow for a rich set of options: when the firing of an actor can have two or more different modes, configuration parameters (produced data type, execution time, placement, code version, etc.) may change depending on the mode, enabling static analysis of the modeled system with many different objectives. Our goal here being to provide a formal presentation of the modeling language, its mechanism for changing modes dynamically in an execution, and its properties, we do not detail how such parameters are associated to modes.

Mode Propagation. Like in SADF, in our proposal, some actors, called *selectors*, are in charge of identifying reconfigurations and notifying the impacted actors, called *followers*. But unlike SADF, we do not require that selectors broadcast the selection information to all their followers. Instead, we define the propagation of modes transitively from a selector to its followers. In Fig. 1a, the double-circled display actor is a good candidate to be the selector responsible for the three user-defined modes λ_1, λ_2, and λ_3, since it reads the user input that will decide of the configuration. It does not require a specific channel connected to the fusion actor, the mode information will reach it through the channels represented with dashed arrows.

The advantage of this approach is that we do not need channels between a selector and its followers which are not its direct successors. This overcomes the issues caused by these channels. The propagation by transitivity also provides means to automatically check the absence of indecision in a model.

3 The Polygraph Modeling Language

We denote by $\mathbb{Z}$ the set of integers, by $\mathbb{N} = \{n \in \mathbb{Z} \,|\, n \geqslant 0\}$ the set of natural integers, and by $\mathbb{Q}$ the set of rational numbers. A number $r \in \mathbb{Q}$ rounded down (resp., up) to a closest integer is denoted by $\lfloor r \rfloor$ (resp., $\lceil r \rceil$), and the fractional part of r is denoted $\lfloor r \rceil = r - \lfloor r \rfloor$.

For a set A, we denote by A^* the set of all finite *words* over A (i.e. sequences of elements of A), and by A^+ the set of non-empty words.[1] The length of a word $w = a^1 \cdots a^n \in A^*$ is denoted $|w| = n$, and the ith element of w is denoted $w[i] = a_i$. For any $a \in A$ and for any $n \in \mathbb{N}$ we denote $n * a$ the word composed of n occurrences of a. For any word $w \in A^*$ and $0 \leqslant l \leqslant |w|$, the suffix of w of length l is denoted suffix(w, l). For any two words w and w', the concatenation of w and w' is denoted by $w \cdot w'$ or ww'.

3.1 Background

A *system graph* is a connected finite directed graph $G = (V, E)$ with set of vertices (or *actors*) V and set of edges (or *channels*) $E \subseteq V \times V$. We consider that V and E are indexed respectively by $\{1, \cdots, |V|\}$ and $\{1, \cdots, |E|\}$, and denote by v_j the actor of index j and by e_i the channel of index i. For an actor v_j, let $\text{in}(v_j) = \{\langle v_k, v_j \rangle \in E \,|\, v_k \in V\}$ denote the set of *input channels* of v_j; $\text{out}(v_j) = \{\langle v_j, v_k \rangle \in E \,|\, v_k \in V\}$ the set of *output channels* of v_j.

For any pair of a channel e_i and an actor v_j, we associate a *rate* γ_{ij} which is a rational number whose absolute value defines the partial production or consumption effect on e_i of each firing of v_j, and whose sign indicates if the effect is a partial production ($\gamma_{ij} > 0$) or consumption ($\gamma_{ij} < 0$). By convention, the rate γ_{ij} must be 0 if v_j is not connected to e_i, or connected to both ends of e_i. Indeed, for a *self-loop* $e_i = \langle v_j, v_j \rangle$ connecting v_j to itself, the global production/consumption effect of v_j on the channel must be 0 for the model to be consistent. Therefore the associated production and consumption rates must be equal. Their exact value does not matter and can be any integer. The rates

[1] In other words, A^* is the *free monoid* on A, and A^+ is the *free semigroup* on A.

are given by a matrix with one row per channel and one column per actor, as illustrated in Fig. 1b for $\mathcal{P}_1$.

Definition 1 (Topology matrix). *A matrix* $\mathbf{\Gamma} = (\gamma_{ij}) \in \mathbb{Q}^{|E|\times|V|}$ *is a* topology matrix *of a system graph* G *if for every channel* $e_i = \langle v_k, v_l\rangle \in E$*, we have:*

- *the rate* $\gamma_{ij} = 0$ *for all* $j \neq k, l$*;*
- *if* $k \neq l$*, then the rates* $\gamma_{ik} > 0$ *and* $\gamma_{il} < 0$ *are irreducible fractions, and at least one of them has a denominator equal to 1 (i.e. is an integer); let* $q_i \geqslant 1$ *be the greatest of their denominators, we define* $r_i = 1/q_i$ *the* smallest fraction portable *by* e_i*;*
- *if* $k = l$*, then* $\gamma_{ik} = 0/1 = 0$*, and we define* $q_i = r_i = 1$*.*

A *channel state* is a vector of rational numbers giving for each channel its state, tracking the partial production or consumption effect of the successive firings, which must thus be a multiple of its smallest portable fraction (c.f. Fig. 1b). The number of tokens in a channel is defined as the integer part of its rational state, and a token is actually produced (resp. consumed) by a firing when this integer part increases (resp. decreases) at this firing.

Definition 2 (Channel state). *A vector* $\mathbf{c} = (c_i) \in \mathbb{Q}^{|E|\times 1}$ *is a* channel state *of a system graph* G *with topology matrix* $\mathbf{\Gamma}$ *if for every channel* $e_i = \langle v_j, v_k\rangle \in E$*, we have* $c_i = zr_i$ *for some* $z \in \mathbb{Z}$*. We say that* $\lfloor c_i \rfloor$ *is the* number of tokens *occupying channel* e_i*.*

A *polygraph* is composed[2] of a system graph, a topology matrix, and a subset of *timed actors* $V_F \subseteq V$ with certain *synchronous constraints* Θ. These constraints require that each timed actor fires at a given *frequency*, synchronously with respect to the ticks of a *global clock*. It is possible to choose a suitable time unit and a global clock with a suitable frequency, such that each $v_j \in V_F$ has to fire the same number of times $t_j \in \mathbb{N}$ during this time unit. In $\mathcal{P}_1$, with a time unit of 100ms and a global clock at 120 Hz, the vector $\mathbf{t} = (t_j)$ gives that value t_j for each $v_j \in V_F$. The current tick of the global clock and the information about the timed actors which have already fired at this tick are represented[3] by a synchronous state θ. The detailed semantic of these synchronous constraints [5] is not essential for the comprehension of the extension we propose, as further discussed in Remark 5. For lack of space, we only recall basic notation and definitions that are mandatory to present the contributions of this paper.

Definition 3 (Polygraph, state). *A* polygraph *is a tuple* $\mathcal{P} = \langle G, \mathbf{\Gamma}, \Theta\rangle$ *containing a system graph* G*, a topology matrix* $\mathbf{\Gamma}$*, and* synchronous constraints Θ*. A* state *of a polygraph* $\mathcal{P}$ *is a tuple* $s = \langle \mathbf{c}, \theta\rangle$ *containing a channel state* $\mathbf{c}$*, and a* synchronous state θ*. We denote by* S *the set of all possible states of* $\mathcal{P}$*.*

[2] Θ corresponds to ω and φ in [5, Def. 4], while initial marking $\mathbf{m}$ is not integrated into the polygraph definition in this paper.

[3] θ corresponds to τ and $\mathbf{a}$ in [5, Def. 5].

The only possible transitions from one state to another are the firing of an actor or a tick of the global clock. Starting from an *initial state*, a sequence of states resulting from such successive transitions is called an *execution*.

Definition 4 (Fire, Tick). *For a polygraph $\mathcal{P}$, the mapping* fire : $V \times S \longrightarrow S$ *maps an actor v_j and a state $s = \langle \mathbf{c}, \theta \rangle$ to the state $s' = \langle \mathbf{c}', \theta' \rangle$ such that for each $e_i \in E$ we have $c'_i = c_i + \gamma_{ij}$, and θ' is the resulting synchronous state. The mapping* tick : $S \longrightarrow S$ *maps a state $s = \langle \mathbf{c}, \theta \rangle$ to the state $s' = \langle \mathbf{c}', \theta' \rangle$ such that we have $\mathbf{c}' = \mathbf{c}$, and θ' is the resulting synchronous state (see [5] for detail).*

Remark 1. Let $\delta_i^+(s) \in \mathbb{N}$ denote the amount of tokens produced on a channel $e_i = \langle v_j, v_k \rangle$ by a firing of v_j in state $s = \langle \mathbf{c}, \theta \rangle$. By Definitions 2 and 4, we have $\delta_i^+(s) = \lfloor c_i + \gamma_{ij} \rfloor - \lfloor c_i \rfloor$. Similarly, for the number of tokens consumed on e_i by a firing of v_k in state s, denoted $\delta_i^-(s) \in \mathbb{N}$, we have $\delta_i^-(s) = \lfloor c_i \rfloor - \lfloor c_i + \gamma_{ik} \rfloor$.

Not all transitions from a state $s = \langle \mathbf{c}, \theta \rangle$ to a state $s' = \langle \mathbf{c}', \theta' \rangle$ are valid. First, the synchronous constraints impose an order on some firing and tick transitions. We write $\theta \vdash \theta'$ when these synchronous constraints (formally defined in [5]) are satisfied for the transition from s to s'. In addition, the policy to read from a channel e_i is read-blocking. Thus, the transition from s to s' is called *valid*, and denoted $s \vdash s'$, if $\theta \vdash \theta'$ and $\forall e_i \in E, c_i \geqslant 0 \wedge c'_i \geqslant 0$.

Definition 5 (Execution). *An* execution *of a polygraph $\mathcal{P}$ is a sequence of states $\sigma = s^1 \cdots s^n \in S^+$, such that s^1 is the* initial state *of σ, and for each $1 \leqslant l < n$, we have either $s^{l+1} = \text{fire}(v_j, s^l)$ for some $v_j \in V$, or $s^{l+1} = \text{tick}(s^l)$. An execution σ is said to be* valid *if $s^l \vdash s^{l+1}$ for all $1 \leqslant l < n$.*

Remark 2. The number of firings of actors in an execution $\sigma = s^1 \cdots s^n$ can be represented by a *tracking vector* $\mathbf{x}^\sigma = (x_j^\sigma) \in \mathbb{N}^{|V| \times 1}$, such that for each v_j, the component x_j^σ gives the number of l such that $1 \leqslant l \leqslant n$ and $s^{l+1} = \text{fire}(v_j, s^l)$. We say that the fth such firing is of *rank* f.

To perform a static performance analysis of a polygraph, there should be a valid periodic behavior of the system. In other words, only the valid executions $\sigma = s^1 \cdots s^n \in S^+$ returning to their initial state $s^1 = s^n$ are relevant. From [5, Th. 1, 2], the existence of such executions can be decided in general. In Fig. 2, a small example polygraph $\mathcal{P}_2$ and an execution σ_2 are represented.

Example 1. Figure 2a presents a polygraph $\mathcal{P}_2$ with 3 actors and 3 channels. For simplicity, it has no synchronous constraints. Figure 2b illustrates, step-by-step, the states of an execution σ_2 with consecutive firings of v_3, v_2, v_1, v_2. The first five columns give the firing actor, the number of its firings so far, and the states of the channels. The latter show the states c_i of channels e_i and illustrate by circles the tokens occupying each channel. The last four columns will be explained later. The first row provides the initial state. For instance, the first firing of v_2 consumes one token from e_2 (since its state changes from $2/2 = 1$ to $1/2$) and produces one token on e_3. Note that σ_2 is valid and returns to its initial state after the first 4 steps, and can thus be repeated infinitely.

Definition 6 (Live execution). *For a polygraph $\mathcal{P}$, a valid execution $\sigma = s^1 \cdots s^n \in S^+$ is called* live *if $s^1 = s^n$. In this case, polygraph $\mathcal{P}$ is said to be* live from s^1.

Remark 3. We say that two valid executions $\sigma, \sigma' \in S^+$ of a polygraph $\mathcal{P}$ are equivalent, denoted by $\sigma \simeq \sigma'$, if their tracking vectors and initial states are equal, that is, $\mathbf{x}^\sigma = \mathbf{x}^{\sigma'}$ and $\sigma[1] = \sigma'[1]$, and the number of ticks is the same. If $\mathcal{P}$ is live from a state s^1, by Th. 2 in [4,5] there is a minimal live execution σ, such that $\sigma[1] = s^1$. Moreover, any other live execution σ' with $\sigma'[1] = s^1$ is equivalent to l repetitions of σ (for some $l \geqslant 1$), that is, $\mathbf{x}^{\sigma'} = l \cdot \mathbf{x}^\sigma$ [4, Cor. 2]. Futhermore, any valid execution σ'' with $\sigma''[1] = s^1$ can be extended to a live execution σ' [4, Th. 2], thus, equivalent to a certain number of repetitions of a minimal live execution σ. This property will be used to justify the algorithm in Sect. 4.

3.2 Additional Properties of Polygraph Executions

For a given valid execution $\sigma = \langle \mathbf{c}^1, \theta^1 \rangle \cdots \langle \mathbf{c}^n, \theta^n \rangle$ and a channel $e_i = \langle v_j, v_k \rangle$ with $j \neq k$, we can consider the total number of tokens produced (resp. consumed) on e_i by the firings of v_j (resp. v_k) along σ, denoted $\delta_i^+(\sigma)$ (resp. $\delta_i^-(\sigma)$). Formally, by Definitions 2, 4 and 5, we have:

$$\delta_i^+(\sigma) = \sum_{\substack{l\,:\,v_j \text{ fires on} \\ \langle \mathbf{c}^l, \theta^l \rangle \text{ in } \sigma}} (\lfloor c_i^{l+1} \rfloor - \lfloor c_i^l \rfloor), \quad \delta_i^-(\sigma) = -\sum_{\substack{l\,:\,v_k \text{ fires on} \\ \langle \mathbf{c}^l, \theta^l \rangle \text{ in } \sigma}} (\lfloor c_i^{l+1} \rfloor - \lfloor c_i^l \rfloor). \qquad (1)$$

The number of tokens occupying e_i along σ is modified only by productions (by v_j) and consumptions (by v_k), thus using (1) we have:

$$\lfloor c_i^n \rfloor - \lfloor c_i^1 \rfloor = \sum_{1 \leqslant l < n} (\lfloor c_i^{l+1} \rfloor - \lfloor c_i^l \rfloor) = \delta_i^+(\sigma) - \delta_i^-(\sigma).$$

It follows that $\lfloor c_i^1 \rfloor + \delta_i^+(\sigma) = \delta_i^-(\sigma) + \lfloor c_i^n \rfloor$. These two expressions compute the total *number of tokens transiting through channel e_i along* σ, that we denote by $\eta_i^\sigma \in \mathbb{N}$. We call these tokens the *footprint* of σ on channel e_i, and each of these tokens is identified by a *rank* $1 \leqslant l \leqslant \eta_i^\sigma$. They can be seen as the tokens initially occupying e_i and the $\delta_i^+(\sigma)$ tokens produced along σ. On the other hand, the same tokens can be seen as the $\delta_i^-(\sigma)$ tokens consumed along σ and the tokens occupying e_i after σ. In execution σ_2 of Fig. 2, four tokens transit through e_3 along σ_2, thus the footprint has $\eta_1^\sigma = 4$ tokens, and each token is shown as ①–④ for the states when they are occupying e_3.

The next result shows that η_i^σ, $\delta_i^+(\sigma)$, $\delta_i^-(\sigma)$ depend only on the number of firings of v_j and v_k in σ and the initial state of e_i, and not on the order of transitions in σ.

Proposition 1. *Let $\mathcal{P}$ be a polygraph, and $\sigma = \langle \mathbf{c}^1, \theta^1 \rangle \cdots \langle \mathbf{c}^n, \theta^n \rangle \in S^+$ be a valid execution of $\mathcal{P}$ with tracking vector $\mathbf{x}^\sigma$. Let $e_i = \langle v_j, v_k \rangle \in E$ be a channel with $j \neq k$, and denote $r = \lfloor c_i \rceil$. Then we have: $\eta_i^\sigma = \lfloor c_i^1 \rfloor + \delta_i^+(\sigma) = \delta_i^-(\sigma) + \lfloor c_i^n \rfloor$, $\delta_i^+(\sigma) = \lfloor x_j^\sigma \gamma_{ij} + r \rfloor$, $\delta_i^-(\sigma) = \lceil x_k^\sigma |\gamma_{ik}| - r \rceil$.*

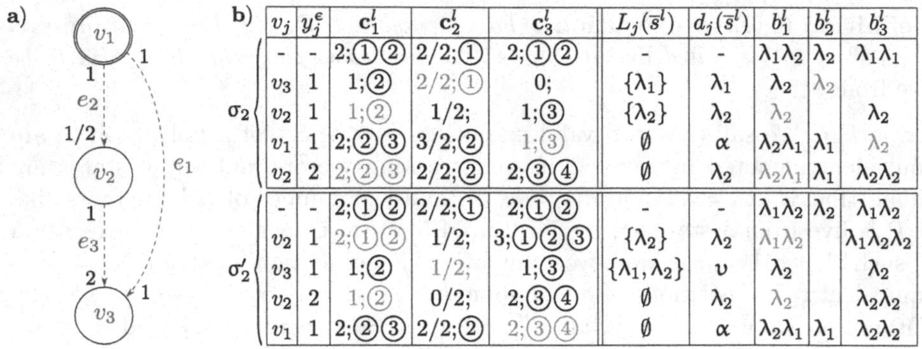

	v_j	y_j^ϵ	$\mathbf{c}_1^l$	$\mathbf{c}_2^l$	$\mathbf{c}_3^l$	$L_j(\overline{s}^l)$	$d_j(\overline{s}^l)$	b_1^l	b_2^l	b_3^l
σ_2	-	-	2;①②	2/2;①	2;①②	-	-	$\lambda_1\lambda_2$	λ_2	$\lambda_1\lambda_1$
	v_3	1	1;②	2/2;①	0;	$\{\lambda_1\}$	λ_1	λ_2	λ_2	
	v_2	1	1;②	1/2;	1;③	$\{\lambda_2\}$	λ_2	λ_2		λ_2
	v_1	1	2;②③	3/2;②	1;③	$\emptyset$	α	$\lambda_2\lambda_1$	λ_1	λ_2
	v_2	2	2;②③	2/2;②	2;③④	$\emptyset$	λ_2	$\lambda_2\lambda_1$	λ_1	$\lambda_2\lambda_2$
σ_2'	-	-	2;①②	2/2;①	2;①②	-	-	$\lambda_1\lambda_2$	λ_2	$\lambda_1\lambda_2$
	v_2	1	2;①②	1/2;	3;①②③	$\{\lambda_2\}$	λ_2	$\lambda_1\lambda_2$		$\lambda_1\lambda_2\lambda_2$
	v_3	1	1;②	1/2;	1;③	$\{\lambda_1, \lambda_2\}$	υ	λ_2		λ_2
	v_2	2	1;②	0/2;	2;③④	$\emptyset$	λ_2	λ_2		$\lambda_2\lambda_2$
	v_1	1	2;②③	2/2;②	2;③④	$\emptyset$	α	$\lambda_2\lambda_1$	λ_1	$\lambda_2\lambda_2$

Fig. 2. (a) A polygraph $\mathcal{P}_2$, with v_1 the unique selector of modes $\Lambda_1 = \{\lambda_1, \lambda_2\}$ and its followers v_2 and v_3, and (b) two step-by-step live executions σ_2 and σ_2' of $\mathcal{P}_2$.

Proof. The first fact was shown above. We claim that the sums of $\delta_i^+(\sigma)$, $\delta_i^-(\sigma)$ in (1) can be rewritten as follows: $\delta_i^+(\sigma) = \sum_{f=1}^{x_j^\sigma}(\lfloor c_i^1 + f\gamma_{ij}\rfloor - \lfloor c_i^1 + (f-1)\gamma_{ij}\rfloor)$ and $\delta_i^-(\sigma) = -\sum_{f'=1}^{x_k^\sigma}(\lfloor c_i^1 + f'\gamma_{ik}\rfloor - \lfloor c_i^1 + (f'-1)\gamma_{ik}\rfloor)$.

Indeed, at each step, $c_i^{l+1} = c_i^1 + f\gamma_{ij} + f'\gamma_{ik}$ where f and f' are the number of firings, resp., of v_j and v_k in the prefix of length $l+1$ in σ. At most one of γ_{ij} and γ_{ik} is not an integer[4]; by symmetry, we can assume $\gamma_{ik} \in \mathbb{Z}$. Then in the first sum we have $\lfloor c_i^{l+1}\rfloor = \lfloor c_i^1 + f\gamma_{ij}\rfloor$ for all l, that implies the proposed rewriting. In the second sum, the rewriting follows from the fact: $\forall p, p' \in \mathbb{Q}, \forall m, m' \in \mathbb{Z}, \lfloor p+m\rfloor - \lfloor p+m'\rfloor = \lfloor p'+m\rfloor - \lfloor p'+m'\rfloor$.

We simplify the first sum $\delta_i^+(\sigma) = \lfloor c_i^1 + x_j^\sigma\gamma_{ij}\rfloor - \lfloor c_i^1\rfloor = \lfloor x_j^\sigma\gamma_{ij} + r\rfloor$ as required since $r = \lfloor c_i \rceil = \lfloor c_i^1\rfloor - c_i^1$, and the second sum $\delta_i^-(\sigma) = \lfloor c_i^1\rfloor - \lfloor c_i^1 + x_k^\sigma\gamma_{ik}\rfloor = -\lfloor x_k^\sigma\gamma_{ik} + r\rfloor$. The third formula follows from the fact: $\forall p \in \mathbb{Q}, -\lfloor p\rfloor = \lceil -p\rceil$. □

For the footprint of σ on e_i, we can consider a mapping $o_i^\sigma : \{1, \ldots, \eta_i^\sigma\} \to \{0, \ldots, \delta_i^+(\sigma)\}$ (resp. $\iota_i^\sigma : \{1, \ldots, \eta_i^\sigma\} \to \{0, \ldots, \delta_i^-(\sigma)\}$) associating to each token in the footprint the rank of the firing of v_j (resp. v_k) that produced (resp. consumed) that token in σ. We call that rank the *production* (resp. *consumption*) *rank* of the token. By convention, a rank 0 is assigned to a token that was not produced (resp. consumed) by a firing in σ. In Fig. 2, since the 1st firing of v_2 consumes ① on e_2 and produces ③ on e_3, we have $\iota_2^\sigma(1) = 1$ and $o_2^\sigma(3) = 1$.

Proposition 2. *In the assumptions of Proposition 1, we have:*

1. $\forall 1 \leqslant l \leqslant \lfloor c_i^1\rfloor,\ o_i^\sigma(l) = 0;\quad \forall\lfloor c_i^1\rfloor < l \leqslant \eta_i^\sigma,\ o_i^\sigma(l) = \lceil (l - c_i^1) / \gamma_{ij} \rceil;$
2. $\forall 1 \leqslant l \leqslant \delta_i^-(\sigma),\ \iota_i^\sigma(l) = 1 + \lfloor (l-1+r) / |\gamma_{ik}| \rfloor;\quad \forall \delta_i^-(\sigma) < l \leqslant \eta_i^\sigma,\ \iota_i^\sigma(l) = 0.$

Proof. The formulas with rank 0 follow from the definition. Given an index l with $\lfloor c_i^1\rfloor < l \leqslant \eta_i^\sigma$, let us compute the rank f of firing of v_j producing the lth token

[4] We see here the reason for that condition in Definition 1: if both $\gamma_{ij}, \gamma_{ik} \notin \mathbb{Z}$, this and the following results do not hold, and the order of transitions can be important.

of the footprint. Considering the prefixes σ' of σ with $f = x_j^{\sigma'} \in \{1, 2 \ldots, x_j^{\sigma}\}$ firings of v_j we have to find the shortest prefix σ' producing that token. In other words, by Proposition 1, we have to find the smallest f such that $l \leqslant \delta_i^+(\sigma') = \lfloor c_i^1 + f\gamma_{ij} \rfloor$. Since $l \in \mathbb{Z}$, we look for the smallest f such that $l \leqslant c_i^1 + f\gamma_{ij}$, or equivalently, $f \geqslant (l - c_i^1)/\gamma_{ij}$. Thus, $o_i^{\sigma}(l) = \lceil (l - c_i^1) \,/\, \gamma_{ij} \rceil$.

Following the same logic, for $1 \leqslant l \leqslant \delta_i^-(\sigma)$, we look for the shortest prefix σ' of σ consuming the lth token of the footprint. By Proposition 1, we have to find the smallest f such that $l \leqslant \delta_i^-(\sigma') = \lceil f|\gamma_{ik}| - r \rceil$. Equivalently, we look for the smallest f such that $l - 1 < f|\gamma_{ik}| - r$, i.e. $f > (l - 1 + r)/|\gamma_{ik}|$. In other words, we look for the biggest f such that $f - 1 \leqslant (l - 1 + r)/|\gamma_{ik}|$. Thus, $f - 1 = \lfloor (l - 1 + r)/|\gamma_{ik}| \rfloor$. It follows that $\iota_i^{\sigma}(l) = 1 + \lfloor (l - 1 + r) \,/\, |\gamma_{ik}| \rfloor$. □

Remark 4. For two valid executions $\sigma, \sigma' \in S^+$ that are equivalent (i.e. $\sigma \simeq \sigma'$, cf. Remark 3), by Proposition 1, for all channels[5] $e_i = \langle v_j, v_k \rangle \in E$ with $j \neq k$, we have $\eta_i^{\sigma} = \eta_i^{\sigma'}$, $o_i^{\sigma} = o_i^{\sigma'}$, and $\iota_i^{\sigma} = \iota_i^{\sigma'}$. For example in Fig. 2, we have $\sigma_2' \simeq \sigma_2$, and the footprints and production/consumption ranks are the same in these executions.

3.3 Mode Extension of the Polygraph Modeling Language

In the rest of the paper, when there is no risk of confusion, we will use the term *polygraph* for an extended polygraph for short.

Extended Polygraph. A *mode* identifies a reconfiguration of a polygraph's behavior. When firing, an actor has a mode for that firing, called *decided mode.* In the channels, the tokens are labeled with modes. An extended polygraph has a *nominal mode* denoted α, an *undefined mode* denoted υ, and a set of *user modes* denoted Λ_M with $\Lambda_M \cap \{\alpha, \upsilon\} = \varnothing$. The *mode set* is the set $\Lambda = \Lambda_M \cup \{\alpha, \upsilon\}$.

Every actor v_j is associated with a subset of user modes $\Lambda_j \subseteq \Lambda_M$. The set Λ_j contains the modes selectable by actor v_j, and is called its *selection set.* An actor v_j with $\Lambda_j \neq \varnothing$ is called a *selector*, and the subset of such actors is denoted by $V_M \subseteq V$. When firing, a selector v_j chooses a *selected mode* $\lambda \in \Lambda_j$ with which it labels the tokens it produces. A non-selector labels the tokens it produces with its decided mode. We assume that the Λ_j form a partition of Λ_M (cf. (i) in Definition 7). Hence a given user mode can be selected by one and only one selector. In addition, a selection makes sense only if there are at least two elements to select from (cf. (i)).

Every actor v_k is associated with a non-empty subset of *enabling modes* $\mathrm{M}_k \subseteq \Lambda$. The decided mode for a firing of v_k should always belong to M_k, unless it is undefined. We assume (cf. (ii) in Definition 7) that either $\mathrm{M}_k = \{\alpha\}$, or there exists a unique selector $v_j \in V_M$ with $\mathrm{M}_k = \Lambda_j$. In the latter case, v_j is said to be the *selector of* v_k, and v_k is said to be a *follower of* v_j, denoted $v_j \rightsquigarrow v_k$, and the decided mode of v_k can only be a mode selectable by v_j. The only exception

[5] For the case of self-loops, excluded in the proposition, a similar result can be proved by separately considering matrices $\mathbf{\Gamma}^+, \mathbf{\Gamma}^-$ with production and consumption rates.

is the undefined mode υ, which becomes the decided mode of v_k when its mode cannot be decided. Note that a selector can be a follower of another selector.

The decided mode of a firing of actor v_k is determined based on the labels of the tokens consumed by this firing from a subset of its input channels, denoted $\Psi_k \subseteq \text{in}(v_k)$, called the *deciding set of* v_k, and whose elements are called *deciding channels* of v_k. If $\mathrm{M}_k = \{\alpha\}$, we require (cf. (ii) in Definition 7) that $\Psi_k = \varnothing$, since v_k does not need information to decide its mode. If $v_j \rightsquigarrow v_k$, to determine its decided mode, v_k must have at least one deciding channel. If all the tokens it consumes from its deciding channels are labeled with the same user mode, this mode becomes its decided mode. If conflicting modes are read, the decided mode of v_k is undefined. In order to obtain user modes in its enabling set $\mathrm{M}_k = \Lambda_j$, v_k's deciding channels come either from v_j or another follower v_l of v_j (cf. (ii)).

To ensure a follower receives tokens labeled with a mode selected by its selector, there must be a directed path from that selector to that follower, composed exclusively of deciding channels (cf. (iii) in Definition 7). Moreover, if there is a cycle of followers composed of deciding channels, some follower can receive conflicting modes from (the shortest path from) its selector and from its predecessor in the cycle. We exclude such a backward propagation of mode selections (cf. (iv)).

Definition 7 (Extended polygraph). *An* extended polygraph *is a tuple* $\overline{\mathcal{P}} = \langle \mathcal{P}, \Lambda, \{\langle \Lambda_j, \mathrm{M}_j, \Psi_j \rangle\}_j \rangle$ *where* $\mathcal{P}$ *is a polygraph,* $\Lambda = \Lambda_M \cup \{\alpha, \upsilon\}$ *is a mode set, and the tuples* $\langle \Lambda_j, \mathrm{M}_j, \Psi_j \rangle$ *contain respectively the selection set, enabling set, and deciding set of actor* $v_j \in V$*, such that:*

(i) $\Lambda_M = \coprod_{v_j \in V} \Lambda_j$; $\forall v_j \in V, |\Lambda_j| = 0$ *or* $|\Lambda_j| \geqslant 2$; $V_M = \{v_j \in V \mid \Lambda_j \neq \varnothing\}$;
(ii) for any v_k*, either* $\mathrm{M}_k = \{\alpha\} \wedge \Psi_k = \varnothing$*,*
or $\exists v_j \in V_M$, $\mathrm{M}_k = \Lambda_j \wedge \varnothing \neq \Psi_k \subseteq \{\langle v_l, v_k \rangle \in E \mid j = l \vee \mathrm{M}_l = \Lambda_j\}$;
(iii) if $\mathrm{M}_k = \Lambda_j$*, there is a path* $v_j = v_{l_1}, \cdots, v_{l_n} = v_k$ *of deciding channels;*
(iv) for any $v_j \in V_M$*, there is no cycle* $v_{k_1}, \cdots, v_{k_p} = v_{k_1}$ *in which* $\mathrm{M}_{k_l} = \Lambda_j$ *and all channels are deciding.*

In addition to a state of a polygraph (cf. Definition 3), a state of an extended polygraph $\overline{\mathcal{P}}$ contains an *actor mode mapping* $m : V \longrightarrow \Lambda$, which stores for an actor v_j the decided mode of its last firing, denoted $m_j = m(v_j)$. To capture the mode labels associated to tokens in the channels, the state of $\overline{\mathcal{P}}$ also has a *token labeling* $b : E \longrightarrow \Lambda^*$ mapping a channel e_i to a sequence of modes, denoted $b_i = b(e_i)$. In a given state $s = \langle \mathbf{c}, \theta \rangle$, in channel e_i, there are $\lfloor c_i \rfloor$ tokens (cf. Definition 2), so there is a mode label for each of them in FIFO order (see for example the three rightmost columns for the executions of Fig. 2).

Definition 8 (State). *A* state *of an extended polygraph* $\overline{\mathcal{P}}$ *is a tuple* $\overline{s} = \langle s, m, b \rangle$ *where* $s = \langle \mathbf{c}, \theta \rangle \in S$ *is a state of* $\mathcal{P}$*,* m *is an actor mode mapping such that* $\forall v_j \in V$ *we have* $m_j \in \mathrm{M}_j \cup \{\upsilon\}$*, and* b *is a token labeling for* s *such that* $\forall e_i \in E$ *we have* $|b_i| = \lfloor c_i \rfloor$*. We denote by* $\overline{S}$ *the set of all possible states for* $\overline{\mathcal{P}}$*, and by* $\nabla : \overline{S} \longrightarrow S$ *the forgetful mapping that maps a state* $\overline{s} = \langle s, m, b \rangle$ *to* $\nabla(\overline{s}) = s$*.*

Our next goal is to extend the fire and tick transitions between states of $\mathcal{P}$ to transitions between states of $\overline{\mathcal{P}}$. We first define, given a state $\overline{s} = \langle s, m, b\rangle \in \overline{S}$, a new state $\overline{s}' = \langle s', m', b'\rangle \in \overline{S}$ resulting from the firing of an actor v_j in state $\overline{s}$. We assume that $s = \langle \mathbf{c}, \theta\rangle$ and $\overline{s} = \langle \mathbf{c}', \theta'\rangle$. As mentioned in Sect. 3.1, only valid executions are relevant. For this reason, we only define partial mappings for the transitions in $\overline{\mathcal{P}}$ such that $\nabla(\overline{s}) \vdash \nabla(\overline{s}')$.

Decided Mode. We first define how the decided mode for a firing of v_j in $\overline{s}$ is determined. Only the mode labels of the $\delta_i^-(s)$ tokens consumed from each deciding channel e_i will influence the decision. The set of the relevant modes is thus defined by $L_j(\overline{s}) = \{b_i[k] \mid e_i \in \Psi_j, 1 \leq k \leq \delta_i^-(s)\}$.

If the set $L_j(\overline{s})$ is restricted to a singleton $\{\lambda\}$, then λ is the decided mode of v_j (Case 2 in the following Definition 9). If $L_j(\overline{s}) = \varnothing$, it means that $L_j(\overline{s})$ does not provide information to decide, and v_j will keep its last mode m_j (Case 1). The last possible case is that $|L_j(\overline{s})| \geqslant 2$, which means that $L_j(\overline{s})$ provides incoherent information, since several modes are possible. As explained in Sect. 2, this is an *indecision*, and v_j will switch to the undefined mode υ (Case 3).

For a non-follower v_j, since $\Psi_j = \varnothing$ (cf. (ii) in Definition 7), the set $L_j(\overline{s})$ is empty (Case 1 in Definition 9), and the decided mode always remains the same (nominal if the previous mode was nominal). Finally, if a predecessor of v_j propagated to v_j an undefined mode via one of its deciding channels, the decision for v_j is taken either by Case 2 or Case 3, and in both situations v_j also enters an undefined mode. Hence, the undefined mode is propagated to successors.

Definition 9 (Decided mode). *Let $\overline{\mathcal{P}}$ be an extended polygraph, $v_j \in V$ an actor, and $\overline{s} = \langle s, m, b\rangle \in \overline{S}$ a state with $s = \langle \mathbf{c}, \theta\rangle \in S$ such that $\forall e_i \in \mathrm{in}(v_j)$, $c_i \geqslant |\gamma_{ij}|$. Given the set $L_j(\overline{s})$, the* decided mode *$d_j(\overline{s})$ of v_j for its firing in state $\overline{s}$ is defined as follows:*

1. *if $L_j(\overline{s}) = \varnothing$, then $d_j(\overline{s}) = m_j$;*
2. *if $L_j(\overline{s}) = \{\lambda\}$ for some λ, then $d_j(\overline{s}) = \lambda$;*
3. *if $|L_j(\overline{s})| \geqslant 2$, then $d_j(\overline{s}) = \upsilon$.*

Extended Transitions. We can now define the resulting state $\overline{s}'$ after the firing of v_j in state $\overline{s}$ as an extension of a firing in $\mathcal{P}$ (cf. Case 1 in Definition 10 below). The mode of v_j is set to its decided mode $m_j' = d_j(\overline{s})$, while for the other actors, their mode is unchanged (cf. Case 2).

By Definition 2 and Remark 1, for every input channel e_i of v_j, the firing of v_j consumes the first $\delta_i^-(s)$ tokens, so the token labeling b_i' for the remaining tokens is the suffix of b_i of length $|b_i| - \delta_i^-(s)$ (cf. Case 3). Since we only define a partial mapping for states where the firing of an actor does not result in a negative channel state, the resulting token labeling is always well defined.

When firing, v_j arbitrarily chooses a mode, and labels all the produced tokens with that mode. If v_j is not a selector, then it can only choose its decided mode. Otherwise, v_j is a selector, and can select any mode from its selection set (cf. (ii)). In Definition 10, we make the choice to represent the arbitrarily chosen mode λ

as an additional parameter of the partial firing mapping, so that different choices can lead to different resulting states. Then for each output channel e_i, since the number of tokens produced is $\delta_i^+(s)$, a suffix $(\delta_i^+(s) * \lambda)$ is added to the token labeling sequence (cf. Case 4).

Definition 10 (Extended firing). *For an extended polygraph $\overline{\mathcal{P}}$, the partial mapping* fire : $V \times \overline{S} \times \Lambda \nrightarrow \overline{S}$ *is defined for the tuples $\langle v_j, \overline{s}, \lambda \rangle$ such that (i) $\nabla(\overline{s}) \vdash \text{fire}(v_j, \nabla(\overline{s}))$, and (ii) $\lambda = d_j(\overline{s})$ if $v_j \notin V_M$ or $\lambda \in \Lambda_j$ if $v_j \in V_M$. In this case, if we denote $\overline{s} = \langle s, m, b \rangle$ and $\langle s', m', b' \rangle = \text{fire}(v_j, \overline{s}, \lambda)$, we have:*

1. $s' = \text{fire}(v_j, s)$;
2. $m'_j = d_j(\overline{s})$, *and* $m'_k = m_k$ *for any* $k \neq j$;
3. $\forall e_i \in \text{in}(v_j)$, $b'_i = \text{suffix}(b_i, |b_i| - \delta_i^-(s))$;
4. $\forall e_i \in \text{out}(v_j)$, $b'_i = b_i \cdot (\delta_i^+(s) * \lambda)$.

Definition 11 (Extended tick). *For an extended polygraph $\overline{\mathcal{P}}$, the partial mapping* tick : $\overline{S} \nrightarrow \overline{S}$ *is defined for the tuples $\langle v_j, \overline{s}, \lambda \rangle$ such that $\nabla(\overline{s}) \vdash \text{tick}(\nabla(\overline{s}))$. In this case, if we denote $\overline{s} = \langle s, m, b \rangle$ and $\langle s', m', b' \rangle = \text{tick}(\overline{s})$, we have $s' = \text{tick}(s)$, $m' = m$, and $b' = b$.*

Remark 5. Deffinitions 9, 10 and 11 show that the extended transitions in $\overline{\mathcal{P}}$ impact, or depend on the synchronous constraints θ in the same way as the underlying transitions in $\mathcal{P}$ do. There is no additional dependence or impact on synchronous constraints introduced by the mode extension. An extended firing only relies on the channel states $\mathbf{c}$ in $s = \langle \mathbf{c}, \theta \rangle \in S$ to determine the mode changes. Therefore, the mode extension is orthogonal to synchronous constraints. We thus chose not to detail them here. In other words, the mode extension is about *which* tokens are consumed or produced by a firing, not *when* they are.

Extended Execution. An execution of $\overline{\mathcal{P}}$ relies on the extended firing and the extended tick. By construction, the underlying execution in $\mathcal{P}$ is valid.

Definition 12 (Extended execution). *An* execution *of an extended polygraph $\overline{\mathcal{P}}$ is a sequence $\overline{\sigma} = \overline{s}^1 \cdots \overline{s}^n \in \overline{S}^+$, such that $\forall 1 \leqslant k < n$ we have either $\overline{s}^{k+1} = \text{fire}(v_j, \overline{s}^k, \lambda)$ for some $v_j \in V$ and $\lambda \in \Lambda$, or $\overline{s}^{k+1} = \text{tick}(\overline{s}^k)$. The forgetful mapping is extended to any execution $\overline{\sigma} = \overline{s}^1 \cdots \overline{s}^n$ as follows: $\nabla(\overline{\sigma}) = \nabla(\overline{s}^1) \cdots \nabla(\overline{s}^n)$. In addition, if $\sigma = \nabla(\overline{\sigma})$, for all channels $e_i \in E$ we denote $\eta_i^{\overline{\sigma}} = \eta_i^{\sigma}$, $o_i^{\overline{\sigma}} = o_i^{\sigma}$, and $\iota_i^{\overline{\sigma}} = \iota_i^{\sigma}$.*

Coherence. As explained above, the decision of the next mode captures a drift in mode propagation by assigning an undefined mode to actors. We propose in the next section an algorithm to verify that, given a polygraph $\overline{\mathcal{P}}$ with an initial state $\overline{s}^1$, the decided mode is never undefined in any execution starting from $\overline{s}^1$. To show its soundness, we need to show (cf. Theorem 1 below) that the decided modes of all actors are pre-determined by the initial state and the modes selected by the selectors, even if the order of transitions is changed.

To formalize this idea, for an execution $\overline{\sigma} = \overline{s}^1 \cdots \overline{s}^n \in \overline{S}^+$ and for each actor v_j, we define two mappings $\mu_j^{\overline{\sigma}}$ and $\chi_j^{\overline{\sigma}}$ giving for each $l \in \{1, \dots, x_j^{\sigma}\}$ the decided mode $\mu_j^{\overline{\sigma}}(l)$ and the selected mode $\chi_j^{\overline{\sigma}}(l)$ for the lth firing of v_j in $\overline{\sigma}$. Hence, if the fth firing of v_j occurs in state $\overline{s}^l$ such that $\overline{s}^{l+1} = \text{fire}(v_j, \overline{s}^l, \lambda)$, we have $\mu_j^{\overline{\sigma}}(f) = d_j(\overline{s}^l)$ and $\chi_j^{\overline{\sigma}}(f) = \lambda$. By Definition 10, they are equal for non-selectors.

Theorem 1. *Let $\overline{\mathcal{P}}$ be an extended polygraph, and $\overline{\sigma} \in \overline{S}^+$, $\overline{\sigma}' \in \overline{S}^+$ be two executions of $\mathcal{P}$ such that $\nabla(\overline{\sigma}) \simeq \nabla(\overline{\sigma}')$ and $\overline{\sigma}[1] = \overline{\sigma}'[1]$. Assume that for any selector $v_j \in V_M$ we have $\chi_j^{\overline{\sigma}} = \chi_j^{\overline{\sigma}'}$. Then for any actor $v_k \in V$ we have $\mu_k^{\overline{\sigma}} = \mu_k^{\overline{\sigma}'}$.*

Sketch of Proof. By definition of $\simeq$ (see Remark 3), the tracking vectors of $\overline{\sigma}$ and $\overline{\sigma}'$ are equal, so each actor v_j fires the same number of times $x_j^{\sigma} = x_j^{\sigma'}$ in $\overline{\sigma}$ and $\overline{\sigma}'$, while the order of firings can be different. Assume the result does not hold. We can then choose the very first firing of an actor in $\overline{\sigma}$ for which the property does not hold. Assume this is the fth firing of actor v_k (referred to below as *problematic*) for which the decided mode is not the same: $\mu_k^{\overline{\sigma}}(f) \neq \mu_k^{\overline{\sigma}'}(f)$. Hence for all previous firings (of all actors) in $\overline{\sigma}$, the required property holds.

To choose the decided mode of its fth firing, v_k considers the tokens either initially present in the channel or produced by a firing of some actor occurring *before* this firing of v_k in $\overline{\sigma}$. By Proposition 2, a given token of the footprint of a channel is produced by the firings of the same rank of the producer, and consumed by the firings of the same rank of the consumer of the channel in both executions $\nabla(\overline{\sigma})$ and $\nabla(\overline{\sigma}')$ (and thus in $\overline{\sigma}$ and $\overline{\sigma}'$). Thus, the fth firing of v_k in $\overline{\sigma}$ and $\overline{\sigma}'$ consumes the initial tokens of the same rank in the footprint, that is, exactly the same number and on the same position. Since $\overline{\sigma}[1] = \overline{\sigma}'[1]$, there cannot be any difference of modes for these tokens between $\overline{\sigma}$ and $\overline{\sigma}'$. Regarding the tokens produced by a firing of a selector in $\overline{\sigma}$, since the ranks of such tokens in the footprint are the same in $\overline{\sigma}$ and $\overline{\sigma}'$ and since the selector's choice is the same in $\overline{\sigma}$ and $\overline{\sigma}'$, there cannot be any difference of token modes either. Regarding the tokens produced by a firing of a non-selector in $\overline{\sigma}$ *before* the problematic firing of v_k, there cannot be any difference since each such token is produced by a firing for which the property holds and therefore the token was labeled with the same decided mode in $\overline{\sigma}$ and $\overline{\sigma}'$. The contradiction finishes the proof. □

4 Method and Tool Support to Check Coherence

In this work, we design and implement in DIVERSITY an algorithm to check whether or not an indecision can occur in a live execution of a polygraph. DIVERSITY is a customizable model analysis tool based on symbolic execution, available in the *Eclipse Formal Modeling Project* [12].

The input of our algorithm is a polygraph $\overline{\mathcal{P}}$ and an initial state $\overline{s}^1$ such that $\mathcal{P}$ is live from $\nabla(\overline{s}^1)$. Assume σ_0 is a minimal live execution of $\mathcal{P}$ from $\nabla(\overline{s}^1)$. The algorithm performs symbolic execution of all executions $\overline{\sigma}$ of $\overline{\mathcal{P}}$ with initial state $\overline{s}^1$ such that $\nabla(\overline{\sigma})$ is a repeated execution of σ_0 (up to a certain number of times). This exploration is based on a straightforward implementation of Definitions 10, 11 and 12. We call *current state* the state $\overline{s}^l$ resulting from the last such application, with $\overline{s}^l = \overline{s}^1$ initially. In order to represent all possible choices modeled by the selected mode arguments of the extended fire transitions, for any firing of rank f of a selector v_j in these executions, we use a symbolic parameter a_{jf} representing that mode and on which we compute constraints (the initial constraint being that $a_{jf} \in \Lambda_j$). The produced tokens are labelled with a_{jf}. The resulting symbolic state represents all possible choices of selected modes and resulting constraints (stating that the mode labels of some tokens—having the same a_{jf}—are equal).

Each time an actor fires, we compute the conditions given in Definition 9. By construction at least one of them is satisfiable. If the condition corresponding to Item 3 is satisfiable, it means that there exists a valuation of the formal parameters for which the decided mode is undefined. In this case the computation ends with a verdict *no* stating that there is at least one live execution with an indecision. Otherwise, the exploration continues.

From Proposition 1, for any actor v_j and channel $e_i \in \text{in}(v_j)$, the $\lfloor c_i^1 \rfloor$ tokens initially occupying e_i are consumed after a known number of firings of v_j. Hence, from Remark 3, it is possible to successively execute σ_0 (with all possible choices of decided modes) a number of times $l > 0$ such that all tokens initially occupying input channels are consumed. Assume we reach some state $\overline{s}^n$; as σ_0 is live, we have $\triangledown(\overline{s}^n) = \triangledown(\overline{s}^1)$, so the number of tokens in the channels is the same as in the initial state. The labels of all tokens present in the channels at that stage are expressed by some a_{jf}. Finally, our algorithm executes σ_0 one last time, overall to a repetition of $l + 1$ minimal live executions σ_0. This last step, starting from some symbolic state $\overline{s}^n$, necessarily comes to a symbolic state equivalent to $\overline{s}^n$ (since by Proposition 2 the constraints on the mode labels of tokens—having the same a_{jf}—will be semantically the same, even if the indices j of a_{jf} will be shifted). If no indecision is detected by executing an extension of σ_0 from state $\overline{s}^n$, and since it leads to an equivalent state, we can stop iterations: any additional step will not detect an indecision. The computation ends with a verdict *yes*.

The proposed technique is *sound* by construction: if an indecision is detected, it really occurs since the algorithm simulates a possible execution of $\overline{\mathcal{P}}$. To show its *completeness*, we should check that if an indecision can occur for some execution of $\overline{\mathcal{P}}$, the *no* verdict will be returned.

We claim that it is indeed sufficient to explore extensions of live executions as per our algorithm, and check that no indecision occurs in them. First, from Theorem 1, the only parameters influencing the decided modes are the labels of the tokens initially occupying the channels, and the modes selected by the firings of selectors. The labels of the initial tokens are an input of the problem and do not change in the executions to consider. The symbolic parameters used to label the tokens produced by the firing of selectors cover all possible choices. Hence, all possible executions $\overline{\sigma}$ such that $\triangledown(\overline{\sigma})$ is a repeated execution of σ_0 (any finite number of times, as argued above) are covered by our exploration. By Remark 3 and Theorem 1, we deduce that a possible indecision in any execution of $\overline{\mathcal{P}}$ will be thus detected by our technique on an execution $\overline{\sigma}$ such that $\nabla(\overline{\sigma})$ is equivalent to a repeated execution of σ_0.

N°	example	♯ actors (♯ timed act.)	min live exec. len.	verdict	♯ firings simulated	♯ min. live execs.	time
1	Fig. 1	5 (4)	22	yes	44	2	95ms
2	Fig. 1(†)	5 (4)	220	yes	440	2	432ms
3	Fig. 2	3 (2)	8	yes	16	2	9ms
4	Fig. 4	15 (0)	1358	yes	2716	2	4s668ms
5	Fig. 4(†)	15 (0)	2702	yes	5404	2	14s716s
6	Fig. 4(†)	15 (0)	13580	yes	27160	2	1m41s
7	Fig. 4(‡)	15 (0)	1358	no	8	0	6ms
8	MP4-SP	5 (2)	299	yes	598	2	557ms
9	MP4-SP(†)	5 (2)	598	yes	6008	2	7s451ms
10	MP4-SP(§)	5 (2)	299	no	237	0	189ms

Fig. 3. Experiments on examples, where (†) denotes token rate modification preserving consistency, (‡) denotes a modified number of initial tokens, and (§) denotes marking an existing channel as deciding. The last three columns show the verdict, the number of firings and the number of full live executions executed by DIVERSITY.

We have applied our algorithm to different examples and summarized the results in Fig. 3. The three examples introduced in this paper were analyzed, and are referenced by Figure number (for Fig. 2 the tested model received synchronous constraints). The example denoted MP4-SP is a translation to Polygraph of the classical MPEG4-SP SADF decoder (see [13] for original graph). For some examples, transformations were applied to the initial model, in order to show how execution time increases linearly with the number of firings, or to voluntarily introduce an indecision. Correctness of verdicts was checked manually. Experiments were run on an Intel core i7-7920HQ@3.10 GHz, 32 GB RAM.

5 Discussion and Related Work

In [9], the authors introduced Synchronous Data Flow (SDF), a restriction of Kahn Process Networks [8], overcoming the undecidability of the existence of an admissible schedule (in the general case), and allowing static performance analysis. The key was the introduction of a linear behavior using static integer rates. For a more precise performance prediction, it is useful to allow rates to change dynamically during an execution to find tighter bounds on the evaluated memory footprint, throughput, and latency. The main difficulty to introduce such dynamic behavior resides in the capability to approximate the desired nonlinear behavior while preserving the good properties of a linear equation system.

Our proposition is one of many other approaches attempting to tackle this issue [1–3,10]. In Sect. 2, we mentioned SADF [14], and referenced a recent and extensive survey of similar approaches [6], showing that SADF is the most expressive while retaining the scheduling properties. Compared to SADF, Polygraph can express global synchronous constraints, simplifies the reconfiguration mechanisms by removing control channels, and offers a different approach to capture the dynamic changes in communication. Since the rational rates are the same in all modes, consistency and liveness can be checked as for static models. By adding configuration information per mode on the tokens, the existing examples with variable rates provided in [13] can be modeled in Polygraph without loss of behavioral information.

For example, in the translation of the MP3 decoder of Fig. 4, the actor H is a selector and determines the frame type for the left and right channels, and produces 2 granules of 576 components labeled with the determined frame types (*e.g.* FSL stands for short frame on left channel and long frame on right channel). Actor S is a follower of H, and it is also a selector, determining the amount and type of blocks to distribute to the block processing pipelines starting with actors AR_i. For example, if S consumes a granule labeled FSL on its 1st firing, it will not consume another granule for its next 95 firings (input rates 1/96), and from the 1st firing to the 96th, the left channel will receive 96 short blocks each of size 6, and the right channel will receive 32 long blocks each of size 18. In the model, both channels receive 96 tokens, the first 32 are labeled BSL for short block on left and long block on right, and the remaining 64 tokens are labeled $BS0$ for short block on left and empty block on right. As in SADF, depending on the mode for a firing, the execution time can change and be set to 0 for actors that do not process for the determined frame and block types.

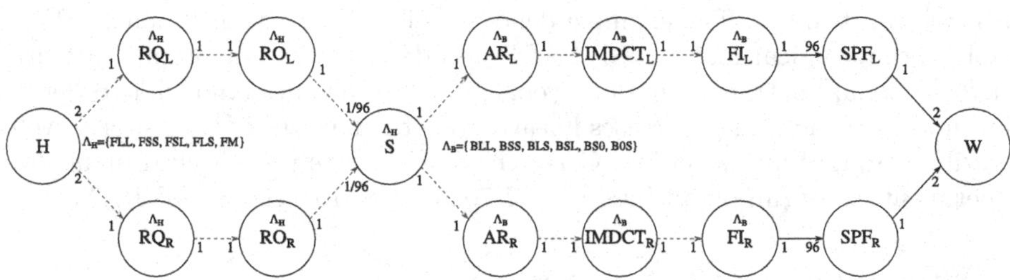

Fig. 4. A MP3 decoder modeled as a polygraph.

6 Conclusion

To cover the needs of modeling distributed and reconfigurable CPS, we have introduced dynamic behavior in Polygraph, such that for an extended polygraph, the consistency and liveness properties of the underlying static polygraph are not impacted by the extension. This allows for a single verification of these properties for a static model, and the static performance analysis of many alternative extended versions.

An adaptation of the existing approaches for the static performance analysis of similar languages will be the main part of our future work. In addition, we want to consider hierarchical and composable modeling of polygraphs, allowing the design of large scale complex distributed CPS.

Acknowledgement. Part of this work has been realized in the FACE/OPTEEM projects, involving CEA List and Renault. The Polygraph formalism has been used as a theoretical foundation for the software methodology in the project.

References

1. Bhattacharya, B., Bhattacharyya, S.S.: Parameterized dataflow modeling for DSP systems. IEEE Trans. Signal Process. **49**(10), 2408–2421 (2001)
2. Bilsen, G., Engels, M., Lauwereins, R., Peperstraete, J.A.: Cyclo-static data flow. In: Proceedings of ICASSP, vol. 5, pp. 3255–3258 (1995)
3. Buck, J.T.: Static scheduling and code gen. from dynamic dataflow graphs with integer-valued control streams. In: Proceedings of ACSSC, vol. 1, pp. 508–513 (1994)
4. Dubrulle, P., Gaston, C., Kosmatov, N., Lapitre, A., Louise, S.: Polygraph: a data flow model with frequency arithmetic (submitted)
5. Dubrulle, P., Gaston, C., Kosmatov, N., Lapitre, A., Louise, S.: A data flow model with frequency arithmetic. In: Hähnle, R., van der Aalst, W. (eds.) FASE 2019. LNCS, vol. 11424, pp. 369–385. Springer, Cham (2019). https://doi.org/10.1007/978-3-030-16722-6_22
6. Geilen, M., Falk, J., Haubelt, C., Basten, T., Theelen, B., Stuijk, S.: Performance analysis of weakly-consistent scenario-aware dataflow graphs. J. Signal Process. Syst. **87**(1), 157–175 (2017)
7. Geilen, M., Stuijk, S.: Worst-case performance analysis of synchronous dataflow scenarios. In: Proceedings of CODES+ISSS, pp. 125–134. ACM (2010)
8. Kahn, G., MacQueen, D., Laboria, I.: Coroutines and Networks of Parallel Processes. IRIA Research Report, IRIA Laboria (1976)
9. Lee, E.A., Messerschmitt, D.G.: Static scheduling of SDF programs for digital signal processing. IEEE Trans. Comput. **C–36**(1), 24–35 (1987)
10. Oh, H., Ha, S.: Fractional rate dataflow model for efficient code synthesis. J. VLSI Signal Process. Syst. Signal Image Video Technol. **37**(1), 41–51 (2004)
11. Plishker, W., Sane, N., Kiemb, M., Anand, K., Bhattacharyya, S.S.: Functional DIF for rapid prototyping. In: Proceedings of International Symposium on RSP, pp. 17–23 (2008)
12. The List Institute, CEA Tech: The DIVERSITY tool. http://projects.eclipse.org/proposals/eclipse-formal-modeling-project/
13. Theelen, B.D., et al.: Scenario-aware dataflow. Technical Reports, ESR-2008-08, TUE (2008)
14. Theelen, B.D., Geilen, M.C., Basten, T., Voeten, J.P., Gheorghita, S.V., Stuijk, S.: A scenario-aware data flow model for combined long-run average and worst-case performance analysis. In: Proceedings of MEMOCODE, pp. 185–194. IEEE (2006)
15. Wiggers, M.H., Bekooij, M.J., Smit, G.J.: Buffer capacity computation for throughput constrained streaming applications with data-dependent inter-task communication. In: Proceedings of RTAS, pp. 183–194. IEEE (2008)

Ontology-Mediated Probabilistic Model Checking

Clemens Dubslaff(✉), Patrick Koopmann, and Anni-Yasmin Turhan

Technische Universität Dresden, Dresden, Germany
{clemens.dubslaff,patrick.koopmann,anni-yasmin.turhan}@tu-dresden.de

Abstract. Probabilistic model checking (PMC) is a well-established method for the quantitative analysis of dynamic systems. Description logics (DLs) provide a well-suited formalism to describe and reason about terminological knowledge, used in many areas to specify background knowledge on the domain. We investigate how such knowledge can be integrated into the PMC process, introducing *ontology-mediated PMC*. Specifically, we propose a formalism that links ontologies to dynamic behaviors specified by guarded commands, the de-facto standard input formalism for PMC tools such as Prism. Further, we present and implement a technique for their analysis relying on existing DL-reasoning and PMC tools. This way, we enable the application of standard PMC techniques to analyze knowledge-intensive systems. Our approach is implemented and evaluated on a multi-server system case study, where different DL-ontologies are used to provide specifications of different server platforms and situations the system is executed in.

1 Introduction

Probabilistic model checking (PMC, see, e.g., [6,17] for surveys) is an automated technique for the quantitative analysis of dynamic systems. PMC has been successfully applied in many areas, e.g., to ensure that the system meets quality requirements such as low error probabilities or an energy consumption within a given bound. The de-facto standard specification for the dynamic (probabilistic) system under consideration is given by *stochastic programs*, a probabilistic variant of Dijkstra's guarded command language [14,21] used within many PMC tools such as Prism [24]. Usually, the behavior described by a stochastic program is part of a bigger system, or might be even used within a collection of systems that have an impact on the operational behavior as well. There are different ways in which this can be taken into consideration by using stochastic programs: one could (1) integrate additional knowledge about the surrounding system directly

The authors are supported by the DFG through the Collaborative Research Centers CRC 912 (HAEC) and TRR 248 (see https://perspicuous-computing.science, project ID 389792660), the Cluster of Excellence EXC 2050/1 (CeTI, project ID 390696704, as part of Germany's Excellence Strategy), and the Research Training Groups QuantLA (GRK 1763) and RoSI (GRK 1907).

W. Ahrendt and S. L. Tapia Tarifa (Eds.): IFM 2019, LNCS 11918, pp. 194–211, 2019.
https://doi.org/10.1007/978-3-030-34968-4_11

into the stochastic program, or (2) use the concept of nondeterminism that models all possible behaviors of the surrounding system. The second approach might lead to analysis results that are too coarse with respect to desired properties and increases the well-known state-space explosion problem. Also the first approach has its drawbacks: although guarded command languages are well-suited to specify operational behaviors, they are not specialized to describe static knowledge. This, e.g., makes it cumbersome to describe knowledge-intensive contexts within guarded commands. We therefore propose a third approach where we separate the specification of the dynamic behavior of a system from the specification of the additional knowledge that influences the behaviors. This allows to use different, specialized formalisms for describing the complex properties of the system analyzed. Further, such an approach adds flexibility, as we can exchange both behavioral and knowledge descriptions, e.g., to analyze the same behavior in different contexts, or to analyze different behaviors in the same context.

A well-established family of formalisms for describing domain knowledge are description logics (DLs), fragments of first-order logic balancing expressivity and decidability [1,3]. While the worst-case complexity for reasoning in DLs can be very high, modern optimized DL reasoning systems often allow reasoning even for very large knowledge bases in short times [30]. Logical theories formulated in a DL are called ontologies, and may contain universal statements defining and relating concepts from the application domain and assertional axioms about specific individuals.

In this paper, we propose *ontology-mediated probabilistic model checking* as an approach to include knowledge described in a DL ontology into the PMC process. The center of this approach are *ontologized (stochastic) programs* which can be subject of probabilistic model checking. Following the separation of concerns described above, ontologized programs use different formalisms for specifying the operational behavior and the ontology, loosely coupled through an interface. Specifically, ontologized programs are stochastic programs that use *hooks* to refer to the ontology within the behavior description, which are linked to DL expressions via the interface. The semantics of ontologized programs follows a product construction of the operational semantics for the stochastic program, combined with annotations in which states are additionally associated with DL knowledge bases. To analyze ontologized programs, we present a technique to rewrite ontologized programs into (plain) stochastic programs without explicit references to the ontology, preserving those properties of the program that are relevant for the analysis. A similar transformation is done to those analysis properties that depend on an ontology, i.e., include hooks. This translation approach enables the full potential of standard PMC tools such as PRISM [24] including advanced analysis properties [8,23] also for the analysis of ontologized programs with properties that refer to background knowledge captured in the ontology.

We implemented the technique in a tool chain in which the operational behavior is specified in the input language of PRISM, and where the ontology is given as an OWL knowledge base [28]. Since our approach is independent of any particular DL, the implementation supports any OWL-fragment that is supported by modern DL reasoners. In the translation process we use *axiom pinpointing* to minimize the use of external DL reasoning, and to enable a practical implementation.

We evaluated the implementation based on a heterogeneous multi-server scenario and show that our approach facilitates the analysis of knowledge-intensive systems when varying behavior and ontology.

Missing proofs and details about the evaluation can be found in the technical report [16] that also explains the use of ontology-mediated probabilistic model checking for the analysis of context-dependent systems.

2 Preliminaries

We recall well-known notions and formalisms from probabilistic model checking and description logics required to ensure a self-contained presentation throughout the paper. By $\mathbb{Q}$, $\mathbb{Z}$, and $\mathbb{N}$ we denote the set of rationals, integers, and nonnegative integers, respectively. Let S be a countable set. We denote by $\wp(S)$ the powerset of S. A probability *distribution* over S is a function $\mu\colon S \to [0,1] \cap \mathbb{Q}$ with $\sum_{s\in S} \mu(s) = 1$. The set of distributions over S is denoted by $Distr(S)$.

2.1 Markov Decision Processes

The operational model used in this paper is given in terms of *Markov decision processes (MDPs)* (see, e.g., [32]). MDPs are tuples $\mathcal{M} = \langle Q, Act, P, q_0, \Lambda, \lambda\rangle$ where Q and Act are countable sets of *states* and *actions*, respectively, $P\colon Q \times Act \rightharpoonup Distr(Q)$ is a partial probabilistic transition function, $q_0 \in Q$ an initial state, and Λ a set of labels assigned to states via the labeling function $\lambda\colon Q \to \wp(\Lambda)$. Intuitively, in a state $q \in Q$, we nondeterministically select an action $\alpha \in Act$ for which $P(q,\alpha)$ is defined, and then move to a successor state q' with probability $P(q,\alpha,q')$. Formally, a *path in* $\mathcal{M}$ is a sequence $\pi = q_0\,\alpha_0\,q_1\,\alpha_1\ldots$ where $P(q_i,\alpha_i)$ is defined and $P(q_i,\alpha_i,q_{i+1}) > 0$ for all i. The probability of a finite path is the product of its transition probabilities. Resolving nondeterministic choices gives then rise to a probability measure over *maximal paths*, i.e., paths that cannot be extended. Amending $\mathcal{M}$ with a *weight function* $wgt\colon Q \to \mathbb{N}$ turns $\mathcal{M}$ into a *weighted MDP* $\langle \mathcal{M}, wgt\rangle$. The weight of a finite path $\pi = q_0\,\alpha_0\,q_1\ldots q_n$ is defined as $wgt(\pi) = \sum_{i\leq n} wgt(q_i)$.

MDPs are suitable for a quantitative analysis using probabilistic model checking (PMC, cf. [6]). A property to be analyzed is usually defined using temporal logics over the set of labels, constituting a set of maximal paths for which the property is fulfilled after the resolution of nondeterministic choices. By ranging over all possible resolutions of nondeterminism, this enables a best- and worst-case analysis on the property. Standard analysis tasks ask, e.g., for the minimal and maximal probability of a given property, or the expected weight reaching a given set of states. An *energy-utility quantile* [5] is an advanced property that is used to reason about trade-offs: given a probability bound $p \in [0,1]$ and a set of goal states, we ask for the minimal (resp. maximal) weight required to reach the goal with probability at least p when ranging over some (resp. all) resolutions of nondeterminism.

2.2 Stochastic Programs

A concise representation of MDPs is provided by a probabilistic variant of Dijkstra's *guarded-command language* [14,21], compatible with the input language of the PMC tool PRISM [24]. Throughout this section, we fix a countable set *Var* of *variables*, on which we define *evaluations* as functions $\eta\colon \mathit{Var} \to \mathbb{Z}$. We denote the set of evaluations over *Var* by $\mathit{Eval}(\mathit{Var})$.

Arithmetic Constraints and Boolean Expressions. Let z range over $\mathbb{Z}$ and v range over *Var*. The set of *arithmetic expressions* $\mathbb{E}(\mathit{Var})$ is defined by the grammar

$$\alpha ::= z \mid v \mid (\alpha + \alpha) \mid (\alpha \cdot \alpha).$$

Variable evaluations are extended to arithmetic expressions in the natural way, i.e., $\eta(z) = z$, $\eta(\alpha_1 + \alpha_2) = \eta(\alpha_1) + \eta(\alpha_2)$, and $\eta(\alpha_1 \cdot \alpha_2) = \eta(\alpha_1) \cdot \eta(\alpha_2)$. $\mathbb{C}(\mathit{Var})$ denotes the set of *arithmetic constraints* over *Var*, i.e., terms of the form $(\alpha \bowtie z)$ with $\alpha \in \mathbb{E}(\mathit{Var})$, $\bowtie \in \{>, \geq, =, \leq, <, \neq\}$, and $z \in \mathbb{Z}$. For a given evaluation $\eta \in \mathit{Eval}(\mathit{Var})$ and constraint $(\alpha \bowtie z) \in \mathbb{C}(\mathit{Var})$, we write $\eta \models (\alpha \bowtie z)$ iff $\eta(\alpha) \bowtie z$ and say that $(\alpha \bowtie z)$ is *entailed by* η. Furthermore, we denote by $\mathbb{C}(\eta)$ the constraints entailed by η, i.e., $\mathbb{C}(\eta) = \{c \in \mathbb{C}(\mathit{Var}) \mid \eta \models c\}$.

For a countable set X and x ranging over X, we define *Boolean expressions* $\mathbb{B}(X)$ over X by the grammar $\phi ::= x \mid \neg\phi \mid \phi \wedge \phi$. Furthermore, we define the *satisfaction relation* $\models \subseteq \wp(X) \times \mathbb{B}(X)$ in the usual way (with $Y \subseteq X$) as $Y \models x$ if $x \in Y$, $Y \models \neg\psi$ iff $Y \not\models \psi$, and $Y \models \psi_1 \wedge \psi_2$ iff $Y \models \psi_1$ and $Y \models \psi_2$. For an evaluation $\eta \in \mathit{Eval}(\mathit{Var})$ and $\phi \in \mathbb{B}(\mathbb{C}(\mathit{Var}))$, we write $\eta \models \phi$ iff $\mathbb{C}(\eta) \models \phi$. Well-known Boolean connectives such as disjunction $\vee$, implication $\rightarrow$, etc. and their satisfaction relation can be deduced in the standard way using syntactic transformations, e.g., through de Morgan's rule.

Stochastic Programs. We call a function $u\colon \mathit{Var} \to \mathbb{E}(\mathit{Var})$ *update*, and a distribution $\sigma \in \mathit{Distr}(\mathit{Upd})$ over a given finite set *Upd* of updates *stochastic update*. The effect of an update $u\colon \mathit{Var} \to \mathbb{E}(\mathit{Var})$ on an evaluation $\eta \in \mathit{Eval}(\mathit{Var})$ is their composition $\eta \circ u \in \mathit{Eval}(\mathit{Var})$, i.e., $(\eta \circ u)(v) = \eta(u(v))$ for all $v \in \mathit{Var}$. This notion naturally extends to *stochastic updates* $\sigma \in \mathit{Distr}(\mathit{Upd})$ by $\eta \circ \sigma \in \mathit{Distr}(\mathit{Eval}(\mathit{Var}))$, where for any $\eta' \in \mathit{Eval}(\mathit{Var})$ we have

$$(\eta \circ \sigma)(\eta') = \sum_{u \in \mathit{Upd}, \eta \circ u = \eta'} \sigma(u).$$

A *stochastic guarded command* over a finite set of updates *Upd*, briefly called *command*, is a pair $\langle g, \sigma \rangle$ where $g \in \mathbb{B}(\mathbb{C}(\mathit{Var}))$ is a *guard* and $\sigma \in \mathit{Distr}(\mathit{Upd})$ is a stochastic update. Similarly, a *weight assignment* is a pair $\langle g, w \rangle$ where $g \in \mathbb{B}(\mathbb{C}(\mathit{Var}))$ is a guard and $w \in \mathbb{N}$ a *weight*. A *stochastic program* over *Var* is a tuple $\mathbf{P} = \langle Var, C, W, \eta_0 \rangle$ where C is a finite set of commands, W a finite set of weight assignments, and $\eta_0 \in Eval(Var)$ is an initial variable evaluation. For simplicity, we write $Upd(\mathbf{P})$ for the set of all updates in C.

The semantics of $\mathbf{P}$ is now defined as the weighted MDP

$$\mathcal{M}[\mathbf{P}] = \langle S, Act, P, \eta_0, \Lambda, \lambda, wgt \rangle$$

where

- $S = Eval(Var)$,
- $Act = Distr(Upd(\mathbf{P}))$,
- $\Lambda = \mathbb{C}(Var)$,
- $\lambda(\eta) = \mathbb{C}(\eta)$ for all $\eta \in S$,
- $P(\eta, \sigma, \eta') = (\eta \circ \sigma)(\eta')$ for any $\eta, \eta' \in S$ and $\langle g, \sigma \rangle \in C$ with $\lambda(\eta) \models g$, and
- $wgt(\eta) = \sum_{\langle g,w \rangle \in W, \lambda(\eta) \models g} w$ for any $\eta \in S$.

Note that $\mathcal{M}[\mathbf{P}]$ is indeed a weighted MDP and that $P(\eta, \sigma)$ is a probability distribution with finite support for all $\eta \in Eval(Var)$ and $\sigma \in Distr(Upd(\mathbf{P}))$.

2.3 Description Logics

We recall basic notions of description logics (DLs) (see, e.g., [1,3] for more details). Our approach presented in this paper is general enough to be used with any expressive DL, and our implementation supports the expressive DL $\mathcal{SROIQ}$ underlying the web ontology standard OWL-DL [20]. For illustrative purposes, we present here a small yet expressive fragment of this DL called $\mathcal{ALCQ}$. Let $\mathsf{N_c}$, $\mathsf{N_r}$ and $\mathsf{N_i}$ be pairwise disjoint countable sets of *concept names*, *role names*, and *individual names*, respectively. For $A \in \mathsf{N_c}$, $r \in \mathsf{N_r}$, and $n \in \mathbb{N}$, $\mathcal{ALCQ}$ *concepts* are then defined through the grammar

$$C ::= A \mid \neg C \mid C \sqcap C \mid \exists r.C \mid {\geq} nr.C.$$

Further concept constructors are defined as abbreviations: $C \sqcup D = \neg(\neg C \sqcap \neg D)$, $\forall r.C = \neg \exists r.\neg C$, ${\leq} nr.C = \neg {\geq} (n+1)r.C$, $\bot = A \sqcap \neg A$ (for any A), and $\top = \neg \bot$. *Concept inclusions* (CIs) are statements of the form $C \sqsubseteq D$, where C and D are concepts. A common abbreviation is $C \equiv D$ for $C \sqsubseteq D$ and $D \sqsubseteq C$. *Assertions* are of the form $A(a)$ or $r(a, b)$, where A is a concept, $r \in \mathsf{N_r}$, and $a, b \in \mathsf{N_i}$. CIs and assertions are commonly referred to as *DL axioms*, and we use $\mathbb{A}$ to denote the set of all DL axioms. A *knowledge base* $\mathcal{K}$ is a finite set of DL axioms.

CIs model background knowledge on notions and categories from the application domain. Assertions are used to describe the facts that hold for particular objects from the application domain.

Example 1. We can define the state of a multi-server platform, in which different servers run processes with different priorities, using the following assertions:

$$\mathsf{hasServer(platform, server1)} \quad \mathsf{hasServer(platform, server2)} \tag{1}$$

$$\mathsf{runsProcess(server2, process1)} \quad \mathsf{runsProcess(server2, process2)} \tag{2}$$

$$\mathsf{hasPriority(process1, highP)} \quad \mathsf{hasPriority(process2, highP)} \quad \mathsf{High(highP)}, \tag{3}$$

and specify further domain knowledge using the following CIs:

$$\exists \mathsf{runsProcess}.\top \sqsubseteq \mathsf{Server} \tag{4}$$
$$\geq 4\mathsf{runsProcess}.\top \sqsubseteq \mathsf{Overloaded} \tag{5}$$
$$\geq 2\mathsf{runsProcess}.\exists \mathsf{hasPriority}.\mathsf{High} \sqsubseteq \mathsf{Overloaded} \tag{6}$$
$$\mathsf{PlatformWithOverload} \equiv \exists \mathsf{hasServer}.\mathsf{Overloaded}. \tag{7}$$

These CIs express that if something runs a process (of some kind) then it is a server (4), and something that runs more than 4 processes is overloaded (5), that something is already overloaded when it runs 2 processes with a high priority (6), and that PlatformWithOverload is a platform that has an overloaded server (7)./

The semantics of DLs is defined in terms of *interpretations*, which are tuples $\langle \Delta^\mathcal{I}, \cdot^\mathcal{I} \rangle$ of a set $\Delta^\mathcal{I}$ of *domain elements*, and an *interpretation function* $\cdot^\mathcal{I}$ that maps every $A \in \mathsf{N_c}$ to some $A^\mathcal{I} \subseteq \Delta^\mathcal{I}$, every $r \in \mathsf{N_r}$ to some $r^\mathcal{I} \subseteq \Delta^\mathcal{I} \times \Delta^\mathcal{I}$, and every $a \in \mathsf{N_i}$ to some $a^\mathcal{I} \in \Delta^\mathcal{I}$. Interpretation functions are extended to complex concepts in the following way:

$$(\neg C)^\mathcal{I} = \Delta^\mathcal{I} \setminus C^\mathcal{I} \qquad\qquad (C \sqcap D)^\mathcal{I} = C^\mathcal{I} \cap D^\mathcal{I}$$
$$(\exists r.C)^\mathcal{I} = \{d \in \Delta^\mathcal{I} \mid \exists e : \langle d, e\rangle \in r^\mathcal{I} \wedge e \in C^\mathcal{I}\}$$
$$(\geq nr.C)^\mathcal{I} = \{d \in \Delta^\mathcal{I} \mid \#\{\langle d, e\rangle \in r^\mathcal{I} \mid e \in C^\mathcal{I}\} \geq n\}$$

Satisfaction of a DL axiom α in an interpretation $\mathcal{I}$, in symbols $\mathcal{I} \models \alpha$, is defined as $\mathcal{I} \models C \sqsubseteq D$ iff $C^\mathcal{I} \subseteq D^\mathcal{I}$, $\mathcal{I} \models A(a)$ iff $a^\mathcal{I} \in A^\mathcal{I}$, and $\mathcal{I} \models r(a, b)$ iff $\langle a^\mathcal{I}, b^\mathcal{I}\rangle \in r^\mathcal{I}$. An interpretation $\mathcal{I}$ is a *model* of a DL knowledge base $\mathcal{K}$ iff $\mathcal{I} \models \alpha$ for all $\alpha \in \mathcal{K}$. $\mathcal{K}$ is *inconsistent* if it does not have a model, and it *entails an axiom* α, in symbols $\mathcal{K} \models \alpha$, iff $\mathcal{I} \models \alpha$ for all models $\mathcal{I}$ of $\mathcal{K}$.

Example 2. Returning to Example 1, we have $\mathcal{K} \models \mathsf{Overloaded}(\mathsf{server2})$ as server server2 runs two prioritized processes, and $\mathcal{K} \models \mathsf{PlatformWithOverload}(\mathsf{platform})$ as platform has server2 as an overloaded server. /

3 Ontologized Programs

We introduce our notion of ontologized programs. In general, an ontologized program comprises the following three components:

The Program is a specification of the operational behavior given as an abstract stochastic program, which may use *hooks* to refer to knowledge relative to the ontology.

The Ontology is a DL knowledge base representing additional knowledge that may influence the behavior of the program.

The Interface links program and ontology by providing mappings between the language used in the program and the DL of the knowledge base.

We provide a formal definition of ontologized programs (Sect. 3.1) and define their semantics in terms of weighted MDPs (Sect. 3.2). To illustrate these definitions, we extend Example 1 towards a scenario for probabilistic model checking: we consider a generic multi-server platform on which processes can be assigned to servers, scheduled to complete a given number of jobs. The program specifies the dynamics of this scenario, i.e., how jobs are executed, how processes are assigned to servers or moved, and when processes terminate and when they are spawned. The ontology gives details and additional constraints for a specific multi-server platform. In this setting, probabilistic model checking can be used to analyze different aspects of the system, depending on the operational behavior and the different hardware and software configurations specified by the ontology.

3.1 Ontologizing Stochastic Programs

We introduce ontologized programs formally and illustrate their concepts by our running example. In preparation of the definition, we fix a set H of labels called *hooks*. We define *abstract stochastic programs* as an extension of stochastic programs where the guards used in guarded commands and in weights can be picked from the set $\mathbb{B}(\mathbb{C}(\mathit{Var}) \cup H)$. For instance, with a hook $\mathtt{migrate} \in H$, the following guarded command may appear in an abstract stochastic program:

$$(\mathtt{migrate} \wedge \mathtt{server\_proc1} = 2) \mapsto \begin{cases} 1/2 : \mathtt{server\_proc1} := 1 \\ 1/2 : \mathtt{server\_proc1} := 3 \end{cases}$$

This command states that, if the hook `migrate` is active and Process 1 runs on Server 2, then we move Process 1 to Server 1 or to Server 3 with a 50% probability each. For a given abstract program $\mathbf{P}$, we refer to its hooks by $H(\mathbf{P})$.

Definition 1. *An* ontologized program *is a tuple* $\mathbf{O} = \langle \mathbf{P}, \mathcal{K}, \mathbf{I} \rangle$ *where*

- $\mathbf{P} = \langle \mathit{Var}_{\mathbf{P}}, C, W, \eta_0 \rangle$ *is an abstract stochastic program,*
- $\mathcal{K}$ *is a DL knowledge base describing the* ontology,
- $\mathbf{I} = \langle \mathit{Var}_{\mathbf{O}}, H_{\mathbf{O}}, \mathcal{F}_{\mathbf{O}}, \mathsf{pD}, \mathsf{Dp} \rangle$ *is a tuple describing the* interface, *where* $\mathit{Var}_{\mathbf{O}}$ *is a set of variables,* $H_{\mathbf{O}}$ *is a set of hooks,* $\mathcal{F}_{\mathbf{O}}$ *is a set of* DL axioms *called* fluent axioms, *and two mappings* $\mathsf{pD}\colon H_{\mathbf{O}} \to \wp(\mathbb{A})$ *and* $\mathsf{Dp}\colon \mathcal{F}_{\mathbf{O}} \to \mathbb{B}(\mathbb{C}(\mathit{Var}_{\mathbf{O}}))$,

and for which we require that $\mathbf{I}$ *is* compatible with $\mathbf{P}$ *in the sense that* $H(\mathbf{P}) \subseteq H_{\mathbf{O}}$ *and* $\mathit{Var}_{\mathbf{O}} \subseteq \mathit{Var}_{\mathbf{P}}$. *Given an ontologized program* $\mathbf{O}$, *we refer to its abstract stochastic program by* $\mathbf{P}_{\mathbf{O}}$, *to its ontology by* $\mathcal{K}_{\mathbf{O}}$, *and to its interface by* $\mathbf{I}_{\mathbf{O}}$.

We illustrate the above definition and its components by our multi-server system example, for which we consider instances running n processes on m servers.

Program. The stochastic program $\mathbf{P}_{\mathbf{O}}$ specifies the protocol how processes are scheduled to complete their jobs when running on the same server, and when ontology-dependent migration of processes to other servers should be performed. Job scheduling could be performed, e.g., by selecting processes uniformly via tossing a fair coin or in a round-robin fashion. Here, the hook `migrate` $\in H$ is used to determine when a server should migrate processes to other servers. The program further specifies guarded weights, e.g., amending states marked with `migrate` by the costs to migrate processes.

Ontology. The knowledge base $\mathcal{K}_\mathbf{O}$ models background knowledge about a particular server platform. For instance, it could use the example axioms from Example 1 to specify hardware characteristics of the servers using the CIs (5)–(7), architecture specifics using the assertions in (1), and distribute different priorities among a set of predefined processes using the assertions in (3). To establish a link with the hook `migrate` in the interface, we use an additional CI to describe the conditions that necessitate a migration in the platform:

$$\mathsf{NeedsToMigrate} \equiv \mathsf{PlatformWithOverload}.$$

In more complex scenarios, migration can depend on a server and can be specified by more complex CIs. This modeling makes it easy to define different migration strategies within the different ontologies. Each of them can be used by simply referring to the `migrate` hook in the program.

Note that the guarded command language uses variables (over integers) to refer to servers and processes, while the knowledge base uses individual names for them. The program and the ontology thus have different views on the system, mapped to each other via the interface.

Interface. To interpret the states of the program $\mathbf{P}_\mathbf{O}$ in DL, the interface specifies a set $\mathcal{F}_\mathbf{O}$ of "fluent" DL axioms that describe the dynamics of the system. The function Dp maps each element $\alpha \in \mathcal{F}_\mathbf{O}$ to an expression $\mathsf{Dp}(\alpha) \in \mathbb{B}(\mathbb{C}(\mathit{Var}))$, identifying states in the program language in which α holds. It is thus a mapping from the DL to the abstract program language. In our example, $\mathcal{F}_\mathbf{O}$ would contain assertions of the form $\mathsf{runsProcess}(\mathsf{server}i, \mathsf{process}j)$, which are mapped using $\mathsf{Dp}(\mathsf{runsProcess}(\mathsf{server}i, \mathsf{process}j)) = (\mathtt{server\_proc}j = i)$ to constraints over the states of the abstract program. This allows to represent each program state as a DL knowledge base with axioms from $\mathcal{F}_\mathbf{O}$ and $\mathcal{K}_\mathbf{O}$. Note that the mapping Dp can only refer to variables that are used by the program, as we require $\mathit{Var}_\mathbf{O} \subseteq \mathit{Var}_\mathbf{P}$. Hence, for every axiom $\alpha \in \mathcal{F}_\mathbf{O}$, $\mathsf{Dp}(\alpha)$ has a well-defined meaning within the abstract program. However, the program may use additional variables that are only relevant for the operational behavior.

To interpret the hooks in the DL, we additionally need a mapping pD from the program language into the DL. Specifically, pD assigns to each hook $\ell \in H_\mathbf{O}$ a set $\mathsf{pD}(\ell)$ of DL axioms. In our running example, the hook `migrate` would, e.g., be mapped as $\mathsf{pD}(\mathtt{migrate}) = \{\mathsf{NeedsToMigrate}(\mathsf{platform})\}$. All hooks in the program are mapped by the interface due to the condition $H(\mathbf{P}) \subseteq H_\mathbf{O}$. However, further hooks can be defined that are only relevant for the analysis tasks to be performed. For instance, we might use a hook `critical` to mark critical situations in our system, and analyze the probability of the ontologized program to enter a state in which this hook is activated.

To illustrate the idea of the mappings, consider a virtual communication flow between the program and the ontology. If the ontology wants to know which axioms in $\alpha \in \mathcal{F}_{\mathbf{O}}$ hold in the current state, it "asks" the abstract program whether the expression $\mathsf{Dp}(\alpha)$ is satisfied. For the program to know which hooks $\ell \in H_{\mathbf{O}}$ are active in the current state, it "asks" the ontology whether an axiom in $\mathsf{pD}(\ell)$ is entailed. In the next section, we formalize this intuition and define the semantics of ontologized programs via induced MDPs.

3.2 Semantics of Ontologized Programs

The semantics is formally defined using *ontologized MDPs.* In order to account for both the program $\mathbf{P}_{\mathbf{O}}$ and the ontology $\mathcal{K}_{\mathbf{O}}$, the ontologized MDP induced by $\mathbf{P}_{\mathbf{O}}$ has to provide two views on its states. The first view is from the perspective of $\mathbf{P}_{\mathbf{O}}$: for a stochastic programs, a system state is characterized by an evaluation over $Var_{\mathbf{P}}$. For instance, a state q might be associated with the following evaluation η_q:

$$\texttt{server\_proc1} = 2 \qquad \texttt{server\_proc2} = 2 \qquad \texttt{server\_proc3} = 0,$$

stating that Process 1 and Process 2 run on Server 2, while Process 3 is currently not running. The second view is from the perspective of the ontology: state q is characterized by a knowledge base $\mathcal{K}_q$ that contains all axioms in $\mathcal{K}_{\mathbf{O}}$ and

$$\mathsf{runsProcess}(\mathsf{server2}, \mathsf{process1}) \qquad \mathsf{runsProcess}(\mathsf{server2}, \mathsf{process2}).$$

$\mathcal{K}_q$ entails $\mathsf{NeedsToMigrate}(\mathsf{platform})$, and therefore the state q should be labeled with the hook `migrate`. We make this intuition formal in the following definition.

Definition 2. *An* ontologized state *is a tuple of the form $q = \langle \eta_q, \mathcal{K}_q \rangle$, where η_q is an evaluation and $\mathcal{K}_q$ a DL knowledge base. Let $\mathbf{O}$ be an ontologized program as in Definition 1. An ontologized state q* conforms to $\mathbf{O}$ *iff*

1. $\mathcal{K}_q \subseteq \mathcal{K}_{\mathbf{O}} \cup \mathcal{F}_{\mathbf{O}}$,
2. $\mathcal{K}_{\mathbf{O}} \subseteq \mathcal{K}_q$, and
3. for every $\alpha \in \mathcal{F}_{\mathbf{O}}$, we have $\alpha \in \mathcal{K}_q$ iff $\eta_q \models \mathsf{Dp}(\alpha)$.

Intuitively, an ontologized state *conforms to* $\mathbf{O}$ if it conforms to the mapping Dp provided by the interface, as well as to the axioms specified by the ontology $\mathcal{K}_{\mathbf{O}}$. It follows from Condition 3 in Definition 2 that for every evaluation η and ontologized program $\mathbf{O}$, there is a unique ontologized state q that conforms to $\mathbf{O}$ such that $\eta_q = \eta$. We refer to this unique ontologized state as $q = e(\mathbf{O}, \eta)$, which is defined by $\eta_q = \eta$ and $\mathcal{K}_q = \mathcal{K}_{\mathbf{O}} \cup \{\alpha \in \mathcal{F}_{\mathbf{O}} \mid \eta \models \mathsf{Dp}(\alpha)\}$. This observation allows us to define updates on ontologized states in a convenient manner. Specifically, the result of applying an update u on an ontologized state q is defined as $u(q) = e(\mathbf{O}, u(\eta_q))$. Intuitively, we first apply the update on the evaluation η_q of q, and then compute its unique extension to an ontologized state conforming to $\mathbf{O}$. Our definition naturally extends to stochastic updates, leading to distributions over ontologized states.

Let q denote the ontologized state from above and consider the update $u = \{\texttt{server\_proc1} \mapsto 1\}$. For $q' = u(q)$, we obtain $u(\eta_q) = \eta_{q'}$ as

$$\texttt{server\_proc1} = 1 \qquad \texttt{server\_proc2} = 2 \qquad \texttt{server\_proc3} = 0,$$

and $\mathcal{K}'_q = \mathcal{K}_{\mathbf{O}} \cup \mathcal{F}'$, where $\mathcal{F}'$ contains

$$\mathsf{runsProcess}(\mathsf{server1}, \mathsf{process1}) \qquad \mathsf{runsProcess}(\mathsf{server2}, \mathsf{process2}).$$

While $\mathcal{K}_q \models \mathsf{NeedsToMigrate}(\mathsf{platform})$, there is no such entailment in $\mathcal{K}_{q'}$, so that the hook `migrate` should become inactive in state q'.

In the ontologized MDP, states are labeled with constraints $\mathbb{C}(\mathit{Var}_{\mathbf{O}})$ and with hooks $H_{\mathbf{O}}$. The hooks $h \in H_{\mathbf{O}}$ included in the label of a state q are determined by whether $\mathcal{K}_q \models \mathsf{pD}(h)$ is satisfied. This is captured using the labeling function of the MDP, since the labels determine relevant properties of a state for both model checking and update selection.

Definition 3. *Let* $\mathbf{O} = \langle \mathbf{P}, \mathcal{K}, \mathbf{I} \rangle$ *be an ontologized program as in Definition 1. The* weighted MDP induced by $\mathbf{O}$ *is* $\mathcal{M}[\mathbf{O}] = \langle Q, \mathit{Act}, P, q_0, \Lambda, \lambda, \mathit{wgt} \rangle$ *where*

- $Q = \{e(\mathbf{O}, \eta) \mid \eta \in \mathit{Eval}(\mathit{Var}_{\mathbf{P}})\}$,
- $\mathit{Act} = \mathit{Distr}(\mathit{Upd}(\mathbf{P}))$,
- $q_0 = e(\mathbf{O}, \eta_0)$,
- $\Lambda = H_{\mathbf{P}} \cup \mathbb{C}(\mathit{Var}_{\mathbf{P}})$,
- $\lambda(q) = \mathbb{C}(\eta_q) \cup \{\ell \in H_{\mathbf{O}} \mid \mathcal{K}_q \models \mathsf{pD}(\ell)\}$ *for every* $q \in Q$,
- $P(q_1, \sigma, q_2) = (\eta_{q_1} \circ \sigma)(\eta_{q_2})$ *for any* $q_1, q_2 \in Q$ *and* $\langle g, \sigma \rangle \in C$ *with* $\lambda(q_1) \models g$, *and*
- $\mathit{wgt}(q) = \sum_{\langle g, w \rangle \in W, \lambda(q) \models g} w$ *for all* $q \in Q$.

The above definition closely follows the standard semantics for stochastic programs (see Sect. 2.2), while amending knowledge information to each state in such a way that hooks are assigned to states as specified by the interface **I**. Thus, the weighted MDP induced by a ontologized program is well defined.

Remark on Inconsistent States. Note that our formalism allows for states of the induced MDP to have logically inconsistent knowledge bases assigned. We call those states *inconsistent*. We can identify and mark inconsistent states easily using a hook $\ell_\bot \in H$ for which we set $\mathsf{pD}(\ell_\bot) = \{\top \sqsubseteq \bot\}$. Depending on the application, inconsistent states might or might not be desirable. In general, there are different ways in which such states can be handled within our framework: (1) Inconsistent states could stem from errors in specification of the operational behavior or in the ontology. We would then want to provide users with tool support for detecting whether the program can enter an inconsistent state. Existing model-checking tools can directly be used for this, as they just have to check whether a state labeled with $\ell_\bot$ is reachable. (2) The stochastic program can detect inconsistent states using the hook $\ell_\bot$, and act upon them accordingly to resolve the inconsistency. This could be useful, e.g., for modeling exception handling or interrupts within the program to deal with unexpected situations. (3) Both the nondeterministic and probabilistic choices in the MDP can be restricted to only enter consistent states. The ontology then has a direct impact on the state space of the MDP. This can be seen as a desirable feature of ontologized programs, as different ontologies may pose different constraints on possible states a system may enter, which can be quite naturally expressed using DL axioms.

4 Analysis of Ontologized Programs

For the quantitative analysis of ontologized programs, we make use of a probabilistic model checking (PMC) tool in combination with a DL reasoner. Specifically, the DL reasoner is used to decide which hooks are assigned to each state in the MDP. This in turn depends on the axioms entailed by the knowledge base assigned to the state. Constructing the ontologized states explicitly is not feasible in practice, as there can be exponentially many. One might think about using advanced techniques to represent the set of MDP states concisely by PMC tools such as PRISM to mitigate the exponential blowup, e.g., through symbolic representations via MTBDDs [27]. However, such a representation does not provide a guarantee to concisely represent ontologized states and does not directly enable a method how to assign hooks. Furthermore, DL reasoning itself can be costly. For the DL $\mathcal{SROIQ}$ underlying the OWL-DL standard, reasoning is N2EXPTIME-complete [22], and already for its fragment $\mathcal{ALCQ}$ introduced in Sect. 2.3, it is EXPTIME-complete [35]. Even though there exist optimized reasoners that can deal with large OWL-DL ontologies [30], if we want to perform model checking efficiently, we should avoid invoking the reasoner exponentially many times.

In settings where ontologies are used to enrich queries over databases [9], a common technique is to *rewrite* queries by integrating all relevant information from the ontology. This allows for a direct evaluation of the rewritten query using standard database systems [10]. We propose a similar technique here, where we rewrite the ontologized program into a stochastic program that can be directly evaluated using PMC tools. To do this efficiently, our technique aims at reducing the amount of reasoning required and to reduce the size of the resulting program.

Formalizing this idea, we define a translation t from ontologized programs $\mathbf{O}$ into stochastic programs $t(\mathbf{O})$ that do not contain any hooks in guards. The translation is based on an assignment $\mathsf{hf}\colon H_{\mathbf{O}} \to \mathbb{B}(\mathbb{C}(\mathit{Var}_{\mathbf{O}}))$ of hooks $\ell \in H_{\mathbf{O}}$ to corresponding *hook formulas* $\mathsf{hf}(\ell)$, such that the MDPs induced by $\mathbf{O}$ and by $t(\mathbf{O})$ correspond to each other except for the hooks. This correspondence is captured in the following definition.

Definition 4. *Given two weighted MDPs, $\mathcal{M} = \langle S, \mathit{Act}, P, s_0, \Lambda, \lambda, \mathit{wgt}\rangle$ and $\mathcal{M}' = \langle S', \mathit{Act}', P', s_0', \Lambda', \lambda', \mathit{wgt}'\rangle$, such that $\mathit{Act} = \mathit{Act}'$, and a partial function $\mathsf{hf}\colon \Lambda \rightharpoonup \mathbb{B}(\Lambda')$ mapping labels in Λ to formulas over Λ', the weighted MDPs $\mathcal{M}$ and $\mathcal{M}'$ are* equivalent modulo hf *iff there exists a bijection $b\colon S \to S'$ such that*

1. $b(s_0) = s_0'$,

2. *for every* $s_1, s_2 \in S$ *and* $\alpha \in Act$, $P(s_1, \alpha)$ *is defined iff* $P'(b(s_1), \alpha)$ *is defined, and* $P(s_1, \alpha, s_2) = P'(b(s_1), \alpha, b(s_2))$,
3. *for every* $s \in S$, $wgt(s) = wgt'(b(s))$, *and*
4. *for every* $\ell \in \Lambda$ *and* $s \in S$ *holds that* $\ell \in \lambda(s)$ *iff* $\lambda(b(s)) \models \mathsf{hf}(\ell)$.

This notion extends to stochastic programs and ontologized programs via their induced MDPs: an ontologized program $\mathbf{O}$ and a stochastic program $\mathbf{P}$ are equivalent modulo hf iff $\mathcal{M}[\mathbf{O}]$ and $\mathcal{M}[\mathbf{P}]$ are equivalent modulo hf.

If an ontologized program $\mathbf{O}$ and a stochastic program $\mathbf{P}$ are equivalent modulo hf, all analysis tasks on $\mathbf{O}$ can be reduced to analysis on $\mathbf{P}$, as we just have to replace any label ℓ relevant for the analysis by $\mathsf{hf}(\ell)$. In particular, hf allows for a straightforward translation of properties expressed using temporal logics. As a result, we can perform any PMC task that is supported by a PMC tool like PRISM on ontologized programs, provided that the translation function hf and the corresponding stochastic program can be computed practically.

Based on $\mathbf{O}$ we define a function hf that can be efficiently computed using DL reasoning and which can be used to compute a corresponding stochastic program equivalent to the ontologized program modulo hf. Specifically, for every constraint $c \in \mathbb{C}(Var_{\mathbf{P}})$ we set $\mathsf{hf}(c) := c$, and for every hook $\ell \in H_{\mathbf{O}}$, we provide a *hook formula* $\mathsf{hf}(\ell)$. In other words, we only provide for a translation of the hooks, and keep the evaluations in the program the same. The stochastic program $t(\mathbf{O})$ is then obtained from $\mathbf{O}$ by replacing every hook $\ell \in H_{\mathbf{O}}$ by $\mathsf{hf}(\ell)$. This is sufficient, since the labels assigned to an ontologized state q are fully determined by the evaluation of the state: the axioms that are part of the state are determined by the mapping $\mathsf{Dp}\colon \mathcal{F}_{\mathbf{O}} \to \mathbb{B}(\mathbb{C}(Var))$, and the labels that are part of the state are determined by using the mapping $\mathsf{pD}\colon H_{\mathbf{O}} \to \wp(\mathbb{A})$, based on which axioms are entailed by the ontology $\mathcal{K}_q$ assigned to the state.

To compute hf in a goal-oriented manner, we make use of so-called *justifications*. These are defined independently of the DL in question, and there exist tools for computing justifications in various DLs.

Definition 5. *Given a knowledge base* $\mathcal{K}$ *and an axiom (set)* α *s.t.* $\mathcal{K} \models \alpha$, *a subset* $\mathcal{J} \subseteq \mathcal{K}$ *is a* justification of $\mathcal{K} \models \alpha$ *iff* $\mathcal{J} \models \alpha$, *and for every* $\mathcal{J}' \subsetneq \mathcal{J}$, $\mathcal{J}' \not\models \alpha$. *We denote by* $\mathsf{J}(\mathcal{O}, \alpha)$ *the set of all justifications of* $\mathcal{K} \models \alpha$.

Intuitively, a justification for $\mathcal{K} \models \alpha$ is a minimal sufficient axiom set witnessing the entailment of α from $\mathcal{K}$. For the hook formula $\mathsf{hf}(\ell)$, we consider the justifications $\mathcal{J}$ of $\mathcal{K}_{\mathbf{O}} \cup \mathcal{F} \models \mathsf{pD}(\ell)$, as these characterize exactly those subsets $\mathcal{F}' \subseteq \mathcal{F}_{\mathbf{O}}$ for which $\mathcal{K}_{\mathbf{O}} \cup \mathcal{F}' \models \mathsf{pD}(\ell)$. Note that for each such justification $\mathcal{J}$, only the subset $\mathcal{J} \setminus \mathcal{K}_{\mathbf{O}}$ is relevant. We thus define the hook formula $\mathsf{hf}(\ell)$ for $\ell \in H_{\mathbf{O}}$ as

$$\mathsf{hf}(\ell) = \bigvee_{\mathcal{J} \in \mathsf{J}(\mathcal{K}_{\mathbf{O}} \cup \mathcal{F}_{\mathbf{O}}, \mathsf{pD}(\ell))} \; \bigwedge_{\alpha \in (\mathcal{J} \cap \mathcal{F}_{\mathbf{O}})} \mathsf{Dp}(\alpha). \tag{8}$$

Here, we follow the convention that the empty disjunction corresponds to a contradiction $\bot$, while the empty conjunction corresponds to a tautology $\top$.

The final translation $t(\mathbf{O})$ of the ontologized program $\mathbf{O} = \langle \mathbf{P}, \mathcal{K}, \mathbf{I} \rangle$ is then obtained from $\mathbf{P}$ by replacing every hook $\ell \in H_{\mathbf{O}}$ by $\mathsf{hf}(\ell)$. The following theorem is proven in the extended version of the paper [16].

Theorem 1. *The ontologized program* $\mathbf{O}$ *and the stochastic program* $t(\mathbf{O})$ *are equivalent modulo* hf.

5 Evaluation

We implemented the method described in Sect. 4, where we use the input language of PRISM [24] to specify the abstract program, and the standard web ontology language OWL-DL [20] to specify the ontology. Specifically, our tool chain computes a stochastic program based on the ontologized program, on which we can directly perform ontology-mediated PMC using PRISM. We used the OWL-API [19] to parse and access the ontology, and the OWL reasoner Pellet [34] for computing the justifications, where we adapted the implementation slightly to improve its performance. Note that in Eq. 8 for the hook formula, we are only interested in the intersection of the full justification with the set $\mathcal{F}$ of the axioms the program can actually change. This reduces the search space for computing justifications drastically. We adapted the justification algorithm in PELLET to take this into account, which was crucial for computing the hook formulas used in our experiments. Apart from this optimization, we computed the situation formulas exactly as described in Sect. 4.

Our evaluation scenario is based on the multi-server platform example used in this paper, but modeled in more detail. In addition to modeling different capacity constraints of the servers and different priority settings on the processes, we also modeled software compatibility between processes and servers, so that certain processes can only be executed on servers having respective software support. We furthermore used three different types of hooks to link the abstract program with the ontology: (1) a *critical system state hook* to mark states the system should avoid, which we call in the following *critical states*, (2) a *migrate hook* describing when the system should schedule the migration of a process, and (3) *consistency hooks* specifying when it is allowed for a given process to be moved to a particular server, taking into account both capacity and compatibility limitations. We defined four ontologies in total, which differ in their capacity and compatibility constraints, as well as properties of the server and processes. To evaluate also the flexibility regarding the operational behavior in ontologized programs, we furthermore provided two abstract programs differing in their policy in how jobs are processed on each server by using either a randomized or round-robin selection. Weights were used to model the energy consumption of the system and the number of critical states entered. A special counter variable is used to store the *achieved utility* in terms of total number of jobs completed. Ontologies and abstract programs were defined for systems with two and three servers, respectively. Within all these combinations, we obtained $2 \cdot 4 \cdot 2 = 16$ ontologized programs in total, which we translated into stochastic programs expressed in the input language of PRISM. The rewriting of all 16

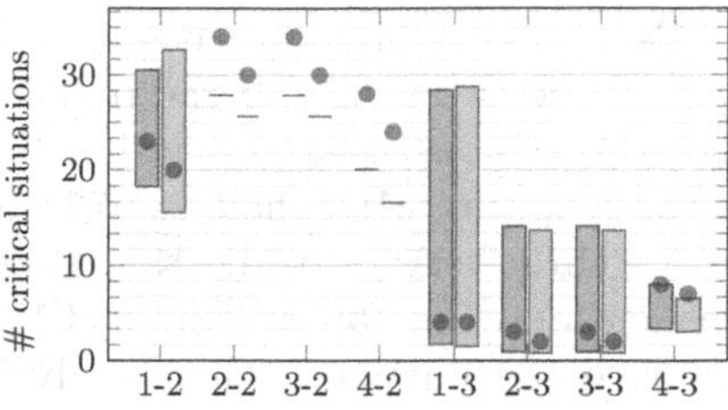

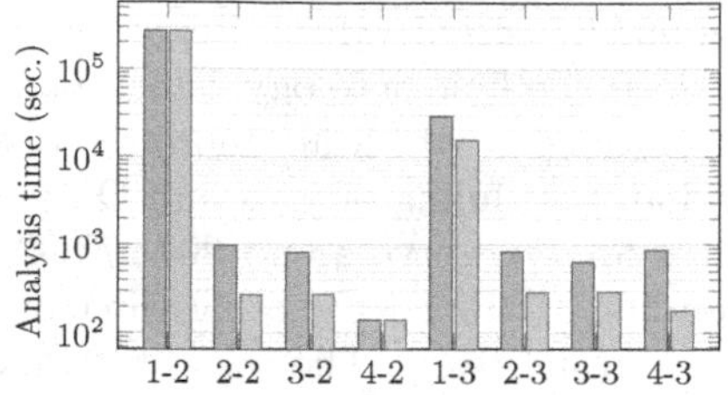

Fig. 1. Selected analysis results (left) and running times (right, logarithmic scale).

ontologized programs into PRISM programs took 130 s in total, including the computation of hook formulas using justifications.

For the analysis, we first considered standard reachability properties, and computed (i) the probability of reaching a critical system state within a given time window, (ii) the expected energy consumption of gaining a specified utility value, and (iii) the expected number of critical states entered before reaching a specified utility value. For each of these properties, we computed the minimal and maximal value when ranging over all nondeterministic choices in the MDP. To show-case our approach for more advanced model-checking tasks, we furthermore considered *energy-utility quantiles* [5]. Specifically, we computed (1) the minimal energy required, and (2) the minimal number of critical states entered, to gain a utility value of at least 20 with probability at least 95%.

All the experiments were carried out[1] using the symbolic MTBDD engine of PRISM 4.2 in the version presented in [23], which also supports advanced PMC tasks such as the computation of energy-utility quantiles [5]. Details about the setup, as well as the evaluation results for all PMC tasks, can be found in the extended version of the paper [16]. We only illustrate some of the results and analysis statistics. On the left in Fig. 1, we see the analysis results for property (iii), where bars span the range of minimal and maximal expected number of critical situations and for the critical situation quantile (2) depicted by dots. The analysis times required to compute these properties are depicted on the right of Fig. 1. The four different ontologies considered in both hardware/software settings are listed in the x-axis, using the notation "o-s", where "o" identifies an ontology and "s" is the number of servers. The blue and red bars show the values for random and round-robin scheduling behavior, respectively, modeled in the stochastic program. In the case of the two-server setup, only in the first ontology there is some freedom in performing migrations as in this ontology all software instances are placed on both servers while in the other ontologies each server has a different software setup. Hence, only in the configuration 1–2 (Ontology 1 with 2 servers) the minimal and maximal expected number of critical situations differ. For the three-server setup, the additional server provides enough freedom for migration strategies, but also there the first ontology has the most impact on

[1] Hardware setup: Intel Xeon E5-2680@2.70 GHz, 128 GB RAM; Turbo Boost and HT enabled; Debian GNU/Linux 9.1.

minimal/maximal values. Regarding the MDPs, we see a big difference as well between the first ontology, which poses very little constraints, and the remaining ontologies, which are more restrictive in terms of consistent states. For the random scheduling of jobs and Ontology 1, the resulting MDP had 23'072'910 states for two servers and 90'027'882 states for three servers, while the corresponding MDPs for the other three ontologies had between 158'368 and 934'122 states, respectively. The sizes of the models have direct impact on their analysis times, explaining the huge analysis times for the setups with Ontology 1 shown in Fig. 1. Our experiments hence show that model-checking speed and results profit from sufficiently precisely and restrictively modeled ontologies.

6 Related Work

Model Checking Context-Dependent Systems. The idea of using different formalisms for behaviors and contexts to facilitate model checking goes back to [13], where a scenario-based *context description language (CDL)* based on message sequence charts is used to describe environmental behaviors. Their aim is to mitigate the state-space explosion problem by resolving nondeterminism in the system to model the environment by parallel composition with CDL ontologies. Modeling and model checking role-based systems with exploiting exogenous coordination has been detailed in [7,12]. Here, components may play different roles in specific contexts (modeled through elements called *compartments*). As the approach above, the formalism to specify contexts is the same as for components, and a parallel composition is used for deployment. Feature-oriented systems describe systems comprising features that can be active or inactive (see, e.g., [15]). We can employ similar principles within our framework to combine ontological elements, as show-cased in our evaluation in Sect. 5. A reconfiguration framework for context-aware feature-oriented systems has been considered in [26]. All the above formalisms use an operational description of contexts, while we intentionally focused on a knowledge-based representation through ontologies that allows for reasoning about complex information and enables the reuse of established knowledge bases.

Description Logics in Golog Programs. There is a relation between our work and work on integrating DLs and ConGolog programs [4,36]. The focus there is on verifying properties formulated in computation tree logic for ConGolog programs, where also DL axioms specify tests within the program and within the properties to be checked. In contrast, we provide a generic approach that allows to employ various PMC tasks using existing tools, and allow for probabilistic programs. Furthermore, ontologies and program statements are not separated as in our approach. However, the main difference is that in the semantics of [4,36], states are identified with interpretations rather than knowledge bases, which are directly modified by the program. This makes reasoning much more challenging, and easily leads to undecidability if syntactic restrictions are not carefully put. Closer to our semantics are the DL-based programs presented in [11,18], where actions consist of additions and removals of assertions in the knowledge base. Again, there is no separation of concerns in terms of program and ontology, and they only support a Golog-like program language that cannot describe probabilistic behavior.

Ontology-Mediated Query Answering. There is a resemblance between the our concept of ontology-mediated PMC and *ontology-mediated query answering* (OMQA) [9,31], which also inspired the title of this paper. OMQA is concerned with the problem of querying a possibly incomplete database, where an ontology is used to provide for additional background knowledge about the domain of the data, so that also information that is only implicit in the database can be queried. Sometimes, additionally a mapping from concept and role names in the ontology to tables in the database is provided, which plays a comparable role to our interface [31]. Similar to our approach, a common technique for OMQA is to rewrite ontology-mediated queries into queries that can be directly evaluated on the data using standard database systems. However, different to our approach, this is in general only possible for very restricted DLs, while for expressive DLs, the complexity of OMQA is often very high [25,29,33].

7 Discussion and Future Work

We introduced ontologized programs, in which stochastic programs specify operational behaviors, and DLs are used to describe additional knowledge, with the aim of facilitating quantitative analysis of knowledge-intensive systems. From an abstract point of view, the general idea is to use different, domain-specific formalisms for specifying the program and knowledge, which are linked through hooks by an interface. We believe that the general idea of specifying operational behavior and static system properties separately, each using a dedicated formalism, would indeed be useful for many other applications. To this end, behaviors could be specified, e.g., by program code of any programming language, UML state charts, control-flow diagrams, etc., amended with hooks referring to additional knowledge, e.g., described by databases where hooks are resolved through database queries. Depending on the chosen formalisms, our method for rewriting ontologized programs could still be applicable in such settings.

Regarding the specific ontologized programs introduced in this paper, several improvements are possible. First, as discussed in Sect. 3.2, we are currently not addressing inconsistent states in the ontologized programs directly, but offer various ways to deal with them in the program or analysis. In future work, we want to investigate integrated mechanisms for handling inconsistent states in an automatized way. Second, one could look at closer integrations between the ontology and the abstract program by means of a richer interface. For example, we could map numerical values directly into the DL by use of *concrete domains* [2], which would allow to express more numerical constraints in the ontology. Furthermore, we want to investigate dynamic switching of ontologies during program execution, to model complex interaction between ontologies as in [15], exploiting the close connection to feature-oriented systems discussed in Sect. 6.

References

1. Baader, F., Calvanese, D., McGuinness, D.L., Nardi, D., Patel-Schneider, P.F. (eds.): The Description Logic Handbook: Theory, Implementation, and Applications. Cambridge University Press, Cambridge (2003)
2. Baader, F., Hanschke, P.: A scheme for integrating concrete domains into concept languages. In: Proceedings of IJCAI 1991, pp. 452–457. Morgan Kaufmann (1991)
3. Baader, F., Horrocks, I., Lutz, C., Sattler, U.: An Introduction to Description Logic. Cambridge University Press, Cambridge (2017)
4. Baader, F., Zarrieß, B.: Verification of Golog programs over description logic actions. In: Fontaine, P., Ringeissen, C., Schmidt, R.A. (eds.) FroCoS 2013. LNCS (LNAI), vol. 8152, pp. 181–196. Springer, Heidelberg (2013). https://doi.org/10.1007/978-3-642-40885-4_12
5. Baier, C., Daum, M., Dubslaff, C., Klein, J., Klüppelholz, S.: Energy-utility quantiles. In: Badger, J.M., Rozier, K.Y. (eds.) NFM 2014. LNCS, vol. 8430, pp. 285–299. Springer, Cham (2014). https://doi.org/10.1007/978-3-319-06200-6_24
6. Baier, C., Katoen, J.P.: Principles of Model Checking. MIT Press, Cambridge (2008)
7. Baier, C., Chrszon, P., Dubslaff, C., Klein, J., Klüppelholz, S.: Energy-utility analysis of probabilistic systems with exogenous coordination. In: de Boer, F., Bonsangue, M., Rutten, J. (eds.) It's All About Coordination. LNCS, vol. 10865, pp. 38–56. Springer, Cham (2018). https://doi.org/10.1007/978-3-319-90089-6_3
8. Baier, C., et al.: Probabilistic model checking and non-standard multi-objective reasoning. In: Gnesi, S., Rensink, A. (eds.) FASE 2014. LNCS, vol. 8411, pp. 1–16. Springer, Heidelberg (2014). https://doi.org/10.1007/978-3-642-54804-8_1
9. Bienvenu, M., Ortiz, M.: Ontology-mediated query answering with data-tractable description logics. In: Reasoning Web, Web Logic Rules, pp. 218–307 (2015)
10. Calvanese, D., De Giacomo, G., Lembo, D., Lenzerini, M., Rosati, R.: Tractable reasoning and efficient query answering in description logics: the DL-lite family. J. Autom. Reasoning **39**(3), 385–429 (2007)
11. Calvanese, D., De Giacomo, G., Lenzerini, M., Rosati, R.: Actions and programs over description logic knowledge bases: a functional approach. In: Knowing, Reasoning, and Acting: Essays in Honour of H. J. Levesque, College Publications (2011)
12. Chrszon, P., Dubslaff, C., Klüppelholz, S., Baier, C.: Family-based modeling and analysis for probabilistic systems – featuring ProFeat. In: Stevens, P., Wąsowski, A. (eds.) FASE 2016. LNCS, vol. 9633, pp. 287–304. Springer, Heidelberg (2016). https://doi.org/10.1007/978-3-662-49665-7_17
13. Dhaussy, P., Boniol, F., Roger, J.C., Leroux, L.: Improving model checking with context modelling. Adv. Softw. Eng. **2012**, 13 (2012)
14. Dijkstra, E.W.: A Discipline of Programming. Prentice-Hall, Upper Saddle River (1976)
15. Dubslaff, C., Baier, C., Klüppelholz, S.: Probabilistic model checking for feature-oriented systems. Trans. Aspect Oriented Softw. Dev. **12**, 180–220 (2015)
16. Dubslaff, C., Koopmann, P., Turhan, A.Y.: Ontology-mediated probabilistic model checking (extended version). LTCS-Report 19–05, TU Dresden, Dresden, Germany (2019). https://lat.inf.tu-dresden.de/research/reports.html
17. Forejt, V., Kwiatkowska, M., Norman, G., Parker, D.: Automated verification techniques for probabilistic systems. In: Bernardo, M., Issarny, V. (eds.) SFM 2011. LNCS, vol. 6659, pp. 53–113. Springer, Heidelberg (2011). https://doi.org/10.1007/978-3-642-21455-4_3

18. Hariri, B.B., Calvanese, D., Montali, M., De Giacomo, G., De Masellis, R., Felli, P.: Description logic knowledge and action bases. J. Artif. Intell. Res. **46**, 651–686 (2013)
19. Horridge, M., Bechhofer, S.: The OWL API: a Java API for OWL ontologies. Semant. Web **2**(1), 11–21 (2011)
20. Horrocks, I., Kutz, O., Sattler, U.: The even more irresistible $\mathcal{SROIQ}$. In: Proceedings of KR 2006, pp. 57–67. AAAI Press (2006)
21. Jifeng, H., Seidel, K., McIver, A.: Probabilistic models for the guarded command language. Sci. Comput. Program. **28**(2), 171–192 (1997)
22. Kazakov, Y.: $\mathcal{RIQ}$ and $\mathcal{SROIQ}$ are harder than $\mathcal{SHOIQ}$. In: Proceedings of the 11th International Conference on Principles of Knowledge Representation and Reasoning (KR 2008), pp. 274–284. AAAI Press (2008)
23. Klein, J., et al.: Advances in probabilistic model checking with PRISM: variable reordering, quantiles and weak deterministic büchi automata. Int. J. Softw. Tools Technol. Transfer **20**(2), 179–194 (2018)
24. Kwiatkowska, M., Norman, G., Parker, D.: PRISM 4.0: verification of probabilistic real-time systems. In: Gopalakrishnan, G., Qadeer, S. (eds.) CAV 2011. LNCS, vol. 6806, pp. 585–591. Springer, Heidelberg (2011). https://doi.org/10.1007/978-3-642-22110-1_47
25. Lutz, C.: Inverse roles make conjunctive queries hard. In: Proceedings of the 20th International Workshop on Description Logics (DL 2007), CEUR Workshop Proceedings, vol. 250 (2007). CEUR-WS.org
26. Mauro, J., Nieke, M., Seidl, C., Yu, I.C.: Context aware reconfiguration in software product lines. In: Proceedings of the 10th International Workshop on Variability Modelling of Software-Intensive Systems (VaMoS 2016), pp. 41–48. ACM (2016)
27. Miner, A., Parker, D.: Symbolic representations and analysis of large probabilistic systems. In: Baier, C., Haverkort, B.R., Hermanns, H., Katoen, J.-P., Siegle, M. (eds.) Validation of Stochastic Systems. LNCS, vol. 2925, pp. 296–338. Springer, Heidelberg (2004). https://doi.org/10.1007/978-3-540-24611-4_9
28. Motik, B., Cuenca Grau, B., Horrocks, I., Wu, Z., Fokoue, A., Lutz, C.: OWL 2 web ontology language profiles. W3C Recommendation, 27 October 2009. http://www.w3.org/TR/2009/REC-owl2-profiles-20091027/
29. Ngo, N., Ortiz, M., Simkus, M.: Closed predicates in description logics: results on combined complexity. In: Proceedings of KR 2016, pp. 237–246. AAAI Press (2016)
30. Parsia, B., Matentzoglu, N., Gonçalves, R.S., Glimm, B., Steigmiller, A.: The OWL reasoner evaluation (ORE) 2015 competition report. J. Autom. Reasoning **59**(4), 455–482 (2017)
31. Poggi, A., Lembo, D., Calvanese, D., De Giacomo, G., Lenzerini, M., Rosati, R.: Linking data to ontologies. J. Data Semant. **4900**, 133–173 (2008)
32. Puterman, M.: Markov Decision Processes: Discrete Stochastic Dynamic Programming. Wiley, New York (1994)
33. Rudolph, S., Glimm, B.: Nominals, inverses, counting, and conjunctive queries or: why infinity is your friend!. J. Artif. Intell. Res. **39**, 429–481 (2010)
34. Sirin, E., Parsia, B., Grau, B.C., Kalyanpur, A., Katz, Y.: Pellet: a practical OWL-DL reasoner. J. Web Semant. **5**(2), 51–53 (2007)
35. Tobies, S.: Complexity results and practical algorithms for logics in knowledge representation. Ph.D. thesis, RWTH Aachen University, Germany (2001)
36. Zarrieß, B., Claßen, J.: Verification of knowledge-based programs over description logic actions. In: IJCAI, pp. 3278–3284. AAAI Press (2015)

Fuzzing JavaScript Environment APIs with Interdependent Function Calls

Renáta Hodován, Dániel Vince, and Ákos Kiss(✉)

Department of Software Engineering, University of Szeged, Dugonics tér 13., Szeged 6720, Hungary
{hodovan,vinced,akiss}@inf.u-szeged.hu

Abstract. The prevalence of the JavaScript programming language makes the correctness and security of its execution environments highly important. The most exposed and vulnerable parts of these environments are the APIs published to the executed untrusted JavaScript programs. This paper revisits the fuzzing technique that generates JavaScript environment API calls using random walks on so-called prototype graphs to uncover potentially security-related failures. We show the limits of generating independent call expressions, the approach of prior work, and give an extension to enable the generation of interdependent API calls that re-use each other's results. We demonstrate with an experiment that this enhancement allows our approach to exercise JavaScript environment APIs in ways that were not possible with the previous approach, and that it can also trigger more issues in a real target.

1 Introduction

> *"For the seventh year in a row, JavaScript is the most commonly used programming language"*
> —Stack Overflow Developer Survey Results 2019

The popularity of JavaScript (standardized as ECMAScript [4]) has been steadily growing over the past few years until it became the most commonly used programming language. Not only is it enabling the client-side execution of web applications in browsers but it is also driving the server-side [21]. Moreover, even resource-constrained IoT devices have become programmable using JavaScript, thanks to memory-aware execution engines [14,26] and application environments built on top of them [23].

Having an easy to learn, well-supported, and flexible language available on all our computing devices opens up great possibilities but it also makes the correctness and security of its execution environments highly important. This is especially true when untrusted code can be executed in these environments, e.g., in web browsers, on modular platforms with a community-maintained package

W. Ahrendt and S. L. Tapia Tarifa (Eds.): IFM 2019, LNCS 11918, pp. 212–226, 2019.
https://doi.org/10.1007/978-3-030-34968-4_12

registry, or on devices with JavaScript-based open application models [5]. In these scenarios, those parts of the execution environments are the most exposed and the most vulnerable, which publish such APIs to the executed JavaScript programs that cross the so-called trust boundary, i.e., which allow calling and passing parameter data from untrusted JavaScript programs into the trusted code of the environment that is typically compiled to machine code and running at elevated privileges.

Random or fuzz testing is a popular automatic technique for uncovering bugs with potential security implications [25]. Fuzzers generate totally or partially random test cases and feed them to their target (a.k.a. system-under-test or SUT) hoping that some of these inputs cause the SUT to malfunction, e.g., lead to an exploitable crash. In the context of JavaScript execution environments (engines, platforms) this means that fuzzers have to generate executable JavaScript programs as test inputs.

In previous work [9], we introduced a graph representation modelling the objects and types of JavaScript engine APIs, and a fuzzing approach for generating test cases consisting of call expressions to those APIs by performing random walks on such graphs. In this paper, we show the limits of generating independent call expressions and extend the previous work to enable the generation of interdependent API calls that re-use each other's results. We demonstrate that this extension can better exercise APIs in a JavaScript environment and trigger more issues in a real project than the original variant.

The rest of the paper is organized as follows: first, in Sect. 2, we give a brief overview of the used graph representation and we also give an algorithm for generating (independent) call expressions from the graph, then in Sect. 3 we describe how to allow the calls to be interdependent. In Sect. 4, we present the results of our experiment with the proposed approach. In Sect. 5, we discuss related work. Finally, in Sect. 6, we give a summary of our work and conclude the paper.

2 Prototype Graphs

In our previous paper [9], we introduced a graph representation for the weak type system of JavaScript, called the *Prototype Graph*. The graph balances between the theoretical possibility that each object in a JavaScript program can have completely different prototype and members, and the observation that in practice they tend to fall into similarity categories in an actual execution environment. As the rest of this paper builds on this representation, for the sake of completeness, we give the original definition of prototype graphs below.

Definition 1 (Prototype Graph). Let a *Prototype Graph* be a labeled directed multigraph (a graph allowing parallel edges with own identity)

$$G = \langle V, E, s, t, l_{prop}, l_{param} \rangle$$

such that

- $V = V_{type} \cup V_{sig}$, set of vertices, where the subsets are disjoint,
  - V_{type} vertices represent 'types', i.e., categories of similar objects,
  - V_{sig} vertices represent 'signatures' of callable types, i.e., functions,
- $E = E_{proto} \cup E_{prop} \cup E_{cstr} \cup E_{call} \cup E_{param} \cup E_{ret}$, set of edges, where all subsets are mutually disjoint,
  - E_{proto} edges represent prototype relation ('inheritance') between types,
  - E_{prop} edges represent the properties ('members') of types,
  - E_{cstr} and E_{call} edges connect callable types to their signatures and represent the two ways they can be invoked, i.e., the construct and call semantics,
  - E_{param} edges represent type information on parameters of callable types,
  - E_{ret} edges represent return types of callable types,
- $s : E \to V$ assigns to each edge its source vertex, under the constraint that $\forall e \in E_{proto} \cup E_{prop} \cup E_{cstr} \cup E_{call} \cup E_{param} : s(e) \in V_{type}$ and $\forall e \in E_{ret} : s(e) \in V_{sig}$,
- $t : E \to V$ assigns to each edge its target vertex, under the constraint that $\forall e \in E_{proto} \cup E_{prop} \cup E_{ret} : t(e) \in V_{type}$ and $\forall e \in E_{cstr} \cup E_{call} \cup E_{param} : t(e) \in V_{sig}$,
- the $\langle V, E_{proto}, s|_{E_{proto}}, t|_{E_{proto}} \rangle$ directed sub-multigraph is acyclic,
- $l_{prop} : E_{prop} \to \Sigma$ labeling function assigns arbitrary symbols ('names') to property edges, under the constraint that $\forall e_1, e_2 \in E_{prop} : s(e_1) = s(e_2) \Rightarrow l_{prop}(e_1) = l_{prop}(e_2) \iff e_1 = e_2$,
- $l_{param} : E_{param} \to \mathbb{N}_0$ labeling function assigns numeric indices to parameter edges, under the constraint that $\forall e_1, e_2 \in E_{param} : t(e_1) = t(e_2) \Rightarrow l_{param}(e_1) = l_{param}(e_2) \iff e_1 = e_2$.

Informally, a prototype graph is a collection of *type* and *sig* vertices connected by six different kind of edges (and multiple edges can run between two vertices). *Proto* and *prop* edges connect *type* vertices, while the others connect *type* and *sig* vertices in one direction or the other. And finally, member (property) name information and function argument order is encoded in edge labels. Vertices have no labeling as all relevant information is encoded in the existence of and labels of edges.

How such a graph can be built automatically is described both in our previous paper and will also be discussed later in Sect. 4. But Fig. 1 already shows an example prototype graph of 7 *type* and 4 *sig* vertices, manually constructed based on a portion of the ECMAScript 5.1 standard [4, Sections 15.2, 15.3]. The graph contains the types of `Object`, `Object.prototype`, `Function`, and `Function.prototype` objects, the global object, two constructor signatures for `Object`, and also the types and call signatures for two additional functions (`Object.create` and `Object.valueOf`).

In our previous work, we have shown how this graph representation encodes property accesses, type-correct parametrization of function and constructor calls, and also how the expressive power of the graph can be extended to deal with literals; and we have formally defined a set of function call expressions that can be generated from a graph. Now, we rephrase our original formal definitions into an algorithm to show how to generate a single function call instead

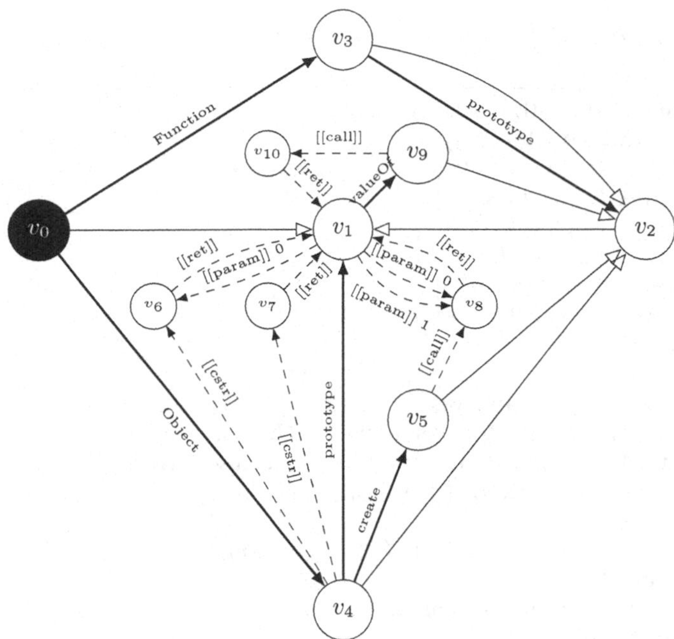

Fig. 1. Example prototype graph manually constructed based on a portion of the ECMAScript 5.1 standard. Large and small nodes represent *type* and *sig* vertices respectively. The single black node on the left represents the type of the global object. (Both colors and vertex labels are for identification and presentation purposes only.) Thick lines with labels represent *prop* edges, thin lines with hollow arrows represent *proto* edges, while dashed lines with double-bracketed labels represent *cstr*, *call*, *param*, and *ret* edges.

of all possible functions function call expressions. The random and recursive graph walking algorithm that collects the labels of visited edges thus generating a test case is named RANDOMCALL and is given in Listing 1. The informal concept behind the formal definition is to first walk forward on *proto*, *prop*, *cstr*, *call*, and *ret* edges to a *sig* vertex, then walk backward on *param* and *proto* edges, and so on... For the sake of brevity, G is always an alias to $\langle V_{type} \cup V_{sig}, E_{proto} \cup E_{prop} \cup E_{cstr} \cup E_{call} \cup E_{param} \cup E_{ret}, \quad s, t, l_{prop}, l_{param} \rangle$ in the algorithm, as in Definition 1; Λ is a function from *type* vertices to a set of literals (i.e., valid JavaScript expressions lying outside the expressiveness of the graph); and v_0 is a designated starting vertex in V_{type}, usually the type of the global object of the JavaScript language. The algorithm is also relying on some helper functions: RANDOMPATH finds a random finite path in a graph between two vertices on *proto*, *prop*, *cstr*, *call*, and *ret* edges and returns the list of edges on the found path; PARAMETERS enumerates the sources of all incoming *param* edges in ascending order of the edge labels (and returns them together with the edge labels); DESCENDANTS returns all vertices transitively available backwards

Listing 1. Algorithm for generating random function call expressions from a prototype graph.

```
procedure RANDOMEXPR(G, Λ, v_from, v_to)
  expr := RANDOM(Λ(v_from))
  forall e_step in RANDOMPATH(G, v_from, v_to) do
    if e_step ∈ E_prop then
      expr += '.' + l_prop(e_step)
    elif e_step ∈ E_call ∪ E_cstr then
      if e_step ∈ E_cstr then
        expr := 'new (' + expr + ')'
      end if
      expr += '('
      forall n, v_param in PARAMETERS(G, t(e_step)) do
        v_param := RANDOM(DESCENDANTS(G, v_param))
        if |Λ(v_param)| > 0 and RANDOM({true,false}) then
          expr += RANDOM(Λ(v_param))
        else
          expr += RANDOMEXPR(G, Λ, v_from, v_param)
        end if
        expr += not last iteration ? ',' : ''
      end forall
      expr += ')'
    end if
  end forall
  return expr
end procedure

procedure RANDOMCALL(G, Λ, v_0)
  return RANDOMEXPR(G, Λ, v_0, RANDOM(V_sig))
end procedure
```

from a starting point (including the starting vertex); and RANDOM randomly selects one element from its parameter set. Finally, $+$ and $+=$ stand for string concatenation.

As an example, below we give some test cases that can be generated with RANDOMCALL(G_{ex}, Λ_{ex}, v_0), where G_{ex} is the graph shown in Fig. 1, v_0 is the type of the global object in that graph (i.e., the `this` of the current lexical scope, marked with black), and $\Lambda_{ex} = \{v_0 \mapsto \{\text{'this'}\}, v_1 \mapsto \{\text{'\{\}'}\}\}$:

- `this.Function.valueOf()`,
- `new (this.Object)(this.Function.valueOf())`,
- `this.Object.valueOf().create(this.Object.prototype.valueOf(),{})`.

Listing 2. Datagram sending example.

```
var client = require('dgram').createSocket('udp4');
client.send(Buffer.from('Some bytes'), 41234,
    'localhost', function (err) { client.close(); });
```

3 Interdependent Function Calls

The above described prototype graph representation and its use to generate test cases for JavaScript engines showed promising results as they had triggered real failures [9]. However, the previous paper has only shown the results of generating expressions that are independent of each other. As it is also shown by the examples at the end of the previous section, even if such expressions were executed in sequence in the same execution context, there was very little possibility for them to have an effect on each other (a notable exception is if an expression changes the properties of a prototype object, as that may have an overarching effect even on future descendants of the prototype).

The fact that the expressions are mostly independent is no shortcoming if the types or objects of the API-under-test can be exercised that way, i.e., without a state carried across multiple expressions. This turns out to be mostly the case for the standard built-in ECMAScript objects [4, Section 15], i.e., if a JavaScript engine is only tested in its purest form (like the *jsc*, *d8*, *jerry*, or *duk* command line utilities of the WebKit/JavaScriptCore, V8, JerryScript, or Duktape projects, respectively). However, JavaScript engines are rarely used on their own, they are usually embedded in some bigger application. To make the embedding useful, the environments or platforms that build on top of JavaScript engines extend the standard ECMAScript API with custom types and objects and functions; and we have found that independent function call expressions are insufficient for the testing of many of these APIs.

For example, both Node.js [21] and IoT.js [23] are JavaScript application environments that allow the extension of the execution context with various modules. Both environments support UDP datagrams via the *dgram* module (as the resource-constrained IoT.js aims at being upward compatible with the desktop and server-targeted Node.js platform), where the proper sending of a datagram requires four steps: the loading of the module, the creation of a socket, the sending of the message, and the closing of the socket. As the example in Listing 2 shows, the established API of the *dgram* module does not allow to express all these steps as a single expression. In this example, the result of the expression that created the socket object needs to be carried over to and reused in the next expression: the same object must be used to send the message as well as to close the socket. However, if expressions are generated independently, there is no way for an object that was created in one expression to be further accessed in another. This means that the RANDOMCALL algorithm has no chance to generate test cases like Listing 2.

Listing 3. Algorithm for generating lists of interdependent random function call expressions from a prototype graph.

```
RANDOMEXPR' := RANDOMEXPR
procedure RANDOMEXPR(G, Λ, v_from, v_to)
  return RANDOMEXPR'(G, Λ, RANDOM(DOMAIN(Λ)), v_to)
end procedure

procedure RANDOMCALLLIST(G, Λ, n)
  list := ''
  forall i in 1..n do
    uid := UNIQUEID()
    v_from := RANDOM(DOMAIN(Λ))
    v_to := RANDOM(V_sig)
    list += 'var ' + uid + '=' + RANDOMEXPR'(G, Λ, v_from, v_to) + ';'
    Λ(RET(G, v_to)) ∪= {uid}
  end forall
  return list
end procedure
```

The *dgram* module is not the only one with an API that needs objects kept across functions calls, and Node.js or IoT.js are not the only platforms that host such APIs. The classic embedders of JavaScript engines, i.e., browsers, and their web API also show similar patterns. Rendering context objects of the DOM interface of HTML canvas elements [29] are also typical examples of objects that have to be reused in multiple function calls.

Therefore, we propose to enhance the prototype graph-based fuzzing approach shown in the previous section by generating multiple expressions for a single test case, capturing the results of the individual expressions, and re-using them in following generations. Fortunately, the prototype graph-based formalism and algorithm have an 'extension point', the Λ function, that allows the generation of expressions that lay outside the expressiveness of the graph. So, we propose to generate variable statements with the graph-generated expressions being the initialisers (and with unique identifiers as variable names), and to change (update) the Λ function after the generation of every variable statement so that it extends the set, which is associated with the type of the variable, with the identifier of the variable. This way the Λ function (and the fuzzing technique) becomes capable of generating not only literals as starting points and parameters of call expressions but also variable references, thus opening the possibility for interdependent API function calls that reuse the result of each other.

The above outlined idea is formalized by the RANDOMCALLLIST algorithm in Listing 3. The algorithm is using some further helper functions in addition to those already introduced: UNIQUEID returns a valid unique JavaScript identifier on every call, and RET returns the target vertex of an outgoing *ret* edge. Additionally, DOMAIN returns the set for which its parameter function is defined,

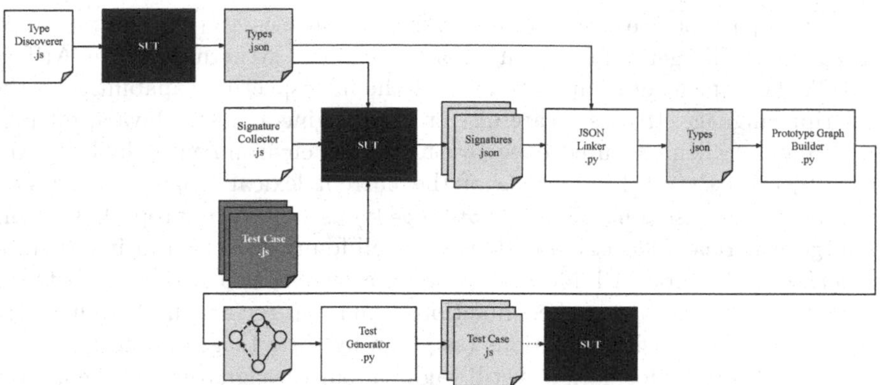

Fig. 2. Architecture overview of the prototype implementation of the JavaScript API fuzzing approach. The white elements are part of the implementation, while the black boxes stand for the SUT. The dark and light gray elements are inputs used and outputs generated during their execution.

while the $\Lambda(.) \cup=$ notation stands for the update of the Λ function, extending its result set (as well as its domain, potentially). (The redefinition or wrapping of RANDOMEXPR at lines 1–4 ensures that the recursion at line 16 of Listing 1, which generates parameters for function calls, can also make use of the updated Λ function.)

To follow up on the example of the previous section, the following code snippets are test cases that can be generated with RANDOMCALLLIST on G_{ex} and Λ_{ex} (with various n inputs):

-
```
var v0=this.Object.valueOf();
var v1=this.Object.prototype.valueOf();
var v2=v0.create(v1,{});
```
-
```
var v0=this.Object.valueOf();
var v1=v0.create(v0,v0);
```

4 Experimental Results

To experiment with prototype graph-based fuzzing and with the approaches that generate independent and interdependent function calls, we have created a prototype implementation that is able to build prototype graphs by automatically discovering the API of its SUT and to generate test cases from the built graph using the algorithms shown above. The architecture overview of the prototype implementation is shown in Fig. 2.

The top part of the architecture overview outlines the automatic graph building steps. To get information about the basic structure of the API of the SUT, the implementation makes use of the introspecting capabilities of the JavaScript language. It uses a carefully crafted engine-agnostic JavaScript program, which – when executed once by the target environment – looks at the global object of the SUT (the `this` of the current lexical scope), retrieves its prototype object (using `Object.getPrototypeOf`) as well as its properties (using `Object.getOwnPropertyNames`), and does so to all found objects transitively, thus *discovering* the target's API. Moreover, the program can also distinguish between regular and callable objects (i.e., functions) and can record the length of the argument list of the visited functions (as given by their `length` property).

The so-retrieved information is still vague about the signatures of the discovered API functions because it finds only the number of arguments without any type details. Therefore, the prototype implementation contains another specifically crafted script that can be loaded into the target environment before the execution of other programs, and wraps all API functions discovered in the previous step to record the types of parameters and return values of actual invocations. With sufficiently many and diverse executions, the result of this *signature collection* step can be used to gather information about possible valid parametrizations of the API.

As the final phase in the graph building process, the implementation links together the information provided by the structure discovery and signature collection steps and builds the data structure that conforms to Definition 1. (Fig. 2 also discloses the implementation detail that those parts of the prototype tool that are executed in the SUT – i.e., discovery and signature collection – are written in JavaScript, while the rest of the steps – like linking the results of the previous steps and building the actual graph, as well as the test case generation from the graph – are written in Python.)

As environment-under-test, we have chosen the IoT.js project [23], a modular application platform for embedded IoT devices built on top of the JerryScript [14] execution engine. We have executed both the discovery script in the environment and signature collection, using the project's own test suite to ensure that the discovered API functions are called diversely enough. Table 1 informs about the size of the so-built graphs (the numbers are given after both the discovery and signature collection steps), while Fig. 3 visualizes them. (Due to their size, the graph plots are not as clean as the manually created one in Fig. 1, but the graph resulting from the discovery step still shows some of the structure of the modular system of the IoT.js API. The graph extended with all the collected signature information is admittedly more entangled.)

The graph built as above (the one extended with all collected signature information) was used to generate test cases for IoT.js (outlined in the lower part of Fig. 2). Each generated test case contained either 20 independent API call expressions or 20 interdependent ones. The fuzzing session ran for 5 days and was driven by the Fuzzinator framework [11], which channelled the generated test cases to the SUT, monitored the execution, and collected unique failures

Table 1. Size metrics of prototype graphs built for IoT.js.

	After discovery step	Extended with collected signatures
$\lvert V_{type}\rvert$	576	1045
$\lvert V_{sig}\rvert$	8	425
$\lvert E_{proto}\rvert$	575	1044
$\lvert E_{prop}\rvert$	1569	2706
$\lvert E_{call}\rvert$	267	626
$\lvert E_{cstr}\rvert$	46	58
$\lvert E_{param}\rvert$	28	692
$\lvert E_{ret}\rvert$	8	425

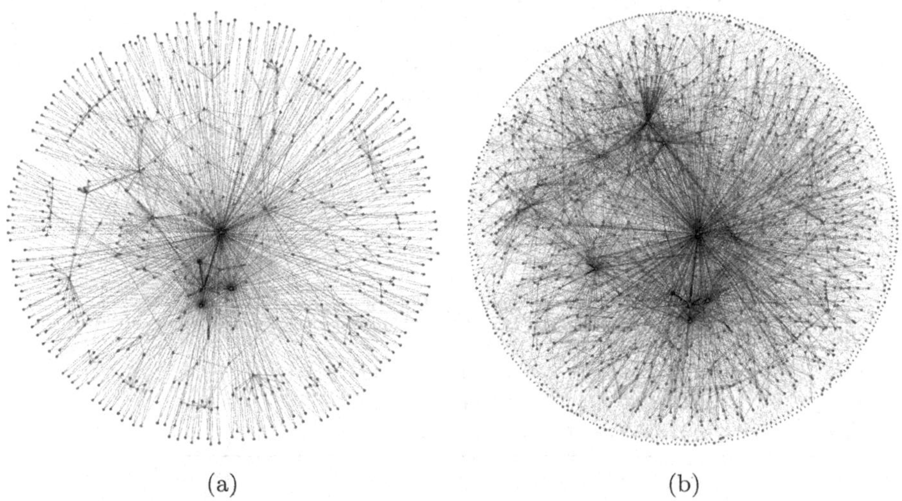

(a) (b)

Fig. 3. Prototype graphs built for the JavaScript API exposed by IoT.js (a) using discovery only and (b) after extending discovery results with signatures seen in executed test cases.

(i.e., determined if multiple test cases triggered the same issue and kept only one of them).

By the end of the fuzzing session, the two test case generation variants have induced 14 different failures altogether in IoT.js. The test cases that contained independent function calls triggered 9 of the issues, while the test cases with interdependent function calls could trigger all of them. Manual investigation has revealed that two failures not found by the original approach could have been potentially triggered by test cases with independent function calls; it is due to the random nature of fuzz testing that they were not hit during our experiment. However, the manual investigation has also revealed that the other three test cases have actually made use of the interdependency of the generated function calls and thus could not have been generated by the original algorithm variant.

Table 2. Issues found in IoT.js by prototype graph-based fuzzing technique generating independent and interdependent function calls.

Issue ID	Independent calls	Interdependent calls
#1904	(✗)	✓
#1905	✓	✓
#1906	✓	✓
#1907	(✗)	✓
#1908	✗	✓
#1909	✓	✓
#1910	✗	✓
#1911	✗	✓
#1912	✓	✓
#1913	✓	✓
#1914	✓	✓
#1915	✓	✓
#1916	✓	✓
#1917	✓	✓

Listing 4. Issue #1908 of IoT.js.

```
var net = require('net')
var v0 = new (net.connect(1).constructor)()
try { v0.connect() } catch ($) { }
try { v0._handle.readStart() } catch ($) { }
```

Listing 5. Issue #1910 of IoT.js.

```
var http_common = require('http_common')
var v0 = http_common.createHTTPParser(1)
v0.execute(Buffer(6083374109688862375))
v0.resume()
```

The found failure-inducing test cases were reduced by the automatic test case reducer tool Picireny [10,12,15] and further beautified by hand, and the so-minimized inputs were reported to the issue tracker of IoT.js. Table 2 sums up these results, showing the public issue IDs of the found problems, and whether a test case generation technique has found it or not. (Check marks show issues found, crosses signal issues not found, while crosses in parentheses mark failures that could have been found, potentially.)

Listing 6. Issue #1911 of IoT.js.

```
var dgram = require('dgram')
var v0 = dgram.createSocket('udp4')
v0.addMembership(decodeURIComponent(), v0)
```

To highlight the results, we also show the test cases of those three issues that were found only by the algorithm that generated interdependent function calls (see Listings 4, 5, and 6). These examples demonstrate that the technique presented in this paper was able to exercise three separate parts of the API of its target environment in a way that was not possible with a previous approach.

5 Related Work

With the growing influence of the JavaScript language, its execution engines are also getting more attention security-wise.

Godefroid et al. published a grammar-based white-box methodology to test the JavaScript engine of Internet Explorer 7 [6]. They exploited the information gathered from symbolic execution of existing test cases and a context-free grammar definition of the input format, and created new test cases to exercise different control paths.

Ruderman created jsfunfuzz [20], a JavaScript fuzzer that manually defined generator rules to create syntactically and semantically correct test cases. This approach also took advantage of the introspection possibility of the language to extract field and method names but it did not try to build a complex model nor to infer function parametrization.

Holler et al. presented LangFuzz [13], a language-independent mutational approach that consists of two steps. First, it parses existing test cases and builds a so-called fragment pool from the created parse trees. After this preprocess step, LangFuzz creates new test cases from the extracted fragments by random recombinations. Although the idea is language-independent, the authors applied it to test SpiderMonkey, the JavaScript engine of the Firefox web browser where they found hundreds of bugs. IFuzzer [27] is an evolutionary approach built upon the idea of LangFuzz. It defines a fitness function using information about the generated test (like complexity metrics) and the feedback of the SUT (like crashes, exceptions, timeouts, etc.) to choose the elements of the next population. Similarly to LangFuzz, IFuzzer was applied to generate JavaScript sources and it exercised the SpiderMonkey engine. BlendFuzz [30] is also a similar solution to LangFuzz as it processes existing sources with ANTLR grammars, which also improves the mutation phase by collecting additional information from parse trees. SkyFire [28] is a tool aiming to generate valuable input seeds for other fuzzing strategies. It infers probabilistic context-sensitive grammars from examples to specify both syntax features and semantic rules and it uses this information for seed generation. SkyFire was used to test the JavaScript engine of Internet Explorer 11.

Guiding random test generation by the SUT's coverage information has gained popularity recently. American Fuzzy Lop [31] (or AFL for short) is one of the most well-known example. It was used, adapted, and improved by many [1–3,16–18,22,24]. AFL is a language-independent mutation-based fuzzing approach. It usually starts with an initial test population and iteratively applies various atomic mutation operators (bit/byte insertion/deletion/replacement, etc.) on its elements. If a mutant covers new edges in the SUT then it will be kept for further iterations, otherwise it will be removed from the population. The main strength of this approach is that it is fast and it can be applied to any file-based SUT without being acquainted with the input format requirements. However, this can be a drawback, too, if the SUT has complex syntax requirements, like JavaScript engines, since it will generate many useless, syntactically incorrect test cases.

Honggfuzz [7] and libFuzzer [19] are also coverage-guided fuzzers that improve the fuzzing performance by running it in-process and by focusing only on some selected methods. Google's OSS-Fuzz [8] platform uses both AFL and libFuzzer to test open-source projects with a large user base.

6 Summary

In this paper, we have revisited a fuzzing (or random testing) technique that used prototype graphs to model the weak type system of the JavaScript programming language and generated function call expressions from such graphs to exercise the APIs of JavaScript execution engines. We have observed that JavaScript-based execution environments (built on top of execution engines) often exposed APIs that had parts which required multiple separate but not independent function calls to be reachable. As the original technique could not generate test cases for those parts of APIs, we have given an extension to the original graph-based approach so that it can generate a series of API calls which can re-use the results of each other.

We have created a prototype tool based on the here-presented algorithms and used it to fuzz test the IoT.js platform. The generated test cases have caused numerous issues in the platform-under-test: we have found 9 unique failures that were triggered by both algorithm variants (showing that the original approach is still a valid fuzzing technique), but there were also 5 unique failures that were caused by test cases generated by the new approach only. Manual investigation showed that at least 3 of these failure-inducing test cases indeed made use of interdependencies between multiple function calls and could not be merged into a single expression. All failures have been reported to the public issue tracker of the tested project along with the issue-triggering test cases.

Since the prototype implementation has already found real issues in a real project, we plan to further experiment with the technique. As a natural continuation of the current work, we plan to target the Node.js platform with this technique, as well as the JavaScript APIs of current web browsers. We foresee that these new targets may impose new requirements both on the implementation and on the formalism of the prototype graph (e.g., because of language constructs introduced by newer JavaScript specification versions they support). We also plan to adapt techniques that can guide prototype graph-based fuzzing – i.e., influence its randomness – as greybox techniques have been proved beneficial in other fuzzing approaches as well. Finally, although JavaScript is one of the most widespread programming languages these days, we would like to investigate the adaptability of the (proto)type graph-based API fuzzing technique to other languages as well.

Acknowledgment. This research was supported by the EU-supported Hungarian national grant GINOP-2.3.2-15-2016-00037 and by grant TUDFO/47138-1/2019-ITM of the Ministry for Innovation and Technology, Hungary.

References

1. Böhme, M., Pham, V.T., Nguyen, M.D., Roychoudhury, A.: Directed greybox fuzzing. In: Proceedings of the 2017 ACM SIGSAC Conference on Computer and Communications Security (CCS 2017), pp. 2329–2344. ACM (2017)
2. Böhme, M., Pham, V.T., Roychoudhury, A.: Coverage-based greybox fuzzing as Markov chain. In: Proceedings of the 2016 ACM SIGSAC Conference on Computer and Communications Security (CCS 2016), pp. 1032–1043. ACM (2016)
3. Chen, Y., Jiang, Y., Liang, J., Wang, M., Jiao, X.: Enfuzz: From ensemble learning to ensemble fuzzing. Computing Research Repository abs/1807.00182 (2018)
4. Ecma International: ECMAScript Language Specification (ECMA-262), 5.1 edn., June 2011
5. Fitbit Inc: Fitbit OS. https://dev.fitbit.com. Accessed May 07 2019
6. Godefroid, P., Kiezun, A., Levin, M.Y.: Grammar-based whitebox fuzzing. In: Proceedings of the 29th ACM SIGPLAN Conference on Programming Language Design and Implementation (PLDI 2008), pp. 206–215. ACM (2008)
7. Google: honggfuzz. http://honggfuzz.com. Accessed 07 May 2019
8. Google: OSS-Fuzz - continuous fuzzing of open source software. https://github.com/google/oss-fuzz. Accessed 07 May 2019
9. Hodován, R., Kiss, Á.: Fuzzing JavaScript engine APIs. In: Ábrahám, E., Huisman, M. (eds.) IFM 2016. LNCS, vol. 9681, pp. 425–438. Springer, Cham (2016). https://doi.org/10.1007/978-3-319-33693-0_27
10. Hodován, R., Kiss, Á.: Modernizing hierarchical delta debugging. In: Proceedings of the 7th International Workshop on Automating Test Case Design, Selection, and Evaluation (A-TEST 2016), pp. 31–37. ACM, November 2016
11. Hodován, R., Kiss, Á.: Fuzzinator: an open-source modular random testing framework. In: Proceedings of the 11th IEEE International Conference on Software Testing, Verification and Validation (ICST 2018), pp. 416–421. IEEE Computer Society, April 2018. https://github.com/renatahodovan/fuzzinator

12. Hodován, R., Kiss, Á., Gyimóthy, T.: Tree preprocessing and test outcome caching for efficient hierarchical delta debugging. In: Proceedings of the 12th IEEE/ACM International Workshop on Automation of Software Testing (AST 2017), pp. 23–29. IEEE, Buenos Aires, May 2017
13. Holler, C., Herzig, K., Zeller, A.: Fuzzing with code fragments. In: 21st USENIX Security Symposium, pp. 445–458. USENIX (2012)
14. JS Foundation, et al.: JerryScript. http://www.jerryscript.net. Accessed 07 May 2019
15. Kiss, Á., Hodován, R., Gyimóthy, T.: HDDr: a recursive variant of the hierarchical delta debugging algorithm. In: Proceedings of the 9th ACM SIGSOFT International Workshop on Automating Test Case Design, Selection, and Evaluation (A-TEST 2018). pp. 16–22. ACM, Lake Buena Vista, November 2018
16. Lemieux, C., Padhye, R., Sen, K., Song, D.: Perffuzz: automatically generating pathological inputs. In: Proceedings of the 27th ACM SIGSOFT International Symposium on Software Testing and Analysis, ISSTA 2018, pp. 254–265. ACM, New York (2018)
17. Lemieux, C., Sen, K.: Fairfuzz: Targeting rare branches to rapidly increase greybox fuzz testing coverage. Computing Research Repository abs/1709.07101 (2017)
18. Li, Y., Chen, B., Chandramohan, M., Lin, S.W., Liu, Y., Tiu, A.: Steelix: program-state based binary fuzzing. In: Proceedings of the 2017 11th Joint Meeting on Foundations of Software Engineering (ESEC/FSE 2017), pp. 627–637. ACM (2017)
19. LLVM Project: libfuzzer – a library for coverage-guided fuzz testing. https://llvm.org/docs/LibFuzzer.html. Accessed 07 May 2019
20. Mozilla Security: jsfunfuzz. https://github.com/MozillaSecurity/funfuzz/. Accessed 07 May 2019
21. Node.js Foundation: Node.js. https://nodejs.org. Accessed 07 May 2019
22. Pham, V., Böhme, M., Santosa, A.E., Caciulescu, A.R., Roychoudhury, A.: Smart greybox fuzzing. Computing Research Repository abs/1811.09447 (2018)
23. Samsung Electronics Co., Ltd., et al.: IoT.js. http://www.iotjs.net. Accessed 07 May 2019
24. Stephens, N., et al.: Driller: augmenting fuzzing through selective symbolic execution. In: Proceedings of the 2016 Network and Distributed System Security Symposium (NDSS 2016). Internet Society (2016)
25. Takanen, A., DeMott, J., Miller, C., Kettunen, A.: Fuzzing for Software Security Testing and Quality Assurance, 2nd edn. Artech House (2018)
26. Vaarala, S., et al.: Duktape. http://duktape.org. Accessed 07 May 2019
27. Veggalam, S., Rawat, S., Haller, I., Bos, H.: IFuzzer: an evolutionary interpreter fuzzer using genetic programming. In: Askoxylakis, I., Ioannidis, S., Katsikas, S., Meadows, C. (eds.) ESORICS 2016. LNCS, vol. 9878, pp. 581–601. Springer, Cham (2016). https://doi.org/10.1007/978-3-319-45744-4_29
28. Wang, J., Chen, B., Wei, L., Liu, Y.: Skyfire: data-driven seed generation for fuzzing. In: 2017 IEEE Symposium on Security and Privacy (SP), pp. 579–594. IEEE Press (2017). https://doi.org/10.1109/SP.2017.23
29. WHATWG: HTML living standard. https://html.spec.whatwg.org. Accessed 07 May 2019
30. Yang, D., Zhang, Y., Liu, Q.: Blendfuzz: a model-based framework for fuzztesting programs with grammatical inputs. In: IEEE International Conference on Trust, Security and Privacy in Computing and Communications (TrustCom), pp. 1070–1076. IEEE, IEEE Computer Society (2012)
31. Zalewski, M.: American fuzzy lop. http://lcamtuf.coredump.cx/afl/. Accessed 07 May 2019

DIONE: A Protocol Verification System Built with DAFNY for I/O Automata

Chiao Hsieh(✉) and Sayan Mitra

University of Illinois at Urbana-Champaign, Champaign, IL 61820, USA
{chsieh16,mitras}@illinois.edu

Abstract. Input/Output Automata (IOA) is an expressive specification framework with built-in properties for compositional reasoning. It has been shown to be effective in specifying and analyzing distributed and networked systems. The available verification engines for IOA are based on interactive theorem provers such as Isabelle, Larch, PVS, and Coq, and are expressive but require heavy human interaction. Motivated by the advances in SMT solvers, in this work we explore a different expressivity-automation tradeoff for IOA. We present DIONE, the first IOA analysis system built with DAFNY and its SMT-powered toolchain and demonstrate its effectiveness on four distributed applications. Our translator tool converts Python-esque DIONE language specification of IOA and their properties to parameterized DAFNY modules. DIONE automatically generates the relevant compatibility and composition lemmas for the IOA specifications,which can then be checked with Dafny on a per module-basis. We ensure that all resulting formulas are expressed mostly in fragments solvable by SMT solvers and hence enables Bounded Model Checking and k-induction-based invariant checking using Z3. We present successful applications of DIONE in verification of an asynchronous leader election algorithm, two self-stabilizing mutual exclusion algorithms, and CAN bus Arbitration. We automatically prove key invariants of all four protocols; for the last three this involves reasoning about arbitrary number of participants. These analyses are largely automatic with minimal manual inputs needed, and they demonstrate the effectiveness of this approach in analyzing networked and distributed systems.

1 Introduction

For modeling and verifying network and distributed systems, compositional approaches are considered essential in achieving modularity and scalability. A recent study on building verified industrial scale systems highlight the importance of compositional reasoning and connecting layers of abstractions, especially for integrating formal methods into software development practices [22]. The Input/Output Automata (IOA) [20] framework comes with an expressive modeling language [8], and a powerful set of simulation and substitutivity results that support reasoning about compositions, abstractions, and substitutions. The framework has been used to model and analyze a wide variety of distributed systems ranging from high-level protocols for mutual exclusion, consensus, leader

W. Ahrendt and S. L. Tapia Tarifa (Eds.): IFM 2019, LNCS 11918, pp. 227–245, 2019.
https://doi.org/10.1007/978-3-030-34968-4_13

election [20], to implementation-level specifications for shared memory and group communication services [4,6,7], and communication protocols like TCP [25].

Currently available mechanized verification engines for IOA are mostly based on interactive theorem provers including Isabelle/HOL [21], Larch Shared Language [3], PVS [19], and recently CoqIOA [1]. All of these provide expressive specification languages based on higher order theories for modeling IOA, but they require a nontrivial amount of human interactions for constructing proofs[1].

In this paper, we aim to achieve higher automation for verification of distributed systems expressed in IOA, by restricting the specifications to less expressive theories with established decision procedures. One predominant option is First Order Theories supported by existing Satisfiability Modulo Theories (SMT) solvers. There has been a wave of advancements in SMT solvers, which in turn has led to the creation of widely diverse program verification engines like CBMC [5], DAFNY [16], and SEAHORN [15]. We therefore believe that theories solvable with SMT solvers can be expressive enough for a broadly useful class of IOA, and an SMT-based IOA verification engine can advance the design and analysis of distributed systems.

Specifically, we build a toolchain based on DAFNY [16], instead of directly interfacing with SMT solvers. DAFNY provides a higher level of abstraction for developing both system specifications and for proof strategies [17]. The IronFleet project [11], for instance, demonstrates how practical consensus protocols can be modeled and verified in DAFNY. The project further develops a DAFNY implementation of the model with formal conformance guarantees, and ultimately generates correct-by-construction C# source code from the implementation. These results suggest that DAFNY is a good candidate for supporting modeling and mostly-automatic verification for distributed protocols as IOA.

In this work, we propose DIONE—a modeling language and verification system built using DAFNY for IOA. The DIONE workflow is similar to that of [3,19]. First, users model the protocol and specify the desired invariant in the DIONE language. For example in Fig. 1, a distributed algorithm from the textbook [9] can be faithfully modeled in DIONE. DIONE frontend then translates DIONE to DAFNY specification language. Additionally, DIONE generates DAFNY lemmas so that proving these lemmas is equivalent to Bounded Model Checking (BMC) and k-induction based invariant checking for the original IOA. There are three major contributions in this work:

(i) We have developed a Python-like language, DIONE, for naturally specifying distributed systems as compositions of parameterized IOA. We have implemented the supporting tools for (a) translating DIONE specifications to DAFNY, and for (b) carrying out automatic proofs for DIONE specifications. Our translator uses modules in DAFNY to automatically generate (nontrivial) composition and compatibility checks for parameterized automata.

(ii) We have demonstrated that DIONE can effectively model diverse distributed protocols: self-stabilizing mutual exclusion algorithms with different network topologies, leader election algorithms, and the CAN bus Arbitration.

[1] Also, none of the tools appear to be maintained for at least two years.

```
# s[0] ∈ {1,3}, s[n-1] ∈ {2, 4}, and N(i) returns neighbors of i #
program StableArray;
{program for process i, i=0 or i=n-1}
do
∃j ∈ N(i): (s[j] = s[i]+1 mod 4) → s[i] := s[i]+2 mod 4
od
{program for process i, 0<i<n-1}
do
∃j ∈ N(i): (s[j] = s[i]+1 mod 4) → s[i] := s[j]
od
```

```
Status: type = IntRange[0:4]
@automaton
def StableArray(N: int):
   where= 2 <= N
   class signature:
      @output
      def trans(i: int): where=(0 <= i < N)
   class states:
      s: Seq[Status]
   initially= len(s)==N and(s[0]==1 or s[0]==3)and(s[N-1]==0 or s[N-1]==2)
   class transitions:
      @output
      @pre((i==0 and s[i+1]==incre(s[i]))or(i==N-1 and s[i-1]==incre(s[i])))
      def trans(i): s[i] = incre(incre(s[i]))
      @output
      @pre(0 < i < N-1 and s[i-1]==incre(s[i]))
      def trans(i): s[i] = s[i-1]
      @output
      @pre(0 < i < N-1 and s[i+1]==incre(s[i]))
      def trans(i): s[i] = s[i+1]
   invariant_of= len(s)==N and(s[0]==1 or s[0]==3)and(s[N-1]==0 or s[N-1]==2)
```

Fig. 1. Textbook description of a self-stabilizing mutual exclusion algorithm [9, Section 17.3.2] (top) and specification in DIONE (bottom).

These showcase how protocols and requirements for an arbitrary number of processes can be modeled with parallel composition and collection types.

(iii) Finally, we have demonstrated that DIONE can achieve a promising level of proof automation. The ratio lengths of DIONE specifications to DAFNY models plus proofs is about 1:3 to 1:5. In the worst case only two out of five lemmas require user specified proof strategies. In particular, (a) for self-stabilization algorithms, our verifier is able to prove invariants for an arbitrary number of processes by k-induction with one or two manually added basic facts about a generic sequence. (b) For the leader election algorithm and CAN bus Arbitration, we show that auxiliary invariants or over-approximation of transitions can be easily integrated to fully automate verification, and over-approximation itself can be automatically validated by the verifier.

Related Work. In addition to the related works mentioned earlier, recently there are several large projects in ensuring correct implementation of distributed protocols including Verdi [27], Chapar [18], Project Everest [2], to name a few. These projects aimed to verify programs in high level language with manually written proofs and synthesize low level implementations. DIONE does not automatically generate low level implementation for now, but it can serve as an alternative high level language and provide different verification approaches.

The translation by Dione resembles the translation to Larch [3] as both are using First Order Theories. Dione benefits from the advancement in SMT solving and program verification. With better understanding on the efficiency and decidability of SMT solving, Dione is designed to achieve higher automation using Dafny. In return, it is difficult to specify user-defined sorts and theories not supported by Dafny in comparison with [3] and other works.

The design decision to translate IOA to Dafny is greatly influenced by the modeling techniques in IronFleet [11]. The objective of IronFleet project and our work however are very different. IronFleet focused on connecting layers of abstractions from specification to implementation. Their proofs of refinement based on Temporal Logic of Actions (TLA) were manually written. In comparison, our work aims to achieve higher automation on invariant checking for IOA and provides an IOA language with Dafny translation to reduce user effort.

More broadly, Tuttle and Goel [26] demonstrated how to use the SMT-based checker, DVF, to verify a consensus protocol. Ivy [23] recently explored using EPR, a decidable fragment of FOL, to model and verify infinite state transition systems. However, the DVF model for the protocol explicitly described the global state transition system instead of the local state of a participant of the protocol, and Ivy defined the execution of a protocol as one RML program within only one while loop; it is likely cumbersome to cleanly model parallel composition in both DVF and Ivy languages. Moreover, it is unclear how to specify which automaton has control over certain actions. On the other hand, our IOA-based language provides a language construct to explicitly specify components of a composition as well as **input** and **output** keywords to denote the controlling automaton of actions. For our purpose of verifying IOA, we believe DVF and Ivy can be used as alternative back-ends for Dione with proper translations.

2 Background: Brief Overview of IOA

Mathematical Notations. Let X be a finite set of *variable* names. To model variables with static types, we assume a function $type(x)$ to return the set of possible values for x. A *valuation*, s, is a mapping from $x \in X$ to a value $s(x) \in type(x)$, and $val(X)$ denotes the set of all possible valuations of X. For a valuation $s \in val(X)$ and a subset of variable names $Y \subseteq X$, we use $s \lceil Y$ to denote the restriction of s to Y.

Input/Output Automata. An IOA [20], $\mathcal{A} = (\Sigma, X, Q, \Theta, \delta)$, is a tuple where (i) $\Sigma = \Sigma^I \dot\cup \Sigma^O \dot\cup \Sigma^H$ is the set of all actions partitioned into Σ^I, Σ^O, and Σ^H representing **input**, **output**, and **internal** actions, respectively. (ii) X is a finite set of *state variable* names. (iii) $Q \subseteq val(X)$ is the set of states (iv) $\Theta \subseteq Q$ is the set of initial states. (v) $\delta \subseteq Q \times \Sigma \times Q$ is the transition relation. An important requirement for an IOA $\mathcal{A}$ is that it is *input enabled.* That is, it cannot block input actions. Formally,

$$\forall s \in Q, a \in \Sigma^I, \exists s' \in Q, (s, a, s') \in \delta$$

A pair of IOA $\mathcal{A}_1$ and $\mathcal{A}_2$ are *compatible* if and only if the following holds: (i) Output actions are disjoint, i.e., $\Sigma_1^O \cap \Sigma_2^O = \emptyset$; (ii) Internal actions are only used by itself, i.e., $\Sigma_1^H \cap \Sigma_2 = \Sigma_2^H \cap \Sigma_1 = \emptyset$; and (iii) Variable names are disjoint, i.e., $X_1 \cap X_2 = \emptyset$. This ensures that a composition of compatible automata (defined next) is also an IOA.

Given two compatible automata $\mathcal{A}_1$ and $\mathcal{A}_2$, we can construct the parallel composition automaton $\mathcal{A}_1 \parallel \mathcal{A}_2 = (\Sigma, X, Q, \Theta, \delta)$ where

(i) $\Sigma^I = (\Sigma_1^I \cup \Sigma_2^I) \setminus (\Sigma_1^O \cup \Sigma_2^O)$; $\quad \Sigma^O = \Sigma_1^O \cup \Sigma_2^O$; $\quad \Sigma^H = \Sigma_1^H \cup \Sigma_2^H$
(ii) $X = X_1 \cup X_2$
(iii) $Q = \{s \in val(X) \mid s \lceil X_1 \in Q_1 \wedge s \lceil X_2 \in Q_2\}$
(iv) $\Theta = \{s \in Q \mid s \lceil X_1 \in \Theta_1 \wedge s \lceil X_2 \in \Theta_2\}$
(v) The transition δ is defined as follows with shorthand expressions $s_1 = s \lceil X_1$, $s_2 = s \lceil X_2$, $s_1' = s' \lceil X_1$, and $s_2' = s' \lceil X_2$:

$$\{(s, a, s') \in Q \times \Sigma \times Q \mid (a \in \Sigma_1 \Rightarrow (s_1, a, s_1') \in \delta_1) \wedge (a \notin \Sigma_1 \Rightarrow s_1 = s_1') \\ \wedge (a \in \Sigma_2 \Rightarrow (s_2, a, s_2') \in \delta_2) \wedge (a \notin \Sigma_2 \Rightarrow s_2 = s_2')\}$$

It can be checked that the composed automaton $\mathcal{A}_1 \parallel \mathcal{A}_2$ is indeed an IOA. The theory of IOA also defines executions, traces, invariance, abstractions, refinements, forward-backward simulation relations, and substitutivity properties. We refer the interested reader to [8,20] for more complete overview.

IOA with Parameters. To concisely model a distributed protocol, a standard practice is to use parameterized automaton specifications. Formal parameters may appear in names of automata, actions, and in all the predicate and transition definitions. This interdependence of parameters and variables make compatibility and composition nontrivial to implement.

For example, it is standard to assume that each participating process is distinguished by a unique address *ip*, and that messages are tagged with source and destination *ips*. We can specify the address as a parameter *ip* of *Addr* type and define a family of automata $\{\mathcal{A}_{ip}\}_{ip \in Addr}$. The complete behavior of the protocol is then modeled by composing automata instantiated with distinct *ips*. For specifying one **output** action sending a message, we can use a tuple $(src, dst, ...)$ to represent a tagged message. However, in order to satisfy compatibility criteria, the set of **output** actions Σ_{ip}^O for sending messages has to be constrained by *ip*, e.g., $\Sigma_{ip}^O = \{(src, dst, ...) | src, dst \in Addr \wedge src = ip\}$, or else the action sets for different automaton instances may intersect. Consequently, it is not obvious whether the compatibility criteria are satisfied when the constraints are more complex, or when a composite automaton is used in another composition. Hence, it is important to have an automated check of the compatibility criteria.

3 Overview of DIONE

In this section, we discuss the design and features of DIONE as well as the translation from DIONE language to DAFNY for model checking.

3.1 DIONE Language

To provide users a familiar modeling language for IOA while allowing DIONE to be extensible, DIONE language borrows the syntax from one of the most popular programming languages, PYTHON. This design decision allows us to potentially embed DIONE into normal PYTHON programs and use existing PYTHON packages such as Z3Py for verification. Further, our tools benefit from existing and advanced compiler/interpreter infrastructure of PYTHON, and in the future an interpreter for DIONE programs could be built on top of PYTHON.

The syntax of DIONE is a strict subset of PYTHON 3.7 syntax. We interpret DIONE code as defining an IOA as in [8]. At the top level of a DIONE program, one can only define either a *type* or an *automaton.*

Data Types. A type definition is simply an assignment with type hints. The left hand side is annotated with the built-in base meta-type, **`bool`**, to indicate the identifier represents a type. On the right hand side, one can provide an existing type to create a type synonym, or use a built-in type constructor to build new types, for example **`Enum`** and **`NamedTuple`** in Fig. 2. The list of built-in types for DIONE can be found in our project website [12].

Automata. An automaton definition uses a PYTHON function definition syntax decorated with either `@automaton` or `@composition` to define a primitive or a composite automaton. The function parameters naturally serve as the parameters of the automaton. One can optionally add an assignment to the `where` variable to bound the parameter values for the automaton. For a primitive automaton, four DIONE program constructs, namely `states`, `initially`, `signature`, and `transitions`, are required to specify state variables, initial states, the signature, and the transition relation as discussed in Sect. 2. For a composition, `components` is required to specify the component automata. For either primitive or composite automaton, one can optionally assign an `invariant_of` variable to specify the invariant.

States. The `states` class is to specify variables X and consists of only variables annotated with types as shown in Fig. 2. The `initially` variable should be assigned with a Boolean expression over state variables and/or automaton parameter. An allowed initial state is when `initially` is evaluated to true.

Signature and Transitions. The `signature` class is for declaring the set of actions used in the automaton. It should contain only functions decorated with `@input`, `@output`, or `@internal`, to declare an action in Σ^I, Σ^O, or Σ^H. Similarly, an assignment to `where` can be added to bound the parameters of the action. The `where` clause is crucial for sharing a same action name across multiple automata. For instance, the **output** action `send` defined in Fig. 3 is constrained with messages sent from its own `ip`. Without the constraint, there can be no compatible automata using `send` as an **output** action because their output sets of actions are not disjoint. With the constraint, other automata

```
Loc: type = nat
Addr: type = Enum[A, B, C]
Msg: type = NamedTuple[src: Addr,
                       dst: Addr,
                       val: int]
@automaton
def Proc(ip: Addr, b: int):
    where = b>=10
    class states:
        pc: Loc
        x: int
    initially = (pc==1 and 0<=x<b)
```

```
type Loc = nat
datatype Addr = A | B | C
datatype Msg = Msg(src: Addr,
                   dst: Addr,
                   val: int)
datatype Parameter = Parameter(
    ip: Addr, b: int)
datatype State = State(pc: Loc, x: int)
predicate aut_where(p: Parameter)
{  p.b ≥ 10  }
predicate initially(
    s: State, p: Parameter)
{  s.pc = 1 ∧ 0 ≤ s.x < p.b  }
```

Fig. 2. DIONE types and states (*Left*) and translated DAFNY (*Right*).

using send as an **output** action are still compatible if the source address is not ip. To define transition relation for the automaton in transitions class, we follow [8] to specify preconditions and effects for actions. As show in Fig. 3, the action is decorated with @pre as the precondition, and the effect of this action is specified within the function body. Currently, DIONE allows only some commonly used PYTHON statements and expressions in the effect. An updated list of supported statements and expressions is available on our website [12].

Composition. The components class is required for specifying a composite automaton. It is a list of component names annotated by the automaton instantiated with actual parameter values. For Fig. 1 as an example, the Sys automaton is composed of three components, p1, p2, and env. Both p1 and p2 are instances of automaton Proc, and env is an instance of Env.

3.2 Translating DIONE to DAFNY

In this section, we informally describe the translation of program constructs from DIONE to DAFNY in our implementation. In particular, we illustrate the insights into systematically translating from notions of sets, subsets, and transitions in Sect. 2 to data types and predicates expressible in DAFNY. We first describe translating all constructs for one automaton with parameters and then we provide the composition of automata with compatibility checks by DAFNY.

Data Types. Benefitting from the rich types available in DAFNY, a broad class of types are supported in DIONE. Primitive types such as **int**, **str**, **nat**, **real**, and **bv**N (bit-vectors with N bits) are translated to equivalent types in DAFNY. Python type **float** however is not supported due to the limitation of DAFNY. Collection types including **Mapping**, **Sequence**, **Set**, and **Counter** are available as **map**, **seq**, **set**, and **multiset** respectively. **NamedTuple**, **Enum**, and **Union** are directly modeled with inductive data types in DAFNY. Currently, we do not allow other kinds of user defined types for simplicity.

```
1 class signature:
2     @output
3     def send(m: Msg):
4         where = (m.src==ip)
5     @input
6     def recv(m: Msg): pass
7     @internal
8     def hide(k: int): pass
9
10 class transitions:
11     @output
12     @pre(m==Msg(ip, B, 10)
13         and pc==1)
14     def send(m):
15         pc = pc + 1
16         x = x + m.val
```

```
1 datatype Action=send(m: Msg)| recv(m: Msg)
2                     | hide(k: int)
3 predicate Output(act: Action ,p: Parameter)
4 { act.send? ∧ act.m.src = p.ip }
5 predicate Input(act: Action ,p: Parameter)
6 { act.recv? }
7 predicate Internal(act: Action ,p: Parameter)
8 { act.hide? }
9 predicate Signature(act: Action ,p: Parameter)
10 {Output(act ,p) ∨ Input(act ,p)
11                 ∨ Internal(act ,p)}
12 predicate pre_send(act: Action , s: State ,
13                   p: Parameter)
14 { act.send? ∧ act.m=Msg(p.ip ,B,10) ∧ s.pc=1 }
15 function eff_send(act: Action , s: State ,
16                  p: Parameter): State
17     requires pre_send(act ,s) {
18     var s: State := s.(pc := s.pc+1);
19     var s: State := s.(x := s.x+act.m.val); s}
```

Fig. 3. DIONE signature and transitions (*Left*) and translated DAFNY (*Right*).

States and Automaton Parameters. The `states` class is used to declare variables of an automaton, or formally *val*(X). Instead of directly using a function or **`map`** in DAFNY for mapping from variable names X to values, we model the state with a record type, a special case of inductive data types with only one constructor. Each field of the record type then corresponds to a variable of the automaton. Similarly, we introduce a new record type `Parameter` to model the parameter space of the automaton. For the example in Fig. 2, we simply define a `Parameter` type (Line 6) and a `State` type (Line 8). The bound over the parameter space is translated into the `aut_where` predicate (Line 9). Initial set of states specified through `(pc==1 and 0<=x<b)` is translated to the `initially` predicate below:

```
predicate initially(s:State,p:Parameter)
{  s.pc = 1  ∧  0 ≤ s.x  < p.b  }
```

Notice that `initially` refers to the parameter and bound the value of `s.x` with `p.b`. Hence, checking $s \in \Theta_p$ is equivalent to asking `initially(s,p)`.

Actions and Transitions. To model the set of actions for a network of automata, we collect all actions declared in the `signature` class from all automata. We then specify an algebraic data type `Action` with each action as an individual constructor. For example, we specify `Action` with two constructors `send` and `recv` at Line 1 in Fig. 3 representing sending and receiving messages where the message `m` is a parameter of the action. For each automaton, the three predicates `input`, `output`, and `internal` symbolically represent Σ_p^I, Σ_p^O, and Σ_p^H. Similarly, the translation makes sure $act \in \Sigma_p^O$ is equivalent to `output(act,p)` and so on. For example, `output` predicate (Line 3) constrains the source `m.src` of sent messages with its own `ip`.

The precondition `@pre` for each transition is represented by a **`predicate`**, and the body of each transition is rewritten to an *effect* function using LET expressions ("**`var`** ... ;" in DAFNY). The translation for the limited kinds

```
1 @automaton
2 def Proc(ip: Addr,
3          b: int):
4     ...
5
6 @automaton
7 def Env():
8     ...
9
10 @composition
11 def Sys():
12     class components:
13         env: Env()
14         p1:  Proc(A,10)
15         p2:  Proc(B,20)
16
17     invariant_of = \
18         0 <= p1.x < 10
```

```
1 module Type { type Msg = ...; type Action = ... }
2 module Proc { import Type
3   type State = ...; datatype Parameter = ...
4   {: All predicates and functions } }
5 module Env { import Type; type State = ...
6   {: All predicates and functions } }
7 module Sys { import Env; import Proc
8   datatype State = State(env: Env.State,
9                          p1: Proc.State,
10                         p2: Proc.State)
11  predicate output(act: Action) {
12     Env.output(act)
13  ∨  Proc.output(act,Proc.Parameter(A,10))
14  ∨  Proc.output(act,Proc.Parameter(B,20)) }
15  // Similar for input,output,internal,etc.
16  predicate invariant_of(s: State)
17  {  0 ≤ s.p1.x < 10  }
18 } // End Sys
```

Fig. 4. DIONE composition (*Left*) and translated DAFNY (*Right*).

of statements in DIONE, such as assignments and if-conditions, to a function producing a new state is not specific to DAFNY. It has been discussed thoroughly in other works such as [19] for PVS. We recommend interested readers to refer to [19] for details. The only major difference is that, we further specify the precondition of the effect function with **requires** clause. This instructs DAFNY verifier to only consider states and actions satisfying the precondition.

Lastly, given all pairs of translated (pre_i, eff_i) for the automaton, the whole transition relation $\delta \subseteq Q \times \Sigma \times Q$ is modeled by the transitions predicate over current state s, a given action act, and next state s' as follows.

```
predicate transitions(s: State, act: Action, s': State)
{ (pre_1(act,s) ∧ s'=eff_1(act,s)) ∨ (pre_2(act,s) ∧ s'=eff_2(act,s)) ∨... }
```

Primitive Automaton with Parameters. A primitive automaton is translated into a DAFNY **module** to group Parameter and State types as well as **functions** and **predicates** defining actions and transitions. Action type and other types shared across multiple automata are declared as a separate **module** and imported to each automaton module. An example layout is shown in Fig. 4. Note that both automata can define its own Parameter and State types without causing naming collision.

Composition and Invariants. Given all component automata and their corresponding **modules**, we define another module and **import** those component **modules**. We then can define State for the composition with State from each component **module**. The State essentially represents the Cartesian product of each component state space. With the new State type, we can then define the necessary predicates, namely initially, input, output, internal, and transitions, according to the composition operation defined in Sect. 2. For Fig. 4 as an example, we can implement output predicate (Line 11) using the disjunction of output from each component to represent $\Sigma^O_{Sys} = \Sigma^O_{Env} \cup \Sigma^O_{Proc(A,10)} \cup \Sigma^O_{Proc(B,20)}$. Do notice that the parameter value for instantiating each component automaton needs to be passed down to the predicates from sub-modules. Finally, translating an invariant of an automaton becomes defining an `invariant_of` predicate with current state as the argument and is similar to defining `initially`.

Checking Compatibility Axioms for IOA. In specifying systems in IOA, several simple mistakes are easily overlooked when designing larger and more complicated systems. We list three required axioms when specifying IOA and provide translated lemmas below to detect simple violations with DAFNY. For simplicity, we do not include parameters here. The first lemma simply states Σ^I, Σ^O, and Σ^H are mutually disjoint. The second lemma checks the IOA is input-enabled, i.e., $\forall s \in Q.a \in \Sigma^I.\exists s' \in Q.(s,a,s') \in \delta$. The third states that two component IOAs assigned with concrete parameters are compatible when $\Sigma^O_1 \cap \Sigma^O_2 = \emptyset$ and $\Sigma^H_1 \cap \Sigma_2 = \Sigma^H_2 \cap \Sigma_1 = \emptyset$.[2]

```
lemma disjoint_actions_proof?(a: Action)
  ensures ¬(input(a) ∧ output(a))
       ∧ ¬(input(a) ∧ internal(a))
       ∧ ¬(output(a) ∧ internal(a))

lemma input_enabled_proof?(a: Action, s: State)
  requires input(a)
  ensures ∃ s' • transitions(s,a,s')

lemma compatibility_proof?(a: Action)
  ensures ¬(P1.output(a) ∧ P2.output(a))
       ∧ ¬(P1.internal(a) ∧ P2.signature(a))
       ∧ ¬(P1.signature(a) ∧ P2.internal(a))
```

3.3 Bounded Model Checking and *k*-Induction with DAFNY

With the system automaton with invariant specification translated to DAFNY, we now discuss how to perform Bounded Model Checking (BMC) to detect violations. Given a bound k, BMC intends to prove that the invariant holds at any state reachable from initial states in k transitions. Formally, given a candidate invariant φ, we check the validity of following proposition:

$$\forall s_0, a_1, s_1, ..., a_k, s_k, (s_0 \in \Theta \wedge \bigwedge_{i=0}^{i<k} \delta(s_i, a_{i+1}, s_{i+1})) \implies \bigwedge_{i=0}^{i<k+1} \varphi(s_i) \quad (1)$$

We can ask DAFNY to prove the following equivalent **lemma**:

```
lemma bmc_proof?(s0: State,a1: Action,s1: State,...,ak: Action,sk: State)
  requires initially(s0) ∧ transitions(s0,a1,s1) ∧...∧ transitions(sk−1,ak,sk)
  ensures  invariant_of(s0) ∧ invariant_of(s1) ∧...∧ invariant_of(sk)
```

The underlying engine of DAFNY translates the lemma further into formulas in First Order Theories supported by SMT solver, Microsoft Z3. If the lemma is proven, then it proves no violation within k transitions. Otherwise, Z3 returns

[2] Question mark '?' and prime symbol ''' are allowed in identifiers in DAFNY.

Table 1. Protocols verified with DIONE. **#A** is the number of primitive and composite automata. **#Ln** (resp., **#Ty**, **#Fn**, **#Lem**) is the total number of lines (resp., custom types, functions, lemmas) in DIONE or DAFNY code. Numbers inside parentheses indicate manually added items for proving. **#k** is the number of transitions for BMC and induction proof. **#PO** is the number of proof obligations reported by DAFNY. **Time** and **Mem** shows the time and peak memory usage to prove with DAFNY.

Protocol	DIONE			Dafny				#k	#PO	Time (s)	Mem (MB)
	#A	#Ty	#Ln	#Ty	#Fn	#Lem	#Ln				
StableArray	1	1	24	4	17(0)	4(1)	115	0	32	4	84.5
StableRing	1	1	20	3	13(0)	5(2)	115	0	66	166	377.6
AsyncLCR	2	2	47	7	26(2)	5(0)	159	0	51	3	100.3
CANArb	3	2	62	6	38(5)	6(0)	333	24	60	287	169.7

a valuation disproving the formula, and we can use the debugger in the DAFNY tool chain to find the valuation of state and action variables. That is, we can reconstruct the execution from a counterexample of Eq. 1.

Similarly, to prove invariant φ by k-induction, we prove Eq. 1 to ensure the states reachable in k-steps are within the invariant, and then prove Eq. 2 to show the invariant is inductive at $(k+1)$-th step:

$$\forall s_0, a_1, s_1, ..., a_{k+1}, s_{k+1}, \left(\bigwedge_{i=0}^{i<k+1} \varphi(s_i) \land \delta(s_i, a_{i+1}, s_{i+1}) \right) \implies \varphi(s_{k+1}) \tag{2}$$

Or in DAFNY:

```
lemma induction_proof?(s0: State,a1: Action,s1: State,...,
          ak: Action,sk: State,ak+1: Action,sk+1: State)
  requires invariant_of(s0) ∧ transitions(s0,a1,s1) ∧...
         ∧ invariant_of(sk) ∧ transitions(sk,ak+1,sk+1)
  ensures  invariant_of(sk+1)
```

4 Case Studies with DIONE

To study the capability of DIONE, we analyze four distributed protocols with different network topologies, applications, and invariant properties using DIONE: The first two, `StableArray` and `StableRing`, are self-stabilizing mutual exclusion algorithms on an array and a ring network, `AsyncLCR` is a classic leader election algorithm on a ring, and `CANArb` is the protocol that arbitrates the access to CAN bus. For each case study, we first describe our DIONE models and invariants, then explain necessary auxiliary lemmas and functions added in the translated DAFNY code for verification, and finally discuss verification results based on BMC and k-induction using the DAFNY verifier. All experiments are conducted with DAFNY 2.2.0 on Ubuntu 18.04 LTS running on Intel Xeon CPU E3-1240 v3 at 3.40 GHz with 4 cores and 8 GB RAM. To obtain the verification results, all invariants for one system are conjuncted together as one big invariant predicate. DAFNY would verify all lemmas specified in a case study including disjointness of actions for primitive automata, compatibility in compositions, BMC, and k-induction for invariant checking. Each reported time and memory usage is the average of running DAFNY three times. All our code, the DIONE translator, the input specifications for the examples in DIONE language,[3] their DAFNY translations, and the proofs[4] are available at our repository.

4.1 Self-stabilization Protocol on a Bidirectional Array

`StableArray` in Fig. 1 is the self-stabilizing algorithm for mutual exclusion on a bidirectional array topology from [9, Section 17.3.2]. The system consists of an array of N processes with at least two processes, i.e., $N \geq 2$. All processes except for process 0 and $N-1$ can remain in any of $\{0, 1, 2, 3\}$ states. Process 0 should stay in $\{1, 3\}$, and process $N-1$ should stay in $\{0, 2\}$. We model the system with a global state variable, s, of sequence type with the length $|s| = N$, and each process state $s[i]$ is of an enumeration type from 0 to 3, and we also specify that $s[0]$ should be 1 or 3 and $s[N-1]$ be 0 or 2. Formally, the following invariant should trivially hold for `StableArray`:

Invariant 1. $|s| = N \wedge (s[0] = 1 \vee s[0] = 3) \wedge (s[N-1] = 0 \vee s[N-1] = 2)$

A process i is considered holding a token if any of its neighbor process j satisfies $s[j] = \mathit{incre}(s[i])$ where incre finds the next value in the enumeration type, equivalently, $\mathit{incre}(n) = (n+1)\%4$. A process i holding a token except for process 0 and $N-1$ can initiate a transition to copy the state from the above mentioned neighbor j. If process 0 or $N-1$ is holding a token, it increments twice, i.e., $s[0] = \mathit{incre}(\mathit{incre}(s[0]))$. For achieving mutual exclusion, a *legal configuration* of the system is when the number of processes holding tokens is exactly one. A desired invariant is that, once in a legal configuration, the system continues to be in the legal configuration. Here we prove a relaxed invariant that the number of processes holding a token is at most one. Formally,

Invariant 2. $$\left|\left\{ i \mid 0 \leq i < N \wedge \begin{pmatrix} i \neq 0 \wedge s[i-1] = \mathit{incre}(s[i]) \vee \\ i \neq N-1 \wedge s[i+1] = \mathit{incre}(s[i]) \end{pmatrix} \right\}\right| \leq 1$$

We can specify the conjunction of Invariant 1 and 2 in DIONE as below:

```
    (len(s)==N and (s[0]==1 or s[0]==3) and (s[N-1]==0 or s[N-1]==2))
and (len({i for i in range(0,len(s)) if (i!=0 and s[i-1]==incre(s[i]) or
                                        i!=N-1 and s[i+1]==incre(s[i]))}) <= 1)
```

Proof Strategy. As shown in Table 1, we are able to automatically prove that the conjunction of Invariant 1 and 2 is an inductive invariant for arbitrarily many processes (N) in 4 s. We however needed to manually introduce one auxiliary fact (lemma) in the translated DAFNY code to make the proof go through by

[3] See https://github.com/cyphyhouse/Dione/tree/master/system_tests/ioa_examples.

[4] See https://github.com/cyphyhouse/Dione/tree/master/system_tests/expected_dafny.

induction. The intuition behind this lemma is that, when some process i makes a transition, only processes $i-1$, i, and $i+1$ can either lose or gain tokens, and all other processes should remain the same. Therefore, the set of processes holding tokens before and after a transition could only differ for these three processes. This extra lemma simply enumerates all eight cases where the size of the set may either increase, decrease, or remain the same, and DAFNY is able to prove this lemma automatically. We then use this lemma over the two states before and after a transition in specifying the proof strategy, DAFNY verifier further infers that those cases where the size increases are impossible and successfully proves that the invariant is inductive.

4.2 Self-stabilization Protocol on a Ring

The second case study `StableRing` is the Dijkstra's famous self-stabilizing algorithm for mutual exclusion on a ring [9, Section 17.3.1]. The system is parameterized with an arbitrary number of N processes and K states where $N < K$. Each process always stays in one of states $0, ..., K-1$. Similarly, we model the system with a global sequence s as the state variable with $|s| = N$ and $0 \leq s[i] < K$ for each process i; the following invariant should be maintained (we skip DIONE versions from now on):

Invariant 3. $|s| = N \wedge \forall i(0 \leq i < N \implies 0 \leq s[i] < K)$

Process i is considered holding a token by checking its predecessor $i-1$ and see if it's in one of two conditions: (1) $i = 0 \wedge s[i] = s[N-1]$ or (2) $i \neq 0 \wedge s[i] \neq s[i-1]$. Any process except process 0 holding a token can initiate a transition to copy the state from its predecessor in the ring, i.e., $s[i] = s[i-1]$. If process 0 is holding a token, it can assign itself the value from process $N-1$ plus one, i.e., $s[0] = (s[N-1]+1)\%K$. Likewise, a legal configuration is defined as that only one process is holding a token. For `StableRing`, we prove the desired invariant that, once in a legal configuration, the system continues to be in the legal configuration. Formally, the following invariant should hold:

Invariant 4.
$$\left|\left\{i \mid 0 \leq i < N \wedge \begin{pmatrix} i = 0 \wedge s[i] = s[N-1] \vee \\ i \neq 0 \wedge s[i] \neq s[i-1] \end{pmatrix}\right\}\right| = 1$$

Proof Strategy. As reported in Table 1, two of five lemmas are manually written to prove Invariant 4. Our first lemma is to establish the axiom that, if an element i is in a set I, then $|I| = 1 \iff I = \{i\}$. This helps DAFNY infer from inductive hypothesis that only one process i was holding a token in the prestate s before a transition. Notice that after transition, process $i' = (i+1)\%N$ will replace process i to hold the token. This leads to only two possible scenarios in the state after transition s': (1) $i' = 0$ and every process state is the same as its predecessor OR (2) $i' \neq 0$ and only process state $s'[i']$ is different from its predecessor. Otherwise, at least two processes will be different from their predecessors and hence holding tokens. The difficulty for DAFNY here is to infer $s'[0] = s'[N-1]$ in scenario 1 to show process 0 is holding a token and $s'[j] = s'[j-1]$ in scenario 2 so that every other process j does not hold a token. Based on this observation, the second simple lemma we add asserts that, if every element is equal to its predecessor in a sequence, then all elements are identical. This lemma can be proven by DAFNY by induction on the length of the sequence. Our proof strategy thus simply splits into two cases $i = N - 1$ and $i \neq N - 1$ and applies the lemma over appropriate (sub-)sequences of s'. DAFNY can then infer the intermediate result mentioned above and prove the invariant inductively.

4.3 Asynchronous Leader Election on a Ring

Our third case study explores the possibility to use DIONE to model parameterized systems via composition and check the correctness. `AsyncLCR` is a simplified version of the leader election algorithm from [20, Section 15.1]. In this system, each process is instantiated with a unique $u \in \mathit{UID}$ for voting. The main algorithm flow is the following: Each process maintains a queue q of votes to be sent to its successor and a *status* variable initialized as `UNKNOWN`. When a vote from its predecessor is delivered, only the vote greater than u is added into the queue. The leader is decided when a process receives a vote v where $v = u$ and sets its status to `CHOSEN`. A process with $\mathit{status} =$ `CHOSEN` can then report itself as the leader and set its *status* to `REPORTED`. The algorithm guarantees that the reported leader process should have the maximum *UID* over all processes. For simplicity, our model first assumes the vote is delivered instantaneously and removes the need of channel automata by merging send and receive into one `send_recv` action. Second, although it is straightforward to model an arbitrary number of processes in DIONE, we only consider three processes to reduce the verification effort in this study. Thus, our model for the system is a composition of three automata $\{P_0, P_1, P_2\}$. Each P_i is an instance of the same automaton design assigned with actual parameters, the index i and the *UID* value u_i. We prove the key invariant described in [20] that no process other than the process with the max *UID* can report itself as the leader. Formally,

Invariant 5. $\bigwedge_{i=0}^{2} (u_i \neq max(u_0, u_1, u_2) \implies P_i.status = \texttt{UNKNOWN})$

Proof Strategy. In Table 1, we reported that two functions and no extra lemmas are needed. These two functions, needed for an auxiliary invariant, are currently not expressible in DIONE. The first required function finds the greatest u_i and returns the index i; here we use a variable i_{max} to represent the return value for simplicity. The second function $between(lo, i, hi)$ checks if lo must pass thru i to reach hi in the ring topology where $lo \neq i$ and $lo \neq hi$. We then use both functions to build the invariant modified from [20]:

Invariant 6. $\bigwedge_{i=0}^{2} \bigwedge_{j=0 \wedge j \neq i}^{2} (i \neq i_{max} \wedge between(i, i_{max}, j)) \implies u_i \notin P_j.q$

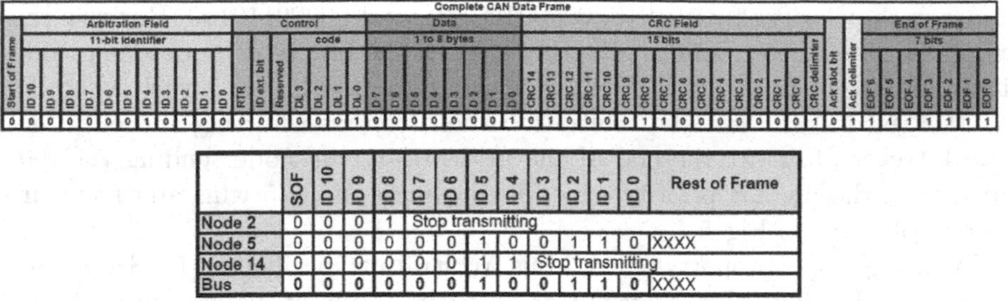

	SOF	ID 10	ID 9	ID 8	ID 7	ID 6	ID 5	ID 4	ID 3	ID 2	ID 1	ID 0	Rest of Frame
Node 2	0	0	0	1	Stop transmitting								
Node 5	0	0	0	0	0	0	1	0	0	1	1	0	XXXX
Node 14	0	0	0	0	0	0	1	1	Stop transmitting				
Bus	0	0	0	0	0	0	1	0	0	1	1	0	XXXX

Fig. 5. Complete CAN data frame structure (Top). Example arbitration with three nodes and CAN Data observed on bus (Bottom).

This invariant is to prove that, when i must reach i_{max} before reaching j, the vote u_i should have been dropped before reaching j; therefore u_i should never appear in the queue of process j. DAFNY is able to prove the conjunction of Invariant 5 and 6 to be inductive without any additional lemma.

4.4 CAN bus Arbitration

In our last case study, we consider a vastly different communication protocol, the arbitration protocol for Controller Area Network (CAN bus). CAN bus is a long lasting and extremely popular communication protocol for Electronic Control Units (ECUs) in automotive. Specifically, the data link layer of CAN bus implements a Carrier-Sense Multiple Access with Collision Detection (CSMA/CD) type of protocols to arbitrate between ECUs and grant access to CAN bus to only one ECU at a certain time. In this section, we first describe this arbitration protocol, then give our DIONE model for the protocol, and finally provide our proof strategy for checking invariant.

CAN bus Arbitration. According to the ISO standard [13, Section 10.4], it is assumed that all ECUs (or nodes) are synchronized with a global clock for bit transmission, and every node implements the same mechanism to *serially* transmit and receive CAN data frame as shown in Fig. 5. The frame starts with a start of frame (SOF bit) bit that must be DOMINANT value (logical 0) followed by a 11-bit arbitration field (ID bits) representing the priority of this frame where a smaller value of ID bits represents a higher priority. Otherwise, a node keeps sending RECESSIVE value (logical 1) when it is not sending data. Further, all nodes are connected to the CAN bus. The CAN bus can be considered as a logical conjunction of an arbitrary number of inputs from all nodes so that it outputs logical 0 if any node sends logical 0 in a cycle.

Arbitration happens only when multiple nodes simultaneously attempt to send a data frame. More precisely, multiple nodes simultaneously transmit SOF and the 11-bit arbitration field of the frames bit by bit in each cycle. Figure 5 shows an arbitration between three nodes, Node 2, 5, and 14, sending CAN frames with priority 0010101010, 00000100110, and 00000110100. Bus row represents the bit values monitored on bus. When the bits sent by different nodes differs, nodes sending logical 0 win over those sending logical 1 such as at ID8 and ID4. Nodes who lost the arbitration then stop transmitting and only send logical 1 ever after. At the end of the arbitration, the node sending the data frame with the highest priority wins. For example, node 5 wins and transmits the rest of frame in Fig. 5.

Finally, a major property of CAN bus Arbitration specified in [13, Section 6.3] states the following: "The transmitter with the frame of highest priority shall gain the bus access". The standard also explicitly explains that the priority of different frames are assumed to be distinct. The statement can paraphrased and formalized as the following equivalent invariant: "The ECU with the frame of highest priority shall keep transmitting in every cycle".

DIONE *Model.* Our DIONE model is designed following specifications in [13]. The system is composed of a `NodeSeq` automaton and a `Bus` channel automaton. The `NodeSeq` automaton is an abstraction of an arbitrary number of nodes. Its state consists of a `pos` to indicate which ID bit is currently transmitted and a sequence of `NodeStates` for individual nodes. Each node has an `arb` variable for the 11-bit arbitration field and a `transmit` variable to denote if this node is transmitting. Initially, `pos` starts at 10 and `transmit` is `True` to model that all nodes start to send at the same time. The `Bus` automaton simply has one state variable `bus` to represent the current bus state at each cycle. This `Bus` automaton can be considered as a broadcast channel where all nodes `send` to and `recv` from the `Bus` automaton.

To model synchronized communication, a cycle is modeled with a `send` action followed by a `recv` action. At the `send` action, `NodeSeq` outputs `msgs` modeling the sequence of bits with each bit sent from one node. Each node either extracts the bit from `arb` at current `pos` via a built-in function `bv_extract`, or sends logical 1 if it already stopped transmitting. `Bus` automaton then reads `msgs`, computes the logical conjunction via universal quantification, and stores the result in `bus`. At the `recv` action, `Bus` automaton publishes the value of `bus` as `msg` back to each node. Upon receiving `msg` from `Bus` in the `recv` action, each node then compares if the received bit is what it transmitted. If a node observes unequal bit values, then this node will set its `transmit` to `False` to stop transmitting. Notice that this requires an iteration through all nodes. Here, we choose to support *list comprehension* syntax in PYTHON and create a new sequence of `NodeState` from the old sequence with each node updated accordingly. This eliminates the need for a loop structure and simplifies the translation. After all nodes are updated, `pos` is decremented until it is negative.

Lastly, given the index i_{min} of the node with the highest priority, i.e., the smallest arbitration field, the invariant simply means the `transmit` of node i_{min} should stay `True`. The invariant is formulated as below:

Invariant 7. $|nodes| \geq 1 \wedge nodes[i_{min}].transmit$

Proof Strategy. In order to prove the invariant for this case study, we have to manually introduce the following code in DAFNY. First, to reflect the synchronized communication, one `send` and one `recv` action compose a cycle; hence assumptions over actions are added to consider only the executions composed of alternating `send` and `recv` actions. Second, four auxiliary functions are added to support translating the aforementioned list comprehension expression. These functions are for generic type of lists and therefore can be reused in more cases. Finally, we have to manually figure an over-approximation of one effect of the `recv` action, and use this approximation in the transition relation instead. Fortunately, we can instruct DAFNY to automatically check whether the approximation is indeed an over-approximation.

With above mentioned manual efforts, DAFNY is able to prove both BMC and induction with $k = 24$. $k = 24$ is simply because there are only 11 bits in arbitration field, and hence the states should stay the same ever after 12 cycles, i.e., 24 transitions. This showcases the potential of DIONE in verifying parameterized system composed with different channel or environment models, and this can be achieved within a manageable amount of manual effort.

5 Conclusion

We presented DIONE, a formal framework for analyzing distributed systems with specification language based on I/O automata and verification methods powered by DAFNY. The key compatibility conditions for IOA models are encoded as lemmas that can be automatically discharged by DAFNY in all of our cases. Our case studies show that a range of different distributed protocols can be naturally modeled in DIONE for Bounded Model Checking and k-induction invariant checking. The translated DAFNY specifications in the case studies were analyzed with DAFNY verifier automatically, with little extra manual annotations. These results are encouraging, and suggest several exciting future directions. (1) In the spirit of [11], IOA specifications could be translated to synthesizable DAFNY code, and hence, to correct-by-construction C# implementations for protocols. (2) Uniform or parameterized verification for distributed systems using small model properties [24] or theory of arrays [10]. Finally, (3) DIONE could be extended to support timed, hybrid, and probabilistic I/O Automata [14].

Acknowledgements. The authors were supported in part by research grants from the National Science Foundation under the Cyber-Physical Systems (CPS) program (award number 1544901 and 1739966).

References

1. Athalye, A.A.R.: CoqIOA: a formalization of IO automata in the Coq proof assistant. Thesis, Massachusetts Institute of Technology (2017)
2. Bhargavan, K., Bond, B., et al.: Everest: towards a verified, drop-in replacement of HTTPS. In: SNAPL 2017, vol. 71, pp. 1:1–1:12. Schloss Dagstuhl-Leibniz-Zentrum fuer Informatik (2017)

3. Bogdanov, A.: Formal verification of simulations between I/O automata. Thesis, Massachusetts Institute of Technology (2001)
4. Chockler, G., Lynch, N., Mitra, S., Tauber, J.: Proving atomicity: an assertional approach. In: Fraigniaud, P. (ed.) DISC 2005. LNCS, vol. 3724, pp. 152–168. Springer, Heidelberg (2005). https://doi.org/10.1007/11561927_13
5. Cordeiro, L., Fischer, B., Marques-Silva, J.: SMT-based bounded model checking for embedded ANSI-C software. In: ASE 2009, pp. 137–148, November 2009
6. Fekete, A., Kaashoek, M.F., Lynch, N.A.: Implementing sequentially consistent shared objects using broadcast and point-to-point communication. J. ACM **45**(1), 35–69 (1998)
7. Fekete, A., Lynch, N.A., Shvartsman, A.A.: Specifying and using a partitionable group communication service. ACM Trans. Comput. Syst. **19**(2), 171–216 (2001)
8. Garland, S.J., Lynch, N.A., et al.: IOA user guide and reference manual (2003)
9. Ghosh, S.: Distributed Systems: An Algorithmic Approach, 2nd Edition, 2nd edn. Chapman & Hall/CRC, Boca Raton (2014)
10. Gurfinkel, A., Shoham, S., Meshman, Y.: SMT-based verification of parameterized systems. In: FSE 2016, pp. 338–348. ACM (2016)
11. Hawblitzel, C., Howell, J., et al.: IronFleet: proving practical distributed systems correct. In: SOSP 2015, pp. 1–17. ACM (2015)
12. Hsieh, C., Mitra, S.: Dione (2019). https://github.com/cyphyhouse/dione
13. ISO: Road vehicles-Controller area network (CAN) - Part 1: Data link layer and physical signalling. Standard, International Organization for Standardization, December 2003
14. Kaynar, D.K., Lynch, N., et al.: Timed I/O automata: a mathematical framework for modeling and analyzing real-time systems. In: RTSS 2003, p. 166. IEEE Computer Society (2003)
15. Komuravelli, A., Gurfinkel, A., Chaki, S.: SMT-based model checking for recursive programs. In: Biere, A., Bloem, R. (eds.) CAV 2014. LNCS, vol. 8559, pp. 17–34. Springer, Cham (2014). https://doi.org/10.1007/978-3-319-08867-9_2
16. Leino, K.R.M.: Dafny: an automatic program verifier for functional correctness. In: Clarke, E.M., Voronkov, A. (eds.) LPAR 2010. LNCS (LNAI), vol. 6355, pp. 348–370. Springer, Heidelberg (2010). https://doi.org/10.1007/978-3-642-17511-4_20
17. Leino, K.R.M.: Automating theorem proving with SMT. In: Blazy, S., Paulin-Mohring, C., Pichardie, D. (eds.) ITP 2013. LNCS, vol. 7998, pp. 2–16. Springer, Heidelberg (2013). https://doi.org/10.1007/978-3-642-39634-2_2
18. Lesani, M., Bell, C.J., Chlipala, A.: Chapar: certified causally consistent distributed key-value stores. In: POPL 2016, pp. 357–370. ACM (2016)
19. Lim, H., Kaynar, D., Lynch, N., Mitra, S.: Translating timed I/O automata specifications for theorem proving in PVS. In: Pettersson, P., Yi, W. (eds.) FORMATS 2005. LNCS, vol. 3829, pp. 17–31. Springer, Heidelberg (2005). https://doi.org/10.1007/11603009_3
20. Lynch, N.A.: Distributed Algorithms. Morgan Kaufmann Publishers Inc., San Francisco (1996)
21. Nipkow, T., Slind, K.: I/O automata in Isabelle/HOL. In: Dybjer, P., Nordström, B., Smith, J. (eds.) TYPES 1994. LNCS, vol. 996, pp. 101–119. Springer, Heidelberg (1995). https://doi.org/10.1007/3-540-60579-7_6
22. O'Hearn, P.W.: Continuous reasoning: scaling the impact of formal methods. In: LICS 2018, pp. 13–25. ACM (2018)
23. Padon, O., McMillan, K.L., et al.: Ivy: safety verification by interactive generalization. In: PLDI 2016, pp. 614–630. ACM (2016)

24. Pnueli, A., Rodeh, Y., et al.: The small model property: how small can it be? Inf. Comput. **178**(1), 279–293 (2002)
25. Smith, M.A.S.: Formal verification of TCP and T/TCP. Ph.D. thesis (1997)
26. Tuttle, M.R., Goel, A.: Protocol proof checking simplified with SMT. In: NCA 2012, pp. 195–202, August 2012
27. Wilcox, J.R., Woos, D., et al.: Verdi: a framework for implementing and formally verifying distributed systems. In: PLDI 2015, pp. 357–368. ACM (2015)

Relating Alternating Relations for Conformance and Refinement

Ramon Janssen[1(✉)], Frits Vaandrager[1], and Jan Tretmans[1,2]

[1] Radboud University, Nijmegen, The Netherlands
{ramonjanssen,f.vaandrager,tretmans}@cs.ru.nl
[2] ESI (TNO), Eindhoven, The Netherlands

Abstract. Various relations have been defined to express refinement and conformance for state-transition systems with inputs and outputs, such as **ioco** and **uioco** in the area of model-based testing, and *alternating simulation* and *alternating-trace containment* originating from game theory and formal verification. Several papers have compared these independently developed relations, but these comparisons make assumptions (*e.g.,* input-enabledness), pose restrictions (*e.g.,* determinism – then they all coincide), use different models (*e.g.,* interface automata and Kripke structures), or do not deal with the concept of *quiescence*. In this paper, we present the integration of the **ioco**/**uioco** theory of model-based testing and the theory of alternating refinements, within the domain of non-deterministic, non-input-enabled interface automata. A standing conjecture is that **ioco** and alternating-trace containment coincide. Our main result is that this conjecture does not hold, but that **uioco** coincides with a variant of alternating-trace containment, for image finite interface automata and with explicit treatment of quiescence. From the comparison between **ioco** theory and alternating refinements, we conclude that **ioco** and the original relation of alternating-trace containment are too strong for realistic black-box scenarios. We present a refinement relation which can express both **uioco** and refinement in game theory, while being simpler and having a clearer observational interpretation.

Keywords: Alternating refinement · ioco · uioco · Interface automata

1 Introduction

Many software systems can be modelled using some kind of state-transition automaton. States in the model represent an abstraction of the states of the system, and transitions between states model the actions that the system may perform. Depending on the kind of state-transition model, an action can be the acceptance of an input, the production of an output, an internal computation of the system, the combination of an input and corresponding output, or just an

Funded by the Netherlands Organisation of Scientific Research (NWO-TTW), project 13859: SUMBAT - SUpersizing Model-BAsed Testing.

W. Ahrendt and S. L. Tapia Tarifa (Eds.): IFM 2019, LNCS 11918, pp. 246–264, 2019.
https://doi.org/10.1007/978-3-030-34968-4_14

abstract, uninterpreted 'action' of the system. Formal relations between state machines are often used to express some notion of refinement, implementation correctness, or conformance: s_1 is related to s_2 expresses that s_1 implements, refines, or conforms to s_2. Many such relations have been defined over the years, expressing different intuitions of what constitutes a conforming implementation or a correct refinement.

In this paper, we focus on state-transition systems where actions are interpreted as either input or output. An input involves a trigger from the environment to the system, where the initiative is taken by the environment, whereas an output is initiated by the system itself. Modelling formalisms with inputs and outputs are, e.g., Input/Output Automata [13], Input-Output Transition Systems [17], and Interface Automata [2]. We use the latter in this paper. We will extensively compare the relations **ioco** and **uioco** from the area of model-based testing, and *alternating simulation* and *alternating-trace containment* originating from game theory and formal verification. Previous papers have compared these independently developed relations, but these comparisons make assumptions (*e.g.,* input-enabledness), pose restrictions (*e.g.,* determinism – then they all coincide), use different models (*e.g.,* interface automata and Kripke structures), or do not deal with the concept of *quiescence*, i.e., the absence of outputs in a state, that is crucial in the relations **ioco** and **uioco**. Based on this comparison, we propose the novel relation of *input-failure refinement*, which links **uioco** and alternating-trace-containment.

ioco. Model-based testing (MBT) is a form of black-box testing where a System Under Test (SUT) is tested for conformance to a model. The model is the basis for the algorithmic generation of test cases and for the evaluation of test results. Conformance is defined with a formal *conformance* or *implementation relation* between SUTs and models. Although an SUT is a black box, we assume it could be modelled by some model instance in a domain of implementation models, so that we can reason about SUTs as if they were formal models.

An often used conformance relation is **ioco** (**i**nput-**o**utput-**co**nformance) [17,18]. The relation **ioco** is based on the assumption that implementations can be modelled as *input-enabled* interface automata, i.e., all states have a transition for all inputs. An implementation **ioco**-conforms to its specification if the implementation never produces an output that cannot be produced by the specification model in the same situation. A particular, virtual output is *quiescence*, actually expressing the absence of real outputs: an implementation may only refuse outputs if the specification can do so. Observing quiescence during a practical test is done by waiting for a time-out. The **ioco**-testing theory has found its way into many MBT tools and practical applications [14,19].

Whereas input-enabledness seems reasonable for real-world systems, it is an inconvenience in mathematical reasoning about **ioco**, in comparing specification models, and in stepwise refinement, since the different domains for implementations and specifications make that **ioco** is not reflexive and not transitive [11].

A variation of **ioco** is **uioco** [4]. This relation is weaker than **ioco** and it was shown to have some beneficial properties with respect to intuition of what conformance means, as well as for formal reasoning about composition, transitivity, and refinement [4,11]. Moreover, a generalization of **uioco** was given in [21] that also applies to non-input-enabled implementations and that is reflexive and transitive, but a complete testing theory including test generation, test execution, and test observations is still missing for this generalization,

Alternating Refinement. Originating from game theory, *alternating refinement relations* describe refinement as a game [3]. Originally, alternating refinement was defined on alternating transition systems, a variant of Kripke structures, which have state propositions instead of input and output labels on transitions. Behaviour of alternating transition systems is determined by *agents*, which are either adversarial or collaborative. In a two-player game of alternating refinement on two models s_1 and s_2, the antagonist controls the collaborative agents of s_1 and the adversarial agents of s_2. The protagonist controls the collaborative agents of s_2 and the adversarial agents of s_1, and tries to ensure that the moves made by the agents in both models match. Alternating refinement holds if the protagonist has a winning strategy, i.e., the protagonist is always able to match moves. There are different ways of 'matching a move', and these determine which alternating refinement relation is obtained. The branching time *alternating simulation* uses a local, single transition-based notion of matching, whereas the linear time *alternating-trace-containment* adopts a global, trace-based approach.

A successful instantiation of alternating simulation is in interface theory, where alternating transition systems are replaced by *Interface Automata* (IA) with inputs and outputs, and where fixed agents are chosen: the software system itself controls the outputs, and the environment control the inputs. This led to the definition of alternating simulation on IA [2]. Unfortunately, alternating simulation is not black-box *observational*, i.e., it is difficult to construct a realistic test and observation scenario with which the differences between unrelated systems can be observed in a black-box setting. Since observable behaviour is often represented by trace-based (linear time) relations, alternating-trace-containment for IA may be of interest, but this relation has not been translated to IA, yet. A translation of alternating-trace-containment to labelled transition systems with inputs and outputs was recently proposed [5], but only for deterministic models.

Relating Relations. The relations **ioco** and **uioco** on one hand, and *alternating-trace containment* and *alternating simulation* on the other hand, were proposed in different communities and for different purposes, yet, they show considerable overlap. In particular, it has been shown that all four relations coincide for deterministic models [1,3,5,20], but for non-determinsitic models such a comparison has not been made, yet. Only a conjecture in [5] claims that alternating-trace-containment and **ioco** also coincide for non-deterministic models.

If we manage to relate these independently defined relations also for non-determinsitic systems, this would indicate that these relations indeed express a generic and natural notion of conformance and refinement. An integration of both paradigms would strengthen both **ioco** theory and interface theory: it would add black-box observability to alternating refinement, and it would provide concepts and algorithms for refinement to **ioco**/**uioco**.

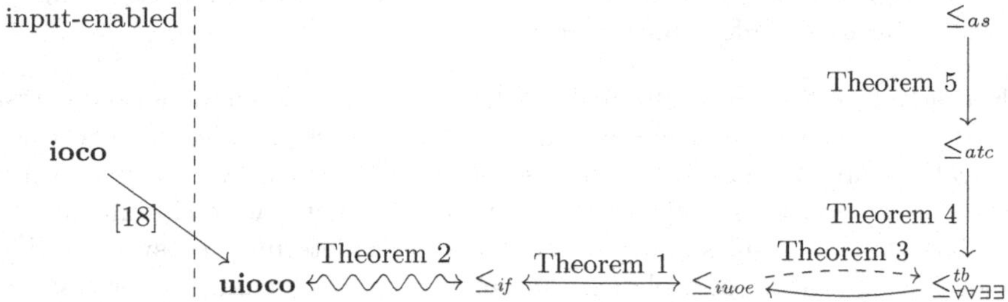

Fig. 1. Overview of the relations treated in this paper. An arrow from relation A to relation B denotes that A is stronger than B. The dashed arrow only holds if the second of the related models is image finite. The wavy arrow only holds if quiescence is explicitly added to the models related by input-failure refinement. Relation **ioco** is only defined if the first argument is input-enabled.

Contributions and Overview. The main contribution of this paper is an integration of the **ioco** theory of model-based testing [17], the theory of interface automata [2], and the theory of alternating refinements [3]. More specifically, we present the following results:

1. *Input-failure refinement* $\leq_{if}$ and *input-universal output-existential refinement* $\leq_{iuoe}$ are two equivalent preorders, which are defined in Sect. 3. They are proved to coincide with **uioco**, after explicitly adding quiescence in the IAs, in Sect. 4. The new preorders are in essence the same as the relation of substitutive refinement in [6], but adapted to our context. The new characterizations serve as a basis for the integration: they increase intuition and understanding and they turn out to be helpful for comparing with alternating refinements.
2. The game-theoretic notion of alternating-trace containment [3,5] is translated to the setting of non-deterministic interface automata in Sect. 5. (Alternating simulation of [3] was already translated in [2]). We show that the resulting alternating-trace containment preorder $\leq_{atc}$ is weaker than alternating simulation preorder $\leq_{as}$ for interface automata, similar to the result of [3] for alternating transition systems, in Sect. 6.
3. We show that $\leq_{atc}$ is not observational and not intuitive as a conformance relation, using a natural testing scenario for interface automata. Motivated by this scenario, we define a slightly weaker game-theoretic refinement relation $\leq^{tb}_{\forall\forall\exists\exists}$. We prove that $\leq^{tb}_{\forall\forall\exists\exists}$ coincides with $\leq_{if}$ and $\leq_{iuoe}$, and, modulo proper treatment of quiescence, with **uioco**, for image-finite interface automata. The tight link with **uioco** and $\leq_{if}$ implies that $\leq^{tb}_{\forall\forall\exists\exists}$ is indeed observational. Moreover, these results disprove the conjecture that **ioco** and alternating-trace containment coincide [5].

4. We provide first steps towards a linear time – branching time spectrum for interface automata in Fig. 1, similar to the well-known linear time – branching time spectrum for labeled transition systems of Van Glabbeek [8]. Based on our classification, we motivate that also **ioco** is too strong to act as intuitive conformance relation.

Recently, [5] established a fundamental connection between model-based testing and 2-player concurrent games, in a setting of deterministic systems, where specifications are game arenas, test cases are game strategies, test case derivation is strategy synthesis, and conformance is alternating-trace containment. Our work show that the results of [5] can be lifted to nondeterministic systems. This enables the application of a plethora of game synthesis techniques for test case generation.

Proofs and more extensive examples can be found in the technical report [12].

2 Preliminaries

We start by introducing the basic definitions of state-based models with inputs and outputs, as a basis for the alternating relations as well as **ioco** and **uioco**. The former are defined on interface automata, whereas the latter are defined on labelled transition systems. These paradigms differ mainly on the handling of internal transitions, which we omit in the scope of this paper. Other differences are minor, so Definition 1 reflects both domains of models from both works.

Definition 1. *An Interface Automaton (IA) is a 5-tuple* (Q, I, O, T, q^0)*, where*

- Q *is a set of states,*
- I *and* O *are disjoint sets of input and output labels,*
- $T \subseteq Q \times (I \cup O) \times Q$ *is a transition relation, and*
- $q^0 \in Q$ *is the initial state.*

The domain of IA is denoted $\mathcal{IA}$*. For* $s \in \mathcal{IA}$*, we write* Q_s*,* I_s*,* O_s*,* T_s *and* q^0_s *to refer to its respective elements, and* $L_s = I_s \cup O_s$ *for the full set of labels. For* $s_1, s_2, \dots, s_A, s_B, \dots$ *a family of IAs, we write* Q_j*,* I_j*,* O_j*,* T_j *and* q^0_j *to refer to the respective elements, and* $L_j = I_j \cup O_j$*, for* $j = 1, 2, \dots, A, B, \dots$*.*

In examples, we represent IA as state diagrams as usual. For the remainder of this paper, we assume that IA have the same input alphabet I and output alphabet O, with $L = I \cup O$, unless explicitly stated otherwise. Symbols a and b represent inputs, and x, y and z represent outputs.

Definition 2. *Let* $s \in \mathcal{IA}$*,* $Q \subseteq Q_s$*,* $q, q' \in Q_s$*,* $\ell \in L$ *and* $\sigma \in L^*$*, where* * *denotes the Kleene star, and* ϵ *denote the empty sequence. We define*

$$
\begin{array}{rlrl}
q \xrightarrow{\epsilon}_s q' & \Leftrightarrow q = q' & q \xrightarrow{\sigma\ell}_s q' & \Leftrightarrow \exists r \in Q_s : q \xrightarrow{\sigma}_s r \wedge (r, \ell, q') \in T_s \\
q \xrightarrow{\sigma}_s & \Leftrightarrow \exists r \in Q_s : q \xrightarrow{\sigma}_s r & \mathrm{trans}(s, q) & = \{(r, \ell, r') \in T_s \mid q = r\} \\
\mathrm{traces}_s(q) & = \{\sigma \in L^* \mid q \xrightarrow{\sigma}_s\} & Q \text{ after}_s\, \sigma & = \{r \in Q_s \mid \exists r' \in Q : r' \xrightarrow{\sigma} r\} \\
\mathrm{traces}(s) & = \mathrm{traces}_s(q_s^0) & s \text{ after } \sigma & = \{q_s^0\} \text{ after}_s\, \sigma \\
\mathrm{out}_s(q) & = \{x \in O \mid q \xrightarrow{x}_s\} & \mathrm{out}_s(Q) & = \{x \in O \mid \exists q \in Q : x \in \mathrm{out}_s(q)\} \\
\mathrm{in}_s(q) & = \{a \in I \mid q \xrightarrow{a}_s\} & \mathrm{in}_s(Q) & = \{a \in I \mid \forall q \in Q : a \in \mathrm{in}_s(q)\}
\end{array}
$$

$$s \textit{ is deterministic} \iff \forall \sigma \in \mathrm{traces}(s) : |s \text{ after } \sigma| = 1$$

We omit the subscript for interface automaton s when clear from the context.

Definition 3. *For $s \in \mathcal{IA}$, a* path *through s is a (finite or infinite) sequence $\pi = q^0\ell^1q^1\ell^2q^2\cdots$ of alternating states from Q_s and labels from L starting with state $q^0 = q_s^0$ and, if the sequence is finite, also ending in a state, such that each triplet $(q^j, \ell^{j+1}, q^{j+1})$ is contained in T_s. The domain of finite paths through s is denoted* paths(s)*. The* trace *of path π is the subsequence of labels that occur in it:* $\mathrm{trace}(\pi) = \ell^1\ell^2\cdots$*. Note that each $\pi \in \mathrm{paths}(s)$ has $\mathrm{trace}(\pi) \in \mathrm{traces}(s)$. We write* $\mathrm{last}(\pi)$ *to denote the last state occurring in a finite path π.*

3 Two Preorders on Interface Automata

We now present two equivalent relations, which serve as a stepping stone to bridge the gap between **ioco** theory and alternating refinements. The first relation has a clear observational interpretation, whereas the second is more elegant and convenient in reasoning, and thus useful in proofs and examples. They essentialy coincide with the relation of substitutive refinement in [6], adapted to our context.

3.1 Input-Failure Refinement

The first relation is based on covariance and contravariance, strongly inspired by interface theory [2]. Outputs are treated covariantly, as in normal trace containment: if s_1 refines s_2, then outputs produced by s_1 are also produced by s_2. Inputs are treated contravariantly, instead: inputs refused by s_1 are also refused by s_2. If s_2 refuses an input, then s_1 may choose to be more liberal than s_2, accepting that input instead. If it does so, the behaviour after that input is unspecified.

We first make the notion of refusing an input explicit.

Definition 4. *For any input symbol a, we define the* input-failure *of a as $\overline{a}$. Likewise, for any set of inputs A, we define $\overline{A} = \{\overline{a} \mid a \in A\}$. The domain of* input-failure traces *is defined as $\mathcal{FT}_{I,O} = L^* \cup L^* \cdot \overline{I}$. Set $S \subseteq \mathcal{FT}_{I,O}$ of* input-failure traces *is* input-failure closed *if, for all $\sigma \in L^*$, $a \in I$ and $\rho \in \mathcal{FT}_{I,O}$, $\sigma\overline{a} \in S \implies \sigma a \rho \in S$. The* input-failure closure *of S is the smallest input-failure closed superset of S, that is,* $\mathrm{fcl}(S) = S \cup \{\sigma a \rho \mid \sigma\overline{a} \in S, \rho \in \mathcal{FT}_{I,O}\}$.

We associate with every IA a set of input-failure traces, to define *input-failure refinement* and *input-failure equivalence*, denoted $\leq_{if}$ and $\equiv_{if}$, respectively.

Definition 5. *Let* $s_1, s_2 \in \mathcal{IA}$. *Then*

$$\begin{aligned} \text{Ftraces}(s_1) &= \text{traces}(s_1) \cup \{\sigma\overline{a} \mid \sigma \in L^*, a \in I, a \notin \text{in}(s_1 \text{ after } \sigma)\} \\ s_1 \leq_{if} s_2 &\iff \text{Ftraces}(s_1) \subseteq \text{fcl}(\text{Ftraces}(s_2)) \\ s_1 \equiv_{if} s_2 &\iff s_1 \leq_{if} s_2 \wedge s_2 \leq_{if} s_1 \end{aligned}$$

Remark that the definition of in(Q) is universally quantified over states in Q. This means that $\sigma\overline{a}$ is an input-failure trace of s if $\sigma \in \text{traces}(s)$ and some state in s after σ refuses input a. For a closed system, all actions are outputs. In that case, input-failure refinement coincides with ordinary trace containment.

The Ftraces provide an observational, trace-based semantics for IA. Intuitively, to observe an input-failure trace of system s_1, we let s_1 interact with its environment. The system produces outputs and consumes inputs from the environment, until we decide to stop, or until the system refuses an input. If the resulting input-failure trace is not in the closure of the Ftraces of specification s_2, then it proves $s_1 \not\leq_{if} s_2$. If no such trace can be found, then $s_1 \leq_{if} s_2$ holds.

Example 1. Figure 2 shows four IA with $I = \{a\}$ and $O = \{x\}$. Clearly, $\overline{a} \notin \text{Ftraces}(s_A)$ holds. Furthermore, $ax\overline{a} \notin \text{Ftraces}(s_A)$ since following trace ax in s_A leads to state q_A^1, and input a is not refused in q_A^1. In contrast, $a\overline{a} \in \text{Ftraces}(s_A)$ holds, since $(s_A \text{ after } a) = \{q_A^1, q_A^2\}$, and input a is not enabled in q_A^2.

Now, let us establish whether s_B, s_C and s_D are input-failure refinements of s_A. We find $s_B \not\leq_{if} s_A$, shown by trace $axax \in \text{Ftraces}(s_B)$ which is not allowed by s_A. Put formally, $axax \notin \text{fcl}(\text{Ftraces}(s_A))$ holds, because $axax$, $ax\overline{a}$ and $\overline{a}$ are not in Ftraces(s_A). Similarly $s_C \not\leq_{if} s_A$ is shown by trace $ax\overline{a} \in \text{Ftraces}(s_C)$. Refusing $\overline{a}$ after ax is not allowed by s_A, or formally, $ax\overline{a} \notin \text{fcl}(\text{Ftraces}(s_A))$. Finally, $s_D \leq_{if} s_A$ does hold, as $\text{Ftraces}(s_D) = \{\epsilon, a, aa, aax\} \cup aax^*\overline{a}$, and all of these traces are in fcl(Ftraces(s_A)): traces ϵ and a are in fcl(Ftraces(s_A)) because they are in Ftraces(s_A), and all other traces are in fcl(Ftraces(s_A)) because $a\overline{a} \in \text{Ftraces}(s_A)$. Intuitively, $a\overline{a} \in \text{Ftraces}(s_A)$ implies that the behaviour after trace aa is underspecified, so s_D is free to choose any behaviour after this trace.

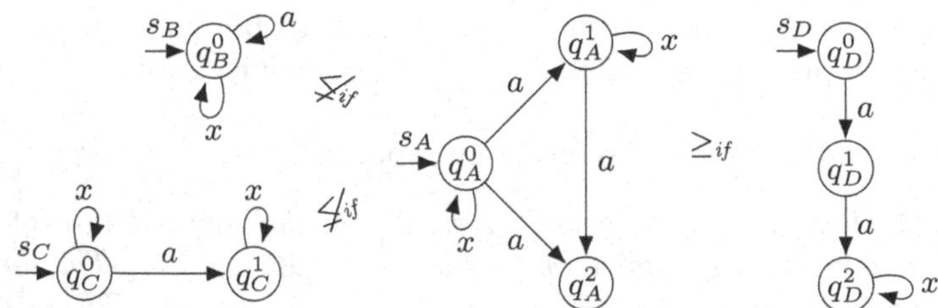

Fig. 2. Specification IA s_A is not input-failure refined by s_B and s_C, but it is by s_D.

The closure of the input-failure traces serves as a canonical representation of the behaviour of an IA, as stated in Proposition 1. That is, if and only if the closures of two models are the same, then they are input-failure equivalent.

Proposition 1. *Let* $s_1, s_2 \in \mathcal{IA}$. *Then*

$$s_1 \leq_{if} s_2 \iff \text{fcl}(\text{Ftraces}(s_1)) \subseteq \text{fcl}(\text{Ftraces}(s_2))$$
$$s_1 \equiv_{if} s_2 \iff \text{fcl}(\text{Ftraces}(s_1)) = \text{fcl}(\text{Ftraces}(s_2))$$

Proposition 1 implies that relation $\leq_{if}$ is reflexive ($s \leq_{if} s$) and transitive ($s_1 \leq_{if} s_2 \wedge s_2 \leq_{if} s_3 \implies s_1 \leq_{if} s_3$), making it suitable for stepwise refinement. Formally, it is thus a preorder.

3.2 Input Universal/Output Existential Traces

The definition of input-failure refinement clearly reflects its observational nature. Yet, reasoning about this relation can be simplified by using an alternative characterization. This characterization is not expressed in terms of explicit input refusals, but it is based upon the existential and universal definitions of the respective operators out and in, from Definition 2.

Definition 6. *Let* $s \in \mathcal{IA}$, *and let* $\sigma = \ell^1 \dots \ell^n \in L^*$. *Then*

$$\sigma \textit{ is s-output-existential} \iff \forall j \in \{1 \dots n\} : \ell^j \in \text{out}(s \text{ after } \ell^1 \dots \ell^{j-1}) \cup I$$
$$\sigma \textit{ is s-input-universal} \iff \forall j \in \{1 \dots n\} : \ell^j \in \text{in}(s \text{ after } \ell^1 \dots \ell^{j-1}) \cup O$$

OE(s) *denotes the set of s-output-existential words in* L^*, *and* IU(s) *the set of s-input-universal words in* L^*.

Definition 7. *Let* $s_1, s_2 \in \mathcal{IA}$. *Then*

$$s_1 \leq_{iuoe} s_2 \iff \text{OE}(s_1) \cap \text{IU}(s_2) \subseteq \text{IU}(s_1) \cap \text{OE}(s_2)$$

Theorem 1. $s_1 \leq_{if} s_2 \iff s_1 \leq_{iuoe} s_2$

Example 2. We revisit Example 1, and we should find the same IA to be related by $\leq_{iuoe}$ as by $\leq_{if}$, by Theorem 1. We find $axax \in \text{OE}(s_B) \cap \text{IU}(s_A)$ and $axax \notin \text{OE}(s_A)$, which confirms $s_B \not\leq_{iuoe} s_A$. We also find $axa \in \text{OE}(s_C) \cap \text{IU}(s_A)$ and $axa \notin \text{IU}(s_C)$, confirming $s_C \not\leq_{iuoe} s_A$. Finally, we find $\text{OE}(s_D) \cap \text{IU}(s_A) = \{\epsilon, a\}$, and these traces are both in IU(s_D) and in OE(s_A), which confirms $s_D \leq_{iuoe} s_A$.

4 Characterizing *uioco*

An often used implementation relation for MBT on interface automata (or labelled transition systems) is **ioco** [17,18]. For **ioco** it is assumed that implementations can be modelled as *input-enabled* interface automata, denoted by $\mathcal{IOTS}$. Moreover, quiescence is assumed to be observable. Formally, quiescence is expressed by adding a fresh output label $\delta \notin L_s$ in all states where no outputs are possible. (Since this changes the output alphabet, we will not assume the globally defined alphabets L, I and O for the remainder of this section.)

Definition 8. *Let $i \in \mathcal{IOTS}$ and $s \in \mathcal{IA}$ with $I_i = I_s$, $O_i = O_s$, and $\delta \notin L_s$.*

1. $\mathcal{IOTS} = \{s \in \mathcal{IA} \mid \forall q \in Q_s, \forall a \in I_s : q \xrightarrow{a}\}$
2. $\Delta(s) = (Q_s, I_s, O_s \cup \{\delta\}, T_\delta, q_s^0) \in \mathcal{IA}$, *with*
   $T_\delta \quad = T_s \cup \{(q, \delta, q) \mid q \in Q_s, \text{out}(q) = \emptyset\}$
3. i **ioco** $s \iff \forall \sigma \in \text{traces}(\Delta(s)) : \text{out}(\Delta(i) \text{ after } \sigma) \subseteq \text{out}(\Delta(s) \text{ after } \sigma)$

A variation of **ioco** is **uioco** [4]. Whereas **ioco** quantifies over all possible traces (with quiescence) in traces($\Delta(s)$), including those where some input in the trace may be underspecified, **uioco** only considers traces where all inputs are never underspecified. We take the generalized definition from [21], which also applies to non-input-enabled implementations. This definition coincides with the original one [4] if restricted to input-enabled implementations.

Definition 9. *Let $i, s \in \mathcal{IA}$ with $I_i = I_s$ and $O_i = O_s$, and let $\preccurlyeq$ denote the prefix relation on traces.*

1. $\text{Utraces}(s) = \{\sigma \in \text{traces}(s) \mid \forall \rho \in L_s^*, a \in I_s : \rho a \preccurlyeq \sigma \implies a \in \text{in}(s \text{ after } \rho)\}$
2. i **uioco** $s \iff \forall \sigma \in \text{Utraces}(\Delta(s)) :$
   $\text{out}(\Delta(i) \text{ after } \sigma) \subseteq \text{out}(\Delta(s) \text{ after } \sigma)$
   $\wedge \text{in}(\Delta(i) \text{ after } \sigma) \supseteq \text{in}(\Delta(s) \text{ after } \sigma)$

Proposition 2. *All $i \in \mathcal{IOTS}$ and $s \in \mathcal{IA}$ have i **ioco** $s \implies i$ **uioco** s. There exist $i \in \mathcal{IOTS}$ and $s \in \mathcal{IA}$ with i **uioco** $s \not\Longrightarrow i$ **ioco** s.*

The next step is to relate **ioco** and **uioco** to the relations defined in the previous sections. The main result of this section is that **uioco** is the same as input-failure refinement (Theorem 2), and thus also as input-universal-output-existential refinement (Theorem 1), if in the latter quiescence is explicitly added. The consequence is that **ioco** and input-failure refinement do not coincide, following Proposition 2. The difference between the two relations is the treatment of specification traces which are not input-universal, as shown in Example 3.

Lemma 1. $\text{Utraces}(s) = \text{IU}(s) \cap \text{traces}(s)$.

Theorem 2. i **uioco** $s \iff \Delta(i) \leq_{if} \Delta(s)$

Example 3. Consider $s_E \in \mathcal{IOTS}$ and $s_F \in \mathcal{IA}$ with $I_E = I_F = \{a\}$ and $O_E = O_F = \{x, y\}$ in Fig. 3, where quiescence has been explicitly added. Implementation s_E is not **ioco**-conformant to specification s_F: if we consider the trace $aa \in \text{traces}(\Delta(s_F))$ then $y \in \text{out}(\Delta(s_E) \text{ after } aa)$ but $y \notin \text{out}(\Delta(s_F) \text{ after } aa)$.

However, trace aa does not disprove **uioco**-conformance, since it is not s_F-input-universal: $aa \notin \text{Utraces}(\Delta(s_F))$, since $a \notin \text{in}(\Delta(s_F) \text{ after } a)$. In fact, s_E **uioco** s_F holds, which we prove via Theorems 1 and 2 by showing that $\Delta(s_E) \leq_{iuoe} \Delta(s_F)$. We first establish that $\text{OE}(\Delta(s_E)) \cap \text{IU}(\Delta(s_F)) = \delta^* + \delta^* a \delta^*$: extending any trace σ in this set by an output ℓ other than δ causes $\sigma\ell \notin \text{OE}(\Delta(s_E))$, and extending it by an input ℓ causes $\sigma\ell \notin \text{IU}(\Delta(s_F))$. Clearly, any trace in $\delta^* + \delta^* a \delta^*$ is also in $\text{IU}(\Delta(s_E))$ and in $\text{OE}(\Delta(s_F))$, so $\Delta(s_E) \leq_{iuoe} \Delta(s_F)$ holds. It follows that $\Delta(s_E) \leq_{if} \Delta(s_F)$ and s_E **uioco** s_F hold.

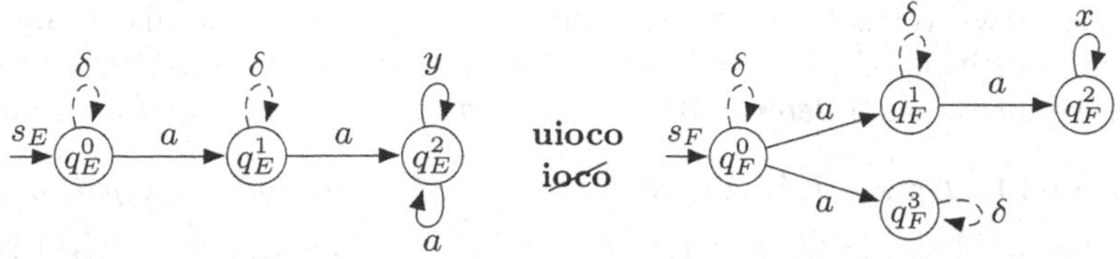

Fig. 3. $s_E \in \mathcal{IOTS}$ and $s_F \in \mathcal{IA}$. The dashed transitions are added by Δ.

5 Game Characterizations

Ordinary trace containment can be seen as a game between a protagonist and antagonist: the antagonist chooses a path in the left-hand model, and the protagonist should find a path in the right-hand model having the same trace. Trace containment then holds if the protagonist can always win. Alur et al. [3] generalized this game to alternating-trace containment, which we will now compare to input-failure refinement, **ioco** and **uioco**.

Alternating-trace containment acts on alternating transition systems. Such a model is parameterized by a set of *agents*, which are either collaborative or adversarial. Every agent can restrict the possible transitions by choosing a *strategy*. If every agent has chosen a strategy, this yields a unique path following these choices. The game of alternating-trace containment on models s_1 and s_2 is then played as follows. First, the antagonist chooses a strategy for the collaborative agents in s_1. Second, the protagonist chooses a matching strategy for the collaborative agents in s_2. Third, the antagonist chooses a strategy for the adversarial agents in s_2, and fourth, the protagonist matches this choice for the adversarial agents in s_1. In this way, the protagonist must ensure that the path in s_1 following these strategies has the same trace as the path in s_2. Again, s_1 is alternating-trace contained in s_2 if the protagonist can always win.

5.1 Alternating-Trace Containment for IA

The agents in [3] have no predefined roles, and any number of them may be defined. In our setting, we instantiate a fixed number of agents to reflect the input-output-behaviour of a software system. In particular, we introduce agents controlling the respective inputs and outputs, similarly to [2,5]. In practice, a system itself acts as an agent controlling its outputs, whereas the environment serves as an agent controlling the inputs of the system. The system and environment may also abstain from performing an action.

Definition 10. *Let $s \in \mathcal{IA}$. An* output strategy *for s is a partial function $f_o : \text{paths}(s) \rightharpoonup O$, such that $f_o(\pi)\downarrow$ implies $f_o(\pi) \in \text{out}(\text{last}(\pi))$ for all π (where $f_o(\pi)\downarrow$ means that $f_o(\pi)$ is defined). An* input strategy *for s is a partial function $f_i : \text{paths}(s) \rightharpoonup I$, such that $f_i(\pi)\downarrow$ implies $f_i(\pi) \in \text{in}(\text{last}(\pi))$. The domains of output and input strategies for s are $\Sigma_o(s)$ and $\Sigma_i(s)$ respectively.*

A system cannot only choose which outputs it produces, but also which transition it takes for a given input or output, in the case of non-determinism. It also chooses how to resolve race conditions, that is, whether to take an input or an output transition, if both the input and output strategy choose an action. To this end we introduce a *determinization strategy* and a *race condition strategy*.

Definition 11. *Let $s \in \mathcal{IA}$. A* determinization strategy *for s is a partial function $f_d : \text{paths}(s) \times L \rightharpoonup Q_s$ satisfying: (a) $q^n \xrightarrow{\ell}$ implies $f_d(q^0\ell^0 \cdots q^n, \ell) \downarrow$, and (b) $f_d(q^0\ell^0 \cdots q^n, \ell) = q^{n+1}$ implies $q^n \xrightarrow{\ell} q^{n+1}$. A* race condition strategy *for s is a function $f_r : \text{paths}(s) \to \{0, 1\}$, where 0 denotes choosing the input in case of a race, whereas 1 denotes choosing the output. The respective domains of determinization and race condition strategies for s are denoted $\Sigma_d(s)$ and $\Sigma_r(s)$.*

The combination of an input strategy, an output strategy, a determinization strategy and a race condition strategy uniquely determines a path through an interface automaton.

Definition 12. *Let $f = \langle f_i, f_o, f_d, f_r\rangle \in \Sigma_i(s) \times \Sigma_o(s) \times \Sigma_d(s) \times \Sigma_r(s)$ for $s \in \mathcal{IA}$, and let function $\text{next}_{s,f} : \text{paths}(s) \to \text{paths}(s)$ be given by*

$$\text{next}_{s,f}(\pi) = \begin{cases} \pi f_i(\pi) f_d(\pi, f_i(\pi)) & \text{if } f_i(\pi)\downarrow \wedge (f_o(\pi)\downarrow \Rightarrow f_r(\pi) = 0) \\ \pi f_o(\pi) f_d(\pi, f_o(\pi)) & \text{if } f_o(\pi)\downarrow \wedge (f_i(\pi)\downarrow \Rightarrow f_r(\pi) = 1) \\ \pi & \text{otherwise} \end{cases}$$

Note that the infinite sequence $\pi_0, \pi_1, \ldots$ with $\pi_0 = q_s^0$ and $\forall j > 0 : \pi_j = \text{next}_{s,f}(\pi_{j-1})$ forms a chain of finite paths ordered by prefix. The outcome *of s and f, notation $\text{outc}_s(f)$, is the limit under prefix ordering of $\pi_0, \pi_1, \ldots$. Observe that $\text{outc}_s(f)$ is either a finite path π with $\text{next}_{s,f}(\pi) = \pi$, or an infinite path.*

A software system is assumed to control its own outputs, as well as nondeterminism as race conditions, so the corresponding strategies are collaborative. Inputs are chosen by the environment, so the input strategy is adversarial. This leads to the following instantiation of alternating-trace containment for IA.

Definition 13. *Let $s_1, s_2 \in \mathcal{IA}$. Then s_1 is* alternating-trace contained *in s_2, denoted $s_1 \leq_{atc} s_2$, if*

$$\begin{aligned} &\forall f_o^1 \in \Sigma_o(s_1), \forall f_d^1 \in \Sigma_d(s_1), \forall f_r^1 \in \Sigma_r(s_1), \\ &\exists f_o^2 \in \Sigma_o(s_2), \exists f_d^2 \in \Sigma_d(s_2), \exists f_r^2 \in \Sigma_r(s_2), \\ &\forall f_i^2 \in \Sigma_i(s_2), \exists f_i^1 \in \Sigma_i(s_1) : \\ &\quad \text{trace}(\text{outc}(f_i^1, f_o^1, f_d^1, f_r^1)) = \text{trace}(\text{outc}(f_i^2, f_o^2, f_d^2, f_r^2)) \end{aligned}$$

Having defined alternating-trace containment for IA, we can now disprove the conjecture in [5]: Alternating-trace containment does not coincide with **ioco**, nor with **uioco**, $\leq_{if}$ or $\leq_{iuoe}$, as shown by Example 4.

Example 4. Consider IA s_G and s_H in Fig. 4. IA s_G is input-enabled, so **ioco** can be applied. Both IA have an output transition in every state, so Δ has no effect, which implies that $\leq_{if}$ and **uioco** coincide, even without explicitly applying Δ. All traces of s_H are input-universal, so **uioco** and **ioco** also coincide.

Then $\text{OE}(s_G) \cap \text{IU}(s_H)$ are the traces in $z^*az^*ax^*$ and $z^*az^*by^*$, and all prefixes of those traces. These are included in $\text{IU}(s_G) \cap \text{OE}(s_H)$, so $s_G \leq_{iuoe} s_H$ holds, and s_G is thus also related to s_H by relations $\leq_{if}$, **uioco** and **ioco**.

Now, let us play the game of alternating-trace containment. The antagonist chooses outputs x and y in states q_G^2 and $q_G^{2\prime}$ respectively, and resolves race conditions such that states q_G^2 or $q_G^{2\prime}$ are reached. In this way, the antagonist could enforce traces aax and aby, so the protagonist must match this with outputs x and y in respectively q_H^2 and $q_H^{2\prime}$. The protagonist should also choose a determinization strategy. Only two choices are possible: from q_H^0 it can make a transition to either q_H^1 or to $q_H^{1\prime}$. Suppose that the protagonist chooses q_H^1. The antagonist must then choose an input strategy, and it chooses to pick input a after path q_H^0, and input b after any path with trace a. Now, all strategies for s_H have been chosen and the outcome is $q_H^0 a q_H^1 b q_H^3$, with trace ab. The protagonist should choose a matching strategy to pick inputs in s_G, but it cannot: if it picks inputs to produce trace ab, then the resulting trace in s_G will be aby instead of ab. The protagonist thus loses the game. Had the protagonist chosen a determininization strategy to $q_H^{1\prime}$, then he would lose in the same manner.

Thus, $s_G \not\leq_{atc} s_H$ holds, even though s_G is related to s_H by relations $\leq_{if}$, $\leq_{iuoe}$, **uioco** and **ioco**. The intuitive reason is that the protagonist must already choose a determinization strategy for s_H, before the antagonist chooses an input strategy for s_H. Would this order of turns be reversed, then the protagonist could win the game for this example. The protagonist could then choose the determinization strategy for s_H such that either trace aax or trace aby is matched, depending on which inputs are chosen by the antagonist in s_G.

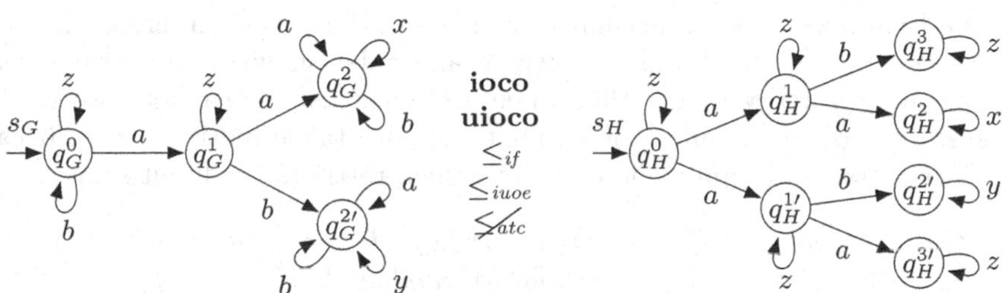

Fig. 4. IA s_G and s_H.

The analysis of $s_G \not\leq_{atc} s_H$ in Example 4 is rather complex. An intuitive experiment showing the difference between s_G and s_H would improve understanding of $\leq_{atc}$, but unfortunately, no observational interpretation of alternating-trace containment is given in [3].

For non-input-enabled IA, another difference between alternating-trace containment and the other relations is shown in Example 5.

Example 5. Consider IA s_I and s_J in Fig. 5. Clearly, $s_I \leq_{iuoe} s_J$ holds, since $\mathrm{OE}(s_I) \cap \mathrm{IU}(s_J)$ are the traces $y^* + y^*xy^*$ and their prefixes, which are in $\mathrm{IU}(s_I)$ and $\mathrm{OE}(s_J)$. Therefore, $s_I \leq_{if} s_J$ and s_I **uioco** s_J hold as well by the same resoning as in Example 4. Since s_I is not input-enabled, **ioco** is not defined.

Now, we play the game of alternating-trace containment. In s_I, the antagonist first picks output x, and then abstains performing an output, so the trace of the outcome in s_I is x. Clearly, the protagonist can match this in s_J. But no matter the determinization strategy he chooses, if the antagonist picks inputs a and b in s_J whenever possible, then the protagonist cannot match these inputs in s_I.

The intuitive reasoning is that the antagonist may choose inputs a and b after paths $q_J^0 x q_J^1$ and $q_J^0 x q_J^{1'}$, respectively, whereas a and b are not universally enabled after trace x. Would the antagonist pick only inputs in $\mathrm{in}(s_J \text{ after } x)$, then the protagonist could win the game.

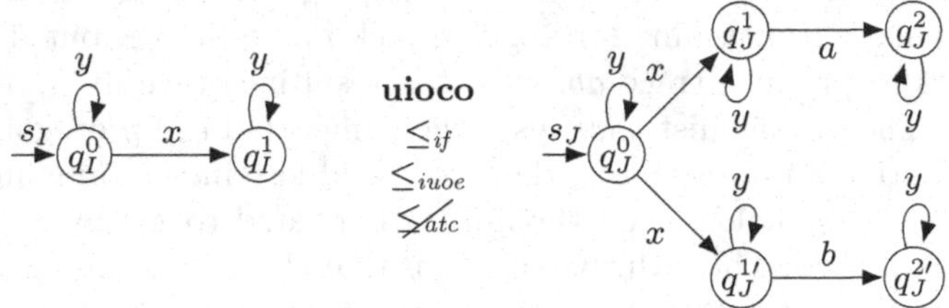

Fig. 5. Interface automata s_I and s_J.

5.2 The Game of Input-Failure Refinement

Based on Examples 4 and 5, we change the rules of the game of alternating-trace containment, in order to obtain a slightly weaker relation with a clearer observational meaning. First, we argue that an environment usually cannot observe the precise state of a system, and thus also not the path taken by the system. It can only observe traces of inputs and outputs, which restricts the input strategies.

Definition 14. *For $s \in \mathcal{IA}$, an input strategy $f_{i,tb}$ is* trace-based *if, for all $\pi_1, \pi_2 \in \mathrm{paths}(s)$, $\mathrm{trace}(\pi_1) = \mathrm{trace}(\pi_2)$ implies $f_{i,tb}(\pi_1) = f_{i,tb}(\pi_2)$. The domain of trace-based input strategies for s is denoted $\Sigma_{i,tb}(s)$.*

A second change is the order of turns. The antagonist must first resolve all its choices, before the protagonist resolves any choices.

Definition 15. *Let $s_1, s_2 \in \mathcal{IA}$. Then $s_1 \leq^{tb}_{\forall\forall\exists\exists} s_2$, if*

$$\forall f^2_{i,tb} \in \Sigma_{i,tb}(s_2), \forall f^1_d \in \Sigma_d(s_1), \forall f^1_o \in \Sigma_o(s_1), \forall f^1_r \in \Sigma_r(s_1),$$
$$\exists f^1_{i,tb} \in \Sigma_{i,tb}(s_1), \exists f^2_d \in \Sigma_d(s_2), \exists f^2_o \in \Sigma_o(s_2), \exists f^2_r \in \Sigma_r(s_2):$$
$$\mathrm{trace}(\mathrm{outc}(f^1_{i,tb}, f^1_o, f^1_d, f^1_r)) = \mathrm{trace}(\mathrm{outc}(f^2_{i,tb}, f^2_o, f^2_d, f^2_r))$$

In contrast to alternating-trace containment, this game has a correspondence with **ioco** theory in the non-deterministic setting. It does not coincide with **ioco**, but with **uioco**. We show this in Theorem 3, via input-failure refinement. A technical detail is that this correspondence only holds in both directions when the right-hand interface automaton is image-finite.

Definition 16. *Interface automaton s is* image-finite *if, for each $q \in Q_s$ and $\ell \in L_s$, q has finitely many ℓ-successors, i.e., set $\{q' \mid (q, \ell, q') \in T_s\}$ is finite.*

Theorem 3. *Let $s_1, s_2 \in \mathcal{IA}$. Then $s_1 \leq^{tb}_{\forall\forall\exists\exists} s_2 \implies s_1 \leq_{iuoe} s_2$. Furthermore, if s_2 is image-finite, then $s_1 \leq^{tb}_{\forall\forall\exists\exists} s_2 \impliedby s_1 \leq_{iuoe} s_2$.*

Example 6. We revisit Example 1 to investigate the game-characterization of input-failure refinement. The IA in Fig. 2 are image-finite so we should find the same related IA. First, consider $s_B \not\leq^{tb}_{\forall\forall\exists\exists} s_A$. The antagonist chooses $f^A_{i,tb}$, f^B_o and f^B_r by following the trace $axax$ in both models. Strategy f^B_d is fixed, since s_B is deterministic. Now, the protagonist should choose strategies so that the traces of the resulting outcomes match. It can match the first three actions axa, but this leads to q^2_A in s_A. Here the protagonist cannot match the last action x, so indeed $s_B \not\leq^{tb}_{\forall\forall\exists\exists} s_A$ holds. We show $s_C \not\leq^{tb}_{\forall\forall\exists\exists} s_A$ similarly. Let the antagonist choose strategies following trace axa. Now, the protagonist ends up in state q^1_A and q^1_C after two actions, where it cannot match the third action a in s_C. Finally, $s_D \leq^{tb}_{\forall\forall\exists\exists} s_A$ holds. Since q^0_D and q^1_D do not have outgoing output transitions and q^2_A has no input transitions, the antagonist can only choose a single action a in s_A, which can easily be matched by the protagonist s_D.

For image-infinite IA, the relation between $\leq^{tb}_{\forall\forall\exists\exists}$ and $\leq_{iuoe}$ is indeed strict, as is proven in [12]. For completeness, we also establish that $\leq^{tb}_{\forall\forall\exists\exists}$ is indeed weaker than $\leq_{atc}$. Strictness follows from Examples 4 and 5.

Theorem 4. $s_1 \leq_{atc} s_2 \implies s_1 \leq^{tb}_{\forall\forall\exists\exists} s_2$.

6 Alternating Simulation

In [3], two alternating refinement relations have been introduced for alternating transition systems: alternating-trace containment and alternating simulation. As shown in [3], alternating simulation is stronger than alternating-trace containment, and both relations coincide for deterministic alternating transition systems. This should also hold for instantiations on interface automata. We thus compare our adaptation of alternating-trace containment to the adaptation of alternating simulation from [2].

Definition 17. [2] *Let s_1, $s_2 \in \mathcal{IA}$. Then $R \subseteq Q_1 \times Q_2$ is an* alternating simulation *from s_1 to s_2 if for all $(q_1, q_2) \in R$,*

- $\text{out}(q_1) \subseteq \text{out}(q_2)$ *and* $\text{in}(q_2) \subseteq \text{in}(q_1)$, *and*
- *for all $\ell \in \text{out}(q_1) \cup \text{in}(q_2)$ and $q'_1 \in (q_1 \text{ after } \ell)$, there is a $q'_2 \in (q_2 \text{ after } \ell)$ such that $q'_1 \mathrel{R} q'_2$.*

The greatest alternating simulation is denoted $\leq_{as}$. *We write* $s_1 \leq_{as} s_2$ *to denote* $q_1^0 \leq_{as} q_2^0$.

Theorem 5 relates the two alternating relations. Example 7 proves strictness.

Theorem 5. *Let* $s_1, s_2 \in \mathcal{IA}$. *Then* $s_1 \leq_{as} s_2 \implies s_1 \leq_{atc} s_2$.

Example 7. Readers familiar with ordinary trace containment and simulation will recognize IA s_M and s_N in Fig. 6 as a standard example that shows the difference between the two relations. These IA also show the difference between the alternating refinement relations, since $s_M \leq_{atc} s_N$ and $s_M \not\leq_{as} s_N$ hold.

Let us first establish $s_M \not\leq_{as} s_N$. Any alternating simulation relation R from s_M to s_N must have $q_M^0 \; R \; q_N^0$. Since q_M^0 and q_N^0 share output x, Definition 17 states that either $q_M^1 \; R \; q_N^1$ or $q_M^1 \; R \; q_N^{1\prime}$ should hold. If $q_M^1 \; R \; q_N^1$ holds, then R is not an alternating simulation, since $\text{out}(q_M^1) = \{x, y\} \not\subseteq \text{out}(q_N^1) = \{x\}$. Likewise, $\text{out}(q_M^1) \not\subseteq \text{out}(q_N^{1\prime}) = \{y\}$ holds, so this disproves alternating simulation.

Clearly, $s_M \leq_{atc} s_N$ holds: any output strategy by the antagonist in s_M yields a unique path through s_M. The protagonist can choose output and determinization strategies in s_N such that the outcome in s_N has the same trace.

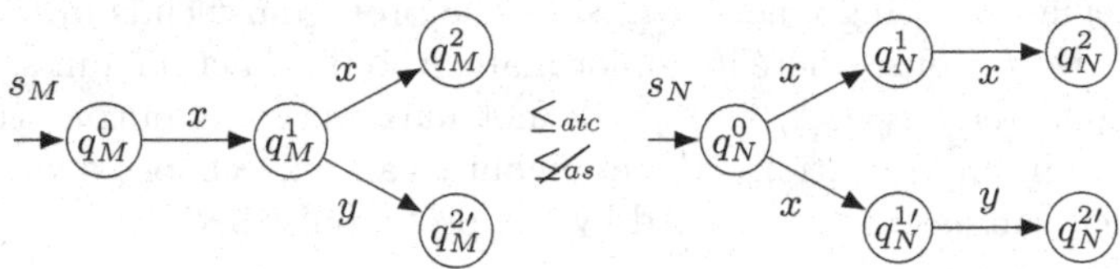

Fig. 6. IA s_M and s_N.

In the deterministic setting, all presented relations coincide. Clearly, **ioco** and **uioco** coincide by their definitions. We show that the remaining relations coincide by proving that the weakest relation implies the strongest.

Theorem 6. *Let* $s_1, s_2 \in \mathcal{IA}$, *such that* s_2 *is deterministic. Then*

$$s_1 \leq_{iuoe} s_2 \implies s_1 \leq_{as} s_2.$$

Efficient algorithms for checking alternating simulation exist [2]. Since all relations treated in this paper coincide if the right-hand IA is deterministic, an approach to decide any of these relations between two IA could be to transform the right-hand IA to a deterministic IA, preserving that relation, and then use the algorithm for alternating simulation. The standard subset-construction for determinization [10,17], however, does not preserve input-failure refinement, as Example 8 shows. We recall the subset-construction in Definition 18.

Definition 18. *Let* $s \in \mathcal{IA}$. *Then* $\text{det}(s) = (\mathcal{P}(Q_s) \setminus \{\emptyset\}, I, O, T_{\text{det}}, \{q_s^0\})$, *with*

$$T_{\text{det}} = \{(Q, \ell, Q \text{ after}_s \ \ell) \mid Q \subseteq Q_s, \ell \in L, (Q \text{ after}_s \ \ell) \neq \emptyset\}.$$

Example 8. Consider the interface automaton s_A from Fig. 2. We perform the subset construction on s_A, and obtain $\det(s_A)$ as shown in Fig. 7. Whereas s_A contains failure trace $a\overline{a}$, $\det(s_A)$ does not. As a consequence, $s_A \not\leq_{if} \det(s_A)$, so the model is changed with respect to input-failure refinement.

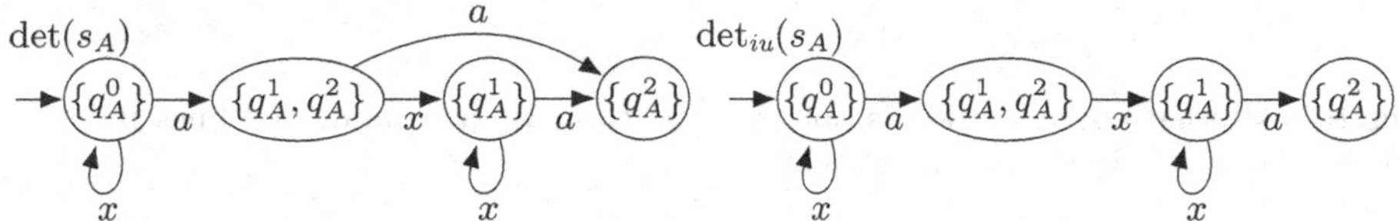

Fig. 7. The subset-construction (standard and input-universal, respectively) performed on s_A. Only the part reachable from the initial state is shown.

We introduce a determinization variant which respects input-universality, in order to preserve input-failure refinement, instead of normal trace containment.

Definition 19. *Let* $s \in \mathcal{IA}$. *Then* $\det_{iu}(s) = (\mathcal{P}(Q_s) \setminus \emptyset, I, O, T_{\det_{iu}}, \{q_s^0\})$, *with*

$$T_{\det_{iu}} = \{(Q, \ell, Q \text{ after}_s\ \ell) \mid \emptyset \neq Q \subseteq Q_s, \ell \in \text{in}_s(Q) \cup \text{out}_s(Q)\}.$$

Example 9. Figure 7 also shows the input-universal determinization $\det_{iu}(s_A)$ of s_A. Since $a \notin \text{in}(q_A^2)$, input a is not universally enabled in $\{q_A^1, q_A^2\}$, which implies that this state has no a-transition in $\det_{iu}(s_A)$. In fact, the reader may check that $s_A \equiv_{if} \det_{iu}(s_A)$ holds. This also follows from Theorem 7.

Theorem 7. *Let* $s \in \mathcal{IA}$. *Then* $s \equiv_{if} \det_{iu}(s)$.

Corollary 1. *Let* $s_1, s_2 \in \mathcal{IA}$. *Then*

$$\begin{aligned} s_1 \leq_{as} \det_{iu}(s_2) &\iff s_1 \leq_{if} s_2 \\ s_1 \leq_{as} \det_{iu}(s_2) &\iff s_1 \leq_{iuoe} s_2 \\ \Delta(s_1) \leq_{as} \det_{iu}(\Delta(s_2)) &\iff s_1 \mathbf{\,uioco\,} s_2 \\ \textit{if } s_2 \textit{ image finite then } s_1 \leq_{as} \det_{iu}(s_2) &\iff s_1 \leq^{tb}_{\forall\forall\exists\exists} s_2 \end{aligned}$$

Completing the lattice in Fig. 1, one may expect alternating simulation to be the strongest relation, in the same way that ordinary simulation is the strongest in the spectrum of Van Glabbeek [8]. But Example 10 shows that alternating simulation is neither stronger nor weaker than **ioco**. This supports the conclusion in [11] that it is hard to **ioco**-implement a given specification: even an alternating simulation refining implementation may not be **ioco**-conformant.

Example 10. Consider IA s_P and s_Q in Fig. 8. They have $\Delta(s_P) \leq_{as} \Delta(s_Q)$, as shown by the alternating simulation relation $\{(q_P^0, q_Q^0), (q_P^1, q_Q^1), (q_P^2, q_Q^2)\}$. However, $s_P \mathbf{\,i\!\!/oco\,} s_Q$ since $\text{out}(s_P \text{ after } ab) = \{x\} \not\subseteq \text{out}(s_Q \text{ after } ab) = \{y\}$.

Vice versa, in Fig. 6, $s_M \mathbf{\,ioco\,} s_N$ clearly holds, whereas $s_M \not\leq_{as} s_N$.

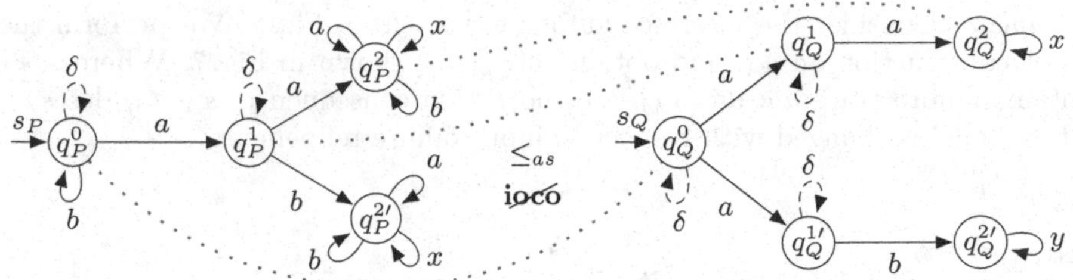

Fig. 8. Alternating simulation is not stronger than **ioco**. The dotted lines indicate states related by alternating simulation.

7 Conclusion and Future Work

We provided strong links between the **ioco** testing theory and alternating refinement theory on interface automata. The overlap between the relations from these independently developed theories indicate that they express a natural notion of refinement. Based on the strong correspondence between elements in testing theory and concepts from game theory [5], the provided links pave the way for using results from game theory in testing with **uioco** and $\leq_{if}$. We have also shown that alternating-trace containment does not lend itself well to an observational interpretation, but that a slight modification of the game rules solves this. Likewise, we deem **ioco** to be too strong for a practical implementation relation, as alternating simulation is not stronger.

To ease the comparison between **ioco** theory and alternating refinements, we introduced two relations which may be of interest in their own right. Input-failure refinement has a direct connection to alternating simulation, and to **uioco** when quiescence is added explicitly. Because of its straightforward observational interpretation, input-failure refinement should be suitable in conformance testing. A next step is to formalize and implement testing algorithms for this relation. The alternative characterization in terms of input-existential and output-universal traces may serve as a tool in formal reasoning.

More conformance and refinement relations for systems with inputs and outputs exist, e.g., in the context of testing theory [7,9] and I/O automata theory [15,16]. It would be interesting to include these works in our spectrum. An additional improvement is to include internal transitions, as commonly found in interface automata and labelled transition systems.

References

1. Aarts, F., Vaandrager, F.: Learning I/O automata. In: Gastin, P., Laroussinie, F. (eds.) CONCUR 2010. LNCS, vol. 6269, pp. 71–85. Springer, Heidelberg (2010). https://doi.org/10.1007/978-3-642-15375-4_6
2. de Alfaro, L., Henzinger, T.A.: Interface automata. In: Gruhn, V. (ed.) Joint 8th European Software Engineering Conference and 9th ACM SIGSOFT Symposium on the Foundations of Software Engineering, volume 26 of SIGSOFT Software Engineering Notes, pp. 109–120. ACM Press (2001)

3. Alur, R., Henzinger, T.A., Kupferman, O., Vardi, M.Y.: Alternating refinement relations. In: Sangiorgi, D., de Simone, R. (eds.) CONCUR 1998. LNCS, vol. 1466, pp. 163–178. Springer, Heidelberg (1998). https://doi.org/10.1007/BFb0055622
4. van der Bijl, M., Rensink, A., Tretmans, J.: Compositional testing with IOCO. In: Petrenko, A., Ulrich, A. (eds.) FATES 2003. LNCS, vol. 2931, pp. 86–100. Springer, Heidelberg (2004). https://doi.org/10.1007/978-3-540-24617-6_7
5. van den Bos, P., Stoelinga, M.: Tester versus bug: a generic framework for model-based testing via games. In: Orlandini, A., Zimmermann, M., (eds.) Proceedings of the 9th International Symposium on GandALF, Saarbrücken, Germany, Volume 277 of Electronic Proceedings in Theoretical Computer Science, pp. 118–132. Open Publishing Association (2018)
6. Chilton, C., Jonsson, B., Kwiatkowska, M.: An algebraic theory of interface automata. Theor. Comput. Sci. **549**, 146–174 (2014)
7. Frantzen, L., Tretmans, J.: Model-based testing of environmental conformance of components. In: de Boer, F.S., Bonsangue, M.M., Graf, S., de Roever, W.-P. (eds.) FMCO 2006. LNCS, vol. 4709, pp. 1–25. Springer, Heidelberg (2007). https://doi.org/10.1007/978-3-540-74792-5_1
8. van Glabbeek, R.J.: The linear time – branching time spectrum I. The semantics of concrete, sequential processes. In: Bergstra, J.A., Ponse, A., Smolka, S.A. (eds.) Handbook of Process Algebra, pp. 3–99. North-Holland (2001)
9. Heerink, L., Tretmans, J.: Refusal testing for classes of transition systems with inputs and outputs. In: Mizuno, T., Shiratori, N., Higashino, T., Togashi, A. (eds.) Formal Description Techniques and Protocol Specification, Testing and Verification FORTE X /PSTV XVII, pp. 23–38. Chapman & Hall (1997)
10. Hopcroft, J.E., Ullman, J.D.: Introduction to Automata Theory, Languages and Computation. Addison-Wesley, Boston (1979)
11. Janssen, R., Tretmans, J.: Matching implementations to specifications: the corner cases of IOCO. In: Proceedings of the 34th ACM/SIGAPP Symposium on Applied Computing, Limassol, Cyprus, pp. 2196–2205. ACM (2019)
12. Janssen, R., Vaandrager, F., Tretmans, J.: Relating alternating relations for conformance and refinement (2019). https://arxiv.org/pdf/1909.13604.pdf
13. Lynch, N.A., Tuttle, M.R.: An introduction to input/output automata. MIT Laboratory for Computer Science (1988)
14. Mostowski, W., Poll, E., Schmaltz, J., Tretmans, J., Wichers Schreur, R.: Model-based testing of electronic passports. In: Alpuente, M., Cook, B., Joubert, C. (eds.) FMICS 2009. LNCS, vol. 5825, pp. 207–209. Springer, Heidelberg (2009). https://doi.org/10.1007/978-3-642-04570-7_19
15. Reingold, N., Wang, D.-W., Zuck, L.D.: Games I/O automata play. In: Cleaveland, W.R. (ed.) CONCUR 1992. LNCS, vol. 630, pp. 325–339. Springer, Heidelberg (1992). https://doi.org/10.1007/BFb0084801
16. Segala, R., Gawlick, R., Søgaard-Andersen, J.F., Lynch, N.A.: Liveness in timed and untimed systems. Inf. Comput. **141**(2), 119–171 (1998)
17. Tretmans, J.: Test generation with inputs, outputs and repetitive quiescence. Softw.-Concepts Tools **17**(3), 103–120 (1996)
18. Tretmans, J.: Model based testing with labelled transition systems. In: Hierons, R.M., Bowen, J.P., Harman, M. (eds.) Formal Methods and Testing. LNCS, vol. 4949, pp. 1–38. Springer, Heidelberg (2008). https://doi.org/10.1007/978-3-540-78917-8_1
19. Tretmans, J.: On the existence of practical testers. In: Katoen, J.-P., Langerak, R., Rensink, A. (eds.) ModelEd, TestEd, TrustEd. LNCS, vol. 10500, pp. 87–106. Springer, Cham (2017). https://doi.org/10.1007/978-3-319-68270-9_5

20. Veanes, M., Bjørner, N.: Alternating simulation and IOCO. Int. J. Softw. Tools Technol. Transf. **14**(4), 387–405 (2012)
21. Volpato, M., Tretmans, J.: Towards quality of model-based testing in the IOCO framework. In: International Workshop on Joining AcadeMiA and Industry Contributions to testing Automation - JAMAICA 2013, pp. 41–46. ACM (2013)

Embedding SMT-LIB into B for Interactive Proof and Constraint Solving

Sebastian Krings(✉) and Michael Leuschel

Institut für Informatik, Universität Düsseldorf,
Universitätsstr. 1, 40225 Düsseldorf, Germany
{sebastian.krings,leuschel}@uni-duesseldorf.de

Abstract. The SMT-LIB language and the B language are both based on predicate logic and have some common operators. However, B supports data types not available in SMT-LIB and vice versa. In this article we suggest a straightforward translation from SMT-LIB to B. Using this translation, SMT-LIB can be analyzed by tools developed for the B method. We show how Atelier B can be used for automatic and interactive proof of SMT-LIB problems. Furthermore, we incorporated our translation into the model checker ProB and applied it to several benchmarks taken from the SMT-LIB repository. In contrast to most SMT solvers, ProB relies on finite domain constraint propagation, with support for infinite domains by keeping track of the exhaustiveness of domain variable enumerations. Our goal was to see whether this kind of approach is beneficial for SMT solving.

1 Introduction and Motivation

B [1] and Event-B [2] are formal software development methods following the correct-by-construction approach. They are supported by a range of tools such as Atelier B [16], the integrated development environment Rodin [3] or the animator and model checker ProB [34]. Most B users rely on a mixture of automatic and interactive proof as well as model checking during development.

The SMT-LIB language and its logics [7] and the B language have several similarities. Both are based on predicate logic, they support the same arithmetic operators and quantifiers. Furthermore, both are strongly typed languages. However, there are considerable differences as well. For instance, B supports several data types not (fully) available in SMT-LIB, such as (finite) sets and sequences. For SMT-LIB, these only exist as a proposal [40]. However, some solvers already provide partial support, e.g., CVC4 [5] supports finite sets [13]. SMT-LIB and certain SMT solvers on the other hand are able to cope with real arithmetic, while B only supports integer arithmetic.

With this article, we bridge the gap between B and the SMT-LIB language, embedding SMT-LIB in the B language. This allows reasoning over both SMT-LIB constraints as well as SMT solving algorithms, using the B method and its tool chain, e.g., one can specify any algorithm working on SMT-LIB constraints using the B language and prove its correctness using Atelier B.

W. Ahrendt and S. L. Tapia Tarifa (Eds.): IFM 2019, LNCS 11918, pp. 265–283, 2019.
https://doi.org/10.1007/978-3-030-34968-4_15

Listing 1. Boolean Example in SMT-LIB

```
(set-logic QF_UF)
(declare-fun p () Bool)
(assert (and p (not p)))
(check-sat)
```

Additionally, as the semantics specified for SMT-LIB are preserved during the translation, one can analyze properties of given SMT-LIB constraints in B. This could be used to perform a meta-level analysis of SMT-LIB.

2 Introductory Examples

First, let us look at two simple examples illustrating the general translation scheme: In Listing 1 we encode the assertion $p \wedge \neg p$, which is obviously unsatisfiable. With the first line, we state that the solver should use the logic QF_UF of quantifier free uninterpreted functions. We do not need to translate this fact to B, since B does not distinguish between different logics. The second line introduces a constant symbol p that is of type boolean. As an SMT constant can have just one value, we translate it to a B constant with the same name.

The type can then be specified using the `PROPERTIES` section of a B machine that contains predicates that have to be true for the constants. In this case, we assert that $p \in BOOL$, where $BOOL$ is the set $\{TRUE, FALSE\}$.

The assertion $p \wedge \neg p$ cannot be written in B as trivially as one might expect, because B does not support the use of booleans as predicates. Hence, the assertion has to be translated as $p \wedge \neg p \Leftrightarrow p = TRUE \wedge \neg p = TRUE$. The complete B machine can be found in Listing 2. Once loaded, ProB detects the unsatisfiability and reports that the properties are inconsistent.

The same basic idea can be used for integer arithmetic as shown in Listings 3 and 4. Here, we solve the indeterminate equation system $6x + 12y + 3z = 30 \wedge 3x + 6y + 3z = 12$. This time, ProB is able to find a valuation for the constants and satisfiability can be reported.

Note that `INTEGER` is the B type for the integers. As with SMT-LIB, the B set of integers represents mathematical integers. The B method tools in general, and ProB's solver in particular, can handle arbitrarily large integers.[1] In contrast to SMT-LIB, B's arithmetic operators do not support an arbitrary number of operands. Hence, `(+ x y z)` has to be translated into `x + y + z`.

3 Translating SMT-LIB to B

Because B provides more involved operators than SMT-LIB, translating SMT-LIB into B is mostly straightforward. New SMT-LIB non-parametric sorts (i.e.

[1] The CLP(FD) library employed by ProB may generate overflows, which ProB tries to catch and provide alternative treatment for. In case this is not possible, ProB reports "unknown".

Listing 2. Boolean Example in B

```
MACHINE BooleanExample
CONSTANTS p
PROPERTIES
 p:BOOL & p=TRUE & not(p=TRUE)
END
```

Listing 3. Integer Example in SMT-LIB

```
(set-logic QF_LIA)
(declare-fun x () Int)
(declare-fun y () Int)
(declare-fun z () Int)
(assert (= (+ (* 6 x) (* 2 y) (* 12 z)) 30))
(assert (= (+ (* 3 x) (* 6 y) (* 3 z)) 12))
(check-sat)
```

new base types) declared by the user are mapped to B *deferred* sets. Deferred sets introduce new base type to B as well, each containing an arbitrary (and possibly infinite) but fixed non-zero number of elements. If a new sort is parametric (i.e. a recursive type) further sets are generated for each concrete combination of parameters used in the input.

For instance, the SMT-LIB declaration `(declare-sort NewSort 0)` corresponds to a B deferred set `NewSort`. In contrast, a parametric sort declared by `(declare-sort Pair 2)` is not included in the B machine. Instead, its instantiations such as `(Pair Int Bool)` are introduced as sets containing pairs taken from `Int` × `Bool`. Nested pairs are used for higher number of arguments.

New function symbols are translated to B constants. The SMT types are thereby mapped to B types, e.g., the `Int` sort is mapped to B's `INTEGER` set. For functions declared using `declare-fun`, we create constants defined as total functions between the parameter types and the result type.

Listing 4. Integer Example in B

```
MACHINE IntegerExample
CONSTANTS x, y, z
PROPERTIES
 x:INTEGER & y:INTEGER & z:INTEGER &
 6*x + 12*y + 3*z = 30 &
 3*x +  6*y + 3*z = 12
END
```

Certain SMT-LIB operators have a direct equivalence in B. With the exception of division, the arithmetic operators can be translated directly. Furthermore, like SMT-LIB, the B language and tools support universal and existential quantification natively.

There is no absolute value function in B. However it can be translated as $|x| = \max(\{-x, x\})$. Integer division and modulo in SMT-LIB are defined following the Euclidean definition by Boute [10], while B uses a floored division [30].[2] Thus in B $-8/3 = -2$ while in SMT-LIB it is -3. Furthermore, in B, $x \mod y$ is only defined if x is non-negative and y is positive. In contrast, the Euclidean definition permits both cases. We express (in Sect. 3.3) SMT-LIB's division and modulo by rewriting it to B's floored division. Another difference is that in SMT-LIB all functions are total, meaning that 2/0 is an (unknown) integer value. So, in SMT-LIB $x/0 = 2$ is a satisfiable formula, while in B it is ill defined. Currently, our B translation of $x/0 = 2$ is not well-defined in B [4],and Atelier-B will generate a well-definedness proof obligation that cannot be discharged.ProB will also raise errors, followed by reporting unknown for the constraint.[3]

Aside from the translations above, certain constructs available in SMT-LIB are not available in B and require more involved translations:

- In B, booleans are values and cannot be used as predicates. We showed how to overcome this limitation in the introductory examples. Listing 2 shows how to turn booleans into predicates simply by comparing them to `TRUE`.
- There is no if-then-else for expressions or predicates in B. The B if-then-else may only be used in substitutions (aka statements). Thus, the if-then-else from SMT-LIB has to be rewritten as we explain in Sect. 3.1.
- Analogously, B features a let substitution but no let predicate. We rewrite let as shown in Sect. 3.2.

Additionally, B has no dedicated data types for arrays or bit vectors. While we experimented with different translations, we found no representation performing well for both constraint solving and proof. Further research in this area is needed and part of our future work.

Another limitation is that there are no real numbers in B [1]. There is experimental support for floats and reals in Atelier B since version 4.1 [16]. However, proof support is far from being useful and there is currently no support in ProB. Hence, we currently do not take them into account in our translation.

3.1 If-Then-Else

As mentioned above, the if-then-else construct in B can only be used in substitutions, not in predicates or expressions. However, the core theory of the SMT-LIB language supports the `ite` function that returns its second or third argument

[2] More precisely, the definition of division in B [1] is $n/m = \min(\{x \mid x \in \mathbb{N} \wedge n < m * succ(x)\})$.

[3] We may improve our translation to remedy this, but our assumption is that most SMT-LIB examples are well-defined according to B.

depending on the truth value of the first one. To mimic the behavior of `ite` we can reuse a translation developed for a translation from TLA$^+$to B [27].

In order to translate (`ite` P E_1 E_2) we first have to look at the type of E_1 and E_2. If both are predicates, the if-then-else can be expressed in terms of implications, that is, (`ite` P E_1 E_2) is translated to $(P \Rightarrow E_1) \wedge (\neg P \Rightarrow E_2)$. Implication is available in B, so the predicate above can be used as a replacement for `ite` in case the arguments are all predicates.

When the `ite` construct is used as an expression rather than a predicate, the translation is more complex. We use the translation suggested by [27]: For both branches of the `if` we create a lambda function that maps 1 to E_1 or E_2 respectively. Afterwards, the union of the two lambda relations is computed:

$$(\lambda t \cdot (t = 1 | E_1)) \cup (\lambda t \cdot (t = 1 | E_2)).$$

This relation has two elements both mapping 1 to a result. In order to mimic the behavior of if-then-else, we now have to assure that one of the lambda relations is empty depending on the value of P:

$$(\lambda t \cdot (t = 1 \wedge P | E_1)) \cup (\lambda t \cdot (t = 1 \wedge \neg P | E_2)).$$

Now, either P or $\neg P$ is false, making the respective lambda expression to be the empty set (and avoiding the evaluation of the corresponding expression E_i). The other lambda expression maps 1 to the result of (`ite` P E_1 E_2). Hence, we just have to apply the relation to 1 to extract the result:

$$(ite\ P\ E_1\ E_2) == (\lambda t \cdot (t = 1 \wedge P | E_1)) \cup (\lambda t \cdot (t = 1 \wedge \neg P | E_2))(1).$$

Observe that B strictly distinguishes between boolean values and predicates. However, there are operators to convert between the two. We considered other encodings of if-then-else, such as using a constant function. However, they often did not harmonize with the inner workings of B and its tools. The encoding presented above exhibits the best performance so far.

Take for example the SMT-LIB formula, where we suppose x to be a natural number: $(ite\ (not\ (=\ x\ 0))\ (div\ 10\ x)\ (div\ 10\ (-\ x\ 1)))$. Our translation is

$$(\lambda t \cdot (t = 1 \wedge x \neq 0 | 10/x)) \cup (\lambda t \cdot (t = 1 \wedge \neg(x \neq 0) | 10/(x - 1)))(1)$$

One may think we could translate this into a simpler B expression:

$$\{TRUE \mapsto 10/x, FALSE \mapsto 10/(x-1)\}(bool(x \neq 0))$$

However, it has the problem that in order to determine the value of the expression, one needs to compute the value of the subexpression $\{TRUE \mapsto 10/x, FALSE \mapsto 10/(x-1)\}$. Thus, when x = 0, we still need to evaluate $10/x$, generating a well-definedness error in B. Similarly, when x = 1 we still need to evaluate $10/(x-1)$, again causing a well-definedness error.

3.2 Let

Similar to the if-then-else, B only has a let substitution and no let for expressions or predicates. SMT-LIB on the other hand includes a let construct available for both expressions and predicates.

According to the SMT-LIB standard [7] a let can always be resolved by inlining its definitions. This step may have to include renaming in order to avoid scoping errors due to capturing by quantifiers.

Regarding performance, inlining may lead to duplicated computation during solving. To some extent this could be countered by ProB's common subexpression detection. However, this would be equal to re-introducing the let internally. In order to avoid duplicating computation we suggest a translation comparable to the one of the if-then-else.

First, let us consider the case of a let where t is a predicate. In this case we rewrite $(let\ ((x_1\ t_1)\ \ldots\ (x_n\ t_n))\ t)$ to

$$\exists x_1, \ldots, x_n \cdot (\bigwedge_{i=1}^{n} x_i = t_i) \wedge t$$

which can be written in B without further translation.

Replacing a let where t is an expression can not be done as easily. As in Sect. 3.1 we create a function that is called on a fixed value. We translate $(let\ ((x_1\ t_1)\ \ldots\ (x_n\ t_n))\ t)$ to

$$\{k, v \mid k = 1 \wedge \exists x_1, \ldots, x_n \cdot v = t \wedge \bigwedge_{i=1}^{n} x_i = t_i\}(1).$$

The set comprehension contains only one element: The pair $(1, v)$ where v is equal to t, the expression copied from inside the let binder. We call this function on 1 to extract v.

As an example, consider $(let\ ((x_1\ 1)\ (x_2\ 2))\ (+\ x_1\ x_2))$. We translate this to $\{k, v \mid k = 1 \wedge \exists x_1, x_2 \cdot v = x_1 + x_2 \wedge x_1 = 1 \wedge x_2 = 2\}(1)$. The existential quantification can be removed by inlining the definition of the quantified variables, simplifying the comprehension to $\{k, v \mid k = 1 \wedge v = 1 + 2\}(1)$, which represents the partial function $1 \mapsto 1 + 2$. The function is applied to 1 in order to extract the desired result, i. e., $\{k, v \mid k = 1 \wedge v = 1 + 2\}(1) = \{(1 \mapsto 3)\}(1) = 3$.

3.3 Formal Definition of Translation

The translation is implemented as an AST walker carrying around a type environment. We will define how AST nodes are translated by gradually defining a translation function τ, mapping SMT-LIB to B. Just as above, we will use mathematical notation instead of B's ASCII syntax. However, the mathematical representation can be expressed in B without further translation.

Sorts are mapped to B types as discussed above. Existential and universal quantifiers are directly available in B. Let and if-then-else are translated as stated above. For the SMT-LIB Core theory, we translate as follows:

$$\tau(true) = TRUE \qquad \tau(false) = FALSE$$
$$\tau((=>\ x_1\ x_2)) = (\tau(x_1) \Rightarrow \tau(x_2)) \qquad \tau((and\ x_1\ x_2)) = (\tau(x_1) \wedge \tau(x_2))$$
$$\tau((or\ x_1\ x_2)) = (\tau(x_1) \vee \tau(x_2)) \qquad \tau((=\ x_1\ x_2)) = (\tau(x_1) = \tau(x_2))$$
$$\tau((distinct\ x_1\ x_2)) = (\tau(x_1) \neq \tau(x_2))$$
$$\tau((xor\ x_1\ x_2)) = ((\neg\tau(x_1) \wedge \tau(x_2)) \ \vee \ (\tau(x_1) \wedge \neg\tau(x_2)))$$

For the SMT-LIB Ints theory, we translate as follows:

$$\tau(NUMERAL) = NUMERAL \qquad \tau(-x) = -\tau(x)$$
$$\tau((-\ x_1\ x_2)) = (\tau(x_1) - \tau(x_2)) \qquad \tau((+\ x_1\ x_2)) = (\tau(x_1) + \tau(x_2))$$
$$\tau((*\ x_1\ x_2)) = (\tau(x_1) * \tau(x_2)) \qquad \tau((abs\ x)) = (\max(\{-\tau(x), \tau(x)\}))$$
$$\tau((<=\ x_1\ x_2)) = (\tau(x_1) \leq \tau(x_2)) \qquad \tau((<\ x_1\ x_2)) = (\tau(x_1) < \tau(x_2))$$
$$\tau((>=\ x_1\ x_2)) = (\tau(x_1) \geq \tau(x_2)) \qquad \tau((>\ x_1\ x_2)) = (\tau(x_1) > \tau(x_2))$$

Division and modulo are rewritten as discussed above, i. e., we express the Euclidean definitions in terms of B's floored division.

$$\tau((div\ x_1\ x_2)) = \tau(fdiv\ (-\ x_1\ (ite\ (<\ x_1 0)\ (ite\ (<\ x_2\ 0)\ (-\ 0\ 1\ x_2)\ (-\ x_2\ 1))\ 0))\ x_2)$$
$$\tau((fdiv\ x_1\ x_2)) = (\tau(x_1)\ /\ \tau(x_2))$$
$$\tau((mod\ x_1\ x_2)) = \tau((-\ x_1\ (*\ x_2\ (div\ x_1\ x_2))))$$

4 Interactive Proof Using Atelier B

In the following section, we illustrate how the B method and its tools could be used for the development and validation of SMT algorithms or SMT optimization rules. As an example, we will verify a translation rule used in CVC4 in case the `-rewrite-divk` command line option has been provided.

The source code is given in Listing 5, taken from CVC4's repository[4]. The given snippet implements a rewriting rule for integer division. Numerator and denominator are given as variables `num` and `den`. For better understandability, we shortened some of the technical detail of CVC4's internal workings, as they do not contribute to the rewriting rule itself.

If the denominator is constant, the division is replaced by a new constant called `intVar`. Depending on the denominator, `intVar` is axiomatically defined using one of two additional constraints: If the denominator is larger than zero, $den * intVar <= num \wedge num < den * (intVar + 1)$ is asserted. Otherwise, $den * intVar <= num \wedge num < den * (intVar - 1)$ is asserted.

[4] At commit a6bd02c5c442b806b5e01fed40ab9d1017e42bc3, see https://github.com/CVC4/CVC4/blob/a6bd02c5c442b806b5e01fed40ab9d1017e42bc3/src/theory/arith/theory_arith_private.cpp#L1231 for the full file and context.

Listing 5. CVC4 Source Code Snippet

```
// Input numerator "num" and denominator "den"
// shortened technical detail, e.g., creation of intVar
if(den.isConst()) {
  if(den != 0) {
    if(den > 0) {
       d_containing.d_out->lemma(nm->mkNode(kind::AND,
           nm->mkNode(kind::LEQ,
               nm->mkNode(kind::MULT, den, intVar), num),
           nm->mkNode(kind::LT, num,
               nm->mkNode(kind::MULT, den,
                   nm->mkNode(kind::PLUS, intVar,
                       nm->mkConst(Rational(1)))))));
    } else {
       d_containing.d_out->lemma(nm->mkNode(kind::AND,
           nm->mkNode(kind::LEQ,
               nm->mkNode(kind::MULT, den, intVar), num),
           nm->mkNode(kind::LT, num,
               nm->mkNode(kind::MULT, den,
                   nm->mkNode(kind::PLUS, intVar,
                       nm->mkConst(Rational(-1)))))));
    }
  }
  return intVar;
}
```

Listing 6. B Encoding

```
DEFINITIONS
    smt_abs(x) == max({-x,x});
    smt_div_mod(m,n,q,r) ==
        (n /= 0 => m = n*q + r & 0 <= r & r <= smt_abs(n) - 1);
    smt_div(x,y,divres) ==
        #(modres).(modres:INTEGER
                  & smt_div_mod(x,y,divres,modres));
    smt_mod(x,y,modres) ==
        #(divres).(divres:INTEGER
                  & smt_div_mod(x,y,divres,modres))
ASSERTIONS
    !(num,den,intVar).(num:INTEGER & den:INTEGER
        & intVar:INTEGER &
        smt_div(num,den,intVar) =>
          (den > 0 =>
              den*intVar <= num & num < den*(intVar + 1)) &
          (den <= 0 =>
              den*intVar <= num & num < den*(intVar - 1)))
```

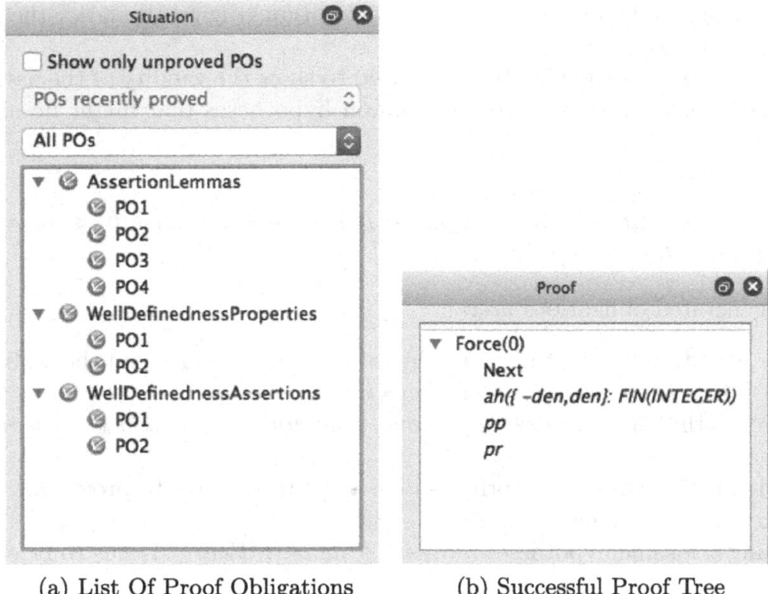

(a) List Of Proof Obligations (b) Successful Proof Tree

Fig. 1. Atelier B screenshots

We want to use B and Atelier B to verify if the additional assertions are implied by the definition of modulo and division in SMT-LIB. Proving the reverse direction could be done in the same way.

In order to prove the rule correct, we translate it to B using the translation defined in Sect. 3. The result can be found in Listing 6. The given B machine defines the absolute value, division and modulo following our translation scheme.

The property we want to prove is then provided as an assertion using B's universal quantifier, written as `!`: For all combinations of integers `num,den,intVar`, corresponding to the variables in CVC4's code, we want to prove that if `intVar` is the result of the division of `num` by `den` it follows that the axioms added by CVC4 are indeed true. The left hand side of the implications represents the two paths that can be taken in the if statement in Listing 5.

Atelier B type checks the machine and automatically generates eight proof obligations. Four of them are concerned with well-definedness and four with the actual assertion. Figure 1a shows the list of proof obligations. The ones named "PO1" to "PO4" in the group "AssertionLemmas" are concerned with the proof of our propagation rule.

The well-definedness proof obligations stem from the usage of the maximum operator in the definition of `smt_abs`. It is only well-defined if there exists a maximum element. Hence, we have to prove that the set $\{-den, den\} \cap \mathbb{N} \in \mathbb{F}(\mathbb{N})$, where $\mathbb{F}(\mathbb{N})$ is the set of all finite subsets of $\mathbb{N}$.

The proof obligation can be discharged by interactively adding the additional hypothesis $\{-den, den\} \in \mathbb{F}(\mathbb{Z})$. Once added, Atelier B's automatic provers can process further and discharge the proof obligation. Figure 1b shows the proof tactic used to perform the proof.

The remaining proof obligations are used to show the validity of the assertion in different steps. All share a set of common hypotheses that might be used in the proof:

- $num \in \mathbb{Z} \wedge den \in \mathbb{Z} \wedge intVar \in \mathbb{Z}$
- $\exists m.(m \in \mathbb{Z} \wedge (den \neq 0 \Rightarrow num = den * intVar + m \wedge 0 \leq m \wedge m \leq \max(\{-den, den\}) - 1))$

The generated obligations are:

PO1. We have to prove that using the hypotheses given above and the additional one $0 + 1 <= den$ it follows that $den * intVar \leq num$.
PO2. Proves that from the same preconditions $num + 1 \leq den * (intVar + 1)$ follows.
PO3. With the additional hypotheses $den + 1 \leq 0$, we have to prove that $den * intVar \leq num$ is true.
PO4. Using the same hypotheses $num + 1 \leq den * (intVar + 1)$ has to be shown.

As you can see the proof obligations mimic the case distinction done in Listing 5. The remaining proofs can be performed automatically this time.

In summary, we have used both interactive and automatic proof methods offered by Atelier B to show that the implemented rewriting rule is compliant with SMT-LIB's local definitions of the operators used.

5 Constraint Solving Using ProB

The ProB kernel can be viewed as a constraint-solver for the basic datatypes of B and the various operators on it. It supports booleans, integers, user-defined base types, pairs, records and inductively: sets, relations, functions and sequences. These datatypes and operations are embedded inside B predicates, which can make use of the usual logical connectives ($\wedge, \vee, \Rightarrow, \Leftrightarrow, \neg$) and typed universal ($\forall x.P \Rightarrow Q$) and existential ($\exists x.P \wedge Q$) quantification. For integers and finite base types ProB uses the finite domain library CLP(FD) [14], whereby each B variable is associated with an interval of possible values. Sets and relations are represented as Prolog terms, with special representations for large known sets and for infinite sets defined by predicates. ProB tries to delay enumeration of values and gives priority to deterministic computations. To cater for large sets and relations, ProB prioritizes operations that are deterministic *and* are guaranteed to produce data values in an efficient representation.

The underlying mechanism is thus deterministic propagation of partial information about variables, interleaved with controlled enumeration of possible values. This is fundamentally different to the DPLL(T) [26] based SMT solvers and the DPLL [17] or CDCL [35] based SAT solvers.

Using SMT solvers and ProB for cooperative constraint solving and proof has been suggested by us [33], where we made the observation that constraint logic programming based solvers and SMT solvers show different strength and weaknesses. On the one hand, SMT solvers are usually faster when it comes to detecting unsatisfiability. They can handle variables with infinite domains, e.g. integers, more easily. On the other hand, constraint logic programming based solvers can often effectively handle intertwined constraints over bounded variables. Furthermore, they always generate a model for a satisfiable formula. In case of constraints specified in B, combining constraint logic programming and SMT solving in ProB has been proven successful [33].

We compare ProB to Z3 [18] and CVC4 [5] on benchmark files taken from the SMT-LIB benchmark repository. We used development snapshot versions of all three solvers.[5] We limit the benchmarks to non-incremental ones taken from the logics including quantifiers and integer arithmetic: QF_IDL, (QF_)LIA, (QF_)NIA. Logics starting with QF are quantifier-free. The different and possibly combined abbreviations for logics are LIA for linear integer arithmetic and NIA for non-linear integer arithmetic. IDL represents integer difference logic, i. e., expressions of the form $r = o_1 - o_2$.

In addition to comparing provers, we also compare several options of ProB's constraint solver. In particular, we compare vanilla ProB to

- A version using random instead of linear enumeration of CLP(FD) domains,
- A version using common sub-expression elimination (CSE), and
- A version featuring an extended rule set of CHR [25] rules used to infer certain facts CLP(FD) is unable to infer on its own.

All benchmarks were run on StarExec [39]. The machines used feature an Intel Xeon E5–2609 Quad-Core CPU running at 2.4 GHz and 256 GB of RAM. Red Hat Enterprise Linux Workstation 6.3 was used as the operating system.

Regarding time and memory limits, we used the same values used in the SMT Competition [6]. The timeout was set to 1500 s (25 min) walltime and CPU time for all solvers. Solvers were enforced to use 100 GB of memory or less.

Table 1 lists the total number of benchmarks detected satisfiable or unsatisfiable by the different solvers. As was to be expected, ProB is outperformed by Z3 and CVC4. Z3 clearly outperforms ProB both when it comes to runtimes and number of solved benchmarks. CVC4 is faster than ProB but solves less benchmarks. However, this is mostly due to the fact that the version of CVC4 used did not fully support non-linear integer arithmetic yet.

ProB being outperformed is especially shown by the high number of benchmarks ProB has to report "unknown" on. In most cases, this is due to infinite sets that would need to be enumerated exhaustively in order to solve the constraint or to prove it unsatisfiable. In certain cases, ProB is able to detect that any further attempt is futile and gives up reporting "unknown".

Furthermore, the table shows that ProB performs better on satisfiable benchmarks. Again, this is due to the CLP(FD) based solving kernel. Using constraint programming, it is easier to find a valuation than to detect unsatisfiability. Especially for infinite domains, the latter might even be impossible.

[5] The development version of ProB is available at http://www3.hhu.de/stups/prob/Download.

Table 1. Benchmarks: Median Runtimes and Deviation (in s)

solver	configuration	# successful tests	⌀ runtime sat	⌀ runtime unsat
Successful tests per solver				
ProB	Vanilla	9081	0.84 (0.04)	1.38 (0.85)
ProB	Random	9081	0.84 (0.04)	1.39 (0.85)
ProB	CSE	9074	0.84 (0.04)	1.38 (0.84)
ProB	CHR	9065	0.87 (0.04)	1.32 (0.73)
Z3	-	16322	0.01 (0.01)	0.56 (0.56)
CVC4	-	7757	3.5 (5.16)	1.29 (1.29)
Common successful tests				
ProB	Vanilla	1328	1.65 (0.83)	1.23 (0.61)
ProB	Random	1328	1.64 (0.82)	1.24 (0.63)
ProB	CSE	1328	1.64 (0.8)	1.22 (0.6)
ProB	CHR	1328	2.61 (2.42)	1.29 (0.68)
Z3	–	1328	0.12 (0.16)	0.02 (0.02)
CVC4	–	1328	0.57 (0.81)	0.05 (0.05)

Figure 2a shows the number of test cases solved by each of the solvers individually as well as the number of test cases multiple solvers were able to solve. We only consider the "vanilla" configuration of ProB, in order not to compare CVC4 and Z3 with a portfolio of ProB-based solvers. As can be seen, CVC4 and Z3 each contribute some test cases they alone were able to solve. Furthermore, there is a large class of test cases both can solve.

Interestingly, the diagram shows an (albeit small) number of benchmarks can only be solved by ProB. We suspect that this is due to the different technologies used by ProB and Z3/CVC4, as benchmarks that are only solved by ProB can easily be classified: they are satisfiable and involve non-linear constraints, variables are highly intertwined and the SMT solvers CVC4 run out of time rather than memory. The efficiency of CLP(FD) for non-linear arithmetic is underlined by the fact that ProB won the NIA division of the 2016 SMT competition[6].

In addition to the result, we measured the runtimes of the different solvers. Table 1 shows how long the solvers took to produce different results. In general, ProB is much faster for satisfiable benchmarks than for unsatisfiable ones. This is to be expected from a tool that has mainly been used to find models of formulas. In contrast, CVC4 and Z3 runtimes do not differ much between satisfiable and unsatisfiable benchmarks.

For better comparability, the table also shows the median runtimes and median absolute deviation on the commonly solved benchmarks. ProB is one to two orders of magnitude slower than the dedicated SMT solvers. However, ProB's run time includes the time spent in the translation phase (Table 2).

[6] See http://smtcomp.sourceforge.net/2016/results-NIA.shtml.

Summarizing, we suspect that, especially for detection of satisfiability, a CLP(FD) based approach can be a useful addition to DPLL(T) based algorithms if used in a solver portfolio. Since we introduced a certain overhead by the translation, a direct implementation should add to the gain.

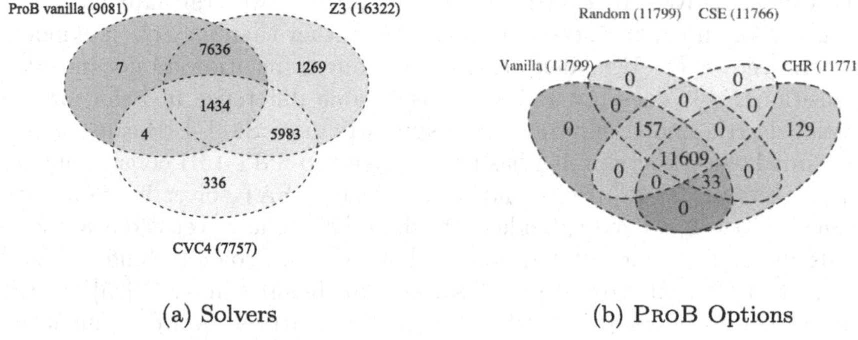

(a) Solvers (b) ProB Options

Fig. 2. Performance comparison

Table 2. Performance comparison: overall results

solver	configuration	sat	unsat	unknown	timeout	memory out
ProB	Vanilla	8625	456	1444	7228	0
ProB	Random	8625	456	1444	7228	0
ProB	CSE	8625	449	1444	7235	0
ProB	CHR	8627	438	1138	7550	0
Z3	–	12472	3850	412	1019	0
CVC4	–	4152	3605	9324	672	0

In addition to the benchmarks above, we evaluated how the different options the ProB kernel can be tweaked with influence its performance on SMT-LIB benchmarks. Figure 2b shows the results.

Of the options mentioned above, only the "CHR" option has a positive influence on the number of solved test cases. However, this influence is neither positive nor negative. On the one hand, the CHR rules help to identify unsatisfiable predicates. There is a significant number of test cases that can only be solved with the option enabled. On the other hand, evaluating propagation rules takes time. There is a set of (mostly satisfiable) benchmarks that used to be solvable within the timeout, but is not solvable with the extended rule set.

6 Related Work

Of course there are other solvers supporting SMT-LIB available. Most prominently, these are Boolector [12], CVC4 [5], veriT [11], Yices [22] and Z3 [18].

Using model checkers to solve SMT-LIB formulas has been suggested at least for certain SMT-LIB formulas. A translation from SMT-LIB formulas featuring bit vectors to SMV has been suggested [24], using the NuSMV [15] symbolic model checker as solver. In contrast to this approach, we translate into the input language of an explicit state model checker rather than a symbolic model checker. However, as the B models generated by our translation do not include state transitions, this does not cause a considerable difference in behavior or performance. Furthermore, our translation supports more SMT-LIB constructs.

Constraint Logic Programming has been applied to SMT-LIB constraints in different projects [21,28,29]. Howe and King present a SAT solver in Prolog as a programming pearl [28] and extended it to SMT [29]. The solver is quite small and easy to understand and extend, showing how certain Prolog techniques lead to an efficient implementation. An SMT solver implemented in CHR [25] rather than pure Prolog has been presented as well [21]. It features an input language comparable to SMT-LIB, however, it can not be applied to SMT-LIB directly.

A translation in the opposite direction, i.e., from Event-B proof obligations to SMT-LIB has been developed [19,23]. Sadly, it proves hard to fully encode B's and Event-B's axioms of set theory. The authors of [19,23] thus suggest to break down set theory and arithmetic into first-order formulas using uninterpreted functions for membership, etc. The resulting constraint is enriched by certain set theoretic axioms conveying background knowledge about Event-B to the SMT solvers. As a result, encoded formulas only approximate the Event-B semantics, but work well in practice.

A comparable approach has been followed in the Isabelle community as well. Blanchette et al. [9] translate Isabelle/HOL to first-order relational logic. Afterwards Kodkod is used, translating to SAT formulas solved using a SAT solver. The Sledgehammer tool to discharge proof obligations in interactive proofs in Isabelle can be connected to SMT solvers as well [8]. The authors report a considerable increase in automatically discharged proof obligations.

Using first-order theorem provers for SMT solving has been considered by Vampire [37]. Recent improvements include the introduction of the FOOL logic, an extension of many-sorted first-order logic by a first-class boolean sort [32]. FOOL is supported by Vampire [31] and includes if-then-else and let and thus simplifies translating SMT-LIB into TPLP, the common input language of first-order theorem provers. In comparison to our approach, our CLP(FD) backend focusses more on model finding for satisfiable formulas rather than proof.

A higher level approach towards embedding B and Event-B into SMT-LIB has also been evaluated [33]. Instead of relying on a first-order encoding, we directly employ Z3's own set theory solver. Thus, we only have to supply axiomatic definitions of operators unavailable in SMT-LIB, e.g., cardinality. Empirical comparison shows that both approaches have their merits and none of them is strictly superior [33]. In particular, Z3 was good at detecting inconsistent predicates but not good at finding solutions (aka models). This finding is also confirmed in one of our projects [38], where we experimented with various encodings and solvers for university timetabling.

7 Future Work

In the future, we would like to further investigate ProB's performance in comparison with SMT solvers to gain a deeper understanding on kinds of constraints and how they relate to the performance of CLP(FD) and DPLL(T). In order to perform a more in-depth comparison, we would like to extend our translation and ProB's constraint solving kernel to support incremental solving. This would enable us to use larger industrial case studies for our evaluation.

We would also like to further evaluate the effectiveness of our translation, considering different representations of SMT-LIB expressions in B. While we have done so for smaller collections of benchmarks, we would like to compare encodings more thoroughly throughout the whole SMT-LIB collection. In particular, we would like to improve our translation for bit vectors and arrays. Another aspect to be considered later is the time we allow the solvers to run. It would be interesting to check if the timeout influences the solvers differently.

Furthermore, we want to evaluate how a combination of ProB with the Atelier B provers performs as a solver portfolio. However, as classical rule based provers, the Atelier B provers are not designed to report models for satisfiable formulas. An efficient integration with ProB into a combined solver is thus more complex than just running the tools in parallel. For the combined solver to be of use, we have to enable ProB to identify predicates that it should submit to the provers and make it react to the two possible outcomes "proof" and "unknown".

The empirical evaluation showed that the enumeration strategies employed by ProB are not fully suitable for solving SMT-LIB. In future work, we want to enrich our constraint solver by further enumeration strategies. This will not only aid the SMT solver but will strengthen the model checker as well.

Along with tuning the enumeration strategy we would like to deepen our understanding of the effectiveness of the additional propagation rules and how they interact with CLP(FD). The evaluation shows that the added rules render certain benchmarks solvable while decreasing the performance on others. As of now, we have no proper way of deciding upfront which rules to enable.

8 Discussion and Conclusion

Summarizing, we have presented a translation from SMT-LIB to B that allows all tools available for the B method to be employed on SMT-LIB files. In addition to Atelier B and ProB, there are other model checkers such as pyB [41] and eboc [36], both using different approaches to constraint solving. A new platform for automatic proof is developed in the BWare [20] project.

We laid the groundwork for an analysis or proof of SMT solving algorithms using the B method by embedding SMT-LIB in B or Event-B. We were able to mimic the semantics of SMT-LIB in B, including constructs like if-then-else. Aside from ProB, the translation allows further B method tools like Atelier B to examine SMT-LIB data structures, expressions and algorithms. We have performed a case study showing how to prove SMT propagation laws using the B method. Hence, our translation could help reasoning about solvers and solving procedures in a structured way.

Furthermore, we made the constraint solving and model finding capabilities of ProB available in the form of a standalone constraint solver that takes the SMT-LIB language as input, making it available in a more general context. This not only enables users to use ProB without having to learn B, it also gives us access to the benchmarks and test cases of the SMT-LIB collection. Our evaluation showed that it is competitive for special types of benchmarks, i.e., it was able to win the NIA track of the 2016 SMT competition. However, the overall performance is rather weak.

Performance aside, using ProB to solve benchmarks taken from the SMT-LIB collection helped us discover different errors and inconsistencies in ProB itself. Deploying ProB on the numerous new test cases has increased our test coverage. In particular, SMT-LIB benchmarks tend to exercise different parts of ProB's kernel than classical B machines due to the diverse usage of constraints.

During benchmarking, we found bugs both in the SMT-LIB translation as well as in ProB's kernel. Usually, these were made obvious by the SMT solvers disagreeing ProB, e.g., Z3 reported unsatisfiability while ProB found a model. Furthermore, several performance bottlenecks have been brought to our attention and have been resolved. In summary, making ProB available as a general purpose SMT solver has helped us to improve ProB itself.

In summary, despite the relatively low number of test cases successfully solved by ProB, we still believe a translation from SMT-LIB to B is beneficial:

- It allows for cross-checking of results using a different approach to solving.
- It enables using SMT-LIB's benchmarks to validate and improve B tools.
- Using Atelier B it provides interactive (assisted) proof. As far as we know, there is currently no other way to interactively tackle SMT-LIB constraints.
- ProB already provides reasoning over sets and strings, features just starting to find their way into SMT-LIB and is competitive for special kinds of benchmarks.

Last, we hope that our article is able to narrow the gap between the SMT solving, the constraint logic programming and the formal methods communities and eases mutual understanding of algorithms and design principles.

References

1. Abrial, J.-R.: The B-Book: Assigning Programs to Meanings. Cambridge University Press, New York (1996)
2. Abrial, J.-R.: Modeling in Event-B: System and Software Engineering. Cambridge University Press, New York (2010)

3. Abrial, J.-R., Butler, M., Hallerstede, S., Voisin, L.: An open extensible tool environment for event-B. In: Liu, Z., He, J. (eds.) ICFEM 2006. LNCS, vol. 4260, pp. 588–605. Springer, Heidelberg (2006). https://doi.org/10.1007/11901433_32
4. Abrial, J.-R., Mussat, L.: On using conditional definitions in formal theories. In: Bert, D., Bowen, J.P., Henson, M.C., Robinson, K. (eds.) ZB 2002. LNCS, vol. 2272, pp. 242–269. Springer, Heidelberg (2002). https://doi.org/10.1007/3-540-45648-1_13
5. Barrett, C., et al.: CVC4. In: Gopalakrishnan, G., Qadeer, S. (eds.) CAV 2011. LNCS, vol. 6806, pp. 171–177. Springer, Heidelberg (2011). https://doi.org/10.1007/978-3-642-22110-1_14
6. Barrett, C., de Moura, L., Stump, A.: SMT-COMP: satisfiability modulo theories competition. In: Etessami, K., Rajamani, S.K. (eds.) CAV 2005. LNCS, vol. 3576, pp. 20–23. Springer, Heidelberg (2005). https://doi.org/10.1007/11513988_4
7. Barrett, C., Fontaine, P., Tinelli, C.: The SMT-LIB standard: version 2.5. Tech. rep., Department of Computer Science, The University of Iowa (2015). www.SMT-LIB.org
8. Blanchette, J.C., Böhme, S., Paulson, L.C.: Extending sledgehammer with SMT solvers. In: Bjørner, N., Sofronie-Stokkermans, V. (eds.) CADE 2011. LNCS (LNAI), vol. 6803, pp. 116–130. Springer, Heidelberg (2011). https://doi.org/10.1007/978-3-642-22438-6_11
9. Blanchette, J.C., Nipkow, T.: Nitpick: a counterexample generator for higher-order logic based on a relational model finder. In: Kaufmann, M., Paulson, L.C. (eds.) ITP 2010. LNCS, vol. 6172, pp. 131–146. Springer, Heidelberg (2010). https://doi.org/10.1007/978-3-642-14052-5_11
10. Boute, R.T.: The Euclidean definition of the functions div and mod. ACM Trans. Program. Lang. Syst. **14**(2), 127–144 (1992)
11. Bouton, T., Caminha B. de Oliveira, D., Déharbe, D., Fontaine, P.: veriT: an open, trustable and efficient SMT-solver. In: Schmidt, R.A. (ed.) CADE 2009. LNCS (LNAI), vol. 5663, pp. 151–156. Springer, Heidelberg (2009). https://doi.org/10.1007/978-3-642-02959-2_12
12. Brummayer, R., Biere, A.: Boolector: an efficient SMT solver for bit-vectors and arrays. In: Kowalewski, S., Philippou, A. (eds.) TACAS 2009. LNCS, vol. 5505, pp. 174–177. Springer, Heidelberg (2009). https://doi.org/10.1007/978-3-642-00768-2_16
13. Cantone, D., Zarba, C.G.: A new fast tableau-based decision procedure for an unquantified fragment of set theory. In: Caferra, R., Salzer, G. (eds.) FTP 1998. LNCS (LNAI), vol. 1761, pp. 126–136. Springer, Heidelberg (2000). https://doi.org/10.1007/3-540-46508-1_8
14. Carlsson, M., Ottosson, G., Carlson, B.: An open-ended finite domain constraint solver. In: Glaser, H., Hartel, P., Kuchen, H. (eds.) PLILP 1997. LNCS, vol. 1292, pp. 191–206. Springer, Heidelberg (1997). https://doi.org/10.1007/BFb0033845
15. Bouton, T., Caminha B. de Oliveira, D., Déharbe, D., Fontaine, P.: veriT: an open, trustable and efficient SMT-solver. In: Schmidt, R.A. (ed.) CADE 2009. LNCS (LNAI), vol. 5663, pp. 151–156. Springer, Heidelberg (2009). https://doi.org/10.1007/978-3-642-02959-2_12
16. ClearSy: Atelier B 4.1 Release Notes. Aix-en-Provence, France (2009). http://www.atelierb.eu/
17. Davis, M., Putnam, H.: A computing procedure for quantification theory. J. ACM **7**(3), 201–215 (1960)

18. de Moura, L., Bjørner, N.: Z3: an efficient SMT solver. In: Ramakrishnan, C.R., Rehof, J. (eds.) TACAS 2008. LNCS, vol. 4963, pp. 337–340. Springer, Heidelberg (2008). https://doi.org/10.1007/978-3-540-78800-3_24
19. Déharbe, D., Fontaine, P., Guyot, Y., Voisin, L.: SMT solvers for Rodin. In: Derrick, J., Fitzgerald, J., Gnesi, S., Khurshid, S., Leuschel, M., Reeves, S., Riccobene, E. (eds.) ABZ 2012. LNCS, vol. 7316, pp. 194–207. Springer, Heidelberg (2012). https://doi.org/10.1007/978-3-642-30885-7_14
20. Delahaye, D., Dubois, C., Marché, C., Mentré, D.: The BWare project: building a proof platform for the automated verification of B proof obligations. In: Ait Ameur, Y., Schewe, K.D. (eds.) ABZ 2014. LNCS, vol. 8477, pp. 290–293. Springer, Heidelberg (2014). https://doi.org/10.1007/978-3-662-43652-3_26
21. Duck, G.J.: SMCHR: satisfiability modulo constraint handling rules. CoRR, abs/1210.5307 (2012)
22. Dutertre, B.: Yices 2.2. In: Biere, A., Bloem, R. (eds.) CAV 2014. LNCS, vol. 8559, pp. 737–744. Springer, Cham (2014). https://doi.org/10.1007/978-3-319-08867-9_49
23. Déharbe, D., Fontaine, P., Guyot, Y., Voisin, L.: Integrating SMT solvers in Rodin. Sci. Comput. Program. **94**(2), 130–143 (2014)
24. Fröhlich, A., Kovásznai, G., Biere, A.: Efficiently solving bit-vector problems using model checkers. In: Proceedings SMT Workshop, pp. 6–15 (2013)
25. Frühwirth, T.: Theory and practice of constraint handling rules. J. Logic Program. **37**(1–3), 95–138 (1998)
26. Ganzinger, H., Hagen, G., Nieuwenhuis, R., Oliveras, A., Tinelli, C.: DPLL(T): fast decision procedures. In: Alur, R., Peled, D.A. (eds.) CAV 2004. LNCS, vol. 3114, pp. 175–188. Springer, Heidelberg (2004). https://doi.org/10.1007/978-3-540-27813-9_14
27. Hansen, D., Leuschel, M.: Translating TLA$^+$ to B for validation with ProB. In: Derrick, J., Gnesi, S., Latella, D., Treharne, H. (eds.) IFM 2012. LNCS, vol. 7321, pp. 24–38. Springer, Heidelberg (2012). https://doi.org/10.1007/978-3-642-30729-4_3
28. Middeldorp, A., Sato, T. (eds.): FLOPS 1999. LNCS, vol. 1722. Springer, Heidelberg (1999). https://doi.org/10.1007/10705424
29. Howe, J.M., King, A.: A pearl on SAT and SMT solving in prolog. Theor. Comput. Sci. **435**, 43–55 (2012)
30. Knuth, D.E.: The art of computer programming, volume 1: Fundamental Algorithms, vol. 1. Addison Wesley Longman Publishing Co., Inc., Redwood City (1997)
31. Kotelnikov, E., Kovács, L., Reger, G., Voronkov, A.: The vampire and the FOOL. In: Proceedings CPP, CPP 2016, pp. 37–48. ACM (2016)
32. Kotelnikov, E., Kovács, L., Voronkov, A.: A first class boolean sort in first-order theorem proving and TPTP. In: Kerber, M., Carette, J., Kaliszyk, C., Rabe, F., Sorge, V. (eds.) CICM 2015. LNCS (LNAI), vol. 9150, pp. 71–86. Springer, Cham (2015). https://doi.org/10.1007/978-3-319-20615-8_5
33. Krings, S., Leuschel, M.: SMT solvers for validation of B and event-B models. In: Ábrahám, E., Huisman, M. (eds.) IFM 2016. LNCS, vol. 9681, pp. 361–375. Springer, Cham (2016). https://doi.org/10.1007/978-3-319-33693-0_23
34. Leuschel, M., Bendisposto, J., Dobrikov, I., Krings, S., Plagge, D.: From animation to data validation: the prob constraint solver 10 years on. In: Boulanger, J.-L. (ed.) Formal Methods Applied to Complex Systems: Implementation of the B Method, pp. 427–446. Wiley ISTE (2014)
35. Marques-Silva, J., Sakallah, K.: GRASP: a search algorithm for propositional satisfiability. IEEE Trans. Comput. **48**(5), 506–521 (1999)

36. Matos, P.J., Fischer, B., Marques-Silva, J.: A lazy unbounded model checker for EVENT-B. In: Breitman, K., Cavalcanti, A. (eds.) ICFEM 2009. LNCS, vol. 5885, pp. 485–503. Springer, Heidelberg (2009). https://doi.org/10.1007/978-3-642-10373-5_25
37. Reger, G., Suda, M., Voronkov, A.: Instantiation and pretending to be an SMT solver with vampire. In: Proceedings SMT Workshop (2012)
38. Schneider, D., Leuschel, M., Witt, T.: Model-based problem solving for university timetable validation and improvement. In: Bjørner, N., de Boer, F. (eds.) FM 2015. LNCS, vol. 9109, pp. 487–495. Springer, Cham (2015). https://doi.org/10.1007/978-3-319-19249-9_30
39. Stump, A., Sutcliffe, G., Tinelli, C.: StarExec: a cross-community infrastructure for logic solving. In: Demri, S., Kapur, D., Weidenbach, C. (eds.) IJCAR 2014. LNCS (LNAI), vol. 8562, pp. 367–373. Springer, Cham (2014). https://doi.org/10.1007/978-3-319-08587-6_28
40. Weissenbacher, G., Kröning, D., Rümmer, P.: A proposal for a theory of finite sets, lists, and maps for the SMT-Lib standard. In: Proceedings SMT Workshop (2009)
41. Witulski, J., Leuschel, M.: Checking computations of formal method tools - a secondary toolchain for ProB. In: Proceedings F-IDE, vol. 149, EPTCS. Electronic Proceedings in Theoretical Computer Science (2014)

An Integrated Approach to a Combinatorial Optimisation Problem

J.Bowles(✉) and M.B.Caminati

School of Computer Science, University of St Andrews, St Andrews KY16 9SX, UK
{jkfb,mbc8}@st-andrews.ac.uk

Abstract. We take inspiration from a problem from the healthcare domain, where patients with several chronic conditions follow different guidelines designed for the individual conditions, and where the aim is to find the best treatment plan for a patient that avoids adverse drug reactions, respects patient's preferences and prioritises drug efficacy. Each chronic condition guideline can be abstractly described by a directed graph, where each node indicates a treatment step (e.g., a choice in medications or resources) and has a certain duration. The search for the best treatment path is seen as a combinatorial optimisation problem and we show how to select a path across the graphs constrained by a notion of resource compatibility. This notion takes into account interactions between any finite number of resources, and makes it possible to express non-monotonic interactions. Our formalisation also introduces a discrete temporal metric, so as to consider only simultaneous nodes in the optimisation process. We express the formal problem as an SMT problem and provide a correctness proof of the SMT code by exploiting the interplay between SMT solvers and the proof assistant Isabelle/HOL. The problem we consider combines aspects of optimal graph execution and resource allocation, showing how an SMT solver can be an alternative to other approaches which are well-researched in the corresponding domains.

1 Introduction

In complex systems it is common for processes to execute in parallel. The underlying composed behavioural model is complex and, unless strictly necessary, it is preferable to avoid computing it. We developed an approach to find optimal paths across multiple models denoting preferred scenarios of execution. The choice of a path across a model may be influenced by external factors, available resources and further constraints on such resources. Models are given as directed

This research is supported by MRC grant MR/S003819/1 and Health Data Research UK, an initiative funded by UK Research and Innovation, Department of Health and Social Care (England) and the devolved administrations, and leading medical research charities.

W. Ahrendt and S. L. Tapia Tarifa (Eds.): IFM 2019, LNCS 11918, pp. 284–302, 2019.
https://doi.org/10.1007/978-3-030-34968-4_16

graphs, and the challenge is to find paths across all graphs satisfying not just all constraints but optimised against one or more arithmetic measures.

Our approach has been inspired by a problem in healthcare where patients with two or more ongoing chronic conditions, also known as *multimorbidity*, do not receive adequate treatment. Typically patients follow treatment guidelines for individual conditions in isolation, and the presence of multimorbidity requires them to follow several guidelines simultaneously. However, there is a lack of guidance on how best to prioritise recommendations for multimorbidity [17]. Patients with multimorbidity are often required to take many medications for their conditions, which can cause adverse drug reactions often leading to unnecessary complications and hospitalisations [15]. It is also possible that taking several medications together decreases the effectiveness of the individual drugs when administered at the same time, or that a patient is intolerant to a combination of medications. In precision therapeutics, the aim is to tailor medical treatment to the individual characteristics of each patient which includes finding the right set of medications for patients with multimorbidities.

Besides the small example in Sect. 2, where the healthcare setting is used for illustrative purposes, we abstract from the medical problem and terminology in this paper, and it suffices to understand each guideline as a directed graph whereby a patient may be at a given node at a particular moment in time, resources are (groups of) medications (aka drugs), and external factors can denote patient specific intolerances, and so on.

Resources have a known value of how effective they are individually for the purpose they are used for (e.g., metformin when used for treating diabetes), as well as a measure of conflict (interaction constraints) with others. Our aim is to find the optimal path across all graphs which maximises effectiveness and minimises conflicts. Such a path selects the drugs across multiple graphs that suit the patient best.

This paper is structured as follows. Section 2 motivates and describes the context of our approach in more detail. Related work is described in Sect. 3. Section 4 describes the abstraction used for capturing guidelines as directed graphs, and how paths and interaction constraints are defined. Our translation to SMT (Satisfiability Modulo Theories) code is shown in Sect. 5 and how verification is done is described in Sect. 6. This is followed by concluding remarks in Sect. 7.

2 Problem Motivation and Informal Description

Assume that a patient with an acute condition is hospitalised on day 0. There are two possible treatments for the condition: a non-surgical treatment and surgery. The two alternatives are represented by the two branches in the directed graph of Fig. 1 (left), where the source node represents the hospitalisation. The right branch represents the choice of surgery with nodes n_3 and n_4 denoting the steps implied by this choice (n_3: pre-surgical testing and n_4: the surgery itself). Each node execution in a treatment graph may correspond to a choice of actions. For example, in the case of pre-surgical testing it involves administering one of two drugs (d_1 or d_2), while in the case of the surgery, only one possibility is present. The left branch (with n_2) models the non-surgical choice, here associated to the prescription of drug d_0 (with no other choice available). The bracketed number besides each node represent its duration: for example, pre-surgical testing (node n_3) lasts 2 days. Furthermore, this particular patient suffers from two chronic conditions: C_1 requires him to take drug d_3 on even days and d_4 on odd days (Fig. 1 middle), and C_2 requires him to take drug d_5 on even days followed by either d_6 or d_7 on odd days whereby d_7 further delays the subsequent administering of d_5 by two days (Fig. 1 right).

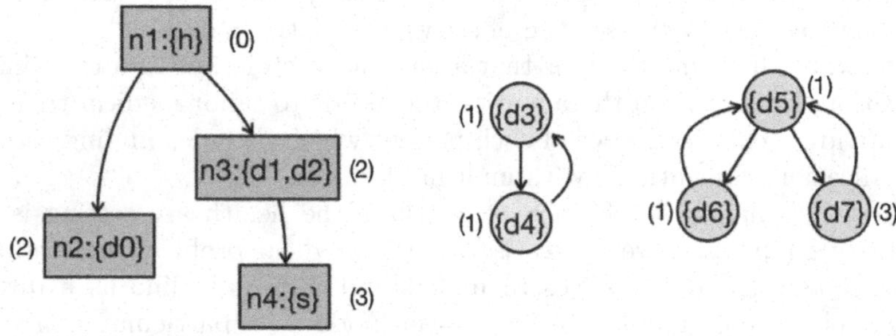

Fig. 1. A simple example problem

Surgery is preferable, but d_1 interacts negatively with d_3 and d_2 with d_4. It is known that d_6 is more effective than d_7 when used for treating C_2. However, d_7 can act as an inhibitor in the reaction between d_1 and d_3, mitigating the ensuing negative effects on the patient. In this fictitious example, we want to determine the best course of action in the hospitalisation of a patient with chronic conditions C_1 and C_2 taking into account drug efficacy and known drug interactions.

The simple example above expresses the family of problems we want to deal with. In what follows, we abstract away from the healthcare application domain expressed above in terms of directed graphs, one for each separate treatment a patient undergoes, and where each node is annotated with a *duration* and a potential choice of *resources*. This makes it possible to reduce the problem to a path finding problem across several directed graphs, respecting constraints on interactions among several resources and their temporal overlapping. In other words, we want to find paths in given directed graphs (*digraphs*, [2,9]) such that:

- P1 for each visited node a resource (e.g., in our context this can be a medication) is selected amongst a set of allowed ones for that node, and
- P2 the interactions between selected resources are minimised and their individual effectiveness maximised in the obtained solution.

The effect of the mutual interactions (see point (P2) above) on the computation of the solution takes into account the duration of each node which, in turn, determines the required temporal distance between possibly interacting resources (e.g., two interacting resources happening at close temporal distance can be given more weight than the same interacting resources happening at distant times). The efficiency of modern SMT solvers makes them feasible to search for a solution satisfying the criteria above. However, only (P2) above makes use of the arithmetic capabilities of the solver, while we otherwise only made use of the basic SAT solver for the remaining computations in our previous work [5–7]. Given that SMT solvers are SAT solvers with awareness of additional facts (e.g., arithmetics), we wonder whether this can be used to better exploit SMT solvers capabilities. In our case, motivations for working in this direction include:

M1 Given that resource interactions are expressed by numerical functions having the resources as arguments, the current basic SAT implementation only allows us to consider binary interactions as opposed to interactions of an arbitrary number of resources.

The limitation to binary interactions arises because the arity of SMT functions is fixed, and more elaborated datatypes such as lists or function operators are not directly available. We will see in Sect. 5 how this limitation can be worked around by the theory of Bit-Vectors through which the SMT-LIB standard [3] extends the basic domain of propositional logic in which a standard SAT solver operates. We use this theory to emulate a variadic function, i.e., a function taking a variable number of variables, thereby granting the possibility of expressing interactions between a variable number of resources. This makes it possible to express the particular case of non-monotonic interactions whereby adding a resource to, say, a pair of conflicting resources not necessarily exacerbates the conflict. The interest in this was illustrated in our healthcare example earlier, where drug d_7 inhibits an interaction between two other drugs.

M2 Expressing the problem of path finding in SAT terms leads to assertions rapidly increasing in complexity with the dimension of the given graphs, and hence unintelligible SAT code.

We addressed the problem through a novel combination of the SMT solver itself and the theorem prover Isabelle [21], formally proving the correctness of the complicated SAT code used for path finding. However, any path naturally admits a discrete linear ordering, which suggests an alternative route to expressing the path finding problem in the SMT-LIB language: the solution, rather than consisting of a function over the nodes being true exactly for all the nodes in the path, can be expressed by a function from the integers into the set of nodes, telling, when its argument has value i, which node is the i-th in the path. This is possible because SMT solvers, contrary to SAT solvers, are aware of the theory of integers (i.e., in the latter, arithmetic operators can only be introduced as uninterpreted operators). For this strategy to work, one must be able to express the requirement that the $i+1$-th node visited in the path belongs to the set of children of the i-th node visited. However, the notion of "set" and "belongs to" are not directly available in SMT solvers: we will see in Sect. 5 how, again, the theory of Bit-Vectors allows us to find a workaround to this problem which, in our previous work, caused increased complexity in the produced SMT code.

Furthermore, we note that sorting path nodes by exploiting the natural number linear ordering allows us to restrict the scope of the sought solution. This is useful since in practice we are often only interested in considering a solution for future steps not too distant from the current one.

3 Related Work and Justification of an SMT Approach

The problem we propose features (as we will more formally express in Sect. 4) path finding across multiple directed (non necessarily acyclic) graphs, resources selection among sets of resources annotating each path-belonging node, overall optimisation of the selected resources under constraints of arbitrary arity, and a dependency of these constraints on the temporal separation of selected resources.

The fact that it combines traits of the distinct, widely explored problems in *combinatorial optimisation* (CO) which are mentioned above does not imply that the corresponding, well-explored solutions for these distinct problems can be easily combined to obtain a solution to the problem considered in this paper. For example, one could try to apply existing, well-known algorithms for the path-finding portion of our problem, and then hope to reduce the remaining portions of the problem to well-understood problems in CO, maybe by applying integer programming (IP), one of the domains of CO richest in methods and algorithms, to the sub-problem of resource subset selection. However, the problem of resources subset selection is not natively expressed in terms of integer variables and functions; and, more importantly, even if one finds a IP rendition of it, that rendition is bound to be, in general, non-linear, due to the fact that our notion of resource interactions aims by the design at dealing with the non-monotonic case (in more formal terms, the function ι we will introduce in (4) is completely arbitrary). This implies that we do not have direct access to the powerful and well-developed methods of integer linear programming (ILP), and have to deal with the more difficult approaches available in the less developed field of non-linear programming, where typically one has to resort to techniques (reconnecting the problem to special cases) such as continuous relaxation, branch and bound algorithms, approximation algorithms, ad-hoc heuristics, fractional programming [1,8,16]. All these approaches typically require significant amounts of work, add complexity to the solutions and require assumptions about the problem specification (for example, concavity/convexity requirements on the continuous relaxation's feasible region).

Before choosing the problem treatment presented in this paper, as explained above in the case of IP, we reviewed many other combinatorial optimisation sub-domains, without finding techniques able to capture all the aspects of the problem we consider. For example, resource scheduling [22, Section 22], an actively researched field, deals with executing a set of activities, each needing to employ some resources, while respecting the resource capacities, temporal constraints, and while optimising a given objective function. While this can accommodate the concepts of nodes (as activities) and resources featured in our problem, the focus about the constraints in resource scheduling is on the capacities of the resources and maybe (through the objective function) on temporal optimisations (e.g., minimising the number of late activities); in contrast, in our problem, the optimisation focuses on the mutual (and non necessarily binary) interaction of resources, as we will see in Sect. 4 (e.g. formula (8) featured there).

The considerations above about the difficulties we encountered in adapting existing techniques in the broad domain of combinatorial optimisation to the several facets of the problem at hand suggests that this problem presents some degree of hardness. This is confirmed by noting that the simpler problem of finding a path in a single graph with the additional constraint of the binary exclusion (e.g., on an either selected or unselected basis, as opposed to our problem featuring a score-based selection criterion) of given sets of node pairs is established to be NP-hard in [14].

Further justification for the adoption of SMT techniques is given by the fact that other authors also employ SAT or SMT solvers for simpler problems. SMT solvers are applied, in [11], to a particular optimal path selection problem in the semi-conductor manufacturing domain; besides the use of Bit-Vector capabilities of the SMT solver, there are little further similarities: the problem there can be described by only one graph, having one single cost annotation for each edge (we have multiple "costs" on each node). Work bearing some similarity with ours is in [19], presenting an graph-theoretical representation of a problem in computational task parallel scheduling, and also featuring a notion of temporal separation between nodes and of resources. Only one graph is needed to represent that problem, however, and the notion of conflict there is quite different from the one presented here. Besides the example above in clock routing, Bit-Vector capabilities of SMT solvers have been employed typically (but not only) to software and hardware validation as, for example, in [12], [13], [23]. This happened before and after the remarkable complexity of Bit-Vector reasoning was emphasised in [18], confirming the practical relevance and convenience of the theory nevertheless [10]. Our work provides a further witness of this phenomenon.

Our own recent works [5–7] propose the use of SMT solvers for finding optimal paths along processes executed in parallel, combined with the problem of picking resources at each selected path node under the constraint of mutual resource interaction. None of them can accommodate either cyclic graphs or interactions with arity greater than 2, which is a first contribution of the present paper; in those works, we expose the issue (largely under-explored in the current literature) of ascertaining the correctness of the SMT code we use, and provide a theorem-prover based solution. As a second contribution, we will show in Sect. 6 that technique is quite general, by applying it to the considered case to obtain correct-by-construction SMT code using the theorem prover Isabelle/HOL. As a final contribution, the approach presented in this paper avoids the issues entailed by more standard techniques in the field of non-linear programming (see the second paragraph of this section) by adopting a holistic attitude, in that it expresses all the constraints and the optimality requirements for our problem as a single stack of SMT assertions, without splitting it into sub-problems.

4 Formal Model of the Problem and of Its Solution

In what follows, $\operatorname{dom} P$, $\operatorname{ran} P$ and $P[X]$ will represent, respectively, the domain, range of a relation P, and the image through P of the set $X \subseteq \operatorname{dom} P$, while 2^Y will denote the power set of a set Y. We are given n finite, simple, directed *graphs* $G_1, \ldots, G_n$; we assume their node sets to be mutually disjoint. Usually, the graphs will also be connected, but we will not assume that. Since each of the graphs G_i is simple, it can be thought of as a finite set of ordered pairs of nodes (j, k) (that is, the set representing the covering relation corresponding to G_i), each representing a directed edge from node j to node k. Therefore, we can define

$$G := \bigcup_{i=1}^{n} G_i,$$

and denote by $V(G')$ the set of nodes touched by any edge in $G' \subseteq G$, that is

$$V : 2^G \to 2^{\operatorname{dom} G \cup \operatorname{ran} G} \qquad V(G') := \bigcup_{(v,v') \in G' \subseteq G} \{v, v'\},$$

G, being a set of ordered pairs, can be regarded as the set-theoretical representation of a relation, and has, therefore, a domain and a range. The requirement for the node sets of distinct graphs to be disjoint can now be expressed as

$$\forall j \in \{1, \ldots, n\}, j' \in \{1, \ldots, n\} \setminus \{j\}. \qquad V(G_j) \cap V(G_{j'}) = \emptyset.$$

We want to describe where a given agent, who is simultaneously executing all the n graphs, is located at a given time (this agent could, for instance, be a patient being following n guidelines recommendations): the agent must start at a given node for each of the graphs, and go through the nodes of some path in each graph, spending, in each of these nodes, an amount of time which is given by a map $d : V(G) \to \mathbb{N}$. The paths will be determined from constraints we will express later on (Sect. 5); for the moment, we focus on how such a description can be achieved.

4.1 Paths Calculation

A representation of an agent's position could be achieved, for example, by n functions (one for each graph), each defined on $\mathbb{N}$ (we assume a *discrete* representation of time) and yielding values in the node set of the relevant graph. However, as we explained in point (M2) of Sect. 2, we would like to exploit the discrete linear ordering naturally definable over a given path. Therefore, rather than introducing n functions yielding the node at which the executing agent is at a given time, we introduce the auxiliary concept of *stage*: rather than directly saying that the agent, at a given time and in a given graph, is at some node, we will split this piece of information into two functions: one expressing the stage of the solution path for graph j which the agent is at time t:

$$s_j : \mathbb{N} \to \mathbb{N} \qquad j = 1 \dots n;$$

and a second one expressing the sorting of nodes belonging to the solution path for the j-th graph:

$$\eta_j : \mathbb{N} \to V(G_j) \qquad j = 1 \dots n.$$

Thus, the description of the solution paths according to the notions of stage and of time are kept separated. The function relating them is

$$\tau_j : \mathbb{N} \to \mathbb{N} \qquad j = 1 \dots n,$$

yielding, for each stage in the solution path of a given digraph $j \in \{1, \dots, n\}$, the time at which that stage starts.

Although these functions are formally defined on the whole $\mathbb{N}$, we will actually restrict their computation to given, finite natural intervals S and T of stages and times, respectively, so that the above families of functions are related by the following assertions:

$$\forall j \in \{1, \dots, n\}, \; t \in T.$$
$$s_j(t+1) = \begin{cases} s_j(t) & \text{if } t+1 < \tau_j(1 + s_j(t)) \\ 1 + s_j(t) & \text{else.} \end{cases} \tag{1}$$

$$\forall j \in \{1, \dots, n\}, \; i \in S.$$
$$\tau_j(i+1) = \tau_j(i) + d(\eta_j(i)). \tag{2}$$

The role of S and T is to put a bound on the scope of future evolution we want to follow. On one hand, this allows to reduce the search space for the SMT solver; on the other hand, the finiteness thus imposed does not prevent to consider theoretically infinite paths (e.g., when cycles are present in the graphs), reconciling their presence with the need of finite computations. One can therefore compute optimal executions for given (S_1, T_1), ending up in some configuration; then have another computational session starting from the reached configuration for some other (S_2, T_2), thus reaching another configuration, etc: although the single sessions involve finite objects, there is no bound on the number of the sessions. This implies that the computations given by (1) and (2) must assume some starting point; that is, at the smallest stage and time, the executing agent must be located in a given node $\overline{\eta_j}$ for each $j \in \{1, \dots, n\}$:

$$\forall j \in \{1, \dots, n\}. \begin{cases} \eta_j(\min S) = \overline{\eta_j} \\ \tau_j(\min S) = \min T \\ s_j(\min T) = \min S \end{cases}$$

Since S and T are not in general constant through any sequence of computational sessions, we had to define our maps (s_j, τ_j, η_j, etc) on the whole $\mathbb{N}$ rather than directly on the subsets S and T; another reason for doing so is that SMT solvers do not directly provide support for partial functions.

Finally, we must impose that η_j actually describes a walk in the directed graph G_j:

$$\forall j \in \{1, \ldots, n\}, \ i \in S. \ \eta_j (i + 1) \in G_j [\{\eta_j (i)\}], \tag{3}$$

which asks that the $i+1$-th node is a child (according to the digraph G_j) of the i-th node in the path selected for the digraph G_j. The notation using the square brackets was introduced at the very beginning of this section.

4.2 Interaction Constraints

In Sect. 4.1, we have set up the problem of representing (through functions η, τ, s) a path in each G_j, and of computing the representing functions. Here we add constraints regulating how the path in distinct digraphs interact, so as to select the paths solving the earlier points (P1) and (P2) in Sect. 2.

We assume a finite set R of resources is given, together with maps $r_j : V(G_j) \to 2^R$ describing the subset of resources available to be chosen for a given node. We now want to solve the problem of picking, for each node appearing in the walks calculated in Sect. 4.1, resources allowed by the maps r_j (see point (P1) in the list of Sect. 2). Additionally, we want to do that such as to maximise the effectiveness of the picked resources along the executed path and to minimise the negative interactions between resources occurring at the same time in distinct simultaneous nodes (see point (P2) in the list of Sect. 2). To achieve this, we must have a database map

$$\iota : 2^R \to \mathbb{Z} \tag{4}$$

providing, for each possible combination of resources, their overall score, which is a numerical representation of how much each single resource in a given subset is effective and of how much different resources in the same subset possibly interact. Since it would be a computational waste to consider resources which cannot be prescribed in any possibly visited node, we add the constraint

$$R = \bigcup_{\substack{X \in \operatorname{ran} r_j \\ j \in \{1,\ldots,n\}}} X, \tag{5}$$

imposing that any resource must appear in $\bigcup (\operatorname{ran} r_j)$ for some digraph j. Now, the solution to the problem just introduced can be represented by maps

$$\rho_j : \mathbb{N} \to R, \ j = 1, \ldots, n$$

associating a stage number to the resource picked at that stage, for each digraph $G_1, \ldots, G_n$. The first requirement to be imposed on ρ is that the resource picked at any stage is in the permitted resources for the node corresponding to that stage:

$$\forall j \in \{1, \ldots, n\}, \ i \in S. \ \rho_j (i) \in r_j (\eta_j (i)), \tag{6}$$

where, as explained in Sect. 4.1, we limit the stages we are looking at to a finite natural interval S.

Finally, we need to optimise the interactions of resources happening at any same instant. To this end, we introduce a map $\Delta : \mathbb{N} \to 2^R$, yielding for each time the subset of all the resources picked in all the nodes happening at the given time in the selected paths across all the digraphs $G_1, \ldots, G_n$. That is, we impose

$$\Delta (t) := \bigcup_{j \in \{1,\ldots,n\}} \{\rho_j (s_j (t))\} \tag{7}$$

for each t in T, and then we require the SMT solver to maximise

$$\sum_{t \in T} \iota (\Delta (t)). \tag{8}$$

5 SMT Translation

This section presents the choices we made to represent the elements expressed mathematically in Sect. 4 in ways amenable to an SMT solver.

For each of the formulas introduced and motivated in that section, we will choose suitable SMT-LIB code to express it, and motivate our choice. The mathematical entities (functions, sets, etc.) used in that section will be given ASCII names in order for them to be invoked in SMT-LIB code: we will make clear which ASCII name corresponds to which mathematical object as soon as it is introduced in this section. However, for the reader's convenience, Table 1 summarises these correspondences.

A typical issue when translating into SMT code is to find a feasible representation, given the fact that SMT solvers are constrained to first-order logic together with a limited list of theories (e.g., integer arithmetics or Bit-Vectors). For example, sets are usually complicated to handle: while it is true that a subset of a given universe can be represented as a monadic boolean predicate over that universe, the problem is that predicates and relations are not themselves first-class objects in first-order logic. Therefore, quantifications, sets of sets, operations on sets and set-valued functions or relations are either not expressible or quickly become too complex, impacting both on performance and readability (and therefore reliability) of the code.

In our case, we do have sets of sets and operations on sets occurring in our treatment, for instance in (7). Our solution is to represent subsets of R as Bit-Vectors of length $|R|$: in this way, we can easily introduce an SMT function `resourceSelectionBV` as a counterpart of Δ:

Table 1. Correspondence between mathematical and SMT-LIB names

Mathematical notation	SMT-LIB notation
Δ	`resourceSelectionBV`
ρ	`stage2ResourceSetBV`
s	`time2Stage`
$t \in T$	`isInTimeBounds t`
$i \in S$	`isInStageBounds i`
τ	`stage2StarTime`
d	`duration`
G_j	`adjMatrix_j`
η	`stage2Node`
$V(G_j)$	`nodeType_j`
r	`node2AllowedResources`
$\subseteq$	`isSubsetBv`

```
(declare-fun resourceSelectionBV (Int) (_ BitVec |R|))
```

where $|R|$ must be replaced by its actual numerical value, since the length of a Bit-Vector cannot be a variable in SMT. This is not a problem because our model considers a fixed, finite universe of available resources (see (5)). Now, the problem of a union set operation appearing in (7) is also solved, because we can express (7) as

Listing 1.1. Assertion for (7)

```
(assert (forall ((t Int)) (=> (isInTimeBounds t)
(= (resourceSelectionBV t) (bvor
        (stage2ResourceSetBV1 (time2Stage_1 t))
        ...
        (stage2ResourceSetBVn (time2Stage_n t)))))))
```

where `stage2ResourceSetBV`, `time2Stage` take the place of ρ and s, respectively. Moreover, `isInTimeBounds t` is the first-order logic way of saying $t \in T$, while `bvor` takes the bit-wise or of its Bit-Vector arguments (there can be any finite number of such arguments, as long as they are Bit-Vectors of the same length), effectively resulting in the union of the sets they represent. Representing an overall selection of resources at a given instant as Bit-Vector is a way of working around the limitation of fixed arity of SMT-LIB functions, in the sense that now we are allowed to specify an interaction between an arbitrary number of resources *among the* $|R|$ *available ones* by setting to one the corresponding bits in the resource selection Bit-Vector. Theoretically, the same could have been attained by describing such an interaction via a number-valued SMT function of $|R|$ boolean arguments; however, in this case the resource selection would have no longer have been a first-class object in SMT, making it the translation of some assertions (e.g., (6) and (7)) clumsier than with Bit-Vectors. An important point to be made is that the assertion above requires representing ρ as a function (`stage2ResourceSetBV`) returning a set of resources, rather than a resource. This is necessary exactly to take the union through `bvor`, and creates no problem as long as we add the specification that *stage2ResourceSetBV* returns a singleton. In Bit-Vector terms, this means requiring that the returned Bit-Vector has exactly one bit set to 1, which can be achieved by the following assertions (one for each digraph):

Listing 1.2. Assertion imposing that `stage2ResourceSetBV`j returns a singleton

```
(assert (forall ((i Int))
(=> (isInStageBounds i)
    (and (isPowerOfTwo (stage2ResourceSetBVj i))
    (not (= (_ bv0 |R|) (stage2ResourceSetBVj i)))))))
```

where, similarly to `isInTimeBounds`, `isInStageBounds` is the first-order logic way of requiring $i \in S$, and `isPowerOfTwo` is defined as

```
(define-fun isPowerOfTwo ((x (_ BitVec |R|))) Bool
(= (_ bv0 |R|) (bvand x (bvsub x (_ bv1 |R|)))))
```

`isPowerOfTwo` works by taking the bitwise "and" of its argument and of its argument diminished by 1. It is easy to check that this yields 0 if and only if at most one bit of the argument (assumed to have length at least two) is 1.

The remaining constraints of Sect. 4 are more straightforward, with (1) translating to

Listing 1.3. Assertions for (1)

```
(assert (forall ((t Int))
  (=> (isInTimeBounds (+ 1 t))
    (= (time2Stage_j (+ 1 t))
       (ite (< (+ 1 t)
            (stage2StarTime_j (+ 1 (time2Stage_j t))))
         (time2Stage_j t) (+ 1 (time2Stage_j t)))))))
```

and (2) to

```
(assert (forall ((i Int)) (=> (isInStageBounds (+ 1 i))
(= (stage2StarTime_j (+ 1 i)) (+ (stage2StarTime_j i)
(duration_j (stage2Node_j i)))))))
```

Here, `stage2StarTime` and `duration` have the roles of τ and of d, respectively. Condition (3) again features a set-theoretical aspect (the membership relation $\in$). Although in this case the formula would be simple enough to represent the relevant sets through predicates, we chose to keep using Bit-Vectors. One reason is that, by doing so, the set of nodes adjacent, in graph G_j, to a given node (appearing as $G_j(\eta_j(i))$ in (3)) becomes exactly the row for that node of the *adjacency matrix* for G_j, thus allowing us to use a well-known formalism. Therefore, we enumerate all the nodes of a given G_j through an SMT map `nodeEnum_j`, and represent the edges touching the k-th node as the k-th row of the adjacency matrix for G_j, which is a Bit-Vector. In other words, G_j gets represented, in our SMT formalism, as a function `adjMatrix_j`, of the form

```
(define-fun adjMatrix_j (nodeType_j) (_ BitVec |V(G_j)|) ... )
```

where nodeType_j is a finite enumeration type encompassing all the nodes of G_j. Now, formula (3) is rendered in SMT-LIB as

```
(assert (forall ((i Int)) (=> (isInStageBounds i)
(= #b1
(extractBit_j (- (nodeEnum_j (stage2Node_j (+ 1 i))) 1)
               (adjMatrix_j (stage2Node_j i)))))))
```

where stage2Node is the SMT name for η, and extractBit_j k v extracts the k+1-th rightmost bit of v as a 1-long Bit-Vector. I.e., extractBit_j 0 v returns the rightmost bit of v, extractBit_j 1 v returns the bit on the left of the rightmost, and so on. This behaviour can be obtained as follows:

Listing 1.4. SMT function extracting the i-th bit from a Bit-Vector of fixed length

```
(define-fun extractBit_j ((i Int)
                          (v (_ BitVec |V(G_j)|)))
                         (_ BitVec 1)
((_ extract 0 0) (bvlshr v ((_ int2bv |V(G_j)|) i))))
```

which works by shifting the bits in v right by k places, and then extracting the last bit. This is done via the SMT-LIB functions bvlshr and extract. It should be observed that one cannot directly use extract because its arguments must be constants. For similar reasons, we needed to define multiple copies of extractBit, one for each digraph, because in general the digraphs will have different numbers of nodes, while in SMT-LIB one cannot overload functions to operate on Bit-Vectors of different sizes.

Condition (6) can be easily translated into SMT-LIB thanks to the fact that we used Bit-Vectors to represent sets of resources:

Listing 1.5. Assertion for (6)

```
(assert (forall ((i Int))
  (=> (isInStageBounds i)
      (isSubsetBv (stage2ResourceSetBV j i)
         (node2AllowedResources_j (stage2Node_j i))))))
```

where node2AllowedResources is the SMT-LIB name of r, and the auxiliary function isSubsetBv encodes the relation $\subseteq$ in terms of Bit-Vectors:

```
(define-fun isSubsetBv ((x (_ BitVec |R|))
                        (X (_ BitVec |R|))) Bool
(= (bvand x (bvnot X)) (_ bv0 |R|)))
```

Note that, referring to constraint (6), we are actually requiring that $\{\rho_j(i)\} \subseteq r_j(\eta_j(i))$ in lieu of $\rho_j(i) \in r_j(\eta_j(i))$. We can do this because we already imposed that node2AllowedResources returns a singleton in the assertion above using isPowerOfTwo.

Note that the following time2Stage, stage2Node, stage2ResourceSetBV, and resourceSelectionBV completely describe the solution to our problem given by the solver. The last two represent sets as Bit-Vectors: in some occasions, it can be convenient to have a solution involving equivalent SMT objects not making use of Bit-Vectors. Such equivalent objects can be obtained from the following assertions, defining counterparts of `resourceSelectionBV` and of `stage2ResourceSetBV` expressed by using an enumeration sort `resourceSort` of cardinality $|R|$ rather than using Bit-Vectors of length $|R|$:

Listing 1.6. Assertions for Bit-Vectors-free solutions

```
(assert (forall ((t Int) (d resourceSort))
(=> (isInTimeBounds t) (= (resourceSelection t d)
(= #b1 (extractBit (- (resourceEnum d) 1)
                   (resourceSelectionBV t)))))))
(assert (forall ((g graphSort) (s Int) (d resourceSort))
(=> (isInStageBounds s) (= (stage2ResourceSet g s d)
(= #b1 (extractBit (- (resourceEnum d) 1)
                   (stage2ResourceSetBV g s)))))))
```

which must be preceded by the obvious declarations of the newly introduced functions `resourceSelection` and `stage2ResourceSet`, omitted here. `extractBit` is definied in a way analogous as that of the similar functions appearing in Listing 1.4.

6 Verification

To achieve a way of formulating our problem as an SMT problem, we have split its description and that of the solution into several first-order functions (`time2Stage`, `stage2Node`, `stage2Resource`, `node2AllowedResources`, etc). While this device made it easier to formulate the assertions for the constraints exposed in Sect. 4, one could wonder whether the SMT assertions faithfully reproduce the problem we started from. One way to gain confidence about this is to re-express those first-order functions inside a theorem prover and then to formally prove the correctness theorems one may want to secure. For example, it can be reassuring to show that, at each time $t \in T$, the selected resource for each graph is among the resources allowed for the node of that graph where the executing agent is at time t. We proved the following Isabelle theorem expressing this property (where `N` represents the set of graph indices $\{1, \ldots, n\}$):

Listing 1.7. A Isabelle/HOL correctness theorem

```
lemma assumes assertionUnion:
"∀ t ∈ T. resourceSelection t =
  Union {stage2Resource j (time2Stage j t)| j. j ∈ N}"
and assertionAllowed: "∀ i ∈ S . ∀ j ∈ N.
  stage2Resource j i ⊆ node2AllowedResources j (stage2Node j i)"
and assertionSomeResource: "∀ i ∈ S. ∀ j∈ N.
(stage2Resource j i) ≠ {}"
and StageInBounds:
  "∀ t∈ T. ∀ j ∈ N. time2Stage j t ∈ S"
and TimeInBounds: "tt ∈ T"
and "J ∈ N" shows
"(node2AllowedResources J (stage2Node J (time2Stage J tt))) ∩
(resourceSelection tt) ≠ {}".
```

The Isabelle formula following the keyword `shows` is the thesis of the lemma, stating the property that we just discussed, and that we wanted to grant: it says that for any chosen graph (indexed by `J`), the intersection between the resources allowed for the visited node at time `tt` and the set of all resources selected at that time is non-empty. Note that we cannot claim, in general, that this intersection is a singleton, because there could be resources allowed in more than one node at a given time. Before the `show` keyword, there are six assumptions (the hypotheses of the lemma), each corresponding to SMT-LIB code parts. Hypothesis `assertionUnion` corresponds to assertion in Listing 1.1, `assertionAllowed` to that in Listing 1.5, `assertionSomeResource` is implied by assertion in Listing 1.2. The theorem says that, upon the further natural assumption that S is given to be compatible with T, `resourceSelection` indeed has the expected property.

The natural objection is that what we just proved applies to an Isabelle/HOL object, and that the mere fact that we christened it with the same name as the SMT object computed in Sect. 5 does not fix the problem that our proof applies to the former, not to the latter. This is because the hypotheses of the Isabelle/HOL theorem above suffer from the same problem: they apply to Isabelle/HOL objects which are totally unrelated to the homonymous SMT-LIB objects introduced and computed in Sect. 5. The idea to overcome this issue is to formally prove that those hypotheses also apply to the SMT-LIB objects of that section. To do so, we will take advantage of the Isabelle in-built SMT-LIB generator provided by the Isabelle component *sledgehammer*, originally intended to be used for automating theorem-proving purposes (a goal we are not interested in, in this paper).

6.1 First Step: Generating SMT-LIB Code from Theorem Hypotheses

We start from re-expressing the theorem in Listing 1.7 without using set-theoretical concepts. This can be done by replacing sets by boolean predicates:

```
lemma fixes
resourceSelection::"'t => 'd => bool" and
node2AllowedResources:: "('g => 'n => 'd => bool)" and
stage2ResourceSet::"'g => 's => 'd => bool" and
time2Stage :: "'g => 't => 's"
assumes assertionUnion: "∀ t d. (T t →
  (resourceSelection t d ↔
    (∃ g. (N g & stage2ResourceSet g (time2Stage g t) d))))"
and assertionAllowed: "∀ g s d.
  (S s & N g & stage2ResourceSet g s d) →
    node2AllowedResources g (stage2Node g s) d"
and assertionSomeResource: "∀ s g.
  (S s & N g) →
    (∃ d. (stage2ResourceSet g s d))"
and "∀t g. T t & N g → S (time2Stage g t)"
```

```
and "T tt" and "N gg"
shows "∃ d. ((resourceSelection tt d) &
(node2AllowedResources gg (stage2Node gg (time2Stage gg tt)) d
))"
```

The fact that Isabelle/HOL is higher-order means that it has no problem in passing from the proof for the original version of the theorem to the proof for the new one. The reason for this translation is that this new version gets translated in computable SMT-LIB code, because it is expressed in first-order logic. To obtain this code, we simply prepend the proof of the new theorem with the line

```
sledgehammer run [provers=z3, minimize=false, timeout=1,
                  overlord=true, verbose=true] (assms)
```

This will result in automatically-generated SMT-LIB assertions, one for each hypothesis of the theorem.

6.2 Second Step: Linking Generated SMT Code to the Existing Code

We can now use the SMT solver to formally prove that the Isabelle-generated SMT assertions and the existing ones introduced in Sect. 5 are equivalent: this will imply that the correctness theorem also applies to the latter. To achieve this, we name the bodies of each assertion we are interested in: for example, let us call `unionPredicateOriginal` the conjunction of the predicates being asserted in Listings 1.1 and 1.6, and `unionPredicateIsabelle` the predicate asserted by the code automatically generated from hypothesis `assertionUnion` in the theorem above. The following assertion returning `unsat` is a proof that the Isabelle-generated assertion, for which the formal theorem above holds, is equivalent to the corresponding ones introduced in Sect. 5:

```
(assert(or(and unionPredicateIsabelle(not unionPredicateOriginal))
 (and (not unionPredicateIsabelle) unionPredicateOriginal)))
```

This gives a method of linking the Isabelle correctness theorem to the code from Sect. 5, the one effectively used for actual computations.

This method is general and can be applied to whichever correctness theorem one could desire for their SMT code (which we already did, e.g., in [5–7]). One aspect of this generality is that the method is not limited to a pair of SMT assertion sets (such as `unionPredicateOriginal` and `unionPredicateIsabelle` above): one could refine her SMT code, for example to improve performance, in a third set of SMT assertions (let us call it `unionPredicateOptimised`, and then show, in the same manner as done with the assertion above, that it is also equivalent to the other two assertion sets. A typical application of this consists in replacing universal quantifiers over a finite set with separate assertions, one for each instantiation of the quantified variable, usually resulting in improved performance: this can be done, for example, with most of the occurrences of `forall` in Sect. 5. In this particular case, the verification method ensures that the instantiation of the quantifying variable has been done correctly. We omit further details for space reasons, and further details can be found in [7].

7 Conclusions

We have presented an approach for finding optimal paths across multiple directed graphs annotated with sets of resources. An optimal path is such that it maximises the value of the resources used across the nodes it traverses (e.g., overall drug efficacy) whilst minimising the value of resource interactions (e.g., an overall measure of the severity of drug interactions). A core feature of our approach is the possibility of enriching the constraint of interacting resources with the awareness of their temporal separation: this is represented by Δ being a function of a discrete time argument. A novelty of our work is the function ι which captures interactions between an arbitrary number of resources, and can be used to represent non-monotonic interactions between resources. For instance, we can model the case where two drugs together are problematic, but adding a further drug reduces some of the effects of the drug interaction. Another novel aspect is the presence of the bounds represented by S and T which split hard computation into sessions of limited time and stage scopes, and where the output can be used as input for the next session. In turn, this capability has permitted us to remove the limitation of acyclic graphs, typically imposed in similar work. All these features give a more realistic framework for our original application domain in healthcare.

We presented a general technique to employ rigorous formal proofs in HOL to verify first-order SMT code, and applied it to prove a particular property of our SMT encoding. A current limitation is that, since first-order logic is used in our approach as a bridge between an SMT solver and a higher-order theorem prover, the verification possibilities brought by the latter must be limited to the aspects of the SMT code which are expressible in first-order logic. In particular, we cannot currently verify the optimality aspect of our code: the optimising feature [4] is a speciality of Z3 [20] not covered by the SMT-LIB standard [3]. However, we emphasise that this limitation has limited practical impact, because typically the SMT code executed in concrete problems features a vast majority of assertions in pure SMT (i.e., expressed in the SMT-LIB standard language), and one line of code adding the requirement for optimality. It is therefore usually clear that the optimality part is correct while, in contrast, the same cannot be guaranteed for the assertions in pure SMT. Future work will explore the development of support for parallel SMT solving (e.g., using the `parallel.enable` option recently introduced in version 4.8.0 of the Z3 SMT solver).

References

1. Avriel, M., Diewert, W.E., Schaible, S., Zang, I.: Generalized Concavity, vol. 63. SIAM, Philadelphia (2010)
2. Bang-Jensen, J., Gutin, G.Z.: Digraphs: Theory, Algorithms and Applications. Springer, Berlin (2007)

3. Barrett, C., Stump, A., Tinelli, C.: The SMT-LIB standard: version 2.0. In: Gupta, A., Kroening, D. (eds.) Proceedings of the 8th International Workshop on Satisfiability Modulo Theories, Edinburgh, UK, vol. 13, p. 14 (2010)
4. Bjørner, N., Phan, A.-D., Fleckenstein, L.: *νz* - an optimizing SMT solver. In: Baier, C., Tinelli, C. (eds.) TACAS 2015. LNCS, vol. 9035, pp. 194–199. Springer, Heidelberg (2015). https://doi.org/10.1007/978-3-662-46681-0_14
5. Bowles, J., Caminati, M.B.: Correct composition of dephased behavioural models. In: Proença, J., Lumpe, M. (eds.) FACS 2017. LNCS, vol. 10487, pp. 233–250. Springer, Cham (2017). https://doi.org/10.1007/978-3-319-68034-7_14
6. Bowles, J.K.F., Caminati, M.B.: A flexible approach for finding optimal paths with minimal conflicts. In: Duan, Z., Ong, L. (eds.) ICFEM 2017. LNCS, vol. 10610, pp. 209–225. Springer, Cham (2017). https://doi.org/10.1007/978-3-319-68690-5_13
7. Bowles, J.K.F., Caminati, M.B.: Balancing prescriptions with constraint solvers. In: Liò, P., Zuliani, P. (eds.) Automated Reasoning for Systems Biology and Medicine. CB, vol. 30, pp. 243–267. Springer, Cham (2019). https://doi.org/10.1007/978-3-030-17297-8_9
8. Burer, S., Letchford, A.N.: Non-convex mixed-integer nonlinear programming: a survey. Surv. Oper. Res. Manag. Sci. **17**(2), 97–106 (2012)
9. Chartrand, G., Lesniak, L., Zhang, P.: Graphs & Digraphs. Chapman and Hall/CRC, Boca Raton (2010)
10. Dershowitz, N., Nadel, A.: Is bit-vector reasoning as hard as nexptime in practice. In: 13th International Workshop on Satisfiability Modulo Theories. Citeseer (2015)
11. Erez, A., Nadel, A.: Finding bounded path in graph using SMT for automatic clock routing. In: Kroening, D., Păsăreanu, C.S. (eds.) CAV 2015. LNCS, vol. 9207, pp. 20–36. Springer, Cham (2015). https://doi.org/10.1007/978-3-319-21668-3_2
12. Falke, S., Merz, F., Sinz, C.: LMBC: improved bounded model checking of C programs using. In: Piterman, N., Smolka, S.A. (eds.) TACAS 2013. LNCS, vol. 7795, pp. 623–626. Springer, Heidelberg (2013). https://doi.org/10.1007/978-3-642-36742-7_48
13. Franzén, A., Cimatti, A., Nadel, A., Sebastiani, R., Shalev, J.: Applying SMT in symbolic execution of microcode. In: Proceedings of the 2010 Conference on Formal Methods in Computer-Aided Design, pp. 121–128. FMCAD Inc. (2010)
14. Gabow, H.N., Maheshwari, S.N., Osterweil, L.J.: On two problems in the generation of program test paths. IEEE Trans. Softw. Eng. **3**, 227–231 (1976)
15. Government, S.: Polypharmacy Guidance (2nd edn.). Scottish Government Model of Care Polypharmacy Working Group, March 2015
16. Hemmecke, R., Köppe, M., Lee, J., Weismantel, R.: Nonlinear integer programming. In: Jünger, M., et al. (eds.) 50 Years of Integer Programming 1958–2008, pp. 561–618. Springer, Berlin (2010). https://doi.org/10.1007/978-3-540-68279-0_15
17. Hughes, L., McMurdo, M.E.T., Guthrie, B.: Guidelines for people not for diseases: the challenges of applying UK clinical guidelines to people with multimorbidity. Age Ageing **42**, 62–69 (2013)
18. Kovásznai, G., Fröhlich, A., Biere, A.: On the complexity of fixed-size bit-vector logics with binary encoded bit-width. In: SMT@ IJCAR, pp. 44–56 (2012)
19. Lombardi, M., Milano, M., Benini, L.: Robust scheduling of task graphs under execution time uncertainty. IEEE Trans. Comput. **62**(1), 98–111 (2013)
20. de Moura, L., Bjørner, N.: Z3: an efficient SMT solver. In: Ramakrishnan, C.R., Rehof, J. (eds.) TACAS 2008. LNCS, vol. 4963, pp. 337–340. Springer, Heidelberg (2008). https://doi.org/10.1007/978-3-540-78800-3_24

21. Nipkow, T., Paulson, L.C., Wenzel, M.: Isabelle/HOL: A Proof Assistant for Higher-order Logic. Springer, London (2002)
22. Rossi, F., Van Beek, P., Walsh, T.: Handbook of Constraint Programming. Elsevier, Amsterdam (2006)
23. Wille, R., Große, D., Haedicke, F., Drechsler, R.: SMT-based stimuli generation in the SystemC verification library. In: 2009 Forum on Specification & Design Languages FDL 2009, pp. 1–6. IEEE (2009)

Computing Bisimilarity Metrics for Probabilistic Timed Automata

Ruggero Lanotte and Simone Tini(✉)

DiSUIT, University of Insubria, Como, Italy
{ruggero.lanotte,simone.tini}@uninsubria.it

Abstract. We are interested in describing timed systems that exhibit probabilistic behaviour and in evaluating their behavioural discrepancies. To this purpose, we consider probabilistic timed automata, we introduce a concept of n-bisimilarity metric and give an algorithm to decide it.

1 Introduction

The framework of *Probabilistic Timed Automata* [2,9,34,39,40], PTAs for short, allows for the description of *timed systems* exhibiting a *probabilistic behaviour*, in an intuitive and succinct way. Technically, PTAs extend classical Timed Automata [3] (TAs) by admitting probability in action transitions.

In various fields, such as games, planning or security, the classical way of *comparing* two systems based on the *equivalence* of their behaviour has been demonstrated to be too strict when probability is taken into consideration. Any tiny variation in the probability values will break the equivalence on systems without any further information on the *distance* of their behaviours. Actually, many implementations can only approximate the specification; thus, the verification task requires appropriate instruments to measure the *quality* of the approximation. *Behavioural metrics* [1,14,26,28,31,35] are successful notions proposed to match this objective. In particular, *bisimilarity metrics* [14,26,28] measure the differences in the behaviour of systems in terms of the probability that they have to fail in mimicking each other in a step-by-step fashion. They can be viewed as the quantitative analogue to the well-known notion of *bisimilarity equivalence*. A useful derived notion is the *n-bisimilarity metric* [13], which takes into account the difference in system's behaviour arising in the first n computation steps.

Contribution. We introduce a notion of n-bisimilarity metric for PTAs, which is a pseudometric denoted $\mathbf{b}^n$ assigning a *distance* in $[0,1]$ to each pair of states (i.e. pairs (*location*, *clock valuation*)), and prove its decidability. Pseudometrics $(\mathbf{b}^n)_{n\geq 0}$ are a non-decreasing chain whose limit assign value 0 to the pairs of states that are equated by the probabilistic bisimilarity of [40]. Given a PTA, we build a *zone graph* supporting its *symbolic simulation*. Usually (see, e.g., [12,49]) symbolic simulations for (non necessarily probabilistic) TAs support study of *reachability* and are based on graphs whose nodes are *regions* or *zones* (which groups multiple regions) expressing *sets of states* and whose edges represent *sets*

W. Ahrendt and S. L. Tapia Tarifa (Eds.): IFM 2019, LNCS 11918, pp. 303–321, 2019.
https://doi.org/10.1007/978-3-030-34968-4_17

of transitions. We will argue that in order *to compare the behaviour of pairs of states*, as in [46] we need more structured zones expressing *sets of pairs of states* and edges representing *sets of pairs of transitions mimicking each other.* In detail, two equally labelled steps $s_1 \xrightarrow{\alpha} \Theta_1$ and $s_2 \xrightarrow{\alpha} \Theta_2$ from states s_1, s_2 to distributions over states Θ_1, Θ_2 will be simulated by a step $z \xrightarrow{\alpha} \Delta$ from the zone z containing the pair (s_1, s_2) to the distribution over zones Δ containing a zone z' for each pair of states s'_1, s'_2 with s'_i in the support of Θ_i. In our setting, the $(n+1)$-steps distance $\mathbf{b}^{n+1}(s_1, s_2)$ between s_1, s_2 depends on the n-steps distance between Θ_1, Θ_2, which is usually computed by employing the *Kantorovich lifting* [27], which lifts to Θ_1, Θ_2 the n-steps distance given by $\mathbf{b}^n$ between the states in their support. We will show that the problem of computing the Kantorovich lifting between Θ_1, Θ_2 is equivalent to a linear problem on Δ.

Up to our knowledge, this is the first paper giving an algorithm for deciding n-bisimilarity metric for systems with an *uncountable set of states and labels* and using symbolic representation. Since in the worst case the zone graph is exponential in size w.r.t. the size of the PTA, our algorithm is exponential time on the size of the PTA, namely the size of the *specification.* This complexity is uncomparable with that of the algorithms for bisimilarity metric proposed in the literature (and briefly discussed below) for other formalisms. Those algorithms are polynomial but work directly on the *semantic model*, i.e. the Probabilistic LTS-like that is assumed to be somehow already derived from the specification. The complexity of our algorithm is coherent with the theory of PTAs, since decidability results of other problems on PTAs are at least exponential time due to the number of regions/zones. Clearly our algorithm could be rephrased by using regions instead of zones (which groups more regions). We opted for using zones, which in the past led to efficient algorithms for TA model checking, and hence a statement of the algorithms in terms of zones has practical advantages.

Related Work. The problem of computing bisimilarity metrics has been studied for several formalisms, such as Labelled Markov Chains [15,23,45], Continuous Time Markov Chains [6] and Probabilistic Automata [8,17]. Since n-steps bisimilarity metrics are trivially decidable for *finite* state models, the efforts were addressed to compute directly the bisimilarity metric. Several iterative algorithms were developed in order to compute its approximation up to any degree of accuracy (e.g. [15,16,30]). Afterwards, in [23] the bisimilarity metrics is exactly computed in polynomial time for finite Markov Chains with rational probability by means of a linear program solved with ellipsoid algorithm. Although ellipsoid method is theoretically better than Simplex algorithm, which has an exponential complexity in the worst case, it is very slow practically and not competitive with Simplex. However, for computing bisimilarity metric, the Simplex method cannot be used to speed up performances in practice, since the linear program to be solved may have an exponential number of constraints. Hence, in [5] a polynomial time on-the-fly algorithm using a greedy strategy was given, which is very efficient in practical experiments. Recent works [8,44,45] improve and generalise some of these algorithms to approximate/compute probabilistic bisimilarity.

Some notions of distance for timed systems without probability have been studied. In particular, [21] extends the *edit distance* between untimed traces to timed words by adding the maximal difference in time stamps. Then, [38] addresses the problem of computing the *Skorokhod distance* between polygonal traces. In [22,33] (bi)similarity metrics on timed transition systems quantifying temporal discrepancies in (bi)similar behaviours are given. In [4] a notion of distance over timed words is studied which applies also to words with a different number of events and is robust w.r.t. switching of the ordering of close events.

Finally, among the papers on decidability of probabilistic timed simulation and bisimulation relations based on PTA models, we mention [20,24,36,42,43,47].

Outline. In Sect. 2 we recall the PTA model and n-bisimilarity metrics. In Sect. 3 we introduce our zone graphs, in Sect. 4 we give our algorithm and, finally, in Sect. 5 we discuss some possible future work.

2 Background

2.1 Probabilistic LTS and Bisimulation Metrics

Probabilistic labelled transition systems [40] (PTSs) extend labelled transition systems by allowing probability on transitions. Let $\mathcal{S}$ denote the set of the *states*, ranged over by $s, s_1, \ldots$. A transition takes a state to a *discrete rational probability distribution* over states, i.e. a mapping $\Theta\colon \mathcal{S} \to \mathbb{Q} \cap [0,1]$ with $\sum_{s \in \mathcal{S}} \Theta(s) = 1$. The *support* of Θ is given by $\mathsf{supp}(\Theta) = \{s \in \mathcal{S} : \Theta(s) > 0\}$. The set of all distributions over $\mathcal{S}$ with *finite support* is denoted $\mathcal{D}(\mathcal{S})$ and ranged over by $\Theta, \Theta_1, \ldots$.

Definition 1 (PTS [40]). *A* PTS *is a triple* $(\mathcal{S}, \mathbf{A}, \rightarrow)$*, where: 1.* $\mathcal{S}$ *is an (uncountable) set of* states*; 2.* $\mathbf{A}$ *is an (uncountable) set of* labels*, ranged over by* $\alpha, \beta, \ldots$*; 3.* $\rightarrow \subseteq \mathcal{S} \times \mathbf{A} \times \mathcal{D}(\mathcal{S})$ *is the* transition relation.

A PTS is *image finite* if $\{\Theta\colon s \xrightarrow{\alpha} \Theta\}$ is finite for all $s \in \mathcal{S}$ and $\alpha \in \mathbf{A}$.

In order to use PTSs as a semantic model for PTAs, the set $\mathbf{A}$ in Definition 1 will contain all reals in $\mathbb{R}^{\geq 0}$, modelling the passage of time in a setting with a continuous notion of time, besides a set of *action labels* denoted by Act.

We need some notation on distributions. For a state s, the *point distribution*$\delta(s)$ is defined by $\delta(s)(s) = 1$ and $\delta(s)(s') = 0$ for $s' \neq s$. The convex combination $\sum_{i \in I} p_i \cdot \Theta_i$ of a family $\{\Theta_i\}_{i \in I}$ of distributions, with I a finite set of indexes, $p_i \in (0,1]$ and $\sum_{i \in I} p_i = 1$, is the distribution with $(\sum_{i \in I} p_i \cdot \Theta_i)(s) = \sum_{i \in I} p_i \cdot \Theta_i(s)$ for all $s \in \mathcal{S}$. We denote $\sum_{i \in I} p_i \cdot \Theta_i$ as $p_1 \cdot \Theta_1 + \cdots + p_n \cdot \Theta_n$ when $I = \{1, \ldots, n\}$.

Bisimulation metrics [14,26,28] on PTSs are defined as *pseudometrics* measuring the discrepancies in the probabilistic behaviour of two states, by quantifying how much they are unable to simulate each other in a step-by-step fashion.

Definition 2 (Pseudometric). *Assume a PTS* $(\mathcal{S}, \mathbf{A}, \rightarrow)$*. A function* $d\colon \mathcal{S} \times \mathcal{S} \to [0,1]$ *is said to be a* 1-bounded pseudometric *if for all states* $s, s', s'' \in \mathcal{S}$*: 1.* $d(s,s) = 0$*, 2.* $d(s,s') = d(s',s)$*, 3.* $d(s,s') \leq d(s,s'') + d(s'',s')$*.*

Here we consider the notion of n-bisimilarity metric, denoted $\mathbf{b}^n$, which measures the distance between states that accumulates in the first n computation steps. The family $(\mathbf{b}^n)_{n\in\mathbb{N}}$ is defined inductively. Since no distance is observable in zero computation steps, $\mathbf{b}^0$ is the constant zero function, denoted $\mathbf{0}$. Then, $\mathbf{b}^{n+1}$ is derived from $\mathbf{b}^n$ by relying on the quantitative analogue to the *bisimulation game*: two states can be at some given distance $\epsilon < 1$ according to $\mathbf{b}^{n+1}$ only if they can mimic each other's transitions and evolve to distributions that are, in turn, at a distance $\leq \epsilon$ according to $\mathbf{b}^n$. To formalize this intuition, we need to lift pseudometrics on states to pseudometrics on distributions.

Definition 3 (Kantorovich metric [27]). *The* Kantorovich lifting *of a pseudometric d on $\mathcal{S}$ is the pseudometric $\mathbf{K}(d)$ on distributions in $\mathcal{D}(\mathcal{S})$ defined by*

$$\mathbf{K}(d)(\Theta_1,\Theta_2) = \sum_{s_1\in\mathsf{supp}(\Theta_1)} \sum_{s_2\in\mathsf{supp}(\Theta_2)} \omega_{s_1,s_2}\cdot d(s_1,s_2)$$

where ω_{s_1,s_2} is the solution of variable y_{s_1,s_2} in the following problem:

$$\begin{array}{ll} \underline{\text{minimize}} & \sum_{s_1\in\mathsf{supp}(\Theta_1)} \sum_{s_2\in\mathsf{supp}(\Theta_2)} y_{s_1,s_2}\cdot d(s_1,s_2) \\ \underline{\text{subject to:}} & \forall s_1\in\mathsf{supp}(\Theta_1)\colon \sum_{s_2\in\mathsf{supp}(\Theta_2)} y_{s_1,s_2} = \Theta_1(s_1) \\ & \forall s_2\in\mathsf{supp}(\Theta_2)\colon \sum_{s_1\in\mathsf{supp}(\Theta_1)} y_{s_1,s_2} = \Theta_2(s_2) \\ & \forall s_1\in\mathsf{supp}(\Theta_1)\ \forall s_2\in\mathsf{supp}(\Theta_2)\colon y_{s_1,s_2}\geq 0. \end{array}$$

Intuitively, each set of values y_{s_1,s_2} respecting the requirements above may be understood as a transportation schedule for the shipment of probability mass from Θ_1 to Θ_2. Then, values ω_{s_1,s_2} give the solution of the optimal transport problem, with $d(s_1,s_2)$ the unit cost for shipping probability mass from s_1 to s_2.

The inductive definitions of $\mathbf{b}^n$'s relies on the following functional.

Definition 4 (n-bisimilarity metric). *The function $\mathbf{B}\colon[0,1]^{\mathcal{S}\times\mathcal{S}}\to[0,1]^{\mathcal{S}\times\mathcal{S}}$ is defined for all functions $d\colon\mathcal{S}\times\mathcal{S}\to[0,1]$ and states $s_1,s_2\in\mathcal{S}$ by*

$$\mathbf{B}(d)(s_1,s_2) = \sup_{\alpha\in\mathbf{A}} \max\{\sup_{s_1\xrightarrow{\alpha}\Theta_1}\ \inf_{s_2\xrightarrow{\alpha}\Theta_2} \mathbf{K}(d)(\Theta_1,\Theta_2),\ \sup_{s_2\xrightarrow{\alpha}\Theta_2}\ \inf_{s_1\xrightarrow{\alpha}\Theta_1} \mathbf{K}(d)(\Theta_1,\Theta_2)\}$$

whereby $\sup\emptyset = 0$ *and* $\inf\emptyset = 1$.
Then, for $n\in\mathbb{N}$ we define the n-bisimilarity metric $\mathbf{b}^n$ *as* $\mathbf{b}^n = \mathbf{B}^n(\mathbf{0})$.

By setting $\mathbf{b}^{n+1} = \mathbf{B}(\mathbf{b}^n)$, we are sure that whenever $\mathbf{b}^{n+1}(s_1,s_2) < 1$, any transition $s_1 \xrightarrow{\alpha} \Theta_1$ is mimicked by a transition $s_2 \xrightarrow{\alpha} \Theta_2$ with $\mathbf{K}(\mathbf{b}^n)(\Theta_1,\Theta_2) \leq \mathbf{b}^{n+1}(s_1,s_2)$, and conversely. Since $\mathbf{B}$ maps pseudometrics to pseudometrics (see, e.g., [26]) and $\mathbf{b}^0$ is clearly a pseudometric, all $\mathbf{b}^n$ are pseudometrics. The monotonicity of $\mathbf{K}$ and sup, inf, max ensure that $(\mathbf{b}^n)_{n\geq 0}$ is a non descending chain. Since image finiteness guarantees that $\mathbf{B}$ is continuous [13] over the lattice of functions in $[0,1]^{\mathcal{S}\times\mathcal{S}}$ ordered pointwise, the limit of this chain is the least (pre)fixed point of $\mathbf{B}$, which will be denoted with $\mathbf{b}$. The kernel of $\mathbf{b}$ is the *probabilistic bisimilarity* [37,40], i.e. $\mathbf{b}(s,s') = 0$ iff s and s' are bisimilar (see, e.g., [28]). Characterisation for $\mathbf{b}$ are provided, for different semantic models, in terms of logics with real value [1,7,14,28] and boolean [18,19] semantics.

2.2 Probabilistic Timed Automata

Assume a set X of non negative real variables, called *clocks*. A *valuation* over X is a mapping $v : \mathsf{X} \to \mathbb{R}^{\geq 0}$. The set of all valuations over X is denoted by V_{X}.

Notation 1 (Notation for clock valuations). *Assume any $v \in \mathsf{V}_{\mathsf{X}}$. Then: 1. for a non-negative real t, we let $v+t$ denote the valuation with $(v+t)(x) = v(x)+t$ for all $x \in \mathsf{X}$; 2. for a set of clocks $B = \{x_1, \ldots, x_n\}$, with $v[B]$ we denote the valuation with $v[B](x) = 0$, if $x \in B$, and $v[B](x) = v(x)$, otherwise.*

The set of *constraints* over X, denoted $\Psi(\mathsf{X})$, is defined by the following grammar, where ψ ranges over $\Psi(\mathsf{X})$, $x, y \in \mathsf{X}$, $c \in \mathbb{Z}$ and $\sim \in \{<, \leq, =, \geq, >\}$:

$$\psi ::= \mathsf{true} \mid \mathsf{false} \mid x \sim c \mid x - y \sim c \mid \psi_1 \wedge \psi_2 \mid \psi_1 \vee \psi_2 \mid \neg\psi$$

We write $v \models \psi$ when *the valuation v satisfies the constraint ψ*. The inductive definition of relation $\models$ is straightforward. Essentially, a clock constraint describes a subset of $(\mathbb{R}^{\geq 0})^{|\mathsf{X}|}$, which is usually referred to as a *clock zone*. Sometimes we will freely use a more compact notation, e.g. $x \in [0, 3]$ for $x \geq 0 \wedge x \leq 3$.

Definition 5 (PTA, [34,39]). *A* Probabilistic Timed Automaton *is a tuple $A = (\mathsf{L}, \mathsf{X}, \mathsf{Act}, \mathsf{inv}, \mathsf{enab}, \mathsf{prob})$, where:*

- L *is a finite set of* locations*;*
- X *is a finite set of* clocks*;*
- Act *is a finite set of* actions*;*
- $\mathsf{inv}\colon \mathsf{L} \to \Psi(\mathsf{X})$ *is the location* invariant *condition;*
- $\mathsf{enab}\colon \mathsf{L} \times \mathsf{Act} \to \Psi(\mathsf{X})$ *is the transition* enabling *condition;*
- $\mathsf{prob}\colon \mathsf{L} \times \mathsf{Act} \to \mathcal{D}(2^{\mathsf{X}} \times \mathsf{L})$ *is a probabilistic* transition function.

By using the notation of [3], we let $|A|$ denote the *size* of A, where the length of clock constraints and function prob assumes binary encoding for constants and probabilities. As a further notation, we let C_A denote the *greatest absolute value of constants appearing in invariants and enabling conditions in A.*

Definition 6 (PTA semantics). *A PTA $A = (\mathsf{L}, \mathsf{X}, \mathsf{Act}, \mathsf{inv}, \mathsf{enab}, \mathsf{prob})$ induces the PTS $\mathcal{L}_A = (\mathcal{S}, \mathbf{A}, \to)$, where:*

- $\mathcal{S} = \{(l, v)\colon l \in \mathsf{L}\,,\, v \in \mathsf{V}_{\mathsf{X}}\,,\, v \models \mathsf{inv}(l)\}$*;*
- $\mathbf{A} = \mathsf{Act} \cup \mathbb{R}^{\geq 0}$*;*
- *we have the* timed transition $(l, v) \xrightarrow{t} \Theta$ *if $t \in \mathbb{R}^{\geq 0}$, Θ is the point distribution $\Theta = \delta((l, v + t))$ and $v + t' \models \mathsf{inv}(l)$ for all $0 \leq t' \leq t$;*
- *we have the* action transition $(l, v) \xrightarrow{a} \Theta$ *if $a \in \mathsf{Act}$, $v \models \mathsf{enab}(l, a)$ and Θ is the distribution such that for each state $(l', v') \in \mathcal{S}$:*

$$\Theta(l', v') = \textstyle\sum_{B \in 2^{\mathsf{X}}} \{\!|\, \mathsf{prob}(l, a)(B, l')\colon v' = v[B] \,|\!\}.$$

A PTS $\mathcal{L}_A$ is image finite, since for s and α we have $|\{\Theta\colon s \xrightarrow{\alpha} \Theta\}| \in \{0, 1\}$.

We say that *two clock constraints ψ and ψ' are equivalent*, written $\psi \equiv \psi'$, if they are satisfied by the same valuations. For a natural k, let $\Psi_k(\mathsf{X})$ denote the set of constraints in $\Psi(\mathsf{X})$ with only integer constants in $[-k, k]$. Hence, all constraints in a PTA A are in $\Psi_{C_A}(\mathsf{X})$. In [12] it is shown that the number of clock constraints in $\Psi_{C_A}(\mathsf{X})$ expressed by using only conjunction are at most exponential on $|A|$, modulo equivalence. The following generalization is immediate.

Proposition 7 (Finiteness of clock constraints). *There exist a finite set of clock constraints $\Psi(C_A, \mathsf{X}) \subset \Psi_{C_A}(\mathsf{X})$, with exponential cardinality on $|A|$, such that each clock constraint in $\Psi_{C_A}(\mathsf{X})$ is equivalent to a disjunction of clock constraints in $\Psi(C_A, \mathsf{X})$. We denote with $N(C_A, \mathsf{X})$ the cardinality of $\Psi(C_A, \mathsf{X})$.*

For practical reasons, it is often convenient to add the existential and universal quantifier and the *time variable* t to clock constraints.

Notation 2 (Notation on constraints). *Assume clocks $B = \{x_1, \dots, x_m\}$. Then: $\exists B.\psi$ stands for $\exists x_1.\cdots.\exists x_m.\psi$; $B = 0$ denotes $\bigwedge_{x\in B} x = 0$; and $\psi[B := B + t]$ denotes the formula ψ where each occurrence of each clock $x \in B$ is substituted with $x+t$. Finally, $\forall x.\psi$ stands for $\neg\exists x.\neg\psi$ and $\psi_1 \Rightarrow \psi_2$ for $\neg\psi_1 \vee \psi_2$.*

3 Zone Graph

We aim to have symbolic simulations of PTAs supporting the computation of n-bisimilarity metrics. Usually, symbolic simulations for (non necessarily probabilistic) TAs base on *zone graphs* [12,49], whose nodes are *zones* of the form (l, ψ) expressing *sets of states* (with the same location and differing only on the clock valuation), and whose edges represent *sets of action transitions*. These graphs are built in order to support *reachability*. By an example, we give the intuition that if we aim to *compare the behaviour of pairs of states*, then we cannot simply consider pairs of classical zones, but, as in [46], we need both more structured graph nodes expressing *sets of pairs of states* and edges representing *sets of pairs of transitions* where the transitions in the same pair mimic each other.

Example 8. Consider two locations $l_1, l_2 \in \mathsf{L}$ with invariant $\mathsf{inv}(l_1) = x \le 5$ and $\mathsf{inv}(l_2) = y \le 5$. Clearly, two states (l_1, v_1) and (l_2, v_2) with $v_1(x), v_2(y) \le 5$ perform the same set of timed transitions if and only if $v_1(x) = v_2(y)$. Therefore, a pair of classical zones $(l_1, \psi_1), (l_2, \psi_2)$ would not carry the information needed to infer that only the pairs of states (l_1, v_1) and (l_2, v_2) with $v_1 \models \psi_1$, $v_2 \models \psi_2$ and $v_1(x) = v_2(y)$ simulate each other, unless we take a pair for each value in $[0, 5]$ thus ending with an infinite graph. Following [46] we propose to use zones representing sets of *pairs of states*, with structure of the form (l_1, l_2, ψ) and the formula ψ expressing the relations between the valuations v_1 and v_2 allowing (l_1, v_1) and (l_2, v_2) to mimic each other. For instance, in our case we consider a zone of the form $(l_1, l_2, 0 \le x \le 5 \wedge x = y)$, with $x = y$ expressing the relation between the clocks x used in $\mathsf{inv}(l_1)$ and y used in $\mathsf{inv}(l_2)$. This technique must be refined if $\mathsf{inv}(l_1)$ and $\mathsf{inv}(l_2)$ refer to the same clocks. For instance, if we rewrite $\mathsf{inv}(l_2)$ as $\mathsf{inv}(l_2) = x \le 5$, then $(l_1, l_2, 0 \le x \le 5 \wedge x = x)$ does not express that the clocks used in l_1 and l_2 must have the same value. In order to distinguish the value of clock x in location l_1 and that in location l_2 we use zone $(l_1, l_2, 0 \le x \le 5 \wedge x = \overline{x})$ where $\overline{x}$ represents the value of x in location l_2.

Example 8 suggests us to use disjoint sets of clocks in order to describe the sets of pairs of states. Let $\overline{\mathsf{X}} = \{\overline{x} \colon x \in \mathsf{X}\}$. For a valuation $v \in \mathsf{V}_{\mathsf{X}}$, let $\overline{v}$ denote the valuation over $\overline{\mathsf{X}}$ with $\overline{v}(\overline{x}) = v(x)$ for each $x \in \mathsf{X}$. Given a constraint $\psi \in \Psi(\mathsf{X})$, let $\overline{\psi}$ denote the constraint ψ with each occurrence of x replaced by $\overline{x}$.

Definition 9 (Zone). *Assume a PTA $A = (\mathsf{L}, \mathsf{X}, \mathsf{Act}, \mathsf{inv}, \mathsf{enab}, \mathsf{prob})$. A zone of A is a triple $z = (l_1, l_2, \psi) \in \mathsf{L} \times \mathsf{L} \times \Psi_{C_A}(\mathsf{X} \cup \overline{\mathsf{X}})$ with $\psi \Rightarrow \mathsf{inv}(l_1) \wedge \overline{\mathsf{inv}(l_2)}$.*

Zone $z = (l_1, l_2, \psi)$ represents all pairs of states $((l_1, v_1), (l_2, v_2))$ with $v_1 \uplus \overline{v_2} \models \psi$, notation $((l_1, v_1), (l_2, v_2)) \in z$. As already explained in Example 8, by arguing on both X and $\overline{\mathsf{X}}$ the constraint ψ allows us to express how v_1 and v_2 are related.

Notation 3 (Notation for zones). *For a formula $\psi \in \Psi(\mathsf{X} \cup \overline{\mathsf{X}})$, we denote with $(\psi)_{|_1}$ the* left projection *$\exists \overline{\mathsf{X}}.\psi$ and with $(\psi)_{|_2}$ the* right projection *$\exists X.\psi$. Then, we lift this notion to zones. For a zone $z = (l_1, l_2, \psi)$, we denote with $(z)_{|_1}$ the* left projection *$(l_1, \exists \overline{\mathsf{X}}.\psi)$ and with $(z)_{|_2}$ the* right projection *$(l_2, \exists X.\psi)$.*

For zones $z = (l_1, l_2, \psi)$ and $z' = (l_1', l_2', \psi')$, we write $(z)_{|_1} \equiv (z')_{|_1}$ if and only if $l_1 = l_1'$ and $(\psi)_{|_1} \equiv (\psi')_{|_1}$, namely their left projections coincide. Analogously, we write $(z)_{|_2} \equiv (z')_{|_2}$ if and only if $l_2 = l_2'$ and $(\psi)_{|_2} \equiv (\psi')_{|_2}$. Finally, we write $z \implies z'$ if $l_1 = l_1'$, $l_2 = l_2'$ and $\psi \Rightarrow \psi'$.

Definition 10 (Zone graph). *A* zone graph *G for a PTA A is a finite set of zones satisfying the following properties:*

1. *for all locations $l_1, l_2 \in \mathsf{L}$: $\bigvee_{(l_1, l_2, \psi) \in \mathsf{G}} \psi \equiv (\mathsf{X} \geq 0 \wedge \mathsf{inv}(l_1) \wedge \overline{\mathsf{X}} \geq 0 \wedge \overline{\mathsf{inv}(l_2)})$;*
2. *for all zones $z = (l_1, l_2, \psi)$ and $z' = (l_1', l_2', \psi')$ in G with $z \neq z'$:*
   (a) if $l_1 = l_1'$ and $l_2 = l_2'$ then $\psi \wedge \psi' \equiv \mathsf{false}$;
   (b) if $l_1 = l_1'$ then either $(\psi)_{|_1} \wedge (\psi')_{|_1} \equiv \mathsf{false}$ or $(\psi)_{|_1} \equiv (\psi')_{|_1}$;
   (c) if $l_2 = l_2'$ then either $(\psi)_{|_2} \wedge (\psi')_{|_2} \equiv \mathsf{false}$ or $(\psi)_{|_2} \equiv (\psi')_{|_2}$.

Essentially, a zone graph for a PTA A is a finite set of zones such that each pair of states (s_1, s_2) in $\mathcal{L}_A$ is in precisely one zone (items 1 and 2a). Moreover, if we take the left (resp. right) projection of two different zones, we get two sets of states that either coincide or do not intersect (item 2b (resp. 2c)). Clearly, zone graphs will be properly completed with edges, see Sect. 3.1.

We can state an upper bound to the size of a zone graph G. In detail, G has at most $|\mathsf{L}|^2 \cdot \mathsf{N}(\mathsf{C}_A, \mathsf{X} \cup \overline{\mathsf{X}})$ zones, which, by Proposition 7, is exponential on $|A|$.

Proposition 11 (Zone graph cardinality). *Assume a zone graph G for a PTA A. Then, G has at most $|\mathsf{L}|^2 \cdot \mathsf{N}(C_A, \mathsf{X} \cup \overline{\mathsf{X}})$ zones.*

3.1 Zone Graphs in Normal Form

We aim to lift the notion of transition from states to zones, thus equipping zone graphs with edges. Given a zone graph G, we will define a notion of action transition $z \xrightarrow{a} \Delta$ from a zone z in G to a distribution over zones Δ with support contained in G, where $z \xrightarrow{a} \Delta$ should represent *a set of pairs of action* *transitions from pairs of states in z to pairs of distributions over states.* Then, we define a notion of timed transition $z \longrightarrow \delta(z')$ from a zone z in G to a zone z' in G representing *a set of pairs of equally labelled timed transitions from pairs of states in z to pairs of states in z'*. In this section, we argue that these action/timed transitions over zones require zone graphs in a proper form. Since we consider PTAs with *diagonal constraints* of the form $x - y \sim c$, we know from [11] that already in the case of TAs the so called *forward* analysis cannot be both *correct* and *always terminating*, therefore we follow the *backward* analysis approach proposed in [32,49] for classical zones. Moreover, it is well known that forward analysis does not take into account precisely the branching structure of PTS and does not work well for bisimulation-like reasoning.

We start with analysing action transitions. Assume an action label $a \in \mathsf{Act}$ and locations $l_1, l_2, l_1', l_2' \in \mathsf{L}$ such that the a-labelled transition leaving from l_i has probability greater than 0 to reset the set of clocks B_i and lead to l_i', namely $\mathsf{prob}(l_i, a)(B_i, l_i') > 0$. Consider a zone graph G and a zone z' with $z' = (l_1', l_2', \psi')$. We let $\mathsf{prec}_a(l_1, l_2, B_1, B_2, z')$ denote the following formula, which can be proved to be a clock constraint in $\Psi_{\mathsf{C}_A}(\mathsf{X} \cup \overline{\mathsf{X}})$ following, e.g., [29,49]:

$$\mathsf{prec}_a(l_1, l_2, B_1, B_2, z') = \mathsf{enab}(l_1, a) \wedge \overline{\mathsf{enab}(l_2, a)} \wedge \exists B_1 \cup \overline{B_2}.(\psi' \wedge B_1 \cup \overline{B_2} = 0).$$

We note that $(l_1, l_2, \mathsf{inv}(l_1) \wedge \overline{\mathsf{inv}(l_2)} \wedge \mathsf{prec}_a(l_1, l_2, B_1, B_2, z'))$ is the zone z containing precisely the pairs of states that, by performing a transition labelled a and resetting B_1 for the left projection and B_2 for the right projection, reach a pair of states in z' with a positive probability. Clearly, in general we are not guaranteed that zone z is in the zone graph G. It may happen that the set of pairs of states $((l_1, v_1), (l_2, v_2))$ with $v_1 \uplus \overline{v_2} \models \mathsf{inv}(l_1) \wedge \overline{\mathsf{inv}(l_2)} \wedge \mathsf{prec}_a(l_1, l_2, B_1, B_2, z')$ is partitioned in several zones in G. In detail, given any zone $z = (l_1, l_2, \psi)$, by the definition of zone (Definition 9) we know for sure that $\psi \models \mathsf{inv}(l_1) \wedge \overline{\mathsf{inv}(l_2)}$, then, if we compare ψ with $\mathsf{prec}_a(l_1, l_2, B_1, B_2, z')$, three cases are possible:

1. $\psi \wedge \mathsf{prec}_a(l_1, l_2, B_1, B_2, z') \equiv \mathsf{false}$. In this case, *no* pair of states in z can reach z' by performing a and resetting B_1 and B_2.
2. $\psi \Rightarrow \mathsf{prec}_a(l_1, l_2, B_1, B_2, z')$. In this case, *all* pairs of states in z can reach z' by performing a and resetting B_1 and B_2.
3. None of the two previous cases holds. Then, *a strict and non-empty* subset of the pairs of states in z can reach z' by performing a and resetting B_1, B_2.

Case 3 is incompatible with having transitions $z \xrightarrow{a} \Delta$ such that *all* pairs of states in z can reach the zones in the support of Δ. Hence, we introduce below (Definition 12) a notion of normal form for zone graphs, where case 3 is excluded.

Let us analyse now timed transitions. Assume a zone $z' = (l_1, l_2, \psi')$ in G. We let $\mathsf{prec}(z')$ denote the formula

$$\exists t \geq 0.(\psi'[\mathsf{X} \cup \overline{\mathsf{X}} := \mathsf{X} \cup \overline{\mathsf{X}} + t] \wedge \forall t' \in [0, t].(\mathsf{inv}(l_1) \wedge \overline{\mathsf{inv}(l_2)})[\mathsf{X} \cup \overline{\mathsf{X}} := \mathsf{X} \cup \overline{\mathsf{X}} + t'])$$

It can be proved that $\mathsf{prec}(z')$ is equivalent to a clock constraint. We note that $(l_1, l_2, \mathsf{prec}(z'))$ is the zone containing precisely the pairs of states that, by performing a timed transition with the same label, reach a pair of states in z'. Again, in order to have transitions $z \longrightarrow \delta(z')$ such that *all* pairs of states in z

can reach pairs of states in z' we need that any zone $z = (l_1, l_2, \psi)$ in G (with the same locations) is such that:

- either $\psi \wedge \mathsf{prec}(z') \equiv \mathsf{false}$, so that *no* pair of states in z can reach z' by performing the same timed transition;
- or $\psi \Rightarrow \mathsf{prec}(z')$, so that *all* pairs of states in z can reach z' by performing the same timed transition.

Definition 12 (Normal form for zone graphs). *A zone graph* G *is in* normal form *if for arbitrary zones* $z = (l_1, l_2, \psi)$ *and* $z' = (l'_1, l'_2, \psi')$ *we have:*

- *for any action* $a \in \mathsf{Act}$ *and clock sets* $B_1, B_2 \in 2^{\mathsf{X}}$, *if* $\mathsf{prec}_a(l_1, l_2, B_1, B_2, z')$ *is defined (namely* $\mathsf{enab}(l_i, a)(B_i, l'_i) > 0$ *for* $i = 1, 2$*), then it holds that:*
  - *either* $\psi \wedge \mathsf{prec}_a(l_1, l_2, B_1, B_2, z') \equiv \mathsf{false}$, *or* $\psi \Rightarrow \mathsf{prec}_a(l_1, l_2, B_1, B_2, z')$.
- *if* $l_1 = l'_1$ *and* $l_2 = l'_2$ *then it holds that:*
  - *either* $\psi \wedge \mathsf{prec}(z') \equiv \mathsf{false}$, *or* $\psi \Rightarrow \mathsf{prec}(z')$.

Any zone graph can be mapped to a normal form, by iteratively taking the zones $z = (l_1, l_2, \psi), z' = (l'_1, l'_2, \psi')$ that violate the requirements in Definition 12 and splitting (l_1, l_2, ψ) into zones $(l_1, l_2, \psi \wedge \mathsf{prec}_a(l_1, l_2, B_1, B_2, z'))$ and $(l_1, l_2, \psi \wedge \neg\mathsf{prec}_a(l_1, l_2, B_1, B_2, z'))$, or $(l_1, l_2, \psi \wedge \mathsf{prec}(z'))$ and $(l_1, l_2, \psi \wedge \neg\mathsf{prec}(z'))$ until the fixpoint is reached. Clearly, this splitting must be applied also to the zones having left/right projection equivalent to that of (l_1, l_2, ψ), thus ensuring that requirements 2b-2c in Definition 10 are not broken.

Proposition 13 (Existence of normal form). *Given a zone graph* G, *a zone graph* $\mathsf{NF}(\mathsf{G})$ *in normal form can be computed in exponential time on* $|A|$.

3.2 Action and Timed Transitions over Zones

We start with defining action transitions over zones. We want to have $z \xrightarrow{a} \Delta$ if and only if, given *an arbitrary* pair of states (s_1, s_2) in z, both s_1 and s_2 perform an a-transition taking them to a pair of distributions over states (Θ_1, Θ_2) s.t. for each pair of states (s'_1, s'_2) with $s'_1 \in \mathsf{supp}(\Theta_1)$ and $s'_2 \in \mathsf{supp}(\Theta_2)$ it holds that the zone z' containing (s'_1, s'_2) is in the support of Δ. Moreover, we want that $\Delta(z') = \prod_{i=1,2} \sum_{s'_i \in (z')|_i \cap \mathsf{supp}(\Theta_i)} \Theta_i(s'_i)$. We say that this is the requirement of *soundness and completeness of action transitions over zones w.r.t. transitions over states.* Note that the arbitrarity of the choice of (s_1, s_2) from z requires that by starting from *all* pairs of states in z, the *same* zones are reached. Namely, for any pairs of states (s_1, s_2) and (s'_1, s'_2) in z with $s_i = (l_i, v_i)$ and $s'_i = (l_i, v'_i)$ and any zone $z' = (l'_1, l'_2, \psi')$, either both $v_1 \uplus \overline{v_2}$ and $v'_1 \uplus \overline{v'_2}$ satisfy $\mathsf{prec}_a(l_1, l_2, B_1, B_2, z')$ for suitable B_1 and B_2, or none of them does. Therefore, we need to consider zones in a zone graph in normal form.

Definition 14 (Action transition over zones). *Assume a zone graph in normal form* G*, a zone* $z = (l_1, l_2, \psi)$ *in* G *and an action* $a \in \mathsf{Act}$*. We write*

$$z \xrightarrow{a} \Delta$$

if $\Delta = \sum_{j=1}^{n} p_j \cdot \delta(z_j)$ *is a distribution over zones in* G *such that for* $j = 1, \dots, n$ *we have* $z_j = (l_1^j, l_2^j, \psi_j)$ *and* $p_j = p_1^j \cdot p_2^j$*, where:*
$p_1^j = \sum_{B_1^j \in 2^{\mathsf{X}}} \{\!|\ \mathsf{prob}(l_1, a)(B_1^j, l_1^j) \colon \exists B_2 \in 2^{\mathsf{X}} \text{ s.t. } \psi \Rightarrow \mathsf{prec}_a(l_1, l_2, B_1^j, B_2, z_j)\ |\!\}$;
$p_2^j = \sum_{B_2^j \in 2^{\mathsf{X}}} \{\!|\ \mathsf{prob}(l_2^j, a)(B_2^j, l_2^j) \colon \exists B_1 \in 2^{\mathsf{X}} \text{ s.t. } \psi \Rightarrow \mathsf{prec}_a(l_1, l_2, B_1, B_2^j, z_j)\ |\!\}$.

We can state the soundness and completeness of relation $z \xrightarrow{a} \Delta$.

Theorem 15 (Soundness/completeness of action transitions). *Assume a zone graph in normal form* G*, a zone* $z = (l_1, l_2, \psi)$ *in* G *and an action* $a \in \mathsf{Act}$*. Then, given a mapping* $\Delta \colon \mathsf{G} \to [0, 1]$*, a zone* z' *in* G *and a probability value* $p \in [0, 1]$*, the following two facts are equivalent:*

1. $z \xrightarrow{a} \Delta$*,* $z' \in \mathsf{supp}(\Delta)$ *and* $\Delta(z') = p$*;*
2. *for an arbitrary pair of states* $(s_1, s_2) \in z$ *there are transitions* $s_1 \xrightarrow{a} \Theta_1$ *and* $s_2 \xrightarrow{a} \Theta_2$ *with* $p = \prod_{i=1,2} \sum_{s_i' \in (z')_{|_i} \cap \mathsf{supp}(\Theta_i)} \Theta_i(s_i')$.

Example 16. Assume locations l_1, l_2, l_1', l_2', a clock x and an action a such that:

- $\mathsf{inv}(l_1) = \mathsf{inv}(l_2) = \mathsf{inv}(l_1') = \mathsf{inv}(l_2') = x \geq 0$
- $\mathsf{enab}(l_1, a) = x \leq 5$ and $\mathsf{enab}(l_2, a) = x \leq 4$
- $\mathsf{prob}(l_1, a) = \frac{1}{3}\delta((\{x\}, l_1')) + \frac{2}{3}\delta((\emptyset, l_1'))$, $\mathsf{prob}(l_2, a) = \frac{1}{2}\delta((\{x\}, l_2')) + \frac{1}{2}\delta((\emptyset, l_2'))$.

Let G be a zone graph in normal form and $z_i \in \mathsf{G}$, for $i \in [0, 5]$, zones with $z_0 = (l_1, l_2, \psi_0)$ and $z_j = (l_1', l_2', \psi_j)$ for $j = 1, \dots, 5$, where:

$\psi_0 \equiv x \in (0, 2] \wedge \overline{x} \in (0, 3]$ $\qquad$ $\psi_1 \equiv x = 0 \wedge \overline{x} = 0$
$\psi_2 \equiv x = 0 \wedge \overline{x} \in (0, 4]$ $\qquad$ $\psi_3 \equiv x \in (0, 5] \wedge \overline{x} = 0$
$\psi_4 \equiv x \in (0, 5] \wedge \overline{x} \in (0, 4]$ $\qquad$ $\psi_5 \equiv \neg(\psi_1 \vee \psi_2 \vee \psi_3 \vee \psi_4) \wedge x \geq 0 \wedge \overline{x} \geq 0$.

We have $z \xrightarrow{a} \Delta$, with $\Delta = {}^1\!/_6 \cdot \delta(z_1) + {}^1\!/_6 \cdot \delta(z_2) + {}^1\!/_3 \cdot \delta(z_3) + {}^1\!/_3 \cdot \delta(z_4)$.

We can state now that $z \xrightarrow{a} \Delta$ is computable.

Proposition 17. *Given a graph* G *in normal form, a zone* z *in* G *and* $a \in \mathsf{Act}$*, the distribution* Δ *with* $z \xrightarrow{a} \Delta$ *is computable in exponential time on* $|A|$*.*

As regards timed transitions, we want to have $z \rightarrow \delta(z')$ if and only if, given *an arbitrary* pair of states (s_1, s_2) in z, s_1 and s_2 can perform the *same* (i.e. equally labelled) timed transition taking to a pair of states in z'. We say that this is the requirement of *soundness and completeness of timed transitions over zones w.r.t. transitions over states.*

Note that the arbitrarity of the choice of (s_1, s_2) from z requires that from *all* pairs of states in z, the *same* zone z' is reached: for any pairs of states (s_1, s_2) and (s_1', s_2') in z with $s_i = (l_i, v_i)$ and $s_i' = (l_i, v_i')$ and zone $z' = (l_1', l_2', \psi')$, either both $v_1 \uplus \overline{v_2}$ and $v_1' \uplus \overline{v_2'}$ satisfy $\mathsf{prec}(z')$, or none of them does. Again, we need a zone graph in normal form.

Definition 18 (Timed transition over regions). *Assume a zone graph in normal form* G *and zones* $z = (l_1, l_2, \psi)$ *and* $z' = (l'_1, l'_2, \psi')$ *in* G. *We write*

$$z \longrightarrow \delta(z')$$

if $l'_1 = l_1$, $l'_2 = l_2$ *and* $\psi \Rightarrow \mathsf{prec}(z')$.

Theorem 19 (Soundness/completeness of timed transitions). *Assume a zone graph in normal form* G *and zones* $z = (l_1, l_2, \psi)$ *and* $z' = (l'_1, l'_2, \psi')$ *in* G *with* $l'_1 = l_1$ *and* $l'_2 = l_2$. *The following facts are equivalent:*

1. $z \longrightarrow \delta(z')$;
2. *for an arbitrary pair of states* $(s_1, s_2) \in z$ *there are timed transition* $s_1 \xrightarrow{t} \delta(s'_1)$ *and* $s_2 \xrightarrow{t} \delta(s'_2)$ *for some* $t \geq 0$ *such that* $(s'_1, s'_2) \in z'$.

Proposition 20 *For a zone graph* G *in normal form and region* z *in* G, *then the set of zones* z' *with* $z \longrightarrow \delta(z')$ *is computable in exponential time on* $|A|$.

4 Computing n-Bisimilarity Metric

In this section we give our algorithm computing $\mathbf{b}^n$ for the states in a PTS $\mathcal{L}_A$ induced by a PTA A. We start with the notion of zone graph with distance, as a zone graph G equipped with a function $d_{\mathsf{G}} \colon \mathsf{G} \to [0,1] \cap \mathbb{Q}$ representing that the "candidate" distance between *all* pairs of states in a zone z is $d_{\mathsf{G}}(z)$.

Definition 21 (Zone graph with distance). *A* zone graph with distance *is a pair* $\mathsf{DG} = (\mathsf{G}, d_{\mathsf{G}})$, *with* G *a zone graph and* d_{G} *a function* $d_{\mathsf{G}} \colon \mathsf{G} \to [0,1] \cap \mathbb{Q}$.

A zone graph with distance $(\mathsf{G}, d_{\mathsf{G}})$ induces the distance over states $\mathbf{b}_{\mathsf{G}} \colon \mathcal{S} \times \mathcal{S} \to [0,1]$ defined by $\mathbf{b}_{\mathsf{G}}(s_1, s_2) = d_{\mathsf{G}}(z)$ whenever $(s_1, s_2) \in z$ and $z \in \mathsf{G}$. Since for each pair of states (s_1, s_2) there is exactly one zone z with $(s_1, s_2) \in z$ (requirements 1-2 in Definition 10), we are sure that $\mathbf{b}_{\mathsf{G}}$ is a well-defined function.

In order to compute $\mathbf{b}^n$ we will construct a zone graph with distance $(\mathsf{G}, d_{\mathsf{G}})$ whose induced distance $\mathbf{b}_{\mathsf{G}}$ coincides with $\mathbf{b}^n$. This construction is given in function Main in Fig. 1, where the graphs for $\mathbf{b}^0, \mathbf{b}^1, \ldots$ are constructed inductively.

The zone graph with distance $(\mathsf{G}, d_{\mathsf{G}})$ for $\mathbf{b}^0$ is defined at lines 1–2 of Main and has precisely one zone (l_1, l_2, ψ) for each pair of locations (l_1, l_2). Note that in order to respect the constraints in the definition of zone graph (Definition 10), we impose $\psi \equiv \mathsf{X} \geq 0 \wedge \mathsf{inv}(l_1) \wedge \overline{\mathsf{X}} \geq 0 \wedge \overline{\mathsf{inv}(l_2)}$. Then, we set $d_{\mathsf{G}}(z) = 0$ for all zones z in G, which gives $\mathbf{b}_{\mathsf{G}}(s_1, s_2) = 0 = \mathbf{b}^0(s_1, s_2)$ for all states s_1, s_2.

As regards $\mathbf{b}^1$, since $\mathbf{b}^1(s_1, s_2) = 0$ for all states s_1, s_2 that perform the same (action and timed) transitions, and $\mathbf{b}^1(s_1, s_2) = 1$ for all s_1, s_2 that do not satisfy this property, we "split" any zone in G in a zone containing the pairs of states that perform the same transitions and a zone containing the other pairs. The distance d_{G} on this last zone is set to 1. The splitting is done by means of functions $\mathsf{Action\_Update}$ and $\mathsf{Timed\_Update}$, called at lines 4 and 5 of Main and dealing with action transitions and timed transitions, respectively.

For $n \geq 2$ we reason inductively. At lines 9–13 of Main we derive the d_{G} for $\mathbf{b}^n$ from that for $\mathbf{b}^{n-1}$. In detail, we introduce the *Kantorovich distance over zones* $\mathbf{K}_{\mathsf{G}}$ (Definition 25) and prove that, given transitions $s_i \xrightarrow{a} \Theta_i$, $i = 1, 2$, computing $\mathbf{K}(\mathbf{b}_{\mathsf{G}})(\Theta_1, \Theta_2)$ is equivalent to computing $\mathbf{K}_{\mathsf{G}}(\Delta)$ for the distribution Δ with $z \xrightarrow{a} \Delta$ in bijection with $s_i \xrightarrow{a} \Theta_i$ according to Theorem 15. Then, since by Theorem 19 any pair of transitions $s_i \xrightarrow{t} \delta(s_i')$, $i = 1, 2$, is in bijection with a transition over zones $z \rightarrow \delta(z')$ with $(s_1', s_2') \in z'$, we conclude that $\mathbf{b}^n(s_1, s_2) = \mathbf{B}(d_{\mathsf{G}})(s_1, s_2)$ is $\max\{\max_{a \in \mathbf{A}}\{\mathbf{K}_{\mathsf{G}}(\Delta) \mid z \xrightarrow{a} \Delta\}, \max\{d_{\mathsf{G}}(z') \mid z \rightarrow z'\}\}$ whenever $s_1 \xrightarrow{\alpha}$ iff $s_2 \xrightarrow{\alpha}$ for all $\alpha \in \mathbf{A} \cup \{\mathbb{R}^{\geq 0}\}$, and $\mathbf{b}^n(s_1, s_2) = 1$ otherwise. In this last case $d_{\mathsf{G}}(s_1, s_2)$ was already set to 1 for the d_{G} for $\mathbf{b}^1$.

4.1 Action Transitions

Function Action_Update in Fig. 1 works on a zone graph with distance $(\mathsf{G}, d_{\mathsf{G}})$ and sets to 1 the distance between all pair of states (s_1, s_2) such that one of them can make an *action* transition that cannot be mimicked by the other. Each zone z is split into z_1, z_2, z_3, z_4, where: (i) z_1 contains the pairs (s_1, s_2) s.t. only s_1 can perform a, (ii) z_2 contains the pairs (s_1, s_2) s.t. only s_2 can perform a, (iii) z_3 contains the pairs (s_1, s_2) s.t. both s_1 and s_2 can perform a, (iv) z_4 contains the pairs (s_1, s_2) s.t. neither s_1 nor s_2 can perform a. Both $d_{\mathsf{G}}(z_1)$ and $d_{\mathsf{G}}(z_2)$ are set to 1, whereas $d_{\mathsf{G}}(z_3)$ and $d_{\mathsf{G}}(z_4)$ are not updated. The splitting does not break the requirements in the definition of zone graph for G. In detail, with reference to Definition 10, requirements 1, 2a, 2b, 2c are guaranteed, resp., by: (i) $\bigvee_{i=1}^{4} \psi_i^a \equiv \mathsf{true}$, (ii) $\psi_i^a \wedge \psi_j^a \equiv \mathsf{false}$ for $i \neq j$, (iii) either $(\psi_i^a)_{|_{1}} \equiv (\psi_j^a)_{|_{1}}$ or $(\psi_i^a)_{|_{1}} \wedge (\psi_j^a)_{|_{1}} \equiv \mathsf{false}$ for $i \neq j$, (iv) either $(\psi_i^a)_{|_{2}} \equiv (\psi_j^a)_{|_{2}}$ or $(\psi_i^a)_{|_{2}} \wedge (\psi_j^a)_{|_{2}} \equiv \mathsf{false}$ for $i \neq j$.

Theorem 22. *Assume a zone graph with distance* $(\mathsf{G}, d_{\mathsf{G}})$*. Then,* $(\mathsf{G}', d_{\mathsf{G}'}) =$ Action_Update$(\mathsf{G}, d_{\mathsf{G}})$ *is a zone graph with distance computed in exponential time on* $|A|$*. Moreover, for arbitrary states* s_1, s_2*, either* $\mathbf{b}_{\mathsf{G}'}(s_1, s_2) = \mathbf{b}_{\mathsf{G}}(s_1, s_2)$*, if* $s_1 \xrightarrow{a}$ *if and only if* $s_2 \xrightarrow{a}$ *holds for all* $a \in \mathsf{Act}$*, or* $\mathbf{b}_{\mathsf{G}'}(s_1, s_2) = 1$*, otherwise.*

4.2 Timed Transitions

Function Timed_Update in Fig. 1 works on a zone graph with distance $(\mathsf{G}, d_{\mathsf{G}})$ and sets to 1 the distance between all pairs of states (s_1, s_2) such that one of them can make a *timed* transition that cannot be mimicked by the other. For any zone $(l_1, l_2, \psi) \in \mathsf{G}$, the clock constraint ψ' defined in line 5 expresses the valuations v_1 and v_2 such that, if we take the states (l_1, v_1) and (l_2, v_2), by waiting t units of time for a suitable real t, the states $(l_1, v_1 + t)$ and $(l_2, v_2 + t)$ are reached and either $v_1 + t$ breaks $\mathsf{inv}(l_1)$, as expressed by formula ψ_2 introduced in line 4, or $v_2 + t$ breaks $\mathsf{inv}(l_2)$, as expressed by ψ_1 in line 3. Therefore, only one among (l_1, v_1) and (l_2, v_2) can perform a timed transition labelled t. Coherently, the distance between (l_1, v_1) and (l_2, v_2) is set to 1 in line 6. It can be proved that ψ' can be mapped to some clock constraint in exponential time. By replacing

Algorithm 1: The function $\mathsf{Action\_Update}$.

$\mathsf{Action\_Update}((\mathsf{G}, d_\mathsf{G})$: zone graph with distance): zone graph with distance

foreach $a \in \mathsf{Act}$ **do**
  foreach $z = (l_1, l_2, \psi) \in \mathsf{G}$ **do**
    $\psi_1^a = \mathsf{enab}(l_1, a) \wedge \neg\overline{\mathsf{enab}(l_2, a)}$; $z_1 = (l_1, l_2, \psi \wedge \psi_1^a)$;
    $\psi_2^a = \neg\mathsf{enab}(l_1, a) \wedge \overline{\mathsf{enab}(l_2, a)}$; $z_2 = (l_1, l_2, \psi \wedge \psi_2^a)$;
    $\psi_3^a = \mathsf{enab}(l_1, a) \wedge \overline{\mathsf{enab}(l_2, a)}$; $z_3 = (l_1, l_2, \psi \wedge \psi_3^a)$;
    $\psi_4^a = \neg\mathsf{enab}(l_1, a) \wedge \neg\overline{\mathsf{enab}(l_2, a)}$; $z_4 = (l_1, l_2, \psi \wedge \psi_4^a)$;
    $\mathsf{G} = \mathsf{G} \setminus \{z\} \cup \{z_1, z_2, z_3, z_4\}$;
    $d_\mathsf{G} := d_\mathsf{G} \setminus \{(z, d_\mathsf{G}(z))\} \cup \{(z_1, 1), (z_2, 1), (z_3, d_\mathsf{G}(z)), (z_4, d_\mathsf{G}(z))\}$;

return $(\mathsf{G}, d_\mathsf{G})$;

Algorithm 2: The function $\mathsf{Timed\_Update}$.

$\mathsf{Timed\_Update}((\mathsf{G}, d_\mathsf{G})$: zone graph with distance): zone graph with distance

foreach $(l_1, l_2, \psi) \in \mathsf{G}$ **do**
  $\mathsf{G} := \mathsf{G} \setminus \{(l_1, l_2, \psi)\}$; $d_\mathsf{G} := d_\mathsf{G} \setminus \{((l_1, l_2, \psi), d_\mathsf{G}(l_1, l_2, \psi))\}$;
  $\psi_1 := (\forall t' \in [0, t].\mathsf{inv}(l_1)[\mathsf{X} := \mathsf{X} + t']) \wedge (\neg\,\mathsf{inv}(l_2)[\overline{\mathsf{X}} := \overline{\mathsf{X}} + t])$;
  $\psi_2 := (\neg\,\mathsf{inv}(l_1)[\mathsf{X} := \mathsf{X} + t]) \wedge (\forall t' \in [0, t].\mathsf{inv}(l_2)[\overline{\mathsf{X}} := \overline{\mathsf{X}} + t'])$;
  $\psi' := \exists t \geq 0. (\psi_1 \vee \psi_2)$;
  $\mathsf{G} := \mathsf{G} \cup \{(l_1, l_2, \psi \wedge \psi')\}$; $d_\mathsf{G} := d_\mathsf{G} \cup \{((l_1, l_2, \psi \wedge \psi'), 1)\}$;
  $\mathsf{G} := \mathsf{G} \cup \{(l_1, l_2, \psi \wedge \neg\psi')\}$; $d_\mathsf{G} := d_\mathsf{G} \cup \{((l_1, l_2, \psi \wedge \neg\psi'), d_\mathsf{G}(l_1, l_2, \psi))\}$;
  foreach $(l_1', l_2', \psi'') \in \mathsf{G}$ *with* $l_i = l_i'$ *and* $(\psi)_{|_i} \equiv (\psi'')_{|_i}$ *and* $i = 1, 2$ **do**
    $\mathsf{G} := (\mathsf{G} \setminus \{(l_1', l_2', \psi'')\}) \cup \{(l_1', l_2', \psi'' \wedge \psi'), (l_1', l_2', \psi'' \wedge \neg\psi')\}$;
    $d_\mathsf{G} := (d_\mathsf{G} \setminus \{((l_1', l_2', \psi''), d_\mathsf{G}(l_1', l_2', \psi''))\}) \cup$
     $\{((l_1', l_2', \psi'' \wedge \psi'), d_\mathsf{G}(l_1', l_2', \psi'')), ((l_1', l_2', \psi'' \wedge \neg\psi'), d_\mathsf{G}(l_1', l_2', \psi''))\}$;

return $(\mathsf{G}, d_\mathsf{G})$;

Algorithm 3: The function Main.

$\mathsf{Main}(n : \mathbb{N})$: Zone graph with distance

$\mathsf{G} := \bigcup_{l_1, l_2 \in \mathsf{L}} (l_1, l_2, \mathsf{X} \geq 0 \wedge \mathsf{inv}(l_1) \wedge \overline{\mathsf{X}} \geq 0 \wedge \overline{\mathsf{inv}(l_2)})$;
$d_\mathsf{G} := \{(z, 0) : z \in \mathsf{G}\}$;
if $n \geq 1$ **then**
  $(\mathsf{G}, d_\mathsf{G}) := \mathsf{Action\_Update}(\mathsf{G}, d_\mathsf{G})$;
  $(\mathsf{G}_{\mathsf{new}}, d_{\mathsf{G}_{\mathsf{new}}}) := \mathsf{Timed\_Update}(\mathsf{G}, d_\mathsf{G})$;
  $\mathsf{G} := \mathsf{NF}(\mathsf{G}_{\mathsf{new}})$;
  $d_\mathsf{G} = \bigcup_{z \in \mathsf{G}} \{(z, d_{\mathsf{G}_{\mathsf{new}}}(z')) : z' \in \mathsf{G}_{\mathsf{new}}$ and $z' \implies z$ (see Notation 3)$\}$;
  foreach $i := 2$ *to* n **do**
    $\mathsf{G}_{\mathsf{new}} := \mathsf{G}$;
    foreach $z \in \mathsf{G}_{\mathsf{new}}$ *(assuming* $\max \emptyset = 0$*)* **do**
      $\epsilon := \max_{a \in \mathsf{Act}} \{\mathbf{K}_\mathsf{G}(\Delta) : z \xrightarrow{a} \Delta\}$; $\epsilon' := \max\{d_\mathsf{G}(z') : z \longrightarrow \delta(z')\}$;
      $d_{\mathsf{G}_{\mathsf{new}}} := d_{\mathsf{G}_{\mathsf{new}}} \cup \{(z, \max(d_\mathsf{G}(z), \epsilon, \epsilon'))\}$;
    $(\mathsf{G}, d_\mathsf{G}) := (\mathsf{G}_{\mathsf{new}}, d_{\mathsf{G}_{\mathsf{new}}})$;

return $(\mathsf{G}, d_\mathsf{G})$;

Fig. 1. The functions $\mathsf{Action\_Update}$, $\mathsf{Timed\_Update}$ and Main.

(l_1, l_2, ψ) in G with $(l_1, l_2, \psi \wedge \psi')$ and $(l_1, l_2, \psi \wedge \neg\psi')$, requirements 1 and 2a in the definition of zone graph Definition 10 are not broken. Since we may break requirements 2b and 2c, we use operations in lines 8–10 to restore them.

Example 23. Assume a zone graph $(\mathsf{G}, d_\mathsf{G})$, locations $l_1, l_2 \in \mathsf{L}$ with invariant $\mathsf{inv}(l_1) = \mathsf{inv}(l_2) = x \in [0,3]$ and zone $z = (l_1, l_2, \psi)$, with $\psi = x \in [0,3] \wedge \overline{x} \in [0,3]$ and $d_\mathsf{G}(z) = \epsilon < 1$. Two states $s_1 = (l_1, v_1)$ and $s_2 = (l_2, v_2)$ with $v_1 \uplus \overline{v_2} \models \psi$ perform the same timed transitions only if $v_1(x) = \overline{v_2}(\overline{x})$. If $v_1(x) \neq \overline{v_2}(\overline{x})$ then the distance between s_1 and s_2 should be set to 1. We explain how this is done by $\mathsf{Timed\_Update}$. First we take formula ψ_1 in line 3 of $\mathsf{Timed\_Update}$ and we note that it is equivalent to $\psi_1' = (t < 0 \vee (x \geq 0 \wedge x + t \leq 3)) \wedge \overline{x} + t \notin [0,3]$. Hence $\exists t \geq 0.\, \psi_1 \equiv \psi_1'' = \exists t \geq 0.(x \geq 0 \wedge x + t \leq 3 \wedge \overline{x} + t \notin [0,3])$. Analogously, for ψ_2 at line 4 we get $\exists t \geq 0.\, \psi_2 \equiv \psi_2'' = \exists t \geq 0.(\overline{x} \geq 0 \wedge \overline{x} + t \leq 3 \wedge x + t \notin [0,3])$. Hence $\psi' = \exists t \geq 0.(\psi_1 \vee \psi_2) \equiv \exists t \geq 0.\psi_1 \vee \exists t \geq 0.\psi_2 \equiv \psi_1'' \vee \psi_2''$, which equates $(x \in [0,3] \wedge \overline{x} < 0) \vee (x \in [0,3] \wedge \overline{x} > x) \vee (\overline{x} \in [0,3] \wedge x < 0) \vee (\overline{x} \in [0,3] \wedge x > \overline{x})$. Therefore, we get $\psi \wedge \psi' \equiv (x \in [0,3] \wedge \overline{x} > x) \vee (\overline{x} \in [0,3] \wedge x > \overline{x})$. Therefore, the effect of $\mathsf{Timed\_Update}$ is to set to 1 the distance between all pairs $(l_1, v_1), (l_2, v_2)$ where either $v_1 \models \mathsf{inv}(l_1)$ and $\overline{v_2}(\overline{x}) > v_1(x)$ or $v_2 \models \mathsf{inv}(l_2)$ and $v_1(x) > \overline{v_2}(\overline{x})$.

Theorem 24. *Assume a zone graph with distance* $(\mathsf{G}, d_\mathsf{G})$*. Then,* $(\mathsf{G}', d_{\mathsf{G}'}) = \mathsf{Timed\_Update}(\mathsf{G}, d_\mathsf{G})$ *is a zone graph with distance computed in exponential time on* $|A|$*. Moreover, for arbitrary states* s_1, s_2*, either* $\mathbf{b}_{\mathsf{G}'}(s_1, s_2) = \mathbf{b}_\mathsf{G}(s_1, s_2)$*, if* $s_1 \xrightarrow{t}$ *if and only if* $s_2 \xrightarrow{t}$ *holds for* $t \in \mathbb{R}^{\geq 0}$*, or* $\mathbf{b}_{\mathsf{G}'}(s_1, s_2) = 1$*, otherwise.*

4.3 Computing Kantorovich Lifting

Let $(\mathsf{G}, d_\mathsf{G})$ be a zone graph with distance in normal form. We know that d_G induces the distance over states $\mathbf{b}_\mathsf{G}$ with $\mathbf{b}_\mathsf{G}(s_1, s_2) = d_\mathsf{G}(z)$ whenever $(s_1, s_2) \in z$ and $z \in \mathsf{G}$. Assume a transition $z \xrightarrow{a} \Delta$. A natural question is if the distribution over regions Δ can be exploited to calculate $\mathbf{K}(\mathbf{b}_\mathsf{G})(\Theta_1, \Theta_2)$, for Θ_1 and Θ_2 the distributions over states such that there are action transitions $s_1 \xrightarrow{a} \Theta_1$ and $s_2 \xrightarrow{a} \Theta_2$ in bijection with $z \xrightarrow{a} \Delta$ according to the result of soundness and completeness on transitions over zones (Theorem 15). Notice that calculating $\mathbf{K}(\mathbf{b}_\mathsf{G})(\Theta_1, \Theta_2)$ would allow us to infer $\mathbf{B}(\mathbf{b}_\mathsf{G})(s_1, s_2)$, namely $\mathbf{b}^{n+1}(s_1, s_2)$ if $\mathbf{b}_\mathsf{G} = \mathbf{b}^n$. Calculating $\mathbf{K}(\mathbf{b}_\mathsf{G})(\Theta_1, \Theta_2)$ requires minimizing (1) subject to (2):

$$\sum_{s_1 \in \mathsf{supp}(\Theta_1) s_2 \in \mathsf{supp}(\Theta_2)} y_{s_1, s_2} \cdot \mathbf{b}_\mathsf{G}(s_1, s_2) \tag{1}$$

$$\sum_{s_2 \in \mathsf{supp}(\Theta_1)} y_{s_1, s_2} = \Theta_1(s_1) \text{ and } \sum_{s_1 \in \mathsf{supp}(\Theta_1)} y_{s_1, s_2} = \Theta_2(s_2) \text{ and } y_{s_1, s_2} \geq 0. \tag{2}$$

We will show that this is equivalent to the following problem.

Definition 25 (Kantorovich lifting for distances on zones). *Given a zone graph with distance in normal form* $(\mathsf{G}, d_{\mathsf{G}})$, *the* Kantorovich lifting $\mathbf{K}_{\mathsf{G}}$ *of* d_{G} *to a distribution over zones* Δ *is defined by:*

$$\mathbf{K}_{\mathsf{G}}(\Delta) = \sum_{z \in \mathsf{supp}(\Delta)} \omega_z \cdot d_{\mathsf{G}}(z)$$

where ω_z *is the solution for variable* y_z *of the following problem:*
<u>*minimize*</u> $\sum_{z \in \mathsf{supp}(\Delta)} y_z \cdot d_{\mathsf{G}}(z)$
<u>*subject to:*</u> $\forall z \in \mathsf{G} : \sum_{z' \in \mathsf{supp}(\Delta) \text{ s.t. } (z')_{|_1} \equiv (z)_{|_1}} y_{z'} = \sum_{z' \in \mathsf{supp}(\Delta) \text{ s.t. } (z')_{|_1} \equiv (z)_{|_1}} \Delta(z')$
$\forall z \in \mathsf{G} : \sum_{z' \in \mathsf{supp}(\Delta) \text{ s.t. } (z')_{|_2} \equiv (z)_{|_2}} y_{z'} = \sum_{z' \in \mathsf{supp}(\Delta) \text{ s.t. } (z')_{|_2} \equiv (z)_{|_2}} \Delta(z')$
$\forall z \in \mathsf{G} : y_z \geq 0.$

In order to show the equivalence between the two problems, it is enough to show that from any set of values y_z satisfying the constraints in Definition 25 we can derive values y_{s_1,s_2} satisfying (2), and conversely. To this purpose, for a zone $z \in \mathsf{supp}(\Delta)$ and $i = 1, 2$, let S^i_z denote the set of states $S^i_z = \mathsf{supp}(\Theta_i) \cap (z)_{|_i}$. By the definition of zone graph (Definition 10), for $z, z' \in \mathsf{supp}(\Delta)$ we have $S^i_z \cap S^i_{z'} \neq \emptyset$ only if $(z)_{|_i} \equiv (z')_{|_i}$, thus implying $S^i_z = S^i_{z'}$ in that case. As a preliminary step, we show that for any $i = 1, 2$ and zone $z \in \mathsf{supp}(\Delta)$ we have

$$s \in S^i_z \text{ implies } \sum_{s' \in S^i_z} \Theta_i(s') = \sum_{\{z' \,:\, s \in S^i_{z'}\}} \Delta(z') \tag{3}$$

We show case $i = 1$ of (3). Since $s \in S^i_z$ and $S^i_z = S^i_{z'}$ when $S^i_z \cap S^i_{z'} \neq \emptyset$, we get $\sum_{\{z' : s \in S^1_{z'}\}} \Delta(z') = \sum_{\{z' : S^1_{z'} = S^1_z\}} \Delta(z') = \sum_{\{z' : S^1_{z'} = S^1_z\}} \sum_{s_1 \in S^1_z} \sum_{s_2 \in S^2_{z'}} \Theta_1(s_1) \cdot \Theta_2(s_2) = \sum_{s_1 \in S^1_z} \sum_{s_2 \in \mathsf{supp}(\Theta_2)} \Theta_1(s_1) \cdot \Theta_2(s_2) = \sum_{s_1 \in S^1_z} \Theta_1(s_1)$.

Let us start with deriving the y_{s_1,s_2}'s from the y_z's. For all zones $z \in \mathsf{supp}(\Delta)$ and states $s_1 \in S^1_z$, $s_2 \in S^2_z$, we define the value $y_{s_1,s_2} = y_z \cdot \frac{\Theta_1(s_1) \cdot \Theta_2(s_2)}{\Delta(z)}$. For all $s_1 \in \mathsf{supp}(\Theta_1)$, let $\hat{z}$ be an arbitrary zone with $s_1 \in S^1_{\hat{z}}$. We have:

$$\begin{aligned}
&\textstyle\sum_{s_2 \in \mathsf{supp}(\Theta_2)} y_{s_1,s_2} \\
&= \textstyle\sum_{\{z :\, s_1 \in S^1_z\}} \sum_{s_2 \in S^2_z} y_z \cdot \frac{\Theta_1(s_1) \cdot \Theta_2(s_2)}{\Delta(z)} \\
&= \Theta_1(s_1) \cdot \textstyle\sum_{\{z :\, s_1 \in S^1_z\}} \frac{y_z}{\Delta(z)} \sum_{s_2 \in S^2_z} \Theta_2(s_2) \\
&= \Theta_1(s_1) \cdot \textstyle\sum_{\{z :\, s_1 \in S^1_z\}} \frac{y_z}{\sum_{s \in S^1_z} \Theta_1(s)} && \text{(by } \Delta(z) = \textstyle\prod_{i=1,2} \sum_{s \in S^i_z} \Theta_i(s_i)) \\
&= \Theta_1(s_1) \cdot \frac{1}{\sum_{s \in S^1_{\hat{z}}} \Theta_1(s)} \textstyle\sum_{\{z :\, s_1 \in S^1_z\}} y_z && \text{(by } S^1_{\hat{z}} = S^1_{z'} \text{ when } s_1 \in S^1_{\hat{z}} \cap S^1_{z'}) \\
&= \Theta_1(s_1) \frac{1}{\sum_{\{z :\, s_1 \in S^1_z\}} \Delta(z)} \textstyle\sum_{\{z :\, s_1 \in S^1_z\}} \Delta(z) && \text{(by (3) and constraints in Def. 25)} \\
&= \Theta_1(s_1).
\end{aligned}$$

The symmetric case is analogous, which confirms that the y_{s_1,s_2}'s respect (2).

Now we show that by starting with y_{s_1,s_2}'s respecting (2) we can derive y_z's satisfying Definition 25. We take $y_z = \sum_{s_1 \in S^1_z, s_2 \in S^2_z} y_{s_1,s_2}$. For $z \in \mathsf{G}$ we have:

$$
\begin{aligned}
&\textstyle\sum_{\substack{z'\in\mathsf{supp}(\Delta):\\ (z)_{|1}\equiv(z')_{|1}}} y_{z'}\\
&= \textstyle\sum_{\substack{z'\in\mathsf{supp}(\Delta):\\ (z)_{|1}\equiv(z')_{|1}}} \sum_{\substack{s_1\in S^1_{z'},\\ s_2\in S^2_{z'}}} y_{s_1,s_2}\\
&= \textstyle\sum_{s_1\in S^1_z} \sum_{\substack{z'\in\mathsf{supp}(\Delta):\\ (z)_{|1}=(z')_{|1}}} \sum_{s_2\in S^2_{z'}} y_{s_1,s_2} && \text{(by } S^1_z = S^1_{z'} \text{ if } (z)_{|1} \equiv (z')_{|1})\\
&= \textstyle\sum_{s_1\in S^1_z} \sum_{s_2\in\mathsf{supp}(\Theta_2)} y_{s_1,s_2}\\
&= \textstyle\sum_{s_1\in S^1_z} \Theta_1(s_1) && \text{(being } \Theta_2 \text{ a distribution)}\\
&= \textstyle\sum_{\substack{z'\in\mathsf{supp}(\Delta)\\ (z)_{|1}\equiv(z')_{|1}}} \Delta(z') && \text{(by (3))}
\end{aligned}
$$

the symmetric case being analogous, which confirms that the y_z's satisfy the constraints in Definition 25. The following result follows.

Theorem 26 (Equivalence of Kantorovich liftings). *Assume a zone graph with distance in normal form* $(\mathsf{G}, d_\mathsf{G})$, *a transition over zones* $z \xrightarrow{a} \Delta$ *and transitions* $s_1 \xrightarrow{a} \Theta_1$, $s_2 \xrightarrow{a} \Theta_2$ *in bijection according to Theorem 15. Then:*

$$\mathbf{K}(\mathbf{b}_\mathsf{G})(\Theta_1, \Theta_2) = \mathbf{K}_\mathsf{G}(\Delta) \in \mathbb{Q}.^{1}$$

Example 27. Consider the zones $z_1, \ldots z_4$ and the distribution Δ in Example 16. Assume that for $i = 1, \ldots, 4$ we have $d_\mathsf{G}(z_i) = \epsilon_i$, with $0 \leq \epsilon_i \leq 1$. We have $\mathbf{K}_\mathsf{G}(\Delta) = \sum_{i=1}^{4} \omega_{z_i} \cdot \epsilon_i$, where ω_{z_i} is the solution for y_{z_i} of the following problem: <u>*minimize*</u> $\sum_{i\in[1,4]} y_{z_i} \cdot \epsilon_i$ <u>*subject to*</u>:
$y_{z_1} + y_{z_2} = 1/6 + 1/6 = 1/3 \quad y_{z_3} + y_{z_4} = 1/3 + 1/3 = 2/3$
$y_{z_1} + y_{z_3} = 1/6 + 1/3 = 1/2 \quad y_{z_2} + y_{z_4} = 1/6 + 1/3 = 1/2 \quad \forall i \in [1, 4] \colon y_{z_i} \geq 0.$
Constraint $y_{z_1} + y_{z_2} = 1/6 + 1/6$ is motivated by $(z_1)_{|1} = x \in (0, 2] = (z_2)_{|1}$ and derives from $\Delta(z_1) = \frac{1}{6} = \Delta(z_2)$. The other constraints are analogous.

Since the number of variables in $\mathbf{K}_\mathsf{G}(\Delta)$ is equal to the cardinality of G, which is exponential on $|A|$, and Kantorovich problem is polynomial [27], we conclude that our algorithm is exponential on $|A|$.

Theorem 28 (Computing Kantorovich lifting). *Assume a zone graph with distance in normal form* $(\mathsf{G}, d_\mathsf{G})$ *and a transition on zones* $z \xrightarrow{a} \Delta$. *Then,* $\mathbf{K}_\mathsf{G}(\Delta)$ *is computable in exponential time on* $|A|$.

4.4 Computing Bisimilarity Metrics

The function $\mathsf{Main}(n)$ in Fig. 1 computes $\mathbf{b}^n$, meaning that it returns a zone graph with distance $(\mathsf{G}, d_\mathsf{G})$ such that $\mathbf{b}_\mathsf{G} = \mathbf{b}^n$. The following theorem states the correctness of Main and its exponential time complexity.

Theorem 29 (Decidability of $\mathbf{b}^n$). *For each* $n \in \mathbb{N}$, *the result* $(\mathsf{G}, d_\mathsf{G})$ *returned by* $\mathsf{Main}(n)$ *is a zone graph with distance in normal form, which is computed in exponential time on* $|A|$ *and linear in the parameter* n, *which means exponential in its binary encoding. Moreover, it holds that* $\mathbf{b}_\mathsf{G} = \mathbf{b}^n$.

[1] Recall that probabilities and $d_\mathsf{G}(z)$ are rationals.

Since checking property $v_1 \uplus \overline{v_2} \models \psi$ is decidable in polynomial time in the length of constraint ψ, it is immediate that given two arbitrary states s_1, s_2 we can use $\mathsf{Main}(n)$ to get the distance $\mathbf{b}^n(s_1, s_2)$.

5 Future Work

We have considered the model of PTA in [39]. Our algorithm can be adapted to other versions proposed in the literature. E.g., the model in [42] admits nondeterminism in action transitions, namely $\mathsf{prob}\colon \mathsf{L} \times \mathsf{Act} \to 2^{\mathcal{D}(2^{\mathsf{X}} \times \mathsf{L})}$. This requires that fixed z and a there is a finite *set* of transitions $z \xrightarrow{a} \Delta$ in the zone graph. In this case it is enough to replace $\max_{a \in \mathsf{Act}}\{\mathbf{K}_{\mathsf{G}}(\Delta) \colon z \xrightarrow{a} \Delta\}$ at line 11 of Main with $\max_{a \in \mathsf{Act}} \min\{\mathbf{K}_{\mathsf{G}}(\Delta) \colon z \xrightarrow{a} \Delta\}$.

We intend to extend our results to compute the *bisimilarity metric* $\mathbf{b}$. Then, following the idea in [5], we intend to implement a more efficient on-the-fly algorithm that works when $\mathbf{b}^n$ has to be computed for a fixed pair of states. Inspired by theory developed in [41,48] and implemented in Uppaal SMC [25], $\mathbf{b}^n$ can be computed with a level of accuracy $\epsilon \in [0, 1]$ fixed a priori for a Stochastic Timed Automata [10] by discretising it in a PTA. Finally, inspired by [22,33] we intend to expand our theory to combine the distance arising from probability with the distance arising from timing characteristics.

References

1. de Alfaro, L., Faella, M., Stoelinga, M.: Linear and branching system metrics. IEEE Trans. Softw. Eng. **35**(2), 258–273 (2009)
2. de Bakker, J.W., Huizing, C., de Roever, W.P., Rozenberg, G. (eds.): REX 1991. LNCS, vol. 600. Springer, Heidelberg (1992). https://doi.org/10.1007/BFb0031984
3. Alur, R., Dill, D.L.: A theory of timed automata. Theor. Comput. Sci. **126**, 183–235 (1994)
4. Asarin, E., Basset, N., Degorre, A.: Distance on timed words and applications. In: Jansen, D.N., Prabhakar, P. (eds.) FORMATS 2018. LNCS, vol. 11022, pp. 199–214. Springer, Cham (2018). https://doi.org/10.1007/978-3-030-00151-3_12
5. Bacci, G., Bacci, G., Larsen, K.G., Mardare, R.: On-the-fly exact computation of bisimilarity distances. In: Piterman, N., Smolka, S.A. (eds.) TACAS 2013. LNCS, vol. 7795, pp. 1–15. Springer, Heidelberg (2013). https://doi.org/10.1007/978-3-642-36742-7_1
6. Bacci, G., Bacci, G., Larsen, K.G., Mardare, R.: On-the-fly computation of bisimilarity distances. Logical Methods Comput. Sci. **13**(2) (2017)
7. Bacci, G., Bacci, G., Larsen, K.G., Mardare, R.: Converging from branching to linear metrics on Markov Chains. Math. Struct. Comp. Sci. **29**(1), 3–37 (2019)
8. Bacci, G., Bacci, G., Larsen, K.G., Mardare, R., Tang, Q., van Breugel: F.: Computing probabilistic bisimilarity distances for probabilistic automata. In: CONCUR. LIPiCS, vol. 140, pp. 9:1–9:17 (2019)
9. Beauquier, D.: On probabilistic timed automata. Theor. Comput. Sci. **292**, 65–84 (2003)
10. Bertrand, N., et al.: Stochastic timed automata. Log. Meth. Comp. Sci. **10** (2014)

11. Bouyer, P.: Forward analysis of updatable timed automata. Formal Meth. Syst, Des. **24**, 281–320 (2004)
12. Bouyer, P., Dufourd, C., Fleury, E., Petit, A.: Updatable timed automata. Theoret. Comput. Sci. **321**(2–3), 291–345 (2004)
13. van Breugel, F.: On behavioural pseudometrics and closure ordinals. Inf. Process. Lett. **112**(19), 715–718 (2012)
14. van Breugel, F., Worrell, J.: A behavioural pseudometric for probabilistic transition systems. Theoret. Comput. Sci. **331**(1), 115–142 (2005)
15. van Breugel, F., Sharma, B., Worrell, J.: Approximating a behavioural pseudometric without discount. Log. Methods Comput. Sci. **4**(2) (2008)
16. van Breugel, F., Worrell, J.: Approximating and computing behavioural distances in probabilistic transition systems. Theor. Comput. Sci. **360**(1), 373–385 (2006)
17. van Breugel, F., Worrell, J.: The complexity of computing a bisimilarity pseudometric on probabilistic automata. In: van Breugel, F., Kashefi, E., Palamidessi, C., Rutten, J. (eds.) Horizons of the Mind. A Tribute to Prakash Panangaden. LNCS, vol. 8464, pp. 191–213. Springer, Cham (2014). https://doi.org/10.1007/978-3-319-06880-0_10
18. Castiglioni, V., Gebler, D., Tini, S.: Logical characterization of bisimulation metrics. In: QAPL 2016. EPTCS, vol. 227, pp. 44–62 (2016)
19. Castiglioni, V., Tini, S.: Logical characterization of branching metrics for nondeterministic probabilistic transition systems. Inf. Comput. **268** (2019)
20. Čerāns, K.: Decidability of bisimulation equivalences for parallel timer processes. In: von Bochmann, G., Probst, D.K. (eds.) CAV 1992. LNCS, vol. 663, pp. 302–315. Springer, Heidelberg (1993). https://doi.org/10.1007/3-540-56496-9_24
21. Chatterjee, K., Ibsen-Jensen, R., Majumdar, R.: Edit distance for timed automata. In: HSCC14, pp. 303–312. ACM (2014)
22. Chatterjee, K., Prabhu, V.S.: Quantitative temporal simulation and refinement distances for timed systems. IEEE Trans. Automat. Contr. **60**(9), 2291–2306 (2015)
23. Chen, D., van Breugel, F., Worrell, J.: On the complexity of computing probabilistic bisimilarity. In: Birkedal, L. (ed.) FoSSaCS 2012. LNCS, vol. 7213, pp. 437–451. Springer, Heidelberg (2012). https://doi.org/10.1007/978-3-642-28729-9_29
24. Chen, T., Han, T., Katoen, J.: Time-abstracting bisimulation for probabilistic timed automata. In: TASE08, pp. 177–184. IEEE (2008)
25. David, A., Larsen, K.G., Legay, A., Mikučionis, M., Poulsen, D.B.: Uppaal SMC tutorial. STTT **17**(4), 397–415 (2015)
26. Deng, Y., Chothia, T., Palamidessi, C., Pang, J.: Metrics for action-labelled quantitative transition systems. QAPL. ENTCS **153**(2), 79–96 (2006)
27. Deng, Y., Du, W.: The kantorovich metric in computer science: a brief survey. QAPL. ENTCS **253**(3), 73–82 (2009)
28. Desharnais, J., Gupta, J., Jagadeesan, R., Panangaden, P.: Metrics for labelled Markov processes. Theoret. Comput. Sci. **318**(3), 323–354 (2004)
29. Dill, D.L.: Timing assumptions and verification of finite-state concurrent systems. In: Sifakis, J. (ed.) CAV 1989. LNCS, vol. 407, pp. 197–212. Springer, Heidelberg (1990). https://doi.org/10.1007/3-540-52148-8_17
30. Ferns, N., Panangaden, P., Precup, D.: Metrics for finite markov decision processes. In: UAI, pp. 162–169. AUAI Press (2004)
31. Giacalone, A., Jou, C., Smolka, S.A.: Algebraic reasoning for probabilistic concurrent systems. In: IFIP TC2 PROCOMET (1990)
32. Henzinger, T., Nicollin, X., Sifakis, J., Yovine, S.: Symbolic model checking for real-time systems. Inf. Comp. **111**(2), 193–244 (1994)

33. Henzinger, T.A., Majumdar, R., Prabhu, V.S.: Quantifying similarities between timed systems. In: Pettersson, P., Yi, W. (eds.) FORMATS 2005. LNCS, vol. 3829, pp. 226–241. Springer, Heidelberg (2005). https://doi.org/10.1007/11603009_18
34. Kwiatkowska, M., Norman, G., Segala, R., Sproston, J.: Automatic verification of real-time systems with discrete probability distributions. Theoret. Comput. Sci. **282**, 101–150 (2002)
35. Kwiatkowska, M., Norman, G.: Probabilistic metric semantics for a simple language with recursion. In: Penczek, W., Szałas, A. (eds.) MFCS 1996. LNCS, vol. 1113, pp. 419–430. Springer, Heidelberg (1996). https://doi.org/10.1007/3-540-61550-4_167
36. Lanotte, R., Maggiolo-Schettini, A., Troina, A.: Weak bisimulation for probabilistic timed automata. Theor. Comput. Sci. **411**(50), 4291–4322 (2010)
37. Larsen, K.G., Skou, A.: Bisimulation through probabilistic testing. Inf. Comput. **94**(1), 1–28 (1991)
38. Majumdar, R., Prabhu, V.S.: Computing the Skorokhod distance between polygonal traces. In: HSCC15, pp. 199–208. ACM (2015)
39. Norman, G., Parker, D., Sproston, J.: Model checking for probabilistic timed automata. Formal Methods Syst. Des. **43**, 164–190 (2013)
40. Segala, R.: Modeling and verification of randomized distributed real-time systems. Ph.D. thesis, MIT (1995)
41. Sen, K., Viswanathan, M., Agha, G.: Statistical model checking of black-box probabilistic systems. In: Alur, R., Peled, D.A. (eds.) CAV 2004. LNCS, vol. 3114, pp. 202–215. Springer, Heidelberg (2004). https://doi.org/10.1007/978-3-540-27813-9_16
42. Sproston, J., Troina, A.: Simulation and bisimulation for probabilistic timed automata. In: Chatterjee, K., Henzinger, T.A. (eds.) FORMATS 2010. LNCS, vol. 6246, pp. 213–227. Springer, Heidelberg (2010). https://doi.org/10.1007/978-3-642-15297-9_17
43. Stoelinga, M.: Alea jacta est: verification of probabilistic, real-time and parametric systems. Ph.D. thesis, University of Nijmegen, The Netherlands (2002)
44. Tang, Q., van Breugel, F.: Computing probabilistic bisimilarity distances via policy iteration. In: CONCUR, pp. 22:1–22:15. LIPIcs (2016)
45. Tang, Q., van Breugel, F.: Algorithms to compute probabilistic bisimilarity distances for Labelled Markov Chains. In: CONCUR, pp. 27:1–27:16. LIPiCS (2017)
46. TaŞiran, S., Alur, R., Kurshan, R.P., Brayton, R.K.: Verifying abstractions of timed systems. In: Montanari, U., Sassone, V. (eds.) CONCUR 1996. LNCS, vol. 1119, pp. 546–562. Springer, Heidelberg (1996). https://doi.org/10.1007/3-540-61604-7_75
47. Yamane, S.: Probabilistic timed simulation verification and its application to stepwise refinement of real-time systems. In: Saraswat, V.A. (ed.) ASIAN 2003. LNCS, vol. 2896, pp. 276–290. Springer, Heidelberg (2003). https://doi.org/10.1007/978-3-540-40965-6_18
48. Younes, H.L.S.: Verification and planning for stochastic processes with asynchronous events. Ph.D. thesis, Pittsburgh, PA, USA (2004)
49. Yovine, S.: Model checking timed automata. In: Rozenberg, G., Vaandrager, F.W. (eds.) EEF School 1996. LNCS, vol. 1494, pp. 114–152. Springer, Heidelberg (1998). https://doi.org/10.1007/3-540-65193-4_20

Sound Probabilistic Numerical Error Analysis

Debasmita Lohar[1(✉)], Milos Prokop[2], and Eva Darulova[1]

[1] MPI-SWS, Saarland Informatics Campus, Saarbrücken, Germany
{dlohar,eva}@mpi-sws.org
[2] University of Edinburgh, Edinburgh, UK
m.prokop@sms.ed.ac.uk

Abstract. Numerical software uses floating-point arithmetic to implement real-valued algorithms which inevitably introduces roundoff errors. Additionally, in an effort to reduce energy consumption, approximate hardware introduces further errors. As errors are propagated through a computation, the result of the approximated floating-point program can be vastly different from the real-valued ideal one. Previous work on soundly bounding (roundoff) errors has focused on worst-case absolute error analysis. However, not all inputs and not all errors are equally likely such that these methods can lead to overly pessimistic error bounds.

In this paper, we present a sound probabilistic static analysis which takes into account the probability distributions of inputs and propagates roundoff and approximation errors probabilistically through the program. We observe that the computed probability distributions of errors are hard to interpret, and propose an alternative metric and computation of refined error bounds which are valid with some probability.

Keywords: Probabilistic analysis · Floating-point · Approximate computing

1 Introduction

Many programs compute only approximate results; sometimes because exact solutions do not exist, or because resource constraints mandate using a cheaper and inexact algorithm or hardware. Approximations can thus increase the efficiency of a program, but they also introduce errors. Many applications are designed to be robust to some noise and tolerate errors—as long as they remain within some acceptable bounds. However, automatically determining how individual approximation errors influence overall program accuracy remains a challenge.

Finite precision, which efficiently approximates real-valued arithmetic, is widely used across a variety of domains from embedded systems to machine learning applications. Verification of the roundoff errors that finite-precision introduces has thus attracted significant interest in the recent past [8,11,15,19,31].

D. Lohar—The author is supported by DFG grant DA 1898/2-1.

W. Ahrendt and S. L. Tapia Tarifa (Eds.): IFM 2019, LNCS 11918, pp. 322–340, 2019.
https://doi.org/10.1007/978-3-030-34968-4_18

These tools compute *worst-case* absolute error bounds fully automatically. Such bounds, however, may often be pessimistic. They may not be achieved in practice and furthermore many applications are tolerant to somewhat larger, but infrequent, errors (e.g. control systems, where one feedback iteration compensates for a larger error of a previous one). In order to capture such differentiated behaviour, we need to compute the *probability* of certain error bounds.

Such an analysis is even more relevant with advances in approximate computing [33], which introduces approximate architectures and storage. These hardware components are more resource efficient but often have probabilistic error behaviours: operations return a large error with a certain probability.

While techniques [5,6,20,21,25,26,28] exist which track or compute probability distributions, they do not consider and support reasoning about *errors* due to finite-precision arithmetic or approximate computing, or they only compute coarse-grained error estimates, instead of error probability distributions [22].

In this paper, we present a sound probabilistic error analysis for numerical kernels which computes uncertain distributions of errors, which soundly overapproximate all possible distributions. Our analysis extends the abstract domain of probabilistic affine forms [4] for error analysis, and combines it with a novel probabilistic version of interval subdivision to obtain both an efficient analysis, as well as useful accuracy.

We instantiate our analysis to track two kinds of errors. First, we consider standard floating-point arithmetic, where inputs are distributed according to a user-given distribution. Since roundoff errors depend on the values' magnitudes, we effectively obtain a probability distribution of errors, even though the error of each individual operation is still specified as worst-case. Secondly, inspired by approximate hardware specifications, in addition to probabilistic input ranges, we consider errors which themselves have probabilistic specifications. That is, with a certain probability the error for each operation can be larger than usual [22,27].

We observe that the computed (discretized) probability distributions of errors are hard to interpret and use by a programmer. We thus propose a new metric which states that with probability p, the error is at most C_p, where C_p should be smaller than the overall worst-case error. We show how to compute C_p from the probability distributions of errors, given a particular p by the user.

We have implemented this analysis in the prototype tool called PrAn and evaluated it on several benchmarks from literature. The results show that the proposed probabilistic error analysis refines worst-case errors and soundly computes a smaller error which holds with a predefined probability. For the standard floating-point error specification, PrAn computes refined error bounds which are on average 17% and 16.2% and up to 49.8% and 45.1% lower than worst-case errors for gaussian and uniform input distributions, respectively. These error bounds hold with at least probability 0.85. For an approximate error specification which assumes individual operations to commit an error of larger magnitude with probability 0.1, the refined errors are, again with probability 0.85, on average even 30.6% and up to 73.1% smaller than worst-case.

Contributions. In summary, in this paper we present:

- the first static analysis for probability distributions of numerical errors,
- an instantiation of this analysis for worst-case floating-point and probabilistic approximate error specifications,
- a procedure to extract useful and human-readable refined error specifications,
- an experimental evaluation demonstrating the effectiveness of our analysis,
- an implementation, which we will release as open source.

2 Background

Floating-point Arithmetic is a widely used representation of real numbers on digital computers. Due to optimized hardware or software support, it is efficient, but due to its finite nature, every operation introduces roundoff errors. These errors are individually small, but can potentially accumulate over the course of a computation. To ensure the correctness of systems using floating-point arithmetic, we have to bound roundoff errors at the program's output.

An exact formalization of floating-point arithmetic is too complex for reasoning about larger programs, such that most automated tools for bounding roundoff errors use the following abstraction which is based on the specification of the IEEE 754 standard [1]:

$$x \circ_{fl} y = (x \circ y)(1 + e) + d\,, \;\; |e| \leq \epsilon_m, |d| \leq \delta_m \tag{1}$$

where $\circ \in \{+, -, *, /\}$ and $\circ_{fl}$ denotes the respective floating-point version. Square root follows similarly and unary minus does not introduce roundoff errors. The machine epsilon ϵ_m bounds the maximum relative error for normal values and for subnormal values the round-off error is expressed as δ_m. The values of ϵ_m and δ_m for single and double precision are 2^{-24}, 2^{-150} and 2^{-53} and 2^{-1075} respectively. Equation 1 assumes rounding-to-nearest rounding mode, which is the usual default, and no overflow (the analyses prove that this cannot occur).

Worst-Case Error Analysis Existing work on bounding roundoff errors computes worst-case absolute errors:

$$\max_{x \in [a,\, b]} \mid f(x) - \tilde{f}(\tilde{x}) \mid$$

where f and x denote the real-valued function and input and $\tilde{f}$ and $\tilde{x}$ their floating-point counterparts. Floating-point roundoffs depend on the magnitude of inputs (see Eq. 1), such that tools compute worst-case errors for some bounded, user-provided input domain. There are two different approaches to bounding roundoff errors: dataflow analysis [7–9, 11, 15], and global optimization [19, 24, 31].

Dataflow analysis, which is relevant to our approach, tracks real-valued ranges and finite-precision errors at each abstract syntax tree (AST) node using the domains of interval arithmetic (IA) [23] or affine arithmetic (AA) [14].

Interval arithmetic computes a bounding interval for each basic operation as $x \circ y = [\min(x \circ y), \max(x \circ y)]$ where $\circ \in \{+, -, *, /\}$ and analogously for square root. It is widely used and efficient to bound ranges of variables, but results in over-approximations, because it does not track correlations between variables.

Affine arithmetic represents a range of possible values by an affine form: $\hat{x} = x_0 + \sum_{i=1}^{n} x_i \eta_i$ where $\eta_i \in [-1, 1]$, x_0 is the mid-point of the range and each *noise term* $x_i \eta_i$ represents a deviation from this mid-point. The interval of values represented by an affine form is given by $[\hat{x}] = [x_0 - rad(\hat{x}), x_0 + rad(\hat{x})]$, $rad(\hat{x}) = \sum_{i=1}^{n} |x_i|$. The symbolic variables η_i track linear correlations between variables, allowing AA to often compute tighter ranges than IA. In AA, linear arithmetic operations are computed term-wise, while nonlinear operations are approximated and thus result in a certain imprecision of the analysis.

IA and AA can be combined with interval subdivision, which subdivides input domains into subintervals of usually equal width and runs the analysis separately on each. The overall error is computed as the maximum error over all subintervals. Interval subdivision is, for instance, implemented in the tools Fluctuat [15] and Daisy [8]. It provides tighter error bounds as smaller input domains usually result in smaller over-approximations.

Probabilistic Affine Arithmetic The worst-case error can be pessimistic as it takes into account only the ranges of the input variables. However, inputs may be distributed according to different distributions. To get a more nuanced view, we need to track probability distributions through the program. One possible approach to track real-valued probability distributions is probabilistic affine arithmetic [4]. Here, we provide a high-level idea of probabilistic AA needed to understand our probabilistic error analysis. For details, we refer the reader to [4].

In standard AA, the symbolic noise terms η_i nondeterministically take a value in the interval $[-1, 1]$. Probabilistic AA extends each noise term η_i to carry a *probability distribution* d_{η_i} with support $[-1, 1]$. Thus, a probabilistic affine form represents a probability distribution which is computed by summing the weighted distributions from each noise term:

$$x_0 + \sum_{i=1}^{n} x_i d_{\eta_i} \tag{2}$$

For representing the probability distributions, probabilistic AA uses Interval Dempster-Shafer structures [13,30] (DSI). DSIs discretize a distribution and represent it as a finite list of focal elements: $d = \{\langle \mathbf{x_1}, w_1 \rangle, \langle \mathbf{x_2}, w_2 \rangle, \cdots, \langle \mathbf{x_n}, w_n \rangle\}$ where $\mathbf{x_i}$ is a closed non-empty interval and $w_i \in]0, 1]$ is the associated probability and $\sum_{k=1}^{n} w_k = 1$. That is, the value of a variable x is (nondeterministically) within the interval $\mathbf{x_1}$ with probability w_1, in interval $\mathbf{x_2}$ with probability w_2, and so on. For example, the DSI

$$d = \{\langle [-1, 0.25], 0.1 \rangle, \langle [-0.5, 0.5], 0.2 \rangle, \langle [0.25, 1], 0.3 \rangle, \langle [0.5, 1], 0.1 \rangle, \langle [0.5, 2], 0.1 \rangle, \langle [1, 2], 0.2 \rangle\}$$

represents the distribution where the probability of selecting a value in the interval $[-1, 0.25]$ is 0.1, in the interval $[-0.5, 0.5]$ is 0.2 and so on. Graphically, this DSI looks as follows:

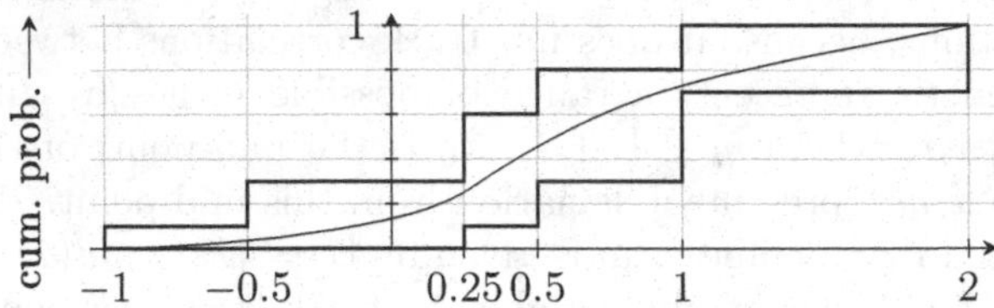

DSIs represent *uncertain* distributions, that is, the set of focal elements in general represents not a single exact distribution, but a set of distributions. Thus DSIs allow us to efficiently and soundly represent the continuous distribution such that the true distribution(s) are guaranteed to be inside the computed DSI. Naturally, the abstraction comes at a cost of certain over-approximations.

To propagate probabilistic affine forms through the program, we note that the affine portion remains the same as standard AA. However, the noise symbols now carry a distribution in the form of a DSI so that we need to define arithmetic operations over DSIs.

The affine form tracks (unknown) dependencies between variables and thus also between DSIs. When two DSIs are independent of each other, arithmetic operations can be computed using standard interval arithmetic. For example, given two independent DSIs, $d_X = \{\langle \mathbf{x_i}, w_i\rangle \mid i \in [1, n]\}$ and $d_Y = \{\langle \mathbf{y_j}, v_j\rangle \mid j \in [1, m]\}$, the resultant DSI structure is: $d_Z = \{\langle \mathbf{z_{i,j}}, r_{i,j}\rangle \mid i \in [1, n], j \in [1, m]\}$ with $\mathbf{z_{i,j}} = \mathbf{x_i} \odot \mathbf{y_j}$ where $\odot \in \{+, -, *, /\}$ and $r_{i,j} = w_i \times v_j$.

If d_X and d_Y are dependent with some unknown dependency, probabilistic AA computes the intervals $(\mathbf{z_{i,j}})$ of d_Z as for the independent case. To compute the corresponding weights, we need to take into account all possible dependencies to obtain a sound over-approximation of the probability distribution. Formally, this means that we need to compute an upper and a lower bound on the cumulative distribution function at every point in the domain. Practically, since our DSIs are discretized, we need to do this computation at every 'step', i.e. for each lower and upper bound in d_Z. For each such 'step', we need to solve an optimization problem, which encodes constraints due to the unknown dependency, effectively encoding all possible dependencies. The resulting linear programming problems can be solved using a Simplex solver.

Probabilistic AA [4] thus propagates discretized uncertain probability distributions through arithmetic computations and provides a sound enclosure on the real-valued probability distribution. So far, probabilistic AA has not been extended to support error propagation.

3 Tracking Probabilistic Errors

In this work we propose to track roundoff and other approximation errors probabilistically, in order to provide less pessimistic error bounds than only a worst-case analysis. Our probabilistic analysis takes into account the distributions of input variables, tracks errors probabilistically throughout the program for a specified uniform floating-point precision, and computes a *sound* over-approximation of the error distribution at the output. We observe that the resulting distributions can be hard to interpret and use. Hence, we further propose and show how to extract an *error metric* from the output distribution. The user of our approach provides a *threshold probability* p, and our technique extracts a tighter refined error bound C_p, which holds with probability p.

We focus here on straight-line arithmetic expressions. Previous techniques for worst-case error bounds reduce reasoning about errors in loops via loop unrolling [7] and loop invariants [9,15,24], and in conditionals by a path-by-path analysis [9,24] to straight-line code. These techniques can also be combined with our probabilistic analysis. We furthermore compute absolute errors. While approaches exist to compute relative errors directly [16], they only compute a result if the output range does not include zero, which however happens often in practice. Whenever the final range does not include zero, our method can compute relative errors from the absolute ones.

Running Example We will use the following program, which computes a third-order approximation of sine, as a running example for this section:

```
x := gaussian(-2.0, 2.0)
0.954929658551372 * x -  0.12900613773279798 * (x * x * x)
```

The user specifies the distribution of input variables: here 'x' is normally distributed in $[-2, 2]$. Suppose the user has further set the threshold probability to $p = 0.85$. The worst-case error for this program in single precision is 4.62e−7. PrAn computes the output distribution and extracts the following error metric: a smaller error of $C_p = 2.67\text{e}{-7}$ occurs with at least probability 0.85. □

Algorithm 1 shows the high-level overview of our analysis. It takes as input the following parameters: a program given as an arithmetic expression (fnc), ranges of the input variables (E), the probability distribution of the variables ($inDist$), a limit on the number of total subdivisions (L), a uniform floating-point precision ($prec$), and a threshold probability (p). Our analysis currently considers the same probability distribution for all variables as well as uniform floating-point precision, but it is straight-forward to extend to consider different distributions and mixed precision.

Algorithm 1 first discretizes each input range distribution into subdomains (line 2). For each subdomain it runs the probabilistic error analysis for the specified floating-point precision $prec$ (line 5). The computed error distribution is then normalized by multiplying the probability of the subdomain occurring (line 6) and merge it with $errDist$ (line 7) that accumulates error distributions for each subdomain to generate the complete error distribution of the output error. Finally from $errDist$ we extract the error metric (line 8) and its actual probability, which may be larger than the requested p and return it (line 9).

In Sect. 3.1 we first describe a simplified version of Algorithm 1, which performs probabilistic interval subdivision but computes errors for each subdomain

Algorithm 1. Tracking Probabilistic Round-off Errors

```
1: procedure PROBABILISTICERROR(fnc, E, inDist, L, prec, p)
2:     subDoms ≐ subdivide(E, inDist, L)
3:     errDist = ϕ
4:     for (dom_i, ρ_i) ← subDoms do
5:         absErr_i = evalProbRoundoff(fnc, dom_i, prec)        ▷ see Algorithm 2
6:         absErr_i = normalizeProb(absErr_i, ρ_i)
7:         errDist = merge(errDist, absErr_i)
8:     (err, prob) = extractErrorMetric(errDist, p)
9:     return (err, prob)        ▷ returns the refined error with probability
```

with standard worst-case roundoff analysis. While interval subdivision is standardly used to decrease overapproximations, to the best of our knowledge, it has not been used previously to compute probabilistic error bounds. Then, we extend this analysis with our novel probabilistic error analysis (Sect. 3.2). Finally we show how our probabilistic error analysis can be further extended to take into account approximate error specifications common in today's approximate hardware (Sect. 3.3).

3.1 Probabilistic Interval Subdivision

First, we consider a relatively simple extension of worst-case error analysis which takes into account the distributions of input variables: for now, we let the function `evalProbRoundoff` compute a worst-case error, instead of a probability distribution, and focus on the interval subdivision where the intervals are subdivided probabilistically (line 2 in Algorithm 1).

Our algorithm first subdivides each input interval equally and for multivariate functions takes their Cartesian product to generate subdomains. The probability of each subdomain is computed by taking the product of the probabilities of the corresponding subintervals. In this way the algorithm generates a set of tuples (dom_i, ρ_i) where a value is in subdomain dom_i with probability ρ_i. On each of these subdomains, we can run the standard worst-case dataflow error analysis from Sect. 2 to compute an error bound $absErr_i$ (here, we use AA for the errors, but IA for the ranges, because it tends to have less over-approximations for nonlinear expressions than standard AA). Hence, the algorithm computes for each subdomain i an error tuple $(absErr_i, \rho_i)$, i.e. with probability ρ_i, the worst-case error is $absErr_i$. From these error tuples ($errDist$), PrAn extracts the error metric.

Extracting the Error Metric We want to extract an error C_p (smaller than the worst-case error), which is satisfied with threshold probability p provided by the user. The function `extractErrorMetric` in Algorithm 1 repeatedly removes tuples with the largest error and subtracts their corresponding probability while the total probability of the remaining tuples remains at least p. Finally, we return the refined error and its probability, which is at least p but may be higher.

Algorithm 2. Probabilistic range and roundoff error analysis

```
procedure EVALPROBROUNDOFF(node, dom, prec)
    if (node = lhs op rhs) then                                   ▷ Binary operation
        realRange = evalRange(lhs, rhs, op, dom)
        errorLhs = evalProbRoundoff(lhs, realRange, prec)
        errorRhs = evalProbRoundoff(rhs, realRange, prec)
        propagatedErr = propagate(errorLhs, errorRhs, op)
        newRange = toDSI(realRange + propagatedErr)
    else                                                          ▷ node is a variable
        newRange = toDSI(dom)
    for (x, w) ← newRange do
        roundoff = maxRoundoff(x, prec)
        errDist.append(roundoff, w)
    return addNoise(propagatedErr, normalize(errDist))
```

Example Recall our running example, which has a worst-case error of 4.62e−7 in single precision. Using probabilistic subdivision PrAn subdivides the input domain into 100 subdomains and computes a reduced error bound of 2.97e−7 which holds with at least probability 0.85 (the worst-case error remains unchanged). If the program is immune to big errors with probability 0.15, the relevant error bound is thus reduced substantially by 35%. □

3.2 Probabilistic Roundoff Error Analysis

The error computed using only probabilistic interval subdivision is pessimistic as the actual error computation still computes worst-case errors. To compute a tighter distribution of errors at the output we propose to track roundoff errors probabilistically throughout the program. To the best of our knowledge, this is the first sound probabilistic analysis of roundoff errors. We first consider an exact error specification, by which we mean that the roundoff error introduced at each individual arithmetic operation is still the worst-case error, following the IEEE754 standard specification (Eq. 1). Even with an exact error specification we obtain an error distribution as the error depends on the ranges, and thus not all values, and not all errors, are equally likely. In this section we first present probabilistic roundoff error analysis and then combine it with probabilistic interval subdivision in order to get tighter error bounds.

The function `evalProbRoundoff` shown in Algorithm 2 extends probabilistic AA to propagate error distributions through the program, by performing a forward dataflow analysis recursively over the program abstract syntax tree (AST). For each AST node (*node*), an input subdomain (*dom*), and a precision (*prec*), it computes the distribution of accumulated roundoff errors. This error distribution is a sound over-approximation, i.e. the true distribution lies within the computed upper and lower bounds. The soundness of our technique follows from the soundness of the underlying probabilistic AA.

For each binary arithmetic operation (*op*), our analysis first computes the real-valued range (line 3) using probabilistic AA as described in Sect. 2. Computing the accumulated errors is more involved and constitutes our extension over probabilistic AA and one of our main contributions. To compute the accumulated errors, the algorithm first computes the errors of its operands (line 4–5) and from these computes the propagated error (*propagatedErr*) (line 6). Our probabilistic error propagation extends rules from standard AA to probabilistic AA. The propagated errors are added to the real-valued range distribution to obtain the finite-precision distribution (line 7), from which we can compute roundoff errors. Before doing so, we convert the probabilistic affine form to the DSI representation (`toDSI`), which is more amenable for roundoff error computation.

Each focal element of the finite-precision range DSI assigns a probability w to an interval x. Hence, we can compute the roundoff error for each focal element following the floating-point abstraction in Eq. 1, and assign the weight w to that error (line 10–12). That is, our procedure computes roundoff errors separately for each focal element, and appends them to generate a new error DSI (line 12). The newly committed error DSI is then normalized to $[-1, 1]$ and added as a fresh noise term to the probabilistic affine form of the propagated errors (line 13).

Probabilistic Error Analysis with Interval Subdivision This probabilistic analysis computes the distribution of the roundoff error at the output, but we observed that it introduces large over-approximations as intervals of the focal elements of the DSI tend to be wide and almost fully overlap with each other. To reduce the over-approximation, we combine the probabilistic error analysis with our probabilistic interval subdivision from Sect. 3.1. Since each subdomain is smaller, this reduces over-approximations in each, and thus also overall.

Extracting the Error Metric To extract the error metric, we first transform the probabilistic affine form of the error to a DSI structure. To extract the error metric we sort the focal elements, and then remove the elements with largest error magnitude from the error DSI similarly to Sect. 3.1, until the total weight of the resultant DSI sums up to the threshold p. PrAn returns the maximum absolute value of the remaining focal elements as the refined error. This extraction effectively tries to find as small error bound as possible which will fall within the probability p.

Example Recall the running sine example. Using only the probabilistic error analysis without subdivision, PrAn first discretizes the input distribution into 100 subdomains as shown in Fig. 1. From this, PrAn computes the probability distribution of the error shown in Fig. 2(a). As the figure shows, the intervals of the DSI are wide and they almost fully overlap with each other. As a result, PrAn cannot refine the error.

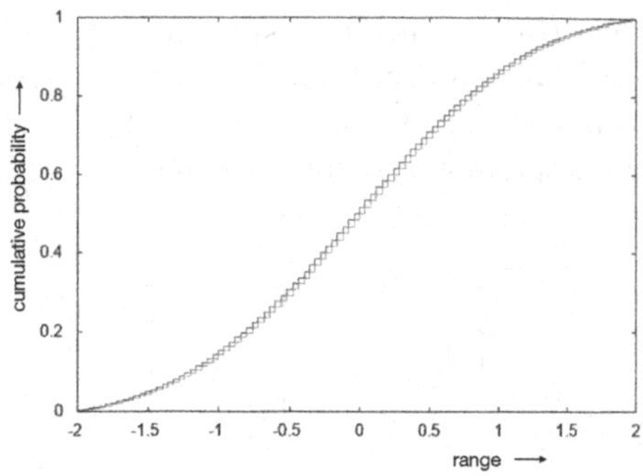

Fig. 1. Input distribution of our example

For the full analysis with probabilistic error analysis and subdivision, we choose 2 initial DSI discretizations and 50 outer interval subdivisions (to keep a fair comparison with 100 overall initial subdivisions). Note that during the computation, the number of DSI discretizations grows and is limited by 100, which we observed to be a good compromise between accuracy and efficiency.

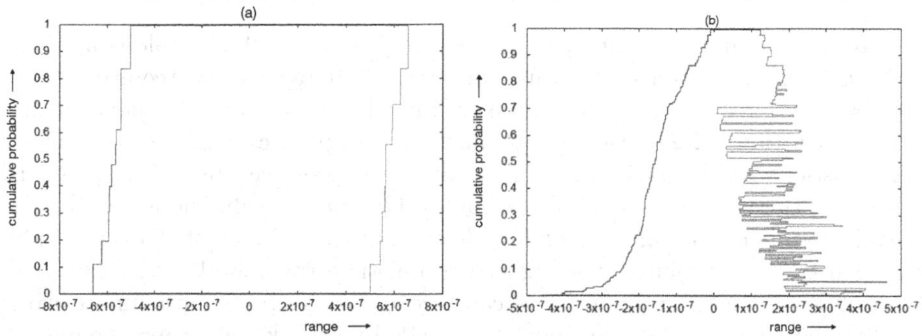

Fig. 2. Error distribution with (a) probabilistic analysis only and (b) full analysis

Figure 2(b) shows the resulting error distribution. It is not a step function, because while for each of the subdomain, PrAn does compute the error DSI as a step function, due to the merging *at the end*, the overall distribution does not have this shape. With our full analysis, PrAn computes a refined error of 2.67e−7 (with threshold probability 0.85). This refined error is smaller than the 2.97e−7, which PrAn computed using only probabilistic interval subdivision. □

Alternatively, we could also compute the probability of the largest errors occurring. To extract this information, the error distribution is conceptually subdivided vertically first as shown in Fig. 3. In this way we can compute the probability of the large error which will be between the outermost extension and the next subdivision. For this, we need to sum all the weights which intersect with the specified interval. We observed this alternative error specification to be less useful in practice due to large overlaps between the focal elements. We thus focus in the remainder on the first type of error metric.

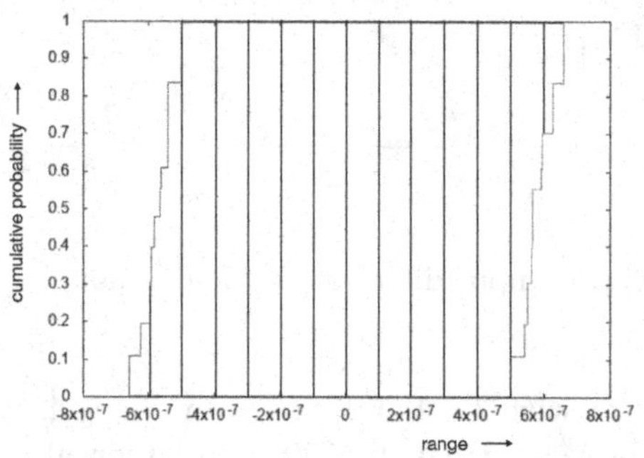

Fig. 3. Alternative vertical subdiv.

3.3 Probabilistic Analysis with Approximate Error Specification

Approximate computing is an emerging design paradigm which exploits approximations to enable better performance in terms of energy or resource utilization. Approximate hardware may, for instance, introduce big, but infrequent, errors in a computation [22,27]. Such approximate error specifications are themselves probabilistic: with a certain probability, the error produced by an operation is larger than the usual worst-case error bound. For such specifications, worst-case analysis considers the large error for all computations, even if it occurs only infrequently, and computes thus highly pessimistic error bounds. With our proposed probabilistic error analysis, we can incorporate such an approximate error specification when the larger errors are bounded with a known upper bound.

To compute a sound probabilistic error bound with approximate specifications we extend the function `maxRoundoff` in Algorithm 2. Previously, we computed one error for each focal element, now we compute multiple errors, depending on the error specification. For example, for a specification where a larger error can occur with a certain probability, we compute two errors and thus two focal elements at line 11 in Algorithm 2: one focal element that keeps track of the big error (with a usually small probability ρ), and one focal element which tracks the regular error (with probability $1 - \rho$).

Example We consider an approximate error specification for our running sine example where an error of size twice the usual machine epsilon ($2 \times \epsilon_m$) occurs with probability $\rho = 0.1$ and the regular roundoff error (ϵ_m) appears with probability 0.9. Our tool PrAn computes 7.34e−7 as the worst-case error with 2

DSI discretizations and 50 outer interval subdivisions. As expected, the absolute error computed with this approximate error specification is larger than the error computed using the exact error specification (4.62e−7) where at each step only an error of ϵ_m appears. Using only probabilistic interval subdivision, PrAn computes a bound of 5.02e−07 with threshold probability 0.85. However, this analysis cannot take advantage of the approximate error specification. Using our full analysis (as described in Sect. 3.2), PrAn computes a refined error bound of 3.86e−7 with threshold probability 0.85. □

3.4 Implementation

We have implemented our proposed probabilistic error analysis technique(s) in the prototype tool PrAn which is implemented on top of the tool Daisy. The analysis itself is implemented using intervals with arbitrary-precision outer bounds (with outwards rounding) using the GNU MPFR library. This ensures soundness in addition to an efficient implementation. We use GLPK [2] as our simplex solver, which uses floating-point arithmetic internally, and may thus introduce roundoff errors into the analysis. A fully satisfactory solution would use a guaranteed LP-solver as Lurupa [17] or LPex [12], but it is unclear whether the analysis performance would suffer.

4 Experimental Evaluation

Benchmarks We have used various benchmarks from the domains of scientific computing, embedded systems and machine learning.[1] Most of the benchmarks are widely used in finite-precision roundoff error estimation [8,9,31]: sine, sineOrder3 and sqroot are polynomial approximations of functions, bsplines are used in embedded image applications, train and rigidBody are linear and nonlinear controller respectively. We also have benchmarks where probabilistic AA has been used previously to compute ranges probabilistically [18]: filter is a 2nd order filter unrolled to specified iterations, cubic is obtained from the GNU library, classIDXs are extracted from a linear support vector classifier, neuron is a simplified version of the DNN that learns 'AND' operator. We have further extracted polyIDXs using sklearn-porter [3] from a polynomial support vector classifier trained on the Iris standard data from Python sklearn library.

Experimental Setup The experiments were performed on a Debian desktop computer with a 3.3 GHz i5 processor and 16 GB RAM. We use 32 bit single precision as the target precision. We consider a threshold probability of 0.85. We have evaluated PrAn with eight different settings denoted by the letters A-H. Settings (A, B) use only the probabilistic interval subdivision from Sect. 3.1 and settings (C, D) use our complete probabilistic analysis with subdivision

[1] All benchmarks are available at https://people.mpi-sws.org/~dlohar/assets/code/Benchmarks.txt.

from Sect. 3.2, assuming an exact error specification. Settings (E, F, G) perform full probabilistic analysis considering an approximate error specification (as in Sect. 3.3), where with probability 0.9 the error is small (ϵ_m) and with probability 0.1 the error has magnitude $2 \times \epsilon_m$ (settings E, F) or magnitude $4 \times \epsilon_m$ (setting G).

For a fair comparison, in settings A-G, we limit the total number of input subdomains from DSI and input interval subdivision to 100. I.e. when probabilistic AA is used (in C-G), each input DSI is subdivided into 2, and the input interval subdivisions are determined such that the overall number of subdomains remains below 100. Note that *during* the computation, the number of DSI subdivisions is limited by 100 (not 2).

Setting (H) considers an approximate error specification as in (G), but performs only probabilistic interval subdivision (Sect. 3.1). We additionally increase the input interval subdomains to 200. With this setting, we evaluate whether probabilistic AA is helpful for approximate error specifications, or simply using more interval subdivisions (which are relatively cheap) is sufficient.

Settings (B, D, F) consider uniformly distributed inputs and the other settings consider gaussian inputs where all inputs are independent. Note that our approach handles any discretized input distribution provided as a DSI, as well as inputs with (unknown) correlations. Our choice of input distribution is arbitrary, as the 'right' distribution is application specific.

Results Table 1 shows the absolute worst-case and refined error values for setting A, C, and E with gaussian inputs. Settings A and C were able to refine the error bounds considering an exact error specification in almost all cases, except those marked with '*'. The train4 benchmark has 9 input variables, which means that with our total limit of subdivisions each input is divided too few times to refine the error. For train3, PrAn could refine the worst-case error only with setting C, i.e. using our full analysis. Using an approximate error specification, PrAn was always able to refine the errors.

For some benchmarks, the full probabilistic error analysis outperforms probabilistic interval subdivision, but for others it is the other way around. When probabilistic error analysis (setting C) is better, it tends to be more significantly better than vice-versa.

We show results with uniform input distributions (settings B, D, F) in Table 2. Settings B and D were also able to reduce the error bounds except the train4 benchmark with uniform inputs. Also with uniform inputs setting B could not reduce the error bound of train3.

In general, which analysis is better is application specific: this depends on the over-approximations committed, which in turn depend on the operations and ranges of an application. A user should consider both variants and use the best result in a portfolio-like approach. Note, however, that for approximate error specifications, a probabilistic error analysis is necessary in order to adequately capture the probabilistic error specification.

Table 1. Worst-case and refined error in different settings with gaussian inputs

	worst-case error			refined error		
	A	C	E	A	C	E
sine	2.40e-7	2.41e-7	4.76e-7	**1.56e-7**	1.68e-7	2.66e-7
sineOrder3	4.62e-7	4.62e-7	7.34e-7	2.97e-7	**2.67e-7**	3.86e-7
sqroot	1.50e-4	1.54e-4	2.42e-4	**8.38e-5**	8.89e-5	1.31e-4
bspline0	8.69e-8	8.69e-8	1.44e-7	**4.36e-8**	4.44e-8	5.51e-8
bspline1	2.09e-7	2.10e-7	3.86e-7	**1.96e-7**	1.97e-7	2.67e-7
bspline2	2.16e-7	2.12e-7	4.21e-7	**1.87e-7**	1.89e-7	2.91e-7
bspline3	5.71e-8	5.71e-8	8.44e-8	**3.33e-8**	3.39e-8	3.72e-8
rigidBody1	1.58e-4	1.73e-4	3.01e-4	**9.99e-5**	1.57e-4	1.98e-4
rigidBody2	1.94e-2	9.70e-3	1.38e-2	1.06e-2	**8.50e-3**	1.05e-2
train1	1.99e-3	2.00e-3	2.94e-3	1.84e-3	**1.67e-3**	2.52e-3
train2	1.37e-3	1.37e-3	2.06e-3	1.32e-3	**1.19e-3**	1.83e-3
train3	2.29e-2	2.29e-2	3.85e-2	2.29e-2*	**2.26e-2**	3.46e-2
train4	2.30e-1	2.30e-1	4.13e-1	2.30e-1*	2.30e-1*	3.75e-1
filter2	1.04e-6	1.04e-6	1.72e-6	8.64e-7	**7.57e-7**	1.13e-6
filter3	2.99e-6	2.87e-6	4.99e-6	2.62e-6	**2.58e-6**	4.52e-6
filter4	6.51e-6	5.20e-6	9.16e-6	6.09e-6	**4.96e-6**	8.69e-6
cubic	1.83e-5	2.02e-5	3.35e-5	**1.73e-5**	1.90e-5	2.80e-5
classIDX0	8.77e-6	9.10e-6	1.45e-5	7.95e-6	**7.92e-6**	1.20e-5
classIDX1	4.63e-6	4.76e-6	7.70e-6	**4.28e-6**	4.38e-6	6.70e-6
classIDX2	7.32e-6	7.60e-6	1.25e-5	**6.35e-6**	6.55e-6	1.02e-5
polyIDX0	5.56e-3	5.80e-3	9.29e-3	2.96e-3	5.32e-3	7.94e-3
polyIDX1	6.81e-4	7.56e-4	1.23e-3	4.51e-4	7.08e-4	1.12e-3
polyIDX2	5.05e-3	5.40e-3	8.73-3	2.84e-3	5.08e-3	7.55e-3
neuron	3.22e-5	7.02e-5	9.87e-5	**3.20e-5**	5.25e-05	7.47e-5

We show the error reduction between the refined and the corresponding worst-case errors in Table 3. The reductions for the exact error specifications are on average 20.9%, 17% and 16.2% with settings A, C and D, respectively. The reduction with gaussian inputs in setting C is in most cases higher than for uniform inputs. We also see that reductions are application specific, and for many benchmarks more substantial than the averages suggest. In some cases our probabilistic analysis even with exact specifications allows to report refined errors with nearly half the magnitude as the worst-case (up to 49.8%), but still with guaranteed probability of at least 0.85.

Our probabilistic analysis achieves even higher reductions with the approximate error specification (settings E and G) with on average 24.9% and 30.6% smaller refined errors than worst-case, respectively. Even if we double the number of total subdivisions (setting H) probabilistic interval subdivision can only reduce the error on average by 25.4%, compared to 30.6% using our full proba-

Table 2. Worst case and refined error in different settings with uniform inputs

	worst-case error			refined error		
	B	D	F	B	D	F
sine	2.72e-7	**2.41e-7**	4.76e-07	2.18e-7	**1.83e-7**	2.66e-7
sineOrder3	4.62e-7	4.62e-7	7.34e-7	3.29e-7	**2.84e-7**	4.04e-7
sqroot	**1.50e-4**	1.54e-4	2.42e-4	**9.02e-5**	9.33e-5	1.39e-4
bspline0	8.69e-8	8.69e-8	1.44e-7	**4.60e-8**	4.77e-8	5.80e-8
bspline1	2.12e-7	**2.10e-7**	3.86e-7	2.00e-7	2.00e-7	2.81e-7
bspline2	2.18e-7	**2.12e-7**	4.21e-7	2.08e-7	**1.93e-7**	2.93e-7
bspline3	5.71e-8	5.71e-8	8.44e-8	3.50e-8	3.50e-8	3.99e-8
rigidBody1	**1.58e-4**	1.73e-4	3.01e-4	**1.50e-4**	1.57e-4	1.98e-4
rigidBody2	1.94e-2	**9.70e-3**	1.38e-2	1.71e-2	**8.55e-3**	1.13e-2
train1	2.00e-3	2.00e-3	2.94e-3	1.91e-3	**1.67e-3**	2.48e-3
train2	1.37e-3	1.37e-3	2.06e-3	1.32e-3	**1.19e-3**	1.80e-03
train3	2.29e-2	2.29e-2	3.85e-2	2.29e-2*	**2.26e-2**	3.46e-2
train4	2.30e-1	2.30e-1	4.13e-1	2.30e-1*	2.30e-1*	3.75e-1
filter1	2.03e-7	2.03e-7	2.62e-7	1.96e-7	**1.86e-7**	1.93e-7
filter2	1.04e-6	1.04e-6	1.72e-6	9.08e-7	**7.74e-7**	1.17e-6
filter3	3.07e-6	**2.87e-6**	4.99e-6	2.96e-6	**2.58e-6**	4.26e-6
filter4	8.23e-6	**5.20e-6**	9.16e-6	8.17e-6	**4.95e-6**	8.69e-6
cubic	**1.85e-5**	2.02e-5	3.35e-5	**1.74e-5**	1.90e-5	2.80e-5
classIDX0	9.10e-6	9.10e-6	1.45e-5	8.52e-6	**7.79e-6**	1.20e-05
classIDX1	4.76e-6	4.76e-6	7.70e-6	4.66e-6	**4.35e-6**	6.79e-6
classIDX2	7.60e-6	7.60e-6	1.25e-5	7.44e-6	**6.36e-6**	1.01e-05
polyIDX0	5.80e-3	**5.19e-3**	9.29e-3	**4.17e-3**	4.78e-3	7.94e-3
polyIDX1	7.55e-4	**5.71e-4**	1.23e-3	7.00e-4	**5.04e-4**	5.04e-4
polyIDX2	5.40e-3	**5.19e-3**	8.38e-3	**3.94e-3**	4.78e-3	7.04e-3
neuron	**6.40e-5**	7.02e-5	9.87e-5	**3.94e-5**	4.86e-5	6.86e-5

bilistic analysis. While for a few cases setting H outperforms setting G (because of overapproximations in the probabilistic analysis), overall probabilistic analysis is successful at capturing the fact that large errors only occur infrequently.

Finally, Table 4 shows the running times of our analysis for settings A, C and E (averaged over 3 runs). The probabilistic error analysis takes more time than the non-probabilistic analysis (i.e. one with only a probabilistic interval subdivision), as expected. We note, however, that the analysis times are nonetheless acceptable for a static analysis which is run only once.

Table 3. Reductions in % in errors w.r.t. the standard worst-case in different settings

	A	C	D	E	G	H		A	C	D	E	G	H
sine	34.9	30.3	24.1	44.1	**52.2**	39.6	*train4*	0.0	0.0	0.0	9.2	**8.3**	0.0
sineOrder3	35.7	42.1	38.5	47.4	**52.9**	34.0	*filter2*	16.9	27.5	25.9	34.5	13.9	**29.7**
sqroot	44.3	42.4	39.5	45.6	**56.6**	45.8	*filter3*	12.4	10.0	10.0	9.6	23.0	**23.8**
bspline0	49.8	48.9	45.1	61.7	**73.1**	56.6	*filter4*	6.5	4.6	4.9	5.1	**47.5**	10.4
bspline1	6.2	6.0	4.7	30.8	**40.2**	9.7	*cubic*	5.8	5.8	5.9	16.2	**41.9**	9.3
bspline2	13.5	11.0	9.4	31.0	**40.6**	17.4	*classIDX0*	9.3	13.0	1.5	17.6	**18.7**	13.6
bspline3	41.6	40.7	38.7	56.0	**67.0**	48.6	*classIDX1*	7.5	8.0	8.6	12.9	5.3	**10.1**
rigidBody1	36.9	8.8	8.8	34.2	34.8	**38.6**	*classIDX2*	13.3	13.8	16.3	18.3	**22.2**	14.8
rigidBody2	45.4	12.4	11.8	24.1	13.5	**49.2**	*polyIDX0*	46.8	8.2	8.0	14.5	14.6	**50.1**
train1	7.5	16.4	16.4	14.4	**20.2**	7.2	*polyIDX1*	33.8	6.3	11.7	8.7	10.6	**37.3**
train2	3.3	12.6	12.7	11.3	**13.6**	1.9	*polyIDX2*	43.9	5.9	8.0	13.6	19.6	**49.2**
train3	0.0	1.3	1.3	10.1	**11.2**	2.2	*neuron*	0.9	25.3	30.8	24.3	**41.7**	13.9

Table 4. Analysis time (averaged over 3 runs) in different settings

	A	C	E		A	C	E
sine	9s	6m 1s	109m 11s	*train4*	0.1s	22s	36s
sineOrder3	5s	3m 7s	6m 46s	*filter2*	0.9s	1m 47s	3m 2s
sqroot	1s	1m 29s	33m 56s	*filter3*	0.9s	4m 19s	11m 16s
bspline0	0.4s	22s	12m 2s	*filter4*	16s	10m 54s	28m 39s
bspline1	0.6s	42s	13m 37s	*cubic*	16s	3m 11s	14m 24s
bspline2	0.8s	50s	16m 6s	*classIDX0*	23s	3m 39s	7m 44s
bspline3	0.4s	18s	1m 20s	*classIDX1*	2s	3m 56s	7m 53s
rigidBody1	0.1s	35s	1m 16s	*classIDX2*	0.1s	3m 39s	7m 1s
rigidBody2	0.4s	1m 14s	10m 59s	*polyIDX0*	0.5s	32m 52s	181m 45s
train1	0.3s	1m 15s	3m 55s	*polyIDX1*	0.8s	33m 26s	193m 19s
train2	0.3s	6m 29s	11m 22s	*polyIDX2*	3s	38m 29s	177m 38s
train3	0.1s	12s	25s	*neuron*	0.5s	1m 11s	4m 17s

5 Related Work

Probabilistic affine arithmetic with Dempster-Shafer Interval structures provide an efficient approach for soundly propagating probability distributions, but it incurs huge over-approximation of the probabilities. An alternative would be exact probabilistic inference [21], however its scalability is very limited [18]. Most probabilistic inference algorithms rely on sampling [6,20,25,26] and thus do not provide guaranteed bounds. Probabilistic affine arithmetic has been also augmented by concentration of measure inequalities [5], which may reduce the amount of over-approximations. It has been used for tracking real-valued ranges in a program (but not errors). This could potentially also help improve the accuracy of our approach, but since the implementation is not available, we leave this to future work.

Sankaranarayanan et al. [28] verify probabilistic properties of programs with many paths with a combination of symbolic execution and volume computation, but do not consider (finite-precision) errors and non-linear programs.

Chisel [22] considers and bounds the probability of errors occurring due to approximate hardware, and is thus in spirit similar to our approach. Chisel, however, only tracks the probability of a large error occurring, whereas our approach provides a more nuanced probability *distribution*, and furthermore tracks the variable ranges probabilistically as well.

Several tools exist for soundly bounding roundoff errors, some are based on affine arithmetic [7–9, 11, 15], and others on a global optimization approach [19, 24, 31]. The tools only compute worst-case roundoff errors, however.

Daumas et al. [10] compute bounds on the probability that accumulated floating-point roundoff errors exceed a given threshold, using known inequalities on sums of probability distributions, and distributions on the individual errors. This approach requires manual proofs and does not consider input distributions.

Statistical error analyses have also been proposed. For instance, the CADNA approach [29] computes a confidence interval on the number of exact digits using repeated simulation with random rounding modes. An approach similar in spirit is to perturb the low-order bits, or rewrite expressions based on real-valued identities to uncover instabilities of programs [32]. The approaches, however, do not provide sound error guarantees.

6 Conclusion

We have presented a probabilistic analysis for tracking errors due to finite-precision arithmetic in straight-line code. Instead of worst-case errors, as usual analyses compute, our analysis computes probability distributions and extracts refined error metrics which determine that a potentially smaller error than the worst-case is satisfied with some probability. We believe that this analysis can be useful for applications which can tolerate larger errors, as long as their probability is bounded. We observe that our refinement is even more useful in the case of probabilistic error specifications common in today's approximate hardware.

References

1. IEEE Standard for Floating-Point Arithmetic. IEEE Std 754-2008 (2008)
2. GLPK (2012). https://www.gnu.org/software/glpk/
3. Project Sklearn-porter (2018). https://github.com/nok/sklearn-porter
4. Bouissou, O., Goubault, E., Goubault-Larrecq, J., Putot, S.: A generalization of p-boxes to affine arithmetic. Computing **94**(2–4), 189–201 (2012)
5. Bouissou, O., Goubault, E., Putot, S., Chakarov, A., Sankaranarayanan, S.: Uncertainty propagation using probabilistic affine forms and concentration of measure inequalities. In: Chechik, M., Raskin, J.-F. (eds.) TACAS 2016. LNCS, vol. 9636, pp. 225–243. Springer, Heidelberg (2016). https://doi.org/10.1007/978-3-662-49674-9_13

6. Carpenter, B., et al.: Stan: a probabilistic programming language. J. Stat. Softw. Art. **76**(1), 1–32 (2017)
7. Damouche, N., Martel, M., Chapoutot, A.: Improving the numerical accuracy of programs by automatic transformation. Int. J. Softw. Tools Technol. Transfer **19**(4), 427–448 (2017)
8. Darulova, E., Izycheva, A., Nasir, F., Ritter, F., Becker, H., Bastian, R.: Daisy - framework for analysis and optimization of numerical programs (tool paper). In: Beyer, D., Huisman, M. (eds.) TACAS 2018. LNCS, vol. 10805, pp. 270–287. Springer, Cham (2018). https://doi.org/10.1007/978-3-319-89960-2_15
9. Darulova, E., Kuncak, V.: Towards a compiler for reals. TOPLAS **39**(2), 8 (2017)
10. Daumas, M., Lester, D., Martin-Dorel, E., Truffert, A.: Improved bound for stochastic formal correctness of numerical algorithms. Innovations Syst. Softw. Eng. **6**(3), 173–179 (2010)
11. De Dinechin, F., Lauter, C.Q., Melquiond, G.: Assisted verification of elementary functions using Gappa. In: ACM Symposium on Applied Computing (2006)
12. Dhiflaoui, M., et al.: Certifying and repairing solutions to large LPs. How good are LP-solvers? In: SODA, pp. 255–256 (2003)
13. Ferson, S., Kreinovich, V., Ginzburg, L., Myers, D.S., Sentz, K.: Constructing probability boxes and Dempster-Shafer structures. Technical report, Sandia National Laboratories (2003)
14. de Figueiredo, L.H., Stolfi, J.: Affine arithmetic: concepts and applications. Numer. Algorithms **37**(1–4), 147–158 (2004)
15. Goubault, E., Putot, S.: Static analysis of finite precision computations. In: Jhala, R., Schmidt, D. (eds.) VMCAI 2011. LNCS, vol. 6538, pp. 232–247. Springer, Heidelberg (2011). https://doi.org/10.1007/978-3-642-18275-4_17
16. Izycheva, A., Darulova, E.: On sound relative error bounds for floating-point arithmetic. In: FMCAD (2017)
17. Keil, C.: Lurupa - rigorous error bounds in linear programming. In: Algebraic and Numerical Algorithms and Computer-assisted Proofs. No. 05391 in Dagstuhl Seminar Proceedings (2006). http://drops.dagstuhl.de/opus/volltexte/2006/445
18. Lohar, D., Darulova, E., Putot, S., Goubault, E.: Discrete choice in the presence of numerical uncertainties. In: EMSOFT (2018)
19. Magron, V., Constantinides, G., Donaldson, A.: Certified roundoff error bounds using semidefinite programming. ACM Trans. Math. Softw. **43**(4), 34 (2017)
20. Minka, T., et al.: Infer.NET 2.6 (2014). http://research.microsoft.com/infernet
21. Gehr, T., Misailovic, S., Vechev, M.: PSI: exact symbolic inference for probabilistic programs. In: Chaudhuri, S., Farzan, A. (eds.) CAV 2016. LNCS, vol. 9779, pp. 62–83. Springer, Cham (2016). https://doi.org/10.1007/978-3-319-41528-4_4
22. Misailovic, S., Carbin, M., Achour, S., Qi, Z., Rinard, M.C.: Chisel: reliability- and accuracy-aware optimization of approximate computational kernels. In: OOPSLA (2014)
23. Moore, R.: Interval Analysis. Prentice-Hall, Upper Saddle River (1966)
24. Moscato, M., Titolo, L., Dutle, A., Muñoz, C.A.: Automatic estimation of verified floating-point round-off errors via static analysis. In: Tonetta, S., Schoitsch, E., Bitsch, F. (eds.) SAFECOMP 2017. LNCS, vol. 10488, pp. 213–229. Springer, Cham (2017). https://doi.org/10.1007/978-3-319-66266-4_14
25. Nori, A.V., Hur, C.K., Rajamani, S.K., Samuel, S.: R2: an efficient MCMC sampler for probabilistic programs. In: AAAI (2014)
26. Sampson, A., Panchekha, P., Mytkowicz, T., McKinley, K.S., Grossman, D., Ceze, L.: Expressing and verifying probabilistic assertions. In: PLDI (2014)

27. Sampson, A., Dietl, W., Fortuna, E., Gnanapragasam, D., Ceze, L., Grossman, D.: EnerJ: approximate data types for safe and general low-power computation. In: PLDI (2011)
28. Sankaranarayanan, S., Chakarov, A., Gulwani, S.: Static analysis for probabilistic programs: inferring whole program properties from finitely many paths. In: PLDI (2013)
29. Scott, N.S., Jézéquel, F., Denis, C., Chesneaux, J.M.: Numerical 'health check' for scientific codes: the CADNA approach. Comput. Phys. Commun. **176**(8), 507–521 (2007)
30. Shafer, G.: A Mathematical Theory of Evidence. Princeton University Press, Princeton (1976)
31. Solovyev, A., Jacobsen, C., Rakamaric, Z., Gopalakrishnan, G.: Rigorous estimation of floating-point round-off errors with symbolic Taylor expansions. In: FM (2015)
32. Tang, E., Barr, E., Li, X., Su, Z.: Perturbing numerical calculations for statistical analysis of floating-point program (in)stability. In: ISSTA (2010)
33. Xu, Q., Mytkowicz, T., Kim, N.S.: Approximate computing: a survey. IEEE Des. Test **33**(1), 8–22 (2016)

Automated Drawing of Railway Schematics Using Numerical Optimization in SAT

Bjørnar Luteberget[1(✉)], Koen Claessen[2], and Christian Johansen[3]

[1] Railcomplete AS, Oslo, Norway
bjlut@railcomplete.no
[2] Chalmers University of Technology, Gothenburg, Sweden
koen@chalmers.se
[3] University of Oslo, Oslo, Norway
cristi@ifi.uio.no

Abstract. Schematic drawings showing railway tracks and equipment are commonly used to visualize railway operations and to communicate system specifications and construction blueprints. Recent advances in on-line collaboration and modeling tools have raised the expectations for quickly making changes to models, resulting in frequent changes to layouts, text, and/or symbols in schematic drawings. Automating the creation of high-quality schematic views from geographical and topological models can help engineers produce and update drawings efficiently. This paper describes three methods for automatically producing *schematic railway drawings* with increasing level of quality and control over the result. The final method, implemented in the tool that we present, can use any combination of the following optimization criteria, which have different priorities in different use cases: width and height of the drawing, the diagonal line lengths, and the number of bends. We show how to encode schematic railway drawings as an optimization problem over Boolean and numerical domains, using combinations of unary number encoding, lazy difference constraints, and numerical optimization into an incremental SAT formulation.

We compare resulting drawings from each of the three approaches, applied to models of real-world engineering projects and existing infrastructure. We also show how to add symbols and labels to the track plan, which is important for the usefulness of the final outputs. Since the proposed tool is customizable and efficiently produces high-quality drawings from railML 2.x models, it can be used (as it is or extended) both as an integrated module in an industrial design tool like RailCOMPLETE, or by researchers for visualization purposes.

The first author was partially supported by the project *RailCons – Automated Methods and Tools for Ensuring Consistency of Railway Designs*, with number 248714 funded by the Norwegian Research Council and Railcomplete AS.

W. Ahrendt and S. L. Tapia Tarifa (Eds.): IFM 2019, LNCS 11918, pp. 341–359, 2019.
https://doi.org/10.1007/978-3-030-34968-4_19

1 Introduction

Engineering schematics of railway track layouts are used for several purposes: serving as construction blueprints, visualizations on train dispatch workstations, infrastructure models in timetabling software, specifications for interlocking control systems, and more. Because of the large distances involved, geographically accurate drawings are not always suitable for communicating an overview that can help with analyzing and reasoning about the railway models. Instead, many disciplines use *schematic* representations of infrastructures to provide a compressed overview, e.g., shortening sections of the railway that have low information density. Figure 1 compares a geographically correct drawing against two alternative schematic renderings (for two purposes) of the same model. Producing schematic drawings like these involves practical and aesthetic trade-offs between intended structure, simplicity, and geographical accuracy.

Perhaps the most well-known railway schematics are the metro maps for passengers, popularized by the iconic Tube Map of the London Underground. When designing metro maps, removing and compressing geographical information better conveys topological structure (e.g., useful for finding transfers) and sequential information along lines (e.g., for finding your stop).

Methods for automatically producing metro maps have been surveyed in [23]. The main approaches are iterative and force-directed algorithms for gradually transforming a geographical network map into a simpler presentation [2,7], and mixed integer programming methods for finding exactly grid-structured and rigidly optimized solutions [14,16]. For railway drawings the convention is to use only horizontal, vertical, and diagonal lines (at 45°). The problem of drawing

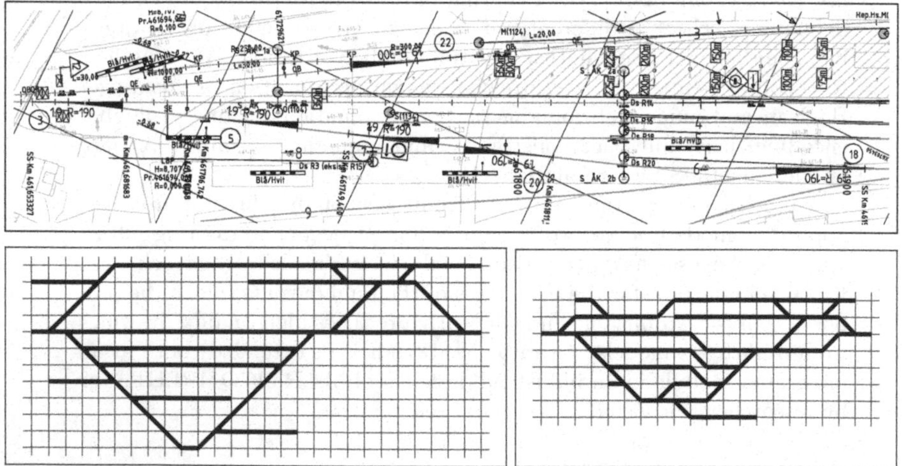

Fig. 1. Example cut-out from a geographical railway drawing (top) and two corresponding full-station schematic layouts, optimized for bends (bottom left) and optimized for height/width (bottom right). See on page 15 our tool's optimization options.

graphs optimized for size and/or bends using only horizontal and vertical lines (so-called orthogonal drawings) can be solved by efficient algorithms [21], but adding diagonal lines in general makes the problem NP-complete [14,15].

Schematic railway drawings used for engineering are usually more strictly constrained than metro maps, but still have large variety in different versions produced for different engineering use cases, project stages, and operational scenarios. Especially in construction projects for new railway lines or upgrades, frequent changes are made in coordinated 2D, 3D, geographical, and schematic models of the railway infrastructure. This can cause much repeated manual work in updating and cross-checking these models after every change in the construction design work in several engineering and construction categories, such as tracks, signaling and interlocking, catenary, cables, telephony.

Automatically producing consistent and high-quality schematics from other models has great potential to increase the efficiency and quality of the documentation, speed up cross-discipline communication during design and construction phases, and also opens up for easier data transfer to other tools. For example, an engineer working on a geographical CAD model may be hindered in performing capacity analysis because importing a network model into a capacity tool may require also inputting a track plan for simulation overview (see, e.g., [12]).

In this paper we develop methods for producing a type of schematic track plan which is suitable for infrastructure within a single corridor, meaning that each point on each track can be located on a common linear axis. We call this a *linear schematic drawing* (see Definition 1). This is a common drawing used for many purposes in construction projects, where drawings typically show placement of tracks and track-side equipment on a single station or along a single corridor. More generally, this problem concerns network structures that are oriented along a linear axis, such as highways, railways, or public transit systems, but may also be extended to encompass routing in electronic design (see e.g. the problem description for VLSI routing in [17]). On larger scales with multiple corridors, the visualization may be split into individual corridors, as in our setting, but for some applications, such as an overview of a national railway network or a city metro network, the single corridor assumption will not work well, and other approaches (see e.g. [14,16]) may be more relevant.

Linear schematic drawings specifically have little coverage in the literature. A specialized algorithm presented in [6] computes corridor-style drawings, but does not guarantee that switch shapes are preserved, and does not offer choice in optimization criteria. For comparison, we apply our method to examples taken from [6] (see Fig. 11). Another algorithmic approach described in [20] has similar goals, but does not automatically produce high-quality results and relies on interactive guidance from the user and manual post-processing.

Graph drawing techniques (see [8,9] for a general overview) have been developed for a great number of different use cases. Most closely related to engineering drawings are the orthogonal layout methods (see e.g. [18,21]) and storyline visualizations (see e.g. [22]). However, most approaches from the graph drawing literature, including orthogonal layout methods, produce outputs that have a distinct style and are not suited to be customized to adhere to engineering drawing conventions.

Instead, we have solved the problem by modeling engineering drawings as mathematical optimization problems using constraints formulated as Boolean satisfiability and difference constraints. We present how different available constraint programming systems can be used to express our constraints, solve optimization problems, and produce high-quality engineering drawings.

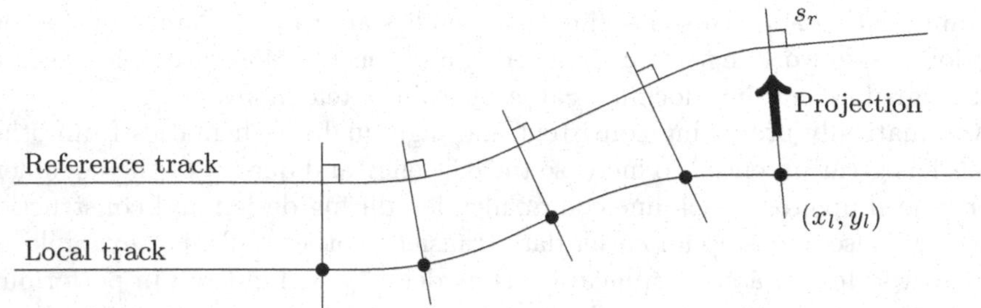

Fig. 2. Linear reference position calculated by projection onto a reference track.

The main contributions of this paper are: (1) We describe and formalize the problem of *linear schematic railway drawings* in Sect. 2. (2) We define three mathematical models for schematic plans, and compare their strengths and weaknesses in Sect. 3. (3) We develop a downloadable tool that can be used by railway engineers to visualize infrastructure, and demonstrate its performance and output on real-world infrastructure models in Sect. 4. Our tool is meant to be used as a module integrated in the RailCOMPLETE engineering framework; but it can also be used as a standalone tool by researchers and developers working on new techniques for analysis and verification, e.g. on interlockings or capacity and timetabling, who can greatly benefit from low-effort, high-quality visualizations in order to improve communication, usability, and for lowering the barrier for adoption of their tools and techniques. Our tool takes input railML files, which are widely available among railway engineers as it is a standard description format for railway infrastructure. The tool also has options for placing symbols besides a track in the schematics.

2 Problem Definition and Formalization

2.1 Linear Positioning System

It is a common practice in railway engineering to use a linear reference positioning system, which assigns a scalar value to each point on, or beside, a railway track. The value corresponds approximately to the traveling distance along a railway corridor from a reference point (which is often a known point on the central station of the network). For a single track, the linear reference system may simply be the arc length from the start of the track's center-line curve. Double tracks and side tracks are typically mapped to the linear reference position by geometrically projecting each point onto a reference curve. The projection's target curve may either be a selected *reference track* (see Fig. 2), or another curve that does not necessarily coincide with a track, such as the geometrical center-line of the corridor. For the rest of this paper, we assume that all locations are already given in such a linear reference system.

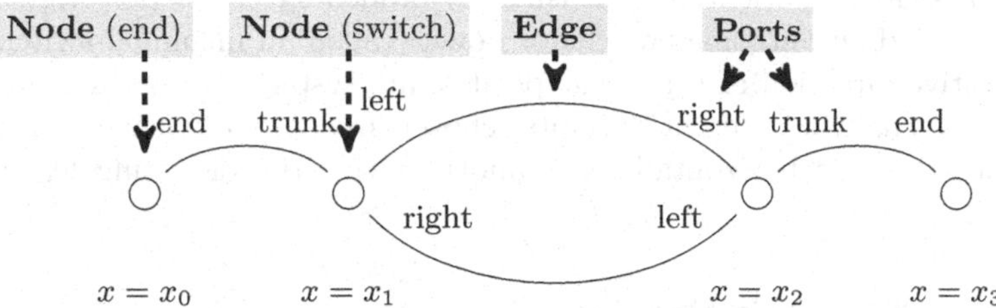

Fig. 3. Graph representation of linearized track plan. Nodes are ordered by an x coordinate, and have a given type which determines which ports it has, e.g., a switch node has *trunk*, *left*, and *right* ports. Edges connect ports on distinct nodes.

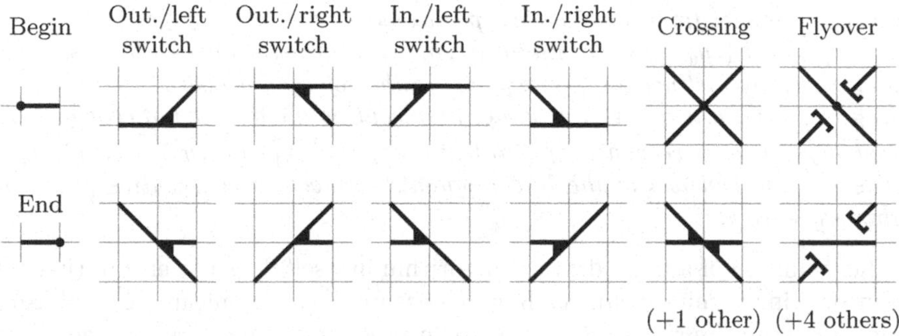

Fig. 4. Node classes and their drawing variants. Begin/end nodes have one variant each. Switches are divided into four classes (each with two variants) based on their orientation (incoming or outgoing) and their course (deviating left or right). Crossings have three variants, and flyovers have six variants (symmetric variants omitted).

2.2 Track Network Representation

Different track segments are connected together at *switches* in a graph-like network. The mathematical definition of a graph is too abstract for many engineering use cases. Some applications use a *double node graph* [11], or describe tracks as nodes with two distinct sides [1]. For a schematic plan, we model switches and crossings as graph nodes which have a given set of *ports* (Fig. 3 presents all our modeling elements). Each end of each edge connects to a specific port on a specific node. Model boundaries and track ends are also represented as nodes with a single port.

Each location where tracks start/end or intersect with other tracks is represented as a node of a given class. The classes used in this paper are ends, switches, crossings, and flyovers (shown in Fig. 4 with all their representative variants). Each class comes with a different set of drawing requirements. For example, a switch is oriented such that its branching edges (left/right) point either up (called an outgoing switch) or down (called an incoming switch), seen in the positive direction of the linear positioning system, and each switch class can be drawn in two different variants, chosen freely, one with the trunk and straight leg directed horizontally and another with the deviating leg directed horizontally.

2.3 Linear Schematic Drawing

A linear schematic drawing algorithm is a core concept in our formalization.

Definition 1. *A linear schematic track drawing algorithm* $d : (N, E) \rightarrow L$ *assigns a set of line segments* L *to each edge in the set* E *of edges connecting the set of nodes* N*, where:*

- $N = \{n_i = (c_i, s_i)\}$*, where* $c_i \in C$ *is a node class, and* $s_i \in \mathbb{R}$ *is a linear position distinct from other nodes' positions.*
- $E = \{e_j = (n_a, p_a, n_b, p_b)\}$*, where* $n_a, n_b \in N$ *are two nodes where* $s_a < s_b$ *and* p_a, p_b *are distinct, available ports on the referenced nodes.*
- $L = \{(e_j, l_j)\}$*, where* l_j *is a polyline, representing the drawing of edge* $e_j \in E$*, and defined by a sequence of points in* $\mathbb{R}^2$*,* $\langle (x_1^j, y_1^j), (x_2^j, y_2^j), \ldots, (x_n^j, y_n^j) \rangle$*. The polyline consists of the line segments connecting consecutive points in this sequence.*

The definition of a track drawing algorithm in itself does not ensure that the output drawing is suitable for reading. To ensure a usable output we establish a set of *criteria for drawing quality* based on engineering conventions and aesthetic judgements. We divide the criteria into *hard constraints*, that all drawings must satisfy and that we can base mathematical models on, and *soft constraints*, which are optimization criteria that can be prioritized differently in different use cases. We base our models on the following hard constraints provided by railway signaling engineers (from Railcomplete AS):

(A) **Octilinearity:** the lines representing tracks should be either horizontal, or diagonal at 45°. This property contributes to the neat look of a schematic drawing, while also giving a visual clue that the drawing is not fully geometrically accurate. When loops are present in the infrastructure, vertical lines may also be allowed, such as in the *balloon loop* used on many tram lines.

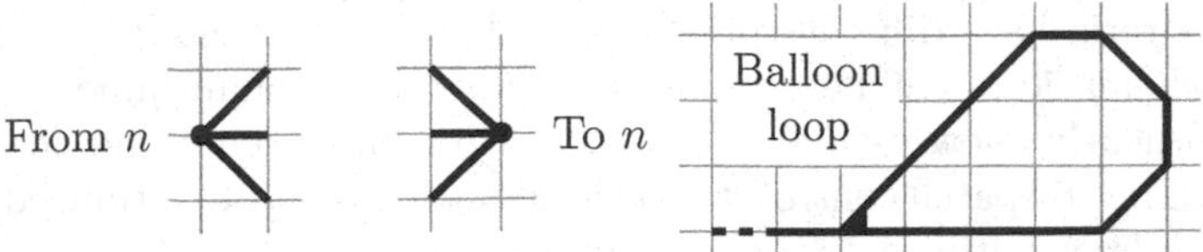

(B) **Linear order:** the reference mileages of locations on the infrastructure should be ordered left-to-right on the schematic drawing to give a clear sense of sequence, which is useful when navigating the infrastructure and reasoning about train movements.

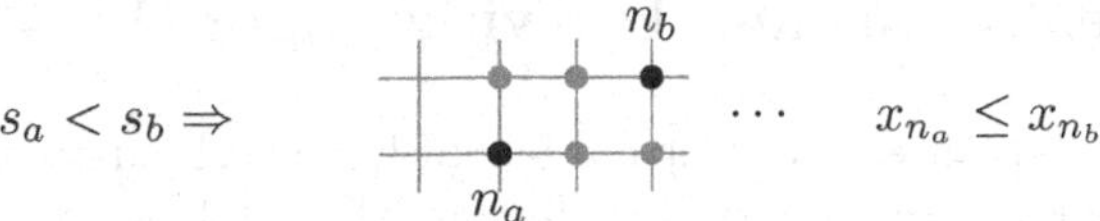

(C) **Node shapes:** switches split the track on the *trunk* side into a left and a right leg on the *branch* side. Left and right should be preserved so that the layout can be traced back to the geography. Since one of the legs of the switch is typically straight and the other is curved, it is also desirable to preserve the straight leg's direction relative to the trunk.

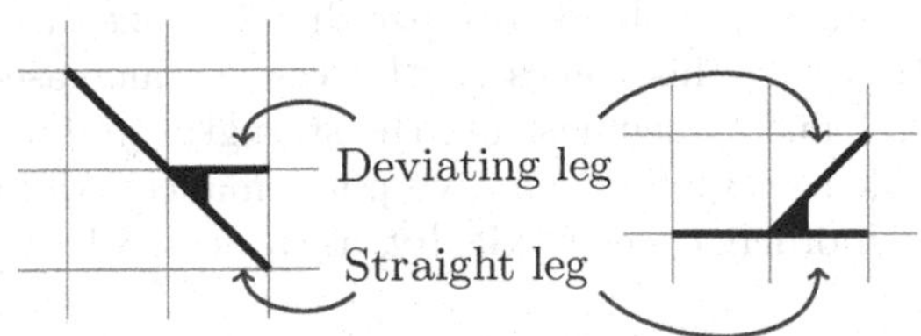

(D) **Uniform horizontal spacing:** parallel tracks are typically required to be drawn at a specific distance from each other, which we normalize and say that y coordinates take integer values. Note that x coordinates have no such restriction, but consecutive nodes will often be placed at integer-valued distances to fulfill the octilinearity constraint.

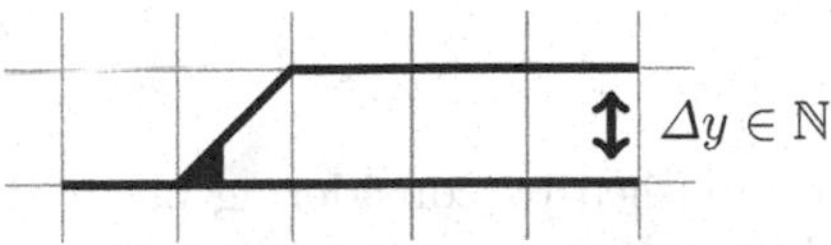

Even with the above constraints fulfilled, there is no guarantee that the drawing output of an algorithm can be deemed of high-quality. For this we use the following soft constraints as optimization criteria:

(i) **Width** and **height** of the drawing.
(ii) **Diagonal line length**, the sum of length of non-horizontal line segments.
(iii) **Number of bends**, i.e. the number of direction changes on lines.

These criteria have different priorities in different use cases. For example, a signaling schematic might be optimized to have a minimum amount of diagonal lines to neatly show several concurrent train movements and their relative progress, while a dispatch control station schematic might be optimized for width to fit more infrastructure into a computer screen.

Several or all of the criteria can be combined into an optimization objective, either by a scoring function, or more commonly, by simply ordering the objectives and performing lexicographical optimization on each objective in turn. Our tool (detailed in Sect. 4) provides options for ranking the objectives.

3 Model Definitions and Drawing Algorithms

This section describes three different models of linear schematic drawings. First, we present a linear programming formulation where edges can have up to two bends. The resulting optimization problem is efficiently solvable, but has some drawbacks in visual quality. Second, we introduce Boolean choice variables to mitigate the shortcomings of the linear programming formulation, and use instead a SAT solver and lazy solving of difference constraints to optimize the Boolean/numerical model (keeping the maximum of two bends per edge). Finally, we present a different Boolean model with unbounded number of bends per edge, which makes this formulation able to optimize drawing size further than the two previous models. However, this comes at the cost of increased running time. Comparison Figs. 7, 8, and 11 demonstrate the strengths and weaknesses of each approach, while Table 1 shows their relative performance. All models use a pre-processing step which orders edges vertically, as in Sect. 3.1.

3.1 Vertical Ordering Relation on Edges

From the nodes and edges defined as inputs to the linear schematic drawing algorithm, it is possible to derive a vertical ordering relation $<_E$ on the set of edges. This relation is a strict partial order relating edges whose linear position intervals intersect, i.e., it relates each pair of edges e_a from n_{a_l} to n_{a_r}, and e_b from n_{b_l} to n_{b_r}, where:

$$]s_{a_l}, s_{a_r}[\ \cap \ ]s_{b_l}, s_{b_r}[\ \neq \emptyset.$$

Such a relation can be established by considering paths starting in each of the branch-side ports of each switch, crossing, and flyover (cf. Fig. 4). For example, an outgoing switch with branch-side edges e_a and e_b connecting to its right and left ports, respectively, will obviously have $e_a <_E e_b$. Each edge connected to the outgoing edges from the other side of e_a and e_b will also be ordered vertically, and so on until either of the following termination conditions are fulfilled:

(C1) The two sets of edges meet in another node.
(C2) One of the sides has no more edges to follow.

More precisely, we define $<_E$ by the following. Let $G = (N, E)$ be the graph from Definition 1. We first look in the positive direction on the linear reference axis. We define a vertical order relation $<_E^i$ for each node $n_i \in N$. If n_i has less than two ports on the side of increasing linear position, $<_E^i$ is empty. However, if the node has two ports on the side of increasing linear position, let the edges connected to these ports be e_l, the lower edge, and e_h, the higher edge. For example, in an outgoing switch node (cf. Fig. 4), these correspond to the right and left ports, respectively.

For any node n_j with $s_i < s_j$, define the directed graph $H_{]i,j[}$ containing:

- The subset of nodes from G with positions in the open interval $]s_i, s_j[$, along with any number of fresh nodes (i.e. the nodes n_i and n_j are not included).
- The subset of edges from G which have at least one end connected to a node from the open interval $]s_i, s_j[$, directed in the direction of increasing linear position. If an edge connects to a node from G which is not included in $H_{]i,j[}$, that connection is replaced with a connection to a distinct fresh node.

We are looking for those nodes n_j such that, in $H_{]i,j[}$, the set of reachable edges when starting from e_l are disjoint from the set of reachable edges when starting from e_h (termination condition (C1)), see Fig. 5(a). Also, the linear position interval of each edge reachable from e_l should have a non-empty intersection with at least one edge reachable from e_h, and vice versa (termination condition (C2)). The node n_j which has the highest position s_j while still fulfilling the above criteria, is called the *termination position.*

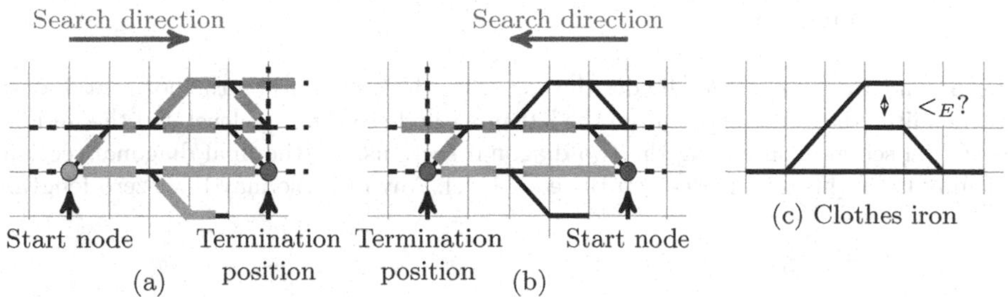

Fig. 5. A search procedure starting in each node produces a set of tuples for the edge vertical order relation $<_E$. Figures (a) and (b) show two different start nodes and search directions, where the lighter, orange edges are all below darker, magenta edges. Figure (c) shows an input on which the procedure cannot decide an ordering. (Color figure online)

Each edge e_x reachable from e_l in $H_{]i,j[}$ is below all edges e_y reachable from e_h in $H_{]i,j[}$ whenever this pair of edges has intersecting linear position intervals, in which case we have $e_x <_E^i e_y$.

For the direction of decreasing linear position we apply the same argument with horizontal directions reversed (see Fig. 5(b)). Finally, the relation $<_E$ is defined as the union of the relations from each node,

$$<_E = \bigcup_{n_i \in N} <^i_E .$$

Remark 1. Unconnected graph components must still be explicitly ordered, and the same for some connected topologies such as the clothes iron example in Fig. 5(c). These are usually easy to decide from, e.g., a geographical model, and this situation occurs rarely, in our experience.

3.2 Level-Based Linear Programming Encoding

We start out by giving a constraint system on linear equations over continuous numerical variables which fulfills the hard requirements from Sect. 2.3 and can be solved efficiently by linear programming (we used the CBC solver v2.9[1]). Later, the shortcomings of this model will motivate the introduction of Boolean and integer-valued variables and a SAT problem formulation.

For each node n_i we use two real variables, x_i and y_i, representing the schematic coordinates of nodes. For each edge e_i we use one real variable l_i representing the edge's *level*. This builds in an assumption that each edge is drawn in three parts as explained in Fig. 6. We introduce the following constraints:

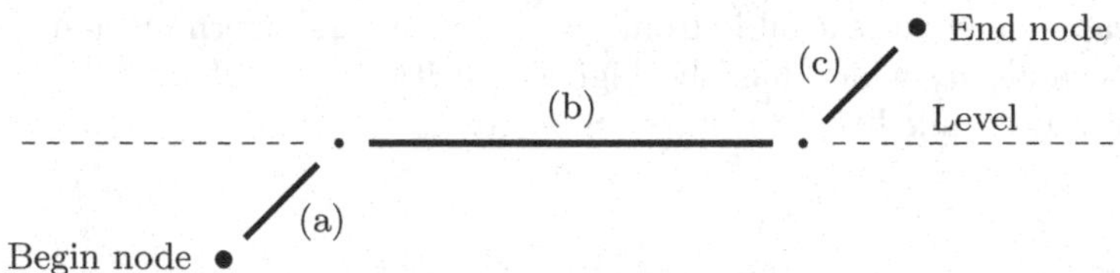

Fig. 6. The *edge level model* divides the edge into three sections on the horizontal axis: (a) the initial diagonal section from the left-most node to the edge level, (b) the middle horizontal section connecting the two diagonal sections, (c) the final diagonal section reaching the right-most node from the edge level. Any of these may have zero length.

1. Node location ordering for successive nodes n_i, n_j gives $x_i \leq x_j$, corresponding to the linear order requirement (from Sect. 2.3(B)).
2. Node location distance for nodes n_i, n_j connected by an edge e_k, where $s_i < s_j$, gives $x_i + |l_k - y_i| + |y_j - l_k| + q_k \leq x_j$, where q_k is 0 if the edge connects an outgoing switch to an incoming switch with the same branching direction, and 1 otherwise. This creates room for a horizontal line segment if needed. The sign of the absolute value terms is determined statically (not part of the linear programming) by the node class and variant. This constraint corresponds to the octilinearity requirement (from Sect. 2.3(A)).
3. Edge level ordering for edges: $e_i <_E e_j$ gives $l_i + 1 \leq l_j$, corresponding to the node shape requirement (from Sect. 2.3(C)).

[1] Part of the COIN-OR project 2018: https://projects.coin-or.org/Cbc.

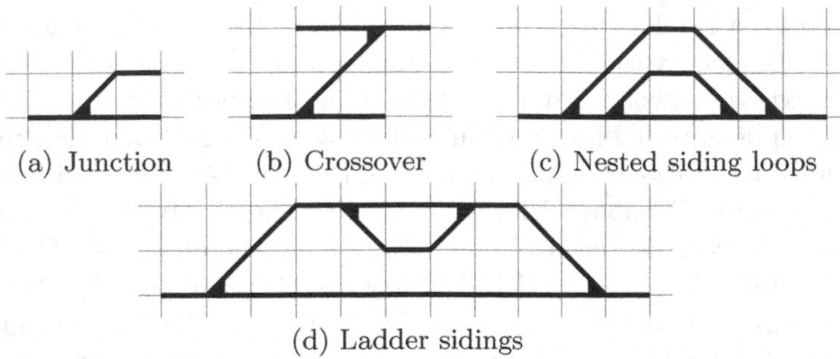
(a) Junction (b) Crossover (c) Nested siding loops

(d) Ladder sidings

Fig. 7. Output examples for the linear programming method. The junction (a) and nested sidings (c) are correctly drawn. The crossover (b) uses 2 units for the diagonal, where 1 would be sufficient, because each edge requires a *level* distinct from other edges with intersecting linear position intervals. The ladder sidings (d) are unnecessarily wide because node shape variants are not included (compare with Fig. 8(b)).

4. Edge levels are related by switches, i.e.: each switch node n_i constrains the trunk-side edge e_j and the straight branch-side edge e_k to be at the same level as the node ($y_i = l_j = l_k$) corresponding to the node shape requirement.

Note that the uniform horizontal spacing constraint (from Sect. 2.3(D)) is implicit in these equations. Now we have the following criteria available for optimization:

- **Width of the drawing.** Take the node n_i with the lowest s_i, and the node n_j with the highest s_j. Then the width of the drawings is $x_j - x_i$.
- **Height of the drawing.** The height of the drawing is not directly expressible in this model, but can be approximated by summing the vertical level difference of edges. For pairs of edges e_i, e_j where $e_i <_E e_j$, the vertical level difference distance is $l_j - l_i$.

Some output examples from the linear programming solution are shown in Fig. 7. Although efficiently solvable, this linear programming solution has a main drawback in that it is not able to choose between different alternatives for drawing a node. For example, in the so-called ladder configuration shown in Fig. 7(d), much space is wasted on diagonal lines going to the top-most level, when the two topmost switches could have been rotated to produce a simpler drawing. Also, each edge needs to have a y value distinct from other edges with intersecting x intervals, even if it is drawn only with diagonals, such as in Fig. 7(b), which contributes to inefficient use of space. Both these shortcomings will be improved by the level-based Boolean formulation in the next section.

3.3 Level-Based SAT Encoding

We reformulate the problem using variables from the Boolean and bounded integer domains. Since we are dealing with small integers, we can transform the problem into a Boolean satisfiability problem (SAT) by encoding numerical variables into Boolean variables and use incremental SAT solvers which can be efficient for lexicographical optimization on small discrete domains, as ours.

Integers can be encoded into SAT in various ways. Eager encodings represent numbers and constraints directly using a set of Boolean variables and constraints and creates an equisatisfiable SAT instance. Most commonly used is the binary encoding (one Boolean for each bit) and the unary encoding (one Boolean for each distinct number). See [4] for details. Lazy encodings, as used in SMT solvers (see [3,13] for an introduction), can avoid some of the work of transforming and solving a large SAT problem by abstracting the numerical constraints into marker Boolean variables. Only when the SAT solver sets markers to true, another procedure (the *theory solver*) will go to work on the numerical constraints and report unsatisfiable combinations back to the SAT solver.

Although the SAT problem itself does not directly concern numbers, much less numerical optimization, an *incremental* interface to a SAT solver allows solving many similar problems consecutively. For a set of constraints ϕ, we can perform numerical optimization on some number x by solving the sequence of formulas $\phi \wedge (x < m_1)$, $\phi \wedge (x < m_2)$, ..., where the sequence m_i is a linear or binary search over the range of x, locating the smallest value that satisfies the constraints. Querying the solver successively with such similar formulas incrementally is much faster than solving the instances separately.

We used the MiniSAT [10] solver v2.2.0 with unary encoding of bounded integers and also lazy representation of unbounded integers with difference constraints, i.e. constraints of the form $x_i - x_j \leq k$, where k is a constant. Difference constraints are suitable as a first-line refinement in SMT solvers (see e.g. [5]) because they can be efficiently solved.

We keep the assumption from the previous subsection that each edge is assigned to a single level, and extend the problem representation as follows:

1. Distances between nodes are represented as a saturating unary number of size 2, i.e. $\Delta x \in \{0, 1, \geq 2\}$. This allows us to distinguish between short ($\Delta x \leq 1$) and long ($\Delta x \geq 2$) edges.
2. For each edge e_j, we use Booleans q_j^{up} and q_j^{down} to indicate a short edge pointing up/down, respectively, seen in the direction of increasing x.
3. Node vertical coordinates y_i and edge levels l_j are represented by unbounded integers on which we can conditionally impose difference constraints.
4. Variant selection $r_i \in R(c_j)$ for each node i indicates the node's variant from the available shapes $R(c_j)$ of the node class $c_j \in C$ listed in Fig. 4.
5. Edge direction values, $d_i^{\text{begin}}, d_i^{\text{end}} \in \{\text{Up}, \text{Straight}, \text{Down}\}$, for the beginning and end of each edge e_i, are based on node variant values.

We need the following constraints:

- Each edge must be at least 1 unit long on the x axis.
- Edge ordering constraints for $e_a <_E e_b$:

$$l_a \leq l_b, \quad (\neg q_a^{\text{up}} \wedge \neg q_b^{\text{down}}) \Rightarrow l_a + 1 \leq l_b$$

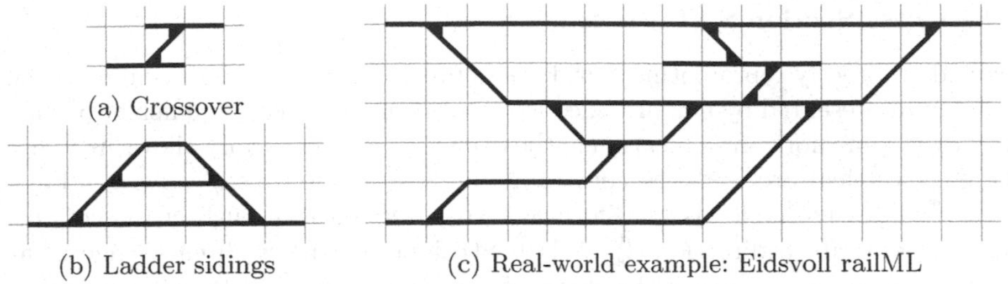

Fig. 8. Output examples for the level-based SAT method. The crossover (a) requires only a 1 unit diagonal edge (improving Fig. 7(b)). The ladder sidings (b) now use diagonal switch variants to improve width, height, and bends (improving Fig. 7(d)). The Eidsvoll station (c) demonstrates real-world infrastructure imported from railML.

If an edge is a short edge (such as a crossover between two adjacent tracks) it does not require its own level, and we use instead the same level as the one of its end nodes which has the *highest* value. This allows to produce a better crossover drawing, as in Fig. 8(a) instead of Fig. 7(b).

- An edge i is short (q^{up} or q^{down}) if both ends have the same direction and the vertical distance between nodes is one:

$$q_i^{\text{up}} \Rightarrow (d_i^{\text{begin}} = \text{Up}) \wedge (d_i^{\text{end}} = \text{Up}) \wedge (y_a + 1 = y_b)$$

$$q_i^{\text{down}} \Rightarrow (d_i^{\text{begin}} = \text{Down}) \wedge (d_i^{\text{end}} = \text{Down}) \wedge (y_a - 1 = y_b)$$

- Direction on edge i decides vertical level constraints:

$$(d_i^{\text{begin}} = \text{Straight}) \Rightarrow (y_a = l_i), \quad (d_i^{\text{begin}} = \text{Up}) \Rightarrow y_a + 1 \leq l_i,$$
$$(d_i^{\text{begin}} = \text{Down}) \Rightarrow ((q_i^{\text{up}} \Rightarrow (y_a \geq l_i)) \wedge (\neg q_i^{\text{up}} \Rightarrow (y_a \geq l_i + 1)))$$

  And correspondingly for d^{end}.
- The sum of Δx values over the edge must match the shape of the edge:

$$\left(q^{\text{up}} \vee q^{\text{down}}\right) \Rightarrow \Sigma_{j \in (a,b)} \Delta x_j \leq 1$$

$$\left(\neg q^{\text{up}} \wedge \neg q^{\text{down}} \wedge \left(d^{\text{begin}} \neq \text{Straight} \vee d^{\text{end}} \neq \text{Straight}\right)\right) \Rightarrow \Sigma_{j \in (a,b)} \Delta x_j \geq 2$$

Since the shape of an edge is now explicit through d^{begin} and d^{end}, we can optimize for the number of bends to produce Fig. 8(b) instead of Fig. 7(d).

The level-based representations do not represent the shapes of edges explicitly at each coordinate, and thus cannot insert bends at arbitrary locations, something which is needed to pack drawings together more tightly. A straightforward grid-based SAT encoding could associate each point on a grid with a choice of any node, and each cell with a choice of edge shape. With this encoding, however, drawings with only about 30 nodes take hours to optimize. We do not describe this method in more detail here, but we have implemented it and tested its performance compared to the other methods, as shown in Table 1.

3.4 Cross-Section SAT Encoding

Instead of directly representing a grid, we define a vertical cross-section c_k of the drawing, represented by a unary-encoded integer $y^k_{e_i}$ capturing the height of each edge e_i at some horizontal location in the drawing. This naturally allows us to use the edge vertical order $<_E$ as constraints on unary numbers $y^k_{e_i} <_E y^k_{e_j}$. Each pair of successive nodes is transformed into a sequence of such cross-sections, and we associate a direction $d^k_{e_i} \in \{\text{Up}, \text{Straight}, \text{Down}\}$ with each edge e_i at each cross-section c_k, giving the shape of the edge to the *left* (lower x value) of the cross-section. Cross-sections can be enabled or disabled (represented by b_k) to optimize the width of the drawing. Finally, the *ahead* Boolean $a^k_{e_i}$ for each edge at each cross-section marks whether the shape of the edge has already been constrained for the next cross-section to the right (higher x value), which allows nodes to impose edge shape constraints in both x-axis directions.

With this representation, we can impose constraints as follows:

1. Edge vertical order:
$$(e_i <_E e_j) \Rightarrow \bigwedge_{c_k} y^k_{e_i} \leq y^k_{e_j}$$

2. A begin node at cross-section c_k constrains the edge shape to the right, and makes the y value unequal to the y value of other edges $e_j \in c_k$.
$$a^k_{e_i} \wedge d^k_{e_i} = \text{Straight}, \quad \bigwedge_{e_j \in c_k} y^k_{e_i} \neq y^k_{e_j},$$
and similar for end nodes, in the opposite direction:
$$\neg a^k_{e_i} \wedge d^k_{e_i} = \text{Straight}, \quad \bigwedge_{e_j \in c_k} y^k_{e_i} \neq y^k_{e_j}.$$

3. A switch node at cross-section c_k constrains the edge shape in both directions by constraining the incoming edges e_i according to the node class variant. For example, for an outgoing left switch we have one incoming edge e_{i1}:
$$\neg a^k_{e_i 1} \wedge d^k_{e_i 1} \neq \text{Up}$$
The incoming edges e_i are replaced by the outgoing edges e_j in the cross-section representation. For example, for an outgoing left switch (see Fig. 9) we have two outgoing edges e_{j1}, e_{j2} as the left and right ports, respectively:
$$a^k_{e_{j1}} \wedge a^k_{e_{j2}},$$
and we have two choices of shape:
$$(d^k_{e_i} = \text{Straight}) \Rightarrow \left(y^k_{e_i} = y^k_{e_{j2}} \wedge d^k_{e_{j2}} = \text{Straight} \wedge d^k_{e_{j1}} = \text{Left}\right)$$
$$(d^k_{e_i} = \text{Down}) \Rightarrow \left(y^k_{e_i} = y^k_{e_{j1}} \wedge d^k_{e_{j2}} = \text{Down} \wedge d^k_{e_{j1}} = \text{Straight}\right)$$
Constraints are similar for other node classes.

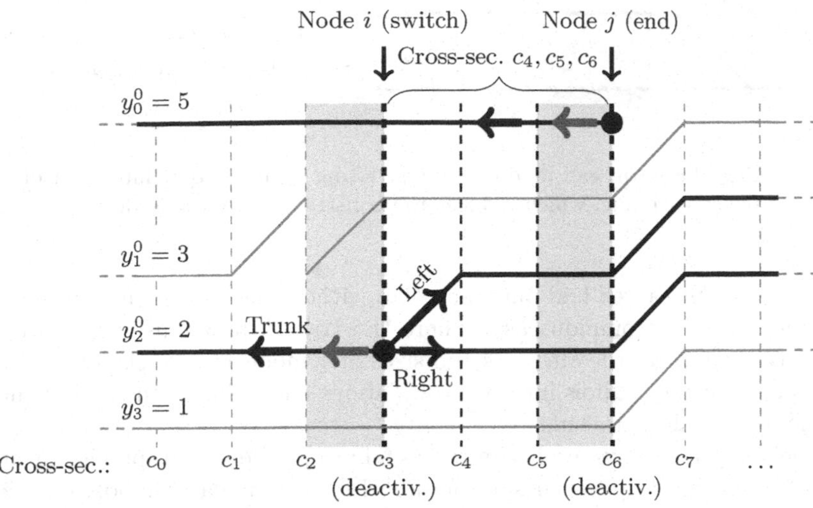

Fig. 9. Cross-section SAT representation. Dashed vertical lines show cross-sections c_i. Edges have a y value and a direction to the left of each cross-sec. Thick red arrows are constraints imposed by node type. Gray columns correspond to deactivated cross-sections, where shape constraints are propagated to the next or previous column. (Color figure online)

4. Disabled cross-sections propagate all their values:

$$\neg b_k \Rightarrow \bigwedge_{e_i \in c_k} \{y^k_{e_i} = y^{k+1}_{e_i} \wedge a^k_{e_i} = a^{k+1}_{e_i} \wedge d^k_{e_i} = d^{k+1}_{e_i}\}$$

5. Enabled cross-sections require consistency between edge shapes and y values:

$$b_k \Rightarrow \bigwedge_{e_i \in c_k} \{(\neg a^k_{e_i} \wedge d^{k+1}_{e_i} = \mathrm{Up}) \Rightarrow y^k_{e_i} + 1 = y^{k+1}_{e_i}\}$$

And correspondingly for *Straight* and *Down* directions.

6. Enabled cross-sections realize rightward-constrained *ahead* values a:

$$b_k \Rightarrow \bigwedge_{e_i \in c_k} \{(a^k_{e_i} \Rightarrow y^k_{e_i} = y^{k+1}_{e_i}) \wedge (a^k_{e_i} \Rightarrow d^k_{e_i} = d^{k+1}_{e_i}) \wedge \neg a^{k+1}_{e_i}\}$$

With this formulation we can choose freely between prioritizing width, height, or bends, and the resulting plans have lower total width than for the level-based methods, since the grid-based method has the added freedom of inserting bends at any location along an edge. See Fig. 11 for a comparison.

3.5 Symbols and Labels

A railway engineering schematic often features a large amount of different symbols and labels (see the example in Fig. 1). In some cases, the symbols and labels

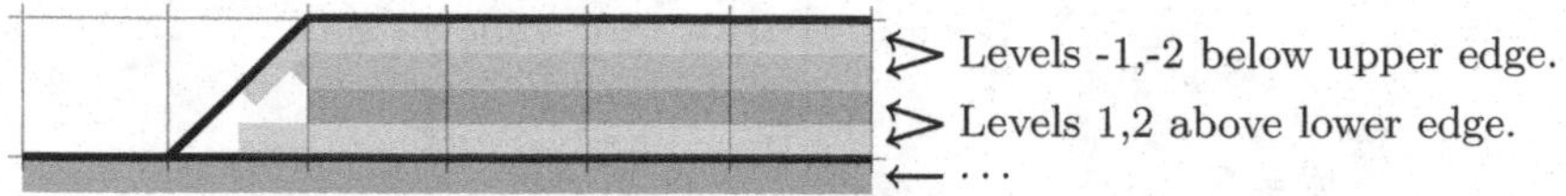

Fig. 10. Label placement can be done by restricting symbols to fit into a set of levels above and below each line, which reduces the constraints to linear ordering.

can be placed onto a well laid-out track plan without needing to change the track plan, but there are common cases where the track layout must be drawn in a way that accounts for the amounts and sizes of symbols and labels. Our tool has options for placing symbols into two rows above and below each track, which is suitable for signaling drawings.

Label placement in general is known as a hard problem in graph visualization. We use a simplified approach suitable for thin rectangular symbols (e.g. as in Fig. 1), and assign each symbol to a level above or below the track (see Fig. 10). Difference constraints on x values ensure that symbols are ordered and not overlapping. When constraints are satisfied, we use linear programming to minimize the deviation from proportional distance between nodes, so that symbols are close to each other on the drawing if they are physically close.

4 Tool Usage

A command-line tool that can generate the drawings as described in this paper is available online[2]. The tool can import railML files as track network input and track-side object symbols, or use a custom format for directly specifying topology. The tool offers two choices of built-in symbol appearances: "*simple*" for generic lamp-like signals and detector, and "*ERTMS*" for ERTMS-style marker boards and detectors (see the bottom part of Fig. 11). Extracting other object types from railML and producing other symbol styles can be done by post-processing JSON output, or by extending the tool using the Lua scripting language. The tool can produce output in JSON format (for custom visualization or post-processing), SVG (for use in web pages and web applications), or TikZ (for use in LaTeX documents).

We have implemented and compared the performance of the above SAT-based methods, summarized in Table 1 (the linear programming formulation is omitted for space, since it has lower quality output). The Direct/SAT encoding has too poor performance to be of practical value. The Levels/SAT encoding is the fastest, and produces good output when optimizing for bends first. Cross-sec./SAT is slower, but is more capable for optimizing for height and width.

[2] https://github.com/luteberget/railplot.

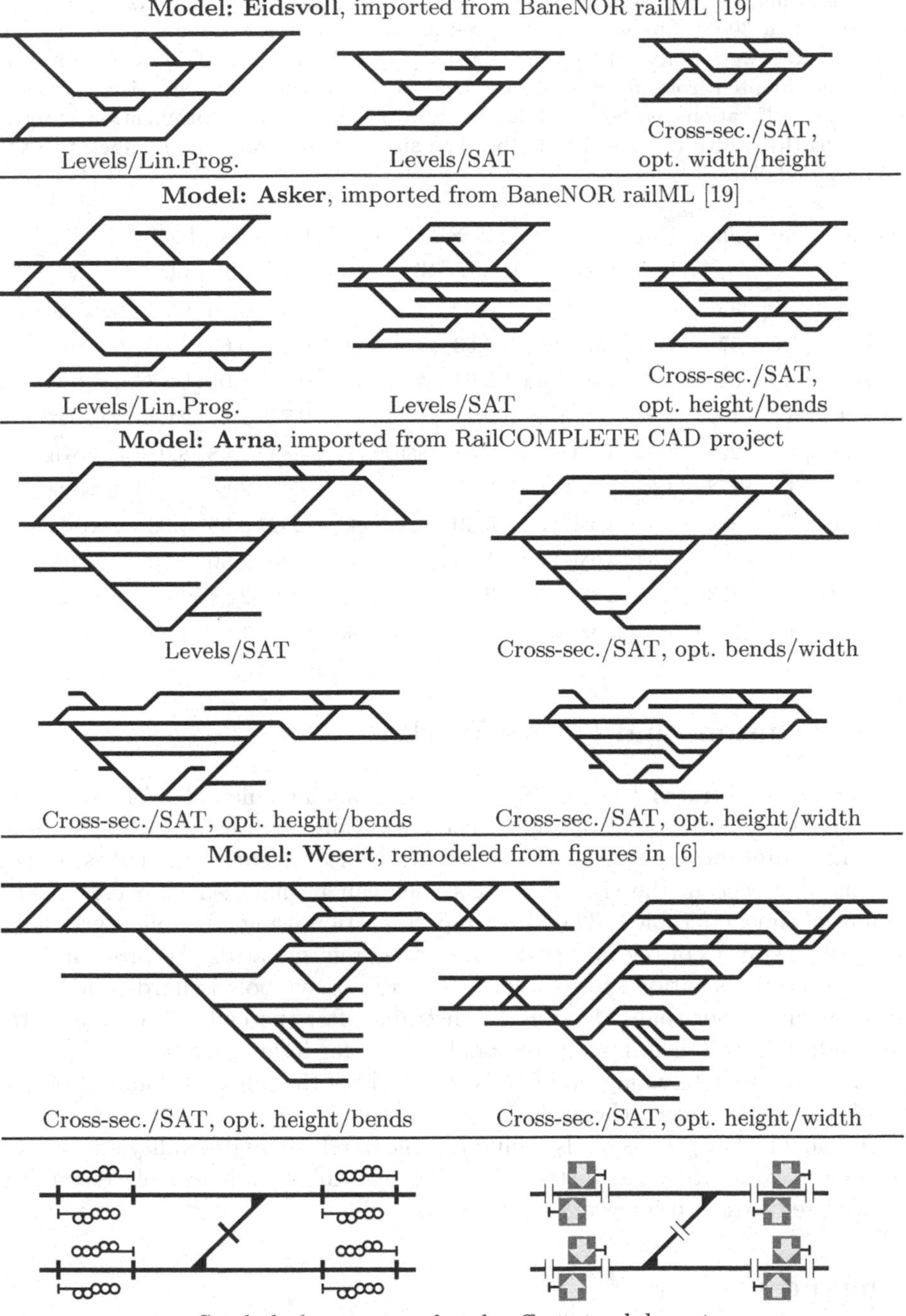

Fig. 11. Comparison of three optimization models on various infrastructure models: Levels/Lin.Prog. (see Sect. 3.2), Levels/SAT (see Sect. 3.3), Cross-sec./SAT (see Sect. 3.4). Symbols and labels placed on the drawing may also affect layout (see Sect. 3.5).

Table 1. Running times in seconds on a mid-range workstation. Time-outs (T/O) indicate exceeding 300 s. Model sizes are given as the sum of the number of nodes and edges. Models were obtained from BaneNOR [19], a RailCOMPLETE CAD project (RC), and adapted from [6]. Scaling test models (T) named $n \times m$ consist of n serially connected stations, each spreading out to m parallel tracks. Optimization criteria are height (h), width (w) and bends (b). The size columns show the number of SAT variables and clauses (v/c).

Model	Src.	Size	Direct/SAT		Levels/SAT		Cross-sec./SAT			
			hwb	Size (v/c)	bhw	Size (v/c)	hwb	hbw	bhw	Size (v/c)
Eidsvoll	[19]	35	60.7	57k/153k	0.02	2.3k/0.7k	0.05	0.06	0.33	4.0k/28k
Arna	RC	57	294	167k/493k	0.03	4.9k/1.3k	0.26	0.65	1.06	11k/100k
Asker	[19]	64	T/O	104k/295k	0.04	5.6k/2.0k	0.61	1.02	0.87	14k/124k
Weert	[6]	102	T/O	304k/969k	0.18	11k/4.0k	0.72	19.3	21.4	29k/327k
5×10	T	228	T/O	2.8M/13M	0.58	35k/2.7k	5.83	7.48	8.08	46k/364k
5×20	T	478	T/O	2.8M/12M	3.37	97k/7.7k	279	299	T/O	265k/4.2M
10×5	T	203	T/O	3.0M/14M	0.40	28k/2.0k	0.52	0.59	1.08	20k/83k
20×5	T	403	T/O	3.0M/14M	1.73	70k/4.0k	1.95	2.50	3.36	44k/165k
10×10	T	453	T/O	2.6M/12M	2.74	86k/5.5k	21.9	22.4	40.7	96k/727k
15×15	T	1053	T/O	2.3M/10M	22.7	255k/15k	T/O	T/O	T/O	N/A

5 Conclusions and Future Work

We have demonstrated the feasibility of using an incremental SAT solver to automatically produce and optimize schematic railway drawings using several different optimization criteria. However, the choice of encoding makes a significant difference in the size of models that can be handled in a reasonable amount of time, cf. Table 1. The direct representation using an explicit grid fails to handle instances of relevant scale. Only after reformulating the problem in a more structured solution space, where the order of symbols is hard-coded into the problem, rather than added as a constraint after the fact, we were able to solve industrial-size instances in reasonable time for interactive use (i.e., under 1s). A remaining interesting problem is the study of the inherent computational complexity of the linear schematic drawing problem.

Our goal is that professionals should be able to rely on high-quality automatic schematics, which requires further tailoring of symbol and text placement to specific use cases, and integration with GUI tools.

References

1. IRS 30100: RailTopoModel - railway infrastructure topological model. The International Union of Railways (UIC) (2016)
2. Avelar, S.: Schematic maps on demand - design, modeling and visualization. Ph.D. thesis, ETH Zürich (2002)

3. Barrett, C., Tinelli, C.: Satisfiability modulo theories. In: Clarke, E., Henzinger, T., Veith, H., Bloem, R. (eds.) Handbook of Model Checking, pp. 305–343. Springer, Cham (2018). https://doi.org/10.1007/978-3-319-10575-8_11
4. Björk, M.: Successful SAT encoding techniques. JSAT **7**(4), 189–201 (2011)
5. Bozzano, M., et al.: An incremental and layered procedure for the satisfiability of linear arithmetic logic. In: Halbwachs, N., Zuck, L.D. (eds.) TACAS 2005. LNCS, vol. 3440, pp. 317–333. Springer, Heidelberg (2005). https://doi.org/10.1007/978-3-540-31980-1_21
6. Brands, A.: Automatic generation of schematic diagrams of the Dutch railway network. M.Sc. thesis, Radboud University (2016)
7. Cabello, S., de Berg, M., van Kreveld, M.J.: Schematization of networks. Comput. Geom. **30**(3), 223–228 (2005)
8. Di Battista, G., Eades, P., Tamassia, R., Tollis, I.G.: Algorithms for drawing graphs: an annotated bibliography. Comput. Geom. **4**, 235–282 (1994)
9. Di Battista, G., Eades, P., Tamassia, R., Tollis, I.G.: Graph Drawing: Algorithms for the Visualization of Graphs. Prentice-Hall, Upper Saddle River (1999)
10. Eén, N., Sörensson, N.: An extensible SAT-solver. In: Giunchiglia, E., Tacchella, A. (eds.) SAT 2003. LNCS, vol. 2919, pp. 502–518. Springer, Heidelberg (2004). https://doi.org/10.1007/978-3-540-24605-3_37
11. Hürlimann, D.: Objektorientierte Modellierung von Infrastrukturelementen und Betriebsvorgängen im Eisenbahnwesen. Ph.D. thesis, ETH Zurich (2002)
12. Luteberget, B., Claessen, K., Johansen, C.: Design-time railway capacity verification using SAT modulo discrete event simulation. In: FMCAD. IEEE (2018)
13. Nieuwenhuis, R., Oliveras, A., Tinelli, C.: Solving SAT and SAT modulo theories: from an abstract Davis–Putnam–Logemann–Loveland procedure to DPLL(T). J. ACM **53**(6), 937–977 (2006)
14. Nöllenburg, M., Wolff, A.: Drawing and labeling high-quality metro maps by mixed-integer programming. IEEE Trans. Vis. Comput. Graph. **17**(5), 626–641 (2011)
15. Nöllenburg, M.: Automated drawing of metro maps. Technical report 25, Universität Karlsruhe, Karlsruhe (2005)
16. Oke, O., Siddiqui, S.: Efficient automated schematic map drawing using multiobjective mixed integer programming. Comput. OR **61**, 1–17 (2015)
17. Ozdal, M.M.: Routing algorithms for high-performance VLSI packaging. Ph.D. thesis (2005)
18. Papakostas, A., Tollis, I.G.: Algorithms for area-efficient orthogonal drawings. Comput. Geom. **9**(1–2), 83–110 (1998)
19. Bane NOR: Model of the Norwegian rail network (2016). http://www.banenor.no/en/startpage1/Market1/Model-of-the-national-rail-network/
20. Seyedi-Shandiz, S.: Schematic representation of the geographical railway network used by the Swedish transport administration. M.Sc. thesis, Lund University (2014)
21. Tamassia, R.: On embedding a graph in the grid with the minimum number of bends. SIAM J. Comput. **16**(3), 421–444 (1987)
22. van Dijk, T.C., Lipp, F., Markfelder, P., Wolff, A.: Computing storyline visualizations with few block crossings. In: Frati, F., Ma, K.-L. (eds.) GD 2017. LNCS, vol. 10692, pp. 365–378. Springer, Cham (2018). https://doi.org/10.1007/978-3-319-73915-1_29
23. Wolff, A.: Drawing subway maps: a survey. Inf. Forsc. Entwick. **22**(1), 23–44 (2007)

Asynchronous Testing of Synchronous Components in GALS Systems

Lina Marsso[1(✉)], Radu Mateescu[1], Ioannis Parissis[2], and Wendelin Serwe[1]

[1] Univ. Grenoble Alpes, Inria, CNRS, Grenoble INP, LIG, 38000 Grenoble, France
lina.marsso@inria.fr

[2] Univ. Grenoble Alpes, Grenoble INP, LCIS, 26000 Valence, France

Abstract. GALS (Globally Asynchronous Locally Synchronous) systems, such as the Internet of Things or autonomous cars, integrate reactive synchronous components that interact asynchronously. The complexity induced by combining synchronous and asynchronous aspects makes GALS systems difficult to develop and debug. Ensuring their functional correctness and reliability requires rigorous design methodologies, based on formal methods and assisted by validation tools. In this paper we propose a testing methodology for GALS systems integrating: (1) synchronous and asynchronous concurrent models; (2) functional unit testing and behavioral conformance testing; and (3) various formal methods and their tool equipments. We leverage the conformance test generation for asynchronous systems to automatically derive realistic scenarios (input constraints and oracle), which are necessary ingredients for the unit testing of individual synchronous components, and are difficult and error-prone to design manually. We illustrate our approach on a simple, but relevant example inspired by autonomous cars.

1 Introduction

A reactive system controls its environment by observing it (via input sensors) and modifying it (via output commands) to obtain the desired behavior. A simple example is the control of the room temperature by commanding a heater. The synchronous approach [16] to reactive systems programming supposes that the system operates triggered by a clock, such that at each clock instant the system instantaneously computes the outputs from the inputs and its internal state. The simplicity of this abstraction is the reason for the success of the synchronous approach, which has been widely used for over two decades for the design and analysis of safety critical systems in various application domains (e.g., avionics, railway transportation, nuclear plants, etc.).

However, modern complex systems, such as autonomous cars or the Internet of Things, are increasingly large and distributed, consisting of multiple components that execute independently and interact with each other. As the assumption of a global clock is less realistic, these systems are better described as GALS

Grenoble INP—Institute of Engineering Univ. Grenoble Alpes.

W. Ahrendt and S. L. Tapia Tarifa (Eds.): IFM 2019, LNCS 11918, pp. 360–378, 2019.
https://doi.org/10.1007/978-3-030-34968-4_20

(Globally Asynchronous, Locally Synchronous) [4,36], i.e., composed of concurrent synchronous reactive systems interacting with each other asynchronously, by means of message passing with non-zero communication delays. For instance, in an autonomous car, the perception devices (radar, lidar, cameras, etc.) and the engine controls are separate components, located in various places of the car, operating independently and connected through communication links. Each of these components might be considered and implemented as a synchronous reactive system, but the complete autonomous car is rather a GALS system. Notice that the GALS approach allows the smooth integration and reuse of existing and time-proven synchronous components when designing new systems that no longer fit into the framework of synchronous programming.

GALS systems are intrinsically complex, and the simultaneous presence of synchronous and asynchronous aspects makes their development and debugging difficult. Hence, to ensure their functional correctness and reliability, it is necessary to follow a rigorous design approach, based on formal methods and assisted by efficient validation and verification tools. Such design approaches and tools exist for the separate modeling and analysis of synchronous or asynchronous parts of a GALS system, but their integration can further improve the effective design of a GALS system.

In this paper we propose a testing methodology for GALS systems integrating: (1) synchronous and asynchronous concurrent models, (2) functional unit testing and behavioral conformance testing, and (3) various formal methods and their tool equipments. The idea is to exploit the information gathered by the analysis of a globally asynchronous system to automate and finely tune the analysis of its individual synchronous components. First, we model the GALS system in GRL (GALS Representation Language) [24,25], a formal language connected to the CADP verification toolbox[1] [10] for asynchronous systems. Using CADP, we validate the asynchronous aspects of the GRL model, e.g., by checking temporal logic formulas expressing desired (global) correctness properties. Next, we use TESTOR [27] to automatically generate conformance tests, which can be used to assess whether an actual implementation of the GALS system conforms to the GRL model. Then, we project such a conformance test on a synchronous component C and translate it automatically into a scenario (i.e., input constraints in Lutin [34] and an oracle in Lustre [18]), required to automate the testing of C using Lurette [22], the test generation tool of the Lustre V6 toolbox[2] [18,34]. Because these scenarios are automatically generated from the GRL model of the GALS system, they correspond by construction to relevant (and often complex) executions of the synchronous component.

We illustrate our approach on a simple, but relevant example, namely an autonomous car, which has to reach a destination, following roads on a map, in the presence of moving obstacles. The car is modeled as a GALS system, comprising synchronous components for perception, decision, and action.

---

[1] http://cadp.inria.fr.

[2] http://www-verimag.imag.fr/DIST-TOOLS/SYNCHRONE/lustre-v6/.

The remainder of the paper is organized as follows. In Sect. 2, we introduce the formal GRL model of an autonomous car. In Sect. 3, we describe the application of analysis techniques for asynchronous systems to the overall GALS system, in particular model checking and conformance test generation. In Sect. 4, we recall techniques for the functional testing of synchronous components. In Sect. 5, we present the main contribution of this paper, namely the integration of asynchronous conformance testing with automated synchronous testing to improve the latter. In Sect. 6, we compare our approach to existing GALS validation approaches. Finally, in Sect. 7 we give concluding remarks and suggest future research directions.

2 GRL Model of an Autonomous Car

To illustrate our approach, we consider the behavioral model of a (simplified) autonomous car interacting with its physical environment, i.e., a given set of moving obstacles (pedestrians, cyclists, other cars, etc.) evolving with the car on a (geographical) map. To limit the complexity, each obstacle executes a fixed number of random or statically chosen movements. The autonomous car itself consists of four synchronous components:

(i) a *GPS* keeps the current position of the car updated,
(ii) a *radar* detects the presence of the obstacles close to the car and builds a perception grid summarizing information about perceived obstacles,
(iii) a *decision* (or trajectory) controller computes an itinerary from the current position to the destination, avoiding streets containing obstacles, and
(iv) an *action* controller commands the engine and direction to follow the itinerary computed by the decision controller, using the perception grid built by the radar to avoid collisions.

These four components communicate in various ways:

- the GPS sends the current position to the decision controller upon request,
- the radar periodically sends the perception grid to the action controller, and
- the action controller requests a new itinerary from the decision controller.

GRL (GALS Representation Language) [24, 25] is a formal language designed to model GALS systems. It integrates the synchronous reactive model underlying dataflow languages and the asynchronous interleaving semantics of concurrency underlying process algebras. Figure 1 shows the architecture of our GRL model of the autonomous car. Each synchronous component (`ACTION`, `RADAR`, `DECISION`, and `GPS`) is represented in GRL as a **block**, depicted as a (light blue) rectangle with solid border in Fig. 1. These blocks exchange data via asynchronous communication media (`POSITION`, `PATH`, `CURRENT_GRID`), each of which is represented in GRL as a **medium**, depicted as a (pink) ellipse with dashed border in Fig. 1. The interaction between blocks also respects constraints (`MAP_MANAGEMENT`), each one being represented in GRL as an **environment**, depicted as a (light pink)

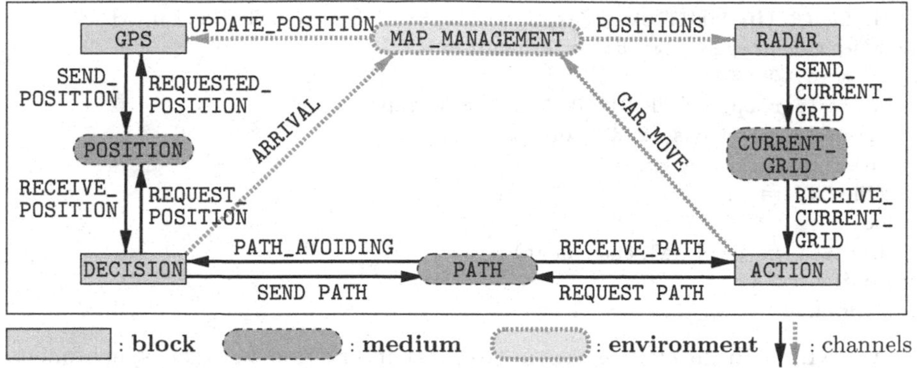

Fig. 1. Architecture of the GRL model of an autonomous car (Color figure online)

ellipse with thick dashed border in Fig. 1. The overall model of the car is represented in GRL as a **system**, which describes the composition and interactions of blocks, media, and environments. In the sequel, we present excerpts of a block, a medium, and an environment of our GRL model (1271 lines).[3]

The map is represented as a directed graph, in which edges correspond to streets and nodes correspond to crossroads; for simplicity, we assume that the car or an obstacle occupies a street completely (a longer street can be represented by several edges in the graph). A set of functions is defined to explore this graph, to compute itineraries, etc. The GRL model is instantiated by providing global constants encoding the map, the initial position and destination of the car, and the set of obstacles with their initial positions and lists of movements.

A GRL **block** defines the deterministic code executed by the synchronous component at each *activation* (i.e., clock instant). For instance, the radar of our autonomous car is modeled by the GRL block `RADAR`, which has a **static** variable `previous_grid` to keep track of the perception grid computed during the previous activation. This grid is considered to be initially empty (i.e., it has the value `Grid (NIL)`). At each activation, the radar receives the current positions of the car and all the obstacles as input from the environment (**in** parameter `POSITIONS`).[4] It then computes the current perception `grid` indicating, for each possible direction the car might take, whether at least `radar_visibility` steps are free of any obstacle. If there is a change between `previous_grid` and `grid`, both the variable `previous_grid` and the output `CURRENT` are updated; otherwise the output is set to the particular value `already_sent` indicating that the grid did not change. At the end of the activation, the computed grid is sent to the connected medium (**send** parameter `CURRENT`).

[3] The complete GRL model, test purpose, the MCL properties, SVL and XTL scripts, and other resources related to the example are available as a demo in the GRL distribution at http://convecs.inria.fr/software/grl.

[4] Currently, for the interaction between a block and an environment, GRL requires to wrap several inputs or outputs into a single structured input or output.

```
block RADAR (in POSITIONS: Car_Obstacle_Pos) [send CURRENT: Grid] is
  static var previous_grid: Grid := Grid (NIL)
  var grid: Grid
  grid := perception (POSITIONS, radar_visibility);
  if grid != previous_grid then
    previous_grid := grid;
    CURRENT := grid
  else
    CURRENT := Grid (already_sent)
  end if
end block
```

A GRL **medium** enables (asynchronous) interaction between synchronous blocks. Explicitly representing media makes it possible to finely model a large panel of behaviors (i.e., message buffering, message loss, nondeterminism, etc.). A medium is connected to each block by at most two channels, called **receive** and **send** channels. Note that a **receive** channel corresponds to the reception of some value in a variable prefixed by "?". Each channel has an associated Boolean condition (tested with a **when** clause), stating whether a message is available. For instance, the following GRL medium `CURRENT_GRID` enables the block `RADAR` to send the current perception grid (via the **receive** channel `INPUT`) to the block `ACTION` (via the **send** channel `OUTPUT`); the transmission takes place only when the perception grid has not already been sent.

```
medium CURRENT_GRID [receive INPUT: Radar_Grid,
                     send OUTPUT: Radar_Grid] is
   static var buffer: Radar_Grid := Grid (NIL)
   select
      when ?INPUT ->
         if INPUT != Grid (already_sent) then buffer := INPUT end if
   [] when OUTPUT -> OUTPUT := buffer
   end select
end medium
```

A GRL **environment** provides blocks with inputs and receives their outputs. Block activations are particular inputs, enabling an environment to precisely control the activations of synchronous blocks, e.g., to control the relative clock speeds and/or drifts. The following fragment of the GRL environment `MAP_MANAGEMENT` ensures that: (1) the positions of the car (`map.c`) and obstacles (`grid`) are shared with the block `RADAR` (by sending this information to `RADAR` as input `POSITIONS`); (2) this information is updated when the car or the obstacles move (by receiving these moves from blocks `ACTION` and `RADAR` as outputs `CAR_MOVE` and `OBSTACLE_MOVE`, respectively); and (3) the blocks are only activated as long as the car neither arrived at destination, nor crashed. Note that an environment may be nondeterministic, e.g., it may contain nondeterministic choices, modelled in GRL using the **select** statement.

```
environment MAP_MANAGEMENT (block RADAR, ...
                            in OBSTACLE_MOVE: Obstacle,
                            in CAR_MOVE: Control, ...
```

```
                                   out POSITIONS: Car_Obstacle_Pos, ...) is
   static var grid: Grid := Grid (NIL),
          map: Localization := Localization (initial_street, initial_map),
          crash: Bool := false, car_arrived: Bool := false, ..
   var collison_detected: Bool, ...
   if not (crash or car_arrived) then
      select
         -- send updated inputs (car and obstacle positions) to the radar
         when POSITIONS -> POSITIONS := pos (map.c, grid)
      [] -- car movement
         when ?CAR_MOVE ->
            -- update car position in the map
            map := move_car (map, CAR_MOVE);
            -- check for collisions (car and an obstacle on the same street)
            collision_detected := intersection (grid, map);
            if collision_detected then crash := true end if
      [] -- potential obstacle movement
         when ?OBSTACLE_MOVE ->
            if OBSTACLE_MOVE != null_obstacle then
              -- update obstacle positions in the grid
              grid := move_obstacle_grid (grid, OBSTACLE_MOVE)
            else
              -- no effective movement
              grid := grid
            end if
      ...
      end select
   end if
end environment
```

GRL defines the semantics of a GALS system as an LTS (Labeled Transition System), whose states represent the memories of all blocks, media, and environments of the system [24, Chapter 4]. The initial state is the initial memory, in which each static variable has its (mandatory) initial value. Each transition going out of a state corresponds to the atomic execution of a block, which consists in reading the values of input and receive channels, executing the code of that block activation, and producing the values for the outputs and send channels of the block. The transition is labeled with all these values, and its target state corresponds to the updated memories of the participating components, i.e., the block and its connected mediums and environments. Thus, the atomic executions of synchronous blocks are interleaved in the LTS, which reflects the GALS nature of the system.

For technical reasons, we rely in this paper on the semantics of GRL as induced by the current translation-based implementation of GRL (see below). In this semantics [24, Chapter 5], the execution of a synchronous block activation is split into an input transition followed by an output transition. These two transitions are executed atomically, i.e., without interleaving of any other transitions corresponding to an activation of another block.

3 Model Checking and Conformance Test Generation

When considering a complete GALS system from the outside, all parts based on the synchronous programming paradigm are hidden. Thus, the overall GALS system is amenable for classic analysis techniques developed for asynchronous systems. GRL is equipped with the GRL2LNT [24,25] translator to LNT [11], the modern formal modeling language recommended as input for the CADP verification toolbox [10]. Using GRL2LNT and CADP, for a map (with 22 streets and 8 crossroads) and two obstacles, each with a first random movement and a second statically chosen movement, we generated (in about 4 min on a standard laptop) the LTS corresponding to our GRL autonomous car model (3,568,781 states and 5,619,802 transitions; 287,103 states and 406,780 transitions after strong bisimulation minimization).

3.1 Model Checking

We first validated our GRL model by checking several safety and liveness properties characterizing the correct behavior of the autonomous car. We expressed the properties in MCL [29], which is the data-handling, action-based, branching-time temporal logic of the on-the-fly model checker of CADP. For simplicity, we describe here the properties in natural language, only giving and commenting the MCL code of the first one to illustrate the flavor (see footnote 3).

- The position of the car is correctly updated after any movement of the car. This safety property specifies that on all transition sequences, an update of the car position (action "`UPDATE_POSITION ?current_street`", where `current_street` is the street on which the car is) followed by a car movement (action "`CAR_MOVE ?control`", where `control` is a movement command) must be followed by an update of the car position consistent with `current_street`, `control`, and the map. This can be expressed in MCL using the necessity modality below, which forbids the transition sequences containing inconsistent position updates:

```
[ true* .
  { UPDATE_POSITION ?current_street:String } .
  (not ({ CAR_MOVE ... } or { UPDATE_POSITION ... }))* .
  { CAR_MOVE ?control:String } .
  (not ({ CAR_MOVE ... } or { UPDATE_POSITION ... }))* .
  { UPDATE_POSITION ?new_street:String where
    not (Consistent_Move (current_street, control, new_street)) }
] false
```

  The values of the current position, movement, and new position of the car present on the actions `UPDATE_POSITION` and `CAR_MOVE` are captured in the variables `current_street`, `control`, and `new_street` of the corresponding action predicates (surrounded by `{ }`) and reused in the **where** clause of the last action predicate. The predicate `Consistent_Move` defines all valid combinations for `current_street`, `control`, and `new_street` allowed by the map.

- A same message from one of the autonomous car components must be considered only once. For instance, the radar should not send twice the same perception grid, i.e., two successive occurrences of action SEND_CURRENT_GRID must carry different values of the grid, reflecting the changes in perception due to obstacle or car movements.
- Inevitably (by avoiding the non-progressing iterations of the synchronous blocks), the system should reach a state where either the car arrived, a collision occurred between the car and an obstacle, or all obstacles have finished their list of movements.

3.2 Conformance Test Generation

Conformance testing aims at establishing whether an SUT (System Under Test) conforms to a formal model, i.e., whether the SUT is an implementation of the model. For concurrent asynchronous systems, both the formal model and the SUT are represented as IOLTSs (Input-Output LTSs), i.e., LTSs whose actions are separated into controllable inputs and observable outputs, even if the IOLTS of the SUT is not necessarily known. A popular relation used for conformance testing is **ioco** [37], which specifies that an SUT conforms to a model if after executing each trace of the model, the SUT exhibits only the outputs and quiescences (i.e., deadlocks, outputlocks, and livelocks) allowed by the model. A classical conformance testing approach consists in deriving from the formal model a suite of *test cases*, which are then executed on the SUT to check the conformance using black-box testing techniques. This approach is based on the hypothesis of synchronous communication between tester and SUT; adaptations are required if this hypothesis is not satisfied (e.g., in the case of remote interaction using buffered channels) [13,32]. To focus the testing process and help the test-case extraction, *test purposes* are used to describe the goal states, i.e., those states of the model to be reached during execution of the test case on the SUT. Executing a test case may produce one of three possible verdicts: *pass* when a goal state has been reached, *fail* when the observed behavior of the SUT is not conform to the model, and *inconclusive* if the goal states become unreachable.

The online-testing tool TESTOR [27] is capable of extracting controllable test cases on the fly. Concretely, starting from the GRL model of a GALS system, a description of the input actions, and a test purpose, TESTOR explores the model and generates automatically a set of test cases or a *complete test graph* (CTG) [23] to be executed on a physical implementation of the system. Intuitively, a CTG denotes a set of traces containing visible actions and quiescence that should be executable by the SUT to assess its conformance with the model and a test purpose. The quiescence is represented in the CTG as self-loops labeled by a special output action δ on the quiescent states. TESTOR handles possibly nondeterministic models and ensures by construction that the complete test graph provides only inputs that allow to reach a goal state (if possible).

For the GRL model of the autonomous car (see Sect. 2), the only controllable inputs are the movements of obstacles; the observable outputs make it possible to study the behavior of the car. An example test purpose ($T2$) is to specify the situation where a collision occurs between a car and an obstacle. The test purpose is expressed as an LTS (in the AUT format), where a transition representing the collision (action `COLLISION`) should lead to a goal state, i.e., having an outgoing transition labelled by an `ACCEPT` action. We also defined four other examples of test purposes ($T1$, $T3$, $T4$, and $T5$) constraining the car and obstacles interaction on the map. For these test purposes, TESTOR generates the complete test graphs in less than a minute (see Table 1).

4 Testing Techniques for Synchronous Components

Functional testing of a reactive system requires to provide a *sequence* of inputs and observe the corresponding sequence of outputs. In general, the previously observed outputs must be taken into account when computing the next input, so as to provide the reactive system with a realistic behavior of the physical environment the reactive system is controlling. Furthermore, the decision about success or failure of a test also requires the sequence of (input, output) pairs, because the reactive system might change its function to adapt to its environment. Hence, testing a reactive system requires specific techniques and tool support to automate the testing process [21].

In this section, we briefly present the testing tool Lurette [22] for synchronous programs. Using formal specifications of the input constraints and an oracle, Lurette automates both, the generation of appropriate inputs for the SUT and the decision about the test result. Lurette takes three inputs:

(i) a specification in Lutin [34] to dynamically constrain the inputs;
(ii) an oracle in Lustre [18] implementing the test decision; and
(iii) some parameters controlling the execution and the coverage-computation of the generated and executed input sequences.

Lurette interacts with the SUT, generates the input sequences with their corresponding outputs in a file, and displays the test decisions.

We illustrate the usage of Lurette to test an implementation of a radar in the C language, which might be a part of an implementation of our GALS autonomous car example described in Sect. 2. Usually, a radar builds an occupancy grid with respect to its position (this grid reflects the visibility of the radar); in an autonomous car, the position of the radar is the position of the car. To simplify, in our example, the radar takes as input the position of the car and the obstacles (provided by the GRL environment on channel `POSITIONS`), and the radar outputs the perception grid (sent to the medium `CURRENT_GRID`).

As in Sect. 3, we consider a fixed instance with two obstacles (`leo` and `lilly`). Testing the synchronous radar component consists in providing a sequence of inputs and observing the generated sequence of outputs. Each of the radar's inputs (position of the car and the obstacles) can take one out of the 21 streets of the map, yielding 21^3 possible inputs. Fortunately, not all sequences of these inputs are realistic, because the car is not flying and has to respect the constraints of the map. However, relevant tests of the radar should include situations where the radar detects obstacles.

The input constraints for the radar should enforce that the positions of the car and the obstacles evolve in a realistic manner, i.e., respecting the map. The following Lutin code corresponds to a simple scenario, where the car starts on street 9 and possibly moves to street 12, and `lilly` (respectively, `leo`) appears on street 5 (respectively, street 14) and moves back and forth to street 12 (respectively, street 11). This scenario can be described by an automaton with five states and seven transitions; the corresponding constraints on the inputs of the radar can be encoded in Lutin as a node `input_constraints` with four outputs (the three inputs of the radar plus the state `s` of the automaton). Although simple, the scenario covers the apparition and movement of obstacles, and the case where the perception grid should remain unchanged.

```
node input_constraints () returns (car, leo, lilly, s: int) =
  let not_visible: int = 2000 in
  (* initial state: car on street 9 and no visible obstacles *)
  car = 9 and lilly = not_visible and leo = not_visible and s = 0 fby
  loop {
    | (* s = 0 -> car on street 9, lilly on street 5, leo on street 14, s = 1 *)
      (pre s = 0) and car = 9 and lilly = 5 and leo = 14 and s = 1
    | (* s = 0 -> car on street 12, lilly on street 5, leo on street 14, s = 2 *)
      (pre s = 0) and car = 12 and lilly = 5 and leo = 14 and s = 2
    | (* s = 1 -> car on street 9, leo on street 11, lilly on street 12, s = 3 *)
      (pre s = 1) and car = 9 and lilly = 12 and leo = 11 and s = 3
    | (* s = 1 -> car on street 12, leo on street 11, lilly on street 5, s = 4 *)
      (pre s = 1) and car = 12 and lilly = 5 and leo = 11 and s = 4
    | (* s = 2 -> car on street 12, leo on street 11, lilly on street 5, s = 4 *)
      (pre s = 2) and car = 12 and lilly = 5 and leo = 11 and s = 4
    | (* s = 3 -> car on street 12, leo on street 14, lilly on street 18, s = 1 *)
      (pre s = 3) and car = 9 and lilly = 5 and leo = 14 and s = 1
    | (* s = 4 -> car on street 12, leo on street 14, lilly on street 5, s = 2 *)
      (pre s = 4) and car = 12 and lilly = 5 and leo = 14 and s = 2
  }
```

At each iteration, Lurette generates inputs by executing one transition of the Lutin node. Note that if the input values are not explicitly constrained in the Lutin specification, random numbers will be generated. Although larger and more complex scenarios can be written manually, this task is tedious and error-prone, in particular due to the representation of street names by natural numbers (the input language of Lutin supports only Boolean and numerical types), and may easily introduce redundant definitions or equivalent states.

The role of oracles is to determine whether the generated outputs are correct or not. An oracle should contain all possible pairs of inputs with the corresponding expected outputs, and signal an error for each unexpected output.

In addition to checking correctness, Lurette supports additional Boolean outputs (called coverage variables) to measure coverage. While testing the SUT, Lurette records the coverage variables that were at least once true, and computes the ratio of covered versus uncovered variables. This information is stored in a file, and updated by any subsequent run of Lurette for the same SUT, input constraints, and oracle.

A small example of an oracle for the previous scenario is given by the following Lustre node `oracle`, describing the expected output (perception grid) for each given input vector (the positions of the car and obstacles). As the Lutin node, the oracle takes, besides the inputs and outputs of the radar, as input also the state `s` to keep track of the evolution (according to the same small automaton mentionned previously). The oracle outputs the verdict `res`, i.e., whether the observed outputs are those expected for the state and the inputs. For instance, in state 3, `lilly` (in street 12) and `leo` (in street 11) should both be detected by the car (in street 9), whereas they should not be detected in the initial state. The oracle also computes two coverage variables `pass` and `blocked`: the former measures the coverage of state 2 (representing the situation where the car arrives at destination and all obstacles appeared), and the latter measures the coverage of the situation where the car is blocked by the obstacles.

```
const invisible = 2000, already_sent = 3000;
node oracle (s, car, lilly, leo, perception_leo, perception_lilly: int)
returns (res, pass, blocked: bool);
let res = true ->
  ((* lilly and leo are visible from the street 9 *)
    (s = 0 and car = 9 and lilly = invisible and leo = invisible and
     perception_lilly = invisible and perception_leo = invisible)
   or (* the perception did not change, it is already sent *)
    (s = 1 and car = 9 and lilly = 5 and leo = 14 and
     perception_lilly = already_sent and perception_leo = already_sent)
   or (* leo and lilly are visible from the street 9 *)
    (s = 3 and car = 9 and lilly = 12 and leo = 11 and
     perception_lilly = 12 and perception_leo = 11)
   or ... );
   (* true if the car reached the destination (state 2) *)
   pass = false -> if s = 2 then true else pre pass;
   (* true, if the car is blocked by the obstacles *)
   blocked = false -> if s = 3 then true else pre pass;
tel
```

Even more than for the Lutin constraints, manually deriving the oracle is complicated, mainly due to the dependency on the map and the necessity to enumerate all possible movements. For instance, to detect the `already_sent`, one should manually follow the scenario's evolution. Because one can easily forget some cases, an automated generation of these input constraints and the oracle is more convenient, as we illustrate in the next section.

5 Test Projection and Exploration

Each synchronous component of a GALS system is constrained by the other synchronous components, communication media, and environments present in the system. In this section we explicitly exploit these constraints to improve the unit testing of a synchronous component taken separately.

The idea is to automatically derive inputs for synchronous testing tools by projecting the complete test graph generated for the entire GALS system on the inputs and outputs of the synchronous component. In this way, the inputs provided to the synchronous component are realistic and relevant, because they are chosen according to possible execution scenarios of the overall GALS system. Furthermore, the synchronous tests generated in this way contain all possible inputs leading to the goals of test purposes (e.g., a possible input leading to collision in the case of $T2$).

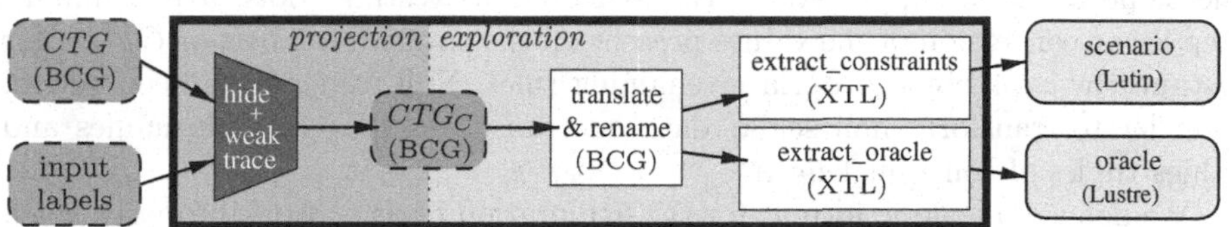

Fig. 2. Overview of the derivation of synchronous test scenarios by projection and exploration of an asynchronous complete test graph CTG

Figure 2 gives an overview of the approach. In a first step, a conformance complete test graph for the overall GALS system is projected on the synchronous component C to be tested, resulting in a test graph for C. In a second step, this test graph is translated and renamed to be compatible with the synchronous testing tool Lurette. In the last step, the test graph is explored (using XTL [28] scripts), generating the input constraints and the oracle for testing C separately. In the remainder of this section, we present the approach in more detail, illustrating how it improves the testing of the radar of our autonomous car example.

5.1 Test Graph Projection

Projecting a complete test graph CTG on a synchronous component C consists in hiding all transitions labeled with an action that is neither an input nor an output of C, and reducing the resulting graph for weak trace equivalence, yielding the projected test graph CTG_C. The reduction removes all internal transitions (created by the hiding), so that all actions of CTG_C are either an input or an output of C. A precondition for a successful projection is that all inputs and outputs of C, as well as the verdict transitions, are present and visible in CTG. Notice that projecting onto the interface of C enables synchronous interaction between the tester and an SUT of C, avoiding all issues related to the asynchronous communication [13,32] present in the GALS model.

In the example of the autonomous car, the radar takes as input the positions of the car and of the obstacles. The positions of the obstacles are also a controllable input of the overall GALS system (see Sect. 3). But the position of the car is computed by the scenario depending on the output of another synchronous component, namely the action controller. The output of the radar is the perception grid, which is, inside the GALS system, sent to the action controller. Hiding, in the complete test graph *CTG*, all transitions but those corresponding to these inputs and outputs, and reducing the result with respect to weak trace equivalence yields the LTS $\texttt{CTG}_{\texttt{RADAR}}$. Columns 6 & 7 of Table 1 give the number of states and transitions of $\texttt{CTG}_{\texttt{RADAR}}$ for the five test purposes considered.

5.2 Translating and Renaming

Because some of the data types used in the GALS model might not be exactly the same as those supported by the synchronous testing tools, a preliminary step is the conversion of the values present on the transition labels of CTG_C, for instance by applying appropriate renaming rules. Null values have been added, in order to transform non scalar data on transitions into variable names and values tuples of constant length.

We defined a generic format for the exploration tools to work properly. Each input transition is renamed into "`INPUT` $!s_1\ !v_1\ \ldots\ !s_m\ !v_m$", where s_i is the name of the input and v_i its value; each output transition is similarly renamed into "`OUTPUT` $!s_1\ !v_1\ \ldots\ !s_n\ !v_n$". For instance, the projected complete test graph $\texttt{CTG}_{\texttt{RADAR}}$ contains non-scalar data structures, in particular, the perception grid computed by the radar is represented as a list and streets are identified by their names (i.e., character strings). To be usable with the synchronous test generator Lurette [22], these lists need to be transformed into tuples of constant length, and the street names need to be translated into the corresponding (numeric) constants.

5.3 Test Graph Exploration

By construction, the projected CTG_C is an LTS describing the interaction with the SUT, and as such contains both, the sequence of inputs for the SUT and the verdict concerning the test outcome (i.e., the test oracle). Because the test inputs and oracle should be provided to Lurette using two different languages (Lutin for the input constraints and Lustre for the oracle), two explorations of (the renamed) CTG_C are required.

The input constraints are generated by encoding CTG_C as a possibly nondeterministic node in Lutin with the XTL [28] script `extract_constraints` (87 lines). This node has the same inputs as C and an additional input variable `s` corresponding to the current state of CTG_C, initialized to the initial state. The main loop of the node contains a nondeterministic choice, with a branch for each transition in CTG_C. A branch corresponding to a transition T is executed if `s` is equal to the source state of T, and as result of execution it sets `s` to the target state of T. A branch for an output transition specifies that the inputs are kept unchanged, which corresponds to the behavior expected for the special output transition δ on quiescent states. A branch for an input transition updates the corresponding inputs. A branch for a verdict transition (i.e., a `pass` or `inconclusive` self-loop on a state of CTG_C), resets the variable `s` to the

Table 1. Sizes and run-time performance for the tests generated for the test purposes

	TP		CTG		$\text{CTG}_{\texttt{RADAR}}$		Constraints (Lutin)	Oracle (Lustre)	Time (s)	Mem. (MB)
	States	Trans.	States	Trans.	States	Trans.				
$T1$	5	4	15,466	29,665	89	281	286	295	29	200
$T2$	4	3	102,985	211,455	584	3617	3622	1916	1237	231
$T3$	5	4	15,444	29,957	83	258	263	282	26	200
$T4$	5	4	2,278	4,959	218	1119	1124	557	86	193
$T5$	5	5	21,930	42,788	105	356	361	344	36	201

initial state of the CTG, thus avoiding to generate the same inputs (as a self-loop would) and covering faster the whole CTG. Thus, the Lutin node describes exactly the set of input sequences contained in CTG_C.

An input of the radar is a new position of the car and the obstacles (lilly and leo). Because the exploration takes into account all transitions of $\text{CTG}_{\texttt{RADAR}}$, the generated Lutin node incorporates all evolutions of the car and the obstacles that are relevant for the considered test purpose. The generated Lutin nodes are quite long (see Table 1) and complex, because they contain nondeterministic choices, induced by the random movements of the obstacles. Writing similar Lutin nodes by hand would probably have been difficult and error-prone.

Because a synchronous block C is executed atomically, i.e., not interleaved with other synchronous components, a sequence of input transitions for C is immediately followed by the expected sequence of output transitions. Because the target state s of the last transition in such a sequence of inputs is also the source state of the first transition in the sequence of outputs, we call such a state s a *corner state*. For the radar, the sequence of input transitions corresponding to new positions of the car or the obstacles is followed by an output transition corresponding to the expected perception grid. The oracle is generated with the XTL script `extract_oracle` (263 lines), by encoding CTG_C as a deterministic node in Lustre, which, to each corner state and its set of inputs/outputs, associates a Boolean verdict, indicating whether the outputs are the expected ones. This node is also defined for the verdict states of CTG_C. For a *pass* (respectively, *fail*) verdict it always returns true (respectively, false). For an *inconclusive* verdict it returns true iff the outputs are unchanged. In order to observe the coverage of the generated tests, for each verdict state (`pass` and `inconclusive`) and each other state of the CTG, a coverage variable is introduced in the Lustre node generated for the oracle. These coverage variables are true if at least one of the executions passed by the corresponding state of the CTG (see Sect. 4).

```
node oracle (s, car, lilly, leo, perception_leo, perception_lilly: int)
returns (res, pass, inconclusive, s0, ... s86: bool);
let
  res = true -> (
    if s = 6 then
```

```
  (car = 11 and lilly = 13 and leo = 6 and
   perception_lilly = 13 and perception_leo = 2000)
    ... );
pass = false -> if s = 83 then true else pre pass;
inconclusive = false -> if s = 7 then true else pre inconclusive;
s0 = false -> if s = 0 then true else pre s0; ...
s86 = false -> if s = 86 then true else pre s86; ...
```

The generated oracles are quite long (see Table 1) and complex, because they contain all oracle verdicts and coverage criteria. For each of the five test purposes, we executed the generated scenarios on the radar SUT using Lurette (the last columns of Table 1 indicate the time and memory consumed by the overall testing process). This enabled us to discover (and fix) a mistake in the SUT related to the incorrect management of the special value `already_sent`.

6 Related Work

Similar to our approach, test purposes for sub-systems can be obtained by projecting symbolic executions of the overall system [7]. A major difference of our approach is that we handle GALS systems (rather than systems homogeneously modeled by IOSTSs), requiring to integrate various formal methods and tools.

The differences between testing synchronous and asynchronous systems in terms of test-suite length, abstraction level, mutation score, non-determinism, and suitability for real-time systems are discussed in [26, Chap. 12]. This analysis enabled to improve the overall testing of a GALS system by taking advantage of the synchronous properties of the components (using a two-level approach combining an overall asynchronous automaton with a dedicated synchronous automaton creating the link to the concrete implementation). In our setting, these properties are taken care of directly by the GRL semantics.

Milner's proposal [30] to encode asynchronism in a synchronous process calculus has been used to specify GALS systems using synchronous programming approaches [14,17,19,31]. Here we follow the opposite way, by specifying the global aspects of a GALS system in an asynchronous language, which enables us to take advantage of the existing tools for asynchronous systems and to leverage them to improve the testing of the synchronous components.

Following a bottom-up approach [15], which manually defines contracts for the synchronous components (to be verified locally, for instance using SCADE [2]), the overall GALS system can be verified by translating the network of component contracts and verification properties into Promela (for verification with SPIN [20]) or timed automata (for timing analysis with UPPAAL [1]). Our approach is top-down and completely automatic, deriving test cases for the synchronous components from a model of the overall GALS system.

A graphical tool set [33], based on the specification of the synchronous components as communicating reactive state machines, translates the system and its properties specified as observers into Promela for verification with SPIN. This tool set focuses on the verification of the overall GALS system, whereas we aim at improving the unit testing of the synchronous components.

Encapsulating synchronous components makes the overall GALS system amenable for analysis with asynchronous verification tools. This approach has been followed for a combination of the synchronous language SAM, the asynchronous language LNT, and the CADP toolbox [12], and a combination of the synchronous language SIGNAL, the asynchronous language Promela, and the model checker SPIN [6]. Compared to these two approaches, we retain a finer modeling of the synchronous components in the overall GALS system and consider the verification of both, the overall GALS system and its synchronous components. Our approach to derive synchronous test scenarios might be adaptable to these language combination techniques.

Focusing on communication media for GALS hardware circuits, the asynchronous connections between synchronous blocks can be encoded into variants of Petri nets dedicated to the analysis of hardware circuits [3]. On the contrary, our approach targets the test of synchronous components of more generic GALS systems, relying on less precise models of the communication signals.

7 Conclusion

We presented an automatic approach integrating both asynchronous and synchronous testing tools to derive complex, but relevant unit test cases for the synchronous components of a GALS system. From a formal model of the system in GRL [25] and a test purpose, the conformance testing tool TESTOR [27] automatically generates a complete test graph [23] capturing the asynchronous behavior of the system relevant to the test purpose. Such a complete test graph is then projected on a synchronous component C and explored using XTL [28] scripts to provide a synchronous test scenario (input constraints in Lutin [34] and an oracle in Lustre [18]) required to test C with the Lurette tool [22]. All these steps have been automated in an SVL [9] script. The approach substantially relieves the burden of handcrafting these test scenarios, because, by construction, the derived scenarios constrain the inputs provided to C to relevant values, covering a test purpose, which might arise during the execution of the GALS system. We illustrated the approach on an autonomous car example.

As future work, we plan to consider the behavioral coverage of GALS systems, which can be achieved by identifying a test suite (ideally as small as possible) covering the whole state space of a GALS system. Such a test suite could be generated by deriving purposes from the action-based, branching-time temporal properties of the model (similar to [8] in the state-based, linear-time setting), by synthesizing purposes according to behavioral coverage criteria [35], or by constructing a complete test suite for a fault domain of the GALS system [5].

Acknowledgements. This work was supported by the Région Auvergne-Rhône-Alpes within the ARC6 programme.

References

1. Behrmann, G., David, A., Larsen, K.G., Möller, O., Pettersson, P., Yi, W.: Uppaal: present and future. In: Decision and Control. IEEE (2001)
2. Berry, G.: SCADE: synchronous design and validation of embedded control software. In: Ramesh, S., Sampath, P. (eds.) Next Generation Design and Verification Methodologies for Distributed Embedded Control Systems, pp. 19–33. Springer, Dordrecht (2007). https://doi.org/10.1007/978-1-4020-6254-4_2
3. Burns, F.P., Sokolov, D., Yakovlev, A.: A structured visual approach to GALS modeling and verification of communication circuits. IEEE Trans. CAD Integr. Circuits Syst. **36**(6), 938–951 (2017)
4. Chapiro, D.M.: Globally-asynchronous locally-synchronous systems. Doctoral thesis, Stanford University, Department of Computer Science (1984)
5. da Silva Simão, A., Petrenko, A.: Generating complete and finite test suite for ioco: is it possible? In: Schlingloff, H., Petrenko, A.K. (eds.) MBT 2014. EPTCS, vol. 141, pp. 56–70 (2014)
6. Doucet, F., Menarini, M., Krüger, I.H., Gupta, R.K., Talpin, J.: A verification approach for GALS integration of synchronous components. ENTCS **146**(2), 105–131 (2006)
7. Faivre, A., Gaston, C., Le Gall, P.: Symbolic model based testing for component oriented systems. In: Petrenko, A., Veanes, M., Tretmans, J., Grieskamp, W. (eds.) FATES/TestCom -2007. LNCS, vol. 4581, pp. 90–106. Springer, Heidelberg (2007). https://doi.org/10.1007/978-3-540-73066-8_7
8. Falcone, Y., Fernandez, J.-C., Jéron, T., Marchand, H., Mounier, L.: More testable properties. STTT **14**(4), 407–437 (2012)
9. Garavel, H., Lang, F.: SVL: a scripting language for compositional verification. In: Kim, M., Chin, B., Kang, S., Lee, D. (eds.) FORTE 2001. IIFIP, vol. 69, pp. 377–392. Springer, Boston, MA (2002). https://doi.org/10.1007/0-306-47003-9_24
10. Garavel, H., Lang, F., Mateescu, R., Serwe, W.: CADP 2011: a toolbox for the construction and analysis of distributed processes. STTT **15**(2), 89–107 (2013)
11. Garavel, H., Lang, F., Serwe, W.: From LOTOS to LNT. In: Katoen, J.-P., Langerak, R., Rensink, A. (eds.) ModelEd, TestEd, TrustEd. LNCS, vol. 10500, pp. 3–26. Springer, Cham (2017). https://doi.org/10.1007/978-3-319-68270-9_1
12. Garavel, H., Thivolle, D.: Verification of GALS systems by combining synchronous languages and process calculi. In: Păsăreanu, C.S. (ed.) SPIN 2009. LNCS, vol. 5578, pp. 241–260. Springer, Heidelberg (2009). https://doi.org/10.1007/978-3-642-02652-2_20
13. Graf-Brill, A., Hermanns, H.: Model-based testing for asynchronous systems. In: Petrucci, L., Seceleanu, C., Cavalcanti, A. (eds.) FMICS/AVoCS -2017. LNCS, vol. 10471, pp. 66–82. Springer, Cham (2017). https://doi.org/10.1007/978-3-319-67113-0_5
14. Guernic, P.L., Talpin, J., Lann, J.L.: POLYCHRONY for system design. J. Circuits Syst. Comput. **12**(3), 261–304 (2003)
15. Günther, H., Milius, S., Möller, O.: On the formal verification of systems of synchronous software components. In: Ortmeier, F., Daniel, P. (eds.) SAFECOMP 2012. LNCS, vol. 7612, pp. 291–304. Springer, Heidelberg (2012). https://doi.org/10.1007/978-3-642-33678-2_25
16. Halbwachs, N.: Synchronous Programming of Reactive Systems. Kluwer, Boston (1993)

17. Halbwachs, N., Baghdadi, S.: Synchronous modelling of asynchronous systems. In: Sangiovanni-Vincentelli, A., Sifakis, J. (eds.) EMSOFT 2002. LNCS, vol. 2491, pp. 240–251. Springer, Heidelberg (2002). https://doi.org/10.1007/3-540-45828-X_18
18. Halbwachs, N., Caspi, P., Raymond, P., Pilaud, D.: The synchronous dataflow programming language LUSTRE. Proc. IEEE **79**(9), 1305–1320 (1991)
19. Halbwachs, N., Mandel, L.: Simulation and verification of asynchronous systems by means of a synchronous model. In: ACSD 2006, pp. 3–14. IEEE (2006)
20. Holzmann, G.J.: The SPIN Model Checker: Primer and Reference Manual. Addison-Wesley, Boston (2003)
21. Jahier, E., Halbwachs, N., Raymond, P.: Engineering functional requirements of reactive systems using synchronous languages. In: 8th IEEE International Symposium on Industrial Embedded Systems, vol. 8, pp. 140–149 (2013)
22. Jahier, E., Raymond, P., Baufreton, P.: Case studies with Lurette V2. STTT **8**(6), 517–530 (2006)
23. Jard, C., Jéron, T.: TGV: theory, principles and algorithms - a tool for the automatic synthesis of conformance test cases for non-deterministic reactive systems. STTT **7**(4), 297–315 (2005)
24. Jebali, F.: Formal framework for modelling and verifying globally asynchronous locally synchronous systems. Ph.D. thesis, Grenoble Alpes University, France, September 2016
25. Jebali, F., Lang, F., Mateescu, R.: Formal modelling and verification of GALS systems using GRL and CADP. FAoC **28**(5), 767–804 (2016)
26. Lorber, F.: It's about time – model-based mutation testing for synchronous and asynchronous timed systems. Ph.D. thesis, Institute of Software Technology, Graz University of Technology, Austria (2016)
27. Marsso, L., Mateescu, R., Serwe, W.: TESTOR: a modular tool for on-the-fly conformance test case generation. In: Beyer, D., Huisman, M. (eds.) TACAS 2018. LNCS, vol. 10806, pp. 211–228. Springer, Cham (2018). https://doi.org/10.1007/978-3-319-89963-3_13
28. Mateescu, R., Garavel, H.: XTL: a meta-language and tool for temporal logic model-checking. In: Margaria, T. (ed.) STTT 1998, pp. 33–42. BRICS (1998)
29. Mateescu, R., Thivolle, D.: A model checking language for concurrent value-passing systems. In: Cuellar, J., Maibaum, T., Sere, K. (eds.) FM 2008. LNCS, vol. 5014, pp. 148–164. Springer, Heidelberg (2008). https://doi.org/10.1007/978-3-540-68237-0_12
30. Milner, R.: Calculi for synchrony and asynchrony. Theoret. Comput. Sci. **25**, 267–310 (1983)
31. Mousavi, M.R., Guernic, P.L., Talpin, J.-P., Shukla, S.K., Basten, T.: Modeling and validating globally asynchronous design in synchronous frameworks. In: DATE 2004, pp. 384–389. IEEE (2004)
32. Noroozi, N., Khosravi, R., Mousavi, M.R., Willemse, T.A.C.: Synchrony and asynchrony in conformance testing. Softw. Syst. Model. **14**(1), 149–172 (2015)
33. Ramesh, S., Sonalkar, S., D'silva, V., Chandra R., N., Vijayalakshmi, B.: A toolset for modelling and verification of GALS systems. In: Alur, R., Peled, D.A. (eds.) CAV 2004. LNCS, vol. 3114, pp. 506–509. Springer, Heidelberg (2004). https://doi.org/10.1007/978-3-540-27813-9_47
34. Raymond, P., Roux, Y., Jahier, E.: Lutin: a language for specifying and executing reactive scenarios. EURASIP J. Embed. Syst. (2008). https://link.springer.com/article/10.1155/2008/753821#citeas

35. Taylor, R.N., Levine, D.L., Kelly, C.D.: Structural testing of concurrent programs. IEEE Trans. Softw. Eng. **18**(3), 206–215 (1992)
36. Teehan, P., Greenstreet, M., Lemieux, G.: A survey and taxonomy of GALS design styles. IEEE Des. Test Comput. **24**(5), 418–428 (2007)
37. Tretmans, J.: Conformance testing with labelled transition systems: implementation relations and test generation. Comput. Netw. ISDN Syst. **29**(1), 49–79 (1996)

Isabelle/SACM: Computer-Assisted Assurance Cases with Integrated Formal Methods

Yakoub Nemouchi, Simon Foster(✉), Mario Gleirscher, and Tim Kelly

University of York, York, UK
{yakoub.nemouchi,simon.foster,mario.gleirscher,tim.kelly}@york.ac.uk

Abstract. Assurance cases (ACs) are often required to certify critical systems. The use of integrated formal methods (FMs) in assurance can improve automation, increase confidence, and overcome errant reasoning. However, ACs can rarely be fully formalised, as the use of FMs is contingent on models that are validated by informal processes. Consequently, assurance techniques should support both formal and informal artifacts, with explicated inferential links between them. In this paper, we contribute a formal machine-checked interactive language for the computer-assisted construction of ACs called Isabelle/SACM. The framework guarantees well-formedness, consistency, and traceability of ACs, and allows a tight integration of formal and informal evidence of various provenance. To validate Isabelle/SACM, we present a novel formalisation of the Tokeneer benchmark, verify its security requirements, and form a mechanised AC that combines the resulting formal and informal artifacts.

1 Introduction

Assurance cases (ACs) are structured arguments, supported by evidence, intended to demonstrate that a system meets its requirements, such as safety or security, when applied in a particular operational context [24,30]. They are recommended by several international standards, such as ISO26262 for automotive applications. An AC consists of a hierarchical decomposition of claims, through appropriate argumentation strategies, into further claims, and eventually supporting evidence. Several AC languages exist, including the Goal Structuring Notation (GSN) [24], Claims, Arguments, and Evidence (CAE) [2], and the Structured Assurance Case Metamodel (SACM)[1] [30], a standard that unifies several notations.

AC creation can be supported by model-based design, which utilises architectural and behavioural models over which requirements can be formulated [30]. However, ACs can suffer from logical fallacies and inadequate evidence [20]. A proposed solution is formalisation in a machine-checked logic to enable verification of consistency and well-foundedness [28]. As confirmed by avionics standard

[1] *OMG Structured Assurance Case Metamodel*: http://www.omg.org/spec/SACM/.

W. Ahrendt and S. L. Tapia Tarifa (Eds.): IFM 2019, LNCS 11918, pp. 379–398, 2019.
https://doi.org/10.1007/978-3-030-34968-4_21

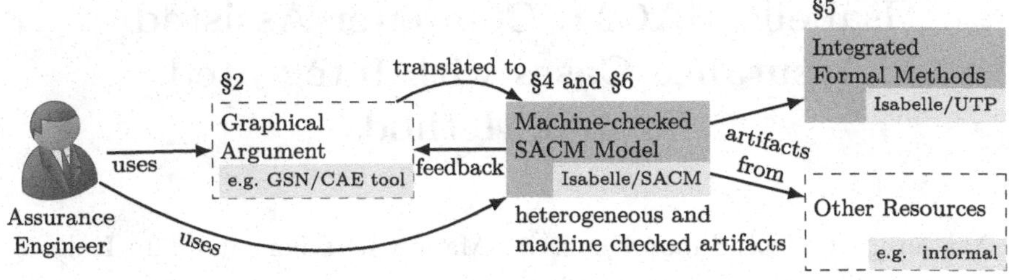

Fig. 1. Overview of our approach to integrative model-based assurance cases

DO-178C, the evidence gathering process can also benefit from the rigour of formal methods (FMs). However, it is also the case that (1) ACs are intended primarily for human consumption, and (2) that formal models must be validated informally [21]. Consequently, ACs usually combine informal and formal content, and so tools must support this. Moreover, there is a need to integrate several FMs [26], potentially with differing computational paradigms and levels of abstraction [22], and so it is necessary to manage the resulting heterogeneity [19].

Vision. Our vision, illustrated in Fig. 1, is a unified framework for machine-checked ACs with heterogeneous artifacts and integrated FMs. We envisage an assurance backend for a variety of graphical assurance tools [9,30] that utilise SACM as a unified interchange format, and an array of FM tools provided by our Isabelle-based verification platform, Isabelle/UTP [16,17]. Our framework aims to improve existing assurance processes by harnessing formal verification to produce mathematically grounded ACs with guarantees of consistency and adequacy of the evidence. In the context of safety regulation, it can help with AC evaluation through machine-checking and automated verification.

Contributions. A first step in this direction is made by the contributions of this paper, which are: (1) Isabelle/SACM, an implementation of SACM in Isabelle [25], (2) a front-end for Isabelle/SACM called interactive assurance language (IAL), which is an interactive DSL for the definition of machine-checked SACM models, (3) a novel formalisation of Tokeneer [1] in Isabelle/UTP, (4) the verification of the Tokeneer security requirements[2], and (5) the definition of an AC with the claims that Tokeneer meets its security requirements. Our Tokeneer AC demonstrates how to integrate formal artifacts, resulting from Isabelle/UTP (4), and informal artifacts, such as the Tokeneer documentation.

Isabelle provides a sophisticated executable document model for presenting a graph of hyperlinked formal artifacts, like definitions, theorems, and proofs. It provides automatic and incremental consistency checking, where updates to artifacts trigger rechecking. Such capabilities can support efficient maintenance

[2] Supporting materials, including Isabelle theories, can be found on our website.

and evolution of model-based ACs [30]. Moreover, the document model allows both formal and informal content [32], and provides access to an array of automated proof tools [31,32]. Additionally, Brucker et al. [4] extend Isabelle with DOF, a framework with a textual language for embedding of meta-models into the Isabelle document model, which we harness to embed SACM.

Isabelle/UTP [16,17] harnesses Unifying Theories of Programming [22] (UTP) to provide formal verification facilities for a variety of languages, with paradigms as diverse as concurrency [13], real-time [14], and hybrid computation [15]. Moreover, verification techniques such as Hoare logic, weakest precondition calculus, and refinement calculus are all available through a variety of proof tactics. This makes Isabelle/UTP an obvious choice for modelling and verification of Tokeneer, and more generally as a platform for integrated FMs based on unifying semantics.

The paper is organised as follows. In Sect. 2 we outline preliminaries: SACM, Isabelle, and DOF. In Sect. 3 we describe the Tokeneer system. In Sect. 4 we begin our contributions by describing Isabelle/SACM, which consists of the embedding of SACM into DOF (Sect. 4.1), and IAL (Sect. 4.2). In Sect. 5 we model and verify Tokeneer in Isabelle/UTP. In Sect. 6 we describe the mechanisation of the Tokeneer AC in Isabelle/SACM. In Sect. 7 we highlight related work, and in Sect. 8 we conclude.

2 Preliminaries

SACM. ACs are often presented using a notation like GSN [24] (Fig. 2). Here, claims are rectangles, which are linked with "supported by" arrows, strategies are parallelograms, and the circles are evidence ("solutions"). The other shapes denote various types of context, which are linked to by the "in context of" arrows. SACM is an OMG standard metamodel for ACs [30]. It unifies, extends, and refines several predecessor notations, including GSN [24] and CAE [2] (Claims, Arguments, and Evidence), and is intended as a definitive reference model.

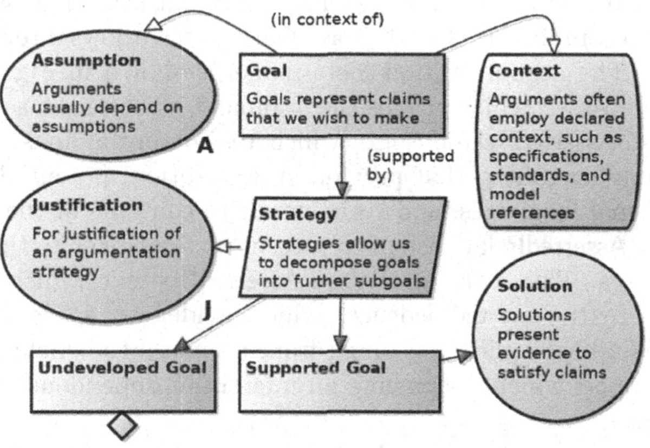

Fig. 2. Goal Structuring Notation

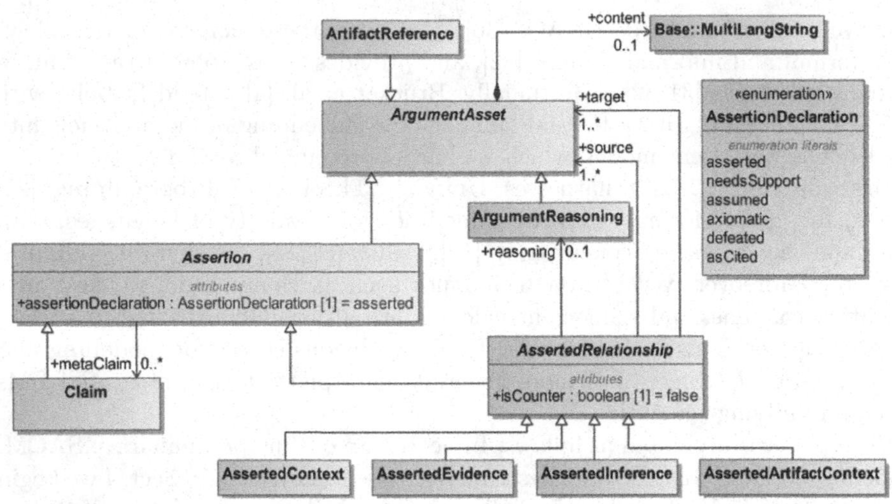

Fig. 3. SACM argumentation meta-model (See footnote 1)

SACM models three crucial concepts: arguments, artifacts, and terminology. An argument is a set of claims, evidence citations, and inferential links between them. Artifacts represent evidence, such as system models, techniques, results, activities, participants, and traceability links. Terminology fixes formal terms for use in claims. Normally, claims are in natural languages, but in SACM they can also contain structured expressions, which allows integration of formal languages.

The argumentation meta-model is shown in Fig. 3. The base class is ArgumentAsset, which groups the argument assets, such as Claims, ArtifactReferences, and AssertedRelationships (which are inferential links). Every asset may contain a MultiLangString that provides a description, potentially in multiple natural and formal languages, and corresponds to contents of the shapes in Fig. 2.

AssertedRelationships represent a relationship that exists between several assets. They can be of type AssertedContext, which uses an artifact to define context; AssertedEvidence, which evidences a claim; AssertedInference which describes explicit reasoning from premises to conclusion(s); or AssertedArtifactSupport which documents an inferential dependency between the claims of two artifacts.

Both Claims and AssertedRelationships inherit from Assertion, because in SACM both claims and inferential links are subject to argumentation and refutation. SACM allows six different classes of assertion, via the attribute assertionDeclaration, including axiomatic (needing no further support), assumed, and defeated, where a claim is refuted. An AssertedRelationship can also be flagged as isCounter, where counter evidence for a claim is presented.

Isabelle. Isabelle/HOL is an interactive theorem prover for higher order logic (HOL) [25], based on the generic framework Isar [31]. The former provides a functional specification language, and an array of automated proof tools [3]. The latter has an interactive, extensible, and executable document model [32], which describes Isabelle theories. Plugins, such as Isabelle/HOL, DOF, Isabelle/UTP, and Isabelle/SACM have document models that contain conservative extensions to Isar.

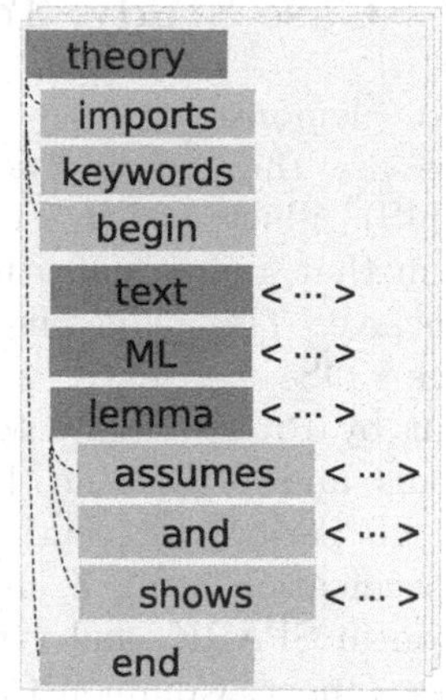

Fig. 4. Document model (Color figure online)

Figure 4 illustrates the document model. The first section for *context definition* describes *imports* of existing theories, and *keywords* which extend the concrete syntax. The second section is the body enclosed between *begin-end* which is a sequence of commands. The concrete syntax of commands consists of (1) a predeclared keyword (in blue), such as the command `ML`, (2) a "semantics area" enclosed between `<...>`, and (3) optional subkeywords (in green). Commands generate formal document artifacts. For example, the command `lemma` creates a new theorem within the underlying theory context. When a document is edited by removal, addition, or alteration of formal artifacts, it is immediately executed and checked by Isabelle, with feedback provided to the frontend. This includes consistency checks for the context and well-formedness checks for the commands. Isabelle is therefore ideal for ACs, which have to be maintainable, well-formed, and consistent. In Sect. 4.2 we extend this document model with commands that define our assurance language, IAL.

Moreover, informal artifacts in Isabelle theories can be combined with formal artifacts using the command `text <...>`. It is a processor for markup strings containing a mixture of informal artifacts and hyperlinks to formal artifacts through *antiquotations* of the form `@{aqname ...}`. For example, `text <The reflexivity theorem @{thm HOL.refl}>` mixes natural language with a hyperlink to the formal artifact `HOL.refl` through the antiquotation `@{thm HOL.refl}`. This is important since antiquotations are also checked by Isabelle as follows: (1) whether the referenced artifact exists within the underlying theory context; (2) whether the type of the referenced artifact matches the antiquotation's type.

DOF. A foundation for our work is DOF and its Isabelle Ontology Specification Language (IOSL) [4]: a textual language to model *document classes*, which extends the document model with new structures. We use the command `doc_class` from IOSL to add new document classes for each of the SACM classes. Instances of DOF classes sit at the meta-logical level, so they can be referenced using antiquotations, and carry an enriched version of Isabelle's markup string.

3 Case Study: Tokeneer

To demonstrate our approach, we use the Identification Station (TIS)[3] illustrated in Fig. 5, a system that guards entry to a secure enclave. The pioneering work on the TIS assurance was carried out by Praxis High Integrity Systems and SPRE Inc. [1]. Barnes et al. performed security analysis, specification using Z, implementation in SPARK, and verification of the security properties. After independent assessment, Common Criteria (CC) Evaluation Assurance Level (EAL) 5 was achieved. Tokeneer is therefore a successful example of using FMs to assure a system against CC Though now more than fifteen years old, it remains an important benchmark for formal methods and assurance techniques.

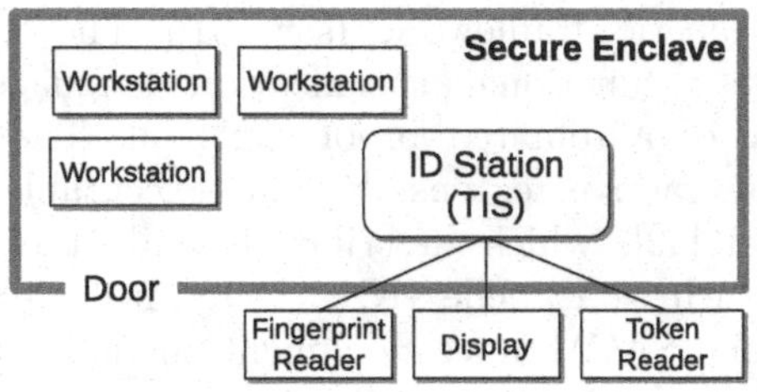

Fig. 5. Tokeneer system overview

The physical infrastructure consists of a door, fingerprint reader, display, and card (token) reader. The main function is to check the credentials on a presented token, read a fingerprint if necessary, and then either unlatch the door, or deny entry. Entry is permitted when the token holds at least three data items: (1) a user identity (ID) certificate, (2) a privilege certificate, with a clearance level, and (3) an identification and authentication (I&A) certificate, which assigns a fingerprint template. When the user first presents their token the three certificates are read and cross-checked. If the token is valid, then a fingerprint is taken, which, if validated against the I&A certificate, allows the door to be unlocked once the token is removed. An optional authorisation certificate is written upon successful authentication, which allows the fingerprint check to be skipped.

The security of the TIS is assured by demonstrating six Security Functional Requirements (SFRs) [7], of which the first three are shown below:

SFR1. If the latch is unlocked, then TIS must possess either a user token or an admin token. The user token must either have a valid authorisation certificate, or valid ID, Privilege, and I&A Certificates, together with a template that allowed to successfully validate the user's fingerprint. Or, if the user token does not meet this, the admin token must have a valid authorisation certificate, with role of "guard".

SFR2. If the latch is unlocked automatically by TIS, then the current time must be close to being within the allowed entry period defined for the User requesting access.

SFR3. An alarm will be raised whenever the door/latch is insecure.

Our objective is to construct a machine-checked assurance case that argues that the TIS fulfils these security properties, and integrate evidential artifacts from our mechanised model of the TIS behaviour in Isabelle/UTP.

[3] Project website: https://www.adacore.com/tokeneer.

4 Isabelle/SACM

Here, we encode SACM as a DOF ontology (Sect. 4.1), and use it to provide an interactive machine-checked AC language (Sect. 4.2). Our embedding implements ACs as meta-logical entities in Isabelle, rather than as formal elements embedded in the HOL logic, as this would prevent the expression of informal reasoning and explanation. Therefore, antiquotations to formal artifacts can be freely mixed with natural language and other informal artifacts.

4.1 Modelling: Embedding SACM in Isabelle

We embed the SACM meta-model in Isabelle using IOSL, and we focus on modelling `ArgumentAsset`[4] and its child classes from Fig. 3, as these are the most relevant classes for the TIS assurance argument that we develop in Sect. 6. The class `ArgumentAsset` has the following textual model:

```
doc_class ArgumentAsset = ArgumentationElement +
  content_assoc:: MultiLangString
```

Here, `doc_class` defines a new class, and automatically generates an antiquotation type, `@{ArgumentAsset <...>}`, which can be used to refer to entities of this type. `ArgumentationElement` is a class which `ArgumentAsset` inherits from, but is not discussed further. `content_assoc` models the content association in Fig. 3. To model `MultiLangString` in Isabelle/SACM, we use DOF's markup string. Thus, the usage of antiquotations is allowed for artifacts with the type `MultiLangString`.

`ArgumentAsset` has three subclasses: (1) `Assertion`, which is a unified type for claims and their relationships; (2) `ArgumentReasoning`, which is used to explicate the argumentation strategy being employed; and (3) `ArtifactReference`, that evidences a claim with an artifact. Since DOF extends the Isabelle/HOL document model, we can use the latter's types, such as sets and enumerations (algebraic datatypes), in modelling SACM classes, as shown below:

```
datatype assertionDeclarations_t =
  Asserted|Axiomatic|Defeated|Assumed|NeedsSupport|AsCited
doc_class Assertion = ArgumentAsset +
  assertionDeclaration::assertionDeclarations_t
doc_class ArgumentReasoning  = ArgumentAsset +
  structure_assoc::"ArgumentPackage option"
doc_class ArtifactReference = ArgumentAsset +
  referencedArtifactElement_assoc::"ArtifactElement set"
```

Here, `datatype` defines a HOL enumeration type, `assertionDeclarations_t` is the defined enumeration type, `set` is the set type, and `option` is the optional type. Attribute `assertionDeclaration` is of type `assertionDeclarations_t`, which specifies the status of instances of type `Assertion`. Examples of `Assertions` in SACM are claims, justifications, and both kinds of arrows from Fig. 2. The attribute

[4] We model all parts of SACM in DOF, but omit details for sake of brevity.

structure_assoc is an association to the class ArgumentPackage, which is not discussed here. Finally, the attribute referencedArtifactElement_assoc is an association to ArtifactElements from the ArtifactPackage, allowing instances of type ArgumentAsset to be supported by evidential artifacts.

The class Claim from Fig. 3 inherits from the class Assertion. This means that Claim inherits the attributes gid, content_assoc, and assertionDeclaration of type assertion Declarations_t. The other child class of Assertion is:

```
doc_class AssertedRelationship = Assertion +
  isCounter::bool
  reasoning_assoc:: "ArgumentReasoning option"
```

This models the relationships between instances of type ArgumentAsset, such as the "supported by" and "in context of" arrows of Fig. 2. isCounter specifies whether the target of the relation is supported or refuted by the source, and reasoning_assoc is an association to ArgumentReasoning, which models GSN strategies in SACM. The child classes of AssertedRelationship also have the attributes source and target, both of type ArgumentAsset.

4.2 Interactive Assurance Language (IAL)

IAL is our assurance language with a concrete syntax consisting of various Isabelle commands that extend the document model in Fig. 4. Each command generates SACM class instances and performs a number of checks: (1) standard Isabelle checks (Sect. 2); (2) OCL constraints imposed on the attributes by SACM (provided by DOF); (3) well-formedness checks against the meta-model, i.e. instances comply to the type restrictions imposed by the SACM datatypes.

IAL instantiates doc_classes from Sect. 4.1 to create SACM models in Isabelle, for example, the command CLAIM creates an instance of the class Claim. Attributes and associations of a class have a concrete syntax represented by an Isabelle (green) subcommand. For example, the association content_assoc:: MultiLangString is represented by CONTENT <...>; where <...> is DOF's markup string. A selection of IAL commands is given below.

```
CLAIM isABS isCITE ASSERTED <gid> CONTENT <MultiLangString>
ASSERTED_INFERENCE <gid> SOURCE <gid>* TARGET <gid>*
ASSERTED_CONTEXT <gid> SOURCE <gid>* TARGET <gid>*
ASSERTED_EVIDENCE <gid> SOURCE <gid>* TARGET <gid>*
```

CLAIM creates an instance of type Claim with an identifier (gid), and content described by a MultiLangString. The antiquotation @{Claim <<gid>>} can be used to reference the created instance. The subcommands isABS, isCITE and ASSERTED are optional. ASSERTED_INFERENCE creates an inference between several instances of type ArgumentAsset. It has subcommands SOURCE and TARGET that are both lists of antiquotations pointing to ArgumentAssets. The use of antiquotations to reference the instances ensures that Isabelle will do the checks explained in Sect. 2. ASSERTED_CONTEXT similarly asserts that an instance should be treated as context for another, and ASSERTED_EVIDENCE associates evidence with a claim. All instances created by IAL are *semi-formal*, since they can contain both informal content and references to formal content that are machine checked.

Figure 6 shows the interactive nature of IAL. It represents an inferential link between the semi-formal artifacts `Claim_A` and `Claim_C`. The semi-formal artifact `Rel_A`, which is the inferential link between `Claim_A` and `Claim_C`, is created via the command `ASSERTED_INFERENCE`. However, `Claim_C` does not exist, and so the error message at the top is issued. The command `text` is then used to reference `Rel_A` using the antiquotation `@{AssertedInference Rel_A}`. This also leads to an error, shown at the bottom, since `Rel_A` was not introduced to the context of the document model, due to the error at the top.

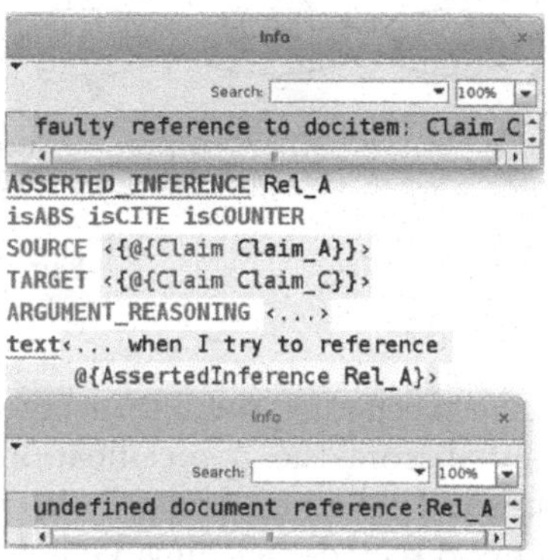

Fig. 6. Interactive DSL

We have now developed Isabelle/SACM and our IAL. In the next section we consider the modelling verification of the Tokeneer system.

5 Modelling and Verification of Tokeneer

Here, we present a novel mechanisation of Tokeneer in Isabelle/UTP [16,17] to provide evidence for the AC. In [7], the SFRs are argued semi-formally, but here we provide a formal proof. We focus on the verification of SFR1[5], the most challenging of the six SFRs, and describe the necessary model elements.

5.1 Modelling and Mechanisation

The TIS specification [6] describes an elaborate state space and a collection of relational operations. The state is bipartite, consisting of (1) the digital state and (2) the monitored and controlled variables shared with the real world. The TIS monitors the time, enclave door, fingerprint reader, token reader, and several peripherals. It controls the door latch, an alarm, a display, and a screen.

The specification describes a state transition system, illustrated in Fig. 7 (cf. [6, page 43]), where each transition corresponds to an operation. Several operations are omitted due to space constraints. Following enrolment, the TIS becomes quiescent (awaiting interaction). ReadUserToken triggers if the token is presented, and reads its contents. Assuming a valid token, the TIS determines whether a fingerprint is necessary, and then triggers either BioCheckRequired or BioCheckNotRequired. If required, the TIS then reads a fingerprint (ReadFingerOK), validates it (ValidateFingerOK), and finally writes an authorisation certificate to the token (WriteUserTokenOK). If the access credentials are available (waitingEntry), then a final check is performed (EntryOK), and once the user removes their token (waitingRemoveTokenSuccess), the door is unlocked (UnlockDoor).

[5] The administrator (role "guard") part is verified but omitted for space reasons.

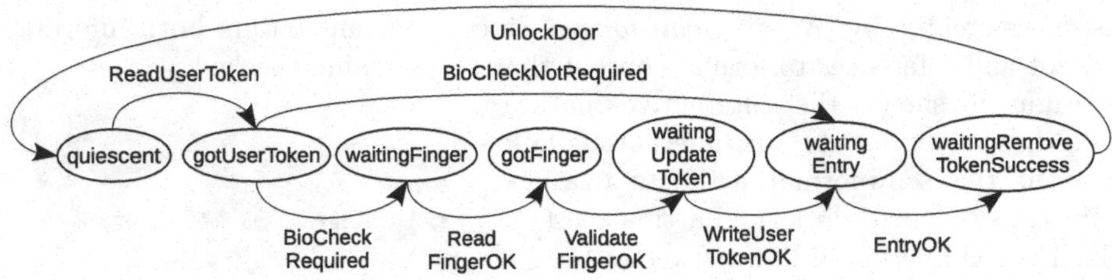

Fig. 7. TIS main states

We mechanise the TIS using hierarchical state space types, with invariants adapted from the Z specification [6]. We define the operations using guarded command language [10] (GCL) rather than the Z schemas directly, to enable syntax-directed reasoning. GCL has a denotational semantics in UTP's relational calculus [22], so that it is possible to prove equivalence with the corresponding Z operations. We use a GCL variant that follows the following syntax:

$$\mathcal{P} ::= \textbf{\textit{skip}} \mid \textbf{\textit{abort}} \mid \mathcal{P} \mathbin{;} \mathcal{P} \mid \mathcal{E} \longrightarrow \mathcal{P} \mid \mathcal{P} \sqcap \mathcal{P} \mid \mathcal{V} := \mathcal{E} \mid \mathcal{V}{:}[\mathcal{P}]$$

Here, $\mathcal{P}$ is a program, $\mathcal{E}$ is an expression, and $\mathcal{V}$ is a variable. The language provides sequential composition, guarded commands, non-deterministic choice, and assignment. We adopt a frame operator $a{:}[P]$, which states that P changes only variables in the namespace a [16,17]. This enables modular reasoning about the TIS internal and real-world states, which is a further novelty of our work.

State Types. We first describe the state space of the TIS state machine:

$$IDStation \triangleq \begin{bmatrix} currentUserToken : TOKENTRY, currentTime : TIME, \\ userTokenPresence : PRESENCE, status : STATUS, \\ issuerKey : USER \nrightarrow KEYPART, \cdots \end{bmatrix}$$

$$Controlled \triangleq \left[\, latch : LATCH, alarm : ALARM, \cdots \right]$$

$$Monitored \triangleq \begin{bmatrix} now : TIME, finger : FINGERPRINTTRY, \\ userToken : TOKENTRY, \cdots \end{bmatrix}$$

$$RealWorld \triangleq [mon : Monitored, ctrl : Controlled]$$

$$SystemState \triangleq [rw : RealWorld, tis : IDStation]$$

We define state types for the TIS state, controlled variables, monitored variables, real-world, and the entire system, respectively. The controlled variables include the physical latch, the alarm, the display, and the screen. The monitored variables correspond to time (*now*), the door (*door*), the fingerprint reader (*finger*), the tokens, and the peripherals. *RealWorld* combines the physical variables, and *SystemState* composes the physical world (*rw*) and the TIS (*tis*).

Variable *currentUserToken* represents the last token presented to the TIS, and *userTokenPresence* indicates whether a token is currently presented. The variable *status* is used to record the state the TIS is in, and can take the values

indicated in the state bubbles of Fig. 7. Variable *issuerKey* is a partial function representing the public key chain, which is needed to authorise user entry.
Operations. We now specify a selection of the operations over *IDStation*[6]:

$$\mathit{BioCheckRequired} \triangleq \left(\begin{array}{l}\mathit{status} = \mathsf{gotUserToken} \wedge \mathit{userTokenPresence} = \mathsf{present} \\ \wedge\ \mathit{UserTokenOK} \wedge (\neg\, \mathit{UserTokenWithOKAuthCert})\end{array}\right) \longrightarrow \mathit{status} := \mathsf{waitingFinger} \fatsemi \mathit{currentDisplay} := \mathsf{insertFinger}$$

$$\mathit{ReadFingerOK} \triangleq \left(\begin{array}{l}\mathit{status} = \mathsf{waitingFinger} \wedge \mathit{fingerPresence} = \mathsf{present} \\ \wedge\ \mathit{userTokenPresence} = \mathsf{present}\end{array}\right) \longrightarrow \mathit{status} := \mathsf{gotFinger} \fatsemi \mathit{currentDisplay} := \mathsf{wait}$$

$$\mathit{UnlockDoorOK} \triangleq \left(\begin{array}{l}\mathit{status} = \mathsf{waitingRemoveTokenSuccess} \\ \wedge\ \mathit{userTokenPresence} = \mathsf{absent}\end{array}\right) \longrightarrow \begin{array}{l}\mathit{UnlockDoor} \fatsemi \mathit{status} := \mathsf{quiescent} \fatsemi \\ \mathit{currentDisplay} := \mathsf{doorUnlocked}\end{array}$$

Each operation is guarded by execution conditions and consist of several assignments. *BioCheckRequired* requires that the current state is $\mathsf{gotUserToken}$, the user token is $\mathsf{present}$, and sufficient for entry (*UserTokenOK*), but there is no authorisation certificate ($\neg\, \mathit{UserTokenWithOKAuthCert}$). The latter two predicates essentially require that (1) the three certificates can be verified against the public key store, and (2) additionally there is a valid authorisation certificate present. Their definitions can be found elsewhere [6]. *BioCheckRequired* updates the state to $\mathsf{waitingFinger}$ and the display with an instruction to provide a fingerprint. *UnlockDoorOK* requires that the current state is $\mathsf{waitingRemoveTokenSuccess}$, and the token has been removed. It unlocks the door, using the elided operation *UnlockDoor*, returns the status to $\mathsf{quiescent}$, and updates the display.

These operations act only on the TIS state space. During their execution monitored variables can also change, to reflect real-world updates. Mostly these changes are arbitrary, with the exception that time must increase monotonically. We therefore promote the operations to *SystemState* with the following schema.

$$\mathit{UEC}(\mathit{Op}) \triangleq \mathit{tis}:[\mathit{Op}] \fatsemi \mathit{rw}:[\mathit{mon{:}now} \leq \mathit{mon{:}now}' \wedge \mathit{ctrl}' = \mathit{ctrl}]$$

In Z, this functionality is provided by the schema *UserEntryContext* [6], from which we derive the name *UEC*. It promotes *Op* to act on *tis*, and composes this with a relational predicate that constrains the real-world variables (*rw*); this separation enables modular reasoning. The behaviour of all monitored variables other than *now* is arbitrary, and all controlled variables are unchanged. Then, we promote each operation, for example $\mathit{TISReadTokenOK} \triangleq \mathit{UEC}(\mathit{ReadTokenOK})$. The overall behaviour of the entry operations is given below:

$$\mathit{TISUserEntryOp} \triangleq \left(\begin{array}{l}\mathit{TISReadUserToken} \sqcap \mathit{TISValidateUserToken} \\ \sqcap\ \mathit{TISReadFinger} \sqcap \mathit{TISValidateFinger} \\ \sqcap\ \mathit{TISUnlockDoor} \sqcap \mathit{TISCompleteFailedAccess} \sqcap \cdots\end{array}\right)$$

[6] Most TIS operations have been mechanised, using the same names as in [6].

In each iteration of the state machine, we non-deterministically select an enabled operation and execute it. We also update the controlled variables, which is done by composition with the following relational update operation.

$$\begin{aligned} \mathit{TISUpdate} \triangleq\ & rw\!:\![mon\!:\!now \leq mon\!:\!now'] \mathbin{;} rw\!:\!ctrl\!:\!latch := tis\!:\!currentLatch \mathbin{;} \\ & rw\!:\!ctrl\!:\!display := tis\!:\!currentDisplay \end{aligned}$$

This allows time to advance, allows other monitored variables to change, and copies the digital state of the latch and display to the corresponding controlled variables. The system transitions are described by $\mathit{TISUserEntryOp} \mathbin{;} \mathit{TISUpdate}$.

5.2 Formal Verification of SFR1

We first formalise the TIS state invariants necessary to prove SFR1:

$$\begin{aligned} \mathit{Inv}_1 &\triangleq \begin{array}{l} status \in \left\{ \begin{array}{l} \mathsf{gotFinger}, \mathsf{waitingFinger}, \mathsf{waitingUpdateToken} \\ \mathsf{waitingEntry}, \mathsf{waitingUpdateTokenSuccess} \end{array} \right\} \\ \Rightarrow (\mathit{UserTokenWithOKAuthCert} \vee \mathit{UserTokenOK}) \end{array} \\ \mathit{Inv}_2 &\triangleq \begin{array}{l} status \in \{\mathsf{waitingEntry}, \mathsf{waitingRemoveTokenSuccess}\} \\ \Rightarrow (\mathit{UserTokenWithOKAuthCert} \vee \mathit{FingerOK}) \end{array} \\ \mathit{TIS\text{-}inv} &\triangleq \mathit{Inv}_1 \wedge \mathit{Inv}_2 \wedge \cdots \end{aligned}$$

Inv_1 states that whenever the TIS is in a state beyond *gotUserToken*, then either a valid authorisation certificate is present, or else the user token is valid; it corresponds to the first invariant in the *IDStation* schema [6, page 26]. Inv_2 states that whenever in state *waitingEntry* or *waitingRemoveTokenSuccess*, then either an authorisation certificate or a valid finger print is present. Inv_2 is actually not present in [6], but we found it necessary to satisfy SFR1[7]. We elide the additional eight invariants that deal with administrators, the alarm, and audit data [6].

Unlike [6], which imposes the invariants by construction, we prove that each operation preserves the invariants using Hoare logic, similar to [27]:

Theorem 5.1. $\{\mathit{TIS\text{-}inv}\}\ \mathit{TISUserEntryOp}\ \{\mathit{TIS\text{-}inv}\}$

This theorem shows that the state machine never violates the 10 state invariants, and we can assume that they hold, to satisfy any requirements. This involves discharging verification conditions for a total of 22 operations in Isabelle/UTP, a process that is automated using our proof tactic `hoare_auto`.

We use this to assure SFR1, which is formalised by the formula FSFR1, that characterises the conditions under which the latch will become unlocked having been previously locked. We can determine these states by application of the weakest precondition calculus [10], which mirrors the (informal) Z schema

[7] There seems to be no invariant that ensures the presence of a valid fingerprint in [6]. We also believe that a necessary invariant regarding admin roles is missing.

domain calculations in [7, page 5]. Specifically, we characterise the weakest precondition under which execution of *TISUserEntryOp* followed by *TISUpdate* leads to a state satisfying $rw{:}ctrl{:}latch = \mathsf{unlocked}$. We formalise this in the theorem below.

Theorem 5.2 (FSFR1)

$$\left(\begin{array}{l} \mathit{TIS\text{-}inv} \land \mathit{tis{:}currentLatch} = \mathsf{locked} \\ \land\ (\mathit{TISUserEntryOp} \mathbin{⨾} \mathit{TISUpdate})\ \mathbf{wp}\,(\mathit{rw{:}ctrl{:}latch} = \mathsf{unlocked}) \end{array}\right)$$
$$\Rightarrow ((\mathit{UserTokenOK} \land \mathit{FingerOK}) \lor \mathit{UserTokenWithOKAuthCert})$$

Proof. Automatic, by application of weakest precondition and relational calculus.

We conjoin the **wp** formula with $tis{:}currentLatch = \mathsf{locked}$ to capture behaviours when the latch was initially locked. The only operation that unlocks the door for users is *UnlockDoorOK*, as confirmed by the calculated unlocking precondition:

$$status = \mathsf{waitingRemoveTokenSuccess} \land userTokenPresence = \mathsf{absent}$$

that is, access is permitted and the token has been removed. We conjoin this with *TIS-Inv*, since we know it holds in any state. We show that this composite precondition implies that either a valid user token and fingerprint were present (using Inv_2), or else a valid authorisation certificate. We have now verified a formalisation of SFR1. In the next section we place this in the context of an AC.

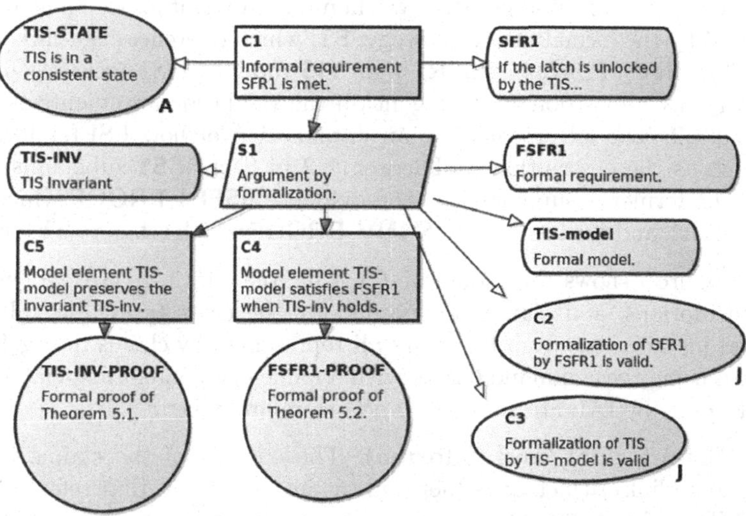

Fig. 8. TIS claim formalization

6 Mechanising the Tokeener Assurance Case

Here, we use Isabelle/SACM to model an AC with the claim that TIS satisfies **SFR1**, using Theorems 5.1 and 5.2 from Sect. 5 as evidential artifacts. The GSN diagram for the AC is shown in Fig. 8, which is inspired by the "formalisation pattern" [9]. Figure 8 is translated to IAL and the result is show in Figs. 9 and 10, which illustrate (1) a machine checked AC; (2) integration of informal, formal, and semi-formal artifacts; and (3) use of Isabelle/UTP verification techniques.

The Formalisation Pattern. [9] shows how results from a formal method can be used to provide evidence to an AC that claims to satisfy a given requirement {R}. The strategy used to decompose the claim "Informal requirement {R} is met by {S}" is contingent on the validation of both the formal model of {R} and the formal model of {S}. Consequently, the pattern breaks down the satisfaction of {R} into 3 claims stating that (1) the formal model of {S} is validated, (2) the formalisation of {R} correctly characterises {R}, and (3) the formal model of {S} satisfies the formalisation of {R}. The former two claims usually have an informal process argument. In Fig. 8, we adapt this pattern as follows. Firstly, instead of using two validation claims, we use two justification elements, **C2** and **C3**. This is to preserve the well-formedness of the AC – the "requirement validation" claims have a type different from the "requirement satisfaction" claims. An example of a "requirement satisfaction" claim is **C4**. Secondly, we add the "requirement satisfaction" claim **C5** for the state invariant of TIS.

In Fig. 8, we apply our adapted pattern to **C1**. This claim states that the informal requirement SFR1 is met, and references **SFR1**, with its natural language description, and the assumption **TIS-STATE**. The latter is important, as the AC's requirements are only satisfied when the invariant in Sect. 5 holds. **C1** is decomposed by the formalisation strategy, **S1**, which references the three formal artifacts **TIS-INV** (*TIS-Inv*), **FSFR1** and **TIS-model** (*TISUserEntryOp*) from Sect. 5. This decomposition is contingent on the validation arguments expressed by **C3** and **C2**. The latter could be an explanation of how FSFR1 formalises SFR1, such as the description of Theorem 5.2 in Sect. 5. **S1** subclaims are **C4** and **C5**. The former is supported by the evidence **FSFR1-PROOF** which refers to Theorem 5.2, and the latter by **TIS-INV-PROOF** which refers to Theorem 5.1.

Claims. Figure 9 shows the model of **C1**–**C5** from Fig. 8. In SACM, justifications, asusmptions, and claims are unified by the class `Assertion`. Thus, the claims and justifications from Fig. 8 are all represented by claims in Fig. 9. They are created using the command `CLAIM`, with a name and content associated. Since the checks done by IAL are successful, no errors are issued.

Formal, Semi-formal, and Informal. The `CONTENT` of the claims in Fig. 9 integrate hyperlinks, which are generated by antiquotations that reference semi-formal artifacts, i.e. instances created by IAL, formal artifacts, i.e. theorems and proof techniques created by Isabelle/HOL commands, and informal artifacts, i.e., natural language. For example, the `CONTENT` of `C4` combines natural language with the antiquotation `@{const <FSFR1>}` to insert a hyperlink to the formal artifact

FSFR1. Also, C1 refers to the semi-formal artifact SFR1, and SFR1 copies the natural language requirement from the Tokeneer documentation.

```
EXPRESSION SFR1 CONTENT‹If the latch is unlocked by the TIS, then the TIS must be ...›

CLAIM C1 CONTENT‹Informal Requirement @{Expression SFR1} is met.›

CLAIM C2 ASSUMED
  CONTENT‹Formalization of the informal security requirement @{Expression SFR1}
        by the formal requirement @{const FSFR1} is valid.›

CLAIM C3 ASSUMED
  CONTENT‹Formalization of system element @{Resource TIS} by model @{const TIS_model} is valid.›

CLAIM C4 NEEDS_SUPPORT
  CONTENT‹The model element @{const TIS_model} satisfies the formal requirement @{const FSFR1}.›

CLAIM C5 NEEDS_SUPPORT
  CONTENT‹The model element @{const TIS_model} preserves the invariant @{const TIS_inv}.›

ASSERTED_INFERENCE S1
  SOURCE‹{@{Claim C2}, @{Claim C3},
        @{Claim C4}, @{Claim C5} }›
  TARGET‹{@{Claim C1} }› ARGUMENT_REASONING‹Argument by formalization›

ASSERTED_CONTEXT AC1
  SOURCE‹{@{ArtifactReference ISABELLE_2018_REF}, @{ArtifactReference TIS_INV_DEF_ACT_REF},
        @{ArtifactReference TIS_FSFR1_DEF_ACT_REF}, @{ArtifactReference TIS_MODEL_DEF_ACT_REF} }›
  TARGET‹{@{AssertedInference S1} }›

ASSERTED_EVIDENCE AE1
  SOURCE‹{@{ArtifactReference TIS_FSFR1_PROOF_REF} }› TARGET‹{@{Claim C4} }›
  ARGUMENT_REASONING‹The claim @{Claim C4} is established by @{thm FSFR1_proof}.›

ASSERTED_EVIDENCE AE2
  SOURCE‹{@{ArtifactReference TIS_INV_PROOF_REF} }› TARGET‹{@{Claim C5} }›
  ARGUMENT_REASONING‹The claim @{Claim C5} is established by @{thm TIS_inv_proof}.›
```

Fig. 9. TIS argument: claims and their relations in Isabelle/SACM

Relations Between Claims. The strategy **S1** from Fig. 8, connecting the elements **C1**–**C5**, is modelled by S1 in Fig. 9. S1 is created using the command ASSERTED_INFERENCE, which uses antiquotations to reference the premise claims C4, C5, C2 and C3, i.e., the SOURCE, and the conclusion claim C1, i.e., the TARGET. C4 and C5 are left undeveloped, and hence marked as NEEDS_SUPPORT: the argument should be completed later. Moreover, C2 and C3 are marked as ASSUMED, meaning that this argument is contingent on their satisfaction elsewhere.

Context. We model the relations between the context elements **TIS-INV**, **FSFR1**, **TIS-model** and the strategy **S1** from Fig. 8. This is done in Fig. 9 using the command ASSERTED_CONTEXT which creates the relation AC1. It uses antiquotations to connect S1 with: (1) ISABELLE_2018_REF, which is an "SACM reference" to the artifact RESOURCE ISABELLE_2018, which is created in Fig. 10 and models the verification tool; and (2) TIS_FSFR1_DEF_ACT_REF, TIS_INV_DEF_ACT_REF. and TIS_MODEL_DEF_ACT_REF, which are all artifact references to their corresponding artifacts created in Fig. 10 using `ACTIVITY`. From the point of view of SACM, artifacts created using `ARTIFACT_REFERENCE` are references to the artifacts, and not the artifacts themselves. Similarly, relationships created using `ASSERTED_CONTEXT` and `ASSERTED_EVIDENCE` link `Assertions` to artifact references.

Evidence. We model the relationships from Fig. 8 that link **C4**, **C5** to **FSFR1-PROOF** and **TIS-INV-PROOF** respectively. This is done in Fig. 9 by `AE1` and `AE2`, which are created using the command `ASSERTED_EVIDENCE`. They support claims `C4` and `C5` by the "SACM references" `TIS_FSFR1_PROOF_REF` and `TIS_INV_PROOF_REF`, respectively. One can see that `TIS_FSFR1_PROOF_REF` and `TIS_INV_PROOF_REF` point to `TIS_FSFR1_PROOF_ACT` and `TIS_INV_PROOF_ACT` using antiquotations. The latter are created in Fig. 10 using the command `ACTIVITY`, which records an activity with a `StartTime` and `EndTime`. They also have a `CONTENT` with antiquotations pointing to the formal artifacts `@{thm FSFR1_proof}` and `@{thm TIS_inv_proof}`, which are Theorems 5.2 and 5.1, respectively. Also, the antiquotations `@{method hoare_auto}` and `@{method rel_auto}` reference the formal artifacts `hoare_auto` and `rel_auto`, which are Isabelle/UTP proof tactics.

```
ACTIVITY TIS_MODEL_DEF_ACT StartTime ‹25/03/2019› EndTime‹28/03/2019› PROPERTIES‹{}›
  CONTENT‹Definition of the formal model @{const TIS_model}.›

ACTIVITY TIS_INV_DEF_ACT StartTime ‹29/03/2019› EndTime‹29/03/2019› PROPERTIES‹{}›
  CONTENT‹Definition of the state invariant @{const TIS_inv}.›

ACTIVITY TIS_INV_PROOF_ACT StartTime ‹29/03/2019› EndTime‹29/03/2019› PROPERTIES‹{}›
  CONTENT‹Proof of the state invariant preservation @{thm TIS_inv_proof} by @{method hoare_auto}.›

ACTIVITY TIS_FSFR1_DEF_ACT StartTime ‹02/04/2019› EndTime‹02/04/2019› PROPERTIES‹{}›
  CONTENT‹Definition of the formal requirement @{const FSFR1}.›

ACTIVITY TIS_FSFR1_PROOF_ACT StartTime ‹02/04/2019› EndTime‹10/04/2019› PROPERTIES‹{}›
  CONTENT‹Discharging the proof obligation related to @{thm FSFR1_proof} by @{method rel_auto}.›

RESOURCE TIS PROPERTIES ‹{}› LOCATION‹@{url "https://www.adacore.com/tokeneer/"}›
  CONTENT‹Website with the specification documents for the TIS.›

RESOURCE Isabelle2018 PROPERTIES ‹{}› LOCATION‹@{url "https://isabelle.in.tum.de/"}›
  CONTENT‹Website of the Isabelle Interactive Theorem Prover.›

ARTIFACT_REFERENCE ISABELLE_2018_REF REFERENCED_ARTIFACTS‹{@{Resource Isabelle2018} }›
ARTIFACT_REFERENCE TIS_MODEL_DEF_ACT_REF REFERENCED_ARTIFACTS‹{@{Activity TIS_MODEL_DEF_ACT} }›
ARTIFACT_REFERENCE TIS_INV_DEF_ACT_REF REFERENCED_ARTIFACTS‹{@{Activity TIS_INV_DEF_ACT} }›
ARTIFACT_REFERENCE TIS_FSFR1_DEF_ACT_REF REFERENCED_ARTIFACTS‹{@{Activity TIS_FSFR1_DEF_ACT} }›
ARTIFACT_REFERENCE TIS_FSFR1_PROOF_REF REFERENCED_ARTIFACTS‹{@{Activity TIS_FSFR1_PROOF_ACT} }›
ARTIFACT_REFERENCE TIS_INV_PROOF_REF REFERENCED_ARTIFACTS‹{@{Activity TIS_INV_PROOF_ACT} }›
```

Fig. 10. TIS argument: artifacts and their relations in Isabelle/SACM

7 Related Work

Woodcock et al. [34] highlight defects of the Tokeneer SPARK implementation, indicate undischarged verification conditions, and perform robustness tests generated by the Alloy SAT solver [23] model. Using De Bono's lateral thinking, these test cases go beyond the anticipated operational envelope and stimulate anomalous behaviours. In shortening the feedback cycle for verification and test engineers, theorem proving can help using this approach more intensively.

Despite its age, we see Tokeneer as a highly relevant benchmark specification, particularly since it is one of the grand challenges of the "Verified Software Initiative" [33]. As we have argued elsewhere [19], such benchmarks allow us to conduct objective analyses of assurance techniques to aid their transfer to other domains. The issues highlighted in [34] are systematic design problems that can be fixed by a change of the benchmark (e.g. by a two-way biometric identification on both sides of the enclave entrance). However, this is out of scope of our work and does not harm Tokeneer in its function as a benchmark.

Rivera et al. [27] present an Event-B model of the TIS, verify this model, generate Java code from it using the Rodin tool, and test this code by JUnit tests manually derived from the specification. The tests validate the model in addition to the Event-B invariants derived from the same specification, and aim to detect errors in the Event-B model caused by misunderstandings of the specification. Using Rodin, the authors verify the security properties (Sect. 3) using Hoare triples. Our work uses a similar abstract machine specification, but with weakest precondition as the main tool for the requirements. Beyond the replication of the Tokeneer case study, [27] deals with the relationship between the model and the code via testing, whereas we focus on the construction of certifiable assurance arguments from formal model-based specifications. Nevertheless, we believe Isabelle's code generation features could be similarly applied.

We believe that our work is the first to put formal verification effort into the wider context of structured assurance argumentation, in our case, a machine-checked security case using Isabelle/SACM. We have also recently applied our technique to collision avoidance for autonomous robots [18]; a modern benchmark.

Several works bring formality to assurance cases [8,9,11,29]. AdvoCATE is a powerful graphical tool for the construction of GSN-based safety cases [9]. It uses a formal foundation called argument structures, which prescribe well-formedness checks for the graph structure, and allow instantiation of assurance case patterns. Our work likewise ensures well-formedness, and additionally allows the embedding of formal content. Denney's formalisation pattern [9] is an inspiration for our work. Our framework is an assurance backend, which complements AdvoCATE with a deep integration of modelling and specification formalisms.

Rushby shows how assurance arguments can be embedded into formal logic to overcome logical fallacies [29]. Our framework similarly allows reasoning using formal logic, but additionally allows us to combine formal and informal artifacts. We were also inspired by the work on evidential toolbus [8], which allows the combination of evidence from several formal and semi-formal analysis tools. Isabelle similarly allows integration of a variety of formal analysis tools [31].

8 Conclusions

We have presented Isabelle/SACM, a framework for computer-assisted assurance cases with integrated formal methods. We showed how SACM is embedded into Isabelle as an ontology, and provided an interactive assurance language that generates valid instances. We applied it to part of the Tokeneer security case, including verification of one of the security functional requirements, and embedded these results into a mechanised assurance argument. Isabelle/SACM enforces the usage of formal ontological links which represent the provenance between the assurance arguments and their claims, a feature inherited from DOF. Isabelle/SACM combines features from Isabelle/HOL, DOF, and SACM in a way that allows integration of formal methods and ACs [18].

In future work, we will connect Isabelle/SACM to a graphical AC tool, such as ACME [30], which will make the platform more accessible. We will consider the integration of AC pattern execution [9], to facilitate AC production. We will also complete the mechanisation of the TIS security case, including the overarching argument for how the formal evidence can satisfy the requirements of CC [5]. In parallel, we are developing our verification framework, Isabelle/UTP [16,17] to support a variety of software engineering notations. We recently demonstrated formal verification facilities for a statechart-like notation [12,13], and are also working towards tools to support hybrid dynamical languages [15] like Modelica and Simulink. Our overarching goal is a comprehensive assurance framework supported by a variety of integrated formal methods in order to support complex certification tasks for cyber-physical systems such as autonomous robots [18,19].

Acknowledgements. This work is funded by EPSRC projects CyPhyAssure[8], (grant reference EP/S001190/1), and RoboCalc (grant reference EP/M025756/1), and additionally German Science Foundation (DFG) grant 381212925.

References

1. Barnes, J., Chapman, R., Johnson, R., Widmaier, J., Cooper, D., Everett, B.: Engineering the Tokeneer enclave protection software. In: Proceedings of IEEE International Symposium on Secure Software Engineering (ISSSE) (2006)
2. Bishop, P.G., Bloomfield, R.E.: A methodology for safety case development. In: Redmill, F., Anderson, T. (eds.) Industrial Perspectives of Safety-Critical Systems, pp. 194–204. Springer, London (1998). https://doi.org/10.1007/978-1-4471-1534-2_14
3. Blanchette, J.C., Bulwahn, L., Nipkow, T.: Automatic proof and disproof in Isabelle/HOL. In: Tinelli, C., Sofronie-Stokkermans, V. (eds.) FroCoS 2011. LNCS (LNAI), vol. 6989, pp. 12–27. Springer, Heidelberg (2011). https://doi.org/10.1007/978-3-642-24364-6_2
4. Brucker, A.D., Ait-Sadoune, I., Crisafulli, P., Wolff, B.: Using the isabelle ontology framework. In: Rabe, F., Farmer, W.M., Passmore, G.O., Youssef, A. (eds.) CICM 2018. LNCS (LNAI), vol. 11006, pp. 23–38. Springer, Cham (2018). https://doi.org/10.1007/978-3-319-96812-4_3
5. Common Criteria Consortium: Common criteria for information technology security evaluation - part 1: introduction and general model. Technical report CCMB-2017-04-001 (2017). https://www.commoncriteriaportal.org

[8] CyPhyAssure Project: https://www.cs.york.ac.uk/circus/CyPhyAssure/.

6. Cooper, D., et al.: Tokeneer ID station: formal specification. Technical report, Praxis High Integrity Systems, August 2008. https://www.adacore.com/tokeneer
7. Cooper, D., et al.: Tokeneer ID station: security properties. Technical report, Praxis High Integrity Systems, August 2008. https://www.adacore.com/tokeneer
8. Cruanes, S., Hamon, G., Owre, S., Shankar, N.: Tool integration with the evidential tool bus. In: Giacobazzi, R., Berdine, J., Mastroeni, I. (eds.) VMCAI 2013. LNCS, vol. 7737, pp. 275–294. Springer, Heidelberg (2013). https://doi.org/10.1007/978-3-642-35873-9_18
9. Denney, E., Pai, G.: Tool support for assurance case development. Autom. Softw. Eng. **25**, 435–499 (2018)
10. Dijkstra, E.W.: Guarded commands, nondeterminacy and formal derivation of programs. Commun. ACM **18**(8), 453–457 (1975)
11. Diskin, Z., Maibaum, T., Wassyng, A., Wynn-Williams, S., Lawford, M.: Assurance via model transformations and their hierarchical refinement. In: MODELS. IEEE (2018)
12. Foster, S., Baxter, J., Cavalcanti, A., Miyazawa, A., Woodcock, J.: Automating verification of state machines with reactive designs and Isabelle/UTP. In: Bae, K., Ölveczky, P.C. (eds.) FACS 2018. LNCS, vol. 11222, pp. 137–155. Springer, Cham (2018). https://doi.org/10.1007/978-3-030-02146-7_7
13. Foster, S., Cavalcanti, A., Canham, S., Woodcock, J., Zeyda, F.: Unifying theories of reactive design contracts. Theoretical Computer Science, September 2019
14. Foster, S., Cavalcanti, A., Woodcock, J., Zeyda, F.: Unifying theories of time with generalised reactive processes. Inf. Process. Lett. **135**, 47–52 (2018)
15. Foster, S., Thiele, B., Cavalcanti, A., Woodcock, J.: Towards a UTP semantics for modelica. In: Bowen, J.P., Zhu, H. (eds.) UTP 2016. LNCS, vol. 10134, pp. 44–64. Springer, Cham (2017). https://doi.org/10.1007/978-3-319-52228-9_3
16. Foster, S., Zeyda, F., Nemouchi, Y., Ribeiro, P., Wolff, B.: Isabelle/UTP: mechanised theory engineering for unifying theories of programming. Archive of Formal Proofs (2019). https://www.isa-afp.org/entries/UTP.html
17. Foster, S., Zeyda, F., Woodcock, J.: Unifying heterogeneous state-spaces with lenses. In: Sampaio, A., Wang, F. (eds.) ICTAC 2016. LNCS, vol. 9965, pp. 295–314. Springer, Cham (2016). https://doi.org/10.1007/978-3-319-46750-4_17
18. Gleirscher, M., Foster, S., Nemouchi, Y.: Evolution of formal model-based assurance cases for autonomous robots. In: Ölveczky, P.C., Salaün, G. (eds.) SEFM 2019. LNCS, vol. 11724, pp. 87–104. Springer, Cham (2019). https://doi.org/10.1007/978-3-030-30446-1_5
19. Gleirscher, M., Foster, S., Woodcock, J.: New opportunities for integrated formal methods. ACM Comput. Surv. (2019, in Press). Preprint: https://arxiv.org/abs/1812.10103
20. Greenwell, W., Knight, J., Holloway, C.M., Pease, J.: A taxonomy of fallacies in system safety arguments. In: Proceedings of the 24th International System Safety Conference, July 2006
21. Habli, I., Kelly, T.: Balancing the formal and informal in safety case arguments. In: VeriSure Workshop, colocated with CAV, July 2014
22. Hoare, C.A.R., He, J.: Unifying Theories of Programming. Prentice-Hall, Upper Saddle River (1998)
23. Jackson, D.: Alloy: a lightweight object modelling notation. ACM Trans. Softw. Eng. Methodol. **11**(2), 256–290 (2000)
24. Kelly, T.: Arguing safety - a systematic approach to safety case management. Ph.D. thesis, University of York (1998)

25. Nipkow, T., Paulson, L.C., Wenzel, M.: Isabelle/HOL – A Proof Assistant for Higher-Order Logic. LNCS, vol. 2283. Springer, Heidelberg (2002). https://doi.org/10.1007/3-540-45949-9
26. Paige, R.F.: A meta-method for formal method integration. In: Fitzgerald, J., Jones, C.B., Lucas, P. (eds.) FME 1997. LNCS, vol. 1313, pp. 473–494. Springer, Heidelberg (1997). https://doi.org/10.1007/3-540-63533-5_25
27. Rivera, V., Bhattacharya, S., Cataño, N.: Undertaking the tokeneer challenge in event-B. In: FormaliSE 2016. ACM Press (2016)
28. Rushby, J.: Logic and epistemology in safety cases. In: Bitsch, F., Guiochet, J., Kaâniche, M. (eds.) SAFECOMP 2013. LNCS, vol. 8153, pp. 1–7. Springer, Heidelberg (2013). https://doi.org/10.1007/978-3-642-40793-2_1
29. Rushby, J.: Mechanized support for assurance case argumentation. In: Nakano, Y., Satoh, K., Bekki, D. (eds.) JSAI-isAI 2013. LNCS (LNAI), vol. 8417, pp. 304–318. Springer, Cham (2014). https://doi.org/10.1007/978-3-319-10061-6_20
30. Wei, R., Kelly, T., Dai, X., Zhao, S., Hawkins, R.: Model based system assurance using the structured assurance case metamodel. Syst. Softw. **154**, 211–233 (2019)
31. Wenzel, M., Wolff, B.: Building formal method tools in the Isabelle/Isar framework. In: Schneider, K., Brandt, J. (eds.) TPHOLs 2007. LNCS, vol. 4732, pp. 352–367. Springer, Heidelberg (2007). https://doi.org/10.1007/978-3-540-74591-4_26
32. Wenzel, M.: Isabelle/jEdit as IDE for domain-specific formal languages and informal text documents. In: Proceedings of the 4th Workshop on Formal Integrated Development Environment (F-IDE), pp. 71–84 (2018). https://doi.org/10.4204/EPTCS.284.6
33. Woodcock, J.: First steps in the verified software grand challenge. IEEE Comput. **39**(10), 57–64 (2006)
34. Woodcock, J., Aydal, E.G., Chapman, R.: The tokeneer experiments. In: Roscoe, A.W., Jones, C.B., Wood, K.R. (eds.) Reflections on the Work of C.A.R. Hoare, pp. 405–430. Springer, London (2010). https://doi.org/10.1007/978-1-84882-912-1_17

Practical Abstractions for Automated Verification of Message Passing Concurrency

Wytse Oortwijn(✉) and Marieke Huisman(✉)

University of Twente, Enschede, The Netherlands
{w.h.m.oortwijn,m.huisman}@utwente.nl

Abstract. Distributed systems are notoriously difficult to develop correctly, due to the concurrency in their communicating subsystems. Several techniques are available to help developers to improve the reliability of message passing software, including deductive verification and model checking. Both these techniques have advantages as well as limitations, which are complementary in nature. This paper contributes a novel verification technique that combines the strengths of deductive and algorithmic verification to reason elegantly about message passing concurrent programs, thereby reducing their limitations. Our approach allows to verify data-centric properties of message passing programs using concurrent separation logic (CSL), and allows to specify their communication behaviour as a process-algebraic model. The key novelty of the approach is that it formally bridges the typical abstraction gap between programs and their models, by extending CSL with logical primitives for proving deductively that a program refines its process-algebraic model. These models can then be analysed via model checking, using mCRL2, to reason indirectly about the program's communication behaviour. Our verification approach is compositional, comes with a mechanised correctness proof in Coq, and is implemented as an encoding in Viper.

1 Introduction

Distributed software is notoriously difficult to develop correctly. This is because distributed systems typically consist of multiple communicating components, which together have too many concurrent behaviours for a programmer to comprehend. Software developers therefore need formal techniques and tools to help them understand the full system behaviour, with the goal to guarantee the reliability of safety-critical distributed software. Two such formal techniques are *deductive verification* and *model checking*, both well-established in research [2,7] and proven successful in practice [12,14]. Nevertheless, both these techniques have their limitations. Deductive verification is often labour-intensive as it requires the system behaviour to be specified manually, via non-trivial code annotations, which is especially difficult for concurrent and distributed systems. Model checking, on the other hand, suffers from the typical abstraction gap [28]

W. Ahrendt and S. L. Tapia Tarifa (Eds.): IFM 2019, LNCS 11918, pp. 399–417, 2019.
https://doi.org/10.1007/978-3-030-34968-4_22

```
send (⟨4, 7, 5⟩, 1);
xs := recv 2;
assert xs = ⟨4, 5, 6, 7, 8⟩;
```

(a) Thread 1

```
while (true) {
  (ys, t) := recv;
  if (t = 1) then
    send (ys + ⟨8, 6⟩, 3);
  else send (ys, 2);
}
```

(b) Thread 2

```
while (true) {
  (zs, t) := recv;
  zs' := ParSort(zs);
  send (zs', t);
}
```

(c) Thread 3

Fig. 1. Our message passing example, consisting of three communicating threads.

(i.e., discrepancies between the program and the corresponding model), as well as the well-known state-space explosion problem.

This paper contributes a scalable and practical technique for automated verification of message passing concurrency that reduces these limitations, via a sound combination of deductive verification and model checking. Our verification technique builds on the insight that deductive and algorithmic verification are complementary [3,32,34]: the former specialises in verifying data-oriented properties (e.g., the function `sort`(xs) returns a sorted permutation of xs), while the latter targets temporal properties of control-flow (e.g., any `send` must be preceded by a `recv`). Since realistic distributed software deals with both computation (data) and communication (control-flow), such a combination of complementary verification techniques is needed, to handle all program aspects.

More specifically, our verification approach uses concurrent separation logic (CSL) to reason about data properties of message passing concurrent programs, and allows to specify their communication behaviour as a process-algebraic model. The key innovation is that CSL is used not only to specify data-oriented properties, but also to formally link the program's communication behaviour to the process-algebraic specification of its behaviour, thereby bridging the typical abstraction gap between programs and their models. These process-algebraic models can then be analysed algorithmically, e.g., using mCRL2 [8,13], to reason indirectly about the communication behaviour of the program. These formal links preserve *safety properties*; the preservation of liveness properties is left as future work. This approach has been proven sound using the Coq proof assistant, and has been implemented as an encoding in the Viper concurrency verifier [22].

Running Example. To further motivate the approach, consider the example program in Fig. 1, consisting of three threads that exchange integer sequences via synchronous message passing. The goal is to verify whether the asserted property in Thread 1's program holds. This program is a simplified version of a typical scenario in message passing concurrency: it involves computation as well as communication and has a complicated communication pattern, which makes it difficult to see and prove that the asserted property indeed holds.

Clarifying the program, Thread 1 first sends the sequence $\langle 4, 7, 5\rangle$ to the environmental threads as a message with tag 1, and then receives any outstanding integer sequence tagged 2. Thread 2 continuously listens for incoming messages of any tag with a wildcard receive, and redirects these messages, possibly with slightly modified content depending on the message tag. Thread 3 is a computing service: it sorts all incoming requests and sends back the result with the original tag. `ParSort` is assumed to be the implementation of an intricate, heavily optimised parallel sorting algorithm. Note that the asserted property holds because the **send** on line 7 is always executed, no matter the interleaving of threads.

Two standard potential approaches for verifying this property are deductive verification and model checking. However, neither of these approaches provides a satisfying solution. Techniques for deductive verification, e.g., concurrent separation logic, have their power in modularity and compositionality: they require modular independent proofs for the three threads, and allow to compose these into a single proof for the entire program. This would not work in our example scenario, as the asserted property is inherently global. One could attempt to impose global invariants on the message exchanges [38], but these are generally hard to come by. Finding a global invariant for this example would already be difficult, since there is no obvious relation between the contents of messages and their tags. Other approaches use ideas from assume-guarantee reasoning [30,36] to somehow intertwine the independent proofs of the threads' programs, but these require extra non-trivial specifications of thread-interference and are difficult to integrate into (semi-)automatic verifiers.

Alternatively, one may construct a model of this program and apply a model checker, which fits more naturally with the temporal nature of the program's communication behaviour. However, this does not give a complete solution either. In particular, certain assumptions have to be made while constructing the model, for example that `ParSort` is correctly implemented. The correctness property of `ParSort` is data-oriented (it relates the output of `ParSort` to its input) and thus in turn fits more naturally with deductive verification. But even when one uses both these approaches—deductive verification for verifying `ParSort` and model checking for verifying communication behaviour—there still is no formal connection between their results: perhaps the model incorrectly reflects the program's communication behaviour.

Contributions and Outline. This paper contributes a novel approach that allows to make such formal connections, by extending CSL with primitives for proving that a program *refines* a process-algebraic model, with respect to send/receive behaviour. Section 2 introduces the syntax and semantics of programs and process-algebraic models. Notably, our process algebra language is similar to mCRL2, but has a special *assertion primitive* of the form $?b$, that allows to encode Boolean properties b into the process itself, as logical assertions. These properties can be verified via a straightforward reduction to mCRL2, and can subsequently be used (relied upon) inside the deductive proof of the program, via special program annotations of the form **query** b, (allowing to "query" for properties b proven on the process level). Section 3 illustrates in detail how this works on the example program of Fig. 1, before Sect. 4 discusses the underlying logical machinery and its soundness proof. This soundness argument has been mechanised using Coq, and the program logic has been encoded in Viper. Section 5 discusses various extensions of the approach. Finally, Sect. 6 relates our work to existing approaches and Sect. 7 concludes.

2 Programs and Processes

This section introduces the programming language (Sect. 2.1) and the process algebra language of models (Sect. 2.2) that are used to formalise the approach.

2.1 Programs

The syntax of our simple concurrent pointer language, inspired by [6,25], is as follows, where $x, y, z, \dots \in \mathit{Var}$ are *variables* and $v, w, \dots \in \mathit{Val}$ are *values.*

Definition 1 (Expressions, Conditions, Commands)

$$\begin{aligned} e \in \mathit{Expr} &::= v \mid x \mid e + e \mid e - e \mid \cdots \\ b \in \mathit{Cond} &::= \mathsf{true} \mid \mathsf{false} \mid \neg b \mid b \wedge b \mid e = e \mid e < e \mid \cdots \\ C \in \mathit{Cmd} &::= \mathbf{skip} \mid C; C \mid C \parallel C \mid x := e \mid x := [e] \mid [e] := e \mid \mathbf{send}\ (e, e) \mid \\ &\quad\ (x, y) := \mathbf{recv} \mid x := \mathbf{recv}\ e \mid x := \mathbf{alloc}\ e \mid \mathbf{dispose}\ e \mid \\ &\quad\ \mathbf{if}\ b\ \mathbf{then}\ C\ \mathbf{else}\ C \mid \mathbf{while}\ b\ \mathbf{do}\ C \mid \mathbf{atomic}\ C \mid \mathbf{query}\ b \end{aligned}$$

This language has instructions to handle dynamically allocated memory, i.e., heaps, as well as primitives for message passing, to allow reasoning about both shared-memory and message passing concurrency models, and their combination.

The notation $[e]$ is used for *heap dereferencing*, where e is an expression whose evaluation determines the heap location to dereference. Memory can be dynamically allocated on the heap using the **alloc** e instruction, where e will be the initial value of the fresh heap cell, and be deallocated using **dispose**.

The command **send** (e_1, e_2) sends a message e_1 to the environmental threads, where e_2 is a *message tag* that can be used for message identification. Messages are received in two ways: $x :=$ **recv** e receives a message with a tag that matches the expression e, whereas $(x, y) :=$ **recv** receives *any* message and writes the message tag to the extra variable y, i.e., a *wildcard* receive.

The specification command **query** b is used to connect process-algebraic reasoning to deductive reasoning: it allows the deductive proof of a program to rely on (or *assume*) a Boolean property b, which is proven to hold (or *guaranteed*) via process-algebraic analysis. This is a ghost command that does not interfere with regular program execution.

The function $\mathsf{fv} : \mathit{Expr} \to 2^{\mathit{Var}}$ is used to determine the set of free variables of expressions as usual, and is overloaded for conditions. Substitution is written $e_1[x/e_2]$ (and likewise for conditions) and has a standard definition: replacing each occurrence of x by e_2 in e_1.

$$(\mathbf{send}\ (e_1, e_2), h, \sigma) \xrightarrow{\mathsf{send}(\llbracket e_1 \rrbracket\sigma, \llbracket e_2 \rrbracket\sigma)} (\mathbf{skip}, h, \sigma)$$

$$((x, y) := \mathbf{recv}, h, \sigma) \xrightarrow{\mathsf{recv}(v, v')} (\mathbf{skip}, h, \sigma[x \mapsto v, y \mapsto v'])$$

$$(x := \mathbf{recv}\ e, h, \sigma) \xrightarrow{\mathsf{recv}(v, \llbracket e \rrbracket\sigma)} (\mathbf{skip}, h, \sigma[x \mapsto v]) \qquad (\mathbf{query}\ b, h, s) \xrightarrow{\mathsf{qry}} (\mathbf{skip}, h, s)$$

$$\frac{(C_1, h, \sigma) \xrightarrow{\mathsf{send}(v_1, v_2)} (C_1', h, \sigma) \qquad (C_2, h, \sigma) \xrightarrow{\mathsf{recv}(v_1, v_2)} (C_2', h, \sigma')}{(C_1 \parallel C_2, h, \sigma) \xrightarrow{\mathsf{comm}(v_1, v_2)} (C_1' \parallel C_2', h, \sigma')}$$

Fig. 2. An excerpt of the small-step operational semantics of programs.

Semantics. The denotational semantics of expressions $\llbracket e \rrbracket\sigma$ and conditions $\llbracket b \rrbracket\sigma$ is defined in the standard way, with $\sigma \in Store \triangleq Var \to Val$ a *store* that gives an interpretation to variables. Sometimes $\llbracket e \rrbracket$ is written instead of $\llbracket e \rrbracket\sigma$ when e is closed, and likewise for $\llbracket b \rrbracket$.

The operational semantics of commands is defined as a labelled small-step reduction relation $\xrightarrow{\cdot} \subseteq Conf \times Label \times Conf$ between configurations $Conf \triangleq Cmd \times Heap \times Store$ of programs. Heaps $h \in Heap \triangleq Loc \rightharpoonup_{\mathsf{fin}} Val$ are used to model shared memory and are defined as finite partial mappings, with $Loc \subseteq Val$ an infinite domain of heap locations. The transition labels represent the atomic (inter)actions of threads, and are defined as follows.

$$l \in Label ::= \ \mathsf{send}(v, v) \mid \mathsf{recv}(v, v) \mid \mathsf{comm}(v, v) \mid \mathsf{cmp} \mid \mathsf{qry}$$

Transitions labelled $\mathsf{send}(v, v')$ indicate that the program sends a value v from the current configuration, together with a tag v'. These can be received by a thread, as a transition labelled $\mathsf{recv}(v, v')$. By doing so, the sending and receiving threads *communicate*, represented by the comm label. Internal computations that are not related to message passing are labelled cmp, e.g., heap reading or writing. The only exception to this are the reductions of **query** commands, which are given the label qry instead, for later convenience in proving soundness.

Figure 2 gives an excerpt of the reduction rules for message exchanging. All other rules are standard in spirit [21,35] and are therefore deferred to [1]. For ease of presentation, a synchronous message passing semantics is used for now. However, our approach can easily be extended to asynchronous message passing.

2.2 Processes

In this work the communication behaviour of programs is specified as a process algebra with data, whose language is defined by the following grammar.

Definition 2 (Processes)

$$P, Q ::= \ \varepsilon \mid \delta \mid \mathsf{send}(e, e) \mid \mathsf{recv}(e, e) \mid ?b \mid b : P \mid P \cdot P \mid P + P \mid P \parallel P \mid \Sigma_x\, P \mid P^*$$

Successful termination

$$\varepsilon\downarrow \qquad P^*\downarrow \qquad \frac{P\downarrow \quad Q\downarrow}{P\cdot Q\downarrow} \qquad \frac{P\downarrow}{P+Q\downarrow} \qquad \frac{P[x/v]\downarrow}{\Sigma_x P\downarrow} \qquad \frac{[\![b]\!] \quad P\downarrow}{b : P\downarrow}$$

Operational semantics

$$\mathsf{send}(e_1,e_2) \xrightarrow{\mathsf{send}([\![e_1]\!],[\![e_2]\!])} \varepsilon \qquad \mathsf{recv}(e_1,e_2) \xrightarrow{\mathsf{recv}([\![e_1]\!],[\![e_2]\!])} \varepsilon \qquad \frac{[\![b]\!]}{?b \xrightarrow{\mathsf{assn}} \varepsilon}$$

$$\frac{P \xrightarrow{\alpha} P'}{P\cdot Q \xrightarrow{\alpha} P'\cdot Q} \qquad \frac{P\downarrow \quad Q \xrightarrow{\alpha} Q'}{P\cdot Q \xrightarrow{\alpha} Q'} \qquad \frac{P[x/v] \xrightarrow{\alpha} P'}{\Sigma_x P \xrightarrow{\alpha} P'} \qquad \frac{[\![b]\!] \quad P \xrightarrow{\alpha} P'}{b : P \xrightarrow{\alpha} P'}$$

$$\frac{P \xrightarrow{\alpha} P'}{P^* \xrightarrow{\alpha} P'\cdot P^*} \qquad \frac{P \xrightarrow{\mathsf{send}(v_1,v_2)} P' \quad Q \xrightarrow{\mathsf{recv}(v_1,v_2)} Q'}{P \parallel Q \xrightarrow{\mathsf{comm}(v_1,v_2)} P' \parallel Q'}$$

Fault semantics

$$\frac{\neg[\![b]\!]}{?b \longrightarrow ↯} \qquad \frac{P\downarrow \quad Q \longrightarrow ↯}{P\cdot Q \longrightarrow ↯} \qquad \frac{P[x/v] \longrightarrow ↯}{\Sigma_x P \longrightarrow ↯} \qquad \frac{[\![b]\!] \quad P \longrightarrow ↯}{b : P \longrightarrow ↯} \qquad \frac{P \longrightarrow ↯}{P^* \longrightarrow ↯}$$

Fig. 3. An excerpt of the small-step operational semantics of processes.

Clarifying the standard connectives, ε is the empty process without behaviour, and δ is the deadlocked process that neither progresses nor terminates. The process $\Sigma_x P$ is the infinite summation $P[x/v_0] + P[x/v_1] + \cdots$ over all values $v_0, v_1, \ldots \in \mathit{Val}$. Sometimes $\Sigma_{x_0,\ldots,x_n} P$ is written to abbreviate $\Sigma_{x_0} \cdots \Sigma_{x_n} P$. The guarded process $b : P$ behaves as P if the guard b holds, and otherwise behaves as δ. The process P^* is the Kleene iteration of P and denotes a sequence of zero or more P's. The infinite iteration of P is derived to be $P^\omega \triangleq P^* \cdot \delta$.

Since processes are used to reason about send/receive behaviour, this process algebra language exclusively supports two actions, $\mathsf{send}(e_1, e_2)$ and $\mathsf{recv}(e_1, e_2)$, for sending and receiving data elements e_1, together with a message tag e_2.

Finally, $?b$ is the *assertive process*, which is very similar to guarded processes: $?b$ is behaviourally equivalent to δ in case b does not hold. However, assertive processes have a special role in our approach: they are the main subject of process-algebraic analysis, as they encode the properties b to verify, as logical assertions. Moreover, they are a key component in connecting process-algebraic reasoning with deductive reasoning, as their properties can be relied upon in the deductive proofs of programs via the **query** b ghost command.

The function fv is overloaded to determine the set of unbound variables in process terms. As always, any process P is defined to be *closed* if $\mathsf{fv}(P) = \emptyset$.

Semantics. Figure 3 presents the operational semantics of processes, which is defined in terms of a labelled binary reduction relation $\stackrel{\cdot}{\longrightarrow} \subseteq \mathit{Proc} \times \mathit{ProcLabel} \times$

Proc between processes. The labels of the reduction rules are defined as follows.

$$\alpha \in \mathit{ProcLabel} ::= \mathsf{send}(v,v) \mid \mathsf{recv}(v,v) \mid \mathsf{comm}(v,v) \mid \mathsf{assn}$$

The labels *send*, *recv* and *comm* are used in the same manner as those of program transitions, whereas *assn* indicates reductions of assertional processes.

The reduction rules are mostly standard [10,13]. Processes are assumed to be closed as a well-formedness condition, preventing the need to include stores. Moreover, it is common to use an explicit notion of *successful termination* in process algebras with ε [4]. The notation $P\downarrow$ intuitively means that P has the choice to have no further behaviour and thus to behave as ε. The send and recv actions communicate in the sense that they synchronise as a *comm* transition.

The property of interest for process-algebraic verification is to check for absence of faults. Any closed process P *exhibits a fault*, denoted $P \longrightarrow \lightning$, if P is able to violate an assertion. Furthermore, any process P is defined to be *safe*, written $P\checkmark$, if P can never reach a state that exhibits a fault, while following the reduction rules of the operational semantics.

Definition 3 (Process safety). *The* $\checkmark$ *predicate is coinductively defined such that, if* $P\checkmark$ *holds, then* $P \not\longrightarrow \lightning$, *and* $P \xrightarrow{\alpha} P'$ *implies* $P'\checkmark$ *for any* α *and* P'.

Given any closed process P, determining whether $P\checkmark$ holds can straightforwardly and mechanically be reduced to an mCRL2 model checking problem. This is done by modelling an explicit fault state that is reachable whenever an assertive process is violated, as a distinctive $\lightning$ action. Checking for fault absence is then reduced to checking the μ-calculus formula $[\mathsf{true}^* \cdot \lightning]\mathsf{false}$ on the translated model, meaning "no faulty transitions are ever reachable".

Process bisimilarity is defined as usual, and preserves faults and termination.

Definition 4 (Bisimulation). *A binary relation* $\mathscr{R} \subseteq \mathit{Proc} \times \mathit{Proc}$ *is a* bisimulation relation *over closed processes if, whenever* $P\mathscr{R}Q$, *then*

- $P\downarrow$ *if and only if* $Q\downarrow$.
- $P \longrightarrow \lightning$ *if and only if* $Q \longrightarrow \lightning$.
- *If* $P \xrightarrow{\alpha} P'$, *then there exists a* Q' *such that* $Q \xrightarrow{\alpha} Q'$ *and* $P'\mathscr{R}Q'$.
- *If* $Q \xrightarrow{\alpha} Q'$, *then there exists a* P' *such that* $P \xrightarrow{\alpha} P'$ *and* $P'\mathscr{R}Q'$.

Two closed processes P and Q are defined to be *bisimilar*, or *bisimulation equivalent*, denoted $P \cong Q$, if there exists a bisimulation relation $\mathscr{R}$ such that $P\mathscr{R}Q$. Any bisimulation relation constitutes an equivalence relation. In our Coq encoding [1], we have proven soundness of various standard bisimulation equivalences for this language. As usual, bisimilarity is a congruence for all process-algebraic connectives. Moreover, process safety is closed under bisimilarity.

3 Verification Example

Before discussing the logical details of our approach, let us first demonstrate it on the example program of Fig. 1. Application of the technique consists of the following three steps:

1. Constructing a process-algebraic model that captures the program's send/recv behaviour;
2. Analysing the model to determine whether the value received by Thread 1 is always the sorted sequence $\langle 4, 5, 6, 7, 8 \rangle$, via a reduction to an mCRL2 model checking problem; and
3. Deductively verifying whether the program correctly implements the process-algebraic model with respect to send/receive behaviour, by using concurrent separation logic.

The remainder of this section discusses each of these three steps in detail.

Step 1: Constructing a Process-Algebraic Model. The communication behaviour of the example program can straightforwardly be captured as a process $\mathsf{P} = \mathsf{P}_1 \parallel \mathsf{P}_2 \parallel \mathsf{P}_3$ (assuming that the expression language is rich enough to handle sequences), so that P_i captures Thread i's send/receive behaviour, where

$$\mathsf{P}_1 \triangleq \mathsf{send}(\langle 4, 7, 5 \rangle, 1) \cdot \Sigma_{xs}\, \mathsf{recv}(xs, 2) \cdot ?(xs = \langle 4, 5, 6, 7, 8 \rangle)$$

$$\mathsf{P}_2 \triangleq \mathsf{P}_2'^{\omega}, \text{ with } \mathsf{P}_2' \triangleq \Sigma_{ys,t}\, \mathsf{recv}(ys, t) \cdot (t = 1 : \mathsf{send}(ys +\!\!+ \langle 8, 6 \rangle, 3) + t \neq 1 : \mathsf{send}(ys, 2))$$

$$\mathsf{P}_3 \triangleq \mathsf{P}_3'^{\omega}, \text{ with } \mathsf{P}_3' \triangleq \Sigma_{zs,t}\, \mathsf{recv}(zs, t) \cdot \mathsf{send}(\texttt{sort}(zs), t)$$

Observe that P_1 encodes the property of interest as the assertion $?(xs = \langle 4, 5, 6, 7, 8 \rangle)$. The validity of this assertion is checked by mCRL2 on the translated model, as described in the next paragraph. Moreover, `sort` is assumed to be the functional description of a sorting algorithm. Such a description can axiomatically be defined in mCRL2. The `sort` mapping can easily act as a functional specification for the implementation of more intricate sorting algorithms like `ParSort`. Deductive verifiers are generally well-suited to relate such functional specifications to implementations via pre/postcondition reasoning:

```
ensures \result = sort(xs);
seq⟨nat⟩ ParSort(seq⟨nat⟩ xs) { ··· }
```

Step 2: Analysing the Process-Algebraic Model. The composite process P can straightforwardly be translated to mCRL2 input and be analysed. Our translation can be found online at [1]. This translation has been done manually, yet it would not be difficult to write a tool that does it mechanically (we are actively working on this).

Notably, assertive processes $?b$ are translated into $\mathsf{check}(b)$ actions. The action $\mathsf{check}(\mathsf{false})$ can be seen as the encoding of $\lightning$. Checking for process safety $\mathsf{P}\checkmark$ can be reduced to checking the μ-calculus formula $\phi = [\mathsf{true}^* \cdot \mathsf{check}(\mathsf{false})]\mathsf{false}$, stating that no $\mathsf{check}(\mathsf{false})$ action can ever be performed, or equivalently that the process is free of faults. mCRL2 can indeed confirm that P is fault-free by checking ϕ, and thus that the asserted property holds. In Step 3 we formally prove that the program adheres to the communication behaviour described by P, which allows to project these model checking results onto program behaviour.

$\{\mathsf{Proc}(\mathsf{P}_1)\}$
send $(\langle 4,7,5\rangle, 1)$;
$\{\mathsf{Proc}(\Sigma_x\, \mathsf{recv}(x,2) \cdot ?(x = \langle 4,5,6,7,8\rangle))\}$
$xs :=$ **recv** 2;
$\{\mathsf{Proc}(?(xs = \langle 4,5,6,7,8\rangle))\}$
query $xs = \langle 4,5,6,7,8\rangle$;
$\{\mathsf{Proc}(\varepsilon) * xs = \langle 4,5,6,7,8\rangle\}$
assert $xs = \langle 4,5,6,7,8\rangle$;
$\{\mathsf{Proc}(\varepsilon) * xs = \langle 4,5,6,7,8\rangle\}$

(a) Proof of Thread 1's program

$\{\mathsf{Proc}(\mathsf{P}_3)\}$
while (true) **invariant** $\mathsf{Proc}(\mathsf{P}_3'^{\omega})$ {
  $\{\mathsf{Proc}(\mathsf{P}_3'^{\omega})\}$
  $\{\mathsf{Proc}(\mathsf{P}_3' \cdot \mathsf{P}_3'^{\omega})\}$
  $(zs, t) :=$ **recv**;
  $\{\mathsf{Proc}(\mathsf{send}(\mathtt{sort}(zs), t) \cdot \mathsf{P}_3'^{\omega})\}$
  $zs' := \mathtt{ParSort}(zs)$;
  $\{\mathsf{Proc}(\mathsf{send}(\mathtt{sort}(zs), t) \cdot \mathsf{P}_3'^{\omega}) *$
    $zs' = \mathtt{sort}(zs)\}$
  send (zs', t);
  $\{\mathsf{Proc}(\mathsf{P}_3'^{\omega})\}$
}

(b) Proof of Thread 3's program

Fig. 4. Proofs for Threads 1 and 3 of our example. Thread 2 is proven likewise.

Step 3: Connecting Processes to Program Behaviour. The final step is to deductively prove that Fig. 1's program refines P, with respect to communication behaviour, using CSL. To do this, we extend CSL with predicates of the form $\mathsf{Proc}(P)$, which express that the remaining program will communicate as prescribed by the process P—the program's model. More specifically, the proof system enforces that every **send** (e, e') instruction must be prescribed by a $\mathsf{Proc}(\mathsf{send}(e, e') \cdot P)$ predicate in the logic, and likewise for **recv**, thereby enforcing that the process-algebraic model can perform a matching send or recv action. These actions are then *consumed* in the logic, while following the structure of the program. Similarly, **query** b annotations must be prescribed by a $\mathsf{Proc}(?b \cdot P)$ predicate, and allow to assume b in the logic as result of Step 2, by which $?b$ is consumed from the Proc predicate.

Figure 4 illustrates this, by giving the intermediate steps of the proofs of Threads 1 and 3. An extra **query** annotation has been added in Thread 1's program for obtaining the asserted property from P_1. Moreover, the annotated **invariant** in Thread 3 is a loop invariant that states that $\mathsf{Proc}(\mathsf{P}_3'^{\omega})$ prescribes the communication behaviour of every loop iteration.

Another feature of the logic is that $\mathsf{Proc}(P)$ predicates can be *split* and *merged* along parallel compositions inside P, in the style of CSL. This is used in the top-level proof of the example program, shown in Fig. 5. The $*$ connective is the *separating conjunction* from separation logic, which now expresses that different threads will use different parts of the model. This makes the approach both modular and compositional, by allowing the program's top-level proof to be composed out of the individual independent proofs of its threads.

We encoded the program logic into the Viper concurrency verifier and used it to fully mechanise the deductive proof of the example program. The Viper files are available online at [1]. This encoding primarily consists of an axiomatic domain for processes, containing constructors for the process-algebraic connectives, supported by standard axioms of process algebra (which we have proven

$$\{\mathsf{Proc}(\mathsf{P}_1 \parallel \mathsf{P}_2 \parallel \mathsf{P}_3)\}$$
$$\{\mathsf{Proc}(\mathsf{P}_1) * \mathsf{Proc}(\mathsf{P}_2) * \mathsf{Proc}(\mathsf{P}_3)\}$$

$\{\mathsf{Proc}(\mathsf{P}_1)\}$	$\{\mathsf{Proc}(\mathsf{P}_2)\}$	$\{\mathsf{Proc}(\mathsf{P}_3)\}$
Thread 1's program	*Thread 2's program*	*Thread 3's program*
$\{\mathsf{Proc}(\varepsilon)\}$	$\{\mathsf{Proc}(\mathsf{P}_2'^{\omega}) * \mathsf{false}\}$	$\{\mathsf{Proc}(\mathsf{P}_3'^{\omega}) * \mathsf{false}\}$

$$\{\mathsf{Proc}(\varepsilon) * \mathsf{Proc}(\mathsf{P}_2'^{\omega}) * \mathsf{false} * \mathsf{Proc}(\mathsf{P}_3'^{\omega}) * \mathsf{false}\}$$
$$\{\mathsf{false}\}$$

Fig. 5. The top-level specification of the example program.

sound in our Coq encoding). The Proc assertions are then encoded as unary predicates over these process types. Viper can verify correctness of the example program in under 3 s.

4 Formalisation

This section discusses the assertion language and entailment rules of the program logic (Sect. 4.1), the Hoare-triple rules for message passing and querying (Sect. 4.2), and their soundness (Sect. 4.3).

4.1 Program Logic

The program logic extends intuitionistic concurrent separation logic [17,35], where the assertion language is defined by the following grammar.

Definition 5 (Assertions)

$$\mathcal{P}, \mathcal{Q} ::= b \mid \forall x.\mathcal{P} \mid \exists x.\mathcal{P} \mid \mathcal{P} \vee \mathcal{Q} \mid \mathcal{P} * \mathcal{Q} \mid \mathcal{P} \mathrel{-\!\!*} \mathcal{Q} \mid e \hookrightarrow_{\pi} e \mid \mathsf{Proc}(P) \mid P \approx Q$$

The assertion $e_1 \hookrightarrow_{\pi} e_2$ is the standard *heap ownership assertion* and expresses the knowledge that the heap holds the value e_2 at heap location e_1. Moreover, $\pi \in (0, 1]_{\mathbb{Q}}$ is a *fractional permission* in the style of Boyland [5] and determines the type of ownership: write access to e_1 is provided in case $\pi = 1$, and read access is provided in case $0 < \pi < 1$.

The $\mathcal{P} * \mathcal{Q}$ connective is the *separating conjunction* from CSL, and expresses that the ownerships captured by $\mathcal{P}$ and $\mathcal{Q}$ are *disjoint*, e.g., it is disallowed that both express write access to the same heap location. The $\mathrel{-\!\!*}$ connective is known as the *magic wand* and describes hypothetical modifications of the current state.

The assertion $\mathsf{Proc}(P)$ expresses the ownership of the right to send and receive messages as prescribed by the process P. Here P may contain free variables and may be replaced by any process bisimilar to P. To handle such replacements, the assertion $P \approx Q$ can be used, which expresses that P and Q are bisimilar in the current context. To give an example, one may wish to deduce that $\mathsf{Proc}(0 < x : P) * x = 2$ entails $\mathsf{Proc}(P)$. Even though $0 < x : P$ has free variables, it is used in a context where x equals 2, and therefore $0 < x : P \approx P$ can be established. We now discuss the entailment rules for these deductions.

$\hookrightarrow$-SPLIT-MERGE
$e_1 \hookrightarrow_{\pi_1+\pi_2} e_2 \dashv\vdash e_1 \hookrightarrow_{\pi_1} e_2 * e_1 \hookrightarrow_{\pi_2} e_2$

Proc-SPLIT-MERGE
$\mathsf{Proc}(P \parallel Q) \dashv\vdash \mathsf{Proc}(P) * \mathsf{Proc}(Q)$

Proc-$\approx$
$\mathsf{Proc}(P) * P \approx Q \vdash \mathsf{Proc}(Q)$

$\approx$-BISIM
$$\frac{P \cong Q}{\vdash P \approx Q}$$

$\approx$-REFL
$\vdash P \approx P$

$\approx$-SYMM
$P \approx Q \vdash Q \approx P$

$\approx$-TRANS
$P \approx Q * Q \approx R \vdash P \approx R$

$\approx$-COND-TRUE
$b \vdash b : P \approx P$

$\approx$-COND-FALSE
$b \vdash \neg b : P \approx \delta$

Fig. 6. An excerpt of the entailment rules of the program logic.

Proof Rules. Figure 6 shows an excerpt of the proof rules, which are given as sequents of the form $\vdash \mathcal{P}$ and $\mathcal{P} \vdash \mathcal{Q}$. All other proof rules are deferred to [1]. The notation $\mathcal{P} \dashv\vdash \mathcal{Q}$ is shorthand for $\mathcal{P} \vdash \mathcal{Q}$ and $\mathcal{Q} \vdash \mathcal{P}$. All proof rules are sound in the standard sense.

The $\hookrightarrow$-SPLIT-MERGE rule expresses that heap ownership predicates can be *split* (in the left-to-right direction) and *merged* (right-to-left) along π, allowing heap ownership to be distributed over different threads. Likewise, Proc-SPLIT-MERGE allows to split and merge process predicates along the parallel composition, to allow different threads to communicate as prescribed by the different parts of the process-algebraic model. Process terms inside Proc predicates may be replaced by bisimilar ones via Proc-$\approx$. This rule can be used to rewrite process terms to a canonical form used by some other proof rules. The $\approx$ connective enjoys properties similar to $\cong$: it is an equivalence relation with respect to $*$, as shown by $\approx$-REFL, $\approx$-SYMM and $\approx$-TRANS, and is a congruence for all process-algebraic connectives. Finally, $\approx$ allows to use contextual information to resolve guards, via $\approx$-COND-TRUE and $\approx$-COND-FALSE.

Semantics of Assertions. The semantics of assertions is given as a modelling relation $\iota, \sigma, P \models \mathcal{P}$, where the models are abstractions of program states (these can also be seen as partial program states). These state abstractions consist of three components, the first being a *permission heap*. Permission heaps $\iota \in \mathit{PermHeap} \triangleq \mathit{Loc} \rightharpoonup_{\mathsf{fin}} (0,1]_{\mathbb{Q}} \times \mathit{Val}$ extend normal heaps by associating a fractional permission to each occupied heap cell. The second component is an ordinary store σ, and the last component is a *closed* process P that determines the state of the process-algebraic model that may be described by $\mathcal{P}$.

The semantics of assertions relies on the notions of disjointness and disjoint union of permission heaps. Two permission heaps ι_1, ι_2 are said to be *disjoint*, written $\iota_1 \perp \iota_2$, if they agree on their contents and the pairwise addition of the fractional permissions they store are again valid fractional permissions. Furthermore, the *disjoint union* of ι_1 and ι_2, which is written $\iota_1 \uplus \iota_2$, is defined to be the pairwise union of all their disjoint heap cells.

Definition 6 (Disjointness of permission heaps)

$$\iota_1 \perp \iota_2 \triangleq \forall \ell \in \mathit{dom}(\iota_1) \cap \mathit{dom}(\iota_2) \,.\, \iota_1(\ell) \perp_{\mathsf{cell}} \iota_2(\ell), \text{ where}$$
$$(\pi_1, v_1) \perp_{\mathsf{cell}} (\pi_2, v_2) \triangleq v_1 = v_2 \wedge \pi_1 + \pi_2 \in (0,1]_{\mathbb{Q}}$$

Definition 7 (Disjoint union of permission heaps)

$$\iota_1 \uplus \iota_2 \triangleq \lambda \ell \,.\, \begin{cases} \iota_1(\ell) & \text{if } \ell \in \mathit{dom}(\iota_1) \setminus \mathit{dom}(\iota_2) \\ \iota_2(\ell) & \text{if } \ell \in \mathit{dom}(\iota_2) \setminus \mathit{dom}(\iota_1) \\ (\pi_1 + \pi_2, v) & \text{if } \iota_1(\ell) = (\pi_1, v) \wedge \iota_2(\ell) = (\pi_2, v) \wedge \pi_1 + \pi_2 \in (0,1]_{\mathbb{Q}} \end{cases}$$

As one would expect, $\uplus$ is associative and commutative, and $\perp$ is symmetric. Intuitively, if $\iota_1 \perp \iota_2$, then $\iota_1 \uplus \iota_2$ does not lose information w.r.t. ι_1 and ι_2.

The semantics of assertions also relies on a closure operation for closing process terms. The *σ-closure* of any process P is defined as $P[\sigma] \triangleq P[x/\sigma(x)]_{\forall x \in \mathsf{fv}(P)}$.

Definition 8 (Semantics of assertions). *The interpretation of assertions $\iota, \sigma, P \models \mathcal{P}$ is defined by structural induction on $\mathcal{P}$, such that*

$$\begin{array}{lll}
\iota, \sigma, P \models b & \textit{iff} & [\![b]\!]\sigma \\
\iota, \sigma, P \models \forall x.\mathcal{P} & \textit{iff} & \forall v \,.\, \iota, \sigma[x \mapsto v], P \models \mathcal{P} \\
\iota, \sigma, P \models \exists x.\mathcal{P} & \textit{iff} & \exists v \,.\, \iota, \sigma[x \mapsto v], P \models \mathcal{P} \\
\iota, \sigma, P \models \mathcal{P} \vee \mathcal{Q} & \textit{iff} & \iota, \sigma, P \models \mathcal{P} \vee \iota, \sigma, P \models \mathcal{Q} \\
\iota, \sigma, P \models \mathcal{P} * \mathcal{Q} & \textit{iff} & \exists \iota_1, P_1, \iota_2, P_2 \,.\, \iota_1 \perp \iota_2 \wedge \iota = \iota_1 \uplus \iota_2 \wedge P \cong P_1 \parallel P_2 \wedge \\
& & \qquad \iota_1, \sigma, P_1 \models \mathcal{P} \wedge \iota_2, \sigma, P_2 \models \mathcal{Q} \\
\iota, \sigma, P \models \mathcal{P} \mathrel{-\!\!*} \mathcal{Q} & \textit{iff} & \forall \iota', P' \,.\, (\iota \perp \iota' \wedge \iota', \sigma, P' \models \mathcal{P}) \Rightarrow \iota \uplus \iota', \sigma, P \parallel P' \models \mathcal{Q} \\
\iota, \sigma, P \models e_1 \hookrightarrow_{\pi} e_2 & \textit{iff} & \exists \pi' \,.\, \iota([\![e_1]\!]\sigma) = (\pi', [\![e_2]\!]\sigma) \wedge \pi \leq \pi' \\
\iota, \sigma, P \models \mathsf{Proc}(Q) & \textit{iff} & \exists Q' \,.\, P \cong Q[\sigma] \parallel Q' \\
\iota, \sigma, P \models Q_1 \approx Q_2 & \textit{iff} & Q_1[\sigma] \cong Q_2[\sigma]
\end{array}$$

All assertions are interpreted intuitionistically in the standard sense [35], except for the last two cases, which cover the process-algebraic extensions. Both cases rely on σ-closures to resolve any free variables that may have been introduced by some other proof rules (e.g., the Hoare rule for **recv** may do this).

Process ownership assertions $\mathsf{Proc}(Q)$ are satisfied if there exists a (necessarily closed) process Q', which is the "framed" process that is maintained by the environmental threads, such that P is bisimilar to $Q[\sigma] \parallel Q'$. The intuition here is that P must have at least the behaviour that is described by Q. Finally, $Q_1 \approx Q_2$ is satisfied if Q_1 and Q_2 are bisimilar with respect to the current state.

4.2 Program Judgments

Judgments of programs are of the usual form $\mathcal{I} \vdash \{\mathcal{P}\}\, C\, \{\mathcal{Q}\}$ and indicate partial correctness of the program C, where $\mathcal{I} \in \mathit{Assn}$ is known as the *resource invariant* [6]. Their intuitive meaning is that, starting from an initial state satisfying

HT-SEND

$$\mathcal{I} \vdash \{\mathsf{Proc}(\mathsf{send}(e_1, e_2) \cdot P)\}\, \mathbf{send}\ (e_1, e_2)\, \{\mathsf{Proc}(P)\}$$

HT-RECV

$$\frac{x \notin \mathsf{fv}(\mathcal{I}) \cup \mathsf{fv}(P) \qquad y \notin \mathsf{fv}(e)}{\mathcal{I} \vdash \{\mathsf{Proc}(\Sigma_y\, \mathsf{recv}(y, e) \cdot P)\}\, x := \mathbf{recv}\ e\, \{\mathsf{Proc}(P[y/x])\}}$$

HT-RECV-WILDCARD

$$\frac{x_1, x_2 \notin \mathsf{fv}(\mathcal{I}) \cup \mathsf{fv}(P) \qquad \{x_1, y_1\} \cap \{x_2, y_2\} = \emptyset}{\mathcal{I} \vdash \{\mathsf{Proc}(\Sigma_{y_1, y_2}\, \mathsf{recv}(y_1, y_2) \cdot P)\}\, (x_1, x_2) := \mathbf{recv}\, \{\mathsf{Proc}(P[y_1/x_1][y_2/x_2])\}}$$

HT-QUERY

$$\mathcal{I} \vdash \{\mathsf{Proc}(?b \cdot P)\}\, \mathbf{query}\ b\, \{\mathsf{Proc}(P) * b\}$$

Fig. 7. An excerpt of the proof rules for program judgments.

$\mathcal{P} * \mathcal{I}$, the invariant $\mathcal{I}$ is maintained throughout execution of C, and any final state upon termination of C will satisfy $\mathcal{Q} * \mathcal{I}$.

Figure 7 gives an overview of the new proof rules that are specific to handling processes. All other rules are standard in CSL and are therefore deferred to [1].

The HT-SEND rule expresses that, as a precondition, any **send** command in the program must be prescribed by a matching send action in the process-algebraic model. Furthermore, it reduces the process term by ensuring a $\mathsf{Proc}(P)$ predicate, with P the leftover process after the performance of send. The HT-RECV rule is similar in the sense that any $x := \mathbf{recv}\ e$ instruction must be matched by a $\mathsf{recv}(y, e)$ action, but now y can be any message. Process-algebraic summation is used here to quantify over all possible messages to receive, and in the post-state of HT-RECV this message is bound to x—the received message. For wildcard receives both the message *and* the tag are quantified over using summation. Finally, HT-QUERY allows to "query" for properties that are verified during process-algebraic analysis.

4.3 Soundness

The soundness statement of the logic relates axiomatic judgments of programs (Sect. 4.2) to the operational meaning of programs (Sect. 2.1). This soundness argument guarantees freedom of data-races, memory safety, and compliance of pre- and postconditions, for any program for which a proof can be derived. The proof rules of Fig. 7 ensure that every proof derivation encodes that the program synchronises with its process-algebraic model. To formulate the soundness statement, this axiomatic notion of synchronisation thus needs to have a matching operational notion of synchronisation. This is defined in terms of an *instrumented semantics* that executes programs in lock-step with their process-algebraic models. The transition rules are shown in Fig. 8 and are expressed as a labelled binary reduction relation $\cdot \xrightarrow{l}\!\!\!\!\rightarrow \cdot$ between extended program configurations.

$$\frac{P \xrightarrow{\mathsf{send}(v_1,v_2)} P' \qquad (C,h,\sigma) \xrightarrow{\mathsf{send}(v_1,v_2)} (C',h',\sigma')}{(C,P,h,\sigma) \xrightarrow{\mathsf{send}(v_1,v_2)}\!\!\!\!\!\rightarrow (C',P',h',\sigma')} \qquad \frac{P \xrightarrow{\mathsf{recv}(v_1,v_2)} P' \qquad (C,h,\sigma) \xrightarrow{\mathsf{recv}(v_1,v_2)} (C',h',\sigma')}{(C,P,h,\sigma) \xrightarrow{\mathsf{recv}(v_1,v_2)}\!\!\!\!\!\rightarrow (C',P',h',\sigma')}$$

$$\frac{P \xrightarrow{\mathsf{comm}(v_1,v_2)} P' \qquad (C,h,\sigma) \xrightarrow{\mathsf{comm}(v_1,v_2)} (C',h',\sigma')}{(C,P,h,\sigma) \xrightarrow{\mathsf{comm}(v_1,v_2)}\!\!\!\!\!\rightarrow (C',P',h',\sigma')} \qquad \frac{P \xrightarrow{\mathsf{assn}} P' \qquad (C,h,\sigma) \xrightarrow{\mathsf{qry}} (C',h',\sigma')}{(C,P,h,\sigma) \xrightarrow{\mathsf{qry}}\!\!\!\!\!\rightarrow (C',P',h',\sigma')}$$

$$\frac{(C,h,\sigma) \xrightarrow{\mathsf{cmp}} (C',h',\sigma')}{(C,P,h,\sigma) \xrightarrow{\mathsf{cmp}}\!\!\!\!\!\rightarrow (C',P,h',\sigma')}$$

Fig. 8. The lock-step execution of programs and process-algebraic models.

The semantics of program judgments is defined in terms of an auxiliary predicate $\mathsf{safe}(C,\iota,\sigma,P,\mathcal{I},\mathcal{Q})$, stating that C: (i) executes safely for any number of execution steps with respect to the abstract program state (ι,σ,P); (ii) will preserve the invariant $\mathcal{I}$ throughout its execution; and (iii) will satisfy the postcondition $\mathcal{Q}$ upon termination. To elaborate on (i), a *safe execution of* C means that C is race free, memory-safe, and synchronises with P with respect to $\dot{\twoheadrightarrow}$.

To relate abstract program state to concrete state, a concretisation operation $\lfloor\cdot\rfloor : \mathit{PermHeap} \rightarrow \mathit{Heap}$ is used. The *concretisation* $\lfloor\iota\rfloor$ of a permission heap ι is defined to be the heap $\lambda\ell\,.\,\lfloor\iota(\ell)\rfloor_{\mathsf{cell}}$, with $\lfloor(\pi,v)\rfloor_{\mathsf{cell}} \triangleq v$ for any π.

Definition 9 (Execution safety). *The* safe *predicate is coinductively defined so that, if* $\mathsf{safe}(C,\iota,\sigma,P,\mathcal{I},\mathcal{Q})$ *holds, then*

- *If* $C = \mathbf{skip}$, *then* $\iota,\sigma,P \models \mathcal{Q}$.
- *C cannot perform a* data-race *or* memory violation *from the current state (the exact formal meaning of these notions are deferred to [1]).*
- *For any* $\iota_I,\iota_F,P_I,C',h',\sigma'$ *and* l, *if*
  i. $\iota \perp \iota_I$ *and* $\iota \uplus \iota_I \perp \iota_F$, *and*
  ii. $\neg\mathsf{locked}(C)$ *implies* $\iota_I,\sigma,P_I \models \mathcal{I}$, *and*
  iii. $(P \parallel P_I)\checkmark$ *and* $(C,\lfloor\iota \uplus \iota_I \uplus \iota_F\rfloor,\sigma) \xrightarrow{l} (C',h',\sigma')$,

  then there exists ι',ι'_I,P',P'_I *such that*
  1. $\iota' \perp \iota'_I$ *and* $\iota' \uplus \iota'_I \perp \iota_F$ *and* $h' = \lfloor\iota' \uplus \iota'_I \uplus \iota_F\rfloor$, *and*
  2. $\neg\mathsf{locked}(C')$ *implies* $\iota'_I,\sigma,P'_I \models \mathcal{I}$, *and*
  3. $(P' \parallel P'_I)\checkmark$ *and* $(C,P \parallel P_I,\lfloor\iota \uplus \iota_I \uplus \iota_F\rfloor,\sigma) \xrightarrow{l}\!\!\!\!\rightarrow (C',P' \parallel P'_I,h',\sigma')$, *and*
  4. $\mathsf{safe}(C',\iota',\sigma',P',\mathcal{I},\mathcal{Q})$.

The above definition is based on the similar well-known inductive notion of *configuration safety* of Vafeiadis [35]. Vafeiadis's definition however is coinductive rather than inductive, as this matches more naturally with the coinductive definitions of bisimilarity and process safety. Moreover, it encodes that the program refines the process with respect to send/receive behaviour: any execution step of the program (*iii*) must be matched by the model (*3*), and vice versa, by definition of $\xrightarrow{\cdot}\!\!\!\rightarrow$. Furthermore, the $\mathsf{locked}(C)$ predicate determines whether C is locked. Any program is defined to be *locked* if it executes an atomic (sub)program.

Definition 10 (Semantics of program judgments)

$$\mathcal{I} \models \{\mathcal{P}\}\, C\, \{\mathcal{Q}\} \triangleq \forall \iota, \sigma, P \,.\, P \checkmark \implies \iota, \sigma, P \models \mathcal{P} \implies \mathsf{safe}(C, \iota, \sigma, P, \mathcal{I}, \mathcal{Q}).$$

Theorem 1 (Soundness). $\mathcal{I} \vdash \{\mathcal{P}\}\, C\, \{\mathcal{Q}\} \implies \mathcal{I} \models \{\mathcal{P}\}\, C\, \{\mathcal{Q}\}$.

The soundness proof has been fully mechanised using Coq. The Coq development can be found online at [1].

5 Extensions

So far the presented approach only deals with synchronous message passing. However, the principles of the approach allow for easy extensions to also reason about asynchronous message passing, message loss and duplication, and collective operations like barriers and broadcasts, in MPI style [20].

The semantics of asynchronous message passing is that **send**s do not block while waiting for a matching **recv**, but instead push the message onto a message queue that is accessible by both threads. The specification language of mCRL2 is rich enough to model such queues, for example as a separate process $\mathsf{Queue}(\eta)$ with η some data-structure that stores messages in order (e.g., a mapping). Then, rather than letting send and recv communicate directly, they should instead communicate with Queue to push and pop messages into η. So to lift the verification approach to programs with an asynchronous communication semantics, one only has to make minor changes to the mCRL2 translation of processes.

Message loss can be integrated in a similar way, by introducing an extra process that "steals" pending messages. For example, one could analyse the process $P \parallel (\Sigma_{x,t}\, \mathsf{recv}(x, t))^{\omega}$ to reason about P's behaviour with the possibility of message loss. Message duplication can be modelled likewise as an extra process that sends multiple copies of any message it receives. Collective operations may require some extra bookkeeping, for example to administer which threads have already received a broadcasted message. However, all collective operations can be implemented using only sends and receives [19], which means that our approach also extends well to collective communication.

Finally, the current biggest limitation of our approach is that mCRL2 is primarily an explicit-state model checker, which limits its ability to reason symbolically about send/receive behaviour. Nonetheless, mCRL2 also comes with a symbolic back-end [24] that, at the time of writing, can handle specifications of limited complexity. We already have some preliminary results on reasoning symbolically about process-algebraic models, and are actively collaborating with the developers of mCRL2 to improve this.

6 Related Work

There are many modern program logics [9,23,29,33] that provide protocol-like specification mechanisms, to formally describe how shared state is allowed to evolve over time. Notably, Sergey et al. [31] employ this notion in a distributed setting, by using state-transition systems combined with invariants as abstractions for the communication behaviour of distributed programs. All these program logics are however purely theoretical, or can at best be semi-automatically applied via a shallow embedding in Coq. Our approach distinguishes itself by focusing on usability rather than expressivity and targets automated concurrency verifiers instead, like the combination of mCRL2 and Viper.

Francalanza et al. [11] propose a separation logic for message passing programs, where the assertion language has primitives for expressing the contents of communication channels. However, their approach circumvents the need to reason about different thread interleavings by targeting deterministic code, thereby sidestepping an important issue that we address: most problems in realistic distributed programs are the result of intricate thread interleavings. Lei et al. [18] propose a separation logic for modular verification of message passing programs. They achieve modularity via assume-guarantee reasoning, but thereby require users of the logic to manually specify thread interference, which is often non-trivial and non-intuitive. Villard et al. [37] propose a similar approach also based on separation logic, but here the main focus is on transferring heap ownership between threads, using message passing techniques.

Also related are session types [15,16], which are a well-studied type discipline for describing protocols of message passing interaction between processes over communication channels (i.e., sessions). As with our approach, these protocols are specifications of the communication behaviour of processes, and are usually expressed using process algebra, most often (variants of) the π-calculus. However, our approach has a slightly different aim: it uses process algebra not only to structure the communication behaviour, but also to reason about it, and to combine this reasoning with well-known deductive techniques for concurrency verification (viz. CSL) in a sound and practical manner.

This paper builds upon our earlier work [26,27], in which process-algebraic abstractions are used to describe how the heap evolves over time in shared-memory concurrent programs (befitting the notion of protocols given earlier). However, in this paper the abstractions have a different purpose: they instead capture message passing behaviour in a distributed setting. Our abstraction language is therefore different, for example by supporting summation and primitives for communication. Furthermore, in contrast to earlier work, this approach allows to use the result of process-algebraic analysis at intermediate points in the proof derivation of a program, via the novel **query** annotation.

7 Conclusion

This paper demonstrates how a combination of complementary verification techniques can be used to reason effectively about distributed applications, by naturally combining data-oriented reasoning via deductive verification, with temporal reasoning using algorithmic techniques. The approach is illustrated on a small, but intricate example. Our technique uses CSL to reason about data-centric properties of message passing programs, which are allowed to have shared state, and combines this with standard process-algebraic reasoning to verify properties of inter-thread communication. This combination of approaches is proven sound using Coq, and can easily be extended, e.g., to handle asynchronous- and collective communication, message loss, and message duplication.

As future work, we plan to extend process-algebraic reasoning to deal with a reasonable subset of MPI [20], with the goal to develop a comprehensive verification framework that targets real-world programming languages. Moreover, we are actively collaborating with the mCRL2 developers to improve support for symbolic reasoning. We will also apply our approach on larger case studies.

Acknowledgements. This work is partially supported by the NWO VICI 639.023.710 Mercedes project and by the NWO TOP 612.001.403 VerDi project.

References

1. Supplementary material for the paper. https://github.com/utwente-fmt/iFM19-MessagePassingAbstr
2. Ahrendt, W., Beckert, B., Bubel, R., Hähnle, R., Schmitt, P., Ulbrich, M.: Deductive Software Verification - The KeY Book. Springer, Heidelberg (2016). https://doi.org/10.1007/978-3-319-49812-6
3. Ahrendt, W., Chimento, J., Pace, G., Schneider, G.: Verifying data- and control-oriented properties combining static and runtime verification: theory and tools. FMSD **51**(1), 200–265 (2017). https://doi.org/10.1007/s10703-017-0274-y
4. Baeten, J.: Process Algebra with Explicit Termination. Eindhoven University of Technology, Department of Mathematics and Computing Science (2000)
5. Boyland, J.: Checking interference with fractional permissions. In: Cousot, R. (ed.) SAS 2003. LNCS, vol. 2694, pp. 55–72. Springer, Heidelberg (2003). https://doi.org/10.1007/3-540-44898-5_4
6. Brookes, S.: A semantics for concurrent separation logic. Theoret. Comput. Sci. **375**(1–3), 227–270 (2007). https://doi.org/10.1016/j.tcs.2006.12.034
7. Brookes, S., O'Hearn, P.: Concurrent separation logic. ACM SIGLOG News **3**(3), 47–65 (2016). https://doi.org/10.1145/2984450.2984457
8. Bunte, O., et al.: The mCRL2 toolset for analysing concurrent systems. In: Vojnar, T., Zhang, L. (eds.) TACAS 2019. LNCS, vol. 11428, pp. 21–39. Springer, Cham (2019). https://doi.org/10.1007/978-3-030-17465-1_2
9. Dinsdale-Young, T., Dodds, M., Gardner, P., Parkinson, M.J., Vafeiadis, V.: Concurrent abstract predicates. In: D'Hondt, T. (ed.) ECOOP 2010. LNCS, vol. 6183, pp. 504–528. Springer, Heidelberg (2010). https://doi.org/10.1007/978-3-642-14107-2_24
10. Fokkink, W., Zantema, H.: Basic process algebra with iteration: completeness of its equational axioms. Comput. J. **37**(4), 259–267 (1994). https://doi.org/10.1093/comjnl/37.4.259
11. Francalanza, A., Rathke, J., Sassone, V.: Permission-based separation logic for message-passing concurrency. Log. Methods Comput. Sci. **7**, 1–47 (2011). https://doi.org/10.2168/lmcs-7(3:7)2011

12. de Gouw, S., Rot, J., de Boer, F.S., Bubel, R., Hähnle, R.: OpenJDK's Java.utils.Collection.sort() is broken: the good, the bad and the worst case. In: Kroening, D., Păsăreanu, C.S. (eds.) CAV 2015. LNCS, vol. 9206, pp. 273–289. Springer, Cham (2015). https://doi.org/10.1007/978-3-319-21690-4_16
13. Groote, J.F., Mousavi, M.R.: Modeling and Analysis of Communicating Systems. MIT Press, Cambridge (2014)
14. Grumberg, O., Veith, H. (eds.): 25 Years of Model Checking: History, Achievements, Perspectives. Springer, Heidelberg (2008). https://doi.org/10.1007/978-3-540-69850-0
15. Honda, K., et al.: Structuring communication with session types. In: Agha, G., et al. (eds.) Concurrent Objects and Beyond. LNCS, vol. 8665, pp. 105–127. Springer, Heidelberg (2014). https://doi.org/10.1007/978-3-662-44471-9_5
16. Honda, K., Vasconcelos, V.T., Kubo, M.: Language primitives and type discipline for structured communication-based programming. In: Hankin, C. (ed.) ESOP 1998. LNCS, vol. 1381, pp. 122–138. Springer, Heidelberg (1998). https://doi.org/10.1007/BFb0053567
17. Hur, C., Dreyer, D., Vafeiadis, V.: Separation logic in the presence of garbage collection. In: LICS, pp. 247–256 (2011). https://doi.org/10.1109/LICS.2011.46
18. Lei, J., Qiu, Z.: Modular reasoning for message-passing programs. In: Ciobanu, G., Méry, D. (eds.) ICTAC 2014. LNCS, vol. 8687, pp. 277–294. Springer, Cham (2014). https://doi.org/10.1007/978-3-319-10882-7_17
19. Luo, Z., Zheng, M., Siegel, S.: Verification of MPI programs using CIVL. In: EuroMPI. ACM (2017). https://doi.org/10.1145/3127024.3127032
20. MPI: A Message-Passing Interface standard. http://www.mpi-forum.org/docs. Accessed Apr 2019
21. Milner, R.: Communication and Concurrency. Prentice-Hall Inc., Upper Saddle River (1989)
22. Müller, P., Schwerhoff, M., Summers, A.J.: Viper: a verification infrastructure for permission-based reasoning. In: Jobstmann, B., Leino, K.R.M. (eds.) VMCAI 2016. LNCS, vol. 9583, pp. 41–62. Springer, Heidelberg (2016). https://doi.org/10.1007/978-3-662-49122-5_2
23. Nanevski, A., Ley-Wild, R., Sergey, I., Delbianco, G.A.: Communicating state transition systems for fine-grained concurrent resources. In: Shao, Z. (ed.) ESOP 2014. LNCS, vol. 8410, pp. 290–310. Springer, Heidelberg (2014). https://doi.org/10.1007/978-3-642-54833-8_16
24. Neele, T., Willemse, T.A.C., Groote, J.F.: Solving parameterised Boolean equation systems with infinite data through quotienting. In: Bae, K., Ölveczky, P.C. (eds.) FACS 2018. LNCS, vol. 11222, pp. 216–236. Springer, Cham (2018). https://doi.org/10.1007/978-3-030-02146-7_11
25. O'Hearn, P.: Resources, concurrency and local reasoning. Theoret. Comput. Sci. **375**(1–3), 271–307 (2007). https://doi.org/10.1007/978-3-540-28644-8_4
26. Oortwijn, W., Blom, S., Gurov, D., Huisman, M., Zaharieva-Stojanovski, M.: An abstraction technique for describing concurrent program behaviour. In: Paskevich, A., Wies, T. (eds.) VSTTE 2017. LNCS, vol. 10712, pp. 191–209. Springer, Cham (2017). https://doi.org/10.1007/978-3-319-72308-2_12
27. Oortwijn, W., Blom, S., Huisman, M.: Future-based static analysis of message passing programs. In: PLACES, pp. 65–72 (2016). https://doi.org/10.4204/EPTCS.211.7
28. Peled, D., Gries, D., Schneider, F. (eds.): Software Reliability Methods. Springer, New York (2001). https://doi.org/10.1007/978-1-4757-3540-6

29. da Rocha Pinto, P., Dinsdale-Young, T., Gardner, P.: TaDA: a logic for time and data abstraction. In: Jones, R. (ed.) ECOOP 2014. LNCS, vol. 8586, pp. 207–231. Springer, Heidelberg (2014). https://doi.org/10.1007/978-3-662-44202-9_9
30. de Roever, W., et al.: Concurrency Verification: Introduction to Compositional and Noncompositional Methods. Cambridge University Press, Cambridge (2001)
31. Sergey, I., Wilcox, J., Tatlock, Z.: Programming and proving with distributed protocols. In: POPL, vol. 2 (2017). https://doi.org/10.1145/3158116
32. Shankar, N.: Combining model checking and deduction. Handbook of Model Checking, pp. 651–684. Springer, Cham (2018). https://doi.org/10.1007/978-3-319-10575-8_20
33. Svendsen, K., Birkedal, L., Parkinson, M.: Modular reasoning about separation of concurrent data structures. In: Felleisen, M., Gardner, P. (eds.) ESOP 2013. LNCS, vol. 7792, pp. 169–188. Springer, Heidelberg (2013). https://doi.org/10.1007/978-3-642-37036-6_11
34. Uribe, T.E.: Combinations of model checking and theorem proving. In: Kirchner, H., Ringeissen, C. (eds.) FroCoS 2000. LNCS (LNAI), vol. 1794, pp. 151–170. Springer, Heidelberg (2000). https://doi.org/10.1007/10720084_11
35. Vafeiadis, V.: Concurrent separation logic and operational semantics. MFPS, ENTCS **276**, 335–351 (2011). https://doi.org/10.1016/j.entcs.2011.09.029
36. Vafeiadis, V., Parkinson, M.: A marriage of rely/guarantee and separation logic. In: Caires, L., Vasconcelos, V.T. (eds.) CONCUR 2007. LNCS, vol. 4703, pp. 256–271. Springer, Heidelberg (2007). https://doi.org/10.1007/978-3-540-74407-8_18
37. Villard, J., Lozes, É., Calcagno, C.: Proving copyless message passing. In: Hu, Z. (ed.) APLAS 2009. LNCS, vol. 5904, pp. 194–209. Springer, Heidelberg (2009). https://doi.org/10.1007/978-3-642-10672-9_15
38. Wolper, P., Lovinfosse, V.: Verifying properties of large sets of processes with network invariants. In: Sifakis, J. (ed.) CAV 1989. LNCS, vol. 407, pp. 68–80. Springer, Heidelberg (1990). https://doi.org/10.1007/3-540-52148-8_6

Formal Verification of an Industrial Safety-Critical Traffic Tunnel Control System

Wytse Oortwijn(✉) and Marieke Huisman(✉)

University of Twente, Enschede, The Netherlands
{w.h.m.oortwijn,m.huisman}@utwente.nl

Abstract. Over the last decades, significant progress has been made on formal techniques for software verification. However, despite this progress, these techniques are not yet structurally applied in industry. To reduce the well-known industry–academia gap, industrial case studies are much-needed, to demonstrate that formal methods are now mature enough to help increase the reliability of industrial software. Moreover, case studies also help researchers to get better insight into industrial needs.

This paper contributes such a case study, concerning the formal verification of an industrial, safety-critical traffic tunnel control system that is currently employed in Dutch traffic. We made a formal, process-algebraic model of the informal design of the tunnel system, and analysed it using mCRL2. Additionally, we deductively verified that the implementation adheres to its intended behaviour, by proving that the code refines our mCRL2 model, using VerCors. By doing so, we detected undesired behaviour: an internal deadlock due to an intricate, unlucky combination of timing and events. Even though the developers were already aware of this, and deliberately provided us with an older version of their code, we demonstrate that formal methods can indeed help to detect undesired behaviours within reasonable time, that would otherwise be hard to find.

1 Introduction

Despite tremendous progress over the last decades on both the theory and practice of formal techniques for software verification [13], these techniques are not yet structurally applied in industrial practice, not even in the case of safety-critical software. Even though formal methods have shown to be able to increase software reliability [6,8,10], their application is often time consuming and may additionally require expert knowledge. Nevertheless, especially in the case of safety-critical software where reliability demands are high, industry can benefit *greatly* from the current state-of-the-art in formal verification research.

To make this apparent, industrial case studies are needed, that show industry and society that formal methods are now ready to help increase software dependability in practice. In turn, such industrial case studies also help researchers and

W. Ahrendt and S. L. Tapia Tarifa (Eds.): IFM 2019, LNCS 11918, pp. 418–436, 2019.
https://doi.org/10.1007/978-3-030-34968-4_23

developers of verification tools to get insight into the needs of industry. By doing so, researchers can improve and adapt their techniques to industrial needs, and thereby reduce the well-known gap between academia and industry.

This paper discusses such an industrial case study. It elaborates on our experiences and results of the formal verification of a safety-critical component of a *control system for a traffic tunnel* that is currently in use in the Netherlands. This particular software component is responsible for handling emergencies. When a fire breaks out inside the tunnel, or a traffic accident occurs, it should start an emergency procedure that evacuates the tunnel, starts the fans to blow away any smoke, turns on the emergency lights to guide people out, and so on. Naturally, the Dutch government imposes very high reliability demands on the traffic tunnel control software, and in particular on this emergency component, which are specified in a document of requirements that is over 500 pages in length [16].

The tunnel control software is developed by Technolution [22], a Dutch software and hardware development company located in Gouda. Technolution has hands-on experience in developing safety-critical, industrial software[1]. The development process of the traffic tunnel control system came together with a very elaborate process of quality assurance/control, to satisfy the high demands on reliability. Significant time and energy has been spent on software design and specification, code inspection, peer reviewing, unit and integration testing, etc.

In particular, during the design phase, the intended behaviour of the tunnel control software has been worked out in great detail: all system behaviours have been specified in pseudo code beforehand. Moreover, these pseudo code descriptions together have been structured further into a finite state machine, whose transitions describe how the different software behaviours change the internal state of the system. Nevertheless, both the pseudo code and this finite state machine have been specified *informally*, and do not have a precise, checkable formal semantics. Throughout the software development process, no formal methods or techniques have been used to assist in the major effort of quality control.

In this case study, we investigate how formal methods can help Technolution to find potential problems in their specification and (Java) implementation, with realistic effort, and preferably at an early stage of development. Technolution is above all interested in establishing whether: **(1)** the specification is *itself* consistent, by not being able to reach problematic states, e.g., deadlocks in the finite state machine; and **(2)** whether the Java code implementation is written correctly with respect to the pseudo code specification of the intended behaviour.

To address both these properties, we use a combination of existing verification techniques, to deal with their different nature. More specifically, for **(1)** we construct a *formal model* of the pseudo code specification and the underlying finite state machine. This model is specified as a process algebra with data, using the mCRL2 modelling language. After that, we use the mCRL2 *model checker* to verify whether the model adheres to certain requirements (e.g., deadlock freedom and strong connectivity), which we formalise in the modal μ-calculus.

[1] To illustrate, Technolution also delivers commercial software written in Rust.

For (**2**), we use VerCors [3] to *deductively* verify whether the control system is correctly implemented with respect to the pseudo code specification. This is done by proving that the implementation is a *refinement* of our mCRL2 model, using our earlier work on model-based deductive verification [17,18].

Our verification effort actually led to the detection of undesired behaviour: the system can potentially reach an internal state in which the calamity procedure is not invoked when an emergency has occurred, due to an intricate, unlucky combination of timing and events. Even though Technolution was well-aware of this—they deliberately provided us with an older version of their specification and implementation—we demonstrate that formal methods *can* indeed help to find such undesired behaviours at an early stage of development. We also demonstrate that formal techniques are able to provide results within reasonable time, that are otherwise hard to find manually. To illustrate, this undesired behaviour was found within approximately 7 working days.

1.1 Contributions and Outline

This paper contributes a successful industrial verification case study that concerns real-world, safety-critical code, and discusses our verification effort and results. The contributions of the case study itself are:

- A formal process-algebraic model of the informal pseudo code description of the tunnel control software, that is defined using mCRL2.
- An analysis of this mCRL2 model, via state-space exploration, and by checking desired μ-calculus properties on the model, like deadlock-freedom.
- A machine-checked proof that the (Java) implementation adheres to the pseudo code specification, by proving that the program refines our mCRL2 model. This refinement proof is done using the automated verifier VerCors.

Here we should note that the actual Java implementation of the tunnel control system is confidential, as well as the documents from the design phase, and therewith also the mCRL2 model and VerCors files that we produced. We therefore sometimes slightly simplify their presentation for the purpose of this paper, for example by using different variable/method/transition names. Nevertheless, the presentation of the case study does not deviate very much from the original, so this paper still gives an accurate overview of our approach and results.

Outline. The remainder of this paper is organised as follows. Section 2 gives preliminaries on the use of mCRL2 and VerCors. Then, Sect. 3 gives more detail on how the tunnel control system is informally specified by Technolution, by discussing the structure of the pseudo code and the finite state machine. Section 4 explains how we modelled this informal specification in mCRL2, after which Sect. 5 discusses its analysis. Section 6 explains how VerCors is used to deductively prove that the tunnel control system correctly implements our mCRL2 model. Section 7 relates our work to existing approaches and industrial case studies, before Sect. 8 concludes.

```
sort AccessType ≜ read | write;

act lock, unlock : AccessType;

proc
  S1 ≜ lock(read)·S2(1) + lock(write)·S3;
  S2(n : ℕ>0) ≜
    n < N → lock(read) · S2(n + 1) +
    1 < n → unlock(read) · S2(n − 1) +
    n = 1 → unlock(read) · S1;
  S3 ≜ unlock(write) · S1;

init S1;
```

(a) The mCRL2 model of a RW lock.

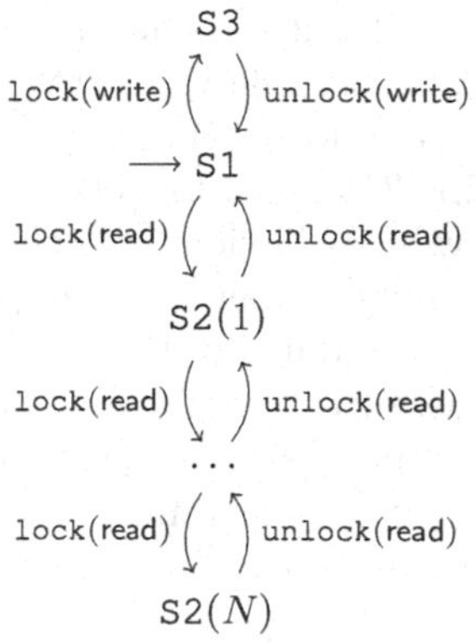

S3
lock(write) unlock(write)
→ S1
lock(read) unlock(read)
S2(1)
lock(read) unlock(read)
...
lock(read) unlock(read)
S2(N)

(b) The underlying state machine.

Fig. 1. An mCRL2 specification of a RW lock, and the underlying state space.

2 Preliminaries

This section gives preliminaries on the use of mCRL2 (Sect. 2.1) and VerCors (Sect. 2.2).

2.1 Modelling and Analysis with mCRL2

During the case study, we modelled the (informal) tunnel control software specification as a process algebra with support for data. This was done using the specification language of mCRL2 [11]. mCRL2 is a toolset that comes with an ACP-style process-algebraic modelling language, and contains more than sixty tools to support visualisation, simulation, minimisation, state-space generation and model checking of these mCRL2 processes [4]. The model checking back-end takes as input an mCRL2 model, together with a temporal property specified in the modal μ-calculus, and determines whether the model satisfies this property. By default this is done via exhaustive (symbolic) state space analysis.

We further illustrate how this modelling and analysis works by means of a small example, that is presented in Fig. 1. This example demonstrates how a simple read–write (RW) lock can be specified and verified with mCRL2. A RW lock can be acquired multiple times for read-only purposes, but can also provide exclusive write access for a single client: a multiple-reader/single writer lock.

Figure 1b shows the corresponding state machine. Initially the RW lock is unlocked (S1). From here the lock can be acquired once for the purpose of writing (S3), via a lock(write) action, and can subsequently be released again via unlock(write). Similarly, from S1, the lock can be acquired/released multiple times for reading purposes. The state S2(n) represents a read lock that has been acquired n times, where n is bounded to some constant threshold N.

Figure 1a presents the mCRL2 encoding of this locking protocol. The specification language of mCRL2 has various built-in data types (like positive numbers;

see line 7), but also allows defining custom abstract data types, as **sort**'s. Line 1 defines a sort that enumerates the different kinds of accesses that can be granted by the RW lock: read-only (read) access, and read/write (write) access.

Line 3 defines the *actions* for the locking protocol, which represent the basic, observable behaviours of the system. In this example, there are only two observable events, namely `locking` and `unlocking`. In mCRL2, actions can be parameterised by data. In this case, both actions are parameterised by *AccessType*.

These two actions can be composed into *processes* (lines 5–11). This example defines three processes, corresponding to the three locking states: `S1` (unlocked), `S2` (locked for reading purposes), and `S3` (locked for read/write purposes).

Processes are of the following form, where e is an expression:

$$P, Q ::= \varepsilon \mid \delta \mid a(\overline{e}) \mid \tau \mid P \cdot Q \mid P + Q \mid b \rightarrow P \mid X(\overline{e}) \qquad \text{(processes)}$$

Of course, the mCRL2 modelling language is actually much richer than the above language [11], for example by supporting parallel compositions. Yet this is the fraction of the mCRL2 language that we will use throughout the paper.

Clarifying the constructs: ε is the *empty* process, without behaviour, whereas δ is the *deadlocked* process, which neither progresses nor terminates. The process $a(\overline{e})$ is an *action invocation*, with $\overline{e}$ a sequence of arguments, while τ is a special, reserved action that models internal, *un*observable system events. $P \cdot Q$ is the sequential composition of P and Q, whereas $P + Q$ is their non-deterministic choice. The process $b \rightarrow P$ is the *conditional* process, that behaves as P if b is a Boolean expression that evaluates to *true*, and behaves as δ if b evaluates to *false*. Finally, $X(\overline{e})$ is the invocation of a process named X, with input arguments $\overline{e}$.

Moving back to the example, the `S1` process can either perform a `lock`(read) action, followed by the process invocation `S2(1)`, or can do a `lock`(write), after which `S3` is invoked (see line 6). Here the $\cdot$ connective has the highest precedence, followed by $\rightarrow$, and then $+$. Process `S3` (line 11) is only able to release the write lock and therewith to continue as `S1`. Finally, `S2`(n) allows to (re)acquire/release read locks, depending on n being small/large enough, respectively, on lines 8–10.

For the actual case study, we modelled the tunnel control system in a similar way: by studying the state machine specification, and encoding it into mCRL2.

Modal μ-calculus. After having constructed a model, mCRL2 allows to analyse it, by checking whether it satisfies a given temporal specification. These specifications are written in the *modal μ-calculus*, a powerful formalism that allows to specify properties about sequences of actions, i.e., traces of the input model.

Properties in the modal μ-calculus are defined by the following language.

$$\begin{aligned} \alpha, \beta &::= \mathit{true} \mid a(\overline{e}) \mid \neg\alpha \mid \alpha \cdot \beta \mid \alpha + \beta \mid \alpha^* && \text{(action formulae)} \\ \phi, \psi &::= b \mid \neg\phi \mid \phi \wedge \psi \mid \langle\alpha\rangle\phi \mid [\alpha]\phi \mid \mu x.\phi \mid \nu x.\phi && \text{(state formulae)} \end{aligned}$$

The actual specification language of mCRL2 is again much richer; we refer to [11] for a complete overview and a more detailed description.

Properties in the modal μ-calculus are defined in terms of *action* and *state* formulae. Action formulae α describe sequences of actions $a(\overline{e})$, where *true* stands for any action. Such descriptions are negatable: $\neg\alpha$ expresses any sequence except for α. Action formulae can also sequentially be composed, $\alpha_1 \cdot \alpha_2$, or alternatively be composed, $\alpha_1 + \alpha_2$, and α^* is the *repetition* (Kleene iteration) of α.

State formulae ϕ, ψ express properties that should hold in the current state. These properties may for example be built from pure Boolean expressions b, but may also contain *modalities*, $\langle\alpha\rangle\phi$ and $[\alpha]\phi$, to express that ϕ must hold after a certain sequence of actions α has been observed. More specifically, $\langle\alpha\rangle\phi$ is the *may modality*, which expresses that, from the current state, the model is able to perform a sequence of actions complying with α, after which ϕ directly holds. Its dual is the *must modality*, $[\alpha]\phi$, which expresses that, from the current state, after the performance of any action sequence α, the property ϕ directly holds.

State formulae may also contain *fixpoint operators*, μ and ν, to specify infinite system behaviour. Here $\mu x.\phi$ is the *least fixpoint* of ϕ, i.e., the smallest reachable set of states satisfying ϕ, where x is the fixpoint variable. These are used to express liveness properties. Its dual is the *greatest fixpoint*, $\nu x.\phi$, used to express safety properties, representing the largest reachable set of states satisfying ϕ.

Below we give three example properties that hold for our RW lock model:

$$[\texttt{unlock}(\mathsf{read})]\mathit{false} \tag{1}$$

$$\nu x.(\,\langle \mathit{true}^* \cdot \texttt{lock}(\mathsf{write})\rangle \mathit{true} \wedge [\mathit{true}^*]x\,) \tag{2}$$

$$\nu x.(\,[(\neg\texttt{unlock}(\mathsf{write}))^* \cdot \texttt{lock}(\mathsf{read})]\mathit{false} \wedge [\mathit{true}^* \cdot \texttt{lock}(\mathsf{write})]x\,) \tag{3}$$

Property (1) states that read locks cannot be released from the initial state, as initially no locks have been acquired. Furthermore, (2) expresses that it always remains possible to acquire the write lock. Finally, (3) states that, when holding the write lock, no read lock can be obtained until the write lock is released.

2.2 Deductive Verification with VerCors

Besides modelling the tunnel software specification in mCRL2, we also used deductive techniques to automatically prove that the code implementation adheres to this specification. This is done using VerCors [3], an automated deductive verifier that targets programs written in high-level languages, like Java and (subsets of) C, that are annotated with JML-like (pre/postcondition) specifications.

VerCors actually specialises in concurrency verification, and is, among other things, able to reason about: fork/join concurrency in Java, GPU kernels in the context of OpenCL, and OpenMP directives for loop parallelisation. Nevertheless, we use VerCors in a purely sequential setting for the purpose of this case study, as the tunnel software does not use any concurrency.

In particular, we use our earlier work on model-based verification [17,18], to mechanically establish that the code implementation of the tunnel control system correctly implements (*refines*) our mCRL2 specification. This resolves a well-known problem in model checking, known as the *abstraction problem*: is the model a *sound* behavioural abstraction of the modelled system?

```
1 shared int r_count;
2
3 modifies r_count;
4 guard 0 < r_count;
5 effect r_count = \old(r_count)−1;
6 action unlock(read);
7
```

(a) The action contract for unlock(read).

```
8 requires Proc(unlock(read) · P + Q);
9 ensures Proc(P);
10 void releaseRead() {
11   action unlock(read) {
12     r_count := r_count − 1;
13   }
14 }
```

(b) Simple read lock release method.

Fig. 2. A simple example of our model-based verification approach, showing the action contract of the unlock(read) action (a), and a code implementation (b).

This refinement approach considers process-algebraic models to be abstract descriptions of shared-memory behaviour. Any (say, Java) implementation of the RW lock would use shared memory to implement the locking functionality, for example by maintaining a shared integer field *r_count* to administer how many times a read lock has currently been acquired. These shared-memory behaviours are specified in terms of *action* and *process contracts*, which are essentially pre/-postcondition extensions to the mCRL2 language. Figure 2a shows a possible action contract for the unlock(read) action, that consists of: a **modifies** clause that determines which shared fields are modified; a **guard** clause that determines the condition under which the action is allowed to be performed; and an **effect** clause that logically describes the effect on shared memory of performing the action. In this case, performing unlock(read) has the effect of decreasing *r_count* by one in the implementation, given that it was positive beforehand.

These actions and their contracts can be related to program code by means of code annotations. Figure 2b shows the (simplified) annotations that would be required for a simple implementation of releasing read locks. The program and process are related via *process ownership predicates*, Proc(P), which express that the remaining program is allowed to behave as specified by (the action sequences of) P, with respect to shared memory behaviour. As a precondition, a process of the form unlock(read) $\cdot P + Q$ is required by releaseRead, for some P and Q. This implies that the method has the choice to behave as unlock(read), and the remaining program to execute according to P (as is ensured on line 9).

Furthermore, *action blocks* are used to relate process-algebraic actions to program code. Lines 11–13 show an action block specification that links the performance of unlock(read) on process level, to the decrement of *r_count* in program code. VerCors checks that all modifications to *r_count* are made within such action blocks, and also automatically verifies whether the decrement of *r_count* on line 12 is actually allowed according to the process-algebraic specification. These checks enable VerCors to prove that a process-algebraic model is a sound abstraction of the shared-memory behaviour of the modelled program.

For the actual case study, we enriched the actions of our mCRL2 model of the tunnel system with action contracts in a similar way, which we derived from the informal pseudo code. Moreover, we added annotations to the program code, and used VerCors to verify that the implementation adheres to the model.

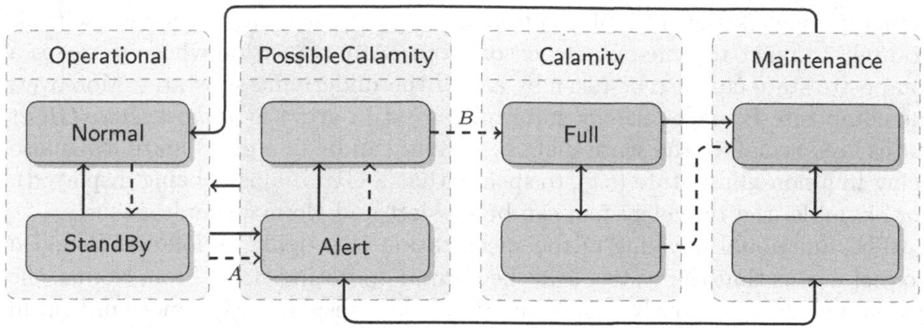

Fig. 3. A simplified visual representation of the FSM. The two transitions that are later written-out as pseudo code in Fig. 4 are labelled A and B.

3 Informal Tunnel Software Specification

Before detailing how mCRL2 and VerCors are applied on the actual case study, let us first discuss the informal specification of the traffic tunnel control system.

Technolution invested significantly in an extensive design phase, to ensure the quality of the control system and to cope with the high reliability demands. During this phase, the intended behaviour of the control software was written-out in pseudo code, together with domain experts. These pseudo code specifications were further structured into a finite state machine (FSM). The states of this FSM are the operational states of the tunnel system (e.g., operating normally, under repair, evacuating, etc.), while the transitions are the pseudo code descriptions of the system behaviour. The FSM thus illustrates how the different behaviours/events of the tunnel system should change its operational state.

Moreover, during the development phase, significant time and effort were invested in ensuring that the code was correctly implemented with respect to this specification. This was done primarily via unit testing and code reviewing.

This section gives more detail on how the tunnel control software was (informally) specified. Section 3.1 discusses the structure of the FSM, after which Sect. 3.2 elaborates on the pseudo code specification, i.e., the transitions of the FSM.

3.1 Structure of the FSM

Figure 3 illustrates the structure of the FSM specification of the tunnel control system. This illustration is simplified for confidentiality reasons: the actual FSM contains many more states and transitions. Nevertheless, the overall structure and the described behaviour are close to the original FSM specification.

The operational states are organised in a 2-layer hierarchy. For example, the composite state Operational contains two sub-states: Normal and StandBy. Transitions come in two flavours. Solid transitions (→) represent *manual interactions*, made by human operators through control panels. Dashed transitions (⇢) are *automatic events* that are taken autonomously by the control system itself, for example to react to time-outs or sensor input. Any transition whose source is a composite state can also be taken by any of the underlying substates. Moreover, the composite PossibleCalamity state (displayed in grey) is a *ghost state*. Ghost states are special, in the sense that the system can be in a ghost state while also being in a non-ghost state (e.g., to specify that a GUI dialog is being displayed). For example, the tunnel system can be in Alert and Normal simultaneously.

The functional meaning of the specification is roughly as follows. Being in Normal means that the system is in the normal operating state. From Normal the system may autonomously go in StandBy state, as result of, e.g., smoke or heat in the traffic tunnel that is detected via sensor reading. If the system finds enough reason to suspect a real calamity, it may autonomously decide to go from Operational to the Alert state. The Alert state can also manually be entered, when a human operator presses the emergency button on a control panel. The PossibleCalamity composite ghost state starts a timer upon entering. While in this state, if a human operator does not intervene in time by manually cancelling the alert status (thereby going back to the Operational state), the system will automatically launch the Calamity programme, for example to evacuate the traffic tunnel. Such calamities can be recovered from via Maintenance: manually repairing or resolving the calamity's cause. By doing so, the system can manually be brought back to the Normal operating state. However, it may also re-enter Alert in case new potential calamities are detected during maintenance.

3.2 Pseudo Code Specification

Figure 4 gives an idea of the structure of the pseudo code specification of the tunnel system. These pseudo code descriptions were provided by the Dutch Ministry of Infrastructure and Water Management, as part of a national standard on traffic tunnels [16]. The figure highlights two transitions of Fig. 3, labelled as A and B, that describe interesting, important key system behaviours. Transition A specifies how the control system should autonomously request a calamity status when it suspects the traffic tunnel to be in an emergency situation. This will cause the system to go into the Alert ghost state, and therewith start the timer. Transition B specifies what should happen when this timer expires.

Elaborating on the textual format, all autonomous/manual system behaviours are specified in pseudo code style. Any such system behaviour corresponds to a transition in the FSM (denoted by **`transition`**) and is given a unique identifier (**`name`**). The internal state of the system is determined by the values of a set of *pseudo-variables*, which are prefixed with a # in the figure. The **`effect`** clauses exactly describe how the transition changes the internal state. The **`condition`** clauses specify under which conditions these state changes are allowed.

Transition A is able to request the calamity procedure to be initiated, by setting `#request_calamity` to `true`, given that `#possible_calamity_detected` has been set to `true` by some other system behaviour, e.g., as result of sensor reading. Such a request will also configure a timer, named

```
transition: A (autonomous)
name: 'ProceedToAlertStatus'
condition:
  #possible_calamity_detected = true &&
  #request_calamity = false &&
  #state = Operational;
effect:
  #request_calamity := true;
  #calamity_timeout := now() + __calamity_timeout_frame;

transition: B (autonomous)
name: 'StartCalamityProgrammeAfterTimeout'
condition:
  #state != Calamity &&
  #request_calamity = true &&
  now() > #calamity_timeout;
effect:
  #request_calamity := false;
  #state := Calamity::Full;
  invoke CalamityProgramme();
```

Fig. 4. The format of the textual specification of the tunnel system.

`#calamity_timeout`, for cancelling the request. Transition *B* specifies what should happen when this timer expires: in that case the system should enter the operational state Calamity (if not already in there) and start the `CalamityProgramme()`.

The control software of every Dutch traffic tunnel is required to comply with these specifications. This is checked by an external code review committee.

4 Modelling the Tunnel Control System Using mCRL2

Even though the tunnel control software has been specified extensively, prior to our work there had been no formal, structural effort to establish whether the specification *itself* obeys the desired properties. For Technolution, the main properties of interest concern *reliability* and *recoverability*: does the system always go into the Calamity state in real emergency situations? And is it always possible to recover from calamities, and thereby go back to the Normal operational state?

To automatically check for such desired properties, we modelled the pseudo code specifications and the underlying FSM as a process in the mCRL2 language. Figure 5 shows the main structure of our mCRL2 model. This is again a simplified representation; the actual model consists of roughly 700 lines of code.

mCRL2 allows new data types to be defined using the **sort** keyword. We use data sorts to explicitly model the different operational states that the tunnel system might be in, as the structured sort *State*, defined on line 2. Also explicitly

```
1  sort
2    State ≜ struct Normal | StandBy | Alert | Full | ⋯;
3    Var ≜ struct possibleCalamityDetected | requestCalamity | ⋯;
4    Val ≜ struct true | false | unknown | ⋯;
5
6  act enter : State;
7
8  proc
9    %% Encoding of transition A (autonomous)
10   ProceedToAlertStatus(state : State, σ : Var → Val, phase : Nat) ≜
11     σ(possibleCalamityDetected) ∧ ¬σ(requestCalamity) ∧
12       isInOperational(state) →
13         enter(Alert) · System(state, σ[requestCalamity := true], phase);
14
15   %% Encoding of transition B (autonomous)
16   StartCalamityProgrammeAfterTimeout(state, σ, phase) ≜
17     ¬isInCalamity(state) ∧ σ(requestCalamity) →
18       enter(Full) · System(Full, σ[requestCalamity := false], phase);
19
20   %% Encoding of the top-level specification
21   System(state : State, σ : Var → Val, phase : Nat) ≜
22     %% First phase: handling GUI input
23     (phase = 1) →
24       (CancelPossibleCalamity(state, σ, phase) +
25       omitted + τ · System(state, σ, 2)) +
26     %% Second phase: handling internal/external controls and function calls
27     (phase = 2) → ( omitted + τ · System(state, σ, 3)) +
28     %% Third phase: processing autonomous system behaviour
29     (phase = 3) →
30       (ProceedToAlertStatus(state, σ, phase) +
31       StartCalamityProgrammeAfterTimeout(state, σ, phase) +
32       omitted + τ · System(state, σ, 4)) +
33     %% Fourth phase: processing sensor data and update all variables
34     (phase = 4) → (τ · System(state, updateVars(σ), 1));
35
36 init System(Maintenance, σ_init, 1);
```

Fig. 5. The main structure of the mCRL2 formalisation of the specification.

modelled are the various "pseudo-variables" that are used in the textual specification (defined on line 3), together with a domain of values for these variables (on line 4). These three data types are used to model the internal state of the tunnel control system.

Line 6 covers the definition of actions, which model the basic, observable units of computation. One of the main challenges was to determine which observable behaviours of the tunnel system to model explicitly. We experienced that modelling too many behaviours leads to state space explosions, while modelling too few hampers analysis. As the main properties of interest are properties of operational state reachability, the most important observable events to model are the transitions between the operational states. These are modelled as `enter(`s`)` actions, where $s \in State$ is the operational state that is being entered.

The traffic tunnel control system is modelled as the `System(`$state, \sigma, phase$`)` process (lines 21–34), whose arguments determine the internal state of the tunnel. In particular, *state* determines its operational state, whereas σ provides a valuation for all pseudo-variables. The third argument, *phase*, is maintained for technical reasons. This is because the overall system is specified and implemented as a (busy) working loop, that continuously cycles through four different phases, to (1) handle GUI input, (2) process internal requests, (3) autonomously make decisions, and (4) read from sensors and update all variables accordingly. These phases have been made explicit in our model, using *phase*. Every phase has the non-deterministic choice to advance to the next phase, as an internal τ action.

The earlier highlighted transitions A and B both describe autonomous behaviour, and thus are both handled in phase 3 (lines 30–31). Their behaviours are modelled on lines 9–18, and closely follow the pseudo code specification.

Finally, line 36 specifies the initial state of the control system. The system initialises in Maintenance state, and starts by handling phase 1 events. The mapping σ_{init} is a constant that holds the initial valuation of pseudo-variables.

5 Analysing the Tunnel Control System with mCRL2

Now that we have a formal model of the tunnel system specification in mCRL2, we can study its state space, and determine whether it satisfies desired properties, formulated in the modal μ-calculus, with relatively little effort. Technolution was primarily interested in verifying these properties: (i) Deadlock freedom and strong connectivity: are all operational states reachable at any point during execution? (ii) Reliability: does the system automatically go to Full after detecting an emergency, unless this is manually cancelled? (iii) Recoverability: can calamities always be recovered from, by getting the system back to Normal?

A major challenge during analysis was to keep the model's state space small enough to be able to analyse it in a reasonable time. In particular, we needed to improve our mCRL2 model various times, as earlier versions suffered from state space explosions resulting from the explicit modelling of time. Recall that the informal specification includes software behaviours that depend on time, for example the timers that are maintained by the PossibleCalamity ghost state. In earlier versions of our model, these timers were modelled explicitly, as discrete values: natural numbers that were bounded by some threshold. However, their analysis was only feasible with thresholds no larger than three time units, which is insufficient. We later solved this scalability issue by modelling time *implicitly*, by constructing the model in such a way that certain actions must happen before others. More specifically, instead of having certain actions depend on timers or timeouts to happen before others, we let them happen non-deterministically, but in such a way that the original order of action occurrences is preserved.

Our latest model has an underlying state space of roughly 4.200 states and 25.400 transitions, which takes about 4 min to generate[2]. This clearly shows that the tunnel system specification comprises far too many behaviours for software designers/developers to comprehend, without the help of automated tooling. In fact, mCRL2 helped us further, by allowing to minimise this state space modulo branching bisimilarity [12], leaving only 27 states and 98 transitions. This reduction gave us better insight into the system's behaviour.

Together with Technolution, we formulated several dozens of desired properties as μ-calculus formulae, and checked these on the reduced mCRL2 model. An example of such a formula is given below, expressing that the StandBy state can only ever be reached via the Normal state of operation.

$$\nu x.(\ [(\neg \texttt{enter(}\mathsf{Normal}\texttt{)})^* \cdot \texttt{enter(}\mathsf{StandBy}\texttt{)}]\mathit{false} \wedge \tag{4a}$$

$$[\mathit{true}^* \cdot \texttt{enter(}\mathsf{StandBy}\texttt{)}]x\ ) \tag{4b}$$

More precisely, this greatest fixed-point formula expresses that StandBy cannot be reached via any path of non-"enter(Normal)" actions (by 4a), and that this reachability property remains preserved each time StandBy is entered (4b).

In addition to checking these properties, we also inspected the state space of the minimised model and discussed its structure with Technolution. Ultimately, our verification exposed an intricate violation of the requirement of reliability. We found that the control system can reach a potentially dangerous situation, in which the Calamity state cannot automatically be entered after having detected a potential emergency (unless a human operator manually interferes), due to an intricate, unlucky combination of timing and events. The following reliability property exposes this behaviour, by stating that, while being in the Alert ghost state, it must always be possible to *directly* enter Full, unless the alert status is manually cancelled. This property does not hold for our mCRL2 model.

$$[\mathit{true}^* \cdot \texttt{enter(}\mathsf{Alert}\texttt{)}]\,\nu x.(\tag{5a}$$

$$[\neg(\texttt{cancel} + \texttt{enter(}\mathsf{Full}\texttt{)})^*]\langle\texttt{enter(}\mathsf{Full}\texttt{)}\rangle \mathit{true} \wedge \tag{5b}$$

$$[\mathit{true}^* \cdot \texttt{enter(}\mathsf{Alert}\texttt{)}]x\ ) \tag{5c}$$

Nevertheless, this is precisely the violating behaviour that Technolution hoped we would find. This is because they already found it, by chance, and deliberately provided us with an older version of their specification and implementation. Our case study therefore shows that formal techniques can indeed help to find such problematic behaviours in a more reliable and structural manner, and at an early stage of development, within reasonable time: we found it within 7 working days.

[2] On a Macbook with an Intel Core i5 CPU with 2.9 GHz, and 8Gb internal memory.

```
shared bool possibleCalamityDetected, requestCalamity;
shared State state;

modifies state;
effect state = s;
action enter(State s);

// The encoding of transition A, as a single action
accesses possibleCalamityDetected, state;
modifies requestCalamity;
guard possibleCalamityDetected ∧ ¬requestCalamity;
guard isInOperational(state);
effect requestCalamity;
action ProceedToAlertStatus;

accesses state;
modifies requestCalamity;
guard ¬isInCalamity(state) ∧ requestCalamity;
effect ¬requestCalamity;
action flipCalamityRequest;

// The encoding of transition B, as a sequential composition of two actions
process StartCalamityProgrammeAfterTimeout ≜
  flipCalamityRequest · enter(Full);
```

Fig. 6. The VerCors encoding of transitions A and B, as processes with contracts.

6 Specification Refinement Using VerCors

As a next step, we use VerCors to deductively verify that the code implementation adheres to the FSM and pseudo code specification. This is done by proving that the code correctly implements (refines) our mCRL2 model, using our earlier work on model-based verification. Such a proof also adds value to the model, as it establishes that the model is a sound abstraction of the program's behaviour.

As explained in Sect. 2.2, the process algebra language that VerCors uses is an extension of mCRL2, in which all process and action definitions are enriched with pre/postcondition-style contracts. These contracts are used to connect/link processes and actions to program code: they logically describe how the performance of an action corresponds to an update to shared memory, very much like the **`effect`** and **`condition`** clauses used in the pseudo code specification. With these contracts we can mechanically prove with VerCors that every execution of the program corresponds to an action trace (a run) in the mCRL2 model. These links between programs and models preserve safety properties (i.e., $\nu x.\phi$).

For this project, we manually encoded our mCRL2 model into the process algebra language of VerCors[3]. Figure 6 shows an excerpt of this encoding, in

[3] Both these languages can be translated into one another, and we are actively working on mechanising these translations.

which transitions A and B are again highlighted. The VerCors encoding consists of a large number of action declarations, corresponding to the FSM transitions, with contracts that closely follow the pseudo code specifications. Moreover, this version does not use a valuation σ for the pseudo variables, like in Sect. 4, but rather connects to the actual shared fields in the program code (e.g., lines 1–2). The variables *state* and *phase* have been translated likewise. Our VerCors encoding is intended, but not (yet) proven, to be equivalent to the mCRL2 version.

Line 6 defines the `enter(s)` action, whose performance has the effect of modifying the shared variable *state*, by assigning s to it. Lines 9–14 give the specification of transition A, as a single action, with a contract that closely follows the corresponding textual specification. Transition B is defined to be composed out of two actions: `flipCalamityRequest` for setting the *requestCalamity* flag to *false*, and `enter` for changing the operating state of the tunnel to Full.

Program Annotations. The next step is to deductively prove that the implementation adheres to the VerCors encoding of the specification, as explained in Sect. 2.2. The actual tunnel control system is implemented in Java. However, we converted this implementation to PVL—an object-oriented toy input language of VerCors—since our model-based verification approach is currently best supported by the PVL front-end (we are currently improving its support for Java).

Figure 7 shows and highlights the annotations of the PVL code implementations of transitions A (lines 2–16) and B (lines 19–35). The **yields bool** *branch* annotations on lines 2 and 19 indicate that *branch* is an extra *output* parameter that only exists for the sake of specification. In the figure, *branch* represents which branch has been executed by the program, and is used in the postconditions to ensure the matching, corresponding process-algebraic choice.

The contract of proceedToAlertStatus states that it will execute as prescribed by the process `ProceedToAlertStatus`$\cdot P+Q$ for some P and Q (line 3), and depending on the execution branch taken, is left with either P (line 4) or with Q (line 5) upon termination. The contract of startCalamityProgrammeAfterTimeout follows the same specification pattern, as well as most of the other methods. Since this model-based verification approach is compositional, we could use it to verify that the entire implementation complies with the process-algebraic specification.

Our deductive verification effort did not directly reveal any problems or violations in the implementation: all methods comply with their specified behaviour. This is expected, as the implementation has been unit tested and code reviewed very rigorously. Nevertheless, this compliance between specification and implementation is now confirmed, by means of a machine-checked proof.

However, this verification did help us, as tool developers, to better understand the needs from industry, and to identify weaknesses in our approach and tooling. To give an example, for future use, Technolution finds it important that our model-based verification technique is applicable on Java code, instead of PVL, and in a more automated manner. We are now actively working on this.

```
// The annotated code implementation of Transition A
yields bool branch;
requires Proc(ProceedToAlertStatus · P + Q);
ensures branch ⇒ Proc(P);
ensures ¬branch ⇒ Proc(Q);
void proceedToAlertStatus() {
 branch := false;
 if (possibleCalamityDetected ∧ ¬requestCalamity ∧
       state = Normal ∨ state = StandBy) {
   action ProceedToAlertStatus {
     requestCalamity := true;
   }
 }
 calamityTimeout := now() + __calamity_timeout_frame();
 branch := true;
}

// The annotated code implementation of Transition B
yields bool branch;
requires Proc(StartCalamityProgrammeAfterTimeout · P + Q);
ensures branch ⇒ Proc(P);
ensures ¬branch ⇒ Proc(Q);
void startCalamityProgrammeAfterTimeout() {
 branch := false;
 if ("state is in calamity" ∧ requestCalamity) {
   action flipCalamityRequest {
     requestCalamity := false;
   }
   action enter(Full) {
     state := Full;
     calamityProgramme();
   }
   branch := true;
 }
}
```

Fig. 7. Relating the tunnel specification to the implementation using VerCors.

7 Related Work

Various earlier successes have been reported in the use of model checking in industrial case studies. mCRL2, for example, maintains a gallery of industrial showcases online [15], which includes, among others, the modelling and analysis of firmware for a pacemaker [23], as well as control software used for experiments at the Large Hadron Collider at CERN [14]. Glabbeek et al. formalised the AODV wireless routing protocol in AWN (Algebra for Wireless Networks) [9]—a process algebra for modelling mobile ad-hoc networks—and used it to reason about safety-critical routing properties. Ruijters et al. [20] uses statistical model checking to study different maintenance strategies for railway joint, in collaboration with ProRail—a Dutch national railway infrastructure manager. Moreover, [1] reports on the experiences of the use of TLA+ at Intel.

In the context of deductive verification, in 2015, de Gouw et al. [10] successfully detected an intricate bug in the standard implementation of OpenJDK's TimSort algorithm, which is used daily by billions of users worldwide. Another successful application of deductive verification is the use of Infer at Facebook [5], to detect potential regressions during continuous integration testing. In [2], a formal verification of a cloud hypervisor is reported, using Frama-C. Also OpenJML has been used successfully for the verification of industrial code; [7] discusses several observations and experiences. Moreover, [19] discusses four industrial case studies that have been performed with VeriFast: two Java Card smart card applets, a Linux networking component, and a Linux device driver.

Regarding combinations of deductive verification and model checking, in [21], CBMC and Frama-C have been used to verify embedded software for satellite launching. But apart from this work, we are not aware of any other industrial applications of model checking combined with deductive verification.

8 Conclusion

During our case study, we found that, even though the specification of the tunnel control system is informal, it *is* well-structured, and therefore has the potential to be formalised within reasonable time. In roughly 7 working days, we constructed a formal model of the informal specification, analysed it using mCRL2, and used VerCors to deductively prove that the code implementation adheres to it. This resulted in the detection of undesired behaviour, preventing the control system from automatically starting the calamity procedure after an emergency has been detected. Even though Technolution was already aware of this behaviour, they found it coincidentally. We demonstrate that formal methods can indeed help to find such undesired behaviours more structurally, and within realistic time.

As a follow-up, we will continue to collaborate with Technolution, by being involved in an upcoming project in late 2019, concerning safety-critical software. In this project, we will attempt to apply formal methods *during* the software design and development process, rather than after the deployment phase.

This case study also helped us to learn about the needs from industry, and the shortcomings of our tooling, which we will work on before starting the follow-up project. More specifically, we will improve VerCors's support for Java, and work on automated translations between mCRL2 and the process algebra language of VerCors. We will also investigate if the pseudo code specification language can be formalised into a DSL, that is automatically translatable to mCRL2.

Acknowledgements. This work is partially supported by the NWO VICI 639.023.710 Mercedes project and by the NWO TOP 612.001.403 VerDi project.

References

1. Beers, R.: Pre-RTL formal verification: an intel experience. In: DAC, pp. 806–811 (2008). https://doi.org/10.1145/1391469.1391675
2. Blanchard, A., Kosmatov, N., Lemerre, M., Loulergue, F.: A case study on formal verification of the anaxagoros hypervisor paging system with Frama-C. In: Núñez, M., Güdemann, M. (eds.) FMICS 2015. LNCS, vol. 9128, pp. 15–30. Springer, Cham (2015). https://doi.org/10.1007/978-3-319-19458-5_2
3. Blom, S., Darabi, S., Huisman, M., Oortwijn, W.: The VerCors tool set: verification of parallel and concurrent software. In: Polikarpova, N., Schneider, S. (eds.) IFM 2017. LNCS, vol. 10510, pp. 102–110. Springer, Cham (2017). https://doi.org/10.1007/978-3-319-66845-1_7
4. Bunte, O., et al.: The mCRL2 toolset for analysing concurrent systems. In: Vojnar, T., Zhang, L. (eds.) TACAS 2019. LNCS, vol. 11428, pp. 21–39. Springer, Cham (2019). https://doi.org/10.1007/978-3-030-17465-1_2
5. Calcagno, C., et al.: Moving fast with software verification. In: Havelund, K., Holzmann, G., Joshi, R. (eds.) NFM 2015. LNCS, vol. 9058, pp. 3–11. Springer, Cham (2015). https://doi.org/10.1007/978-3-319-17524-9_1
6. Clarke, E.M.: The birth of model checking. In: Grumberg, O., Veith, H. (eds.) 25 Years of Model Checking. LNCS, vol. 5000, pp. 1–26. Springer, Heidelberg (2008). https://doi.org/10.1007/978-3-540-69850-0_1
7. Cok, D.R.: Java automated deductive verification in practice: lessons from industrial proof-based projects. In: Margaria, T., Steffen, B. (eds.) ISoLA 2018. LNCS, vol. 11247, pp. 176–193. Springer, Cham (2018). https://doi.org/10.1007/978-3-030-03427-6_16
8. Filliâtre, J.: Deductive software verification. STTT **13**(5), 397–403 (2011). https://doi.org/10.1007/s10009-011-0211-0
9. van Glabbeek, R., Höfner, P., Portmann, M., Tan, W.: Modelling and verifying the AODV routing protocol. Distrib. Comput. **29**(4), 279–315 (2016). https://doi.org/10.1007/s00446-015-0262-7
10. de Gouw, S., Rot, J., de Boer, F.S., Bubel, R., Hähnle, R.: OpenJDK's Java.utils.Collection.sort() is broken: the good, the bad and the worst case. In: Kroening, D., Păsăreanu, C.S. (eds.) CAV 2015. LNCS, vol. 9206, pp. 273–289. Springer, Cham (2015). https://doi.org/10.1007/978-3-319-21690-4_16
11. Groote, J.F., Mousavi, M.R.: Modeling and Analysis of Communicating Systems. MIT Press, Cambridge (2014)
12. Groote, J.F., Wijs, A.: An $O(m \log n)$ algorithm for stuttering equivalence and branching bisimulation. In: Chechik, M., Raskin, J.-F. (eds.) TACAS 2016. LNCS, vol. 9636, pp. 607–624. Springer, Heidelberg (2016). https://doi.org/10.1007/978-3-662-49674-9_40
13. Huisman, M., Joosten, S.J.C.: Towards reliable concurrent software. Principled Software Development, pp. 129–146. Springer, Cham (2018). https://doi.org/10.1007/978-3-319-98047-8_9
14. Hwong, Y., Keiren, J., Kusters, V., Leemans, S., Willemse, T.: Formalising and analysing the control software of the compact muon solenoid experiment at the large hadron collider. SCP **78**(12), 2435–2452 (2013). https://doi.org/10.1007/978-3-642-29320-7_12
15. mCRL2—Showcases. https://www.mcrl2.org/web/user_manual/showcases.html. Accessed July 2019

16. Landelijke Tunnelstandaard (National Tunnel Standard). http://publicaties.minienm.nl/documenten/landelijke-tunnelstandaard. Accessed June 2019
17. Oortwijn, W., Blom, S., Gurov, D., Huisman, M., Zaharieva-Stojanovski, M.: An abstraction technique for describing concurrent program behaviour. In: Paskevich, A., Wies, T. (eds.) VSTTE 2017. LNCS, vol. 10712, pp. 191–209. Springer, Cham (2017). https://doi.org/10.1007/978-3-319-72308-2_12
18. Oortwijn, W., Blom, S., Huisman, M.: Future-based static analysis of message passing programs. In: PLACES, pp. 65–72 (2016). https://doi.org/10.4204/EPTCS.211.7
19. Philippaerts, P., Mühlberg, J., Penninckx, W., Smans, J., Jacobs, B., Piessens, F.: Software verification with verifast: industrial case studies. SCP **82**, 77–97 (2014). https://doi.org/10.1016/j.scico.2013.01.006
20. Ruijters, E., Guck, D., van Noort, M., Stoelinga, M.: Reliability-centered maintenance of the electrically insulated railway joint via fault tree analysis: a practical experience report. In: DSN, pp. 662–669. IEEE Computer Society (2016). https://doi.org/10.1109/DSN.2016.67
21. Silva, R., de Oliveira, J., Pinto, J.: A case study on model checking and deductive verification techniques of safety-critical software. In: SBMF, Federal University of Campina Grande (2012)
22. The Technolution. https://www.technolution.eu. Accessed June 2019
23. Wiggelinkhuizen, J.: Feasibility of formal model checking in the Vitatron environment. Master's thesis, Eindhoven University of Technology (2007)

Resource Sharing via Capability-Based Multiparty Session Types

A. Laura Voinea(✉), Ornela Dardha, and Simon J. Gay

School of Computing Science, University of Glasgow, Glasgow, UK
a.voinea.1@research.gla.ac.uk, {Ornela.Dardha,Simon.Gay}@glasgow.ac.uk

Abstract. *Multiparty Session Types (MPST)* are a type formalism used to model communication protocols among components in distributed systems, by specifying *type* and *direction* of data transmitted. It is standard for multiparty session type systems to use access control based on *linear* or *affine* types. While useful in offering strong guarantees of communication safety and session fidelity, linearity and affinity run into the well-known problem of inflexible programming, excluding scenarios that make use of shared channels or need to store channels in shared data structures.

In this paper, we develop *capability-based resource sharing* for multiparty session types. In this setting, channels are split into two entities, the channel itself and the capability of using it. This gives rise to a more flexible session type system, which allows channel references to be shared and stored in persistent data structures. We illustrate our type system through a producer-consumer case study. Finally, we prove that the resulting language satisfies type safety.

Keywords: Session types · Sharing · Concurrent programming

1 Introduction

In the present era of communication-centric software systems, it is increasingly recognised that the structure of communication is an essential aspect of system design. *(Multiparty) session types* [18,19,31] allow communication structures to be codified as type definitions in programming languages, which can be exploited by compilers, development environments and runtime systems, for compile-time analysis or runtime monitoring. A substantial and ever-growing literature on session types and, more generally, behavioural types [20] provides a rich theoretical foundation, now being applied to a range of programming languages [1,16].

Session type systems must control *aliasing* of the endpoints of communication channels, in order to avoid race conditions. If agents A and B both think they

Supported by the UK EPSRC grant EP/K034413/1, "From Data Types to Session Types: A Basis for Concurrency and Distribution (ABCD)", by the EU HORIZON 2020 MSCA RISE project 778233 "BehAPI: Behavioural Application Program Interfaces", and by an EPSRC PhD studentship.

W. Ahrendt and S. L. Tapia Tarifa (Eds.): IFM 2019, LNCS 11918, pp. 437–455, 2019.
https://doi.org/10.1007/978-3-030-34968-4_24

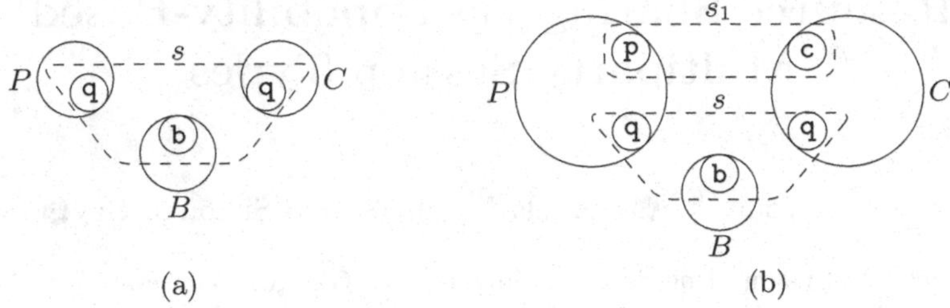

Fig. 1. Producer-consumer system: Producer—P and Consumer—C sharing access to Buffer—B by implementing the same role q. (a) P and C communicate with B in session s; (b) P and C exchange the capability to use channel s[q] in session s_1 and then use it to communicate with B in session s

are running the client side of a protocol with the same server S, then a message sent by A advances the session state without B's knowledge, which interferes with B's attempt to run the protocol.

In order to guarantee unique ownership of channel endpoints and eliminate aliasing, most session type systems use strict *linear typing*. For more flexibility, some others use *affine typing*, which allows channels to be discarded, but they still forbid aliasing. It is possible to allow a session-typed channel to become sharable in the special case in which the session type reaches a point which is essentially stateless. However, in such systems, channels are *linearly typed* for the most interesting parts of their lifetimes—we discuss these possibilities in Sect. 6.

This leads us to our research questions:

Q1 *Are session types intrinsically related to linearity or affinity?*
Q2 *Can we define session type systems without linear types?*
Q3 *How can we check resource (channel) sharing and aliasing, to guarantee communication safety and session fidelity, i.e., type safety?*

The goal of this paper is to investigate questions **Q1**–**Q3**. To give a more flexible approach to resource sharing and access control, we propose a system of multiparty session types (MPST) that includes techniques from the Capability Calculus [11], and from Walker et al.'s work on alias types [35]. The key idea is to split a communication channel into two entities: (1) the channel itself, and (2) its usage *capability*. Both entities are first-class and can be referred to separately. Channels can now be shared, or stored in shared data structures, and aliasing is allowed. However, in order to guarantee communication safety and session fidelity, i.e., type safety, capabilities are used linearly so that only one alias can be used at a time.

This approach has several benefits, and improves on the state of the art: (i) for the first time, it is now possible for a system to have a communication structure defined by shared channels, with the capabilities being transferred from process to process as required; (ii) a capability can be implemented as a simple token, whereas delegation of channels requires a relatively complex implementation, thus making linearity of capabilities more lightweight than linearity of channels.

Example 1 (Producer-Consumer Fig. 1). Producer P and consumer C communicate via buffer B in session $\mathtt{s}$, given in Fig. 1 (a). P and C implement *role* q, and B implements role b. *Shared access* to buffer B is captured by the fact that both P and C implement the same role q and use the same channel $\mathtt{s}[\mathsf{q}]$ to communicate with B.

Following MPST theory, we start by defining a *global type*, describing communications among *all* participants:

$$G_0 = \mathsf{q}{\to}\mathsf{b}{:}\mathsf{add}(\mathtt{Int}).\ \mathsf{q}{\to}\mathsf{b}{:}\mathsf{request}().\ \mathsf{b}{\to}\mathsf{q}{:}\mathsf{send}(\mathtt{Int}).\ G_0$$

In G_0, protocol proceeds as follows: P (playing q) sends an add message to B (playing b), to add data. In sequence, C (playing q) sends a $\mathsf{request}$ message to B, to ask for data. B replies with a send message, sending data to C (playing q), and the protocol repeats as G_0. *Projecting* the global protocol to each role gives us a local session type. In particular, for B, implementing role b, we obtain:

$$S_{\mathsf{b}} = \mathsf{q}?\mathsf{add}(\mathtt{Int}).\ \mathsf{q}?\mathsf{request}().\ \mathsf{q}!\mathsf{send}(\mathtt{Int}).\ S_{\mathsf{b}}$$

where the q annotations show the other role participating in each interaction. For the shared access by P and C (role q), we obtain:

$$S_{\mathsf{q}} = \mathsf{b}!\mathsf{add}(\mathtt{Int}).\ S'_{\mathsf{q}} \qquad\qquad S'_{\mathsf{q}} = \mathsf{b}!\mathsf{request}().\ \mathsf{b}?\mathsf{send}(\mathtt{Int}).\ S_{\mathsf{q}}$$

Finally, the definitions of processes are as follows—we will detail the syntax in Sect. 2.

$$\begin{aligned}
\mathsf{P}\langle v\rangle &= \mathtt{s}[\mathsf{q}][\mathsf{b}]\oplus\langle\mathsf{add}(v)\rangle.\mathsf{P}\langle v+1\rangle\\
\mathsf{C}\langle\rangle &= \mathtt{s}[\mathsf{q}][\mathsf{b}]\oplus\langle\mathsf{request}()\rangle.\mathtt{s}[\mathsf{b}][\mathsf{q}]\&\{\mathsf{send}(\mathsf{i})\}.\mathsf{C}\langle\rangle\\
\mathsf{B}\langle\rangle &= \mathtt{s}[\mathsf{q}][\mathsf{b}]\&\{\mathsf{add}(x)\}.\mathtt{s}[\mathsf{q}][\mathsf{b}]\&\{\mathsf{request}()\}.\mathtt{s}[\mathsf{b}][\mathsf{q}]\oplus\langle\mathsf{send}(x)\rangle.\mathsf{B}\langle\rangle
\end{aligned}$$

Unfortunately, the system of processes above is not typable using standard multiparty session type systems because role q is shared by P and C, thus violating linearity of channel $\mathtt{s}[\mathsf{q}]$. To solve this issue and still allow sharing and aliasing, in our work, instead of associating a channel c with a session type S, we separately associate c with a *tracked* type $\mathtt{tr}(\rho)$, and S with *capability* ρ, $\{\rho\mapsto S\}$. The capability can be passed between P and C as they take turns in using the channel, illustrated in Fig. 1 (b). As a first attempt, we now define the following global type, getting us closer to our framework.

$$\begin{aligned}
G_1 = {} & \mathsf{q}{\to}\mathsf{b}{:}\mathsf{add}(\mathtt{Int}).\ \mathsf{p}{\to}\mathsf{c}{:}\mathsf{turn}(\mathtt{tr}(\rho_{\mathsf{q}})).\ \mathsf{q}{\to}\mathsf{b}{:}\mathsf{request}().\\
& \mathsf{b}{\to}\mathsf{q}{:}\mathsf{send}(\mathtt{Int}).\ \mathsf{c}{\to}\mathsf{p}{:}\mathsf{turn}(\mathtt{tr}(\rho_{\mathsf{q}})).G_1
\end{aligned}$$

However, a type such as $\mathtt{tr}(\rho_{\mathsf{q}})$ is usually too specific because it refers to the capability of a particular channel. It is preferable to be able to give definitions that abstract away from specific channels. We therefore introduce *existential types*, in the style of [35], which package a channel with its capability, in the form $\exists[\rho|\{\rho\mapsto S\}].\mathtt{tr}(\rho)$.

With the existential types in place, we can define our global type G in the following way. It now includes an extra initial message from P to C containing

$P ::= \mathbf{0} \mid P \mid Q \mid (\nu\, s)P$	inaction, parallel composition, restriction
$\mid \mathsf{c}[\mathsf{p}]\oplus\langle l(v)\rangle.P \mid \mathsf{c}[\mathsf{p}]\&_{i\in I}\{l_i(x_i).\, P_i\}$	select, branch
$\mid \mathsf{c}[\mathsf{p}]\oplus\langle l(\mathsf{pack}(\rho, \mathsf{s}[\mathsf{q}]))\rangle.P$	select pack
$\mid \mathsf{c}[\mathsf{p}]\&_{i\in I}\{l_i(\mathsf{pack}(\rho_i, \mathsf{s_i}[\mathsf{q}])).\, P_i\}$	branch pack
$\mid \mathsf{def}\, D\, \mathsf{in}\, P \mid X\langle\tilde{x}\rangle$	recursion, process call
$D ::= X\langle\tilde{x}\rangle = P$	process declaration
$\mathsf{c} ::= x \mid \mathsf{s}[\mathsf{p}]$	variable, channel with role p
$v ::= \mathsf{c} \mid \rho \mid \mathsf{true} \mid \mathsf{false} \mid 0 \mid 1 \mid \ldots$	channel, capability, base value

Fig. 2. Multiparty session π-calculus

the channel used with the buffer. The session types S_{q} and S'_{q} are the same as before.

$$G = \mathsf{p}\!\to\!\mathsf{c}{:}\mathsf{buffer}(\exists[\rho_{\mathsf{q}}|\{\rho_{\mathsf{q}}\mapsto S'_{\mathsf{q}}\}].\mathtt{tr}(\rho_{\mathsf{q}})).\mu\,\mathsf{t}.\mathsf{q}\!\to\!\mathsf{b}{:}\mathsf{add}(\mathtt{Int}).\mathsf{p}\!\to\!\mathsf{c}{:}\mathsf{turn}(\{\rho_{\mathsf{q}}\mapsto S'_{\mathsf{q}}\}).\\ \mathsf{q}\!\to\!\mathsf{b}{:}\mathsf{request}().\mathsf{b}\!\to\!\mathsf{q}{:}\mathsf{send}(\mathtt{Int}).\mathsf{c}\!\to\!\mathsf{p}{:}\mathsf{turn}(\{\rho_{\mathsf{q}}\mapsto S_{\mathsf{q}}\}).\mathsf{t}$$

In Sect. 4 we complete this example by showing the projections to a local type for each role, and the definitions of processes that implement each role. □

Contributions of the paper

(i) **MPST with capabilities**: we present a new version of MPST theory without linear typing for channels, but with linearly-typed capabilities. In Sect. 2 we define a multiparty session π-calculus with capabilities, and its operational semantics, and in Sect. 3 we define a MPST system for it.
(ii) **Producer-Consumer Case Study**: in Sect. 4 we present a detailed account of the producer-consumer case study, capturing the core of resource sharing and use of capabilities.
(iii) **Type Safety**: in Sect. 5 we state the type safety property, and outline its proof.

2 Multiparty Session π-Calculus with Capabilities

Our π-calculus with multiparty session types is based on the language defined by Scalas *et al.* [28]. The syntax is defined in Fig. 2. We assume infinite sets of identifiers for variables (x), sessions (s), capabilities (ρ) and roles (p).

The calculus combines branch (resp., select) with input (resp., output), and a message $l(v)$ consists of a label l and a payload v, which is a value. A message in session s from role p to role q has the prefix $\mathsf{s}[\mathsf{p}][\mathsf{q}]$, where $\mathsf{s}[\mathsf{p}]$ is represented by c in the grammar. The select and branch operations come in two forms. The first form is standard, and the second form handles *packages*, which are the novel feature of our type system. A package consists of a capability ρ and a channel of

$$P \mid \mathbf{0} \equiv P \qquad P \mid Q \equiv Q \mid P \qquad (P \mid Q) \mid R \equiv P \mid (Q \mid R)$$

$$(\nu\, s)\mathbf{0} \equiv \mathbf{0} \qquad (\nu\, s)(\nu\, s')P \equiv (\nu\, s')(\nu\, s)P \qquad (\nu\, s)P \mid Q \equiv (\nu\, s)(P \mid Q) \ \text{ if } s \notin fc(Q)$$

$$\mathsf{def}\, D \,\mathsf{in}\, \mathbf{0} \equiv \mathbf{0} \qquad \mathsf{def}\, D \,\mathsf{in}\, (\nu\, s)P \equiv (\nu\, s)(\mathsf{def}\, D \,\mathsf{in}\, P) \ \text{ if } s \notin fc(P)$$

$$\mathsf{def}\, D \,\mathsf{in}\, (P \mid Q) \equiv (\mathsf{def}\, D \,\mathsf{in}\, P) \mid Q \ \text{ if } dpv(D) \cap fpv(Q) = \emptyset$$

$$\mathsf{def}\, D \,\mathsf{in}\, \mathsf{def}\, D' \,\mathsf{in}\, P \equiv \mathsf{def}\, D' \,\mathsf{in}\, \mathsf{def}\, D \,\mathsf{in}\, P$$
$$\text{if } (dpv(D) \cup fpv(D)) \cap dpv(D') = (dpv(D') \cup fpv(D')) \cap dpv(D) = \emptyset$$

Fig. 3. Structural congruence (processes)

$$\frac{j \in I \text{ and } fv(v) = \emptyset}{\mathsf{s}[\mathsf{p}][\mathsf{q}]\&_{i\in I}\{l_i(x_i).\,P_i\} \mid \mathsf{s}[\mathsf{q}][\mathsf{p}]\oplus\langle l_j(v)\rangle.P \longrightarrow P_j\{v/x_j\} \mid P}\ \text{RCom}$$

$$\frac{j \in I}{\mathsf{s}[\mathsf{p}][\mathsf{q}]\&_{i\in I}\{l_i(\mathsf{pack}(\rho_i, \mathtt{v}_i)).\,P_i\} \mid \mathsf{s}[\mathsf{q}][\mathsf{p}]\oplus\langle l_j(\mathsf{pack}(\rho, \mathtt{v}))\rangle.P \longrightarrow P_j\{\mathtt{v}/\mathtt{v}_i\} \mid P}\ \text{RComP}$$

$$\frac{\tilde{x} = x_1, \ldots, x_n \qquad \tilde{v} = v_1, \ldots, v_n \qquad fv(\tilde{v}) = \emptyset}{\mathsf{def}\, X\langle\tilde{x}\rangle = P \,\mathsf{in}\, (X\langle\tilde{x}\rangle \mid Q) \longrightarrow \mathsf{def}\, X\langle\tilde{x}\rangle = P \,\mathsf{in}\, (P\{\tilde{v}/\tilde{x}\} \mid Q)}\ \text{RCall}$$

$$\frac{P \longrightarrow Q}{(\nu\, s)P \longrightarrow (\nu\, s)Q}\ \text{RRes} \qquad \frac{P \longrightarrow Q}{P \mid R \longrightarrow Q \mid R}\ \text{RPar} \qquad \frac{P \longrightarrow Q}{\mathsf{def}\, D \,\mathsf{in}\, P \longrightarrow \mathsf{def}\, D \,\mathsf{in}\, Q}\ \text{RDef}$$

Fig. 4. Reduction (processes)

type $\mathtt{tr}(\rho)$. We will see in Sect. 3 in the typing rules, the capability is existentially quantified. This enables a channel to be delegated, with the information that it is linked to *some* capability, which will be transmitted in a second message.

As usual, we define structural congruence to compensate for the limitations of textual syntax. It is the smallest congruence satisfying the axioms in Fig. 3. The definition uses the concepts of *free channels* of a process, $fc(P)$; *free process variables* of a process, $fpv(P)$; and *defined process variables* of a process declaration, $dpv(D)$. We omit the definitions of these concepts, which are standard and can be found in [28].

We define a reduction-based operational semantics by the rules in Fig. 4. Rule RCom is a standard communication between roles p and q. Rule RComP is communication of an existential package. Rule RCall defines a standard approach to handling process definitions. The rest are standard contextual rules.

3 Multiparty Session Types with Capabilities

We now introduce a type system for the multiparty session π-calculus. The general methodology of multiparty session types is that system design begins with a *global type*, which specifies all of the communication among various *roles*. Given a global type G and a role p, *projection* yields a *session type* or *local type* $G \upharpoonright \mathsf{p}$ that describes all of the communication involving p. This local type can be further projected for another role q, to give a *partial session type* that describes communication between p and q.

S ::=	*local session type*
$\mathtt{end}$	terminated session
$\mid\ \mathtt{p}\oplus_{i\in I}!l_i(U_i).S_i$	selection towards role p
$\mid\ \mathtt{p}\&_{i\in I}?l_i\,(U_i)\,.S_i$	branching from role p
$\mid\ \mathtt{p}\oplus_{i\in I}!l_i(\exists[\rho_i\vert\{\rho_i\mapsto U_i\}].\mathtt{tr}(\rho_i)).S_i$	pack selection towards role p
$\mid\ \mathtt{p}\,\&_{i\in I}\,?l_i(\exists[\rho_i\vert\{\rho_i\mapsto U_i\}].\mathtt{tr}(\rho_i)).S_i$	pack branching from role p
$\mid\ \mathtt{t}$	type variable
$\mid\ \mu\,\mathtt{t}.S$	recursive session type
G ::=	*global type*
$\mathtt{end}$	termination
$\mid\ \mathtt{p}\to\mathtt{q}{:}\{l_i(U_i).G_i\}_{i\in I}$	interaction
$\mid\ \mathtt{p}\to\mathtt{q}{:}\{l_i(\exists[\rho_i\vert\{\rho_i\mapsto U_i\}].tr(\rho_i)).G_i\}_{i\in I}$	pack interaction
$\mid\ \mathtt{t}$	type variable
$\mid\ \mu\,\mathtt{t}.G$	recursive type
H ::=	*partial session type*
$\mathtt{end}$	terminated session
$\mid\ \oplus_{i\in I}\,!l_i(U_i).H_i$	selection
$\mid\ \&_{i\in I}\,?l_i(U_i).H_i$	branching
$\mid\ \oplus_{i\in I}\,!l_i(\exists[\rho_i\vert\{\rho_i\mapsto U_i\}].\mathtt{tr}(\rho_i)).H_i$	pack selection
$\mid\ \&_{i\in I}\,?l_i(\exists[\rho_i\vert\{\rho_i\mapsto U_i\}].\mathtt{tr}(\rho_i)).H_i$	pack branching
$\mid\ \mathtt{t}$	type variable
$\mid\ \mu\,\mathtt{t}.H$	recursive type
$C\ ::=\ \emptyset\ \mid\ C\otimes\{\rho\mapsto S\}$	*capabilities*
$B\ ::=\ \mathtt{Int}\ \mid\ \mathtt{Bool}$	*ground type*
U ::=	*payload type*
B	ground type
$\mid\ \mathtt{tr}(\rho)$	tracked type
$\mid\ \{\rho\mapsto S\}$	capability type
$\mid\ S$ closed	session type
$\Gamma\ ::=\ \emptyset\ \mid\ \Gamma, x:U\ \mid\ \Gamma,\mathtt{s}[\mathtt{p}]:\mathtt{tr}(\rho)$	*environment*
$\Delta\ ::=\ \emptyset\ \mid\ \Delta, X:\tilde{U}$	*process names*

All branch and select types have the conditions $I \neq \emptyset$ and U_i closed.

Fig. 5. Types, capabilities, environments

Global Types. Figure 5. Each interaction has a source role $\mathtt{p}$ and a target role $\mathtt{q}$. We combine branching and message transmission, so an interaction has a label l_i, a payload of type U_i, or of type $\exists[\rho_i|\{\rho_i\mapsto U_i\}].tr(\rho_i)$, and a continuation type G_i. If there is only one branch then we usually abbreviate the syntax to $\mathtt{p}\to\mathtt{q}{:}l(U).\ G$, respectively $\mathtt{p}\to\mathtt{q}{:}l(\exists[\rho_i|\{\rho_i\mapsto U_i\}].tr(\rho_i)).\ G$. Recursive types are allowed, with the assumption that they are guarded. **Base types** $B, B', \ldots$ can be types like Bool, Int, etc. **Payload types** $U, U_i, \ldots$ are either base types, tracked types, capability types or *closed* session types.

Local (session) Types. Figure 5. The single form of interaction from global types splits into *select* (internal choice) and *branch* (external choice). The *branching type* $\mathtt{p}\&_{i\in I}?l_i\,(U_i)\,.S_i$ describes a channel that can receive a label l_i from role p (for some $i \in I$, chosen by p), together with a *payload* of type U_i; then, the channel must be used as the continuation type S_i. The *selection type* $\mathtt{p}\oplus_{i\in I}!l_i(U_i).S_i$, describes a channel that can choose a label l_i (for any $i \in I$), and send it to p together with a payload of type U_i; then, the channel must be used as S_i. The types for *pack select* and *pack branch* act in a similar manner, and bind the capability ρ_i for the continuation type S_i. Session types also allow guarded recursion.

The relationship between global types and session types is formalised by the notion of projection.

Definition 1. *The projection of G onto a role* q*, written $G\restriction \mathtt{q}$, is:*

$$\mathtt{end}\restriction\mathtt{q} \triangleq \mathtt{end} \qquad \mathtt{t}\restriction\mathtt{q} \triangleq \mathtt{t} \qquad (\mu\,\mathtt{t}.G)\restriction\mathtt{q} \triangleq \begin{cases} \mu\,\mathtt{t}.(G\restriction\mathtt{q}) & \text{if } G\restriction\mathtt{q} \neq \mathtt{t}'\ (\forall \mathtt{t}') \\ \mathtt{end} & \text{otherwise} \end{cases}$$

$$(\mathtt{p}{\to}\mathtt{p}'{:}\{l_i(U_i).G_i\}_{i\in I})\restriction\mathtt{q} \triangleq \begin{cases} \mathtt{p}' \oplus_{i\in I} !l_i(U_i).(G_i\restriction\mathtt{q}) & \text{if } \mathtt{q}=\mathtt{p}, \\ \mathtt{p}\,\&_{i\in I}\,?l_i(U_i).(G_i\restriction\mathtt{q}) & \text{if } \mathtt{q}=\mathtt{p}', \\ \bigsqcap_{i\in I}(G_i\restriction\mathtt{q}) & \text{if } \mathtt{p}\neq\mathtt{q}\neq\mathtt{p}' \end{cases}$$

$$(\mathtt{p}{\to}\mathtt{p}'{:}\{l_i(\exists[\rho_i|\{\rho_i\mapsto U_i\}].\mathtt{tr}(\rho_i)).G_i\}_{i\in I})\restriction\mathtt{q} \triangleq$$
$$\begin{cases} \mathtt{p}' \oplus_{i\in I} !l_i(\exists[\rho_i|\{\rho_i\mapsto U_i\}].\mathtt{tr}(\rho_i)).(G_i\restriction\mathtt{q}) & \text{if } \mathtt{q}=\mathtt{p}, \\ \mathtt{p}\,\&_{i\in I}\,?l_i(\exists[\rho_i|\{\rho_i\mapsto U_i\}].\mathtt{tr}(\rho_i)).(G_i\restriction\mathtt{q}) & \text{if } \mathtt{q}=\mathtt{p}', \\ \bigsqcap_{i\in I}(G_i\restriction\mathtt{q}) & \text{if } \mathtt{p}\neq\mathtt{q}\neq\mathtt{p}' \end{cases}$$

Where the merge operator for session types, $\bigsqcap$, *is defined by:*

$$\mathtt{end}\sqcap\mathtt{end} \triangleq \mathtt{end} \qquad \mathtt{t}\sqcap\mathtt{t} \triangleq \mathtt{t} \qquad \mu t.S \sqcap \mu t.S' \triangleq \mu t.(S\sqcap S')$$

$$\mathtt{p}\,\&_{i\in I}\,?l_i(U_i).S_i \sqcap \mathtt{p}\,\&_{j\in J}\,?l_j(U_j).S'_j \triangleq$$
$$\mathtt{p}\,\&_{k\in I\cap J}\,?l_k(U_k).(S_k\sqcap S'_k)\ \&\ \mathtt{p}\,\&_{j\in I\setminus J}\,?l_i(U_i).S_i\ \&\ \mathtt{p}\,\&_{j\in J\setminus I}\,?l_j(U_j).S'_j$$

$$\mathtt{p}\oplus_{i\in I} !l_i(U_i).S_i \sqcap \mathtt{p}\oplus_{i\in I} !l_i(U_i).S_i \triangleq \mathtt{p}\oplus_{i\in I} !l_i(U_i).S_i$$

$$\mathtt{p}\,\&_{i\in I}\,?l_i(\exists[\rho_i|\{\rho_i\mapsto U_i\}].\mathtt{tr}(\rho_i)).S_i \sqcap \mathtt{p}\,\&_{j\in J}\,?l_j(\exists[\rho_j|\{\rho_j\mapsto U_j\}].\mathtt{tr}(\rho_j)).S'_j \triangleq$$
$$\mathtt{p}\,\&_{k\in I\cap J}\,?l_k(\exists[\rho_k|\{\rho_k\mapsto U_k\}].\mathtt{tr}(\rho_k)).(S_k\sqcap S'_k)\ \&\ \mathtt{p}\,\&_{j\in I\setminus J}\,?l_i(\exists[\rho_i|\{\rho_i\mapsto U_i\}].\mathtt{tr}(\rho_i)).S_i$$
$$\&\ \mathtt{p}\,\&_{j\in J\setminus I}\,?l_j(\exists[\rho_j|\{\rho_j\mapsto U_j\}].\mathtt{tr}(\rho_j)).S'_j$$

$$\mathtt{p}\oplus_{i\in I} !l_i(\exists[\rho_i|\{\rho_i\mapsto U_i\}].\mathtt{tr}(\rho_i)).S_i \sqcap \mathtt{p}\oplus_{i\in I} !l_i(\exists[\rho_i|\{\rho_i\mapsto U_i\}].\mathtt{tr}(\rho_i)).S_i \triangleq$$
$$\mathtt{p}\oplus_{i\in I} !l_i(\exists[\rho_i|\{\rho_i\mapsto U_i\}].\mathtt{tr}(\rho_i)).S_i$$

Projecting end or a type variable t onto any role does not change it. Projecting a recursive type $\mu\,\mathtt{t}.G$ onto q means projecting G onto q. However, if G does not involve q then $G\restriction\mathtt{q}$ is a type variable, $\mathtt{t}'$, and it must be replaced by end to avoid introducing an unguarded recursive type. Projecting an interaction between p and p′ onto either p or p′ produces a select or a branch. Projecting onto a different role q ignores the interaction and combines the projections of the continuations using the merge operator.

The merge operator, $\sqcap$, introduced in [13,36], allows more global types to have defined projections, which in turn allows more processes to be typed. Different external choices from the same role $\mathtt{p}$ are integrated by merging the continuation types following a common message label, and including the branches with different labels. Merging for internal choices is undefined unless the interactions are identical. This excludes meaningless types that result when a sender $\mathtt{p}$ is unaware of which branch has been chosen by other roles in a previous interaction.

Definition 2. *For a session type S, $\mathtt{roles}(S)$ denotes the set of roles occurring in S. We write $\mathtt{p} \in S$ for $\mathtt{p} \in \mathtt{roles}(S)$, and $\mathtt{p} \in S\backslash\mathtt{q}$ for $\mathtt{p} \in \mathtt{roles}(S) \setminus \{\mathtt{q}\}$.*

Partial Session Types. Figure 5 have the same cases as local types, without role annotations. Partial types have a notion of *duality* which exchanges branch and select but preserves payload types.

Definition 3. *$\overline{H}$ is the* dual of *H, defined by:*

$$\overline{\oplus_{i\in I}!l_i(U_i).H_i} \triangleq \&_{i\in I}\,?l_i(U_i).\overline{H_i} \qquad \overline{\&_{i\in I}?l_i\,(U_i)\,.H_i} \triangleq \oplus_{i\in I}\,!l_i(U_i).\overline{H_i}$$

$$\overline{\oplus_{i\in I}\,!l_i(\exists[\rho_i|\{\rho_i\mapsto U_i\}].\mathtt{tr}(\rho_i)).H_i} \triangleq \&_{i\in I}\,?l_i(\exists[\rho_i|\{\rho_i\mapsto U_i\}].\mathtt{tr}(\rho_i)).\overline{H_i}$$

$$\overline{\&_{i\in I}\,?l_i(\exists[\rho_i|\{\rho_i\mapsto U_i\}].\mathtt{tr}(\rho_i)).H_i} \triangleq \oplus_{i\in I}\,!l_i(\exists[\rho_i|\{\rho_i\mapsto U_i\}].\mathtt{tr}(\rho_i)).\overline{H_i}$$

$$\overline{\mathtt{end}} \triangleq \mathtt{end} \qquad \overline{\mathtt{t}} \triangleq \mathtt{t} \qquad \overline{\mu t.H} \triangleq \mu t.\overline{H}$$

Similarly to the projection of global types to local types, a local type can be projected onto a role $\mathtt{q}$ to give a partial type. This yields a partial type that only describes the communications in S that involve $\mathtt{q}$. The definition follows the same principles as the previous definition (cf. Definition 1).

Definition 4. *$S\lceil\mathtt{q}$ is the* partial projection of *S* onto *$\mathtt{q}$:*

$$\mathtt{end}\lceil\mathtt{q} \triangleq \mathtt{end} \qquad \mathtt{t}\lceil\mathtt{q} \triangleq \mathtt{t} \qquad (\mu\mathtt{t}.S)\lceil\mathtt{q} \triangleq \begin{cases}\mu\mathtt{t}.(S\lceil\mathtt{q}) & \text{if } S\lceil\mathtt{q} \neq \mathtt{t}'\ (\forall\mathtt{t}')\\ \mathtt{end} & \text{otherwise}\end{cases}$$

$$(\mathtt{p}\oplus_{i\in I}!l_i(U_i).S_i)\lceil\mathtt{q} \triangleq \begin{cases}\oplus_{i\in I}\,!l_i(U_i).(S_i\lceil\mathtt{q}) & \text{if } \mathtt{q}=\mathtt{p},\\ \sqcap_{i\in I}(S_i\lceil\mathtt{q}) & \text{if } \mathtt{p}\neq\mathtt{q}\end{cases}$$

$$(\mathtt{p}\&_{i\in I}?l_i\,(U_i)\,.S_i)\lceil\mathtt{q} \triangleq \begin{cases}\&_{i\in I}\,?l_i(U_i).S_i\lceil\mathtt{q} & \text{if } \mathtt{q}=\mathtt{p},\\ \sqcap_{i\in I}(S_i\lceil\mathtt{q}) & \text{if } \mathtt{p}\neq\mathtt{q}\end{cases}$$

$$(\mathtt{p}\oplus_{i\in I}\,!l_i(\exists[\rho_i|\{\rho_i\mapsto U_i\}].\mathtt{tr}(\rho_i)).S_i)\lceil\mathtt{q} \triangleq$$
$$\begin{cases}\oplus_{i\in I}\,!l_i(\exists[\rho_i|\{\rho_i\mapsto U_i\}].\mathtt{tr}(\rho_i)).(S_i\lceil\mathtt{q}) & \text{if } \mathtt{q}=\mathtt{p},\\ \sqcap_{i\in I}(S_i\lceil\mathtt{q}) & \text{if } \mathtt{p}\neq\mathtt{q}\end{cases}$$

$$(\mathtt{p}\,\&_{i\in I}\,?l_i(\exists[\rho_i|\{\rho_i\mapsto U_i\}].\mathtt{tr}(\rho_i)).S_i)\lceil\mathtt{q} \triangleq$$
$$\begin{cases}\&_{i\in I}\,?l_i(\exists[\rho_i|\{\rho_i\mapsto U_i\}].\mathtt{tr}(\rho_i)).S_i\lceil\mathtt{q} & \text{if } \mathtt{q}=\mathtt{p},\\ \sqcap_{i\in I}(S_i\lceil\mathtt{q}) & \text{if } \mathtt{p}\neq\mathtt{q}\end{cases}$$

Where the merge operator for partial session types, $\sqcap$, *is defined by:*

$$\mathtt{end} \sqcap \mathtt{end} \triangleq \mathtt{end} \qquad \mathtt{t} \sqcap \mathtt{t} \triangleq \mathtt{t} \qquad \mu \mathtt{t}.H \sqcap \mu \mathtt{t}.H' \triangleq \mu \mathtt{t}.(H \sqcap H')$$

$$\&_{i\in I}?l_i(U_i).H_i \sqcap \&_{i\in I}?l_i(U_i).H'_i \triangleq \&_{i\in I}?l_i(U_i).(H_i \sqcap H'_i)$$

$$\oplus_{i\in I}!l_i(U_i).H_i \sqcap \oplus_{j\in J}!l_j(U_j).H'_j \triangleq$$
$$(\oplus_{k\in I\cap J}!l_k(U_k).(H_k \sqcap H'_k)) \oplus (\oplus_{i\in I\setminus J}!l_i(U_i).H_i) \oplus (\oplus_{j\in J\setminus I}!l_j(U_j).H'_j)$$

$$\&_{i\in I}?l_i(\exists[\rho_i|\{\rho_i \mapsto U_i\}].\mathtt{tr}(\rho_i)).H_i \sqcap \&_{i\in I}?l_i(\exists[\rho_i|\{\rho_i \mapsto U_i\}].\mathtt{tr}(\rho_i)).H'_i \triangleq$$
$$\&_{i\in I}?l_i(\exists[\rho_i|\{\rho_i \mapsto U_i\}].\mathtt{tr}(\rho_i)).(H_i \sqcap H'_i)$$

$$\oplus_{i\in I}!l_i(\exists[\rho_i|\{\rho_i \mapsto U_i\}].\mathtt{tr}(\rho_i)).H_i \sqcap \oplus_{j\in J}!l_j(\exists[\rho_j|\{\rho_j \mapsto U_j\}].\mathtt{tr}(\rho_j)).H'_j \triangleq$$
$$(\oplus_{k\in I\cap J}!l_k(\exists[\rho_k|\{\rho_k \mapsto U_k\}].\mathtt{tr}(\rho_k)).(H_k \sqcap H'_k)) \oplus (\oplus_{i\in I\setminus J}!l_i(\exists[\rho_i|\{\rho_i \mapsto U_i\}].\mathtt{tr}(\rho_i)).H_i)$$
$$\oplus (\oplus_{j\in J\setminus I}!l_j(\exists[\rho_j|\{\rho_j \mapsto U_j\}].\mathtt{tr}(\rho_j)).H'_j)$$

Unlike session type merging, $\sqcap$ can combine different *internal* choices, but *not* external choices because that could violate type safety. Different internal choices can depend on the outcome of previous interactions with other roles, since this dependency can be safely approximated as an internal choice. Different external choices, however cannot capture this dependency.

Example 2 (Projections of Global and Local Types). Consider the global type G of the producer-consumer example from the introduction.

$$G = \mathsf{p}\to\mathsf{c}:\mathsf{buffer}(\exists[\rho_\mathsf{q}|\{\rho_\mathsf{q} \mapsto S'_\mathsf{q}\}].\mathtt{tr}(\rho_\mathsf{q})).\mu\,\mathtt{t}.\mathsf{q}\to\mathsf{b}:\mathsf{add}(\mathtt{Int}).\mathsf{p}\to\mathsf{c}:\mathsf{turn}(\{\rho_\mathsf{q} \mapsto S'_\mathsf{q}\}).$$
$$\mathsf{q}\to\mathsf{b}:\mathsf{request}(\mathtt{Str}).\mathsf{b}\to\mathsf{q}:\mathsf{send}(\mathtt{Int}).\mathsf{c}\to\mathsf{p}:\mathsf{turn}(\{\rho_\mathsf{q} \mapsto S_\mathsf{q}\}).\mathtt{t}$$

It captures the interaction between the producer and consumer entities through roles p, c, and between producer, consumer and buffer through roles q (shared between producer and consumer) and b. Projecting onto p gives the session type

$$S = G \upharpoonright \mathsf{p} = \mathsf{c}\oplus!\mathsf{buffer}(\exists[\rho_\mathsf{q}|\{\rho_\mathsf{q} \mapsto S'_\mathsf{q}\}].\mathtt{tr}(\rho_\mathsf{q})).\mu\,\mathtt{t}.\mathsf{c}\oplus!\mathsf{turn}(\{\rho_\mathsf{q} \mapsto S'_\mathsf{q}\}).$$
$$\mathsf{c}\&?\mathsf{turn}(\{\rho_\mathsf{q} \mapsto S_\mathsf{q}\}).\mathtt{t}$$

and further projecting onto c gives the partial session type:

$$H = S \upharpoonright \mathsf{c} = \oplus!\mathsf{buffer}(\exists[\rho_\mathsf{q}|\{\rho_\mathsf{q} \mapsto S'_\mathsf{q}\}].\mathtt{tr}(\rho_\mathsf{q})).!\mu\,\mathtt{t}.\oplus!\mathsf{turn}(\{\rho_\mathsf{q} \mapsto S'_\mathsf{q}\}).\&?\mathsf{turn}(\{\rho_\mathsf{q} \mapsto S_\mathsf{q}\}).\mathtt{t}$$

$$\frac{\forall i \in I \quad U_i \leqslant_\mathsf{S} U'_i \quad S_i \leqslant_\mathsf{S} S'_i}{\mathsf{p}\&_{i\in I}?l_i\,(U_i)\,.S_i \leqslant_\mathsf{S} \mathsf{p}\,\&_{i\in I\cup J}\,?l_i(U'_i).S'_i}\ \textsc{SBr} \qquad \frac{\forall i \in I \quad U'_i \leqslant_\mathsf{S} U_i \quad S_i \leqslant_\mathsf{S} S'_i}{\mathsf{p}\oplus_{i\in I\cup J}!l_i(U_i).S_i \leqslant_\mathsf{S} \mathsf{p}\oplus_{i\in I}!l_i(U'_i).S'_i}\ \textsc{SSel}$$

$$\frac{\forall i \in I \quad U_i \leqslant_\mathsf{S} U'_i \quad S_i \leqslant_\mathsf{S} S'_i}{\mathsf{p}\,\&_{i\in I}\,?l_i(\exists[\rho_i|\{\rho_i \mapsto U_i\}].\mathtt{tr}(\rho_i)).S_i \leqslant_\mathsf{S} \mathsf{p}\,\&_{i\in I\cup J}\,?l_i(\exists[\rho_i|\{\rho_i \mapsto U'_i\}].\mathtt{tr}(\rho_i)).S'_i}\ \textsc{SBrP}$$

$$\frac{\forall i \in I \quad U'_i \leqslant_\mathsf{S} U_i \quad S_i \leqslant_\mathsf{S} S'_i}{\mathsf{p}\oplus_{i\in I\cup J}!l_i(\exists[\rho_i|\{\rho_i \mapsto U_i\}].\mathtt{tr}(\rho_i)).S_i \leqslant_\mathsf{S} \mathsf{p}\oplus_{i\in I}!l_i(\exists[\rho_i|\{\rho_i \mapsto U'_i\}].\mathtt{tr}(\rho_i)).S'_i}\ \textsc{SSel}$$

$$\frac{B \leqslant_\mathsf{B} B'}{B \leqslant_\mathsf{S} B'}\ \textsc{SB} \qquad \frac{}{\mathtt{end} \leqslant_\mathsf{S} \mathtt{end}}\ \textsc{SEnd} \qquad \frac{S\{\mu\,\mathtt{t}.S/\mathtt{t}\} \leqslant_\mathsf{S} S'}{\mu\,\mathtt{t}.S \leqslant_\mathsf{S} S'}\ \textsc{S}\mu\textsc{L} \qquad \frac{S \leqslant_\mathsf{S} S'\{\mu\,\mathtt{t}.S'/\mathtt{t}\}}{S \leqslant_\mathsf{S} \mu\,\mathtt{t}.S'}\ \textsc{S}\mu\textsc{R}$$

Fig. 6. Subtyping for local session types.

$$\frac{\forall i \in I \quad U_i \leqslant_{\mathsf{S}} U_i' \quad H_i \leqslant_{\mathsf{P}} H_i'}{\&_{i\in I} ?l_i\,(U_i)\,.H_i \leqslant_{\mathsf{P}} \&_{i\in I\cup J}\, ?l_i(U_i').H_i'}\ \textsc{SParBr} \qquad \frac{\forall i \in I \quad U_i' \leqslant_{\mathsf{S}} U_i \quad H_i \leqslant_{\mathsf{P}} H_i'}{\oplus_{i\in I\cup J}\, !l_i(U_i).H_i \leqslant_{\mathsf{P}} \oplus_{i\in I}\, !l_i(U_i').H_i'}\ \textsc{SParSel}$$

$$\frac{\forall i \in I \quad U_i \leqslant_{\mathsf{S}} U_i' \quad H_i \leqslant_{\mathsf{P}} H_i'}{\&_{i\in I}\, ?l_i(\exists[\rho_i|\{\rho_i \mapsto U_i\}].\mathtt{tr}(\rho_i)).H \leqslant_{\mathsf{P}} \&_{i\in I\cup J}\, ?l_i(\exists[\rho_i|\{\rho_i \mapsto U_i'\}].\mathtt{tr}(\rho_i)).H_i'}\ \textsc{SParBrP}$$

$$\frac{\forall i \in I \quad U_i' \leqslant_{\mathsf{S}} U_i \quad H_i \leqslant_{\mathsf{P}} H_i'}{\oplus_{i\in I\cup J}\, !l_i(\exists[\rho_i|\{\rho_i \mapsto U_i\}].\mathtt{tr}(\rho_i)).H_i \leqslant_{\mathsf{P}} \oplus_{i\in I}\, !l_i(\exists[\rho_i|\{\rho_i \mapsto U_i'\}].\mathtt{tr}(\rho_i)).H_i'}\ \textsc{SParSelP}$$

$$\frac{}{\mathbf{end} \leqslant_{\mathsf{P}} \mathbf{end}}\ \textsc{SParEnd} \qquad \frac{H\{\mu\,\mathtt{t}.H/\mathtt{t}\} \leqslant_{\mathsf{P}} H'}{\mu\,\mathtt{t}.H \leqslant_{\mathsf{P}} H'}\ \textsc{SPar}\mu\textsc{L} \qquad \frac{H \leqslant_{\mathsf{P}} H'\{\mu\,\mathtt{t}.H'/\mathtt{t}\}}{H \leqslant_{\mathsf{P}} \mu\,\mathtt{t}.H'}\ \textsc{SPar}\mu\textsc{R}$$

Fig. 7. Subtyping for partial session types.

Definition 5 (Subtyping). Subtyping on session types $\leqslant_{\mathsf{S}}$ *is the largest relation such that (i) if* $S \leqslant_{\mathsf{S}} S'$, *then* $\forall \mathtt{p} \in (\mathtt{roles}(S) \cup \mathtt{roles}(S'))$ $S\lceil \mathtt{p} \leqslant_{\mathsf{P}} S'\lceil \mathtt{p}$, *and (ii) is closed backwards under the coinductive rules in Fig. 6.* Subtyping on partial session types $\leqslant_{\mathsf{P}}$ *is defined coinductively by the rules in Fig. 7.*

Intuitively, the *subtyping relation* says that a session type S is "smaller" than S' when S is "less demanding" than S' i.e., when S allows more internal choices, and imposes fewer external choices, than S'. Clause *(i)* links local and partial subtyping, and ensures that if two types are related, then their partial projections exist. This clause is used later in defining consistency in Definition 8. In the second clause *(ii)* rules SBr, SSel define subtyping on branch/select types, and SBrP, SSelP define subtyping on branch pack/select pack types. SBr and SBrP are covariant in their continuation types as well as in the number of branches offered, whereas SSel, and SSelP are contravariant in both. SB relates base types, if they are related by $\leqslant_{\mathsf{B}}$. SEnd relates terminated channel types. SμL and SμR are standard under coinduction [26, sect. 21], relating types up-to their unfolding.

Capabilities. In our type system linearity is enforced via capabilities, rather than via environment splitting as in most session type systems. Each process has a capability set C associated with it, allowing it to communicate on the associated channels. The tracked type $\mathtt{tr}(\rho)$ is a singleton type associating a channel to capability ρ and to no other, which in turn maps to the channel's session type $\{\rho \mapsto S\}$. Hence two variables with the same capability ρ are aliases for the same channel. Individual capabilities are joined together using the $\otimes$ operator: $C = \{\rho_1 \mapsto S_1\} \otimes \ldots \otimes \{\rho_n \mapsto S_n\}$. The ordering is insignificant. The type system maintains the invariant that $\rho_1, \ldots, \rho_n$ are distinct.

Definition 6 (Terminated capabilities). *A capability set C is* terminated *if for every $\rho \in \mathrm{dom}\,(C)$, $C(\rho) = \mathbf{end}$.*

Definition 7 (Substitution of capabilities).

$$\{\rho \mapsto S\}[\rho'/\rho_2] = \{\rho \mapsto S\} \qquad \{\rho \mapsto S\}[\rho'/\rho] = \{\rho' \mapsto S\}$$

$$\emptyset[\rho'/\rho] = \emptyset \qquad (C_1 \otimes C_2)[\rho'/\rho] = C_1[\rho'/\rho] \otimes C_2[\rho'/\rho]$$

There are two important concepts relating the environment Γ and the capability set C: *completeness* and *consistency*, used in our type system.

Completeness means that if a channel is in Γ and its capability is in C, then Γ also contains the other endpoints of the channel and C contains the corresponding capability. In this case, there is a self-contained collection of channels that can communicate. Consistency means that the opposite endpoints of every channel have dual partial types.

Definition 8 (Completeness and consistency).
(Γ, C) *is* complete *iff for all* $\mathtt{s}[\mathtt{p}]:\mathtt{tr}(\rho_\mathtt{p})$ *with* $\rho_\mathtt{p}:\{\rho_\mathtt{p}\mapsto S_\mathtt{p}\} \in \Gamma$ *and* $\{\rho_\mathtt{p}\mapsto S_\mathtt{p}\} \in C$, $\mathtt{q} \in S_\mathtt{p}$ *implies* $\mathtt{s}[\mathtt{q}] : \mathtt{tr}(\rho_\mathtt{q}), \rho_\mathtt{q} : \{\rho_\mathtt{q}\mapsto S_\mathtt{q}\} \in \Gamma$ *and* $\{\rho_\mathtt{q}\mapsto S_\mathtt{q}\} \in C$.

(Γ, C) *is* consistent *iff for all* $\mathtt{s}[\mathtt{p}] : \mathtt{tr}(\rho_\mathtt{p}), \mathtt{s}[\mathtt{q}] : \mathtt{tr}(\rho_\mathtt{q}), \rho_\mathtt{p} : \{\rho_\mathtt{p}\mapsto S_\mathtt{p}\}, \rho_\mathtt{q} : \{\rho_\mathtt{q}\mapsto S_\mathtt{q}\} \in \Gamma$ *we have* $\overline{S_\mathtt{p} \upharpoonright \mathtt{q}} \leqslant_\mathsf{P} S_\mathtt{q} \upharpoonright \mathtt{p}$.

Definition 9. *Typing judgements are inductively defined by the rules in Fig. 8, and have the form:* $\Gamma \vdash v : T; C$ *for values, or* $\Delta; \Gamma \vdash P; C$ *for processes (with* (Γ, C) *consistent, and* $\forall(\mathtt{c} : \mathtt{tr}(\rho) \in \Gamma; \{\rho\mapsto S\} \in C), S \upharpoonright \mathtt{p}$ *is defined* $\forall \mathtt{p} \in S$*).*

Γ is an environment of typed variables and channels together with their capability typing. Δ, defined in Fig. 5 is an environment of typed process names, used in rules TDef and TCall for recursive process definitions and calls. If a channel $\mathtt{s}[\mathtt{p}]$ is in Γ, with type $\mathtt{tr}(\rho)$, then Γ also contains $\rho : \{\rho\mapsto S\}$ for some session type S. The capability ρ might, or might not, be in C, to show whether or not the channel can be used. If ρ is in C, then it occurs with the same session type: $\{\rho\mapsto S\}$.

Rule TCap takes the type for a capability ρ from the capability set. TVar and TVal are standard. TInact has a standard condition that all session types have reached **end**, expressed as the capability set being terminated. TPar combines the capability sets in a parallel composition. TSub is a standard subsumption rule using $\leqslant_\mathsf{S}$ (Definition 5), the difference being the type in the capability set. TSel (resp. TBr) states that the selection (resp. branching) on channel $\mathtt{c}[\mathtt{p}]$ is well typed if the capability associated with it is of compatible selection (resp. branching) type and the continuations $P_i, \forall i \in I$ are well-typed with the continuation session types. TSelP is similar to TSel, with the notable difference that an existential package is created for the channel being sent, containing the channel and its abstracted capability. Note that the actual capability to use the endpoint remains with process P. TBrP is similar to TBr, with the difference that it unpackages the channel received and binds its capability type in the continuation session type (used to identify the correct capability when received later). TRes requires the restricted environment Γ' and the associated capability set C' to be *complete* (Definition 8). TDef takes account of capability sets as well as parameters, and TCall similarly requires capability sets. The parameters of a defined process include any necessary capabilities, which then also appear in the corresponding C_i, because not all capabilities associated with the channel parameters need to be present when the call is made.

$$\frac{\text{TCap}}{\Gamma \vdash \rho : \{\rho \mapsto S\}; \{\rho \mapsto S\}} \quad \frac{\overset{\text{TVar}}{\mathtt{c} : \mathtt{tr}(\rho), \rho : \{\rho \mapsto S\} \in \Gamma}}{\Gamma \vdash \mathtt{c} : \mathtt{tr}(\rho); \emptyset} \quad \frac{\overset{\text{TVal}}{v \in B}}{\Gamma \vdash v : B; \emptyset} \quad \frac{\overset{\text{TInact}}{C \text{ terminated}}}{\Delta; \Gamma \vdash \mathbf{0}; C}$$

$$\frac{\overset{\text{TPar}}{\Delta; \Gamma \vdash P; C_1 \quad \Delta; \Gamma \vdash Q; C_2}}{\Delta; \Gamma \vdash P \mid Q; C_1 \otimes C_2} \quad \frac{\overset{\text{TSub}}{\Delta; \Gamma \vdash P; C \otimes \{\rho \mapsto U\} \quad U' \leqslant_{\mathsf{S}} U}}{\Delta; \Gamma \vdash P; C \otimes \{\rho \mapsto U'\}}$$

$$\frac{\overset{\text{TSel}}{\Gamma \vdash v : U; C \quad \Delta; \Gamma \vdash P; C' \otimes \{\rho \mapsto S_j\} \quad \mathtt{c} : \mathtt{tr}(\rho), \rho : \{\rho \mapsto S_j\} \in \Gamma \quad j \in I}}{\Delta; \Gamma \vdash \mathsf{c}[\mathsf{p}] \oplus \langle l_j(v) \rangle . P; C \otimes C' \otimes \{\rho \mapsto \mathsf{p} \oplus_{i \in I} ! l_i(U_i).S_i\}}$$

$$\frac{\overset{\text{TBr}}{\Delta; \Gamma, x_i : U_i \vdash P_i; C \otimes C_i \otimes \{\rho \mapsto S_i\} \quad \mathtt{c} : \mathtt{tr}(\rho), \rho : \{\rho \mapsto S_i\} \in \Gamma \quad \forall i \in I}}{\Delta; \Gamma \vdash \mathsf{c}[\mathsf{p}] \&_{i \in I} \{l_i(x_i). P_i\}; C \otimes \{\rho \mapsto \mathsf{p} \&_{i \in I} ? l_i\,(U_i)\,.S_i\}}$$

$$\frac{\overset{\text{TSelP}}{\Gamma \vdash v : \mathtt{tr}(\rho'); \emptyset \quad \Delta; \Gamma \vdash P; C \otimes \{\rho \mapsto S_j, \rho' \mapsto U\} \quad \mathtt{c} : \mathtt{tr}(\rho), \rho : \{\rho \mapsto S_j\} \in \Gamma \quad j \in I}}{\Delta; \Gamma \vdash \mathsf{c}[\mathsf{p}] \oplus \langle l_j(\mathsf{pack}(\rho', v)) \rangle . P; C \otimes \{\rho \mapsto \mathsf{p} \oplus_{i \in I} ! l_i(\exists [\rho' | \{\rho' \mapsto U\}].\mathtt{tr}(\rho')).S_i, \rho' \mapsto U\}}$$

$$\frac{\overset{\text{TBrP}}{\Delta; \Gamma, \mathtt{v_i} : \mathtt{tr}(\rho_i), \rho_i : \{\rho_i \mapsto U_i\} \vdash P_i; C \otimes \{\rho \mapsto S_i\} \quad \forall i \in I \quad \mathtt{c} : \mathtt{tr}(\rho), \rho : \{\rho \mapsto S_i\} \in \Gamma}}{\Delta; \Gamma \vdash \mathsf{c}[\mathsf{p}] \&_{i \in I} \{l_i(\mathsf{pack}(\rho_i, \mathtt{v_i})). P_i\}; C \otimes \{\rho \mapsto \mathsf{p} \&_{i \in I} ? l_i(\exists [\rho_i | \{\rho_i \mapsto U_i\}].\mathtt{tr}(\rho_i)).S_i\}}$$

$$\frac{\overset{\text{TRes}}{\Delta; \Gamma, \Gamma' \vdash P; C \otimes C' \quad (\Gamma' = \{\mathtt{s}[\mathtt{p}] : \mathtt{tr}(\rho_{\mathtt{p}}), \rho_{\mathtt{p}} : \{\rho_{\mathtt{p}} \mapsto S_{\mathtt{p}}\}\}_{\mathtt{p} \in I}, C' = \otimes_{\mathtt{p} \in I} \{\rho_{\mathtt{p}} \mapsto S_{\mathtt{p}}\}) \text{ complete}}}{\Delta; \Gamma \vdash (\nu\, s : \Gamma') P; C}$$

$$\frac{\overset{\text{TDef}}{\Delta, X : \tilde{U}; \tilde{x} : \tilde{U} \vdash P; \tilde{C} \quad \Delta, X : \tilde{U}; \Gamma \vdash Q; C}}{\Delta; \Gamma \vdash \mathsf{def}\, X \langle \tilde{x} : \tilde{U} \rangle = P; \tilde{C}\, \mathsf{in}\, Q; C} \quad \frac{\overset{\text{TCall}}{\forall i \in \{1..n\} \quad \Gamma \vdash v_i : U_i; C_i}}{\Delta, X : U_1, \ldots, U_n; \Gamma \vdash X \langle v_1, \ldots, v_n \rangle; C_1 \otimes \ldots \otimes C_n}$$

Fig. 8. Typing rules

4 Case Study: Producer-Consumer

We now expand on the producer-consumer scenario from Sect. 1 by discussing the process definitions and showing part of the typing derivation. To lighten the notation, we present a set of mutually recursive definitions, instead of using the formal syntax of def ... in.

Recall that the example consists of three processes: the producer, the consumer, and a one-place buffer (Fig. 1). The producer and the consumer communicate with the buffer on a single shared channel. Each of the two must wait to receive the *capability* to communicate on the channel before doing so.

The buffer B is parameterised by channel x and by the capability for it, $\rho_{\mathtt{x}}$, and alternately responds to add and request messages. At the end of the definition, $\{\rho_x \mapsto S_b\}$ shows the held capability and its session type.

$$\mathsf{B}\langle \mathtt{x}{:}\mathtt{tr}(\rho_x), \rho_x{:}\{\rho_x \mapsto S_b\}\rangle = \mathtt{x}[\mathsf{q}]\&\mathsf{add}(\mathsf{i}).\mathtt{x}[\mathsf{q}]\&\mathsf{request}(\mathtt{r}).\mathtt{x}[\mathsf{p}]\oplus\mathsf{send}(\mathsf{i}).\mathsf{B}\langle \mathtt{x}, \rho_x\rangle; \{\rho_x \mapsto S_b\}$$

The producer is represented by two process definitions: Produce and P. Produce is a recursive process with several parameters. Channels x and y are used to communicate with the consumer and the buffer, respectively. Their capabilities are ρ_x and ρ_y. Finally, i is the value to be sent to the buffer. The process sends a value to the buffer (add(i)), transfers the capability for the shared channel y (turn(ρ_y)) and receives it back from the consumer. Process P is the entry point for the producer. It has the same parameters as Produce, except for i. The only action of P is to send the consumer a shared reference to the channel used for communication with the buffer —x[c]$\oplus$buffer(pack(ρ_y, y[b])).

$$\begin{aligned}
&\mathsf{Produce}\langle \mathtt{x} : \mathtt{tr}(\rho_x), \mathtt{y} : \mathtt{tr}(\rho_y), \mathsf{i} : \mathtt{Int}, \rho_x : \{\rho_x \mapsto S_p'\}, \rho_y : \{\rho_y \mapsto S_q\}\rangle = \mathtt{y}[\mathsf{b}]\oplus\mathsf{add}(\mathsf{i}).\\
&\quad \mathtt{x}[\mathsf{c}]\oplus\mathsf{turn}(\rho_y).\ \mathtt{x}[\mathsf{c}]\&\mathsf{turn}(\rho_y).\ \mathsf{Produce}\langle \mathtt{x}, \mathtt{y}, \mathsf{i}{+}1, \rho_x, \rho_y\rangle; \{\rho_x \mapsto S_p'\} \otimes \{\rho_y \mapsto S_q\}\\
&\mathsf{P}\langle \mathtt{x} : \mathtt{tr}(\rho_x), \mathtt{y} : \mathtt{tr}(\rho_y), \rho_x : \{\rho_x \mapsto S_p\}, \rho_y : \{\rho_y \mapsto S_q\}\rangle =\\
&\quad \mathtt{x}[\mathsf{c}]\oplus\mathsf{buffer}(\mathsf{pack}(\rho_y, \mathtt{y}[\mathsf{b}])).\ \mathsf{Produce}\langle \mathtt{x}, \mathtt{y}, 0, \rho_x, \rho_y\rangle; \{\rho_x \mapsto S_p\} \otimes \{\rho_y \mapsto S_q\}
\end{aligned}$$

In a similar way, the consumer is represented by Consume and C. The parameters, however, are different. C has x and its capability ρ_x, for communication with the producer, but it does not have y or ρ_y for communication with the buffer. It receives y from the producer, as part of pack(ρ_y, y[b]), and y is passed as a parameter to Consume. The capability ρ_y is not a parameter of Consume, but it is received in a turn message from the producer.

$$\begin{aligned}
&\mathsf{Consume}\langle \mathtt{x} : \mathtt{tr}(\rho_x), \mathtt{y} : \mathtt{tr}(\rho_y), \rho_x : \{\rho_x \mapsto S_c'\}\rangle = \mathtt{x}[\mathsf{p}]\&\mathsf{turn}(\rho_y).\ \mathtt{y}[\mathsf{b}]\oplus\mathsf{request}(r).\\
&\qquad\qquad \mathtt{y}[\mathsf{b}]\&\mathsf{send}(\mathsf{i}).\ \mathtt{x}[\mathsf{p}]\oplus\mathsf{turn}(\rho_y).\ \mathsf{Consume}\langle \mathtt{x}, \mathtt{y}, \rho_x\rangle; \{\rho_x \mapsto S_c'\}\\
&\mathsf{C}\langle \mathtt{x} : \mathtt{tr}(\rho_x), \rho_x : \{\rho_x \mapsto S_c\}\rangle =\\
&\qquad\qquad \mathtt{x}[\mathsf{p}]\&\mathsf{buffer}(\mathsf{pack}(\rho_y, \mathtt{y}[\mathsf{b}])).\ \mathsf{Consume}\langle \mathtt{x}, \mathtt{y}, \rho_x\rangle; \{\rho_x \mapsto S_c\}
\end{aligned}$$

The complete system consists of the producer, the consumer and the buffer in parallel, with sessions s_1 (roles p and c) and s_2 (roles q and b) scoped to construct a closed process.

$$(\nu\, s_1)((\nu\, s_2)(\mathsf{P}\langle \mathtt{s_1}[\mathsf{p}], \mathtt{s_2}[\mathsf{q}], \rho_p, \rho_q\rangle \mid \mathsf{B}\langle \mathtt{s_2}[\mathsf{b}], \rho_b\rangle) \mid \mathsf{C}\langle \mathtt{s_1}[\mathsf{c}], \rho_c\rangle$$

The session types involved in these processes are projections of the global type G (Sect. 3). They specify how each role is expected to use its channel endpoint. The roles are b for the buffer, q for the combined role of the producer and the consumer as they interact with the buffer, p for the producer, and c for the consumer.

$$\dfrac{\dfrac{\dfrac{\Gamma \vdash \mathtt{x} : \mathtt{tr}(\rho_\mathtt{x}), \mathtt{y} : \mathtt{tr}(\rho_\mathtt{y}), \mathtt{i} : \mathtt{Int}, \rho_\mathtt{x} : \{\rho_\mathtt{x} \mapsto S'_\mathtt{p}\}, \rho_\mathtt{y} : \{\rho_\mathtt{y} \mapsto S_\mathtt{q}\}; \{\rho_\mathtt{x} \mapsto S'_\mathtt{p}, \rho_\mathtt{y} \mapsto S_\mathtt{q}\}}{\Delta; \Gamma \vdash \mathsf{Produce}\langle x, y, \mathsf{i}{+}1, \rho_\mathtt{x}, \rho_\mathtt{y}\rangle; \{\rho_\mathtt{x} \mapsto S'_\mathtt{p}, \rho_\mathtt{y} \mapsto S_\mathtt{q}\}}\,\textsc{TCall}}{\Delta; \Gamma \vdash \mathsf{x[c]}\&\{\mathsf{turn}(\rho_\mathtt{y}).\mathsf{Produce}\langle x, y, \mathsf{i}{+}1, \rho_\mathtt{x}, \rho_\mathtt{y}\rangle\}; \{\rho_\mathtt{x} \mapsto \mathsf{c}\&?\mathsf{turn}(\{\rho_\mathtt{q} \mapsto S_\mathtt{q}\}).S'_\mathtt{p}\}}\,\textsc{TBr} \quad \vdots \quad \dfrac{}{\Gamma \vdash \rho_\mathtt{q} : \{\rho_\mathtt{q} \mapsto S'_\mathtt{q}\}; \{\rho_\mathtt{q} \mapsto S'_\mathtt{q}\}}\,\textsc{TCap} \quad \mathtt{x} : \mathtt{tr}(\rho_\mathtt{x}), \rho_\mathtt{x} : \{\rho_\mathtt{x} \mapsto \mathsf{c}\&?\mathsf{turn}(\{\rho_\mathtt{q} \mapsto S_\mathtt{q}\}).S'_\mathtt{p}\} \in \Gamma}{\Delta; \Gamma \vdash \mathsf{x[c]}\oplus\langle \mathsf{turn}(\rho_\mathtt{q})\rangle.\mathsf{x[c]}\&\{\mathsf{turn}(\rho_\mathtt{y}).\mathsf{Produce}\langle x, y, \mathsf{i}{+}1, \rho_\mathtt{x}, \rho_\mathtt{y}\rangle\}; \{\rho_\mathtt{x} \mapsto S'_\mathtt{p}, \rho_\mathtt{y} \mapsto S'_\mathtt{q}\}}\,\textsc{TSel}$$

$$\dfrac{\vdots \quad \dfrac{\mathsf{i} \in \mathtt{Int}}{\Gamma \vdash \mathsf{i} : \mathtt{Int}; \emptyset}\,\textsc{TVal} \quad \mathtt{y} : \mathtt{tr}(\rho_\mathtt{y}), \rho_\mathtt{y} : \{\rho_\mathtt{y} \mapsto S'_\mathtt{q}\} \in \Gamma}{\Delta; \Gamma \vdash \mathsf{y[b]}\oplus\langle \mathsf{add(i)}\rangle.\mathsf{x[c]}\oplus\langle \mathsf{turn}(\rho_\mathtt{q})\rangle.\mathsf{x[c]}\&\{\mathsf{turn}(\rho_\mathtt{q}).\mathsf{Produce}\langle \mathsf{x}, \mathsf{y}, \mathsf{i}{+}1, \rho_\mathtt{x}, \rho_\mathtt{y}\rangle\}; \{\rho_\mathtt{x} \mapsto S'_\mathtt{p}, \rho_\mathtt{y} \mapsto S_\mathtt{q}\}}\,\textsc{TSel}$$

Fig. 9. Typing derivation for Produce.

$$\dfrac{\dfrac{\Gamma \vdash \mathtt{x} : \mathtt{tr}(\rho_\mathtt{x}), \mathtt{y} : \mathtt{tr}(\rho_\mathtt{y}), \rho_\mathtt{x} : \{\rho_\mathtt{x} \mapsto S'_\mathtt{p}\}, \rho_\mathtt{y} : \{\rho_\mathtt{y} \mapsto S_\mathtt{q}\}; \{\rho_\mathtt{x} \mapsto S'_\mathtt{p}, \rho_\mathtt{y} \mapsto S_\mathtt{q}\}}{\Delta; \Gamma \vdash \mathsf{Produce}\langle x, y, \mathsf{i}, \rho_\mathtt{p}, \rho_\mathtt{q}\rangle; \{\rho_\mathtt{x} \mapsto S'_\mathtt{p}, \rho_\mathtt{y} \mapsto S_\mathtt{q}\}}\,\textsc{TCall} \quad \vdots \quad \dfrac{\mathtt{y} : \mathtt{tr}(\rho_\mathtt{y}), \rho_\mathtt{y} : \{\rho_\mathtt{y} \mapsto S_\mathtt{q}\}}{\Gamma \vdash \mathtt{y} : \mathtt{tr}(\rho_\mathtt{y}); \emptyset}\,\textsc{TVar} \quad \mathtt{x}, \rho_\mathtt{x} : \{\rho_\mathtt{x} \mapsto S_\mathtt{p}\} \in \Gamma}{\Delta; \Gamma \vdash \mathsf{x[c]}\oplus\langle \mathsf{buffer}(\mathsf{pack}(\rho_\mathtt{q}, \mathsf{y[b]}))\rangle.\mathsf{Produce}\langle \mathsf{x}, \mathsf{y}, \mathsf{i}, \rho_\mathtt{x}, \rho_\mathtt{y}\rangle; \{\rho_\mathtt{y} \mapsto \mathsf{p}\oplus!l(\exists[\rho_\mathtt{y}|\{\rho_\mathtt{y} \mapsto S_\mathtt{q}\}].\mathtt{tr}(\rho_\mathtt{y})).S'_\mathtt{p}, \rho_\mathtt{y} \mapsto S_\mathtt{q}\}}\,\textsc{TSelP}$$

Fig. 10. Typing derivation for P.

$$\begin{aligned}
S_\mathtt{b} &= G \restriction \mathtt{b} = \mu\,\mathbf{t}.\mathsf{q}\&?\mathsf{add}(\mathtt{Int}).\mathsf{q}\&?\mathsf{request}(\mathtt{Str}).\mathsf{q}\oplus!\mathsf{send}(\mathtt{Int}).t\\
S_\mathtt{q} &= G \restriction \mathtt{q} = \mu\,\mathbf{t}.\mathsf{b}\oplus!\mathsf{add}(\mathtt{Int}).\mathsf{b}\oplus!\mathsf{request}(\mathtt{Str}).\mathsf{b}\&?\mathsf{send}(\mathtt{Int}).t\\
S_\mathtt{p} &= G \restriction \mathtt{p} = \mathsf{c}\oplus!\mathsf{buffer}(\exists[\rho_\mathtt{q}|\{\rho_\mathtt{q} \mapsto S'_\mathtt{q}\}].\mathtt{tr}(\rho_\mathtt{q})).\mu\,\mathbf{t}.\\
&\qquad\qquad \mathsf{c}\oplus!\mathsf{turn}(\{\rho_\mathtt{q} \mapsto S'_\mathtt{q}\}).\mathsf{c}\&?\mathsf{turn}(\{\rho_\mathtt{q} \mapsto S_\mathtt{q}\}).t\\
S_\mathtt{c} &= G \restriction \mathtt{c} = \mathsf{p}\&?\mathsf{buffer}(\exists[\rho_\mathtt{q}|\{\rho_\mathtt{q} \mapsto S'_\mathtt{q}\}].\mathtt{tr}(\rho_\mathtt{q})).\mu\,\mathbf{t}.\\
&\qquad\qquad \mathsf{p}\&?\mathsf{turn}(\{\rho_\mathtt{q} \mapsto S'_\mathtt{q}\}).\mathsf{p}\oplus!\mathsf{turn}(\{\rho_\mathtt{q} \mapsto S_\mathtt{q}\}).t
\end{aligned}$$

These types occur in the capabilities associated with each process. For example process $\mathsf{P}\langle \mathtt{s}_1[\mathsf{p}], \mathtt{s}_2[\mathsf{q}], \rho_\mathtt{p}, \rho_\mathtt{q}\rangle$ has $\{\rho_\mathtt{q} \mapsto S_\mathtt{q}\} \otimes \{\rho_\mathtt{p} \mapsto S_\mathtt{p}\}$, process $\mathsf{B}\langle \mathtt{s}_2[\mathsf{b}], \rho_\mathtt{b}\rangle$ has $\{\rho_\mathtt{b} \mapsto S_\mathtt{b}\}$, and process $\mathsf{C}\langle \mathtt{s}_1[\mathsf{c}], \rho_\mathtt{c}\rangle$ has $\{\rho_\mathtt{c} \mapsto S_\mathtt{c}\}$.

To illustrate the typing rules, we show the typing derivation for the producer, i.e. processes Produce (Fig. 9) and P (Fig. 10). Full derivations for all of the processes are in the technical report. The derivations use the following definitions.

$$\begin{aligned}
S'_\mathtt{p} &= \mu\,\mathbf{t}.\mathsf{c}\oplus!\mathsf{turn}(\{\rho_\mathtt{q} \mapsto S'_\mathtt{q}\}).\mathsf{c}\&?\mathsf{turn}(\{\rho_\mathtt{q} \mapsto S_\mathtt{q}\}).t\\
S'_\mathtt{q} &= \mathsf{b}\oplus!\mathsf{request}(\mathtt{Str}).\mathsf{b}\&?\mathsf{send}(\mathtt{Int}).S_\mathtt{q}\\
\Delta &= \mathsf{Produce} : (\mathtt{tr}(\rho_\mathtt{p}), \mathtt{tr}(\rho_\mathtt{q}), \mathtt{Int}, \{\rho_\mathtt{p} \mapsto S_\mathtt{p}\}, \{\rho_\mathtt{q} \mapsto S_\mathtt{q}\})\\
\Gamma &= \mathtt{x} : \mathtt{tr}(\rho_\mathtt{p}), \mathtt{y} : \mathtt{tr}(\rho_\mathtt{q}), \mathsf{i} : \mathtt{Int}, \rho_\mathtt{p} : \{\rho_\mathtt{p} \mapsto S_\mathtt{p}\}, \rho_\mathtt{q} : \{\rho_\mathtt{q} \mapsto S_\mathtt{q}\}
\end{aligned}$$

Scenarios with multiple producers/consumers can be represented in a similar way, the capabilities acting as a form of lock for the resource being shared. The full typing derivation for producer consumer case study can be found in the extended version of this paper [33].

5 Technical Results

Following standard practice in the MPST literature, we show type safety and hence communication safety by proving a subject reduction theorem (Theorem 1). In the usual way, session types evolve during reduction—in our system, this is seen in both the Γ environment and the capability set C.

Definition 10 (Typing context reduction). *The* reduction $(\Gamma; C) \longrightarrow (\Gamma'; C')$ *is:*

$$(\mathtt{s[p]}:\mathtt{tr}(\rho_\mathtt{p}),\ \mathtt{s[q]}:\mathtt{tr}(\rho_\mathtt{q}), \rho_\mathtt{p}:\{\rho_\mathtt{p}\mapsto S_\mathtt{p}\}, \rho_\mathtt{q}:\{\rho_\mathtt{q}\mapsto S_\mathtt{q}\}; \{\rho_\mathtt{p}\mapsto S_\mathtt{p}, \rho_\mathtt{q}\mapsto S_\mathtt{q}\}) \longrightarrow$$
$$(\mathtt{s[p]}:\mathtt{tr}(\rho_\mathtt{p}),\ \mathtt{s[q]}:\mathtt{tr}(\rho_\mathtt{q}), \rho_\mathtt{p}:\{\rho_\mathtt{p}\mapsto S_k\}, \rho_\mathtt{q}:\{\rho_\mathtt{q}\mapsto S'_k\}; \{\rho_\mathtt{p}\mapsto S_k, \rho_\mathtt{q}\mapsto S'_k\})$$
$$\text{if}\begin{cases}\mathtt{unf}(S_\mathtt{p}) = \mathtt{q}\oplus_{i\in I}!l_i(U_i).S_i & k\in I\\ \mathtt{unf}(S_\mathtt{q}) = \mathtt{p}\,\&_{i\in I\cup J}\,?l_i(U'_i).S'_i & U_k \leqslant_\mathsf{S} U'_k\end{cases}$$
$$\text{or if}\begin{cases}\mathtt{unf}(S_\mathtt{p}) = \mathtt{q}\oplus_{i\in I}!l_i(\exists[\rho_i|\{\rho_i\mapsto U_i\}].\mathtt{tr}(\rho_i)).S_i & k\in I\\ \mathtt{unf}(S_\mathtt{q}) = \mathtt{p}\,\&_{i\in I\cup J}\,?l_i(\exists[\rho_i|\{\rho_i\mapsto U'_i\}].\mathtt{tr}(\rho_i)).S'_i & U_k \leqslant_\mathsf{S} U'_k\end{cases}$$

$$(\Gamma, \mathtt{c}:\mathtt{tr}(\rho), \rho:\{\rho\mapsto U\}; C\otimes\{\rho\mapsto U\}) \longrightarrow (\Gamma', \mathtt{c}:\mathtt{tr}(\rho), \rho:\{\rho\mapsto U'\}; C'\otimes\{\rho\mapsto U'\})$$
$$\text{if } (\Gamma; C) \longrightarrow (\Gamma'; C') \text{ and } U \leqslant_\mathsf{S} U'$$

Following [28] our Definition 10 also accommodates subtyping ($\leqslant_\mathsf{S}$) and our iso-recursive type equivalence (hence, unfolds types explicitly).

Theorem 1 (Subject reduction). *If* $\Delta; \Gamma \vdash P; C$ *and* $P \longrightarrow P'$*, then there exist* Γ' *and* C' *such that* $\Delta; \Gamma' \vdash P'; C'$ *and* $(\Gamma; C) \longrightarrow^* (\Gamma'; C')$.

The proof is by induction on the derivation of $P \longrightarrow P'$, with an analysis of the derivation of $\Delta; \Gamma \vdash P; C$. A key case is RRes, which requires preservation of the condition in TRes that (Γ, C) is consistent. This is because a communication reduction consumes matching prefixes from a pair of dual partial session types, which therefore remain dual. The full proof is in the extended version of this paper [33].

6 Related Work, Conclusion and Future Work

From the beginning of session types, channel endpoints were treated as linear resources so that each role in a protocol could be implemented by a unique agent. This approach is reinforced by several connections between session types and other linear type theories: the encodings of binary session types and multiparty session types into linear π-calculus types [12,28]; the Curry-Howard correspondence between binary session types and linear logic [6,34]; the connection between multiparty session types and linear logic [7,8].

Some session type systems generalise linearity. Vasconcelos [32] allows a session type to become non-linear, and sharable, when it reaches a state that is invariant with every subsequent message. Mostrous and Vasconcelos [24] define *affine* session types, in which each endpoint must be used at most once and can be discarded with an explicit operator. In Fowler *et al.*'s [15] implementation of session types for the Links web programming language, affine typing allows sessions to be cancelled when exceptions (including dropped connections) occur. Caires and Pérez [5] use monadic types to describe cancellation (i.e. affine sessions) and non-determinism. Pruiksma and Pfenning [27] use adjoint logic to describe session cancellation and other behaviours including multicast and replication.

Usually linearity spreads, because a data structure containing linear values must also be linear. In the standard π-calculus, exceptions to this nature of linearity have been studied by Kobayashi in his work on deadlock-freedom Padovani [25] extends the linear π-calculus with composite regular types in such a way that data containing linear values can be shared among several processes. However, this sharing can occur only if there is no overlapping access to such values, which differs from our work where we have full sharing of values. On the other hand, we work directly with (multiparty) session types, whereas Padovani works with linear π-calculus and obtains his results via the encoding of session types into linear π-types [12].

Session types are related to the concept of *typestate* [29], especially in the work of Kouzapas *et al.* [21,22] which defines a typestate system for Java based on multiparty session types. Typestate systems require linear typing or some other form of alias control, to avoid conflicting state changes via multiple references. Approaches include the permission-based systems used in the Plural and Plaid languages [4,30] and the fine-grained approach of Militão *et al.* [23]. Crafa and Padovani [10] develop a "chemical" approach to concurrent typestate oriented programming, allowing objects to be accessed and modified concurrently by several processes, each potentially changing only part of their state. Our approach is partly inspired by Fähndrich and DeLine's "adoption and focus" system [14], in which a shared stateful resource (in our case, a session channel) is separated from the linear key (capability, in our system) that enables it to be used. In this way the state changes of channels follow the standard session operations, channels can be shared (for example, stored in shared data structures), and access can be controlled by passing the capability around the system.

Balzer *et al.* [2,3] support sharing of binary session channels by allowing locks to be acquired and released at points that are explicitly specified in the session type. Our approach with multiparty sessions is not based on locks, so it doesn't require runtime mechanisms for managing blocked processes and notifying them when locks are released.

We have presented a new system of multiparty session types with capabilities, which allows sharing of resources in a way that generalises the strictly linear or affine access control typical of session type systems. The key technical idea is to separate a channel from the capability of using the channel. This allows channels to be shared, while capabilities are linearly controlled. We use a form of existential typing to maintain the link between a channel and its capability, while both are transmitted in messages. We have proved communication safety, formulated as a subject reduction theorem (Theorem 1). An area of future work is to prove progress and deadlock-freedom properties along the lines of, for example, Coppo *et al.* [9]. Another possibility is to apply our techniques to functional languages with session types [17].

References

1. Ancona, D., et al.: Behavioral types in programming languages. Found. Trends Program. Lang. **3**(2–3), 95–230 (2016). https://doi.org/10.1561/2500000031
2. Balzer, S., Pfenning, F.: Manifest sharing with session types. PACMPL **1**(ICFP), 37:1–37:29 (2017). https://doi.org/10.1145/3110281
3. Balzer, S., Toninho, B., Pfenning, F.: Manifest deadlock-freedom for shared session types. In: Caires, L. (ed.) ESOP 2019. LNCS, vol. 11423, pp. 611–639. Springer, Cham (2019). https://doi.org/10.1007/978-3-030-17184-1_22
4. Bierhoff, K., Aldrich, J.: PLURAL: checking protocol compliance under aliasing. In: ICSE Companion, pp. 971–972. ACM Press (2008). https://doi.org/10.1145/1370175.1370213
5. Caires, L., Pérez, J.A.: Linearity, control effects, and behavioral types. In: Yang, H. (ed.) ESOP 2017. LNCS, vol. 10201, pp. 229–259. Springer, Heidelberg (2017). https://doi.org/10.1007/978-3-662-54434-1_9
6. Caires, L., Pfenning, F.: Session types as intuitionistic linear propositions. In: Gastin, P., Laroussinie, F. (eds.) CONCUR 2010. LNCS, vol. 6269, pp. 222–236. Springer, Heidelberg (2010). https://doi.org/10.1007/978-3-642-15375-4_16
7. Carbone, M., Lindley, S., Montesi, F., Schürmann, C., Wadler, P.: Coherence generalises duality: a logical explanation of multiparty session types. In: CONCUR. LIPIcs, vol. 59, pp. 33:1–33:15. Schloss Dagstuhl – Leibniz-Zentrum für Informatik (2016). https://doi.org/10.4230/LIPIcs.CONCUR.2016.33
8. Carbone, M., Montesi, F., Schürmann, C., Yoshida, N.: Multiparty session types as coherence proofs. In: CONCUR. LIPIcs, vol. 42. Schloss Dagstuhl – Leibniz-Zentrum für Informatik (2015). https://doi.org/10.4230/LIPIcs.CONCUR.2015.412
9. Coppo, M., Dezani-Ciancaglini, M., Yoshida, N., Padovani, L.: Global progress for dynamically interleaved multiparty sessions. Math. Struct. Comput. Sci. **26**(2), 238–302 (2016). https://doi.org/10.1017/S0960129514000188
10. Crafa, S., Padovani, L.: The chemical approach to typestate-oriented programming. ACM Trans. Program. Lang. Syst. **39**(3), 13:1–13:45 (2017). https://doi.org/10.1145/3064849
11. Crary, K., Walker, D., Morrisett, G.: Typed memory management in a calculus of capabilities. In: POPL, pp. 262–275. ACM (1999). https://doi.org/10.1145/292540.292564
12. Dardha, O., Giachino, E., Sangiorgi, D.: Session types revisited. In: PPDP. ACM (2012). https://doi.org/10.1145/2370776.2370794
13. Deniélou, P., Yoshida, N., Bejleri, A., Hu, R.: Parameterised multiparty session types. Log. Methods Comput. Sci. **8**(4) (2012). https://doi.org/10.2168/LMCS-8(4:6)2012
14. Fähndrich, M., DeLine, R.: Adoption and focus: practical linear types for imperative programming. In: PLDI, pp. 13–24. ACM (2002). https://doi.org/10.1145/512529.512532

15. Fowler, S., Lindley, S., Morris, J.G., Decova, S.: Exceptional asynchronous session types: session types without tiers. PACMPL **3**(POPL), 28:1–28:29 (2019). https://doi.org/10.1145/3290341
16. Gay, S.J., Ravara, A. (eds.): Behavioural Types: From Theory to Tools. River Publishers, Gistrup (2017). https://doi.org/10.13052/rp-9788793519817
17. Gay, S.J., Vasconcelos, V.T.: Linear type theory for asynchronous session types. J. Funct. Program. **20**(1), 19–50 (2010). https://doi.org/10.1017/S0956796809990268
18. Honda, K., Yoshida, N., Carbone, M.: Multiparty asynchronous session types. In: POPL, pp. 273–284. ACM Press (2008). https://doi.org/10.1145/1328438.1328472
19. Honda, K., Vasconcelos, V.T., Kubo, M.: Language primitives and type discipline for structured communication-based programming. In: Hankin, C. (ed.) ESOP 1998. LNCS, vol. 1381, pp. 122–138. Springer, Heidelberg (1998). https://doi.org/10.1007/BFb0053567
20. Hüttel, H., et al.: Foundations of session types and behavioural contracts. ACM Comput. Surv. **49**(1), 3 (2016). https://doi.org/10.1145/2873052
21. Kouzapas, D., Dardha, O., Perera, R., Gay, S.J.: Typechecking protocols with Mungo and StMungo. In: PPDP, pp. 146–159. ACM (2016). https://doi.org/10.1145/2967973.2968595
22. Kouzapas, D., Dardha, O., Perera, R., Gay, S.J.: Typechecking protocols with Mungo and StMungo: a session type toolchain for Java. Sci. Comput. Program. **155**, 52–75 (2018). https://doi.org/10.1016/j.scico.2017.10.006
23. Militão, F., Aldrich, J., Caires, L.: Aliasing control with view-based typestate. In: FTFJP, pp. 7:1–7:7. ACM (2010). https://doi.org/10.1145/1924520.1924527
24. Mostrous, D., Vasconcelos, V.T.: Affine sessions. Logical Methods Comput. Sci. **14**(4) (2018). https://doi.org/10.23638/LMCS-14(4:14)2018
25. Padovani, L.: Type reconstruction for the linear π-calculus with composite regular types. Logical Methods Comput. Sci. **11**(4) (2015). https://doi.org/10.2168/LMCS-11(4:13)2015
26. Pierce, B.C.: Types and Programming Languages. MIT Press, Cambridge (2002)
27. Pruiksma, K., Pfenning, F.: A message-passing interpretation of adjoint logic. In: PLACES. Electronic Proceedings in Theoretical Computer Science, vol. 291, pp. 60–79. Open Publishing Association (2019). https://doi.org/10.4204/EPTCS.291.6
28. Scalas, A., Dardha, O., Hu, R., Yoshida, N.: A linear decomposition of multiparty sessions for safe distributed programming. In: ECOOP. LIPIcs, vol. 74, pp. 24:1–24:31. Schloss Dagstuhl – Leibniz-Zentrum für Informatik (2017). https://doi.org/10.4230/LIPIcs.ECOOP.2017.24
29. Strom, R.E., Yemini, S.: Typestate: a programming language concept for enhancing software reliability. IEEE Trans. Softw. Eng. **12**(1), 157–171 (1986). https://doi.org/10.1109/TSE.1986.6312929
30. Sunshine, J., Naden, K., Stork, S., Aldrich, J., Tanter, É.: First-class state change in Plaid. In: OOPSLA, pp. 713–732. ACM (2011). https://doi.org/10.1145/2048066.2048122
31. Takeuchi, K., Honda, K., Kubo, M.: An interaction-based language and its typing system. In: Halatsis, C., Maritsas, D., Philokyprou, G., Theodoridis, S. (eds.) PARLE 1994. LNCS, vol. 817, pp. 398–413. Springer, Heidelberg (1994). https://doi.org/10.1007/3-540-58184-7_118
32. Vasconcelos, V.T.: Fundamentals of session types. Inf. Comput. **217**, 52–70 (2012). https://doi.org/10.1016/j.ic.2012.05.002

33. Voinea, A.L., Dardha, O., Gay, S.J.: Resource sharing via capability-based multiparty session types. Technical report, School of Computing Science, University of Glasgow (2019). http://www.dcs.gla.ac.uk/~ornela/publications/VDG19-Extended.pdf
34. Wadler, P.: Propositions as sessions. In: ICFP, pp. 273–286. ACM (2012). https://doi.org/10.1145/2364527.2364568
35. Walker, D., Morrisett, G.: Alias types for recursive data structures. In: Harper, R. (ed.) TIC 2000. LNCS, vol. 2071, pp. 177–206. Springer, Heidelberg (2001). https://doi.org/10.1007/3-540-45332-6_7
36. Yoshida, N., Deniélou, P.-M., Bejleri, A., Hu, R.: Parameterised multiparty session types. In: Ong, L. (ed.) FoSSaCS 2010. LNCS, vol. 6014, pp. 128–145. Springer, Heidelberg (2010). https://doi.org/10.1007/978-3-642-12032-9_10

A Multi-target Code Generator for High-Level B

Fabian Vu(✉), Dominik Hansen(✉), Philipp Körner(✉), and Michael Leuschel(✉)

Institut für Informatik, Universität Düsseldorf,
Universitätsstr. 1, 40225 Düsseldorf, Germany
{fabian.vu,dominik.hansen,p.koerner,leuschel}@uni-duesseldorf.de

Abstract. Within high-level specification languages such as B, code is refined in many steps until a small "implementable" subset of the language is reached. Then, code generators are used, targeting programming languages such as C or Ada.

We aim to diminish the number of refinement steps needed, by providing an improved code generator. Indeed, many high-level operations and data types, such as sets, can be dealt with in programming languages such as Java and C++. We present a code generator for B named B2Program with two distinct features. Firstly, it targets multiple (high-level) languages via a template-based approach to compilation. In addition to flexibility, this also enables one to safeguard against errors in the individual compilers and standard libraries, by generating multiple implementations of the same formal model. Secondly, it supports higher-level constructs compared to existing code generators. This enables new uses of formal models, as prototypes, demonstrators or simply as very high-level programming languages, by directly embedding formal models as components into software systems. In the article, we discuss the implementation of our code generator, evaluate it using B models taken from literature and compare its performance with simulation in ProB.

1 Introduction and Motivation

Models written in formal specification languages, such as B, can be verified via proof obligation generation and proving (e.g. by using AtelierB [9]) and animation and model checking (e.g. by using ProB [25]). Once a B model is verified, it is often desirable to derive executable code from the model. This might be a standalone binary or code that can be used as a library. Re-implementing the code by hand, however, is cumbersome and might introduce new errors. Instead, for safety-critical applications, code generators are typically applied.

Yet, existing code generators do not work on just any B model but only support a very limited subset of B, often referred to as "B0" [9] or *implementation language*. Refining the model to B0 often requires many refinement steps and, again, is very cumbersome. We can make two observations: firstly, translation of higher-level constructs, e.g. sets, to modern languages is straightforward. This

W. Ahrendt and S. L. Tapia Tarifa (Eds.): IFM 2019, LNCS 11918, pp. 456–473, 2019.
https://doi.org/10.1007/978-3-030-34968-4_25

```
MACHINE Lift
VARIABLES  floor
INVARIANT  floor : 0..100
INITIALISATION floor := 0
OPERATIONS
    inc = PRE floor<100 THEN floor := floor + 1 END;
    dec = PRE floor>0 THEN floor := floor - 1 END
END
```

Listing 1. Example of a State Machine of a Lift Controller in B

allows translation of a larger subset than B0 and reduction of effort due to refinement of the model. Secondly, *flexible output* is desirable: while software can run as low-level program on some embedded systems, there are safety-critical components implemented in different languages, e.g. web applications written in Java or software written in C++.

In this paper, we present B2PROGRAM[1], which is a code generator that, technically, works on any abstraction level and is able to target multiple high-level programming languages using a template-based approach. Following this approach, B2PROGRAM supports higher-level B constructs than other code generators. None of the examples used in Table 2 are in the B0 language, but code can be generated from these models by B2PROGRAM without any refinement steps. Most other code generators would require refining these models to B0 before code generation can be applied.

In the following, we briefly introduce the B method and B language as well as PROB, which is a tool that we build upon. We explain best practices from compiler engineering that are foundations for our own code generator and discuss concerns regarding correctness in Sect. 2. Afterwards, in Sect. 3, our template-based approach to code generation is described in detail. In Sect. 4, the performance of the generated code is compared to PROB and trade-offs in our standard libraries are analysed. Finally, we compare our approach with existing work in Sect. 5.

The B-Method, B and PROB. The B-Method [1] is a method that is mainly used for specification and verification of software systems. The B method enforces a "correct-by-construction" approach. Many safety-critical system applications, e.g. the *Paris Métro Line 14* [10], the New York Canarsie Line [12] and around 95 installations of Alstom's U400 CBTC system contain code generated from verified B models. In some more recent applications such as the *ETCS Hybrid Level 3 Concept* [16] formal B models have been executed at runtime.

Part of the B-Method is the B specification language which is based on set theory and first-order logic. A component in the B language is called a machine, which contains declaration of constants, variables and sets along with initialisation and operations to modify the machine's state. Furthermore, there are constructs relevant for verification, such as preconditions or invariants, i.e. a predicate that must be true in each reachable state. Listing 1 shows a simple

[1] Available at: https://github.com/favu100/b2program.

specification of a lift in B containing substitutions (aka statements), expressions, preconditions and an invariant.

ProB [25] is an animator, constraint solver and model checker for B models. It allows automatic animation along with model checking using different techniques [21,29]. In particular, ProB supports checking invariants and absence of deadlocks, but also custom assertions and LTL formulas.

2 Steps of Code Generation

A compiler is typically separated into two parts [2]: the front-end performing an *analysis*, and the back-end performing code *synthesis*. Within the context of formal methods, the model must be verified before it is passed to the code generator. An overview is given in Fig. 1. In the following, these three phases are described in more detail.

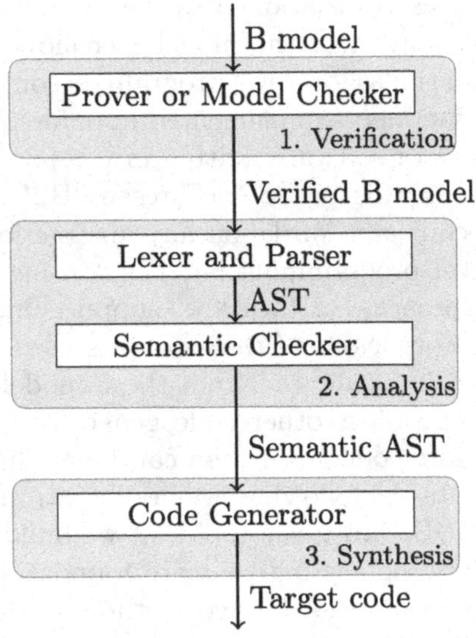

Fig. 1. B model to generated code

Verification of the B Model. Verification can be done either by proving generated POs [9] or by model checking [5]. This is of utmost importance, as generating code from an incorrect model may eventually lead to undesired or incorrect behaviour. Furthermore, well-definedness, as well as the absence of infinite loops and integer overflows has to be checked. This can be done with tools such as ProB or AtelierB.
Note that our code generator currently does not check that verification has been successfully carried out. This phase is currently merely an item on the checklist of a user's workflow.

Analysis Phase. The next step assumes that the given B model already is verified. First, the B model is passed to the lexer, which divides the B code into tokens defined for B, with categories such as identifiers, separators, operators, keywords, literals etc. After this step, the tokens are passed to the parser, which applies the defined context-free grammar rules to create the abstract-syntax tree (AST) for semantic checks. Semantic analysis consists of scoping and type checking. Scoping ensures that variables and operations were defined before they are used. The type checker assigns a type for all appropriate nodes in the AST. After that, the typed AST is checked for type errors (for more details on best practices of compiler front-end design, see [2]).

Synthesis Phase. During the synthesis phase, the semantic AST of the B model is used to generate code. We decided to use a *template-based approach*, which allows taking advantage of similarities of several programming languages. Compared to an approach with intermediate code generation, this renders it easier to target different languages and aligns with the best software engineering principles, e.g. generic programming [3] and don't repeat yourself [18]. Furthermore, an intermediate code representation does not assist the extensibility of the code generator concerning additional target languages in any way.

Correctness of Code Generation. A big question is: how can one trust the output of the code generator, and the underlying hardware and compiler used to process the code generator's output? While there are some efforts to produce formally verified compilers [24], the industry practice is to use at least two different code generators, developed using different techniques and developed by different teams. The purpose of the second piece of code is to validate the output of the main code generator. The second translation is typically run on a different hardware, safeguarding against faults in the hardware as well. If the output of the two translations differ, the system has to go into fail-safe, degraded mode. Our code generator is arguably more complex than the ones derived for B0 [9]. These code generators, however, are also not proven and require to be complemented with a second code generator for high-integrity systems, as described above. Our code generator would hence have to follow this approach when being used for SIL-3 or SIL-4 components.[2] If performance is sufficient, one could investigate using, e.g., ProB as the complementary high-level code generator. One drawback, however, is the dynamic use of heap allocated memory by the respective standard libraries used by our code generator. This will preclude its use in some settings, such as embedded systems, in its current form.

Anyway, the main target of our code generator is not embedded systems, but prototypes, demonstrators, business-critical applications or applications such as data validation. Still, note that our code generator can target different languages. By producing multiple translations for different programming languages, we could safeguard against errors in individual compilers and the respective standard libraries used (but not against errors in the language independent part of our code generator).

3 Code Generation in Practice

In this section, we describe code generation with the use of the semantic B AST generated after the analysis phase and templates written in the language of StringTemplate (https://www.stringtemplate.org).

3.1 Template-Based Code Generation

A *template* is a document with holes, which are filled by a *template engine* using provided parameters. The idea of template-based code generation (cf. Fig. 2) is

[2] SIL stands for Safety Integrity Level. SIL-4 is the highest level of integrity for railway systems. See https://en.wikipedia.org/wiki/Safety_integrity_level.

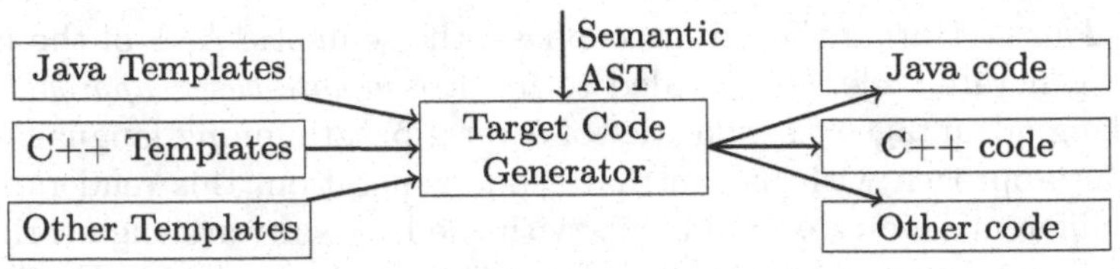

Fig. 2. Template-based code generation

to provide templates for possible operators of the AST. AST nodes are then translated by the template engine to code, by filling out the holes in the associated template; the content of the holes is derived from the concrete attributes and parameters of the AST nodes. A new language can be targeted by providing a new set of templates. Our code generator uses the StringTemplate engine. It was initially applied for generating dynamic web pages [28], but it now complements the ANTLR parser generator and is well-suited for code generation[3]. Parameters of templates in StringTemplate can also be booleans that decide which part of the template is used to generate the resulting code. In StringTemplate all templates for a programming language are stored in a separate file, named group file.

In order to target an additional programming language, the following steps must be followed:

1. Create all templates for the programming language and implement the mapping of semantic AST nodes to the templates. E.g. an operation node is mapped to the operation template with placeholders for the operation name, parameters, return type etc. These placeholders are replaced by strings that are generated from the semantic information of the operation node. So, rendering the operation template with the required placeholders results in the generated code for an operation. Two different AST nodes can also be mapped to the same template e.g. expression nodes and most predicate nodes with binary operators are mapped to the *binary template*. Some templates require information from many AST nodes, as in Sect. 3.2.
   Furthermore, templates in two different programming languages that are associated with the same AST node must have the same name. E.g. an operation node is mapped to a template with the name "operation" in both Java and C++. This is required to keep code generation for both programming languages generic. Thus, there is only one implementation for each AST node in B2Program to generate code for many programming languages.
2. Implement B data types in the target language as described in Sect. 3.4. These types are used by the generated code.
3. Solve the collision problem between keywords and identifiers as described in Sect. 3.6.

[3] https://web.archive.org/web/20170723204548/http://pjmolina.com/metalevel/2010/11/stringtemplate-a-great-template-engine-for-code-generation/.

```
initialisation(machine, properties, values, body) ::= <<
public <machine>() {
    <properties; separator="\n">
    <values>
    <body>
}
>>
```

Listing 2. Template for Generating from the `INITIALISATION`, `PROPERTIES` and `VALUES` Clauses in Java

3.2 Code Generation with StringTemplate and B AST

Based on Listing 2, we explain how Java code is generated from the `INITIALISATION` clause of a B machine. The goal is to generate a valid Java class constructor.

Assume that the `INITIALISATION`, `PROPERTIES` and `VALUES` clauses of a B machine are not implemented in the code generator yet. The template in Listing 2 contains placeholders for the machine name, the body of the `INITIALISATION` clause and the `PROPERTIES` and `VALUES` clause. Until the placeholders are substituted, it only outlines what a Java class constructor may look like.

In addition to the template definition, translation must be implemented for the target language, which is outlined in Listing 3. After the machine name is extracted from the AST and the identifier template is applied, the placeholder *machine* is replaced with the result. The body of the initialisation, which is represented by a *SubstitutionNode* in the AST, is passed to another template that belongs to the *substitution.* Code is generated recursively from this node by generating code from all children of the AST node, each yielding an assignment. It finally results in a string that replaces the placeholder *body*. B2Program has the restriction that the `VALUES` and `PROPERTIES` clauses must assign a value to all constants via "=". The `VALUES` clause is represented by a list of substitutions in the AST. Each of the substitutions are generated like other substitutions. In contrast, the `PROPERTIES` clause contains only a single predicate that must be a conjunction. Then, each conjunct that contains the operator "=" is generated as an assignment.

The final Java constructor code for the B machine in Listing 1 is as follows:

```
public Lift() {
    floor = new BInteger(0);
}
```

The generated code uses the type `BInteger` which has to be implemented as described in Sect. 3.4. Variable declarations are generated beforehand when handling the `VARIABLES` clause of the B machine.

3.3 Extensibility for Other Programming Languages

Adding support for another language, e.g. C++, works similarly to code generation for Java. Some templates in C++ require only a subset of semantic information that is required by the same template in Java. In this case, superfluous

```
private String visitInitialisation(MachineNode node) {
    String machineName = ...
    ST initialisation = group.getInstanceOf("initialisation");
    TemplateHandler.add(initialization, "machine", machineName);
    TemplateHandler.add(initialization, "properties",
        generateConstantsInitializations(node));
    TemplateHandler.add(initialization, "values", generateValues(node));
    if(node.getInitialisation() != null) {
        TemplateHandler.add(initialization, "body",
            machineGenerator.visitSubstitutionNode(...));
    }
    return initialisation.render();
}
```

Listing 3. Implementation within B2Program for the `INITIALISATION`, `PROPERTIES` and `VALUES` Clauses

```
// Java
tuple_create(arg1, arg2) ::= <<
new BTuple\<>(<arg1>, <arg2>)
>>

// C++
tuple_create(leftType, rightType, arg1, arg2) ::= <<
(BTuple\<<leftType>, <rightType> >(<arg1>, <arg2>))
>>
```

Listing 4. Template for Creating a Tuple in Java and C++

information is simply ignored. For some constructs however, additional semantic information may be required to generate C++ code, e.g. type information for the C++ STL. Thus, supporting another programming language requires writing templates for this language and extending the *TemplateHandler* only. So code generation for different programming languages is done by the same *TemplateHandler*, but with different templates. A concrete example are maplets (aka tuples), which are represented by the type `BTuple` in the generated code. `BTuple` is a class containing two generic types (one for the first entry and another for the second). Both templates need placeholders for the actual values. While Java can infer both types from the arguments of the constructor, C++ requires both types written in the code explicitly, as shown in Listing 4.

Listing 5 shows the implementation in B2Program for generating code from a tuple. The highlighted code is added in order to support C++. The additional semantic information does not affect handling the Java template as the function *add* in *TemplateHandler* ensures that there are no additional arguments passed to the Java template. So code generation from a tuple for both languages is done by the same function *generateTuple*. Code generation for the tuple `1|->2` to Java and C++ finally results in:

```
/* Java */ new BTuple<>(new BInteger(1), new BInteger(2))
/* C++  */ (BTuple<BInteger, BInteger>((BInteger(1)), (BInteger(2))))
```

```
private String generateTuple(List<String> args, BType leftType, BType rightType) {
  ST tuple = currentGroup.getInstanceOf("tuple_create");
  TemplateHandler.add(tuple, "leftType", typeGenerator.generate(leftType));
  TemplateHandler.add(tuple, "rightType", typeGenerator.generate(rightType));
  TemplateHandler.add(tuple, "arg1", args.get(0));
  TemplateHandler.add(tuple, "arg2", args.get(1));
  return tuple.render();
}
```

Listing 5. Implementation in B2PROGRAM to Generate Code from a Tuple

```
_ld_x = x;
_ld_y = y;
x = _ld_y;
y = _ld_x;
```

Listing 6. Translation of `x := y || y := x`

3.4 Implementation of B Data Types

The B data types are implemented and provided as a library that is included in the generated code. B2PROGRAM supports the *scalar* types *Integer* and *Boolean* and *compound* types such as *Set*, *Tuple*, *Relation*, *Sequence*, *Struct* and *Record*. Instead of implementing these types ourselves, it would also be possible to use existing equivalent types in the target language (e.g. implementations of `java.util.Set`). But the API of the B types library must contain all operations that can be used in B, e.g. the operation *relational image* in the class `BRelation`. This approach enables the support for high-level data structures, which are not part of B0.

In addition to sequential substitutions, which evaluate statements one after another, B also allows parallel substitutions. The latter is not part of B0 and poses two interesting challenges for code generation. First, it means we need to keep access to the original, unmodified data structures; we cannot modify sets or relations in place. For efficiency, we have used *immutable data structures* (aka persistent data structures, see [20]). Take, for example, the assignment `x := x \/ {max(x)+1}`, where x is a very large set. Using a traditional mutable data structure, we would have to generate a copy of x for read access for other parts of the B operation. With an immutable data structure we can create a new version of x, while keeping the old value of x and while sharing values between the old and new value of x. Second, B variables that are re-used in another expression are assigned to temporary variables first before the actual assignment is executed. [4] An example is the parallel substitution `x := y || y := x`. This statement swaps both values, where a sequential substitution would ensure both `x` and `y` have the same value afterwards. Instead, it is translated to the Java code shown in Listing 6.

[4] Note that assignment does not copy the data structure; it copies just the reference.

Table 1. Supported subset of B types and operators

B type	Class	Supported operators
Integer	BInteger	$x+y$, $x-y$, $x*y$, $x\ mod\ y$, x/y, $-x$, $x<y$, $x\leq y$, $x=y$, $x\neq y$, $x>y$, $x\geq y$, $succ(x)$, $pred(x)$
Boolean	BBoolean	$p\wedge q$, $p\vee q$, $\neg p$, $p\Rightarrow q$, $p\Leftrightarrow q$, $p=q$, $p\neq q$
Set	BSet	$s\cup t$, $\bigcup_{t\in s} t$, $s\cap t$, $\bigcap_{t\in s} t$, $s\setminus t$, $s\times t$, $\lvert s\rvert$, $x\in s$, $x\notin s$, $x..y$, $min(s)$, $max(s)$, $\mathbb{P}(s)$, $\mathbb{P}_1(s)$, $s\subseteq t$, $s\not\subseteq t$, $s\subset t$, $s\not\subset t$, $s=t$, $s\neq t$
Tuple	BTuple	prj_1, prj_2, $s=t$, $s\neq t$
Relation	BRelation	r(s), r[S], $dom(r)$, $ran(r)$, $r^{\sim}$, $S\lhd r$, $S⩤ r$, $r\rhd S$, $r⩥ S$, $r\Leftarrow\!\!\!+\ s$, $r\otimes s$, $r\parallel s$, id, $r\circ s$, $r\,;s$, $r..n$, r^*, r^+, prj_1, prj_2, $fnc(r)$, $rel(r)$, $r=s$, $r\neq s$
Sequence	BRelation	$first(s)$, $last(s)$, $size(s)$, $rev(s)$, $front(s)$, $tail(s)$, $take(s,n)$, $drop(s,n)$, s^t, $conc(S)$, $E\rightarrow s$, $s\leftarrow E$

Scalar Types. Integers have functions for arithmetic operations and comparisons as shown in Table 1. The execution of B2PROGRAM has the option to use *primitive integers*, where the language primitive is used, or *big integers*, which allows arbitrary-sized integer values, for the generated code. Creating `BInteger` as a big integer is done by invoking the constructor with a String. The use of big integers avoids exceptions or unsound behaviour in the presence of under- or overflows, at the cost of performance (memory and speed-wise). If it is proven that in a machine integer overflows cannot occur, primitive integer can be used for better performance. Booleans implement functions for logical operations. All operations on integers and booleans that are part of the B language are supported by B2PROGRAM.

Compound Types. A set in B is represented by a `BSet` in the supported programming languages. The `BSet` class consists of functions for operations on sets (e.g. union, intersection, difference) and an immutable data structure. Thus, applying a binary set operation creates a new `BSet` without changing any of the provided arguments. Deferred sets are also supported by B2PROGRAM. The size of each deferred set is fixed and either defined in the `PROPERTIES` clause or taken from the settings for code generation. This makes it possible to interpret deferred sets as enumerated sets.

A relation in B is represented as `BRelation`. As a relation is a set of tuples in B, all implemented operators for a set are available for relations as well. API functions that are exclusive to relations are implemented in `BRelation`, but not in `BSet`. In earlier implementations, `BRelation` extended `BSet`. But representing `BRelation` as a persistent set of tuples resulted in slow performance of operations on relations. In the current version of B2PROGRAM, `BRelation` is implemented as a persistent map where each element in the domain is mapped to a persistent set containing all belonging mapped elements in the range. This makes it possible to improve the performance of operations on relations significantly.

Functions are special cases of relations where each element in the domain is mapped to at most one element in the range. As long as a function call is well-defined, the associated value of the only matching tuple is returned.

There are two possible errors when applying a function; normally these should be caught during verification (see Sect. 2). Firstly, invoking a function with an argument that is outside of the domain raises an exception at runtime. In contrast, calling a function with a value mapped to more than one element returns the first associated value, without raising an error.

Sequences in B are instances of `BRelation` where the domain is always a contiguous set of integers starting at 1. The implementation of sequence operations assumes that this property is fulfilled. Applying sequence operations on relations that are not sequences should also be caught during verification (see Sect. 2) lest they lead to undefined behaviour at runtime.

Structs and Records are also supported in the generated code. While a struct declares the given fields and field types, a record is an instance of a construct with the given field and the belonging values. In contrast to other compound types, structs are generated at code generation. The generated structs must extend `BStruct` where the needed functions of all structs are implemented. As a struct can have a various number of fields, it would also be possible to implement `BStruct` as a hash map. In this case, each field with its value in a record would be represented as a key-value pair in the hash map. But as the fields can have different types, the implementation would not fulfil type safety. The generated class for a struct contains the belonging fields and functions for accessing or overriding them. The function for overriding is implemented having no side effects on the fields. Instead, a new instance with updated values is returned.

All compound types apart from structs are implemented using generics (aka templates in C++) to specify the type of the elements in `BSet`, `BTuple` and `BRelation`. For example, `BRelation` is a type containing two generic types, one for the type of the elements in the domain and another for the elements in the range. It extends `BSet` where the elements are tuples with the same generic types as the corresponding `BRelation`. Using generics avoids casting and ensures type safety. Table 1 also shows all operations on sets, tuples (i.e., nested pairs), relations and sequences that are supported in B2PROGRAM now. The operations that are not listed in Table 1 are not implemented yet.

3.5 Quantified and Non-deterministic Constructs

Quantified constructs are set comprehensions, lambdas, quantified predicates, quantified expressions as well as `ANY` and "becomes such that" substitutions. They consist of variables constrained by a predicate.

Let $a_1 \dots a_n$ be the bounded variables with $n \in \mathbb{N}$. B2PROGRAM has the restriction that the first n sub-predicates must be joined as a conjunction where the *i-th* conjunct must assign or constrain (e.g. via $\subset$, $\subseteq$, $\in$) the *i-th* bounded variables with $i \in \{1, \dots, n\}$. Moreover, the sets that are used to constrain the bounded variables must be finite in order to avoid infinite loops. Additional conditions are joined to the other n sub-predicates as a conjunction. Furthermore,

```
BSet<BInteger> _ic_set_0 = new BSet<>();
for(BInteger _ic_x :
BSet.interval(new BInteger(0),new BInteger(5))) {
    if((_ic_x.modulo(new BInteger(2)).equal(new BInteger(1))).booleanValue()){
        _ic_set_0 = _ic_set_0.union(new BSet<>(_ic_x));
    }
}
set = _ic_set_0;
```

Listing 7. Generated Java Code for Set Comprehension

the sub-predicates constraining or assigning a variable are only allowed to use other bounded variables if the used bounded variables are constrained or assigned before. These properties provide the opportunity to generate each of the first n predicates as an assignment or a for-loop to iterate over the sets with a conditional check whether the values of the constrained variables satisfy the entire predicate. The restriction is also necessary because otherwise a constraint solver would be needed to solve all quantified constructs in the generated code. E.g. the predicate `x:INTEGER & x > z & x < z*z` can be solved by a constraint solver but is not supported in a quantified construct for this code generator; the type of `x` is infinite and a generated loop would not terminate. We decided against the usage of a constraint solver as it cannot give any performance guarantees.

A fresh variable storing the result of a quantified construct is defined when necessary. Primed variables in "becomes such that" substitutions are generated to temporary variables that are assigned to their belonging variables before constraining the results. Once a solution for the constraint is found, it is assigned or added to the result. The substitution `set := {x|x : 0..5 & x mod 2 = 1}`, for example, results in the Java code shown in Listing 7.

Non-deterministic constructs such as "becomes element of", "becomes such that" and `ANY` substitutions are also implemented in B2Program. "Becomes element of" substitutions generate invocations of a special function `nondeterminism` on the given `BSet` or `BRelation` on the right-hand side. The implementation of `nondeterminism` chooses an element randomly. `ANY` and "becomes such that" substitutions are generated in the same way as quantified constructs with one difference: they are executed with the solution of the predicate that is found first.

3.6 Identifier Clash Problem with Keywords

Different programming languages use different keywords and different regular expressions for identifiers. In particular, some identifiers in B can be keywords in other languages, e.g. `new` in Java. We store the keywords for each target language in a *keywords* template. Identifiers themselves can collide with each other as well, e.g., local variables due to machine inclusion or other local variables and operation names. Thus, some identifiers have to be re-named during code generation, in case scoping rules differ with B.

4 Performance Considerations and Evaluation

In this section, we discuss the performance of the generated code. We target two languages, Java and C++. The actual implementation of the B types, i.e. the representation of integer, boolean and set, has a major impact on performance. This will be discussed in more detail before we compare the results with simulation in ProB.

B Data Type Implementation. There are many subtleties when aiming for a suitable implementation of B Data Types.

Boolean Values are fairly straightforward. They are implemented as classes that wrap a native boolean in both C++ and Java.

Integers can be implemented similarly as long as the absence of over- and underflows is guaranteed. Otherwise, e.g. in C++, this might trigger undefined behaviour. To avoid overflow issues, our code generator also supports arbitrary-sized integer values. In Java, we use the big integer implementation from Clojure [17], as we found operations to be about twice as fast as the one from the Java Class Library. For C++, we use the big integer implementation provided by the GMP library (GNU Multiple Precision Arithmetic Library) [14].

Sets are, as discussed in Sect. 3.4, assumed to be immutable to render a correct translation easier. Java hash sets or sets from the C++ STL, however, are mutable. Initial versions of our code generator used these along with copying upon modification, which did not perform well.[5] Yet, there are immutable set implementations based on Bagwell's Hash Array Mapped Tries [4]. Due to structural sharing, only a small amount of internal nodes has to be copied in order to create a "changed" copy, e.g. where an element is added. Copying six nodes suffices for a perfectly balanced hash trie with 10 billion elements. We have considered several immutable set implementations for Java. By default, we use sets as provided by Clojure, while we use the state-of-the-art library Immer [30] for immutable sets in C++. They are both stable implementations providing very good performance. For both Java and C++, there is the opportunity to change the set implementation at compile-time.

Analogous to the representation of *Sets*, we use persistent hash maps provided by Clojure and the library Immer for *relations*.

Empirical Evaluation. The B data types used in the generated code for the performance analysis are implemented as described above. Generated Java code was executed on the *Java HotSpot(TM) 64-Bit Server VM (build 12.0.1+12, mixed mode, sharing)*. In order to compile C++ code, the *clang compiler (Version: Apple LLVM version 10.0.1 (clang-1001.0.46.4))* was used with the optimisation options `-O1` and `-O2` respectively. As a baseline, we use ProB in the version *1.9.0-nightly (c5a6e9d31022d0bfe40cbcdf68e910041665ec41)*. The complete benchmark code can be found in the B2Program repository.

[5] Several benchmarks ran slower than simulation with ProB.

These benchmarks range from simple machines such as Lift and TrafficLight to complex machines with large state spaces such as CAN bus, Train or Cruise Controller. While Lift and TrafficLight contain arithmetic and logical operations only, Train and CAN bus consist of many set operations. Again, Cruise Controller is a machine having many assignments and logical operations which are more complicated in comparison to other machines. The performance of set operations is also investigated by the benchmarks Sieve, sort_m2_data1000 and scheduler. So the selected benchmarks cover different aspects of the performance.

For the empirical evaluation, an execution trace with a cycle is used for each machine listed in Table 2. The cyclic part of the trace is executed several times within a while loop. Cycles are selected such that each operation is executed at least once. The exceptions are CAN bus and sort_m2_data1000. While the cycle in CAN bus does not contain all operations, sort_m2_data1000 is a quadratic sorting algorithm and does not have any cycles. The state space in sort_m2_data1000 consists of one path from a state representing an unsorted array of 1000 elements to a state representing a sorted array.

Each generated program is executed ten times measuring runtime and memory (maximum resident set size). Table 2 shows the median of all measurements for both runtime and memory. We set a timeout at 30 min execution time. The speedup relative to ProB is given as well. As the translation is only run once, the time utilised by B2Program is not measured. Since execution is long enough, the start-up and parsing time of ProB are not relevant (but are included). Note that ProB does variant checking when executing while loops; this cannot be turned off. ProB was run using the command-line version probcli using the `-execute` command. All measurements are done on a MacBook Air with 8 GB of RAM and a 1.6 GHz Intel i5 processor with two cores.

As can be seen, for most machines, generated Java and C++ code can be one to two orders of magnitudes faster than execution in ProB. This comes to no surprise, as interpretation overhead can be quite large. Furthermore, generated C++ code uses only a small percentage of memory compared to Java and ProB. The reason is that both Java and SICStus Prolog make use of garbage collection and both were running in unconstrained memory. Memory consumption can be heavily reduced at the cost of enormous penalties concerning runtime in Java.

The difference between primitive and big integers concerning runtime is comparatively low impact for most machines. For the traffic light and lift examples however, there is an approximately 5× speed-up. Because the considered loops in the machines are very small, significant overhead is caused by incrementing the loop counter which is also a `BInteger`. There can also be significant performance increases depending on compiler optimisations: as there is neither user input during execution nor program parameters, *clang* is able to optimise aggressively. Similarly, most parts of the cruise controller and the sorting example can be optimised. In the other benchmarks, optimisation is more conservative and increases performance up to a factor of two.

Table 2. Runtimes of PROB and generated code in seconds with number of operation calls (OP calls), Speed-Up Relative to PROB, Memory Usage in KB, BI = Big Integer, PI = Primitive Integer

		PROB	Java BI	Java PI	C++ PI -O1	C++ PI -O2
Lift		PROB	Java BI	Java PI	C++ PI -O1	C++ PI -O2
(2×10^9	Runtime	> 1800	156.63	27.43	78.42	0.00
op calls)	Speed-up	1	> 11.49	> 65.62	> 22.95	> 180 000
	Memory	-	735 188	785 628	756	736
Traffic		PROB	Java BI	Java PI	C++ PI -O1	C++ PI -O2
Light	Runtime	> 1800	47.04	9.05	69.09	0.00
(1.8×10^9	Speed-up	1	> 38.27	> 198.9	> 26.05	> 180 000
op calls)	Memory	-	855 112	447 828	756	736
Sieve		PROB	Java BI	Java PI	C++ PI -O1	C++ PI -O2
(1 op call,	Runtime	76.31	7.71	6.49	14.63	8.94
primes until	Speed-up	1	9.9	11.76	5.22	8.54
2 Million)	Memory	398 980	1 415 428	1 096 284	32 472	35 732
Scheduler		PROB	Java BI	Java PI	C++ PI -O1	C++ PI -O2
(9.6×10^9	Runtime	786.74	10.62	10.49	21.57	10.32
op calls)	Speed-up	1	74.08	74.99	36.47	76.23
	Memory	5 341 316	414 772	398 924	816	820
sort_m2_		PROB	Java BI	Java PI	C++ PI -O1	C++ PI -O2
data1000 [32]	Runtime	17.27	3.27	2.10	0.2	0.03
(500×10^3	Speed-up	1	5.28	8.22	86.35	575.67
op calls)	Memory	577 808	191 280	143 864	1192	1104
CAN Bus		PROB	Java BI	Java PI	C++ PI -O1	C++ PI -O2
(J. Colley,	Runtime	273.58	7.23	6.81	7.23	2.91
15×10^6	Speed-up	1	37.84	40.17	37.84	94.01
op calls)	Memory	167 284	428 084	402 432	968	952
Train [1]		PROB	Java BI	Java PI	C++ PI -O1	C++ PI -O2
(940×10^3	Runtime	241.16	13.31	12.83	18.55	8.10
op calls)	Speed-up	1	18.11	18.8	13	29.77
	Memory	163 476	377 292	376 540	984	1016
Cruise		PROB	Java BI	Java PI	C++ PI -O1	C++ PI -O2
Controller	Runtime	> 1800	21.26	15.26	11.90	0.30
(136.1×10^6	Speed-up	1	> 84.67	> 117.96	> 151.26	> 6000
op calls)	Memory	-	750 816	484 948	864	820

5 Related Work

Low-Level Code Generators. There are a variety of code generators that work on a low-level subset of B or Event-B and emit low-level code. This includes the code generators in ATELIERB [9], which emit C, low-level C++ or Ada code, B2LLVM [7], which generates the LLVM intermediate representation and jBTools [33] that generates low-level Java code. In contrast to B2PROGRAM, these code generators usually only support primitive integers, boolean values as well as enumerated sets which are translated to enums. Higher-level constructs are not supported in order to avoid run-time memory allocation. This also means that most B models cannot be translated without (several) additional refinement steps. Apart from B2LLVM, which can use the LLVM infrastructure in order to emit code in many programming languages, these code generators feature only a single output language.

Automatic Refiner. AtelierB also provides an automatic refiner called BART [31] which can help perform data-refinement and makes it much easier to reach the B0 level. BART can be used to generate code for SIL4 components, as the refinement steps are still validated by AtelierB like regular refinement steps. BART, however, still requires user interaction and may require discharging of proof obligations. We also doubt that BART can be applied to the high-level models in our experiments (cf. Table 2).

Event-B Code Generators. There are also code generators for Event-B to other programming languages. The code generators in the EB2ALL tool-set presented in [27] generate code from Event-B to Java, C, C++ and C#. Like the other code generators for B, these code generators only support a subset of Event-B at implementation level.

In contrast, the code generator EventB2Java presented in [8,32] generates B models from all abstraction levels to Java just like B2Program. While EventB2Java generates JML contracts additionally to Java code, B2Program requires a verified B model as input. JML supports quantified constructs, which is used by EventB2Java to generate code for B quantifications. In contrast to B2Program, EventB2Java does not support non-deterministic constructs and it uses mutable data structures (e.g., java.util.TreeSet). Note that the sorting example from Table 2 stems from [32].[6]

Another code generator for Event-B [11] generates Java, ADA and C for OpenMP and also C for the Functional Mock-up Interface. Code Generation depends on manual annotation of tasks via a Rodin plugin. This code generator also uses a template-based approach to store boilerplate code in templates and re-use them. B2Program does not only use templates to store boilerplate code only, but also to target various programming languages.

Finally, [13] is focused on extracting a scheduling of events from an Event-B model. It does not seem to be publicly available (see Section 3.6.2 of [26]).

Execution in ProB *and TLC.* Another approach to utilise formal models in software is to skip code generation altogether and to directly execute the model using an animator, such as ProB and its Java API [22]. An example model and application is an implementation of the ETCS Hybrid Level 3 principle [16]. There, a Java application interacted with a non-deterministic model using input from different sources in order to calculate new signal states.

The TLC model checker also has library for TLA operators [23]. [15] provided a translation from B to TLA+ and has added some TLC libraries for B data

[6] But note that the timings reported in [32] are incorrect. In our experiments the EventB2Java generated code seems to be about twice as fast as execution with ProB, taking in the order of 8.15 s to sort 1000 elements. In [32] it is reported that sorting a 100,000 element array takes 0.023 s, and a 200,000 element array 0.028 s which is impossible using a quadratic insertion sort.

types. The way TLC deals with quantification is reminiscent of Sect. 3.5. On the other hand, the translation provides limited support for composition and refinement and allows no sequential composition. The speed for lower-level models of TLC is faster than ProB, but one cannot easily use TLC to execute a formal model.

Code Generators for Other State-Based Formal Methods. [6] uses the Xtend technology provided by the Xtext framework for domain specific languages to generate C++ code for ASM formal models. This work [19], contains a code generator for VDM capable of producing Java and C++ code. There seem to be no code generators available for Z, see Sect. 3.9.2 of [26]. The commercial products Matlab/Simulink and Scade come with code generators, which are widely used (despite any guarantees of correctness).

6 Discussion, Conclusion and Future Work

In this paper, we presented B2Program, a code generator for high-level B models. Compared to existing work, more data types can be translated: e.g., sets, tuples, relations, sequences, records, many quantified constructs, and even some instances of non-determinism. Our code generator makes use of efficient immutable data structures to encode sets and relations.

B2Program does not cover the entirety of B. Table 1 shows all supported operators for the supported B types. Those constructs that would require constraint solving techniques to deal with, e.g. infinite sets, are intentionally not supported; we do not wish to embed a constraint solver into the generated code as explained in Sect. 3.5. Substitutions are covered by B2Program completely, except for *becomes such that* constructs that would require a constraint solver. For now, the only supported machine inclusion clauses are `INCLUDES` and `EXTENDS`. Supporting other machine inclusion clauses will be implemented in the future.

The generated code often runs one or two orders of magnitude faster than interpretation using ProB. For some benchmarks, making heavy use of set operations on large sets, the difference is less marked. Initial versions of our code generator used mutable data structures, and was in many cases slower than ProB. Representing relations as a set of tuples using persistent sets was still slower than ProB for the sorting example, possibly because operations on relations such the override operator were still inefficient. But in the current version of B2Program, the performance for operations on relations is improved by representing relations as a persistent map.

Another aspect that makes B2Program unique is the flexible output: using templates with StringTemplate provides the opportunity, to exploit similarities of programming languages. This results in code generation for several target languages with less effort. In the future, we want to explore code generation for other target languages, including declarative languages such as Haskell, Clojure and Prolog. Finally, B2Program might be used to rewrite B models by targeting the B language itself, potentially allowing optimisations for model checking.

To be able to use B2Program for SIL-3 or SIL-4 systems, the independent development of another high-level code generator would be required. But we hope that our code generator will already on its own enable new applications of formal models, putting formal models into the loop and connecting them with other software components and controlling or monitoring systems in real time.

References

1. Abrial, J., Hoare, A.: The B-Book: Assigning Programs to Meanings. Cambridge University Press, Cambridge (2005)
2. Sethi, R., Aho, A.V., Lam, M.S.: The structure of a compiler. In: Compilers Principles, Techniques & Tools, 2nd edn. Addison Wesley, Boston (1986)
3. Backhouse, R., Gibbons, J.: Generic Programming. Springer, Heidelberg (2003)
4. Bagwell, P.: Ideal Hash Trees. Es Grands Champs, 1195 (2001)
5. Baier, C., Katoen, J.-P.: Principles of Model Checking. MIT Press, Cambridge (2008)
6. Bonfanti, S., Carissoni, M., Gargantini, A., Mashkoor, A.: Asm2C++: a tool for code generation from abstract state machines to arduino. In: Barrett, C., Davies, M., Kahsai, T. (eds.) NFM 2017. LNCS, vol. 10227, pp. 295–301. Springer, Cham (2017). https://doi.org/10.1007/978-3-319-57288-8_21
7. Bonichon, R., Déharbe, D., Lecomte, T., Medeiros, V.: LLVM-based code generation for B. In: Braga, C., Martí-Oliet, N. (eds.) SBMF 2014. LNCS, vol. 8941, pp. 1–16. Springer, Cham (2015). https://doi.org/10.1007/978-3-319-15075-8_1
8. Cataño, N., Rivera, V.: EventB2Java: a code generator for event-B. In: Rayadurgam, S., Tkachuk, O. (eds.) NFM 2016. LNCS, vol. 9690, pp. 166–171. Springer, Cham (2016). https://doi.org/10.1007/978-3-319-40648-0_13
9. ClearSy. Atelier B, User and Reference Manuals. Aix-en-Provence, France (2016). http://www.atelierb.eu/
10. Dollé, D., Essamé, D., Falampin, J.: B dans le transport ferroviaire. L'expérience de Siemens Transportation Systems. Technique et Science Informatiques **22**(1), 11–32 (2003)
11. Edmunds, A.: Templates for event-B code generation. In: Ait Ameur, Y., Schewe, K.D. (eds.) ABZ 2014. LNCS, vol. 8477, pp. 284–289. Springer, Heidelberg (2014). https://doi.org/10.1007/978-3-662-43652-3_25
12. Essamé, D., Dollé, D.: B in large-scale projects: the canarsie line CBTC experience. In: Julliand, J., Kouchnarenko, O. (eds.) B 2007. LNCS, vol. 4355, pp. 252–254. Springer, Heidelberg (2006). https://doi.org/10.1007/11955757_21
13. Fürst, A., Hoang, T.S., Basin, D., Desai, K., Sato, N., Miyazaki, K.: Code generation for event-B. In: Albert, E., Sekerinski, E. (eds.) IFM 2014. LNCS, vol. 8739, pp. 323–338. Springer, Cham (2014). https://doi.org/10.1007/978-3-319-10181-1_20
14. Granlund, T.: GNU MP. The GNU Multiple Precision Arithmetic Library, vol. 2, no. 2 (1996)
15. Hansen, D., Leuschel, M.: Translating B to TLA + for validation with TLC. In: Ait Ameur, Y., Schewe, K.D. (eds.) ABZ 2014. LNCS, vol. 8477, pp. 40–55. Springer, Heidelberg (2014). https://doi.org/10.1007/978-3-662-43652-3_4
16. Hansen, D., et al.: Using a formal B model at runtime in a demonstration of the ETCS hybrid level 3 concept with real trains. In: Butler, M., Raschke, A., Hoang, T.S., Reichl, K. (eds.) ABZ 2018. LNCS, vol. 10817, pp. 292–306. Springer, Cham (2018). https://doi.org/10.1007/978-3-319-91271-4_20

17. Hickey, R.: The Clojure programming language. In: Proceedings of DLS. ACM (2008)
18. Hunt, A., Thomas, D.: The evils of duplication. In: The Pragmatic Programmer: From Journeyman to Master, p. 26. The Pragmatic Bookshelf (1999)
19. Jørgensen, P.W.V., Larsen, M., Couto, L.D.: A code generation platform for VDM. In: Battle, N., Fitzgerald, J. (eds.) Proceedings of the 12th Overture Workshop. School of Computing Science, Newcastle University, UK, Technical report CS-TR-1446, January 2015
20. Kaplan, H.: Persistent data structures. In: Handbook of Data Structures and Applications (2004)
21. Krings, S.: Towards infinite-state symbolic model checking for B and event-B. Ph.D. thesis, Heinrich Heine Universität Düsseldorf, August 2017
22. Körner, P., Bendisposto, J., Dunkelau, J., Krings, S., Leuschel, M.: Embedding high-level formal specifications into applications. In: ter Beek, M.H., McIver, A., Oliveira, J.N. (eds.) FM 2019. LNCS, vol. 11800, pp. 519–535. Springer, Cham (2019). https://doi.org/10.1007/978-3-030-30942-8_31
23. Lamport, L.: Specifying Systems: The TLA+ Language and Tools for Hardware and Software Engineers. Addison-Wesley Longman Publishing Co., Inc. (2002)
24. Leroy, X.: Formal certification of a compiler back-end, or: programming a compiler with a proof assistant. In: 33rd Symposium Principles of Programming Languages, POPL, pp. 42–54. ACM Press (2006)
25. Leuschel, M., Butler, M.: ProB: a model checker for B. In: Araki, K., Gnesi, S., Mandrioli, D. (eds.) FME 2003. LNCS, vol. 2805, pp. 855–874. Springer, Heidelberg (2003). https://doi.org/10.1007/978-3-540-45236-2_46
26. Mashkoor, A., Kossak, F., Egyed, A.: Evaluating the suitability of state-based formal methods for industrial deployment. Softw. Pract. Exper. **48**(12), 2350–2379 (2018)
27. Méry, D., Singh, N.K.: Automatic code generation from event-B models. In: Proceedings SoICT 2011, pp. 179–188. ACM ICPS (2011)
28. Parr, T.: Enforcing Strict Model-View Separation in Template Engines. https://www.cs.usfca.edu/~parrt/papers/mvc.templates.pdf. Accessed 14 May 2019
29. Plagge, D., Leuschel, M.: Seven at a stroke: LTL model checking for high-level specifications in B, Z, CSP, and more. Int. J. Softw. Tools Technol. Transf. **12**, 9–21 (2007)
30. Puente, J.P.B.: Persistence for the masses: RRB-vectors in a systems language. In: Proceedings of ACM Programming Languages, vol. 1, no. ICFP, pp. 16:1–16:28 (2017)
31. Requet, A.: BART: a tool for automatic refinement. In: Börger, E., Butler, M., Bowen, J.P., Boca, P. (eds.) ABZ 2008. LNCS, vol. 5238, pp. 345–345. Springer, Heidelberg (2008). https://doi.org/10.1007/978-3-540-87603-8_33
32. Rivera, V., Cataño, N., Wahls, T., Rueda, C.: Code generation for Event-B. STTT **19**(1), 31–52 (2017)
33. Voisinet, J.-C.: JBTools: an experimental platform for the formal B method. In: Proceedings of the Inaugural International Symposium on Principles and Practice of Programming in Java, pp. 137–139 (2002)

Visualization and Abstractions for Execution Paths in Model-Based Software Testing

Rui Wang[1(✉)], Cyrille Artho[2], Lars Michael Kristensen[1], and Volker Stolz[1]

[1] Department of Computing, Mathematics, and Physics, Western Norway University of Applied Sciences, Bergen, Norway
artho@kth.se

[2] School of Computer Science and Communication, KTH Royal Institute of Technology, Stockholm, Sweden
{rwa,lmkr,vsto}@hvl.no

Abstract. This paper presents a technique to measure and visualize execution-path coverage of test cases in the context of model-based software systems testing. Our technique provides visual feedback of the tests, their coverage, and their diversity. We provide two types of visualizations for path coverage based on so-called state-based graphs and path-based graphs. Our approach is implemented by extending the Modbat tool for model-based testing and experimentally evaluated on a collection of examples, including the ZooKeeper distributed coordination service. Our experimental results show that the state-based visualization is good at relating the tests to the model structure, while the path-based visualization shows distinct paths well, in particular linearly independent paths. Furthermore, our graph abstractions retain the characteristics of distinct execution paths, while removing some of the complexity of the graph.

1 Introduction

Software testing is a widely used, scalable and efficient technique to discover software defects [17]. However, generating sufficiently many and diverse test cases for a good coverage of the system under test (SUT) remains a challenge. *Model-based testing* (MBT) [21] addresses this problem by automating test-case generation based on deriving concrete test cases automatically from abstract (formal) models of the SUT. In addition to allowing automation, abstract test models are often easier to develop and maintain than low-level test scripts [20]. However, for models of complex systems, an exhaustive exploration of all possible tests is infeasible, and the decision of how many tests to generate is challenging.

Visualizing the degree to which tests have been executed can be helpful in this context: visualization can show if different parts of the model or SUT have been explored equally well [13], if there are redundancies in the tests [13], and if there are parts of the system that are hard to reach, e. g., due to preconditions that do not hold [3]. In this paper, we focus on the visualization of test paths on the test model, as this provides a higher level of abstraction than the SUT.

W. Ahrendt and S. L. Tapia Tarifa (Eds.): IFM 2019, LNCS 11918, pp. 474–492, 2019.
https://doi.org/10.1007/978-3-030-34968-4_26

The main contribution of this paper is to present a technique to capture and visualize execution paths of the model covered by test cases generated with MBT. Our approach records execution paths with a trie data-structure and visualizes them with the aid of lightweight abstractions as *state-based graphs* (SGs) and *path-based graphs* (PGs). These abstractions simplify the graphs and help us to deal with complexity in moderately large systems. The visual feedback provided by our technique is useful to understand to what degree the model and the SUT are executed by the generated test cases, and to understand execution traces and locate weaknesses in the coverage of the model. Being based on the state machine of the model, the state graph focuses on the behaviors of a system in relation to the test model. The path graph shows paths as transition sequences and eliminates crossing edges.

Our second contribution is to provide a path coverage visualizer based on the Modbat model-based API tester [2]. Our tool extends Modbat and enables the visualization of path coverage without requiring modifications of the models. Users of the tool can choose to visualize all execution paths in the SGs and PGs, or limit visualization to subgraphs of the SGs and PGs for models of large and complex systems. Our third contribution is an experimental evaluation on several model-based test suites. We analyze the number of executed paths against quantitative properties of the graphs. We show how edge thickness and colors help to visualize the frequency of transitions on executed paths, what kinds of paths have higher coverage than others, and what kinds of tests succeed or fail. We also compare the resulting SGs and PGs with *full state-based graphs* (FSGs) and *full path-based graphs* (FPGs). The FSGs and FPGs are the graphs without applying abstractions; they are used only in this paper for comparison with the SGs and PGs. We show that our abstraction technique helps to reduce the number of nodes and edges to get concise and abstracted graphs.

The rest of this paper is organized as follows. Section 2 gives background on extended finite state machines and Modbat. In Sect. 3, we give our definition of execution paths and the trie data structure used for their representation. In Sect. 4, we introduce our approach for the path coverage visualization. In Sect. 5, we present the two types of graphs and the associated abstractions used. Section 6 presents our experimental evaluation of the path coverage visualizer tool and analyzes path coverage of selected test examples. In Sect. 7, we discuss related work, and in Sect. 8 we sum up conclusions and discuss future work.

2 Extended Finite State Machines and Modbat

We use extended finite state machines (EFSMs) as the theoretical foundation for our models and adapt the classical definition [6] to better suit its implementation as an embedded language, and several extensions that Modbat [2] defines.

Definition 1 (Extended Finite State Machine). *An* extended finite state machine *is a tuple* $M = (S, s_0, V, A, T)$ *such that:*

- S *is a finite set of states, including an initial state* s_0.

- $V = V_1 \times \ldots \times V_n$ *is an* n*-dimensional vector space representing the set of values for variables.*
- A *is a finite set of actions* $A : V \to (V, R)$*, where* $res \in R$ *denotes the* result *of an action, which is either* successful, failed, backtracked, *or* exceptional. *A successful action allows a test case to continue; a failed action constitutes a test failure and terminates the current test; a backtracked action corresponds to the case where the enabling function of a transition is* false *[6]; exceptional results are defined as such by user-defined predicates that are evaluated at run-time, and cover the non-deterministic behavior of the SUT. We denote by* $Exc \subset R$ *the set of all possible exceptional outcomes.*
- T *is a transition relation* $T : S \times A \times S \times E$*; for a transition* $t \in T$ *we denote the left-side (origin) state by* $s_{origin}(t)$ *and the right-side (destination) state by* $s_{dest}(t)$*, and use the shorthand* $s_{origin} \to s_{dest}$ *if the action is uniquely defined. A transition includes a possible empty mapping* $E : Exc \to S$*, which maps exceptional results to a new destination state.*

Compared to the traditional definition of an EFSM [6], we merge the enabling and update functions into a single action $\alpha \in A$, and handle inputs and outputs inside the action. Actions deal with preconditions, inputs, executing test actions on the SUT, and its outputs. An action may also include assertions; a failed assertion causes the current test case to fail. Finally, transitions support non-deterministic outcomes in our definition.

Modbat. Modbat is a model-based testing tool aimed at performing online testing on state-based systems [2]. Test models in Modbat are expressed as EFSMs in a domain-specific language based on Scala [18]. The model variables can be arbitrarily complex data structures. Actions can update the variables, pass them as part of calls to the SUT, and use them in test oracles.

Figure 1(left) shows the ChooseTest model that we will use as a simple running example to introduce the basic concepts of Modbat and our approach to execution path visualization and abstraction. A valid execution path in a Modbat model starts from the initial state and consists of a sequence of transitions. The first declared state automatically constitutes the initial state. Transitions are declared with a concise syntax: "*origin*" → "*dest*" := {*action*}. The ChooseTest model in Fig. 1 consists of three states: "*ok*", "*end*", and "*err*". It also uses `require` in the action part as a precondition to check if a call to the random function `choose` returns `0` (10% chance). Only in that case is the transition from "*ok*" to "*err*" enabled. Function `assert` is then used to check if a subsequent call to `choose` returns non-zero. If `0` is returned (10% chance), the assertion fails. Thus, transition "*ok*" → "*err*" is rarely enabled; and if enabled, it fails only infrequently.

Choices. Modbat supports two kinds of *choices*: (1) Before a transition is executed, the choice of the next transition is available. (2) Within an action, choices

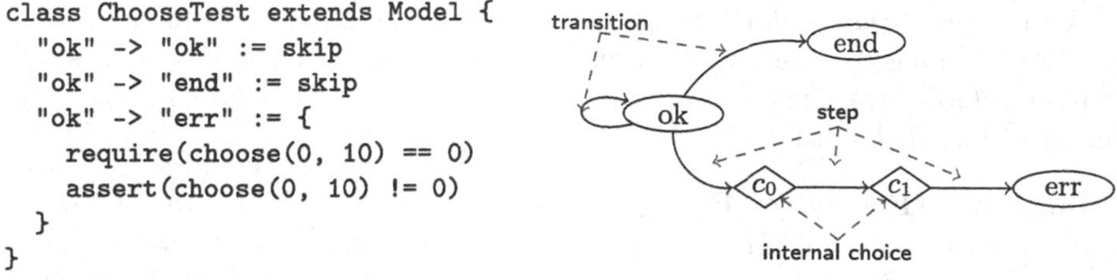

```
class ChooseTest extends Model {
  "ok" -> "ok" := skip
  "ok" -> "end" := skip
  "ok" -> "err" := {
    require(choose(0, 10) == 0)
    assert(choose(0, 10) != 0)
  }
}
```


Fig. 1. Model ChooseTest (left) with steps and internal choices (right).

can be made on parameters that can be used as inputs to the SUT or for computations inside the action. The latter are *internal choices*, which can be choices over a finite set of numbers or functions. These choices are obtained in Modbat by calling the function `choose`. In our example, the action in transition "*ok*" to "*err*" has two internal choices shown as c_0 and c_1 in Fig. 1 (right).

Transitions and Steps. We divide an action into smaller *steps* to distinguish choices between transitions from internal choices inside an action. A step is a maximal-length sequence of statements inside an action that does not contain any choices. Our definition of choices corresponds to the semantics of Modbat, but also that of other tools, such as Java Pathfinder [22], a tool to analyze concurrent software that may also contain non-deterministic choices on inputs.

Action Results. Modbat actions (which execute code related to transitions) have four possible outcomes: successful, backtracked, failed, or exceptional. A successful action allows a test case to continue with another transition, if available. An action is *backtracked* and resets the transition to its original state if any of its preconditions are violated. An action *fails* if an assertion is violated, if an unexpected exception occurs, or if an expected exception does not occur. In our example, the action of transition "*ok*" to "*err*" is backtracked if the `require`-statement in the action evaluates to `false`, and the action *fails* if the `assert`-statement evaluates to `false`. *Exceptional results* are defined by custom predicates that may override the destination state ($s_{dest}(t)$) of a transition t; see above. If no precondition or assertion is violated, and no exceptional result occurs, the action is *successful*.

3 Execution Paths and Representation

Path coverage concerns a sequence of branch decisions instead of only one branch at a time. It is a stronger measurement than branch coverage, since it considers combinations of branch decisions (or statements) with other branch decisions (or statements), which may not have been tested according to the plain branch or statement coverage [16]. It is hard to reach 100% path coverage, as the number of execution paths usually increases exponentially with each additional branch or cycle [15].

A finite *execution path* is a sequence of transitions starting from the initial state and leading to a terminal state. A *terminal state* in our case is a state without outgoing transitions, or a state after a test failed. We denote by $S_{terminal}$ the set of terminal states.

Definition 2 (Execution Path). *Let $M = (S, s_0, V, A, T)$ be an EFSM. A finite execution path p of M is a sequence of transitions, which constitute a path $p = t_0 t_1 \ldots t_n$, $t_n \in T$, such that $s_{origin}(t_0) = s_0$, the origin and destination states are linked: $\forall i, 0 < i \leq n, s_{origin}(t_i) = s_{dest}(t_{i-1})$, and $s_{dest}(t_n) \in S_{terminal}$.*

We first represent the executed paths in a data structure based on the transitions executed by the generated test cases, and then use this to visualize path coverage of a test suite in the form of state-based and path-based graphs.

We record the path executed by each test case in a *trie* [5]. A trie is a prefix tree data structure where all the descendants of a node in the trie have a common prefix. Each trie node n stores information related to an executed transition, including the following: t (executed transition); *ti* (transition information); *trc* (transition repetition counter) to count the number of times transition t has been executed repeatedly without any other transitions executing in between during a test-case execution, with a value of 1 equalling no repetition; *tpc* (transition path counter) to count the number of paths that have this transition t executed *trc* times in a test suite; *Ch*, the set of children of node n; and *lf*, a Boolean variable to decide if the current node is a leaf of the tree. The transition information *ti* consists of the $s_{origin}(t)$ and $s_{dest}(t)$ states of the transition, a transition identifier *tid*, a counter *cnt* to count the number of times this transition is executed in a path, an action result *res*, which could be successful, backtracked, or failed, and sequences of transition-internal choices C for modeling non-determinism.

As an example, consider a test suite consisting of three execution paths: $p_0 = [a \rightarrow b, b \rightarrow b, b \rightarrow c, c \rightarrow d]$, $p_1 = [a \rightarrow b, b \rightarrow b, b \rightarrow b, b \rightarrow c, c \rightarrow d]$, and $p_2 = [a \rightarrow b, b \rightarrow b, b \rightarrow e]$, where a, b, c, d, and e are states. These execution paths can be represented by the trie data structure shown in Fig. 2 where the node labeled root represents the root of the trie. Note that this data structure is not a direct visual representation of the paths and it is not the trie data structure that we eventually visualize in our approach. Each non-root node in the trie in Fig. 2 has been labeled with the transition it represents. As an example, node 1 represents the transition $a \rightarrow b$ and node 2 represents the transition $b \rightarrow b$. This reflects that all the three execution paths stored in the trie have $a \rightarrow b$ followed by $b \rightarrow b$ as a (common) prefix. Each non-root node also has a label representing the transition counters associated with the node. For the transition counters, the value before the colon is *trc* (transition repetition counter), while the value after the colon is *tpc* (transition path counter). For example, the transition $b \rightarrow b$ associated with node 2 has been taken three times in total. Two paths, (p_0 and p_2) execute this transition once (label trc=1:tpc=2), while one path p_1 executes it twice (label trc=2:tpc=1). A parent node and a child node in the trie are connected by a mapping $\langle tid, res \rangle \mapsto n$ in each node which associates a transition identifier and action result (res) with a child (destination) node n.

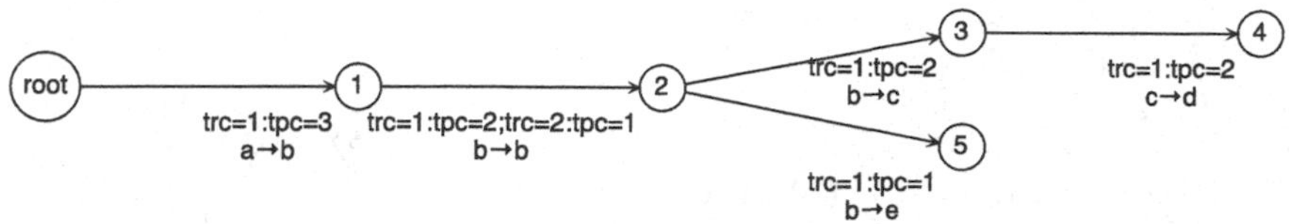

Fig. 2. Example trie data structure representing three executed paths.

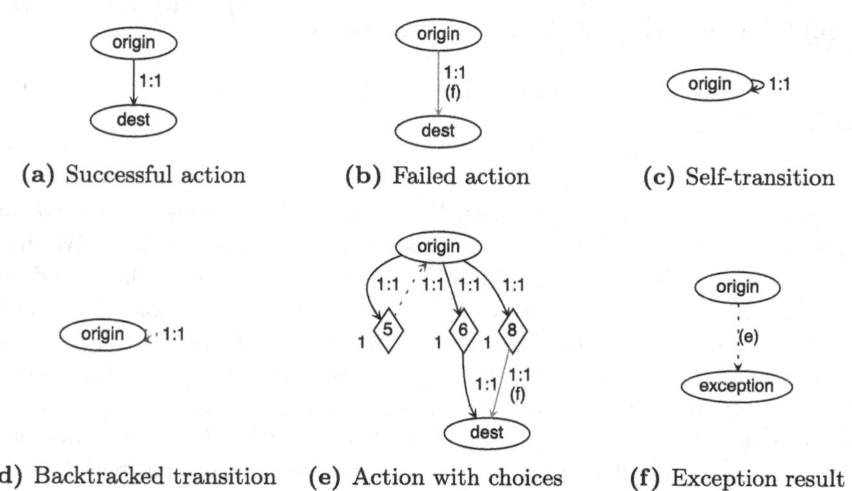

Fig. 3. Basic visualization elements of the state-based graphs (SGs). (Color figure online)

4 Path Coverage Visualization

Our path coverage visualizer can produce two types of directed graphs: state-based graphs (SGs) and path-based graphs (PGs). These two types of graphs are produced based on the data stored in the trie data structure representing the executed paths of the testing model. Figures 3 and 4 illustrate the basic visualization elements of the SGs and PGs, respectively, with the help of the DOT Language [9], which can be used to create graphs with Graphviz tools [4].

The SGs and PGs have common node and edge styles (shape, color and thickness) to indicate different features of the path- execution coverage visualization.

Node Styles. We use three types of node shapes in the graphs for path coverage visualization. Elliptical nodes ⬭ represent states in the SG as shown in Fig. 3. Point nodes • represent the connections between transitions/steps in the PG as shown in Fig. 4. Diamond nodes ◊ visualize internal choices in both the SGs and PGs as shown in Figs. 3e and 4e. Each diamond node has a value inside indicates the chosen value. There is also an optional counter value label aside each diamond node to show how many times this choice has been taken. The edge labels of the format $n : m$ will be discussed later.

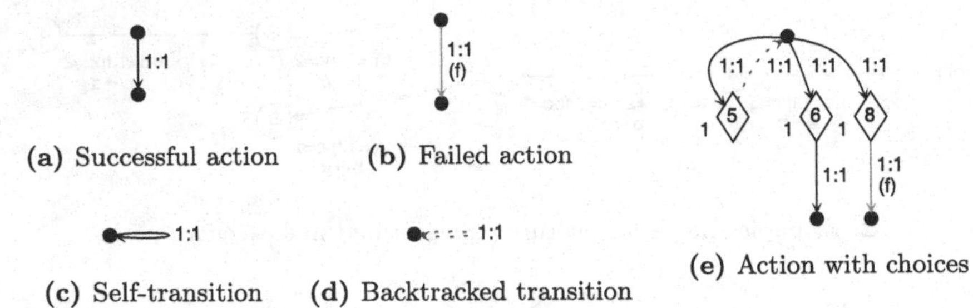

(a) Successful action (b) Failed action (c) Self-transition (d) Backtracked transition (e) Action with choices

Fig. 4. Basic visualization elements of the path-based graphs (PGs). (Color figure online)

Edge Styles. A directed edge in both the SGs and PGs represents an executed transition and its related information as stored in the trie structure. We distinguish different kinds of edges based on the action results, using shape and color styles. Black solid edges are used to represent successful transitions (Figs. 3a and 4a). Blue dotted edges are used to visualize backtracked transitions (Figs. 3d and 4d). Red solid edges labeled (f) are used to visualize failed transitions (shown in Figs. 3b and 4b). Black solid loops represent self-transitions (Figs. 3c and 4c) and are used when $s_{dest}(t)$ and $s_{origin}(t)$ of a transition t are the same state. Black dotted edges labeled (e) are used to represent exceptional results for the SG (shown in Fig. 3f). This allows the visualization to distinguish between the normal destination state $s_{dest}(t)$ and the exception destination state. For the PG, this kind of edge is ignored by merging the point nodes of $s_{origin}(t)$ and the exception destination state of a transition t into one point node. If a transition t consists of multiple *steps* (Figs. 3e and 4e), we only apply the edge styles to the last step edge which connects to $s_{dest}(t)$, while other step edges use a black solid style.

Each edge may have a label for additional information, such as transition identifier *tid*, and values of the counters *trc* and *tpc*. Here we use the format *trc* : *tpc*. It is optional to show these labels. For example, in both Figs. 3 and 4, the values of counters are all 1 : 1 indicates that each transition in a test case is executed only once without any repetitions, and there is only one path that has this transition executed.

The thickness of an edge indicates how frequently a transition is executed for the entire test suite. The thicker an edge is, the more frequently is its transition executed. Let *nTests* be the total number of executed test cases. Then, the thickness of an edge is given by $\ln(\frac{\sum count*100}{nTests} + 1)$, where the value of *count* is the *tpc* value of a transition in each path if there are no internal choices for this transition. If a transition has internal choices, then we use the value of the counter for each internal choice as the value of *count*. Since we merge edges in the graphs corresponding to the same transitions or the same choices from different paths, we then compute the sum of values of *counts* obtained for the transition or choice.

5 State-Based and Path-Based Graphs

We now present the details of the state-based (SG) and path-based (PG) graphs with abstractions that form the foundation of our visualization approach. These abstractions underly the reduced representation of the execution paths.

McCabe [12] proposed basic path testing and gave the definition of a *linearly independent path*. A linearly independent path is any path through a program that contains at least one new edge which is not included in any other linearly independent paths. A subpath q of an execution path p is a subsequence of p (possibly p itself), and an execution path p traverses a subpath q if q is a subsequence of p. In this paper, for the visualization of execution paths, we merge subpaths from different linearly independent paths in both SG and PG with the aid of the trie data structure.

5.1 State-Based Graphs

An SG is a directed graph $SG = (N_s, E_t)$, where $N_s \equiv \{n_{s_0}, n_{s_1}, \ldots, n_{s_i}\}$ is a set of nodes including both elliptical nodes representing states with their names and diamond nodes representing internal choices with their values as discussed in Sect. 4. Elliptical nodes use the name of their state as node identifier; diamond nodes are identified by a tuple $\langle v, cn \rangle$, where v is the value of the choice, and cn is an integer number starting from 1 and increasing with the number of diamond nodes. $E_t \equiv \{e_{t_0}, e_{t_1}, \ldots, e_{t_i}\}$ is a set of directed edges representing both transitions and steps. These edges connect nodes according to node identifiers.

An SG is an abstracted graph of the unabstracted full state-based graph (FSG). An FSG may have redundant edges representing the same transition/step between two states; it may also contain choices with the same choice value appearing more than once. These situations, in general, contribute to making the FSG large, complex and difficult to analyze, especially for large and complex systems. Note that the FSG is only used by us to show its complexity in this paper for comparison with the SG. The FSG for the ChooseTest model (discussed in Sect. 3) is already very dense after only 100 test cases (see Fig. 5).

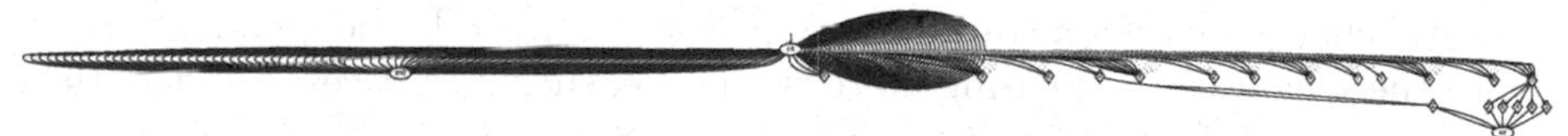

Fig. 5. FSG for 100 test cases of ChooseTest.

In order to reduce the complexity of graphs such as Fig. 5, we abstract the FSG to get the SG, and use edge thickness to indicate the frequency of transitions in the executed paths. We use the ChooseTest model with 1000 executed test cases as an example to show how the SG is obtained in four abstraction steps:

1. *Merge edges of subpaths*: the trie data structure is used to merge subpaths of linearly independent paths when storing transitions in the trie. As discussed for Fig. 2, transition $a \rightarrow b$ followed by $b \rightarrow b$ is a (common) prefix for all the three execution paths p_0, p_1 and p_2. In other words, all these three execution paths traverse the subpaths $a \rightarrow b$ and $b \rightarrow b$. Therefore, to obtain the SG, edges representing transition $a \rightarrow b$ and $b \rightarrow b$ from three execution paths are merged into one edge by the trie data structure. We then use an edge label of the form "*trc* : *tpc*" to show how a transition represented by this edge is executed. (Here, we do not show edge labels due to space limitations.) After merging edges of subpaths, we get only linearly independent paths in the graph. Fig. 6 shows the graph of the ChooseTest model after merging subpaths. There are seven linearly independent paths: $p_0 = [ok \rightarrow end]$, $p_1 = [ok \rightarrow ok, ok \rightarrow end]$, $p_2 = [ok \rightarrow ok, ok \rightarrow err(backtracked), ok \rightarrow end]$, $p_3 = [ok \rightarrow ok, ok \rightarrow err]$, $p_4 = [ok \rightarrow err(backtracked), ok \rightarrow end]$, $p_5 = [ok \rightarrow err(failed)]$ and $p_6 = [ok \rightarrow err]$.
2. *Merge edges of linearly independent paths*: from Fig. 6, it can be noticed that after merging edges of subpaths, the graph may still have redundant edges between two states that represent the same transition with the same action result from different linearly independent paths. For example, there are four edges between the "ok" and "end" states, from four linearly independent paths: p_0, p_1, p_2 and p_4. We merge such edges into one single edge. We also aggregate the path coverage counts. The aggregated counts can be shown as an optional edge label on the form "*trc* : *tpc*", using ";" as the separator, e. g., "1 : 304; 1 : 158; 1 : 177; 1 : 290" for the edge between the "ok" and "end" states after merging p_0, p_1, p_2 and p_4.
3. *Merge internal choice nodes*: internal choice nodes of a transition are merged in two ways. First, based on Step 1, when storing transitions in the trie, each transition has recorded choice lists; we merge choice nodes from different choice lists if these choice nodes have the same choice value and they are a (common) prefix of choice lists. For example, for choice lists $[0, 1, 3]$ and $[0, 1, 3]$ (0, 1, 2, 3 are choice values), we notice that these two choice lists both have choice nodes with value 0 and 1, and they are a (common) prefix for these two lists. We then merge choice nodes with value 0 and 1 to become one choice node, respectively, when storing transitions in the trie. Second, if there are still choice nodes of a transition from different linearly independent paths, with the same value appearing more than once, such as choices in Fig. 6, then we merge them into one choice node during Step 5.1. For both approaches, we get the result of the sum of the values of counters of merged choice nodes. This result denotes the total number of times a choice value appears in the SG, and it can then be shown in addition to the outcome of the choice on the label of the final choice node after merging. Note that to avoid visual clutter, we elide showing the target state for backtracked transitions.
4. *Merge loop edges*: loop edges represent self-transition loops and backtracked transitions; they are merged if they represent the same transition with the same action result.

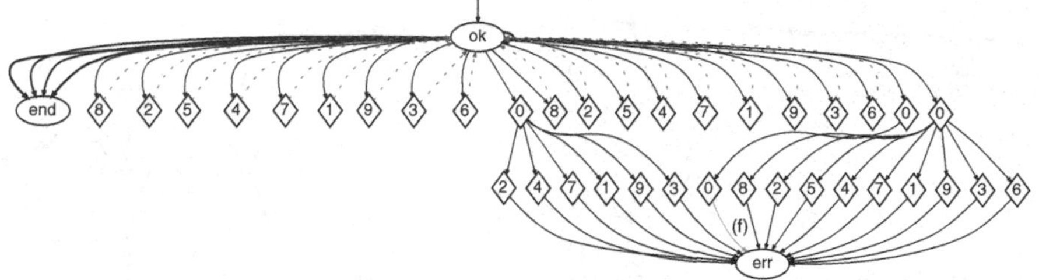

Fig. 6. The graph for 1000 test cases of ChooseTest after merging subpaths.

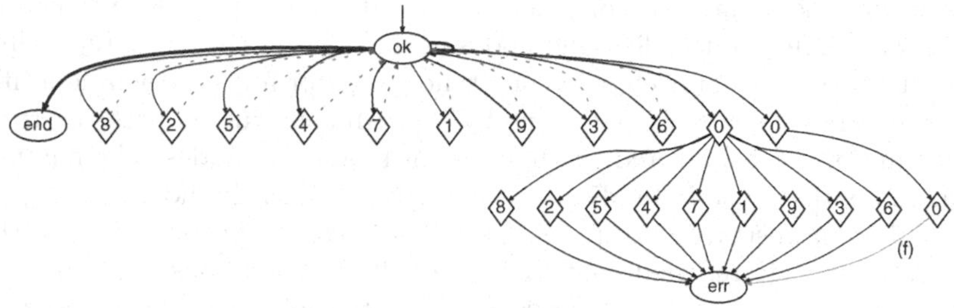

Fig. 7. SG for 1000 test cases of ChooseTest with all abstractions applied.

Figure 7 illustrates the final SG with all abstractions after 1000 test cases. One characteristic of the SG is that it is a concrete instance of its underlying state machine graph. The EFSM shows potential transitions, whereas the SG shows the actually executed steps of actions, and internal choices for non-determinism. For example, Fig. 7 is a concretization of the state machine shown in Fig. 1. As shown in Fig. 1, the transition "*ok*" → "*err*" has a precondition with an internal choice over values 0 to 9 (see Fig. 7). Only choice 0 enables this transition; the transition is backtracked the original state "*ok*" otherwise, as shown with the blue dotted edges. If the transition is enabled by a successful choice with value 0, the assertion, which is another internal choice that fails only for value 0 out of 0 to 9, is executed; its failure is shown by the red solid (failing) edge in Fig. 7.

5.2 Path-Based Graphs

The PG is a directed graph $PG = (N_p, E_t)$, where $N_p \equiv \{n_{p_0}, n_{p_1}, \ldots, n_{p_i}\}$ is a set of nodes, including point nodes representing connections between transitions and diamond nodes representing internal choices with their values (see Sect. 4); and $E_t \equiv \{e_{t_0}, e_{t_1}, \ldots, e_{t_i}\}$ is a set of directed edges representing both transitions and steps. They connect nodes using the identifiers of nodes.

The nodes in PG in contrast to SG do not correspond to states in the EFSM; instead, each node corresponds to a step in a linear independent path through the EFSM. Therefore, each point node is allocated a point node identifier *pn*, an integer starting from 0 (we elide the label in the diagrams here). The value of *pn*

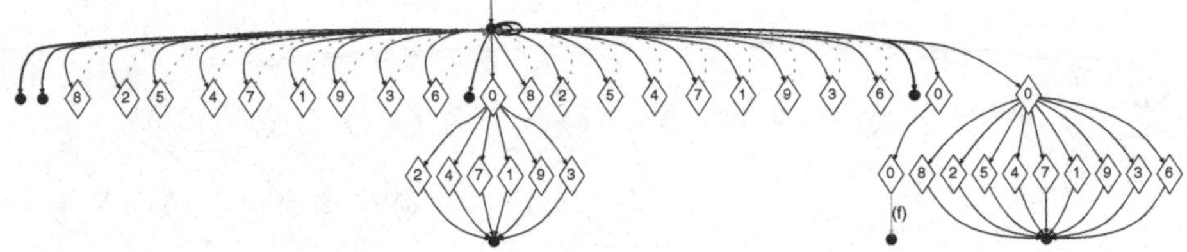

Fig. 8. Path-based graph for 1000 test cases of the ChooseTest model.

increases with the number of point nodes. Each diamond node is identified by a tuple $\langle v, cn \rangle$, similar to the diamond nodes in the SG. For the edges representing transitions, they are connected by point nodes according to their identifiers, which results in constructing paths one by one. All constructed paths start with the same initial point node and end in different final point nodes. The number of constructed paths in the PG indicates the number of linearly independent paths.

An PG is an abstracted graph of the full state-based graph (FPG) without any abstractions. (Here, we do not show the FPG of the ChooseTest model due to space limitations.) As was the case for SG, we apply abstractions to reduce the complexity of the FPG to obtain the PG and use thickness to indicate the frequency of transitions taken by executed paths. The reduction is based on three abstractions:

1. Merge edges of subpaths using the same approach as for step 1 of the SG.
2. Merge internal choice nodes with the first approach of step 3 used to merge choice nodes for the SG.
3. Merge loop edges representing self-transition loops and backtracked transitions as for the SG.

Unlike for the SG, we do not merge edges of linearly independent paths and choice nodes from different linearly independent paths for the PG, since our goal for the PG is to show linearly independent paths after applying the abstractions.

Figure 8 shows the abstracted PG for the ChooseTest model. It can be seen that there are seven black final point nodes from seven paths, which indicate that seven linearly independent paths have been executed. The information about the number of linearly independent paths is one characteristic of the PG, and this information is not easy to derive from the SG shown in Fig. 7.

5.3 User-Defined Search Function

As the SG and PG graphs might become unwieldy for complex testing models, the user can specify a *selection function* to limit the visualization to a subgraph. After completion of the tests, the user can filter the graph into a subgraph by providing a query in the form of a quadruple $\langle tid, res, l, ptid \rangle$ to locate a recorded transition in the trie data structure, where *tid* is the transition identifier for the transition that the user wants to locate; *res* is the action result of this transition;

l is the level of this transition in the trie; *ptid* is the transition identifier for this transition's parent in the trie. With this selection function, users can select a subtrie to generate both SG and PG with the corresponding root node in lieu of an interactive user-interface. It should be noted that this projection only affects visualization, and not the number of executed tests.

6 Experimental Evaluation

We have applied and evaluated our path coverage visualization approach on a collection of Modbat models. The list of models includes the Java server socket implementation, the coordinator of a two-phase commit protocol, the Java array list and linked list implementation, and ZooKeeper [11]. The array and linked list models, as well as the ZooKeeper model, consist of several parallel EFSMs, which are executed in an interleaving way [2].

Table 1 summarizes the results. For each Modbat model, we have considered configurations with 10, 100, 200, 500 and 1000 randomly generated test cases. The table first lists the statistics reported by Modbat: the number of states (S) and transitions (T) covered for each model (including their percentage), and the number of test cases (TC) and failed test cases (FC). The second part of the table shows the metrics of the graphs we generate. For both SGs and PGs, we list: the total number of Nodes (including both state nodes and choice nodes); the total numbers of Edges (E), the number of failed edges (FE), and loops (L). In addition to these graph metrics, for the PGs, our path coverage visualizer calculates the numbers of linearly independent paths (LIP), the longest paths (LP), the shortest paths (SP), the average lengths of paths (AVE), and the corresponding standard deviation (SD).

In Table 1, when comparing the results of the SG and PG obtained from all the models, we can see that for any increase in the number of test cases by going from 10 to 1000, the SG has a smaller number of nodes and edges than the PG. This shows that the SG is constructed in a more abstract way than the PG and is useful for giving an overview of the behavior. For the PG, although there are more nodes and edges in the graph compared to the SG, we can directly see the information about the number of linearly independent paths (LIP column in Table), so that we know how execution paths are constructed and executed from the sequences of transitions executed. This information cannot be easily seen from the SG.

In addition, the results in Table 1 indicate what degree the models are executed by the generated test cases. For example, for the coordinator model, the numbers of nodes and edges in both the PG and SG do not increase after 100 test cases are executed, and there are no failed edges. This gives us confidence about how well this model is explored by the tests. The same situation occurs for the array and linked list models. For the Java server socket and Zookeeper models, the number of failed edges for each model keeps increasing with more tests. This indicates that for these kinds of complex models, there are parts that are hard to reach and explore, so there might be a need to increase the number

Table 1. Experimental results for the Modbat models.

Model	S	T	TC	FC	Path-based (PG)									State-based (SG)			
					Nodes	Edges			Paths					Nodes	Edges		
						E	FE	L	LIP	LP	SP	AVE	SD		E	FE	L
JavaNio ServerSocket	7/ 7 (100%)	17/17 (100%)	10	2	57	79	1	17	8	14	3	9.25	4.18	9	23	1	6
			100	3	177	243	1	48	30	15	2	7.87	3.84	9	23	1	6
			200	8	363	528	4	111	53	29	2	9.68	6.24	10	25	1	7
			500	14	779	1147	8	247	105	29	2	10.51	5.29	11	27	1	8
			1000	28	1269	1904	15	439	168	29	2	10.80	4.79	11	27	1	8
Coordinator Test	7/ 7 (100%)	6/ 6 (100%)	10	0	17	20	0	0	1	6	6	6.00	0.00	17	20	0	0
			100	0	21	27	0	0	1	6	6	6.00	0.00	21	27	0	0
			200	0	21	27	0	0	1	6	6	6.00	0.00	21	27	0	0
			500	0	21	27	0	0	1	6	6	6.00	0.00	21	27	0	0
			1000	0	21	27	0	0	1	6	6	6.00	0.00	21	27	0	0
ArrayList Iterator ListIterator	1/ 1 (100%) 2/ 2 (100%) 2/ 2 (100%)	11/11 (100%) 5/11 (45%) 12/29 (41%)	10	0	174	542	0	276	6	99	12	58.17	38.75	34	85	0	38
ArrayList Iterator ListIterator	1/ 1 (100%) 2/ 2 (100%) 2/ 2 (100%)	11/11 (100%) 9/11 (81%) 13/29 (44%)	100	0	1171	3222	0	1571	75	181	2	23.93	29.74	102	216	0	94
ArrayList Iterator ListIterator	1/ 1 (100%) 2/ 2 (100%) 2/ 2 (100%)	11/11 (100%) 10/11 (90%) 17/29 (58%)	200	1	3369	10474	1	4848	138	181	2	45.35	47.46	204	423	1	184
ArrayList Iterator ListIterator	1/ 1 (100%) 2/ 2 (100%) 2/ 2 (100%)	11/11 (100%) 10/11 (90%) 25/29 (86%)	500	1	10438	29730	1	14024	319	181	2	48.96	43.55	467	955	1	417
ArrayList Iterator ListIterator	1/ 1 (100%) 2/ 2 (100%) 2/ 2 (100%)	11/11 (100%) 10/11 (90%) 27/29 (93%)	1000	14	29056	86871	1	40609	649	406	2	70.87	64.17	896	1812	1	815
LinkedList Iterator ListIterator	1/ 1 (100%) 2/ 2 (100%) 1/ 2 (50%)	18/19 (94%) 8/11 (72%) 5/29 (17%)	10	0	216	718	0	348	9	191	10	56.11	72.01	34	85	0	36
LinkedList Iterator ListIterator	1/ 1 (100%) 2/ 2 (100%) 1/ 2 (50%)	19/19 (100%) 9/11 (81%) 7/29 (24%)	100	0	1190	3348	0	1679	83	191	2	23.51	38.05	148	312	0	131
LinkedList Iterator ListIterator	1/ 1 (100%) 2/ 2 (100%) 2/ 2 (100%)	19/19 (100%) 9/11 (81%) 19/29 (65%)	200	0	6266	17140	0	7549	178	191	2	54.45	49.14	405	824	0	295
LinkedList Iterator ListIterator	1/ 1 (100%) 2/ 2 (100%) 2/ 2 (100%)	19/19 (100%) 9/11 (81%) 22/29 (75%)	500	0	15091	43303	0	19797	406	257	2	60.17	61.56	699	1413	0	522
LinkedList Iterator ListIterator	1/ 1 (100%) 2/ 2 (100%) 2/ 2 (100%)	19/19 (100%) 9/11 (81%) 24/29 (82%)	1000	0	39391	113155	0	52461	825	257	2	74.66	67.19	1404	2819	0	1083
ZKServer ZKClient	4/ 4 (100%) 9/13 (69%)	4/ 4 (100%) 28/54 (51%)	10	0	488	536	0	6	10	27	17	24.60	2.65	158	203	0	6
ZKServer ZKClient	4/ 4 (100%) 11/13 (84%)	4/ 4 (100%) 38/54 (70%)	100	7	4628	5160	7	76	98	31	4	22.57	5.99	862	1110	5	75
ZKServer ZKClient	4/ 4 (100%) 11/13 (84%)	4/ 4 (100%) 39/54 (72%)	200	9	9869	9869	9	138	197	31	4	22.88	5.67	1532	1964	5	135
ZKServer ZKClient	4/ 4 (100%) 11/13 (84%)	4/ 4 (100%) 40/54 (74%)	500	26	27208	31918	25	325	480	31	4	22.79	5.31	3057	3910	10	320
ZKServer ZKClient	4/ 4 (100%) 11/13 (84%)	4/ 4 (100%) 43/54 (79%)	1000	47	63524	76090	44	648	937	31	4	23.01	5.07	5719	7201	16	643

or quality of the tests. Moreover, we can see from Table 1 that for some models such as the ZooKeeper model, there are very large numbers of nodes and edges in both the SG and PG for, e. g., 1000 test cases executed. To deal with such large and complex models, we can use the user-defined search function discussed in Sect. 5.3 to limit the visualization to a subgraph. We do not show any subgraphs due to space limitations.

We use the Java server socket model to further discuss our experimental results based on the graphs obtained. The static visualization of the EFSM (see Fig. 9) shows the transition system and uses red edges to show expected exceptions, since the notion of failed tests does not apply. After applying abstractions, Fig. 10 shows the SG and PG for the Java server socket model with ten test cases executed, including failed transitions in red and labeled with (f).

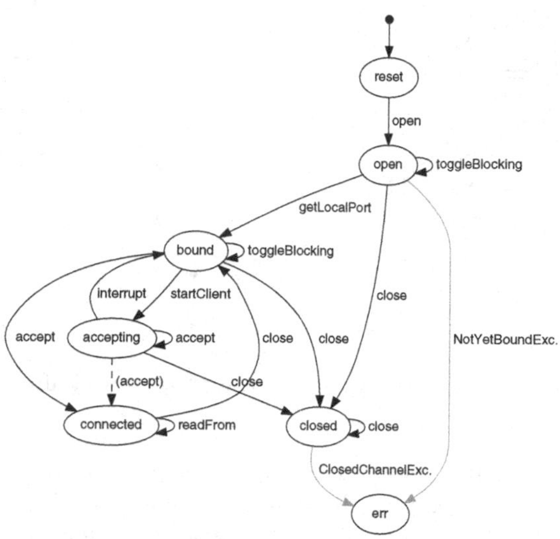

Fig. 9. EFSM for the Java server socket model.

Compared to the EFSM in Fig. 9, the SG in Fig. 10 shows the concrete executions instead of possible executions as shown by the EFSM. We see from the SG that all states have been visited after ten test cases; the SG also provides information about possible exceptions and failures occurred, actual paths and choices taken; the edge thickness indicates how often transitions were taken.

A good path-coverage-based testing strategy requires that the test cases execute as many linearly independent paths as possible. For the PG in Fig. 10, we can directly see that there are eight linearly independent paths. Each linearly independent path has a sequence of edges which represent executed transitions of the path. This gives us a simpler way of showing the paths as transition sequences, at the expense of a graph that has more nodes and edges overall. In addition, all loops, backtracked edges and taken choices are directly shown with their related linearly independent paths in the PG, and there is one linearly independent path which shows a failed test in the graph. Also, like the SG, the edge thickness in the PG indicates how often transitions were taken.

To show how our abstraction reduces the complexity of graphs, we use the Java server socket model as an example. Figure 11 shows the FSG without applying any abstractions for the Java server socket model with 10 test cases executed. This graph should be contrasted with the SG shown in Fig. 10(left). From this FSG, we notice that the FSG has many redundant edges between both state nodes and choice nodes, and it also has more choice nodes, as opposed to the SG

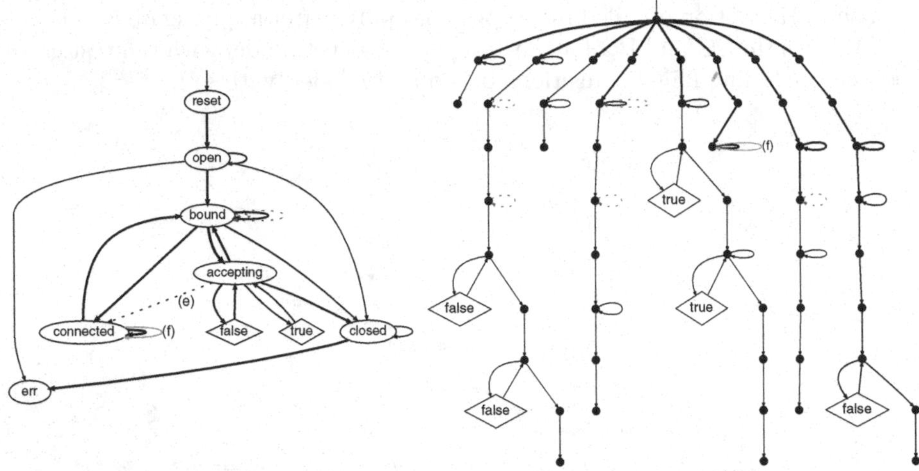

Fig. 10. SG (left) and PG (right) for the above model after ten tests.

in Fig. 10. Here, we do not show the FPG for the Java server socket model due to space limitations, but we give the detailed comparison between the SG and FSG and between the PG and FPG for the Java server socket model in Table 2. For instance, with 1000 test cases, the PG has three times fewer edges than the FPG; the SG has only 11 nodes and 27 edges, as compared to 61 nodes and 5491 edges in the FSG. This comparison shows that with the help of abstractions, the SG and PG are much more concise and less complex than the FSG and FPG.

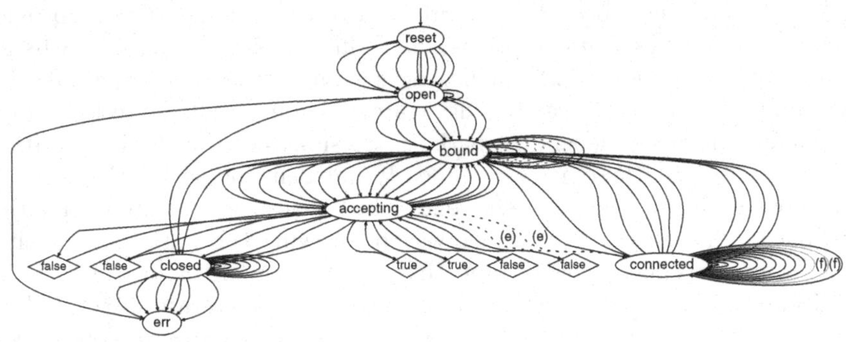

Fig. 11. FSG for the Java server socket model after ten tests.

7 Related Work

Coverage analysis is an important concern in software testing. It can be used as an exit criterion for testing and deciding whether additional test cases are

Table 2. Comparison between PG and FPG, and between SG and FSG of the Java server socket model.

Model	TC	PG				FPG				SG				FSG			
		Nodes	Edges			Nodes	Edges			Nodes	Edges			Nodes	Edges		
			E	FE	L		E	FE	L		E	FE	L		E	FE	L
JavaNio Server-Socket	10	57	79	1	17	70	97	2	21	9	23	1	6	13	109	2	31
	100	177	243	1	48	376	497	3	100	9	23	1	6	15	545	3	145
	200	363	528	4	111	811	1101	8	221	10	25	1	7	26	1239	8	353
	500	779	1147	8	247	1943	2613	14	520	11	27	1	8	40	2910	14	816
	1000	1269	1904	15	439	3721	4982	28	996	11	27	1	8	61	5491	28	1510

needed, and related to which aspects of the SUT. For source code coverage, tools generally only report a verdict on which line of code has been executed how often. In the tool Tecrevis, a visual representation of redundancy in unit tests provides a graphical mapping between each test case and the artifacts in the SUT (here: methods) that indicates which tests exercise the same component [13]. In path coverage, the underlying graph is usually derived from the source code, the *control flow graph*, or from the *call graph* of the SUT when considering function calls. In our approach, we are not directly concerned with visualizing paths of the SUT, but rather, paths on the testing model used for test-case generation. Correspondingly, our graphs are usually more concise than the control flow graph, as not all branches of the SUT may need to be modeled at the level of ESFMs. In particular, with respect to related work and the coverage analysis domain, visualization is usually an orthogonal concern to quantifying coverage, and not often considered.

Visualization makes coverage information understandable. Ladenberger and Leuschel address the problem of visualizing large state spaces in the ProB tool [14]. They introduce *projection diagrams,* which through a user-selectable function partition the states into equivalence classes. A coloring scheme for states and transitions indicates whether the state space has been exhausted, or all collapsed transitions share the same enablement. As their diagrams are based on the actually explored state space, they do not directly visualize coverage of the underlying model as in our approach. Moreover, they do not cover multiple transitions between the same pair of states as in our application scenario; however, this could be accounted for by adjusting the thickness of edges by the number of collapsed edges. Similarly, Groote and van Ham [10] applied an automated visualization to examples from the Very Large Transition System (VLTS) Benchmark set [8]. A relation between the graphical representation of the underlying model (in the form of UML sequence diagrams) and a set of paths from test cases is presented by Rountev et al. [19]. Their goal is deriving test cases, and as such they are not concerned with a representation of the paths.

The basic visualization elements of both SG and PG we have defined in this paper are based on the concept of *simple path* proposed by Ammann and Offutt [1]. An execution path is a simple path if there are no cycles in this path, with the exception that the first and last states may be identical (the entire path itself is a cycle) [1]. Based on this definition, any execution path can be composed of simple paths. Therefore, in this paper, the concept of the simple path is applied by considering only transitions from $s_{origin}(t)$ to $s_{dest}(t)$ (or $s_{origin}(t)$ if t is a self-transition or backtracked transition).

8 Conclusions and Future Work

The main contribution of this paper is to present an approach to capture and visualize test-case-execution paths through models. This is achieved by first recording execution paths with a trie data structure, then visualizing them using state-based graphs (SGs) and path-based graphs (PGs) obtained by applying abstractions. The SG conveys the behavior of the model well. The PG only shows executed paths, without providing detail. It avoids crossing edges, which makes the PG more scalable, even though it contains more nodes and edges as such. Also, the PG directly indicates the number of linearly independent paths.

To obtain the SGs and PGs, we have proposed abstractions as our initial technique to reduce the size and complexity of graphs. We have implemented our approach as a path coverage visualizer for the Modbat model-based API tester. An experimental evaluation on several model-based test suites shows that our abstraction technique reduces the complexity of graphs, and our visualization of execution paths helps to show the frequency of transitions taken by the executed paths and to distinguish successful from failed test cases.

Future work includes investigating other techniques and tools to support more visualization features in the SGs and PGs, using more abstractions for the further reduction of larger graphs and applying the SGs and PGs not only for visualizing execution paths of models, but also for the SUT. Another direction of future work is to investigate approaches to perform state space exploration efficiently for selecting good test suites and visualizing execution paths. Although our current visualization approach has been applied to the Modbat tester, it is also possible to use it for other testing platforms. Furthermore, additional coverage metrics such as branch-coverage of boolean subexpressions within preconditions and assertions, or the more detailed *modified condition/decision coverage* (MC/DC) [7] could be used to refine the intermediate execution steps even further. In essence, many of the coverage techniques available at the SUT-level could be lifted to the model level.

References

1. Ammann, P., Offutt, J.: Introduction to Software Testing. Cambridge University Press, Cambridge (2016)
2. Artho, C.V., et al.: Modbat: a model-based API tester for event-driven systems. In: Bertacco, V., Legay, A. (eds.) HVC 2013. LNCS, vol. 8244, pp. 112–128. Springer, Cham (2013). https://doi.org/10.1007/978-3-319-03077-7_8

3. Artho, C., Rousset, G., Gros, Q.: Precondition coverage in software testing. In: Proceedings of 1st International Workshop on Validating Software Tests (VST 2016), Osaka, Japan. IEEE (2016)
4. AT&T Labs Research. Graphviz - Graph Visualization Software. https://www.graphviz.org
5. Brass, P.: Advanced Data Structures. Cambridge University Press, Cambridge (2008)
6. Cheng, K., Krishnakumar, A.: Automatic functional test generation using the extended finite state machine model. In: Proceedings of 30th International Design Automation Conference, DAC, pp. 86–91, Dallas, USA. ACM (1993)
7. Chilenski, J.J., Miller, S.P.: Applicability of modified condition/decision coverage to software testing. Softw. Eng. J. **9**(5), 193–200 (1994)
8. CWI and INRIA. The VLTS benchmark suite (2019). https://cadp.inria.fr/resources/vlts/. Accessed 20 May 2019
9. Gansner, E., Koutsofios, E., North, S.: Drawing graphs with dot (2006). http://www.graphviz.org/pdf/dotguide.pdf
10. Groote, J.F., van Ham, F.: Interactive visualization of large state spaces. Int. J. Softw. Tools Technol. Transf. **8**(1), 77–91 (2006)
11. Hunt, P., Konar, M., Junqueira, F.P., Reed, B.: Zookeeper: wait-free coordination for internet-scale systems. In: Barham, P., Roscoe, T. (eds.) 2010 USENIX Annual Technical Conference. USENIX Association (2010)
12. Jorgensen, P.C.: Software Testing: A Craftsman's Approach. Auerbach Publications, Boca Raton (2013)
13. Koochakzadeh, N., Garousi, V.: TeCReVis: a tool for test coverage and test redundancy visualization. In: Bottaci, L., Fraser, G. (eds.) TAIC PART 2010. LNCS, vol. 6303, pp. 129–136. Springer, Heidelberg (2010). https://doi.org/10.1007/978-3-642-15585-7_12
14. Ladenberger, L., Leuschel, M.: Mastering the visualization of larger state spaces with projection diagrams. In: Butler, M., Conchon, S., Zaïdi, F. (eds.) ICFEM 2015. LNCS, vol. 9407, pp. 153–169. Springer, Cham (2015). https://doi.org/10.1007/978-3-319-25423-4_10
15. Lawrence, J., Clarke, S., Burnett, M., Rothermel, G.: How well do professional developers test with code coverage visualizations? An empirical study. In: IEEE Symposium on Visual Languages and Human-Centric Computing, pp. 53–60. IEEE (2005)
16. Lu, S., Zhou, P., Liu, W., Zhou, Y., Torrellas, J.: Pathexpander: Architectural support for increasing the path coverage of dynamic bug detection. In: Proceedings of the 39th Annual IEEE/ACM International Symposium on Microarchitecture, pp. 38–52. IEEE Computer Society (2006)
17. Myers, G.J., Badgett, T., Thomas, T.M., Sandler, C.: The Art of Software Testing, vol. 2. Wiley Online Library, Hoboken (2004)
18. Programming Methods Laboratory of École Polytechnique Fédérale de Lausanne. The Scala Programming Language. https://www.scala-lang.org
19. Rountev, A., Kagan, S., Sawin, J.: Coverage criteria for testing of object interactions in sequence diagrams. In: Cerioli, M. (ed.) FASE 2005. LNCS, vol. 3442, pp. 289–304. Springer, Heidelberg (2005). https://doi.org/10.1007/978-3-540-31984-9_22
20. Utting, M., Legeard, B.: Practical Model-Based Testing: A Tools Approach. Morgan Kaufmann Publishers Inc., San Francisco (2007)

21. Utting, M., Pretschner, A., Legeard, B.: A taxonomy of model-based testing approaches. Softw. Test. Verif. Reliab. **22**, 297–312 (2012)
22. Visser, W., Havelund, K., Brat, G., Park, S., Lerda, F.: Model checking programs. Autom. Softw. Eng. J. **10**(2), 203–232 (2003)

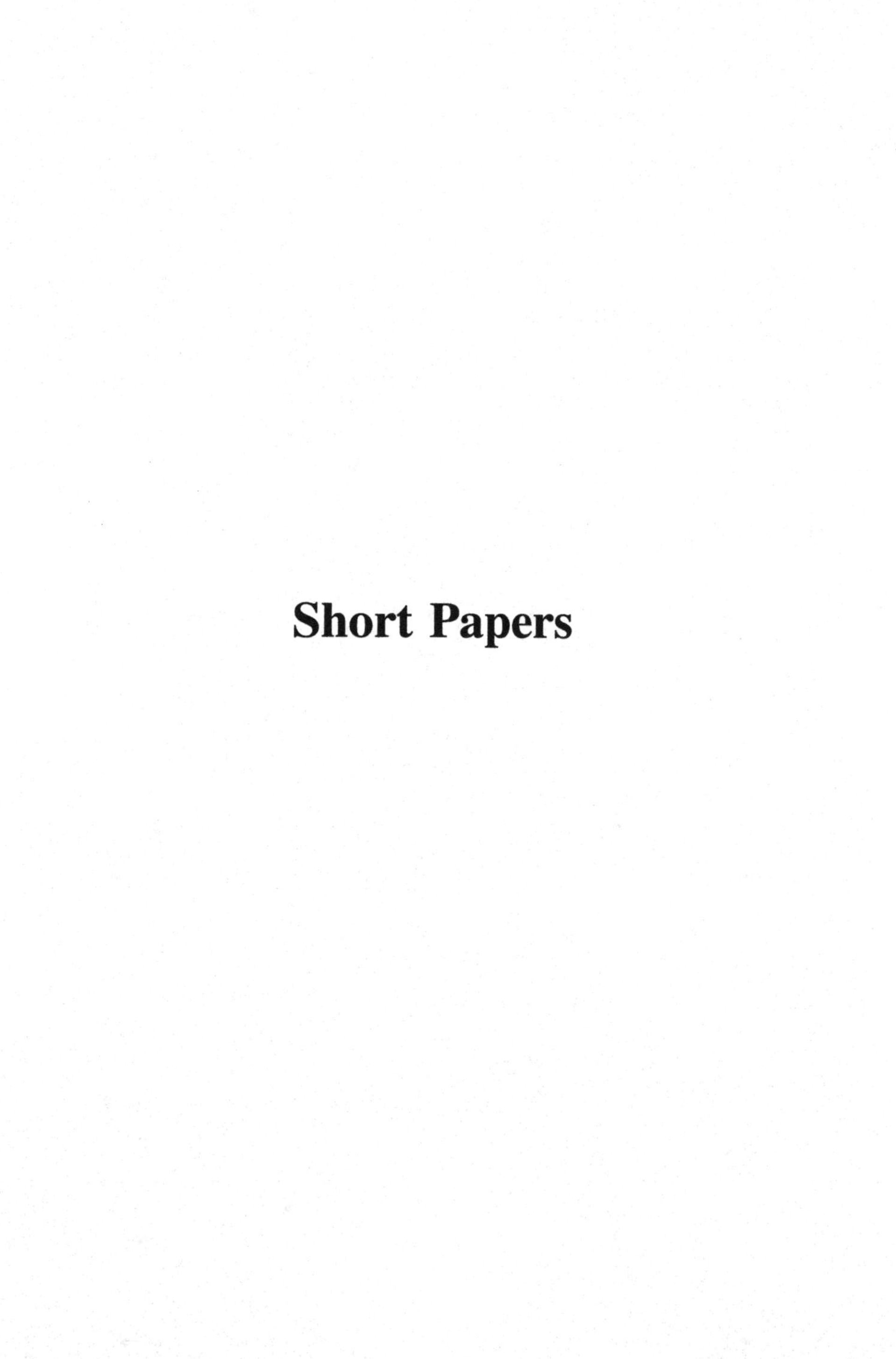

Short Papers

HYPpOTesT: Hypothesis Testing Toolkit for Uncertain Service-Based Web Applications

Matteo Camilli[1(✉)], Angelo Gargantini[2], Rosario Madaudo[3], and Patrizia Scandurra[2]

[1] Faculty of Computer Science, Free University of Bozen-Bolzano, Bolzano, Italy
matteo.camilli@unibz.it
[2] Department of Management, Information and Production Engineering (DIGIP), Università degli Studi di Bergamo, Bergamo, Italy
{angelo.gargantini,patrizia.scandurra}@unibg.it
[3] Altran Italia SPA, Milan, Italy
rosario.madaudo2@altran.it

Abstract. This paper introduces a model-based testing framework and associated toolkit, so called HYPpOTesT, for uncertain service-based web applications specified as probabilistic systems with non-determinism. The framework connects input/output conformance theory with hypothesis testing in order to assess if the behavior of the application under test corresponds to its probabilistic formal specification. The core component is a (on-the-fly) model-based testing algorithm able to automatically generate, execute and evaluate test cases from a Markov Decision Process specification. The testing activity feeds a Bayesian inference process that quantifies and mitigates the system uncertainty by calibrating probability values in the initial specification. This paper illustrates the structure, features, and usage of HYPpOTesT using the U-Store exemplar, i.e., a web-based e-commerce application that exhibits uncertain behavior.

Keywords: Model-based testing · Probabilistic systems · Service-based web applications · Bayesian inference · Uncertainty quantification

1 Introduction

Modern software systems operate in a complex ecosystem of protocols, libraries, services, and execution platforms that change over time in response to: new technologies; repairing activities (due to faults and vulnerabilities); varying resources/services availability; and reconfiguration of the environment. Predictability is very hard to achieve since modern software-intensive systems are often situated in complex ecosystems that can be hard or even impossible to fully understand and specify at design-time. Namely, these systems are often exposed

W. Ahrendt and S. L. Tapia Tarifa (Eds.): IFM 2019, LNCS 11918, pp. 495–503, 2019.
https://doi.org/10.1007/978-3-030-34968-4_27

to multiple sources of uncertainty that can arise from an ambiguous specification not completely known before the system is running. Common examples of applications affected by uncertain and probabilistic behavior are control policies in robotics, speech recognition, security protocols, and service-based web applications (e.g., e-commerce, e-health, online banking, etc.). In this latter case, highly dynamic and changing ecosystems influence a workflow of interacting distributed components (e.g., web-services or microservices) owned by multiple third-party providers with different Quality of Service (QoS) attributes (e.g, reliability, performance, cost, etc.). Testing is the most common validation technique, seen as it generally represents a lightweight and vital process to establish confidence on the developed software systems. Nevertheless, there is little work in the scientific community that focuses on executable testing frameworks for uncertain systems, with notable exceptions in the context of cyber physical systems [11,12].

As part of our ongoing research activity on testing under uncertainty [2,3], this paper introduces HYPpOTesT: a model-based HYPOthesis Testing Toolkit for service-based web applications that considers uncertainty as a first-class concern. Namely, we focus on statistical *hypothesis testing* [5] of uncertain QoS parameters of the System Under Test (SUT), modeled by a Markov Decision Processes (MDP) [7]. MDPs represent a widely adopted formalism for modeling systems exhibiting both probabilistic and nondeterministic behavior. As described in [4], hypothesis testing (differently from functional testing) represents a fundamental activity to assess whether the frequencies observed during model-based testing (MBT) processes correspond to the probabilities specified in the model. Thus, HYPpOTesT has been tailored to deal with the *uncertainty quantification* problem [3] by means of hypothesis testing while executing a model-based exploration of the SUT. The MDP specification, along with assumptions on the uncertain QoS parameters, guides the automatic generation of the test cases so that the probability to stress the uncertain components of the application is maximized. Testing feeds a *Bayesian inference* [5] process that calibrates the uncertain parameters depending on the observed behavior. Bayesian inference is used to compute the Posterior density function associated with specific uncertain parameters θ of the MDP model. As described in [5], Bayesian inference represents an effective technique used to update belief about θ. A Prior density function (or simply Prior) is the probability distribution that would express one's beliefs about θ parameters before some evidence (i.e., experimental data) is taken into account.

This paper focuses on engineering aspects of HYPpOTesT, such as design and implementation concerns. To sum up, our toolkit supports: (*i*) modeling of a service-based web application (SUT) in terms of a MDP using a simple domain-specific language; (*ii*) explicit elicitation of the uncertain QoS parameters using Prior probability distributions; (*iii*) automatic generation, execution, and evaluation of the test cases using an uncertainty-aware (on-the-fly) model-based testing algorithm. Throughout the paper, we adopt an uncertain web-based e-commerce application, U-Store (Uncertain Store), as running example to illustrate the main feature of the toolkit and as exemplar for a preliminary validation of our testing approach.

Table 1. Services composing the U-Store web-based application.

Service	Description
`frontend`	Exposes an HTTP server to serve the website. Generates session IDs for all users
`user`	Provide Customer login, sign up, as well as user's information retrieval
`cart`	Stores selected items in the user's shipping cart (persistent memory) and retrieves it
`catalog`	Provides the list of products from a SQL database, the ability to search products, and get individual products
`shipping`	Gives shipping cost estimates based on the shopping cart and the given address (mock component)
`payment`	Charges the given credit card info (mock component) with the given amount and returns a transaction ID

Related Work. In [1] MDPs are used to model systems exhibiting stochastic failures. The proposed approach aims at finding input-selection (i.e., testing) strategies which maximizes the probability of hitting failures. The approach introduced in [10] is based on Machine Learning and it aims at inferring a behavioral model of the SUT to select those tests which the inferred model is "least certain" about. Results suggest that such a test case generation outperforms conventional random testing. In [12] test case generation strategies based on the uncertainty theory and multi-objective search are proposed in the context of cyber-physical systems. Results in this work showed that this test strategy increases the likelihood to observe more uncertainties due to unknown behaviors of the physical environments. In [11] a testing method that takes into account uncertainty in timing properties of embedded software systems is proposed. This method improves the fault detection effectiveness of tests suites derived from timed automata compared to traditional testing approaches. Summarizing, there are few and recently defined approaches that deal with testing driven by uncertainty awareness. Notable examples has been briefly described. The topic definitely needs further investigation in the area of service-based applications, where QoS attributes are influenced by highly dynamic and uncertain ecosystems.

This paper is organized as follows. Section 2 introduces the running example; Sect. 3 describes our testing toolkit; Sect. 4 reports some experimental results of a preliminary validation of our toolkit; and Sect. 5 concludes the paper.

2 Running Example: The U-Store Web Application

U-Store[1] consists of a number of services that implement specialized pieces of functionalities and interact with each other using HTTP resource APIs. Table 1

[1] Sources and testing results are publicly available at https://github.com/SELab-unimi/ustore-exemplar.

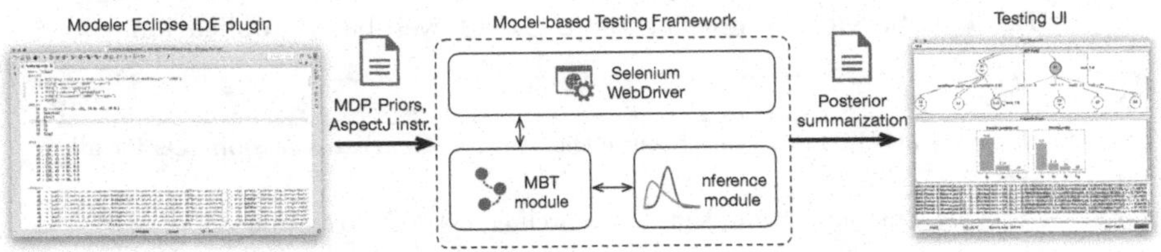

Fig. 1. Main components of the HYPPOTEST toolkit.

lists the services of the U-STORE and provides a brief description of them. From the user perspective, the application behavior can be viewed as a number of *functional statuses* (or states), each one of them with a number of feasible *inputs* that cause services to execute specific tasks. Services tasks generate *outputs* and allow the current state to be changed accordingly.

In this context, both functional and non-functional quality attributes of the web application depend on parameters (e.g., performance, bandwidth, available memory, etc.) typically subject to different sources of uncertainty (e.g., jobs arrival, fault tolerance, scalability, etc.) [6]. As an example, suppose the user navigates the U-STORE towards the *Checkout* web page. After selecting the payment method, the user submits the *buy* request. At this stage, the U-STORE asks the external `payment` service to execute the proper task. The outcome of this operation is inherently influenced by several sources of uncertainty (as those mentioned above), and from the user perspective uncertainty reflects common types of failure or undesired behavior upon the *buy* request, such as unexpected errors and/or high latency.

3 The Hypothesis Testing Toolkit

HYPPOTEST (see Fig. 1) is tailored to perform hypothesis testing of uncertain service-based web applications by combining an uncertainty-aware MBT and Bayesian inference. A description of the three major components follows.

Modeler. The modeler is an ECLIPSE IDE plugin[2] that allows the MDP specification to be created using a textual Domain Specific Language (DSL). As described in [7], a MDP model is composed of finite sets of states, transitions, and actions. Transitions between states occur by taking a nondeterministic choice among the available actions from the current state and then a stochastic choice of the successor state, according to a partial probabilistic transition function. Figure 2 reports an extract of the U-STORE MDP design-time model using our DSL. The keywords reflect the structural elements of the model: actions (line 2), states (line 6), and arcs (line 14). Figure 3 contains a visual representation of this MDP extract. It is worth noting that upon the submit action from state S_6

[2] Publicly available at https://github.com/SELab-unimi/mdp-generator/tree/web-app. The repository contains sources and the complete specification of the U-Store.

(readyToPay) we can have multiple responses from the system. Each one of them is associated with a different probability value reflecting our assumption about the behavior of the `payment` service, typically based on past experience or previous studies. To express uncertainty on the assumptions, the DSL allows the Prior probability density functions to be specified (e.g., line 10). In particular, modelers use *Dirichlet* as conjugate Priors for the uncertain transition probabilities of the MDP model. In fact, as described in [5], the Dirichlet distribution $Dir(\alpha_i)$ is the natural conjugate prior of the categorical distribution, with $\alpha_i = (\alpha_1, ..., \alpha_n)$ vector of concentration parameters. Priors are used to express uncertainty on model parameters describing QoS attributes, such as reliability of the services or the communication channels, response time, and cost in terms of resources usage or energy consumption.

To make our framework able to carry out model-based generation and execution of tests, the structural elements in the model are bound to components in the SUT as informally sketched in Fig. 3. Such a binding is defined by the modeler at design-time. MDP actions are mapped to *controllable actions* while arcs are mapped to *observable events*. Controllable actions are user inputs supplied to the application using the available web UI. A wide range of inputs typically seen in web applications are supported by our DSL, such as click on different UI elements (e.g., link, button, checkbox, etc.), filling in text fields, submit forms, navigating back and forth, and more. As an example, the submit_form controllable action (line 4) allows a form to be submitted. Arguments specify the form *id*, a *timeout*, and the *id* of a specific UI element which contains the result of the executed task. Each arc in the model is mapped to an observable event (e.g., line 22), that is an arbitrary Java boolean expression, where we typically make assertions on the resulting UI element (i.e., a `WebElement` object of the SELENIUM [8] library package `org.openqa.selenium`). After the execution of a controllable action, HYPPOTEST waits until one of the suitable observable events happens and performs the selected transition. These operations are executed by an automatically generated *test harness* (ASPECTJ instrumentation). The MBT module generates test cases using the MDP specification and makes them executable upon the SUT though the test harness.

Model-Based Testing Framework. The main components of the testing framework[3] are: the *MBT module* responsible for test cases generation; the *Selenium WebDriver* responsible for test cases execution; and the *Inference module* responsible for hypothesis testing.

The MBT module dynamically generates test cases from the MDP specification according to an *uncertainty*-aware test case generation strategy. Essentially, this strategy solves a *dynamic decision problem* [7] to compute the *best exploration policy* π^* that returns, for each state s, the actions that maximize the probability to reach the uncertain θ parameters in the model. More technical details on this strategy can be found in [2]. Thus, the testing process stochastically samples the state space by choosing those inputs that allow the uncertain

[3] Sources and instructions are publicly available at https://github.com/SELab-unimi/mbt-module/tree/web-app.

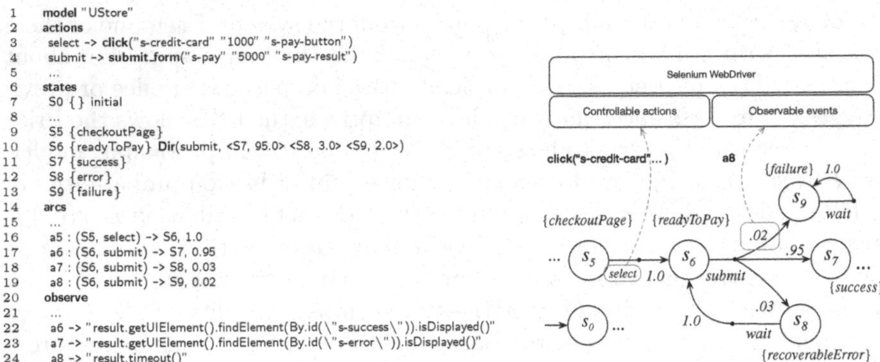

model "UStore"
actions
select -> click("s-credit-card" "1000" "s-pay-button")
submit -> submit_form("s-pay" "5000" "s-pay-result")
...
states
S0 { } initial
...
S5 {checkoutPage}
S6 {readyToPay} Dir(submit, <S7, 95.0> <S8, 3.0> <S9, 2.0>)
S7 {success}
S8 {error}
S9 {failure}
arcs
...
a5 : (S5, select) -> S6, 1.0
a6 : (S6, submit) -> S7, 0.95
a7 : (S6, submit) -> S8, 0.03
a8 : (S6, submit) -> S9, 0.02
observe
...
a6 -> "result.getUIElement().findElement(By.id(\"s-success\")).isDisplayed()"
a7 -> "result.getUIElement().findElement(By.id(\"s-error\")).isDisplayed()"
a8 -> "result.timeout()"
Selenium WebDriver
Controllable actions
Observable events
click("s-credit-card"...)
a8
{failure}
1.0
wait
{checkoutPage}
{readyToPay}
.02
.95
select
1.0
submit
{success}
.03
1.0
wait
{recoverableError}

Fig. 2. U-STORE MDP extract in our DSL.

Fig. 3. Visual representation of the U-STORE MDP extract and of mapping to SUT components.

components of the SUT to be stressed out. To this end, the *test harness* provides a high-level view of the SUT behavior matching the abstraction level of the MDP specification. Technically, it allows the actions selected by the exploration policy π^* to be translated into valid inputs for the SUT by means of the *Selenium WebDriver* that interacts directly with the web UI. At the same time, observable events provide a serialized view on the SUT behavior to keep track of the execution trace and extract meaningful data to perform hypothesis testing. From a theoretical perspective, the MBT module uses the test harness to conduct a input/output *conformance game* [2,9] between the model and the SUT. During the conformance game, hypothesis testing is carried out by the Inference module that incrementally updates beliefs on θ parameters by using the Bayesian inference formulation: $Posterior \propto Likelihood \cdot Prior$. In our context, the Prior and Posterior are conjugate distributions and the Posterior can be obtained by applying a very efficient updating rule [2,5]. In fact, the Posterior is distributed as $Dir(\alpha')$, where $\alpha' = \alpha + (c_1, ..., c_n)$ with c_i number of observations in category i. At termination, the MBT module summarizes the Posteriors (by computing the mean values) and calibrates the θ parameters.

Two termination conditions are currently supported by our testing framework: a traditional condition based on the *number of executed tests*; and termination based on the convergence of the *Bayes factor* [5]. This latter condition, in particular, is a model selection method that allows the testing activity to be terminated when the θ parameters do not substantially change during the inference process. So, by using this latter method the Inference module decides when inferred θ parameters are strongly supported by the data under consideration.

Testing UI. The UI allows information about hypothesis testing to be visualized for human consumption. Three different canvas in the main window show: the MBT model, the Posterior density functions, and a log produced by the MBT module. The MDP model canvas contains an animated visualization of the model. During testing, the UI highlights the current model state and the current action selected by the test case generation strategy. The Probability charts canvas displays the Posterior distributions so that the tester can see how the inference process updates the knowledge on θ parameters while testing goes on. The log canvas shows textual information generated by the MBT module for each uncertain parameter: the number of executed tests, the summarization of the Posterior density functions, and the Bayes factor.

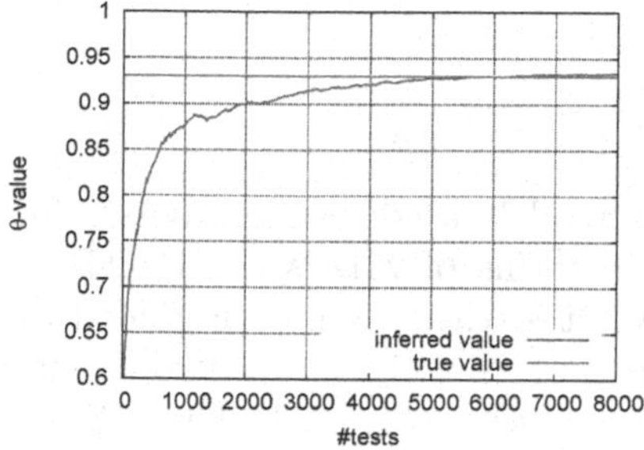

Fig. 4. Inference of a θ parameter.

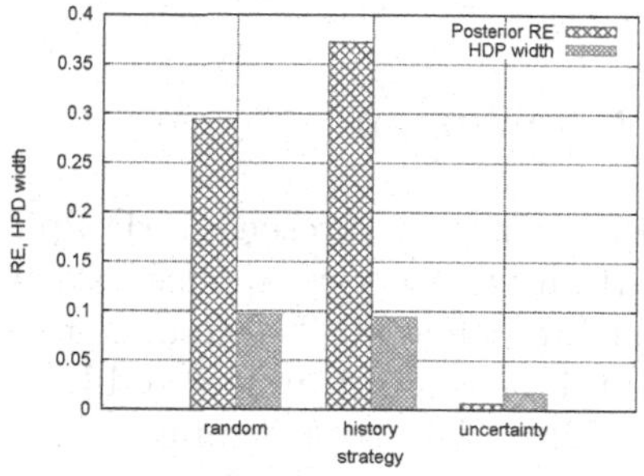

Fig. 5. Inference effectiveness.

4 Evaluation

We are evaluating our testing framework by conducting a large testing campaign of the U-Store application. Here we briefly discuss some significant results and we refer the reader to our implementation for the replicability of the presented data. To measure the effectiveness of HYPpoTest, we artificially induced abnormal conditions due to sources of uncertainty. Namely, the services composing the U-Store application have been configured to simulate service degradation by means of failure rates and random delays. As an example, we forced the uncertain `payment` component to have specific failure/error rates and we executed our testing framework starting from wrong hypothesis (i.e., using an informative Prior having a relative error of 1.5). Figure 4 shows how the uncertain success rate associated with the `payment` service varies during hypothesis testing of the U-Store. The uncertainty-aware strategy allows the probability to test the `payment` component to be maximized during model-based exploration. As long as evidence is collected, the Posterior knowledge is incrementally updated. The termination condition based on the Bayes factor allows the uncertain θ parameter to be inferred with high precision (i.e., the order of magnitude of the Posterior relative error is 10^{-2}) after executing $\sim 8k$ tests.

We also compared the effectiveness of our uncertainty-aware test case generation strategy with two traditional model-based exploration strategies: a completely random walk approach; and a history-based exploration approach.

Figure 5 shows the accuracy in terms of Posterior relative error and Posterior Highest Probability Density (HPD) region width, very often used as a measure of the confidence gained after the inference activity (i.e., the smaller the region width, the higher the accuracy). This comparative evaluation assumes equal effort (i.e., $5k$ tests) spent using different strategies. For each strategy, we started the hypothesis testing activity using a Prior with 0.5 relative error and 0.1 HPD region width. In our running example, the uncertainty-aware strategy used by HYPPOTEST allows inference to be always more precise. On average, we measured a decreased Posterior relative error by a factor of ~ 50.

5 Conclusion

In this paper we presented HYPpOTesT, a model-based testing toolkit for uncertain web service applications modeled in terms of MDPs. HYPpOTesT adopts an online MBT technique that combines test case generation guided by uncertainty-aware strategies and Bayesian inference. Namely, we focused on statistical hypothesis testing of uncertain QoS parameters of the SUT. The U-Store application was used throughout the paper to illustrate the features of the toolkit and as validation benchmark.

As future work, we plan to study different fine grained uncertainty-aware testing methods in order to assess whether delivered confidence out from testing may be better if looking at specific and uncertain model-based properties of interest. We also plan to enhance the toolchain that supports the proposed approach with the ability to perform sensitivity analysis can be apportioned to different experimental designs (e.g., traffic condition, frequency of requests, workload of services).

References

1. Aichernig, B.K., Tappler, M.: Probabilistic black-box reachability checking. In: Lahiri, S., Reger, G. (eds.) RV 2017. LNCS, vol. 10548, pp. 50–67. Springer, Cham (2017). https://doi.org/10.1007/978-3-319-67531-2_4
2. Camilli, M., Bellettini, C., Gargantini, A., Scandurra, P.: Online model-based testing under uncertainty. In: 2018 IEEE 29th International Symposium on Software Reliability Engineering (ISSRE), pp. 36–46, October 2018
3. Camilli, M., Gargantini, A., Scandurra, P., Bellettini, C.: Towards inverse uncertainty quantification in software development (short paper). In: Cimatti, A., Sirjani, M. (eds.) SEFM 2017. LNCS, vol. 10469, pp. 375–381. Springer, Cham (2017). https://doi.org/10.1007/978-3-319-66197-1_24
4. Gerhold, M., Stoelinga, M.: Model-based testing of probabilistic systems. Formal Aspects Comput. **30**(1), 77–106 (2018)
5. Insua, D., Ruggeri, F., Wiper, M.: Bayesian Analysis of Stochastic Process Models. Wiley Series in Probability and Statistics. Wiley, Hoboken (2012)
6. Perez-Palacin, D., Mirandola, R.: Uncertainties in the modeling of self-adaptive systems: a taxonomy and an example of availability evaluation. In: International Conference on Performance Engineering, pp. 3–14 (2014)

7. Puterman, M.L.: Markov Decision Processes: Discrete Stochastic Dynamic Programming. Wiley, New York (1994)
8. Selenium HQ: WebDriver (2019). https://www.seleniumhq.org/. Accessed June 2019
9. Veanes, M., Campbell, C., Schulte, W., Tillmann, N.: Online testing with model programs. SIGSOFT Softw. Eng. Notes **30**(5), 273–282 (2005)
10. Walkinshaw, N., Fraser, G.: Uncertainty-driven black-box test data generation. In: International Conference on Software Testing, Verification and Validation, pp. 253–263 (2017)
11. Wang, C., Pastore, F., Briand, L.: Oracles for testing software timeliness with uncertainty. ACM Trans. Softw. Eng. Methodol. **28**(1), 1:1–1:30 (2018)
12. Zhang, M., Ali, S., Yue, T.: Uncertainty-wise test case generation and minimization for cyber-physical systems. J. Syst. Softw. **153**, 1–21 (2019)

Interactive Visualization of Saturation Attempts in Vampire

Bernhard Gleiss[1(✉)], Laura Kovács[1,2], and Lena Schnedlitz[1]

[1] TU Wien, Vienna, Austria
bgleiss@forsyte.at

[2] Chalmers University of Technology, Gothenburg, Sweden

Abstract. Many applications of formal methods require automated reasoning about system properties, such as system safety and security. To improve the performance of automated reasoning engines, such as SAT/SMT solvers and first-order theorem prover, it is necessary to understand both the successful and failing attempts of these engines towards producing formal certificates, such as logical proofs and/or models. Such an analysis is challenging due to the large number of logical formulas generated during proof/model search. In this paper we focus on saturation-based first-order theorem proving and introduce the SatVis tool for interactively visualizing saturation-based proof attempts in first-order theorem proving. We build SatVis on top of the world-leading theorem prover Vampire, by interactively visualizing the saturation attempts of Vampire in SatVis. Our work combines the automatic layout and visualization of the derivation graph induced by the saturation attempt with interactive transformations and search functionality. As a result, we are able to analyze and debug (failed) proof attempts of Vampire. Thanks to its interactive visualisation, we believe SatVis helps both experts and non-experts in theorem proving to understand first-order proofs and analyze/refine failing proof attempts of first-order provers.

1 Introduction

Many applications of formal methods, such as program analysis and verification, require automated reasoning about system properties, such as program safety, security and reliability. Automated reasoners, such as SAT/SMT solvers [1,5] and first-order theorem provers [9,13], have therefore become a key backbone of rigorous system engineering. For example, proving properties over the computer memory relies on first-order reasoning with both quantifiers and integer arithmetic.

Saturation-based theorem proving is the leading approach for automating reasoning in full first-order logic. In a nutshell, this approach negates a given goal and saturates its given set of input formulas (including the negated goal), by deriving logical consequences of the input using a logical inference system, such as binary resolution or superposition. Whenever a contradiction (false) is

W. Ahrendt and S. L. Tapia Tarifa (Eds.): IFM 2019, LNCS 11918, pp. 504–513, 2019.
https://doi.org/10.1007/978-3-030-34968-4_28

derived, the saturation process terminates reporting validity of the input goal. State-of-the-art theorem provers, such as VAMPIRE [9] and E [13], implement saturation-based proof search using the (ordered) superposition calculus [11]. These provers rely on powerful indexing algorithms, selection functions and term orderings for making saturation-based theorem proving efficient and scalable to a large set of first-order formulas, as evidenced in the yearly CASC system competition of first-order provers [14].

Over the past years, saturation-based theorem proving has been extended to first-order logic with theories, such as arithmetic, theory of arrays and algebraic datatypes [8]. Further, first-class boolean sorts and if-then-else and let-in constructs have also been introduced as extensions to the input syntax of first-order theorem provers [7]. Thanks to these recent developments, first-order theorem provers became better suited in applications of formal methods, being for example a competitive alternative to SMT-solvers [1,5] in software verification and program analysis. Recent editions of the SMT-COMP[1] and CASC system competitions show, for example, that VAMPIRE successfully competes against the leading SMT solvers Z3 [5] and CVC4 [1] and vice-versa.

By leveraging the best practices in first-order theorem proving in combination with SMT solving, in our recent work [3] we showed that correctness of a software program can be reduced to a validity problem in first-order logic. We use VAMPIRE to prove the resulting encodings, outperforming SMT solvers. Our initial results demonstrate that first-order theorem proving is well-suited for applications of (relational) verification, such as safety and non-interference. Yet, our results also show that the performance of the prover crucially depends on the logical representation of its input problem and the deployed reasoning strategies during proof search. As such, users and developers of first-order provers, and automated reasoners in general, typically face the burden of analysing (failed) proof attempts produced by the prover, with the ultimate goal to refine the input and/or proof strategies making the prover succeed in proving its input. Understanding (some of) the reasons why the prover failed is however very hard and requires a considerable amount of work by highly qualified experts in theorem proving, hindering thus the use of theorem provers in many application domains.

In this paper we address this challenge and *introduce the* SATVIS *tool to ease the task of analysing failed proof attempts in saturation-based reasoning.* We designed SATVIS to support interactive visualization of the saturation algorithm used in VAMPIRE, with the goal to ease the manual analysis of VAMPIRE proofs as well as failed proof attempts in VAMPIRE. Inputs to SATVIS are proof (attempts) produced by VAMPIRE. Our tool consists of (i) an explicit visualization of the DAG-structure of the saturation proof (attempt) of VAMPIRE and (ii) interactive transformations of the DAG for pruning and reformatting the proof (attempt). In its current setting, SATVIS can be used only in the context of VAMPIRE. Yet, by parsing/translating proofs (or proof attempts) of other provers into the VAMPIRE proof format, SATVIS can be used in conjunction with other provers as well.

[1] https://smt-comp.github.io/.

When feeding VAMPIRE proofs to SATVIS, SATVIS supports both users and developers of VAMPIRE to understand and refactor VAMPIRE proofs, and to manually proof check soundness of VAMPIRE proofs. When using SATVIS on failed proof attempts of VAMPIRE, SATVIS supports users and developers of VAMPIRE to analyse how VAMPIRE explored its search space during proof search, that is, to understand which clauses were derived and why certain clauses have not been derived at various steps during saturation. By doing so, the SATVIS proof visualisation framework gives valuable insights on how to revise the input problem encoding of VAMPIRE and/or implement domain-specific optimizations in VAMPIRE. We therefore believe that SATVIS improves the state-of-the-art in the use and applications of theorem proving at least in the following scenarios: (i) helping VAMPIRE developers to debug and further improve VAMPIRE, (ii) helping VAMPIRE users to tune VAMPIRE to their applications, by not treating VAMPIRE as a black-box but by understanding and using its appropriate proof search options; and (iii) helping unexperienced users in saturation-based theorem proving to learn using VAMPIRE and first-order proving in general.

Contributions. The contribution of this paper comes with the design of the SATVIS tool for analysing proofs, as well as proof attempts of the VAMPIRE theorem prover. SATVIS is available at:
https://github.com/gleiss/saturation-visualization.

We overview proof search steps in VAMPIRE specific to SATVIS (Sect. 2), discuss the challenges we faced for analysing proof attempts of VAMPIRE (Sect. 3), and describe implementation-level details of SATVIS 1.0 (Sect. 4).

Related Work. While standardizing the input format of automated reasoners is an active research topic, see e.g. the SMT-LIB [2] and TPTP [14] standards, coming up with an input standard for representing and analysing proofs and proof attempts of automated reasoners has received so far very little attention. The TSTP library [14] provides input/output standards for automated theorem proving systems. Yet, unlike SATVIS, TSTP does not analyse proof attempts but only supports the examination of first-order proofs. We note that VAMPIRE proofs (and proof attempts) contain first-order formulas with theories, which is not fully supported by TSTP.

Using a graph-layout framework, for instance Graphviz [6], it is relatively straightforward to visualize the DAG derivation graph induced by a saturation attempt of a first-order prover. For example, the theorem prover E [13] is able to directly output its saturation attempt as an input file for Graphviz. The visualizations generated in this way are useful however only for analyzing small derivations with at most 100 inferences, but cannot practically be used to analyse and manipulate larger proof attempts. We note that it is quite common to have first-order proofs and proof attempts with more than 1,000 or even 10,000 inferences, especially in applications of theorem proving in software verification, see e.g. [3]. In our SATVIS framework, the interactive features of our tool allow one to analyze such large(r) proof attempts.

The framework [12] eases the manual analysis of proof attempts in Z3 [5] by visualizing quantifier instantiations, case splits and conflicts. While both [12] and SATVIS are built for analyzing (failed) proof attempts, they target different architectures (SMT-solving resp. superposition-based proving) and therefore differ in their input format and in the information they visualize. The frameworks [4,10] visualize proofs derived in a natural deduction/sequent calculus. Unlike these approaches, SATVIS targets clausal derivations generated by saturation-based provers using the superposition inference system. As a consequence, our tool can be used to focus only on the clauses that have been actively used during proof search, instead of having to visualize the entire set of clauses, including unused clauses during proof search. We finally note that proof checkers, such as DRAT-trim [15], support the soundness analysis of each inference step of a proof, and do not focus on failing proof attempts nor do they visualize proofs.

2 Proof Search in VAMPIRE

We first present the key ingredients for proof search in VAMPIRE, relevant to analysing saturation attempts.

Derivations and Proofs. An *inference* I is a tuple $(F_1, \ldots, F_n, F)$, where $F_1, \ldots, F_n, F$ are formulas. The formulas $F_1, \ldots, F_n$ are called the *premises* of I and F is called the *conclusion* of I. In our setting, an *inference system* is a set of inferences and we rely on the superposition inference systems [11]. An axiom of an inference system is any inference with $n = 0$. Given an inference system $\mathcal{I}$, a *derivation* from axioms A is an acyclic directed graph (DAG), where (i) each node is a formula and (ii) each node either is an axiom in A and does not have any incoming edges, or is a formula $F \notin A$, such that the incoming edges of F are exactly $(F_1, F), \ldots, (F_n, F)$ and there exists an inference $(F_1, \ldots, F_n, F) \in \mathcal{I}$. A refutation of axioms A is a derivation which contains the empty clause $\perp$ as a node. A derivation of a formula F is called a *proof* of F if it is finite and all leaves in the derivation are axioms.

Proof Search in Vampire. Given an input set of axioms A and a conjecture G, VAMPIRE searches for a refutation of $A \cup \{\neg G\}$, by using a preprocessing phase followed by a saturation phase. In the preprocessing phase, VAMPIRE generates a derivation from $A \cup \{\neg G\}$ such that each sink-node of the DAG[2] is a clause. Then, VAMPIRE enters the saturation phase, where it extends the existing derivation by applying its saturation algorithm using the sink-nodes from the preprocessing phase as the input clauses to saturation. The saturation phase of VAMPIRE terminates in either of the following three cases: (i) the empty clause $\perp$ is derived (hence, a proof of G was found), (ii) no more clauses are derived and the empty clause $\perp$ was not derived (hence, the input is saturated and G is satisfiable), or (iii) an a priory given time/memory limit on the VAMPIRE run is reached (hence, it is unknown whether G is satisfiable/valid).

[2] A sink-node is a node such that no edge emerges out of it.

```
...
[SA] passive: 160. v = a(l11(s(nl8)),$sum(i(main_end),1)) [superposition 70,118]
[SA] active: 163. i(main_end) != -1 [term algebras distinctness 162]
[SA] active: 92. ~'Sub'(X5,p(X4)) | 'Sub'(X5,X4) | zero = X4 [superposition 66,44]
[SA] new: 164. 'Sub'(p(p(X0)),X0) | zero = X0 | zero = p(X0) [resolution 92,94]
[SA] passive: 164. 'Sub'(p(p(X0)),X0) | zero = X0 | zero = p(X0) [resolution 92,94]
[SA] active: 132. v = a(l11(s(s(zero))),2) [superposition 70,124]
[SA] new: 165. v = a(l8(s(s(zero))),2) | i(l8(s(s(zero)))) = 2 [superposition 132,72]
[SA] new: 166. v = a(l8(s(s(zero))),2) | i(l8(s(s(zero)))) = 2 [superposition 72,132]
[SA] active: 90. s(X1) != X0 | p(X0) = X1 | zero = X0 [superposition 22,44]
[SA] new: 167. X0 != X1 | p(X0) = p(X1) | zero = X1 | zero = X0 [superposition 90,44]
[SA] new: 168. p(s(X0)) = X0 | zero = s(X0) [equality resolution 90]
[SA] new: 169. p(s(X0)) = X0 [term algebras distinctness 168]
...
```

Fig. 1. Screenshot of a saturation attempt of VAMPIRE.

Saturation-based proving in VAMPIRE is performed using the following high-level description of the saturation phase of VAMPIRE. The saturation algorithm divides the set of clauses from the proof space of VAMPIRE into a set of *Active* and *Passive* clauses, and iteratively refines these sets using its superposition inference system: the *Active* set keeps the clauses between which all possible inferences have been performed, whereas the *Passive* set stores the clauses which have not been added to *Active* yet and are candidates for being used in future steps of the saturation algorithm. During saturation, VAMPIRE distinguishes between so-called *simplifying* and *generating inferences.* Intuitively, simplifying inferences delete clauses from the search space and hence are crucial for keeping the search space small. A generating inference is a non-simplifying one, and hence adds new clauses to the search space. As such, at every iteration of the saturation algorithm, a new clause from *Passive* is selected and added to *Active*, after which all generating inferences between the selected clause and the clauses in *Active* are applied. Conclusions of these inferences yield new clauses which are added to *Passive* to be selected in future iterations of saturation. Additionally at any step of the saturation algorithm, simplifying inferences and deletion of clauses are allowed.

3 Analysis of Saturation Attempts of VAMPIRE

We now discuss how to efficiently analyze saturation attempts of VAMPIRE in SATVIS.

Analyzing Saturation Attempts. To understand saturation (attempts), we have to analyze the generating inferences performed during saturation (attempts).

On the one hand, we are interested in the *useful* clauses: that is, the derived and activated clauses that are part of the proof we expect VAMPIRE to find. In particular, we check whether these clauses occur in *Active*. (i) If this is the case for a given useful clause (or a simplified variant of it), we are done with processing this useful clause and optionally check the derivation of that clause against the expected derivation. (ii) If not, we have to identify the reason why the clause was not added to *Active*, which can either be the case because (ii.a) the clause (or a simplified version of it) was never chosen from *Passive* to be activated or (ii.b) the clause was not even added to *Passive*. In case (ii.a), we investigate why the clause was not activated. This involves checking which simplified version of the clause was added to *Passive* and checking the value of clause selection in VAMPIRE on that clause. In case (ii.b), it is needed to understand why the clause was not added to *Passive*, that is, why no generating inference between suitable premise clauses was performed. This could for instance be the case because one of the premises was not added to *Active*, in which case we recurse with the analysis on that premise, or because clause selection in VAMPIRE prevented the inference.

On the other hand, we are interested in the *useless* clauses: that is, the clauses which were generated or even activated but are unrelated to the proof VAMPIRE will find. These clauses often slow down the proof search by several magnitudes. It is therefore crucial to limit their generation or at least their activation. To identify the useless clauses that are activated, we need to analyze the set *Active*, whereas to identify the useless clauses, which are generated but never activated, we have to investigate the set *Passive*.

Saturation Output. We now discuss how SATVIS reconstructs the clause sets *Active* and *Passive* from a VAMPIRE saturation (attempt). VAMPIRE is able to log a list of events, where each event is classified as either (i) new C (ii) passive C or (iii) active C, for a given clause C. The list of events produced by VAMPIRE satisfies the following properties: (a) any clause is at most once newly created, added to *Passive* and added to *Active*; (b) if a clause is added to *Passive*, it was newly created in the same iteration, and (c) if a clause is added to *Active*, it was newly created and added to *Passive* at some point. Figure 1 shows a part of the output logged by VAMPIRE while performing a saturation attempt (`SA`).

Starting from an empty derivation and two empty sets, the derivation graph and the sets *Active* and *Passive* corresponding to a given saturation attempt of VAMPIRE are computed in SATVIS by traversing the list of events produced by VAMPIRE and iteratively changing the derivation and the sets *Active* and *Passive*, as follows:

(i) new C: add the new node C to the derivation and construct the edges (C_i, C), for any premise C_i of the inference deriving C. The sets *Active* or *Passive* remain unchanged;
(ii) passive C: add the node C to *Passive*. The derivation and *Active* remain unchanged;
(iii) active C: remove the node C from *Passive* and add it to *Active*. The derivation remains unchanged.

Interactive Visualization. The large number of inferences during saturation in VAMPIRE makes the direct analysis of saturation attempts of VAMPIRE impossible within a reasonable amount of time. In order to overcome this problem, in SATVIS we *interactively* visualize the derivation graph of the VAMPIRE saturation. The graph-based visualization of SATVIS brings the following benefits:

- Navigating through the graph visualization of a VAMPIRE derivation is easier for users rather than working with the VAMPIRE derivation encoded as a list of hyper-edges. In particular, both (i) navigating to the premises of a selected node/clause and (ii) searching for inferences having a selected node/clause as premise is performed fast in SATVIS.
- SATVIS visualizes only the nodes/clauses that are part of a derivation of an activated clause, and in this way ignores uninteresting inferences.
- SATVIS merges the preprocessing inferences, such that each clause resulting from preprocessing has as direct premise the input formula it is derived from.

Yet, a straightforward graph-based visualization of VAMPIRE saturations in SATVIS would bring the following practical limitations on using SATVIS:

(i) displaying additional meta-information on graph nodes, such as the inference rule used to derive a node, is computationally very expensive, due to the large number of inferences used during saturation;
(ii) manual search for particular/already processed nodes in relatively large derivations would take too much time;
(iii) subderivations are often interleaved with other subderivations due to an imperfect automatic layout of the graph.

SATVIS addresses the above challenges using its following interactive features:

- SATVIS displays meta-information only for a selected node/clause;
- SATVIS supports different ways to locate and select clauses, such as full-text search, search for direct children and premises of the currently selected clauses, and search for clauses whose derivation contains all currently selected nodes;
- SATVIS supports transformations/fragmentations of derivations. In particular, it is possible to restrict and visualize the derivation containing only the clauses that form the derivation of a selected clause, or visualize only clauses whose derivation contains a selected clause.
- SATVIS allows to (permanently) highlight one or more clauses in the derivation.

Figure 2 illustrates some of the above feature of SATVIS, using output from VAMPIRE similar to Fig. 1 as input to SATVIS.

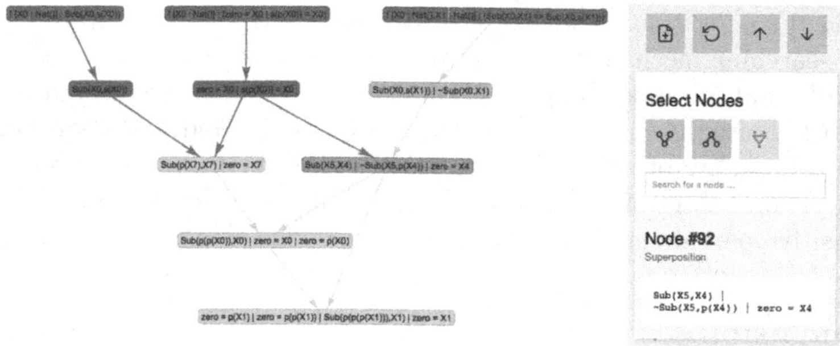

Fig. 2. Screenshot of SatVis showing visualized derivation and interaction menu

4 Implementation of SatVis 1.0

We implemented SatVis as a web application, allowing SatVis to be easily used on any platform. Written in Python3, SatVis contains about 2,200 lines of code. For the generation of graph layouts, we rely on `pygraphviz`[3], whereas graph/derivation visualizations are created with `vis.js`[4]. We experimented with SatVis on the verification examples of [3], using an Intel Core i5 3.1 GHz machine with 16 GB of RAM, allowing us to refine and successfully generate Vampire proofs for non-interference and information-flow examples of [3].

SatVis *workflow.* SatVis takes as input a text file containing the output of a Vampire saturation attempt. An example of a partial input to SatVis is given in Fig. 1. SatVis then generates a DAG representing the derivation of the considered Vampire saturation output, as presented in Sect. 3 and discussed later. Next, SatVis generates the graph layout of for the generated DAG, enriched with configured style information. Finally, SatVis renders and visualizes the Vampire derivation corresponding to its input, and allows interactive visualisations of its output, as discussed in Sect. 3 and detailed below.

DAG Generation of Saturation Outputs. SatVis parses its input line by line using regex pattern matching in order to generate the nodes of the graph. Next, SatVis uses a post order traversal algorithm to sanitize nodes and remove redundant ones. The result is then passed to `pygraphviz` to generate a graph layout. While `pygraphviz` finds layouts for thousands of nodes within less than three seconds, we would like to improve the scalability of the tool further.

It would be beneficial to preprocess and render nodes incrementally, while ensuring stable layouts for SatVis graph transformations. We leave this engineering task for future work.

---

[3] https://pygraphviz.github.io.
[4] https://visjs.org/.

Interactive Visualization. The interactive features of SatVis support (i) various node searching mechanisms, (ii) graph transformations, and (iii) the display of meta-information about a specific node. We can efficiently search for nodes by (partial) clause, find parents or children of a node, and find common consequences of a number of nodes. Graph transformations in SatVis allow to only render a certain subset of nodes from the SatVis DAG, for example, displaying only transitive parents or children of a certain node.

5 Conclusion

We described the SatVis tool for interactively visualizing proofs and proof attempts of the first-order theorem prover Vampire. Our work analyses proof search in Vampire and reconstructs first-order derivations corresponding to Vampire proofs/proof attempts. The interactive features of SatVis ease the task of understanding both successful and failing proof attempts in Vampire and hence can be used to further develop and use Vampire both by experts and non-experts in first-order theorem proving.

Acknowledgements. This work was funded by the ERC Starting Grant 2014 SYMCAR 639270, the ERC Proof of Concept Grant 2018 SYMELS 842066, the Wallenberg Academy Fellowship 2014 TheProSE and the Austrian FWF project W1255-N23.

References

1. Barrett, C., et al.: CVC4. In: Gopalakrishnan, G., Qadeer, S. (eds.) CAV 2011. LNCS, vol. 6806, pp. 171–177. Springer, Heidelberg (2011). https://doi.org/10.1007/978-3-642-22110-1_14
2. Barrett, C., Fontaine, P., Tinelli, C.: The SMT-LIB standard: version 2.6. Technical report, Department of Computer Science, The University of Iowa (2017)
3. Barthe, G., Eilers, R., Georgiou, P., Gleiss, B., Kovacs, L., Maffei, M.: Verifying relational properties using trace logic. In: FMCAD (2019, to appear)
4. Byrnes, J., Buchanan, M., Ernst, M., Miller, P., Roberts, C., Keller, R.: Visualizing proof search for theorem prover development. ENTCS **226**, 23–38 (2009)
5. de Moura, L., Bjørner, N.: Z3: an efficient SMT solver. In: Ramakrishnan, C.R., Rehof, J. (eds.) TACAS 2008. LNCS, vol. 4963, pp. 337–340. Springer, Heidelberg (2008). https://doi.org/10.1007/978-3-540-78800-3_24
6. Gansner, E.R., North, S.C.: An open graph visualization system and its applications to software engineering. Softw. Pract. Exp. **30**(11), 1203–1233 (2000)
7. Kotelnikov, E., Kovács, L., Voronkov, A.: A FOOLish encoding of the next state relations of imperative programs. In: Galmiche, D., Schulz, S., Sebastiani, R. (eds.) IJCAR 2018. LNCS (LNAI), vol. 10900, pp. 405–421. Springer, Cham (2018). https://doi.org/10.1007/978-3-319-94205-6_27
8. Kovács, L., Robillard, S., Voronkov, A.: Coming to terms with quantified reasoning. In: POPL, pp. 260–270. ACM (2017)
9. Kovács, L., Voronkov, A.: First-order theorem proving and Vampire. In: Sharygina, N., Veith, H. (eds.) CAV 2013. LNCS, vol. 8044, pp. 1–35. Springer, Heidelberg (2013). https://doi.org/10.1007/978-3-642-39799-8_1

10. Libal, T., Riener, M., Rukhaia, M.: Advanced proof viewing in ProofTool. In: UITP, pp. 35–47 (2014)
11. Nieuwenhuis, R., Rubio, A.: Paramodulation-based theorem proving. In: Handbook of Automated Reasoning, pp. 371–443 (2001)
12. Rothenberger, F.: Integration and analysis of alternative SMT solvers for software verification. Master's thesis, ETH Zurich, Zürich. Masterarbeit (2016)
13. Schulz, S.: E - a brainiac theorem prover. AI Commun. **15**(2–3), 111–126 (2002)
14. Sutcliffe, G.: TPTP, TSTP, CASC, etc. In: Diekert, V., Volkov, M.V., Voronkov, A. (eds.) CSR 2007. LNCS, vol. 4649, pp. 6–22. Springer, Heidelberg (2007). https://doi.org/10.1007/978-3-540-74510-5_4
15. Wetzler, N., Heule, M.J.H., Hunt, W.A.: DRAT-trim: efficient checking and trimming using expressive clausal proofs. In: Sinz, C., Egly, U. (eds.) SAT 2014. LNCS, vol. 8561, pp. 422–429. Springer, Cham (2014). https://doi.org/10.1007/978-3-319-09284-3_31

SIGmA: GPU Accelerated Simplification of SAT Formulas

Muhammad Osama(✉) and Anton Wijs(✉)

Eindhoven University of Technology, 5600 MB Eindhoven, The Netherlands
{o.m.m.muhammad,a.j.wijs}@tue.nl

Abstract. We present SIGmA (SAT sImplification on GPU Architectures), a preprocessor to accelerate SAT solving that runs on NVIDIA GPUs. We discuss the tool, focussing on its full functionality and how it can be used in combination with state-of-the-art SAT solvers. SIGmA performs various types of simplification, such as variable elimination, subsumption elimination, blocked clause elimination and hidden redundancy elimination. We study the effectiveness of our tool when applied prior to SAT solving. Overall, for our large benchmark set of problems, SIGmA enables MiniSat and Lingeling to solve many problems in less time compared to applying the SatElite preprocessor.

Keywords: Boolean satisfiability · SAT decomposition · Parallel SAT preprocessing · Multi-GPU computing

1 Introduction

Simplifying SAT formulas prior to solving them has proven to be effective in modern SAT solvers [2,5], particularly when applied on SAT formulas encoding software and hardware verification problems [7]. Many techniques based on variable elimination, clause elimination, and equivalence reasoning are being used to simplify SAT formulas [4,6,11]. However, applying variable and clause elimination iteratively to large formulas may actually be a performance bottleneck, or increase the number of literals, negatively impacting the solving time.

Graphics processors (GPUs) have become attractive for general-purpose computing with the availability of the Compute Unified Device Architecture (CUDA) programming model.[1] CUDA is widely used to accelerate applications that are computationally intensive w.r.t. data processing and memory access. For instance, we have applied GPUs to accelerate explicit-state model checking [3,12–15], metaheuristic SAT solving [16], and SAT-based test generation [9]. SIGmA is the first SAT simplifier to exploit GPUs.

This work is part of the GEARS project with project number TOP2.16.044, which is (partly) financed by the Netherlands Organisation for Scientific Research (NWO).
We gratefully acknowledge the support of NVIDIA Corporation with the donation of the GeForce Titan Xp's used for this research.

[1] https://docs.nvidia.com/cuda/cuda-c-programming-guide.

W. Ahrendt and S. L. Tapia Tarifa (Eds.): IFM 2019, LNCS 11918, pp. 514–522, 2019.
https://doi.org/10.1007/978-3-030-34968-4_29

In related work, Eén et al. [4] provided the first powerful preprocessor (SatElite) which applies variable elimination with subsumption elimination. However, the subsumption check is only performed on the clauses resulting from variable elimination, hence no reductions are obtained if there are no variables to resolve. Gebhardt et al. [6] presented the first attempt to parallelise SAT preprocessing on a multi-core CPU using a locking scheme to prevent threads corrupting the SAT formula. Yet, they reported a limited speedup of 1.88$\times$ on average when running on 8 cores. The methods above may still consume considerable time when processing large problems.

Contributions. We present the SIGmA tool to accelerate SAT simplification on CUDA-supported NVIDIA GPUs. In earlier work [10], we presented parallel algorithms for variable elimination, subsumption elimination and self-subsuming resolution. Implementations of these are now publicly available in SIGmA. Moreover, in this work, we have added new implementations for *blocked clause elimination* (BCE) and a new type of elimination we call *hidden redundancy elimination* (HRE). Finally, we propose a generalisation of all algorithms to distribute simplification work over multiple GPUs, if these are available in a single machine. We discuss the potential performance gain of SIGmA and its impact on SAT solving for 344 problems, a larger set than considered previously in [10].

2 SIGmA Functionality and Architecture

SIGmA is developed in CUDA C/C++ version 9.2, runs on Windows and Linux, and requires a CUDA-capable GPU with at least compute capability 3.5 (see Footnote 1). It is freely available at https://gears.win.tue.nl/software. The tool is published with a large set of benchmarks and detailed documentation.

SIGmA accepts as input a SAT formula in Conjunctive Normal Form (CNF), stored in the DIMACS format.[2] A CNF formula is a conjunction of *clauses*, where each clause C_i is a disjunction of *literals*, and each literal ℓ_i is a Boolean variable x or its negation $\bar{x}$ (or $\neg x$). Below, we interpret a formula as a set of clauses, and a clause as a set of literals. The output of SIGmA is a simplified CNF formula in the DIMACS format, and hence can directly be used as input for state-of-the-art SAT solvers.

SIGmA's architecture is depicted in Fig. 1. First, we consider running SIGmA on a single GPU. Once an input formula has been parsed and loaded into the GPU global memory, an Occurrence Table (OT) is created using atomic write operations. This OT stores for each variable x references to all clauses containing either x or $\bar{x}$. Next, a configured combination of simplifications can be applied. The various types of simplification supported by the tool are:

- *Variable elimination* (VE). This eliminates a set of variables by applying *resolution* [11] and *substitution* (also known as gate equivalence reasoning) [4]. When resolution is applied for a variable x, pairs of clauses C_1, C_2 with

[2] See https://www.cs.ubc.ca/~hoos/SATLIB/benchm.html.

$x \in C_1$, $\bar{x} \in C_2$ are combined into a new clause $C = C_1 \cup C_2 \setminus \{x, \bar{x}\}$, called a *resolvent*. We add such a resolvent C to the formula iff C is not a *tautology*, i.e., there exists no variable y for which both $y \in C$ and $\bar{y} \in C$. Substitution detects patterns encoding logical gates, and substitutes the involved variables with their gate-equivalent counterparts. For instance, in the formula $\{\{x, \bar{a}, \bar{b}\}, \{\bar{x}, a\}, \{\bar{x}, b\}, \{x, c\}\}$, the first three clauses together encode a logical AND-gate, hence in the final clause, we can substitute $a \wedge b$ for x. After removal of the AND-gate, we end up with the new formula $\{\{a, c\}, \{b, c\}\}$. SIGmA supports substitution for both AND- and OR-gates. The SAT-encoded representation of the OR gate $x = a \vee b$ is $\{\{\bar{x}, a, b\}, \{x, \bar{a}\}, \{x, \bar{b}\}\}$.
- *Hybrid subsumption elimination* (HSE) [10]. It performs *self-subsuming resolution* followed by *subsumption elimination* [4]. The former can be applied on clauses C_1, C_2 iff for some variable x, we have $C_1 = C_1' \cup \{x\}$, $C_2 = C_2' \cup \{\bar{x}\}$, and $C_2' \subseteq C_1'$. In that case, x can be removed from C_1. The latter is applied on clauses C_1, C_2 with $C_2 \subseteq C_1$. In that case, C_1 is redundant and can be removed. For instance, consider the formula $\mathcal{S} = \{\{a, b, c\}, \{\bar{a}, b\}, \{b, c, d\}\}$. The first clause is self-subsumed by the second clause over variable a and can be strengthened to $\{b, c\}$ which in turn subsumes the last clause $\{b, c, d\}$. The subsumed clause is removed from $\mathcal{S}$ and the simplified formula will be $\{\{b, c\}, \{\bar{a}, b\}\}$.
- *Blocked clause elimination* (BCE) [8]. It removes clauses on which variable elimination can be applied, but doing so results only in tautologies. Consider the formula $\{\{a, b, c, d\}, \{\bar{a}, \bar{b}\}, \{\bar{a}, \bar{c}\}\}$. Both the literals a and c are blocking the first clause, since resolving a produces the tautologies $\{\{b, c, d, \bar{b}\}, \{b, c, \bar{c}, d\}\}$. Likewise, resolving c yields the tautology $\{\{a, b, \bar{a}, d\}$. Hence the blocked clause $\{a, b, c, d\}$ can be removed from $\mathcal{S}$.
- *Hidden redundancy elimination* (HRE) is a new elimination procedure which repeats the following until a fixpoint has been reached: for a given formula $\mathcal{S}$ and clauses $C_1 \in \mathcal{S}, C_2 \in \mathcal{S}$ with $x \in C_1$ and $\bar{x} \in C_2$ for some variable x, if there exists a clause $C \in S$ for which $C \equiv C_1 \otimes_x C_2$ and C is not a tautology, then let $\mathcal{S} := \mathcal{S} \setminus \{C\}$. The clause C is called a *hidden redundancy* and can be removed without altering the original satisfiability. For example, consider the formula
$$\mathcal{S} = \{\{a, \bar{c}\}, \{c, b\}, \{\bar{d}, \bar{c}\}, \{b, a\}, \{a, d\}\}$$
Resolving the first two clauses gives the resolvent $\{a, b\}$ which is equivalent to the fourth clause in $\mathcal{S}$. Also, resolving the third clause with the last clause yields $\{a, \bar{c}\}$ which is equivalent to the first clause in $\mathcal{S}$. HRE can remove either $\{a, \bar{c}\}$ or $\{a, b\}$ but not both.

The general workflow of SIGmA and the challenges are discussed next.

Variable Dependency and Completeness. To exploit parallelism in SIGmA, each simplification is applied on several variables simultaneously. Doing so is non-trivial, since variables may *depend* on each other; two variables x and y are dependent iff there exists a clause C with $(x \in C \vee \bar{x} \in C) \wedge (y \in C \vee \bar{y} \in C)$. If both x and y were to be processed for simplification, two threads might manipulate C at the same time. To guarantee soundness and completeness, we apply

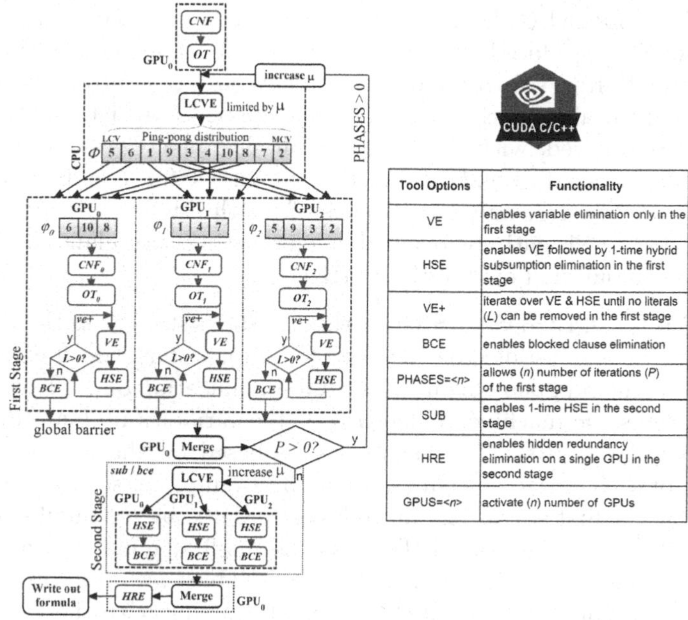

Tool Options	Functionality
VE	enables variable elimination only in the first stage
HSE	enables VE followed by 1-time hybrid subsumption elimination in the first stage
VE+	iterate over VE & HSE until no literals (*L*) can be removed in the first stage
BCE	enables blocked clause elimination
PHASES=<*n*>	allows (*n*) number of iterations (*P*) of the first stage
SUB	enables 1-time HSE in the second stage
HRE	enables hidden redundancy elimination on a single GPU in the second stage
GPUS=<*n*>	activate (*n*) number of GPUs

Fig. 1. SIGmA architecture with supported options.

our *least constrained variable elections* algorithm (LCVE) [10]. This algorithm is responsible for electing a set of mutually independent variables from a set of authorised candidates. The remaining variables relying on the elected ones are frozen. These notions are defined by Definitions 1–4.

Definition 1 (Authorised candidates). *Given a CNF formula* S, *we call* $\mathcal{A}$ *the set of* authorised candidates*:* $\mathcal{A} = \{x \mid 1 \leq h[x] \leq \mu \vee 1 \leq h[\bar{x}] \leq \mu\}$, *where*

- h *is a histogram array* ($h[x]$ *is the number of occurrences of* x *in* S).
- μ *denotes a given maximum number of occurrences allowed for both* x *and its negation* $\bar{x}$, *representing the cut-off point for the LCVE algorithm.*

Definition 2 (Candidate Dependency Relation). *We call a relation* $\mathcal{D}$: $\mathcal{A} \times \mathcal{A}$ *a* candidate dependency relation *iff* $\forall x, y \in \mathcal{A}$, $x \,\mathcal{D}\, y$ *implies that* $\exists C \in S.(x \in C \vee \bar{x} \in C) \wedge (y \in C \vee \bar{y} \in C)$.

Definition 3 (Elected candidates). *Given a set of authorised candidates* $\mathcal{A}$, *we call a set* $\Phi \subseteq \mathcal{A}$ *a set of* elected candidates *iff* $\forall x, y \in \Phi.\, \neg(x \,\mathcal{D}\, y)$.

Definition 4 (Frozen candidates). *Given the sets* $\mathcal{A}$ *and* Φ, *the set of* frozen candidates $\mathcal{F} \subseteq \mathcal{A}$ *is defined as* $\mathcal{F} = \{x \mid x \in \mathcal{A} \wedge \exists y \in \Phi.\, x \,\mathcal{D}\, y\}$.

SIGmA Modes of Operation. SIGmA simplifies formulas in two stages (Fig. 1). In the first stage, variable elimination is applied. Hence, the first stage is executed only if VE is selected, and may in addition apply HSE and/or BCE. Before applying VE, a parallel GPU algorithm is run to estimate the number of resolvents that will be produced, in order to appropriately allocate memory. HSE can be executed after VE to remove or strengthen (self)-subsumed clauses of non-eliminated variables. VE and HSE can be applied iteratively until no more literals can be removed, with the VE+ option. The **phases=<n>** option (outer loop for the first stage in Fig. 1), applies the first stage for a configured number of iterations, with increasingly large values of the threshold μ.

The second stage is entirely focussed on eliminating redundant clauses, using a configured combination of HSE/BCE/HRE.

Multi-GPU Support. By default SIGmA runs on the first GPU of the computing machine, i.e., the one installed on the first PCI-Express bus, which we refer to as GPU_0. The command **gpus=<n>** utilises SAT simplification on n identical GPUs installed in the same machine. When $n > 1$, the variables in Φ are distributed evenly among the GPUs. This distribution is based on the number of literal occurrences of each variable. Figure 1 shows an example of such a distribution, after LCVE in the first stage. The variables are ordered by the number of literals in the formula; the variable with ID 5 has the smallest number, while the last one with ID 2 has the largest number. These variables are distributed over the GPUs in a 'ping-pong' fashion: in the example, starting with the variable with the largest number of literals, the first three variables are distributed over the three GPUs, followed by the next three, which are distributed in reversed order, etc. Finally, in general, in case the number of variables is not a multiple of the number of GPUs, the left-over variables are assigned to GPU_0, which in the example is the case for variable 5. As the number of literals is indicative of the computational effort needed to eliminate a variable, this distribution method achieves good load balancing.

At the end of the distribution, every GPU d gets its own set of elected variables Φ_d. For n GPUs, we say that $\bigcup_{0 \leq d < n} \Phi_d = \Phi$ and for all $0 \leq d, d' < n$ ($d \neq d'$), we have $\Phi_d \cap \Phi_{d'} = \emptyset$. We can now define the subformula of $\mathcal{S}$ assigned to GPU d based on the occurrence list of each variable in Φ_d as follows.

Definition 5 (GPU sub-formula). *Given the input formula $\mathcal{S}$ and a set of elected variables Φ_d, we define subformula $\mathcal{S}_d \subseteq \mathcal{S}$ as*

$$\mathcal{S}_d = \{C \mid C \in \mathcal{S} \land \exists x \in \Phi_d . x \in C \lor \bar{x} \in C\}$$

Definition 6 (non-elected sub-formula). *Given the input formula $\mathcal{S}$ and set of elected variables Φ. The* non-elected sub-formula *$\mathcal{S}_{ne} \subseteq \mathcal{S}$ is defined as*

$$\mathcal{S}_{ne} = \{C \mid C \in \mathcal{S} \land \neg\exists x \in \Phi . x \in C \lor \bar{x} \in C\}$$

The remaining part of $\mathcal{S}$ that belongs to the non-elected variables (Definition 6) can be processed by GPU_0. In Fig. 1, the global barrier acts as a synchronisation point for all GPUs, and in the subsequent *merge* step, all simplified subformulas are sent to GPU_0. HRE cannot be run on multiple GPUs, because the entire formula must be accessed.

Table 1. SIGmA performance analysis with CPU and one GPU configurations.

Mode	-ve+ -sub -bce -hre					-ve -bce -hre			
Method	ve+		bce	hre	all	ve	bce	hre	ve/bce/hre
	ve	hse							
Average Speedup	36.5×	6.4×	29.5×	17×	14×	24×	4×	12×	10×
#Formulas simp. faster					329 (95%)				314 (92%)

Table 2. SIGmA performance analysis with one and two GPU configurations.

Mode	-ve+ -sub -bce					-ve -bce			
Method	ve+		bce	all(-t_c)	all(+t_c)	ve	bce	ve/bce(-t_c)	ve/bce(+t_c)
	ve	hse							
Average Speedup	1.7×	2.64×	1.34×	1.96×	0.85×	2×	5.3×	2.6×	1×
#Formulas simp. faster					79 (22%)				129 (38%)

3 Benchmarks

We evaluated SIGmA using two NVIDIA Titan Xp GPUs. Each GPU has 30 streaming multiprocessors, with 128 cores each, 12 GB global memory and 48 KB shared memory. The GPU machine is running Linux Mint 18.3, has a 3.5 GHz Intel Core i5 CPU, and 32 GB of memory.

We selected 344 SAT problems from the application track of the 2013–2017 SAT competitions.[3] This set consists of all problems from that track that are more than 1 MB in file size. The largest size of problems occurring in this set is 1.2 GB. These problems have been encoded from 46 real-world applications with dissimilar logical properties. Before applying simplifications, any occurring unit clauses (clauses with a single literal) were propagated. Unit clauses immediately lead to simplification. By eliminating them, the results more clearly indicate the impact of SIGmA.

In the experiments, we involved a CPU-only version of SIGmA and the SatELite preprocessor [4] for simplification, and the MiniSat and Lingeling [2] SAT solvers for solving. We chose Minisat as it forms the basis for many CDCL SAT solvers, and Lingeling, since it was the winner of several SAT competitions. The CPU-version of SIGmA applies the same simplifications on the elected variables as the GPU version, but performs them sequentially. All these were executed on the compute nodes of the DAS-5 cluster [1]. Each problem was analysed in isolation on a separate node. Each node has an Intel Xeon E5-2630 2.4 GHz CPU with 128 GB memory, and runs on the CentOS 7.4 operating system. We performed the equivalent of four years of uninterrupted processing on a single node to measure how SIGmA impacts SAT solving.

For all experiments, we set μ initially to 64, which in practice tends to produce good results. Tables 1 and 2 summarise the amount of speedup and the number

[3] See http://www.satcompetition.org.

Table 3. SIGmA performance compared to SatElite and Lingeling simplifiers.

SIGmA (mode)	Counterpart	Speedup	#CNF Simp. faster
SIGmA (CPU:ve+/sub)	SatElite (ve/sub)	36.96×	339 (98%)
SIGmA (GPU:ve+/sub)	SatElite (ve/sub)	69.25×	339 (98%)
SIGmA (GPU:all)	SatElite (ve/sub)	49.32×	326 (94%)
SIGmA (GPU:all)	Lingeling	32.19×	315 (91%)

of problems simplified faster by running SIGmA on one and two GPUs.[4] We compare the single GPU mode of SIGmA with both the CPU-only version and the two GPUs mode of SIGmA. For the CPU-GPU comparison, we used two modes, (`-ve+ -sub -bce -hre`) and (`-ve -bce -hre`) which represent one full iteration of the first stage, followed by the second stage (see Fig. 1). The former is called `all` in Table 1. For the hybrid mode (`-ve+`), we measured the acceleration achieved by using a GPU for both `ve` and `hse` as part of `ve+`. It appears that the speedup obtained by `bce` is influenced by the application of `hse`, while other methods (`ve, hre`) maintain similar speedups. Compared to CPU-only SIGmA, the GPU achieves an acceleration of up to 36.5×. The average speedups of `ve/bce/hre` and `all` modes are 10× and 14×, respectively.

For the comparison of SIGmA's single/multiple GPU modes, we disabled `-hre`, which is only supported in single GPU mode. If we ignore the time needed for data transfer between the GPUs (t_c), SIGmA's runtime scales very well with the number of GPUs. In mode (`-ve+ -sub -bce`), the average acceleration is 2.64×, and overall, the average speedup is 1.96×. When we consider data transfer, the latter drops to 0.85×. Still, disabling `hse` in the second mode (`-ve+ -sub -bce`) positively influences the performance of `bce`. The speedup of this method has improved for the multi-GPU configuration by 5 times higher compared to using a single GPU with `hse` enabled. The overall speedup with and without data transfer has grown to 2.6× and 1×, respectively.

Moreover, in the second mode, SIGmA managed to simplify 129 (38%) problems faster compared to the single GPU mode, even if the communication overhead is taken into account. We expect that hardware improvements of inter-GPU communication in the future will make the multi-GPU mode of SIGmA increasingly attractive.

Table 3 compares SIGmA against the best sequential simplifiers available (SatElite and the preprocessing module of Lingeling, which is very similar to SatElite). Similar to the multi-GPU experiments, we used the heavy mode (`-ve+`) in combination with other simplifications in all of SIGmA's benchmarks. On average, CPU SIGmA is faster than SatElite by 37× since we only consider eliminating elected variables and exclude those occurring in the resolvents (their length grows exponentially by resolution). Moreover, the OT is created once before elimination. The GPU-version, with all simplifications enabled, beats SatElite and Lingeling by accelerations up to 49× and 32× respectively.

[4] Tables with all the data are available at http://gears.win.tue.nl/software.

Table 4. MiniSat solving of original and simplified formulas (timeout: 24 h).

Evaluation	MiniSat (org)	SIGmA+MiniSat				SatElite+MiniSat	
		ve+	ve/bce	ve/hre	ve/bce/hre	ve	ve/sub
#Formulas solved	192 (56%)	228 (66%)	227 (66%)	218 (63%)	230 (67%)	215 (62%)	201 (58%)
Processing time (h)	3989	3201	3256	3354	3214	3474	3754

Table 5. Lingeling solving of original and simplified formulas (timeout: 24 h).

Evaluation	Lingeling (org)	SIGmA+Lingeling			
		ve+	ve/bce	ve/hre	ve/bce/hre
#Formulas solved	252 (73%)	282 (82%)	283 (82.3%)	281 (82%)	283 (82.3%)
Processing time (h)	2566	1826	1862	1880	1854

For the subsequent experiments, we set `phases` to 5, and doubled μ each time before SIGmA performed another iteration of the first stage. With this setup, Table 4 shows the impact of SIGmA in various modes on SAT solving when combined with MiniSat. The processing time includes the solving times of the entire set (344) up to the timeouts, and the simplification and data transfer times in case of SIGmA and SatElite. Based on the experiments, we conclude that the new simplifications (BCE, HRE) proposed in this paper, when combined with all other options, allow 230 problems (67%) to be solved, thereby outperforming all the alternatives. Moreover, the processing time of the (`-ve -bce -hre`) mode (3,214 h) is still shorter than when MiniSat is applied without simplification, and when SatElite is used for simplification. Likewise, Table 5 shows SIGmA's impact on the Lingeling solver. Again, mode (`-ve -bce -hre`) is at least as good as all the alternatives, allowing 283 instances (82.3%) to be solved. The best competitor, mode (`-ve -bce`), took more time to be applied.

4 Conclusion

We have presented the SIGmA tool, the first simplifier for SAT formulas that exploits the power of GPUs. It can be configured to apply a combination of various elimination procedures, among which is a new one (HRE) proposed by us. Experimentally, we have demonstrated the impact of SIGmA on state-of-the-art SAT solving. In particular, our new mode, involving BCE and HRE, positively affects both the solving speed and the ability to solve formulas, when using the MiniSat and Lingeling solvers.

References

1. Bal, H., et al.: A medium-scale distributed system for computer science research: infrastructure for the long term. IEEE Comput. **49**(5), 54–63 (2016)
2. Biere, A.: Lingeling, plingeling and treengeling entering the SAT competition 2013. In: Proceedings of SAT Competition, pp. 51–52 (2013)

3. Bošnački, D., Edelkamp, S., Sulewski, D., Wijs, A.: GPU-PRISM: an extension of PRISM for general purpose graphics processing units. In: PDMC, pp. 17–19. IEEE Computer Society Press (2010)
4. Eén, N., Biere, A.: Effective preprocessing in SAT through variable and clause elimination. In: Bacchus, F., Walsh, T. (eds.) SAT 2005. LNCS, vol. 3569, pp. 61–75. Springer, Heidelberg (2005). https://doi.org/10.1007/11499107_5
5. Eén, N., Sörensson, N.: An extensible SAT-solver. In: Giunchiglia, E., Tacchella, A. (eds.) SAT 2003. LNCS, vol. 2919, pp. 502–518. Springer, Heidelberg (2004). https://doi.org/10.1007/978-3-540-24605-3_37
6. Gebhardt, K., Manthey, N.: Parallel variable elimination on CNF formulas. In: Timm, I.J., Thimm, M. (eds.) KI 2013. LNCS (LNAI), vol. 8077, pp. 61–73. Springer, Heidelberg (2013). https://doi.org/10.1007/978-3-642-40942-4_6
7. Jin, H., Somenzi, F.: An incremental algorithm to check satisfiability for bounded model checking. ENTCS **119**(2), 51–65 (2005)
8. Kullmann, O.: On a generalization of extended resolution. Discrete Appl. Math. **97**, 149–176 (1999)
9. Osama, M., Gaber, L., Hussein, A.I., Mahmoud, H.: An efficient SAT-based test generation algorithm with GPU accelerator. J. Electron. Test. **34**(5), 511–527 (2018)
10. Osama, M., Wijs, A.: Parallel SAT simplification on GPU architectures. In: Vojnar, T., Zhang, L. (eds.) TACAS 2019. LNCS, vol. 11427, pp. 21–40. Springer, Cham (2019). https://doi.org/10.1007/978-3-030-17462-0_2
11. Subbarayan, S., Pradhan, D.K.: NiVER: non-increasing variable elimination resolution for preprocessing SAT instances. In: Hoos, H.H., Mitchell, D.G. (eds.) SAT 2004. LNCS, vol. 3542, pp. 276–291. Springer, Heidelberg (2005). https://doi.org/10.1007/11527695_22
12. Wijs, A.: GPU accelerated strong and branching bisimilarity checking. In: Baier, C., Tinelli, C. (eds.) TACAS 2015. LNCS, vol. 9035, pp. 368–383. Springer, Heidelberg (2015). https://doi.org/10.1007/978-3-662-46681-0_29
13. Wijs, A.: BFS-based model checking of linear-time properties with an application on GPUs. In: Chaudhuri, S., Farzan, A. (eds.) CAV 2016. LNCS, vol. 9780, pp. 472–493. Springer, Cham (2016). https://doi.org/10.1007/978-3-319-41540-6_26
14. Wijs, A., Bošnački, D.: Many-core on-the-fly model checking of safety properties using GPUs. Int. J. Softw. Tools Technol. Transfer **18**(2), 169–185 (2016)
15. Wijs, A., Neele, T., Bošnački, D.: GPUexplore 2.0: unleashing GPU explicit-state model checking. In: Fitzgerald, J., Heitmeyer, C., Gnesi, S., Philippou, A. (eds.) FM 2016. LNCS, vol. 9995, pp. 694–701. Springer, Cham (2016). https://doi.org/10.1007/978-3-319-48989-6_42
16. Youness, H., Ibraheim, A., Moness, M., Osama, M.: An efficient implementation of ant colony optimization on GPU for the satisfiability problem. In: PDP, pp. 230–235. IEEE (2015)

Journal-First Extended Abstracts

Summary of: Dynamic Structural Operational Semantics

Christian Johansen(✉) and Olaf Owe

Department of Informatics, University of Oslo, Oslo, Norway
{cristi,olaf}@ifi.uio.no

Abstract. This short paper summarises the contributions published in the authors' journal article [2].

The journal paper develops the theory of Dynamic Structural Operational Semantics (DSOS or Dynamic SOS) as a framework for describing semantics of programming languages that include dynamic software upgrades. DSOS is built on top of the Modular SOS since it allows a sharp separation of the program execution code from the additional structures needed at run-time. DSOS follows the same modularity and decoupling that MSOS advocates, partly motivated by the long term goal of having machine-checkable proofs for general results like type safety.

Dynamic SOS has been applied on two languages supporting dynamic software upgrades, namely the low-level PROTEUS, which supports updating of variables, functions, records, or types at specific program points, and CREOL, which supports dynamic class upgrades in the setting of concurrent objects. Existing type analyses for software upgrades can be done on top of DSOS too, as we illustrate for PROTEUS.

1 Short Introduction to Dynamic SOS

Dynamic software upgrade constructs have been studied for various programming languages for almost two decades now, however, the approaches are different in presentation and formalization, making it difficult to compare or combine them, especially since each of these approaches concentrates on some particular programming language, paradigm, or constructs. Dynamic software upgrades provide mechanisms for upgrading a program at runtime, during its execution, by changing essential definitions used in executing the program, typically by adding or changing definitions of classes, interfaces, types, or methods, as well as modifying or resetting values of variables. Upgrades may be restricted, semantically or syntactically, so that they may only occur in certain states, called *upgrade points*, where upgrading is meaningful or safe. Dynamic upgrades allow a program to be corrected, improved, maintained or integrated with other programs, without stopping and restarting the execution.

Dynamic upgrades are inherently different from normal programming mechanisms because they are external to the program, using information that is not produced by the program, but is provided at runtime by an external entity or programmer. Yet the interpretation of these dynamic operations in the literature

W. Ahrendt and S. L. Tapia Tarifa (Eds.): IFM 2019, LNCS 11918, pp. 525–528, 2019.
https://doi.org/10.1007/978-3-030-34968-4_30

is given using the same style of operational semantics as for the other language constructs, often employing elaborate definitions, affecting the basic language elements as well as advanced ones. We would like these differences to be apparent in the operational semantics, motivating the development of DSOS.

We focus on *dynamic software updates* as in the sequential PROTEUS [6] and *dynamic class upgrades* for object-oriented languages as in the concurrent CREOL language [3,4]. The two chosen languages illustrate different kinds of dynamic updates. PROTEUS, which is a more low-level language, allows low-level state and code updates as well as control of the possible update points in the code. CREOL is a high-level language for distributed systems supporting actor-like [1] concurrent objects communicating by asynchronous methods calls and with support for high-level synchronization mechanisms including conditional process suspension. Upgrades are done in a distributed manner; each object may upgrade itself at suspension or method completion points. Thus, while the update points are programmer-defined in PROTEUS, they are predefined in CREOL. DSOS can deal with both language settings in a uniform manner.

2 An Illustrative Example

More complex examples can be found in e.g., [6, Fig. 3 & 4] from the Linux kernel or [4, Sec. 3] for complex class upgrades.

Consider a class for keeping track of temperatures. The class implements a simple interface for setting and getting the (latest) temperature. With Java-like syntax it could look like

```
interface Temp {
 void setTemp(int t)
 int getTemp()
}
```

```
class TEMP implements Temp {
 int temp;
 TEMP(int init){this.temp = init;}

 void setTemp(int t){temp = t;}
 int  getTemp(){return temp;}
}
```

Assume we would like to update a running system that uses this class such that it can log the history of past *temp* values and is able to calculate the average temperature value. In CREOL this is done by inserting into the message pool a runtime upgrade message containing upgrade information (using the keyword **upgrade**), which may redefine one or more classes or add new classes and interfaces. With high-level Java-like syntax the upgrade is given below:

```
upgrade {
  interface TempStat extends Temp {
   int  avgTemp()}

  class TEMP implements TempStat{
  int[] log;
  TEMP(int init){this.temp = init; log = empty;} -- initialization
```

```
  void setTemp(int t){temp = t; log.append(t);}

  int avgTemp(){int avg=0; int i=0;
    for all x in log
      {avg = avg + x; i=i+1;}
    return avg/i; }
}}
```

The upgrade introduces a new interface `TempStat` and a new version of class `TEMP` augmented with a `log` variable, as well as a new method `avgTemp` for finding the average temperature. The actual logging is done in a changed version of the original `setTemp` method. The `getTemp` method is unchanged, but the constructor is modified so that the `log` variable is initialized. Type safety is ensured by static checking of classes and of upgrades [7].

3 Dynamic SOS

Dynamic SOS is intended as a framework for studying semantics of programming constructs for dynamic upgrade of software, and thus existing works on dynamic upgrades should be naturally captured; hence our exemplification of DSOS on the semantics of Proteus and Creol. Much of the literature on software updates, however, focuses on type systems and type safety; but their results also hold over Dynamic SOS as a semantic framework.

Compared to the normal flow of control and change of dynamic data that the execution of the program does, we view a dynamic upgrade as a contextual *jump* to a possibly completely different data content. This, in consequence, can alter the normal execution of the program. Moreover, these jumps are strongly related to the upgrade information, which is regarded as outside the scope of the executing program, being externally provided.

One observation that we want to emphasise with DSOS is that *upgrade points* must be identified and marked accordingly in the program code. The marking should be done with special upgrade programming constructs. Here we are influenced by the work on Proteus [6] (which is also taken up in UpgradeJ and the multi-threaded Stump). Opposed to a single marker as in Proteus, we propose to use multiple markers, which allow to capture also incremental upgrades, as in Creol. The purpose of identifying and marking such upgrade points is to ensure type safety after upgrades. The analysis techniques of [6] for safety after upgrades can be reused over DSOS as well. Upgrade markers can be placed by a programmer or automatically by static analysis techniques, as in [6,7].

We are taking a *modular* approach in DSOS, following the work of Mosses [5], thus building on *Modular SOS* (MSOS). This formalism uses notions of category theory, on which our work depends. If normal program execution changes to the dynamic structures are captured by the *morphisms* in the MSOS style, the jumps will be captured in DSOS using *endofunctors*, a concept of higher abstraction, which are still seen as morphisms in an appropriate category. In consequence, the arrow-labelled transition system of MSOS is enriched by adding new kinds of transitions labelled with endofunctors. Moreover, the syntax for writing transition rules is enriched to use endofunctors. Also, the label transformer, that is used to extend a program semantics in the modular way, is enriched accordingly, as well as the label categories used for modelling the upgrade information.

Correctness results are provided, showing that DSOS is a conservative extension of MSOS. In particular, when there are no jumps, a computation in the upgrade transition system is defined exactly as in the arrow-labelled transition system of MSOS. The upgrade label transformer is a special case of the label transformer, i.e., uses a disjoint set of indexes and only discrete label categories.

Modularity of Dynamic SOS is ensured as follows. One defines a basic endofunctor for some dynamic upgrade construct, and this is never changed upon addition of other dynamic upgrade constructs and their upgrade categories and related endofunctors. Moreover, a method of extending the basic endofunctors with the identity functor on the rest of the indexes, ensures modularity when new data or upgrade components are added by the label transformers. When designing a programming language the label transformers may be applied on an already used index, resulting in changing the respective label component, e.g.: (i) we may change a read-only component into a read/write component; (ii) we may decide to have more upgrade functors on one particular component, i.e., to define new ways of updating, maybe needed by new programming constructs; (iii) we may leave one functor unspecified, as the identity functor, and at a later point add a proper functor for the specific component.

The presentation of DSOS thus has two aspects: (i) We first need to introduce the modular way of building programming languages and their semantics, from MSOS; (ii) We then can present the DSOS as an extension of MSOS and the specific concepts introduced for giving semantics to dynamic software upgrades.

References

1. Agha, G., Mason, I.A., Smith, S.F., Talcott, C.L.: A foundation for actor computation. J. Funct. Program. **7**(1), 1–72 (1997)
2. Johansen, C., Owe, O.: Dynamic structural operational semantics. J. Log. Algebr. Methods Program. **107**, 79–107 (2019)
3. Johnsen, E.B., Owe, O.: An asynchronous communication model for distributed concurrent objects. Softw. Syst. Model. **6**(1), 39–58 (2007)
4. Johnsen, E.B., Owe, O., Simplot-Ryl, I.: A dynamic class construct for asynchronous concurrent objects. In: Steffen, M., Zavattaro, G. (eds.) FMOODS 2005. LNCS, vol. 3535, pp. 15–30. Springer, Heidelberg (2005). https://doi.org/10.1007/11494881_2
5. Mosses, P.D.: Modular structural operational semantics. J. Log. Algebr. Program. **60–61**, 195–228 (2004)
6. Stoyle, G., Hicks, M.W., Bierman, G.M., Sewell, P., Neamtiu, I.: Mutatis mutandis: safe and predictable dynamic software updating. ACM Trans. Program. Lang. Syst. **29**(4), 183–194 (2007). Article No. 22
7. Yu, I.C., Johnsen, E.B., Owe, O.: Type-safe runtime class upgrades in creol. In: Gorrieri, R., Wehrheim, H. (eds.) FMOODS 2006. LNCS, vol. 4037, pp. 202–217. Springer, Heidelberg (2006). https://doi.org/10.1007/11768869_16

Summary of: An Evaluation of Interaction Paradigms for Active Objects

Farzane Karami(✉), Olaf Owe, and Toktam Ramezanifarkhani

Department of Informatics, University of Oslo, Oslo, Norway
{farzanka,olaf,toktamr}@ifi.uio.no

Abstract. This short paper summarises the contributions published in [1]. The purpose of this paper is to compare communication paradigms of active object languages considering expressiveness, efficiency, syntactic and semantic complexity including ease of reasoning.

Keywords: Active objects · Asynchronous methods · Distributed Systems · Futures

1 Introduction

The Actor model [2] has been adopted by a number of languages as a natural way of describing distributed systems. The advantages are that it offers high-level system description and that the operational semantics may be defined in a modular manner. The Actor model is based on concurrent units communicating by means of message passing. A criticism of message passing has been that its one-way communication paradigm may lead to complex programming when there are dependencies among the incoming messages.

The Actor-Based Concurrent Language (ABCL) is a family of programming languages based on the Actor model [4]. It makes use of *futures* [3] in order to make the communication more efficient and convenient. A future is a read-only placeholder for a result that is desirable to share by several actors. Future identities can be passed around as first class objects. This model is suitable for modeling of service-oriented systems, and gives rise to efficient interaction, avoiding active waiting and low-level synchronization primitives such as explicit signaling lock operations. The notion of *promises* gives even more flexibility than futures by allowing the programmer to talk about the result of call even before the call has been made.

One may combine the Actor model and object-orientation using the paradigm of concurrent, active objects, and using methods rather than messages as the basic communication mechanism [8]. This opens up for two-way communication.

Work supported by the *IoTSec* and *DiversIoT* projects (Norw. Research Council) and SCOTT (EU, JU).

W. Ahrendt and S. L. Tapia Tarifa (Eds.): IFM 2019, LNCS 11918, pp. 529–533, 2019.
https://doi.org/10.1007/978-3-030-34968-4_31

This is for instance done by the Creol language [6] using so-called *call labels* to talk about calls, implementing method calls and replies by asynchronous method passing. Creol introduced *cooperative scheduling*, allowing mechanisms for suspension and process control. A process may suspend while waiting for a condition or a return value. For instance await f? makes a process suspend until the reply associated with label f appears, resulting in passive waiting.

One may also make use of the future mechanism to generalize this setting so that several objects may share the same method result, given as a future. For instance the ABS language [7] is based on the Creol concurrency model, allowing the call labels of Creol to be first class, thereby supporting futures.

In this setting the two-way communication mechanism is replaced by a more complex pattern, namely that a method call generates a future object where the result value can be read by a number of objects, as long as they know the future identifier. Thus for a simple two-way call, the caller will need to ask or wait for the future. This means that each call has a future identity, and that the programmer needs to keep track of which future corresponds to which call. Our experience is that futures are only needed once in a while, and that basic two-way communication suffices in most cases. Thus the flexibility of futures (and promises) comes at a cost. Moreover, implementation-wise, garbage collection of futures is non-trivial, and static analysis of various aspects, such as deadlock, in presence of futures is more difficult. With futures, even normal calls are more complex due to the overhead of the future mechanism.

In this paper we consider the setting of active objects and compare a future-less programming paradigm to the programming paradigm of future-based interaction. For the future-less programming paradigm we choose a core language derived from Creol, but without call labels nor futures. Comparison of paradigms can be done with respect to several dimensions and criteria. We will use the fairly obvious criteria given by *expressiveness*, *efficiency*, *syntactic complexity*, and *semantic complexity*. Other criteria could also be relevant, such as information security aspects and tool friendliness.

2 Future Mechanisms

Languages may have explicit or implicit support of futures [3,5]. Implicit futures support the "wait by need" principle. However, when considering cooperative scheduling it is essential that the suspension points are explicit, and we therefore focus on explicit support of futures in the comparison below. Languages based on explicit futures have (a subset of) the following mechanisms (providing ABS style syntax):

- creation of a future (f:=o!m(e))
- first class future operations (assignment, parameter passing)
- polling a future, i.e., using an if-statement to check if a future is resolved (if f? then.. else ..)
- waiting for a future while blocking, i.e., active waiting (x:= get f)
- waiting for a future while suspending, i.e., passive waiting (await f?)

Here f is a future variable, m a method, o an object, e a list of actual parameters, and x a program variable. A non-blocking version of get, can be done by await f?; x:= get f, and is abbreviated await x:= get f. In general, polling may lead to complicated branching structures, and is often avoided in languages with support of explicit futures.

3 A High-Level, Future-Less Language for Active Objects

We build on the Creol model for active objects, but avoid call labels (and futures). Object interaction is done by so-called asynchronous method calls, implemented by asynchronous message passing. This means that communication is two-way, passing actual parameters from the caller to the callee object when a method is called, and passing method return values from the callee to the caller when the method execution terminates. We include the Creol primitives for process control and conditional suspension, using the syntax await condition, where condition is a Boolean condition. The syntax for method calls is as follows:

- x:=o.m(e)[s] for a blocking call where s is done while waiting for the future to be resolved, and if needed, active waiting happens after s (as in f:=o!m(e); s; x:= get f, using Creol)
- await x:=o.m(e)[s] for a non-blocking call, where the suspension point is after s (as in f:=o!m(e); s; await x:= get f, using Creol/ABS)
- o!m(e), for calls where no return value is needed.

Here [s] may be empty as in x:=o.m(e)/await x:=o.m(e), or may include additional calls as in for instance await x:=o1.m1(e1)[<calculate e2>; await y:=o2.m2(e2)[s]], where the suspension point is after s, passively waiting for *both* calls to complete. In this manner, programs with nested call-get structures can be expressed without futures. For the comparison we note that the future mechanism involves non-trivial garbage collection. Even if a future is short-lived, it may be complex to detect when it is no longer needed.

4 Comparison

By defining "future" classes supporting the future primitives above, as illustrated below, we show that our high-level core language is expressive enough to define futures, by means objects of (one of the) future classes. This means that efficient two-way interaction is directly supported, without garbage collection and future objects, while futures can be obtained, when needed, by using future objects. In the former case, efficiency is better than in an implementation using futures, in the second case it is similar (modulo optimizations). For programs with a majority of two-way interaction, efficiency is improved by our paradigm. We also note that programming with two-way interaction is conceptually simpler, since the declaration and usage of future variables are avoided. This is also beneficial for static analysis, since in static analysis of future retrieval (get) one typically needs to associate a call statement with each **get** statement. This can in general be difficult, and it is less modular when these associations cross class boundaries. Program reasoning is also more complex in the presence of first class futures [9].

Our language is able to encode futures in a straight forward manner. For instance the ABS code f:=o!m(e) is imitated by f:= new Fut_m(o,e) in our language, where class Fut_m is a predefined class, outlined below with initial code, a local method start, and exported methods:

```
class Fut_m(o,par) {
  Bool res:= false; // is the future resolved?
  T value; // the value of the future when resolved
 {start()} // initial code
  Void start(){await value:=o.m(par); res:=true} // see comment below
  Bool resolved(){return res} // polling
  Bool await_resolved(){await res; return true} // waiting until resolved
  T get(){await res; return value} // waiting for the resolved value
}
```

criteria	FF+CS	FF	LF+P	LF+CS	NF+CS	NF
expressiveness	+	0	0/0	0	0	−
efficiency	−	−	−/0	+	0	−
synt./sem. complexity	−	−	0/0	0	+	+
security aspects	−	−	0/+	+	+	+
static analysis	−	−	−/0	0	+	+
program reasoning	−	−	−/−	−	+	+

Fig. 1. A simplified summary of the evaluation of the different paradigms. The case of local futures with polling (LF+P) is split in two subcases, object-local and method-local futures.

In start we use await when polling is allowed, then the future object will be able to perform incoming call requests, and for instance return the appropriate result of polling requests. (The class parameters should here have the types given by the method m.)

5 Conclusion

We compare seven language paradigms for interaction as the most interesting: (i) first-class futures and cooperative scheduling (FF+CS), (ii) first-class futures without cooperative scheduling (FF), (iii) method-local futures and cooperative scheduling (LF+CS), (iv and v) local futures with polling (LF+P), with subcases for object-local and method-local futures, (vi) no futures and cooperative scheduling (NF+CS), and (vii) no futures (NF). We have focused on these interaction paradigms and evaluated them along the chosen criteria. For a rough overview, some main points of the evaluation results are illustrated in Fig. 1. Here + is better than 0, which is better than −. Languages with built-in first-class and cooperative scheduling futures have the highest expressiveness (marked as "+" in Fig. 1) whereas the ones without (only simulated ones) have somewhat less expressiveness. First-class futures require garbage collection, which is non-trivial in the case of distributed systems. Moreover, they give raise to more messages than languages without first-class futures. We have also seen that first-class futures may cause difficulties with respect to information security. In particular information flow analysis is problematic. Furthermore, the notion of futures, even local futures, make program reasoning more complex than reasoning for future-free languages, by adding a level of indirectness in the reasoning. Static analysis has similar problems, and for first-class futures this is in general more complex than for local futures. For several kinds of static reasoning it is necessary to detect the set of calls that corresponds to a given **get** statement. In general the more constructs a language has, the more expressive it is, but on the negative side, the more complex it is wrt. syntax, semantics, security, and analysis. This is illustrated clearly in the (somewhat oversimplified) table in Fig. 1. There is a trade-off between these different choices depending on the requirements in a given context, considering expressiveness, efficiency, and simplicity. The main benefits of first-class futures are the added flexibility and information sharing, some of which can be compensated by cooperative scheduling. In our treatment, the limitations of future-free programming have been reduced by the addition of delegation and a syntactic tail construct for calls. Consequently, future-free programming can be attractive in a number of settings. A more detailed comparison is made in the full paper [1].

References

1. Karami, F., Owe, O., Ramezanifarkhani, T.: An evaluation of interaction paradigms for active objects. J. Log. Algebr. Methods Program. **103**, 154–183 (2018). https://doi.org/10.1016/j.jlamp.2018.11.008. ISSN 2352-2216
2. Hewitt, C., Bishop, P., Steiger, R.: A universal modular actor formalism for artificial intelligence. In: IJCAI (1973)
3. Baker, H., Hewitt, C.: The incremental garbage collection of processes. In: Proceedings of Symposium on Artificial Intelligence Programming Languages, ACM Sigplan Notices, vol. 12, no. 8, pp. 55–59 (1977)
4. Yonezawa, A. (ed.): ABCL: An Object-Oriented Concurrent System. MIT Press, Cambridge (1990)
5. Halstead, R.H.: MultiLisp: a language for concurrent symbolic computation. TOPLAS **7**, 501–538 (1985)
6. Johnsen, E.B., Owe, O.: An asynchronous communication model for distributed concurrent objects. J. Softw. Syst. Model. **6**(1), 39–58 (2007)
7. Johnsen, E.B., Hähnle, R., Schäfer, J., Schlatte, R., Steffen, M.: ABS: a core language for abstract behavioral specification. In: Aichernig, B.K., de Boer, F.S., Bonsangue, M.M. (eds.) FMCO 2010. LNCS, vol. 6957, pp. 142–164. Springer, Heidelberg (2011). https://doi.org/10.1007/978-3-642-25271-6_8
8. de Boer, F., et al.: A survey of active object languages. ACM Comput. Surv. **50**(5), 1–39 (2017)
9. Din, C.C., Owe, O.: Compositional reasoning about active objects with shared futures. Formal Aspects Comput. **27**(3), 551–572 (2015)

Summary of: On Checking Delta-Oriented Software Product Lines of Statecharts

Michael Lienhardt[1], Ferruccio Damiani[2(✉)], Lorenzo Testa[2], and Gianluca Turin[3]

[1] ONERA —The French Aerospace Lab, Palaiseau, France
michael.lienhardt@onera.fr
[2] University of Turin, Turin, Italy
ferruccio.damiani@unito.it
[3] University of Oslo, Oslo, Norway
gianlutu@ifi.uio.no

Abstract. A Software Product Line (SPL) is a set of programs, called variants, which are generated from a common artifact base. Delta-Oriented Programming (DOP) is a flexible approach to implement SPLs. This short paper summarises the contributions published in [10]. A foundation for rigorous development of delta-oriented product lines of statecharts is provided by defining: a core language for statecharts, DOP on top of it, an analysis ensuring that a product line is well-formed (i.e., all variants can be generated and are well-formed statecharts). An implementation of the analysis has been applied to an industrial case study.

Keywords: Core calculus · Delta-Oriented Programming · Software product line analysis · Statechart

1 Background

A *Software Product Line* (SPL) is a set of programs, called *variants*, which have well documented variability and are generated from a common artifact base [6]. *Delta-Oriented Programming* (DOP) [5,11] [4, Sect. 6.6.1] is a flexible approach to implement SPLs. A delta-oriented SPL consists of a *feature model*, an *artifact base*, and *configuration knowledge*. The feature model provides an abstract description of variants in terms of *features*—each feature represents an abstract description of functionality and each variant is identified by a set of features, called a *product*. The artifact base provides language dependent artifacts that are used to build the variants—it consists of a *base program* (that might be empty or incomplete) and of a set of *delta modules* (*deltas* for short), which are containers of modifications to a program. For example: for Java programs, a delta can add, remove or modify classes and interfaces; for statechart programs, a delta can add, remove or modify states and transitions. Configuration knowledge connects the features in the feature model with the artifacts in the artifact base by associating to each delta an *activation condition* over the features and

W. Ahrendt and S. L. Tapia Tarifa (Eds.): IFM 2019, LNCS 11918, pp. 534–537, 2019.
https://doi.org/10.1007/978-3-030-34968-4_32

specifying an *application ordering* between deltas. Once a user selects a product, the corresponding variant is derived by applying the deltas with a satisfied activation condition to the base program according to the application ordering. Thus configuration knowledge defines a mapping from products to variants, and DOP supports the automatic generation of variants based on a selection of features.

SPL analysis approaches can be classified into three main categories [13]: product-based, family-based and feature-based. *Product-based* analyses work only on generated variants (or models of variants). *Family-based* analyses work on the artifact base, without generating any variant or model of variant, by exploiting feature model and configuration knowledge to derive results about all variants. *Feature-based* analyses work on the reusable artifacts in the artifact base (base program and deltas in DOP) in isolation, without using feature model and configuration knowledge, to derive results on all variants.

2 Contributions of [10]

The toolchain of the HyVar project [2] supports the development of delta-oriented SPLs of statecharts [8] expressed in the format supported by YAKINDU STATECHART TOOLS [3]. A YAKINDU statechart consists of: an *interface definition part*, which declares the elements (e.g., events and typed operations) used by the statechart to interact with the external environment; and a *state definition part*, which defines the structure of the statechart (i.e., a hierarchical state machine that can use the elements declared in the interface definition part). This toolchain has been used to develop product lines of car embedded software systems [2]. It provides: automatic derivation of a statechart variant, C/C++ and Java code generation, linking to external code artifacts, compilation, and support for guaranteeing that all the statechart variants can be generated and are well formed.

In delta-oriented programming, the generation of a variant fails when attempting to apply a delta that contains an operation that cannot be executed (e.g., for an SPL of YAKINDU statecharts, adding an already existing event to the interface definition part, or removing or modifying a non existing state in the state definition part).

In YAKINDU STATECHART TOOLS, a statechart is well formed if the interface definition part is well-formed (e.g., there are no duplicated declarations) and the state definition part is well formed, that is: (i) there are no structural flaws (like, e.g., a dangling transition); (ii) all the elements used to interact with the external environment are declared in the interface definition part; and (iii) the use of each of these elements is correct with respect to its declaration (e.g., each operation is used according to the type declared for it).

The paper [10] provides a formal account of the SPL family-based analysis technique implemented in the HyVar toolchain. Namely, it:

1. defines FEATHERWEIGHT STATECHART LANGUAGE (FSL), a core textual language that captures the key ingredients of YAKINDU statecharts (much as

Featherweight Java [9] captures the key ingredients of class-based object-oriented programming);
2. formalizes for FSL (by a means of a set of typing rules) the well-formedness checks supported by Yakindu Statechart Tools;
3. defines Featherweight Delta Statechart Language (FDSL), a core textual language for delta-oriented SPLs where variants are written in FSL, that captures the key ingredients of the delta operations on Yakindu statecharts supported by the HyVar toolchain;
4. defines (on top of the formalization in points 1, 2 and 3 above) a family-based analysis for guaranteeing that all the variants can be generated and are well formed; and
5. illustrates how the implementation of the analysis in the HyVar toolchain has been applied on the HyVar case study.

The Yakindu statecharts language is defined as an Ecore metamodel [1]. In the HyVar toolchain, the language of deltas on Yakindu statecharts is defined by the DeltaEcore tool suite [12], which supports developers in defining delta languages for Ecore metamodels. The core languages FSL and FΔSL, which capture the key ingredients of delta-oriented programming on Yakindu statecharts, have been designed in order to enable providing a formal account of the SPL analysis (cf. point 4 above).

The proposed family-based well-formedness checking mechanism for delta-oriented SPL of FSL statecharts is inspired by the type checking approach for delta-oriented SPLs of Java-like programs proposed in [7]. In [7], starting from a set of typing rules for IFJ [5] (an imperative version of Featherweight Java [9]), it is shown how to define a family-based type-checking analysis for SPLs written in IFΔJ (a language for delta-oriented SPLs of IFJ programs). In order to enable using the technique proposed for IFΔJ SPLs to define a family-based well-formedness analysis for SPLs written in FΔSL, the notion of well-formed FSL statechart has been formalized by a means of a set of typing rules. Since the structure of an FSL statechart is more complex than the structure of an IFJ program, the technique proposed in [10] had to address this additional complexity. In particular:

- An IFJ program has only classes and attributes, while statecharts have a recursive structure where composite states can contain composite states that can contain states themselves—in the formalization of the analysis this has been addressed by introducing a notion of path to identify where an element is placed in a statechart.
- The elements of an IFJ program have only one dependency slot (classes depend on their super classes, and fields and methods depend on the types and method they use in their declaration), while the elements in a statechart have a more fine grain structure where several parts can be changed (for instance, each part of a transition can be changed)—in the formalization of the analysis this has been addressed by introducing the notion of dependency slots.

3 Conclusion and Future Work

The paper [10] originated in the context of the HyVar project, while enhancing the preliminary version of the HyVar toolchain (that supported delta-oriented SPLs of YAKINDU statecharts) by adding support for an SPL analysis that automatically checks that all the variants can be generated and are well formed. The paper [10] provides a formal account of the well-formedness SPLs analysis technique integrated into the toolchain, and illustrates how the analysis has been applied to an industrial case study.

In future work we would like to further evaluate the implementation by considering other case studies. We also plan to define other static analyses for delta-oriented SPL of YAKINDU statecharts (like, e.g., model checking) and to incorporate them into the HyVar toolchain.

References

1. Eclipse Modeling Framework (EMF). www.eclipse.org/modeling/emf/
2. The HyVar home page. www.hyvar-project.eu
3. Yakindu statechart tools. www.itemis.com/en/yakindu/state-machine/
4. Apel, S., Batory, D., Kästner, C., Saake, G.: Feature-Oriented Software Product Lines: Concepts and Implementation. Springer, Heidelberg (2013). https://doi.org/10.1007/978-3-642-37521-7
5. Bettini, L., Damiani, F., Schaefer, I.: Compositional type checking of delta-oriented software product lines. Acta Informatica **50**(2), 77–122 (2013). https://doi.org/10.1007/s00236-012-0173-z
6. Clements, P., Northrop, L.: Software Product Lines: Practices and Patterns. Addison Wesley Longman, Boston (2001)
7. Damiani, F., Lienhardt, M.: On type checking delta-oriented product lines. In: Ábrahám, E., Huisman, M. (eds.) IFM 2016. LNCS, vol. 9681, pp. 47–62. Springer, Cham (2016). https://doi.org/10.1007/978-3-319-33693-0_4
8. Harel, D.: Statecharts: a visual formalism for complex systems. Sci. Comput. Program. **8**(3), 231–274 (1987). https://doi.org/10.1016/0167-6423(87)90035-9
9. Igarashi, A., Pierce, B., Wadler, P.: Featherweight Java: a minimal core calculus for Java and GJ. ACM TOPLAS **23**(3), 396–450 (2001). https://doi.org/10.1145/503502.503505
10. Lienhardt, M., Damiani, F., Testa, L., Turin, G.: On checking delta-oriented product lines of statecharts. Sci. Comput. Program. **166**, 3–34 (2018). https://doi.org/10.1016/j.scico.2018.05.007
11. Schaefer, I., Bettini, L., Bono, V., Damiani, F., Tanzarella, N.: Delta-oriented programming of software product lines. In: Bosch, J., Lee, J. (eds.) SPLC 2010. LNCS, vol. 6287, pp. 77–91. Springer, Heidelberg (2010). https://doi.org/10.1007/978-3-642-15579-6_6
12. Seidl, C., Schaefer, I., Aßmann, U.: Deltaecore - a model-based delta language generation framework. In: LNI, Modellierung 2014, Wien, Österreich, 19.-21. März 2014, vol. 225, pp. 81–96. GI (2014). http://subs.emis.de/LNI/Proceedings/Proceedings225/article2.html
13. Thüm, T., Apel, S., Kästner, C., Schaefer, I., Saake, G.: A classification and survey of analysis strategies for software product lines. ACM Comput. Surv. (2014). https://doi.org/10.1145/2580950

A Summary of Formal Specification and Verification of Autonomous Robotic Systems

Matt Luckcuck(✉), Marie Farrell(✉), Louise A. Dennis, Clare Dixon, and Michael Fisher

Department of Computer Science, University of Liverpool, Liverpool, UK
{m.luckcuck,marie.farrell}@liverpool.ac.uk

Abstract. Autonomous robotic systems are complex, hybrid, and often safety-critical; this makes their formal specification and verification uniquely challenging. Though commonly used, testing and simulation alone are insufficient to ensure the correctness of, or provide sufficient evidence for the certification of, autonomous robotics. Formal methods for autonomous robotics have received some attention in the literature, but no resource provides a current overview. This short paper summarises the contributions published in [5], which surveys the state-of-the-art in formal specification and verification for autonomous robotics.

1 Introduction and Methodology

This short paper summarises our recently published survey of the formal specification and verification techniques that have been applied to autonomous robotic systems [5], which provides a comprehensive overview and analysis of the state-of-the-art, and identifies promising new research directions and challenges for the formal methods community. Previous work, which draws from this survey, advocates the use of integrated formal methods for autonomous robotic systems [2].

We define an *autonomous system* as an artificially intelligent entity that makes decisions in response to input, independent of human interaction. *Robotic systems* are physical entities that interact with the physical world. Thus, an *autonomous robotic system* is a machine that uses Artificial Intelligence (AI), has a physical presence in and interacts with the real world. Autonomous robotics are increasingly used in commonplace-scenarios, such as driverless cars [3], pilotless aircraft [6], and domestic assistants [1].

For many engineered systems, testing, either by real deployment or via simulation, is deemed sufficient. But autonomous robotics require stronger verification, because of the unique challenges: dependence on sophisticated software control and decision-making, and increasing deployment in safety-critical scenarios. This leads us towards using formal methods to ensure the correctness of, and provide sufficient evidence for the certification of, robotic systems.

Work supported by UKRI Hubs for Robotics and AI in Hazardous Environments: EP/R026092 (FAIR-SPACE), EP/R026173 (ORCA), and EP/R026084 (RAIN).

W. Ahrendt and S. L. Tapia Tarifa (Eds.): IFM 2019, LNCS 11918, pp. 538–541, 2019.
https://doi.org/10.1007/978-3-030-34968-4_33

The corresponding journal paper [5] identifies and investigates the following three research questions:

RQ1: What are the challenges when formally specifying and verifying the behaviour of (autonomous) robotic systems?
RQ2: What are the current formalisms, tools, and approaches used when addressing the answer to **RQ1**?
RQ3: What are the current limitations of the answers to **RQ2** and are there developing solutions aiming to address them?

To answer these questions we performed a systematic literature survey on *formal modelling of (autonomous) robotic systems*, *formal specification of (autonomous) robotic systems*, and *formal verification of (autonomous) robotic systems*. We restricted our search to papers published from 2007 to 2018, inclusive.

In addition to answering the research questions, the survey [5] illustrates opportunities for research applying formal methods (and Integrated Formal Methods (iFM)) to robotics and autonomous systems – either by identifying the popular languages that integration could use, or by showing the gaps that could be filled by iFM. It also provides a brief overview of some popular general software engineering techniques for robotic systems including middleware architectures, testing, and simulation approaches, domain specific languages, graphical notations, and model-driven engineering or XML-based approaches.

2 Answering the Research Questions

This section summarises how the results of our survey address the research questions described in Sect. 1.

To answer **RQ1**, we identified the challenges describe in the surveyed literature and categorised them as *external* or *internal* to the robotic system. External challenges come from the design and environment, independently of how the system is designed internally. We found two major external challenges in the literature: modelling and reasoning about the system's environment, and providing enough evidence for public trust and regulation. Internal challenges stem from how the system is engineered. The three internal challenges that we found in the literature were related to using: agent-based, multi-robot, and adaptive or reconfigurable systems. These challenges, and the tools and techniques used to overcome them, are discussed at length in [5, §3–4].

Tackling internal challenges can have complementary benefits to mitigating external challenges. Reconfigurability is key to safely deploying robots in hazardous environments and much more work needs to materialise in order to ensure the safety of reconfigurable autonomous systems. Therefore, we see a clear link between a robotic system reacting to the changes in its external environment, and reconfigurable systems. Similarly, *rational* agent-based systems that can explain their reasoning provide a good route for providing evidence for public trust or certification bodies. This is because they provide the transparency that is crucial for public trust and certification. A rational agent can provide reasons for its choices, based on input and internal state information.

RQ2, asked what are the current formal methods used for tackling the challenges identified by answering **RQ1**. Thus, we quantify and describe the formalisms, tools, and approaches used in the literature [5, §5–6], summarised in Table 1 (right). We found that state-transition systems and (temporal) logics are the most used formalisms to specify the system and properties, respectively; which may be because they allow abstract specification, which is useful early in development.

Table 1. Summary of the types of formalisms for specifying the system and the properties to be checked, summarising [5, Table 2].

Formalism	System	Property
Set-Based	5	0
State-Transition	33	0
Logics	6	32
Process algebra	3	1
Ontology	4	0
Other	5	8

We found that model-checkers are the most often used verification approach, which complements the wide use of state-transition systems and temporal logics [5, Tables 3–4]. This may be because the model-checking approach is generally easy to explain to stakeholders with no experience of using formal methods. Notably, theorem provers were used a lot less often, we believe that this is due to the level of expert knowledge required to operate them correctly and efficiently.

RQ3, asked what are the limitations of the formalisms and approaches to verification that were identified in the answer to **RQ2** (see [5, §7]). One obvious limitation appears to be a resistance to adopting formal methods in robotic systems development [4]. The perception is that applying formal methods is a complicated additional step in the engineering process, which prolongs development while not adding to the value of the final product. A lack of appropriate tools also often impedes the application of formal methods. There are, however, notable examples of industrial uses of formal methods [7].

There have been a variety of tools developed for the same formalism [5, Table 3] signaling a lack of interoperability between different formalisms and tools. Often, models or specifications of similar components are incompatible and locked into a single tool. Thus, a common framework for translating between, relating, or integrating different formalisms, would help smooth the conversion between formalisms/tools. This would also serve a growing need to capture the behaviour of complex systems using a heterogeneous set of formalisms and integrated formal methods. This is an open problem in formal methods for robotic systems [2].

Another limitation faced in this domain is in formalising the *last link*, the step between a formal model and program code. Ensuring that the program correctly implements the model requires a formalised translation. The lack of clarity about this limitation points to another: a lack of open sharing of models, code, and realistic case studies that are not tuned for a particular formalism.

Field tests and simulations are both useful tools for robotic systems development [5, §2]; but formal verification is crucial, especially at the early stages of development when field tests of the control software are infeasible (or dangerous). A focussed research effort on combining or integrating formal methods should improve their use in robotic systems development, because no single formalism is capable of adequately checking that all aspects of a robotic system behave as expected. Ensuring that these tools are usable by developers and providing similar features in an IDE would also improve their uptake by simplifying their use. Work in this area could lead to an Integrated *Verification* Environment, allowing the use of different formalisms using same developer front-end, connecting them to their respective tools, and providing helpful IDE-like support.

3 Conclusion

The development of autonomous robotic systems is a novel, emerging, and quickly-changing field. Many of these systems are inherently safety- or mission-critical, so it is prudent that formal methods are used to ensure that they behave as intended. To advance research in this area, our survey provides a description of the formalisms and tools that are current being applied to autonomous robotic systems. To provide some guidance for choosing these languages and tools, we describe them and the case study tackled for the surveyed literature [5, Table 1], however a detailed analysis of this is left as future work. The survey also highlights the shortcomings of these approaches and outlines exciting and necessary future directions for the entire formal methods community.

References

1. Dixon, C., Webster, M., Saunders, J., Fisher, M., Dautenhahn, K.: "The fridge door is open"–temporal verification of a robotic assistant's behaviours. In: Mistry, M., Leonardis, A., Witkowski, M., Melhuish, C. (eds.) TAROS 2014. LNCS (LNAI), vol. 8717, pp. 97–108. Springer, Cham (2014). https://doi.org/10.1007/978-3-319-10401-0_9
2. Farrell, M., Luckcuck, M., Fisher, M.: Robotics and integrated formal methods: necessity meets opportunity. In: Furia, C.A., Winter, K. (eds.) IFM 2018. LNCS, vol. 11023, pp. 161–171. Springer, Cham (2018). https://doi.org/10.1007/978-3-319-98938-9_10
3. Fernandes, L.E.R., Custodio, V., Alves, G.V., Fisher, M.: A rational agent controlling an autonomous vehicle: implementation and formal verification. Electron. Proc. Theor. Comput. Sci. **257**(Fvav), 35–42 (2017). https://doi.org/10.4204/EPTCS.257.5
4. Lopes, Y., Trenkwalder, S., Leal, A., Dodd, T., Groß, R.: Supervisory control theory applied to swarm robotics. Swarm Intell. **10**(1), 65–97 (2016). https://doi.org/10.1007/s11721-016-0119-0
5. Luckcuck, M., Farrell, M., Dennis, L.A., Dixon, C., Fisher, M.: Formal specification and verification of autonomous robotic systems. ACM Comput. Surv. **52**(5), 1–41 (2019). https://doi.org/10.1145/3342355
6. Webster, M., Fisher, M., Cameron, N., Jump, M.: Formal methods for the certification of autonomous unmanned aircraft systems. In: Flammini, F., Bologna, S., Vittorini, V. (eds.) SAFECOMP 2011. LNCS, vol. 6894, pp. 228–242. Springer, Heidelberg (2011). https://doi.org/10.1007/978-3-642-24270-0_17
7. Woodcock, J., Larsen, P.G., Bicarregui, J., Fitzgerald, J.: Formal methods: practice and experience. ACM Comput. Surv. **41**(4), 1–36 (2009). https://doi.org/10.1145/1592434.1592436

Summary of: On the Expressiveness of Modal Transition Systems with Variability Constraints

Maurice H. ter Beek[1](✉), Ferruccio Damiani[2], Stefania Gnesi[1], Franco Mazzanti[1], and Luca Paolini[2]

[1] ISTI–CNR, Pisa, Italy
{maurice.terbeek,stefania.gnesi,franco.mazzanti}@isti.cnr.it
[2] University of Turin, Turin, Italy
{ferruccio.damiani,luca.paolini}@unito.it

Abstract. Modal transition systems (MTSs) and featured transition systems (FTSs) are widely recognised as fundamental behavioural models for software product lines. This short paper summarises the contributions published in [3]: MTSs with variability constraints (MTSυs) are equally expressive as FTSs. This is proved by giving sound and complete transformations of the latter into the former, and of the former into the latter. The benefits of this result are twofold. First, it contributes to the expressiveness hierarchy of such basic models studied in the literature. Second, it provides an automatic algorithm from FTSs to MTSυs that preserves the original (compact) branching structure, thus paving the way for model checking FTSs with the variability model checker VMC.

Keywords: SPL · Variability · Behavioural model · Formal specification · Featured transition system · Modal transition system

1 Background

Software systems are more and more often developed and managed as software product lines (SPLs) to tackle the variability inherent to a collection of individual customization [15]. The variability among the instances of highly-configurable, variant-rich systems is expressed in terms of features, which conceptualise pieces of functionality or aspects of a system that are relevant to the stakeholders [1]. Formal models for the specification and verification of SPL behaviour have been the subject of extensive research throughout the last decade.[1]

Behavioural models for SPLs are based on the superimposition of multiple labelled transition systems (LTSs), each of which represents a different variant (a product model), in a single LTS enriched with feature-based variability (a family model). A family's product variant (ordinary LTS) can be derived from the enriched LTS by resolving this variability. This boils down to deciding which

[1] The reader is referred to [3] for a complete list of references.

W. Ahrendt and S. L. Tapia Tarifa (Eds.): IFM 2019, LNCS 11918, pp. 542–546, 2019.
https://doi.org/10.1007/978-3-030-34968-4_34

'variable' behaviour to include in a specific product and which not, based on the combination of features defining the product.

MTSs and FTSs are some of the best known enriched LTS models for SPLs.

An MTS is an LTS that distinguishes between admissible (may) and necessary (must) transitions. MTSs were originally introduced in [14] to capture the refinement of a partial description into a more detailed one, reflecting increased knowledge on the admissible (but not necessary) behaviour. In [5], MTSs were equipped with an additional set of variability constraints, resulting in MTSυs, to compactly model SPL behaviour, whose individual product behaviour, in the form of LTSs, can be obtained by means of a special-purpose refinement relation, or by an equivalent operational derivation procedure.

An FTS is an LTS equipped with a function that labels each transition with a feature expression which needs to hold for this specific transition to be part of executable (product) variant behaviour (according to some feature model). FTSs were introduced in [10,11] to concisely model SPL behaviour, where again the behaviour of its (product) variants is modelled by LTSs. An FTS captures a family of LTSs, one per (product) variant, which can be obtained by projection (pruning away transitions not belonging to the variant).

In [9,16,17], these and other behavioural SPL models (with possibly infinite states) were compared with respect to their expressive power. The expressiveness results in [9] state that MTSs are less expressive than FTSs (with a generalised product-derivation relation), whereas in [17] FTSs are encoded into equivalent sets of multiple MTSs. In [3], we demonstrated instead that finite-state MTSυs are equally expressive as finite-state FTSs, by defining transformations of the latter into the former, of the former into the latter, and proving the soundness and completeness of both transformations, thus contributing to the expressiveness hierarchy of such basic behavioural SPL models studied in [9,16,17].

2 Contributions

In this section, we summarise the main results of [3] and mention their benefits.

We say that a behavioural SPL formalism M' is *at least as expressive as* a behavioural SPL formalism M, denoted by $M \leq M'$, iff there exists a transformation from M into M', denoted by $\tau\colon M \to M'$, such that for all models $\mathcal{M} \in M$, the sets of derived variants $\mathsf{lts}(\mathcal{M})$ and $\mathsf{lts}(\tau(\mathcal{M}))$ coincide. If also the vice-versa holds, we say that M' and M are *equally expressive*, denoted by $M' = M$.

As anticipated, in [3] we formally proved that finite-state MTSυs are equally expressive as finite-state FTSs. To this aim, we extended the automatic technique to transform an FTS into an MTSυ presented in [2], where we moreover merely sketched a proof of the soundness. More precisely, to show that finite-state MTSυs are equally expressive as finite-state FTSs we proved that:

1. FTSs $\leq$ MTSυs by defining an algorithm, FTS2MTSυ that transforms any FTS into an MTSυ and by proving its soundness and completeness (i.e. an MTSυ results with the same set of variant LTSs as the original FTS).

2. MTSυs = FTSs by defining an algorithm, MTSυ2FTS, that transforms any MTSυ into an FTS and by proving its soundness and completeness (i.e. an FTS results with the same set of variant LTSs as the original MTSυ).

Furthermore, in [3] we also pinpoint the specific features of MTSυs that make them at least as expressive as FTSs by illustrating the transformation into an MTSυ of an FTS that was introduced in [9] and for which it was demonstrated that it cannot be encoded as an MTS.

The defined FTS2MTSυ transformation algorithm leads to an MTSυ that generally could be optimised in several ways without changing its behaviour nor its variants, such as reducing the so-called descriptional complexity of the MTSυ (like the number of variability constraints) or improving the efficiency of model checking properties over the MTSυ or deriving variants from it. Notably, the FTS2MTSυ transformation algorithm preserves the original (compact) branching structure of the FTS.[2] This paves the way for using (optimised) versions of the MTSυs for family-based SPL model checking of FTSs with the variability model checker VMC [6,7], which currently accepts only MTSυ. VMC is a tool for modeling and analysing behavioural SPL models, which accepts MTSυs defined as MTS (specified in a high-level modal process algebra) together with a set of variability constraints (specified as propositional logic formulae).

3 Conclusion and Future Work

In [3], we proved that finite-state MTSυs are equally expressive as finite-state FTSs by defining an algorithm to transform any MTSυ into an FTS and vice-versa and proving the soundness and completeness of these transformations. This result complements the expressiveness results that were reported in [9,16] for behavioural SPL formalisms with possibly infinite states, viz. MTSs are less expressive than FTSs (with a generalised product-derivation relation).

Since one of the aims of [3] was to complement the expressiveness hierarchy of fundamental behavioural models for SPLs studied in [9,16], the theoretical result of [3] that MTSυs are equally expressive as FTSs is of interest by itself. However, since the FTS2MTSυ transformation algorithm preserves the original (compact) branching structure of FTSs, this result moreover paves the way for using (optimised) versions of the resulting MTSυs for family-based SPL model checking of FTSs with the variability model checker VMC [6,7].

A related approach, outlined in [4], uses the fact that any FTS can be transformed into an MTS and if the FTS is unambiguous, then the corresponding MTS is live, thus allowing to carry over a result from [5] to facilitate family-based model checking of such FTSs for a rich temporal logic.

In the future, we plan to implement an optimised version of the FTS2MTSυ transformation algorithm (e.g. by creating must transitions whenever possible) as a front-end of VMC and to further explore the approach from [4], to offer SPL model checking of rich temporal logic properties against either FTSs or MTSυs.

[2] The resulting MTSυ has one additional state and dummy transitions to that state [3].

Currently, efficient SPL model checking over FTSs is possible by using dedicated family-based model checkers like ProVeLines [12] or, alternatively, by using highly optimised off-the-shelf model checkers like SPIN or mCRL2, which were recently made amenable to family-based SPL model checking over FTSs [8,13].

References

1. Apel, S., Batory, D.S., Kästner, C., Saake, G.: Springer. Feature-Oriented Software Product Lines (2013). https://doi.org/10.1007/978-3-642-37521-7
2. ter Beek, M.H., Damiani, F., Gnesi, S., Mazzanti, F., Paolini, L.: From featured transition systems to modal transition systems with variability constraints. In: Calinescu, R., Rumpe, B. (eds.) SEFM 2015. LNCS, vol. 9276, pp. 344–359. Springer, Cham (2015). https://doi.org/10.1007/978-3-319-22969-0_24
3. ter Beek, M.H., Damiani, F., Gnesi, S., Mazzanti, F., Paolini, L.: On the expressiveness of modal transition systems with variability constraints. Sci. Comput. Program. **169**, 1–17 (2019). https://doi.org/10.1016/j.scico.2018.09.006
4. ter Beek, M.H., Damiani, F., Lienhardt, M., Mazzanti, F., Paolini, L.: Static analysis of featured transition systems. In: SPLC, pp. 39–51. ACM (2019). https://doi.org/10.1145/3336294.3336295
5. ter Beek, M.H., Fantechi, A., Gnesi, S., Mazzanti, F.: Modelling and analysing variability in product families: model checking of modal transition systems with variability constraints. J. Log. Algebr. Meth. Program. **85**(2), 287–315 (2016). https://doi.org/10.1016/j.jlamp.2015.11.006
6. ter Beek, M.H., Mazzanti, F.: VMC: recent advances and challenges ahead. In: SPLC, pp. 70–77. ACM (2014). https://doi.org/10.1145/2647908.2655969
7. ter Beek, M.H., Mazzanti, F., Sulova, A.: VMC: a tool for product variability analysis. In: Giannakopoulou, D., Méry, D. (eds.) FM 2012. LNCS, vol. 7436, pp. 450–454. Springer, Heidelberg (2012). https://doi.org/10.1007/978-3-642-32759-9_36
8. ter Beek, M.H., de Vink, E.P., Willemse, T.A.C.: Family-based model checking with mCRL2. In: Huisman, M., Rubin, J. (eds.) FASE 2017. LNCS, vol. 10202, pp. 387–405. Springer, Heidelberg (2017). https://doi.org/10.1007/978-3-662-54494-5_23
9. Beohar, H., Varshosaz, M., Mousavi, M.: Basic behavioral models for software product lines: expressiveness and testing pre-orders. Sci. Comput. Program. **123**, 42–60 (2016). https://doi.org/10.1016/j.scico.2015.06.005
10. Classen, A., Cordy, M., Schobbens, P.-Y., Heymans, P., Legay, A., Raskin, J.F.: Featured transition systems: foundations for verifying variability-intensive systems and their application to LTL model checking. IEEE Trans. Softw. Eng. **39**(8), 1069–1089 (2013). https://doi.org/10.1109/TSE.2012.86
11. Classen, A., Heymans, P., Schobbens, P.-Y., Legay, A., Raskin, J.-F.: Model checking lots of systems: efficient verification of temporal properties in software product lines. In: ICSE, pp. 335–344. ACM (2010). https://doi.org/10.1145/1806799.1806850
12. Cordy, M., Classen, A., Heymans, P., Schobbens, P.-Y., Legay, A.: ProVeLines: a product line of verifiers for software product lines. In: SPLC, pp. 141–146. ACM (2013). https://doi.org/10.1145/2499777.2499781
13. Dimovski, A.S., Al-Sibahi, A.S., Brabrand, C., Wąsowski, A.: Family-based model checking without a family-based model checker. In: Fischer, B., Geldenhuys, J. (eds.) SPIN 2015. LNCS, vol. 9232, pp. 282–299. Springer, Cham (2015). https://doi.org/10.1007/978-3-319-23404-5_18

14. Larsen, K.G., Thomsen, B.: A modal process logic. In: LICS, pp. 203–210. IEEE (1988). https://doi.org/10.1109/LICS.1988.5119
15. Pohl, K., Böckle, G., van der Linden, F.: Software Product Line Engineering. Springer (2005). https://doi.org/10.1007/3-540-28901-1
16. Varshosaz, M., Beohar, H., Mousavi, M.: Basic behavioral models for software product lines: revisited. Sci. Comput. Program. **168**, 171–185 (2018). https://doi.org/10.1016/j.scico.2018.09.001
17. Varshosaz, M., Luthmann, L., Mohr, P., Lochau, M., Mousavi, M.: Modal transition system encoding of featured transition systems. J. Log. Algebr. Meth. Program. **106**, 1–28 (2019). https://doi.org/10.1016/j.jlamp.2019.03.003

Summary of: A Framework for Quantitative Modeling and Analysis of Highly (re)configurable Systems

Maurice H. ter Beek[1(✉)], Axel Legay[2], Alberto Lluch Lafuente[3], and Andrea Vandin[3]

[1] ISTI–CNR, Pisa, Italy
maurice.terbeek@isti.cnr.it
[2] UCLouvain, Louvain-la-Neuve, Belgium
[3] DTU, Lyngby, Denmark

Abstract. This short paper summarises the contributions published in [4], where we introduce QFLan, a framework for quantitative modeling and analysis of highly (re)configurable systems, like software product lines. We define a rich domain specific language (DSL) for systems with variability in terms of features, which can be dynamically installed, removed or replaced, capable of modeling probabilistic behavior, possibly subject to quantitative feature constraints. High-level DSL specifications are automatically encoded in a process algebra whose operational behavior interacts with a store of constraints, which allows to separate a system's configuration from its behavior. The resulting probabilistic configurations and behavior converge seamlessly in a semantics based on discrete-time Markov chains, thus enabling quantitative analysis. An accompanying Eclipse-based tool offers a modern integrated development environment to specify such systems and to perform analyses that range from the likelihood of specific behavior to the expected average cost, in terms of feature attributes, of specific system variants. Based on a seamless integration with the statistical model checker MultiVeStA, QFLan allows to scale to larger models with respect to precise probabilistic analysis techniques. We provide a number of case studies that have driven and validated the development of the QFLan framework. In particular, we show the versatility of the QFLan framework with an application to risk analysis of a safe lock system from the security domain.

Extended Abstract

In [1,2], we presented various facets of the probabilistic modeling language QFLan, which is capable of describing a wide spectrum of aspects of (software) product lines (SPL) or configurable (software) systems in general. After a survey in the invited contribution [3], we provide a comprehensive presentation of the QFLan framework, consisting of a high-level modeling language with advanced tool support, in [4] and an accompanying tool paper [7]. Moreover, to illustrate the versatility of the QFLan framework, [4] contains case studies from different

W. Ahrendt and S. L. Tapia Tarifa (Eds.): IFM 2019, LNCS 11918, pp. 547–551, 2019.
https://doi.org/10.1007/978-3-030-34968-4_35

application domains. One of them concerns risk assessment in a security scenario with high variability that makes use of so-called attack trees. We show how to apply QFLan to the seminal example from that area: Schneier's Safe Lock [5,6].

Figure 1 depicts the attack tree from [5]. It specifies a risk assessment for a safe lock system. An attack tree is essentially an and/or tree, whose nodes represent goals, and sub-trees represent sub-goals. In this case, the root represents the main threat under analysis, namely the lock being opened by an attacker. Each of its children are possible ways of enacting such threat. The sub-goal Eavesdrop has two sub-goals that need to be accomplished (thus their combination as *and*-children). Nodes are decorated with an estimation of the cost that the attacker would have to pay to succeed in enacting the corresponding action. The classical analysis of such trees is to compute the minimal cost for an attacker to succeed.

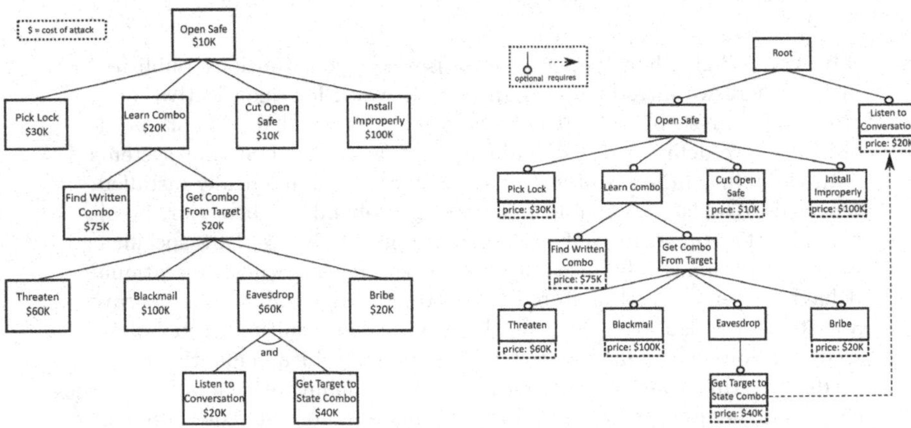

Fig. 1. Schneier's attack tree from [5]

Fig. 2. Feature model representation

Attack trees can easily be modelled as so-called feature models, with the following rationale: a node, representing a goal, can be modeled as a feature of the system which the attacker tries to activate. The sub-goal relation is modeled by the feature hierarchy. The attack tree of Fig. 1 can be modeled as in Fig. 2.

We introduce a slight variation to overcome a well-known limitation of the original attack trees, namely the inability to encode the ordering of events. Indeed, Listen to Conversation should occur before Get Target to State Combo, which we can model with a *requires* cross-tree constraint. A feature model defines which configurations are valid, but not how (i.e., in which order) to configure them. QFLan does model (re)configuration: features can be dynamically installed, removed or replaced as long as at any point in time all constraints are satisfied, including those imposed by the feature model. As noted in [4], the requires cross-tree constraint from Get Target to State Combo to Listen to Conversation implies an order: whenever QFLan tries to install (i.e., the attacker tries to activate) Get Target to State Combo, it fails to do so unless Listen to Conversation was installed (i.e., activated) before. As a matter of fact, the flexibility of the way feature models are specified in QFLan allows us to specify richer relations among sub-goals. For instance, we can specify that Eavesdrop is only successful if the attacker first listens to a conversation and then gets the target to state the combo, thus refining the original *and*-relation among such sub-goals.

A notable advantage of using QFLan for such scenarios is that we can model attacker behavior and study the system's robustness against them. Consider the attackers sketched in Fig. 3 (cf. [4] for their process specifications). An attacker is specified in terms of states and transitions among them, each labeled with the performed action, a weight to probabilistically choose the transition to be executed, and optional variable updates.

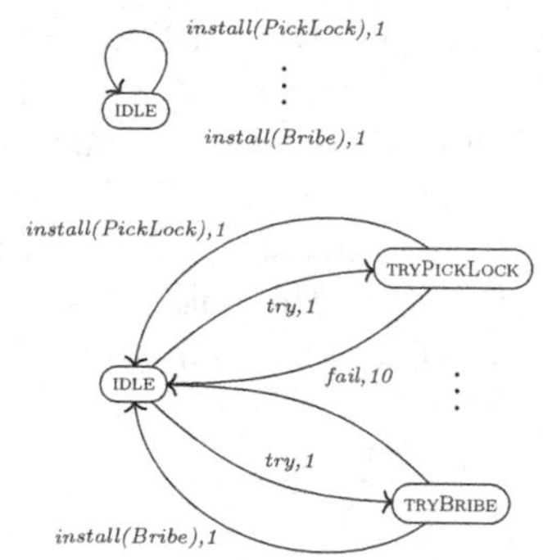

Fig. 3. PowerfulAttacker (top) and FailingAttacker (bottom)

Powerful attacker always succeeds in trying to achieve a goal and has unlimited resources. Failing attacker can fail, may need several attempts (modeled via weights) and has limited resources. Clearly, reasonable attackers stop attacking after a successful attack. This can be expressed in QFLan using two action constraints:

```
begin action constraints
  do(tryAction) -> !has(OpenSafe)          do(install(...)) -> !has(OpenSafe)
end action constraints
```

QFLan's rich specification language allows to express further constraints on the accepted classes of attacks. Consider the following two quantitative constraints:

```
begin quantitative constraints
  { cost(Root) <= 100 }                    { cumul_cost <= 20 }
end quantitative constraints
```

The first restricts to (successful) attacks that cost less than \$100K (i.e., install features with less than that price, cf. the feature model in Fig. 2). The second constraint instead restricts to attacks (independently of their success) that cumulated less than 20 attempts. Noteworthy, using the first constraint we restrict the family of admissible products, while the latter constraint regards only the behavioral part of the model. In fact, `cumul_cost` is not an attribute but a variable, which can be changed through a memory update in the behavior. We use it as a counter to record the number of times that an attack is tried.

For both attackers, we want to know the probability for an attack to succeed in a given amount of time and its average cost. QFLan can run such analyses by querying, at each of the first 40 simulation steps (`eval from 0 to 40 by 1`), the probability of installing the feature `OpenSafe`, the cost of the corresponding variant (cost(`Root`)) and the attempts cumulated by the failing attacker (`cumul_cost`) while trying to install the features corresponding to the sub-goals:

```
begin analysis
  query = eval from 0 to 40 by 1 : { OpenSafe[delta = 0.05] , cost(Root) ,
      cumul_cost }                              default   delta = 1   alpha = 0.05
end analysis
```

QFLan estimates these properties as the mean of n samples obtained from n independent simulations, with n large enough (but minimal) to grant that the size of the $(1-\alpha)\times 100\%$ *confidence interval* for the expected value is bounded by δ, i.e., a confidence interval is specified in terms of two parameters: α and δ.

We consider three configurations: (a) a powerful attacker with constraints as specified above; (b) an attacker that might fail with the same constraints; and (c) an attacker that might fail with less resources, obtained by changing the constraint on the `cumul_cost` to `{ cumul_cost <= 10 }`. This is obtained by running once the analysis on each model variant, each requiring about 12 s.

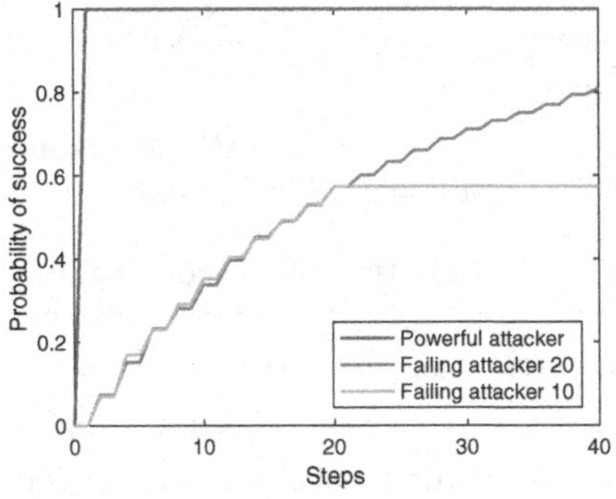

Fig. 4. Probabilities of successful attacks

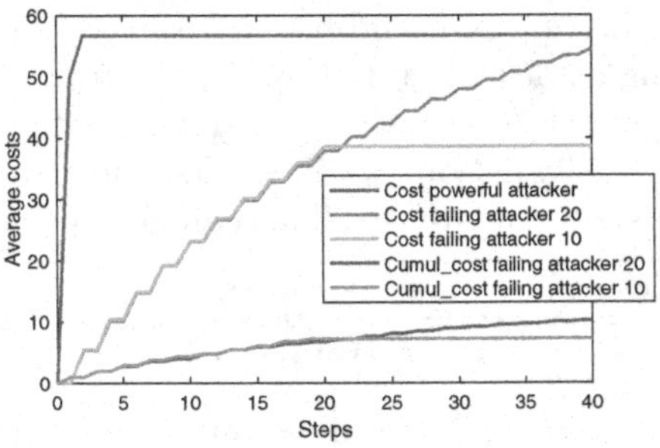

Fig. 5. Costs of successful attacks

Figure 4 plots the probabilities of successful attacks. The powerful attacker succeeds with probability almost 1 after one step, but for the other attackers the probability of success increases slowly. For constraint `{ cumul_cost <= 10 }`, the probability of success stabilizes at ± 0.6 after 20 steps. Indeed, `cumul_cost` increases by 1 every two steps. Instead, for `{ cumul_cost <= 20 }`, the probability reaches 0.8 after 40 steps, but this is not due to the mentioned constraint. In fact, Fig. 5 plots the costs and cumulative attempts for the model variants. The average cumulative attempts for the failing attackers do not diverge enough to attribute the different dynamics of the two attackers to the mentioned constraint. Finally, note that costs evolve similarly to probabilities, but with different scales.

References

1. ter Beek, M.H., Legay, A., Lluch Lafuente, A., Vandin, A.: Quantitative analysis of probabilistic models of software product lines with statistical model checking. EPTCS **182**, 56–70 (2015). https://doi.org/10.4204/EPTCS.182.5

2. ter Beek, M.H., Legay, A., Lluch Lafuente, A., Vandin, A.: Statistical analysis of probabilistic models of software product lines with quantitative constraints. In: SPLC, pp. 11–15. ACM (2015). https://doi.org/10.1145/2791060.2791087
3. ter Beek, M.H., Legay, A., Lluch Lafuente, A., Vandin, A.: Statistical model checking for product lines. In: Margaria, T., Steffen, B. (eds.) ISoLA 2016. LNCS, vol. 9952, pp. 114–133. Springer, Cham (2016). https://doi.org/10.1007/978-3-319-47166-2_8
4. ter Beek, M.H., Legay, A., Lluch Lafuente, A., Vandin, A.: A framework for quantitative modeling and analysis of highly (re)configurable systems. IEEE Trans. Softw. Eng. (2018). https://doi.org/10.1109/TSE.2018.2853726
5. Schneier, B.: Attack trees. Dr. Dobb's J. **24**(12), 21–29 (1999)
6. Schneier, B.: Secrets & Lies: Digital Security in a Networked World. Wiley, New York (2000)
7. Vandin, A., ter Beek, M.H., Legay, A., Lluch Lafuente, A.: QFLan: a tool for the quantitative analysis of highly reconfigurable systems. In: Havelund, K., Peleska, J., Roscoe, B., de Vink, E. (eds.) FM 2018. LNCS, vol. 10951, pp. 329–337. Springer, Cham (2018). https://doi.org/10.1007/978-3-319-95582-7_19

Author Index

Printed in the United States
By Bookmasters